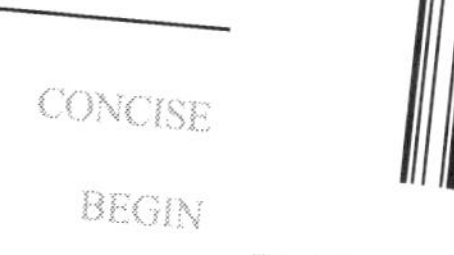

IN A MATTER OF MINUTES!

Find the time required to clean virtually any size building, room, or area, quickly and easily!

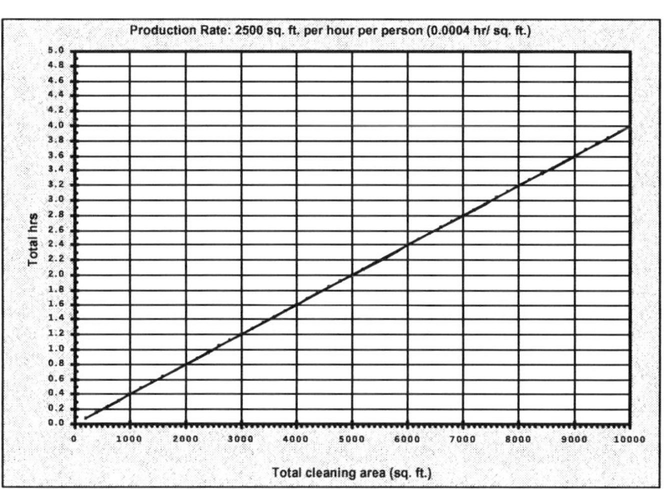

Find a monthly or annual price for price for your cleaning services fast and accurately!

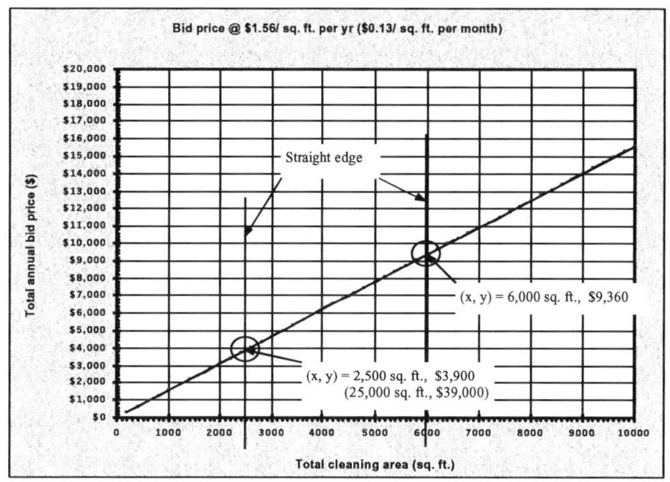

* **Easy To Read Production Rate Charts, For Use In Determining The Cleaning Times Of Tasks Ranging From General Office Cleaning To Floor Care.**

* **Make Quick Work Load Determinations For Situations Involving A Single Individual Or An Entire Cleaning Crew.**

* **Find Cleaning Times For Cleaning Areas Ranging From 100 sq. ft. to 100,000 sq. ft.,.**

* **Determine Bid Prices For Virtually Any Cleaning Service, Such As Floor Care, Pressure Washing, Venetian Blind Cleaning, General Office Cleaning, etc.,.**

* **Determine The Price Of Your Cleaning Services, For Any Cleaning Area Ranging From 100 sq. ft. to 100,000 sq. ft.,.**

Calculate detailed work loads for virtually any set of cleaning tasks using convenient and compact spreadsheets!

WORK LOAD WORKSHEET

ACCOUNT OR FACILITY: ______ Page 1

CLEANING AREA/ ROOM: ______ Date: ______

CLEANING TASK	TOTAL No. units, or AREA (sq. ft)	CLEAN TIME 1 ITEM (min) (INPUT)	CLEAN TIME 1 ITEM (hrs) (INPUT)	PROD. RATE hrs/ sq. ft (INPUT)	FREQUENCY WEEKLY (INPUT)	FREQUENCY MONTHLY (INPUT)	CLEAN TIME 1 ITEM (min) (OUTPUT)	CLEAN TIME 1 ITEM (hrs) (OUTPUT)	TOTAL TIME WEEKLY (hrs)	TOTAL TIME MONTHLY (hrs)	TOTAL TIME ANNUALLY (hrs)
SWEEPING											
DRY MOPPING											
WET MOPPING											
VACUUMING											
EMPTY WASTE BASKET											
EMPTY TRASH CAN											
DUSTING											
WASH WINDOWS											
CLEAN OTHER											
CLEAN OTHER											
CLEAN TOILETS	10	1.8			5		1.80	0.03	1.50	6.50	78.00
CLEAN URINALS	6	1.8			5		1.80	0.03	0.90	3.90	46.80
CLEAN SINKS	10	1.8			5		1.80	0.03	1.50	6.50	78.00
CLEAN MIRRORS	10	1.8			5		1.80	0.03	1.50	6.50	78.00
MOP BATHROOM FLOOR	1250			0.00025	5		18.75	0.31	1.56	6.77	81.25
REPLACE TISSUE PAPER	10	0.9			5		0.90	0.02	0.75	3.25	39.00
REPLACE SANITARY NAPKINS	2	0.9			5		0.90	0.02	0.15	0.65	7.80
REPLACE PAPER TOWELS	5	0.9			5		0.90	0.02	0.38	1.62	19.50
REPLACE AIR FRESHENER	10	0.9			5		0.90	0.02	0.75	3.25	39.00
REPLACE SOAP DISPENSER	10	0.9			5		0.90	0.02	0.75	3.25	39.00
REPLACE/ CLEAN (OTHER)											
REPLACE LIGHTING											
CLEAN STOVE											
CLEAN MICROWAVE											
CLEAN OVEN											
CLEAN REFRIGERATOR											
CLEAN COUNTER TOPS											
CLEAN CUPBOARD DOORS											
CLEAN (OTHER)											

Annualized monthly value e.g., (1.50 * 52)/ 12 = 6.50, not (1.50 * 4) = 6.00

0.00025 hr/ sq. ft., I.e., 1/ 4000 sq. ft./ hr = 0.00025hr/ sq. ft.

RELEVANT TO BEGINNING AND EXPERIENCED CONTRACTORS ALIKE

Prepare concise bid estimates using all of the essential cost factors needed to determine realistic and competitive rates!

Zenith Cleaning services
3300 3rd st
Any Town, USA
phone: xxx-xxxx; fax: xxx-xxxx
e-mail: email@zenclean.com

ACCOUNT: Acme Co.
CONTACT: ______
ADDRESS: ______
PHONE: ______
E-MAIL/ FAX: ______

Date: 01-Jan-01

CLEANING SERVICES BID SUMMARY WORKSHEET

Cleaning services	Total sq. ft.	Frequency	Total labor (hrs)	Labor rate ($/ hr)	Direct labor cost	Direct material costs	Account overhead costs	Total account costs	Profit margin	Bid price (per job)	Bid price (monthly)	Price (per sq. ft./ month)	Price (per sq. ft. / year)
Basic services													
general office cleaning: (monthly basis)	7,200	20/ mo	57.60	9.00	518	50	131	699	121	820	820	0.11	1.37
* all offices	4,500	12/ mo	21.60	9.00	194	30	55	279	49	328	328	0.07	0.88
* all restrooms													
* breakroom													
* warehouse													
* all hallways													
* receptionist area													
Special services													
Hard floor care:													
* Strip & wax (quarterly)	1,500	qrtly	17.00	22.10	376	75	59	510	90	600	200	0.13	1.60
* spray wax & buff (as needed)													
Non-routine cleaning maintenance				14.00									

Terms & conditions	
* Billing	1st of the month
* Payment	5th of the month, 10 day grace period, $25 processing fee following grace period
* Insurance/ bonding	Standard for all employees onsite, proof of ID at all times
* Quote period	Quote good for 30 days from the above date

After you have read
Cleaning Services Bid Estimation,
see the last page for information on ordering other Cleaning Services titles offered by THE KNOUEN GROUP,

such as the companion software for **Cleaning Services Bid Estimation:**

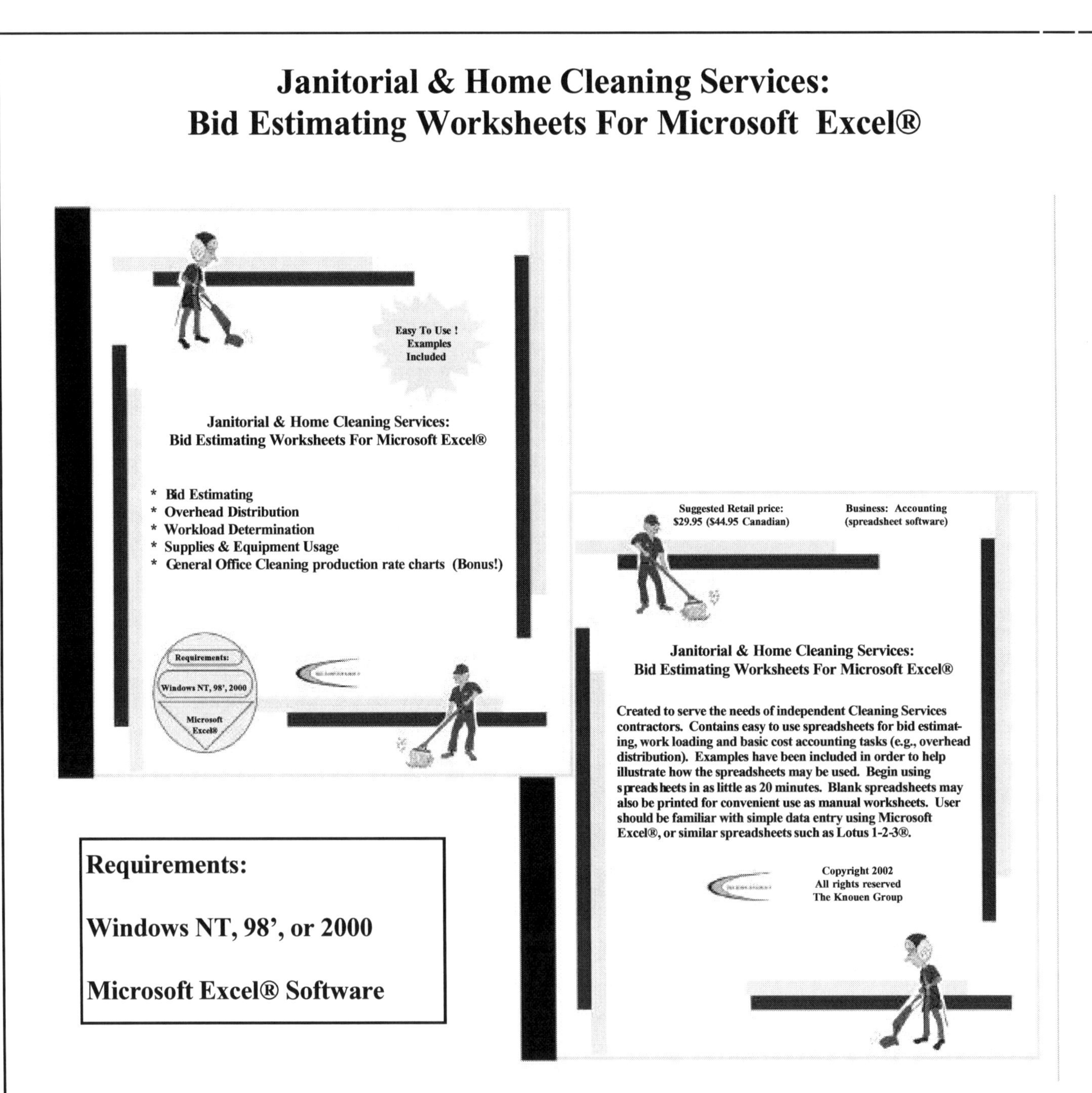

Determine a fair and competitive price for your services, fast and accurately !

CLEANING SERVICES BID ESTIMATION

A Resource Guide To Cleaning Services Bid Estimation, Work Loading And Cost Accounting:

(Charts, Tables And Worksheets For Cleaning Times, Production Rates, Price Per Square Foot, Work Loading, Cost Accounting And Pricing/ Bid Estimation, With Examples, Formulas And Explanations)

First Edition

THE KNOUEN GROUP

Atlanta

Library of Congress Control Number: 2002109211

TABLE OF CONTENTS

Chapter 1

Introduction

This resource guide provides convenient charts and tables to assist the cleaning services novice, as well as experienced professionals in determining:

- ***cleaning times and production rates for various basic cleaning tasks*** *(i.e., per units cleaned, or time per square foot);*

- ***cleaning services rates or pricing*** *(i.e., total price by the job, per month, or total annual price, based on price per square foot and total cleaning square footage);*

- ***cleaning services workload estimates*** *(i.e., total cleaning times and cleaning personnel requirements, for groups of cleaning tasks, based on cleaning frequency, total units cleaned or cleanable surface area and cleaning times or production rates).*

The guide also provides convenient charts for determining **cleaning solution usage** and **cleaning supplies cost estimation**, based on the volume of cleaning solution or generic cost per square foot and the total cleanable surface area involved.

Instructions for the uses of the charts and tables in this guide, as well as forms for preparing bid estimates and work loading estimates are also provided. Sample determinations and calculations are provided to further illustrate the guide's potential uses.

Worksheet forms for overhead costing, total costing, work loading, supply costing and bid estimation, are provided in this guide. Worksheet templates and several worksheet examples along with sample calculations are presented in chapter nine.

While charts and tables providing estimates for cleaning times and production rates for various cleaning tasks, are provided in this guide as a reference or starting point, to preparing bid and work load estimates, the reader is cautioned that actual cleaning times and production rates will vary significantly, with one or more of a variety of factors, including but not limited to:

- ***the relative level of dirt or soiling that occurs between cleanings;***

- ***customer traffic or employee loading or density;***

- ***the types of cleaning surfaces*** *(e.g., carpet type, hard floor type, window type, etc.;*

- ***the size and shape of glass or window fixtures, bathroom fixtures, light fixtures, furniture or appointments being cleaned or serviced;***

- ***the type and size of bulk household supply packages or containers and their ease of handling, as well as the type of household supply dispensers or receptacle and the reloading mechanisms involved*** *(e.g., tissue, paper towels, sanitary napkins, soap, etc.);*

- ***the specific type and suitability of cleaning equipment used, as well as the operator's training and skill level*** *(e.g., cleaning surface diameter or length, rotor speed, cordless or self contained features, self propelled vs manual, cleaning solution or waste solution reservoir capacity etc.,);*

- ***the suitability and effectiveness of the cleaning solutions used, as well as the techniques and tools used for their application*** *(e.g.,* *the use of an effective glass cleaner and a squeegee vs the use of a cloth and soap and water for window cleaning, etc.,);*

- ***the effective and efficient staging and transportation of cleaning equipment and supplies from one cleaning area to the next;***

- ***accessibility to the work surface** (e.g., wide open floor or window surface areas vs areas "broken-up" or separated by partitions, furniture or other obstacles; working in close quarters; the need for interior and exterior height extensions, such as ladders, lifts, scaffolds; access to electrical outlets, etc.,);*

- ***the training, skill, motivation, morale and workload of the workers performing the tasks;***

- ***the effective use of modern team cleaning concepts and efficiencies achieved through thoughtful repetition of each cleaning task, over time;***

- ***the customer's cleaning specifications** (the level of quality required).*

Therefore, the generic charts for production rates in this guide have been designed to assist a cleaning services business, in pinpointing and refining estimates for production rates for any individual cleaning task, or group of tasks, such as "general office cleaning", that can be measured in terms of a production rate (i.e., total time per square foot). Once cleaning tasks have actually been performed, one or more times in the service of clients, or carefully simulated using the actual equipment, tools and supplies that are employed by your business, it is a simple step to establish a realistic production rate for any single task, or group of tasks.

By recording the total square footage of a cleaning surface area ("x") along with the actual, or carefully simulated cleaning time for a given cleaning task or group of tasks ("y") and then using them as a set of (x, y) coordinates, you can quickly find a close match in the generic production rate charts in this guide, for a production rate that can then be used for estimating "at a glance", the time it takes to perform a cleaning task or group of tasks, for any cleanable surface area (i.e., total square footage), with a <u>comparable</u> level of difficulty, going forward.

The generic charts for the cleaning solution usage and material and supply cost estimating, have been prepared for use, in a similar vein.

For example, if you are planning to:

- ***use bulk cleaning chemicals in 5, 10 or 55 gallon drums, based on a manufacturer's recommended usage rate in gallons or quarts per square foot***; or

- ***prepare bulk solutions from concentrates in optimized proportions*** (e.g., adjusted from the manufacturer's recommended ratios, with the intent of improving either economy or effectiveness),

the generic cleaning solution charts can be used to determine the total volume in gallons of a specific chemical or solution needed ("y"), for any cleanable surface area ("x"), that may be encountered in current or prospective cleaning accounts. Once you have a "working" estimate for the usage of a cleaning chemical, you can use the charts in this guide to determine usage for virtually any cleaning surface area.

Similarly, you can calculate the cost of cleaning supplies (i.e., where usage or cost can be expressed as an amount per square foot), for any total cleanable surface area, from the charts provided, in the same manner. For example, once you have recorded typical data for cleaning supply costs for general office or bathroom cleaning areas, for representative numbers of clients or prospective clients, it's a simple task to find a realistic or working estimates for the cost per square foot, for an individual cleaning supply item or groups of items.

Using the generic cleaning supplies cost estimation charts in this guide, you can pinpoint estimates for the cost of cleaning supplies per square foot, that you can use to estimate the total cost of an item or groups of cleaning supplies, for various types of cleaning areas (e.g., bathroom, general office, classroom, or restaurant floor areas, etc.,) or costs for total cleanable area or square footage for various business types (e.g., restaurants, small offices, large offices, warehouses and manufacturing facilities, schools, churches, etc.,), that you have established over time.

These same charts can be used in a similar manner, for estimating the cost of disposable housekeeping supplies, such as paper products, soap and trash liners for typical cleaning areas or types of businesses. In this case the number of employees per square foot and their gender should be taken into consideration (e.g., it is commonly noted by cleaning service professionals, that women will use bathroom paper products at a significantly higher rate than men on average), when formulating categories of housekeeping cost estimates for cleaning areas or business types (e.g., customer traffic patterns, etc.,). A "working" estimate for the cost and usage of housekeeping items, derived from data compiled in the service of clients, can then be used to determine housekeeping supply costs for any total cleaning surface area, for various types of cleaning area and businesses. Such estimates are particularly helpful in preparing bid rates or prices and in tracking or projecting the total costs of housekeeping supplies for current and prospective accounts.

The bid pricing charts in this guide (i.e., price per job, month, or per year ("y") vs the total cleanable surface area, in square feet ("x")), were prepared, to provide cleaning services professionals a convenient reference with which to quickly determine bid prices or rates, or fixed price structures for prospective accounts. For example, the bid pricing tables can be used during telephone and onsite consultations, to assist cleaning services contractors, in providing verbal quotes based on cleaning specification information and cleanable surface area data, provided by a prospective customer, or to translate total monthly rates or price structures into an monthly or annual price per square foot price or rate and visa versa, as requested by a client, etc.,.

First, it is necessary to establish working estimates for a price or rate for various cleaning surface areas, such as open carpeted areas, or office cubicle areas with carpet, or types of businesses such as fast food restaurants with hard floors, or branch banks with carpeting, etc., that are derived in the service of clients, or through market research (e.g., through NOA's (contract bid, notice of award's), published by federal, state and local governments, customer surveys, etc.,). Then the bid estimation charts in this guide can be used to pinpoint a total one time price, or a monthly or annual cleaning services rate, for any size facility or cleanable surface area, of comparable difficulty. Some general pricing guidance for various cleaning tasks or services are provided as a reference, or starting point for the reader.

The forms provided in this guide for use in bid and work loading estimation tasks, may be used as worksheets during an onsite consultation, in the preparation of a formal bid proposal, or to assist a business in projecting revenues, material costs and labor needs for any given project.

Chapter 2

How to use this resource guide

Clear examples with explanations and illustrations are provided for each set of charts and tables provided in this guide. Examples, with explanations and illustrations are also provided for the worksheet forms included in this guide.

Typical production rates and cleaning times for various cleaning tasks

If you haven't read the section in the introduction regarding the typical production rates and cleaning times, you should do so before using the charts and tables in chapter 3, or the generic charts provided in chapter 6, in order to familiarize yourself with the various factors that can affect production rates and cleaning times. Understanding and taking into account these factors, can assist you greatly in establishing initial estimates and then in optimizing or improving average production rates and cleaning times used in your business planning.

Using any published tables or charts for typical production rates, or cleaning times "blindly", without revisiting and refining working estimates, based on actual experience or data, derived in the service of clients, as well as accurate market research, may affect your ability provide competitive bids or fixed price structures, or conversely to turn a profit consistently. Developing the experience and judgment to group cleaning projects, or account types of similar difficulty into categories (mentally, or formally on paper, or in electronic files) and then matching them with working estimates of production rates or cleaning times, is a skill in and of itself. By working methodically with the data that you acquire with experience and using the appropriate charts and tables in this guide, you can greatly improve your skills in this area, as well as achieve greater overall accuracy in general business planning, that is critical to the success of any cleaning services business.

To illustrate the use of a production rate or cleaning time chart, 2 examples are provided here. To estimate the time to vacuum 2,300 sq. ft. of carpet with a vacuum cleaner that has a 12" cleaning surface, simply put a ruler or straight edge across the chart as shown and find the closest estimate for total cleaning time:

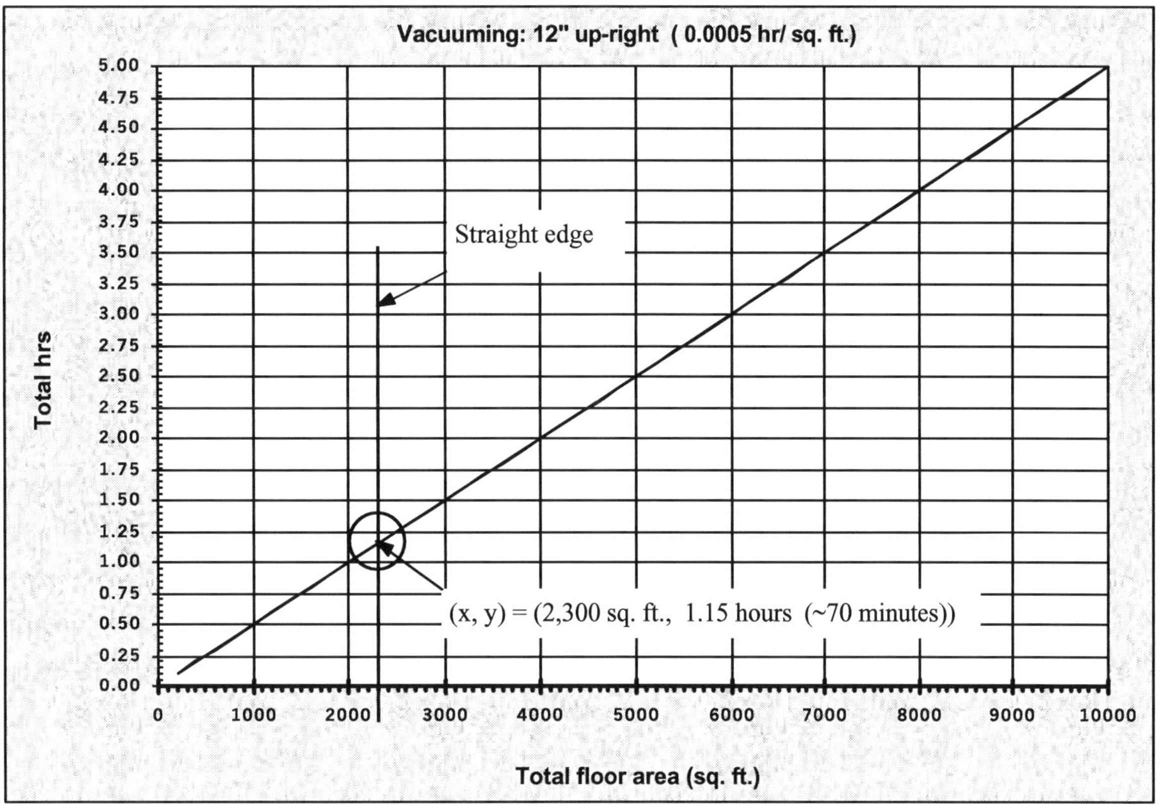

In many instances, such a visual estimate provides adequate accuracy. An exact value for the total vacuuming time, can be obtained by multiplying the production rate provided in the chart title in (hrs/ sq. ft.), by the total square footage of the cleaning surface that is to be cleaned (e.g., 0.0005 hr/ sq. ft. x 2,300 sq. ft.= 1.15 hrs). For cleanable surface areas from 10,000-100,000 sq. ft., simply find the cleaning time for a 1/10th of the cleaning area in question, and multiply the result by 10 (e.g., for 23,000 sq. ft., multiply the cleaning time for 2,300 sq. ft., by 10, or 10 x 1.15 hrs= 11.5 hrs). The companion charts for determining total cleaning time, in minutes, work in the same manner as the charts that are expressed in hours.

The second example illustrated, is the use of a typical cleaning time chart for cleaning a total number of units (e.g., in a large building with multiple bathroom fixtures) is shown below. To estimate the time to clean 60 toilets or commodes (excluding travel times between bathrooms), follow the same procedure used in the vacuum production rate example:

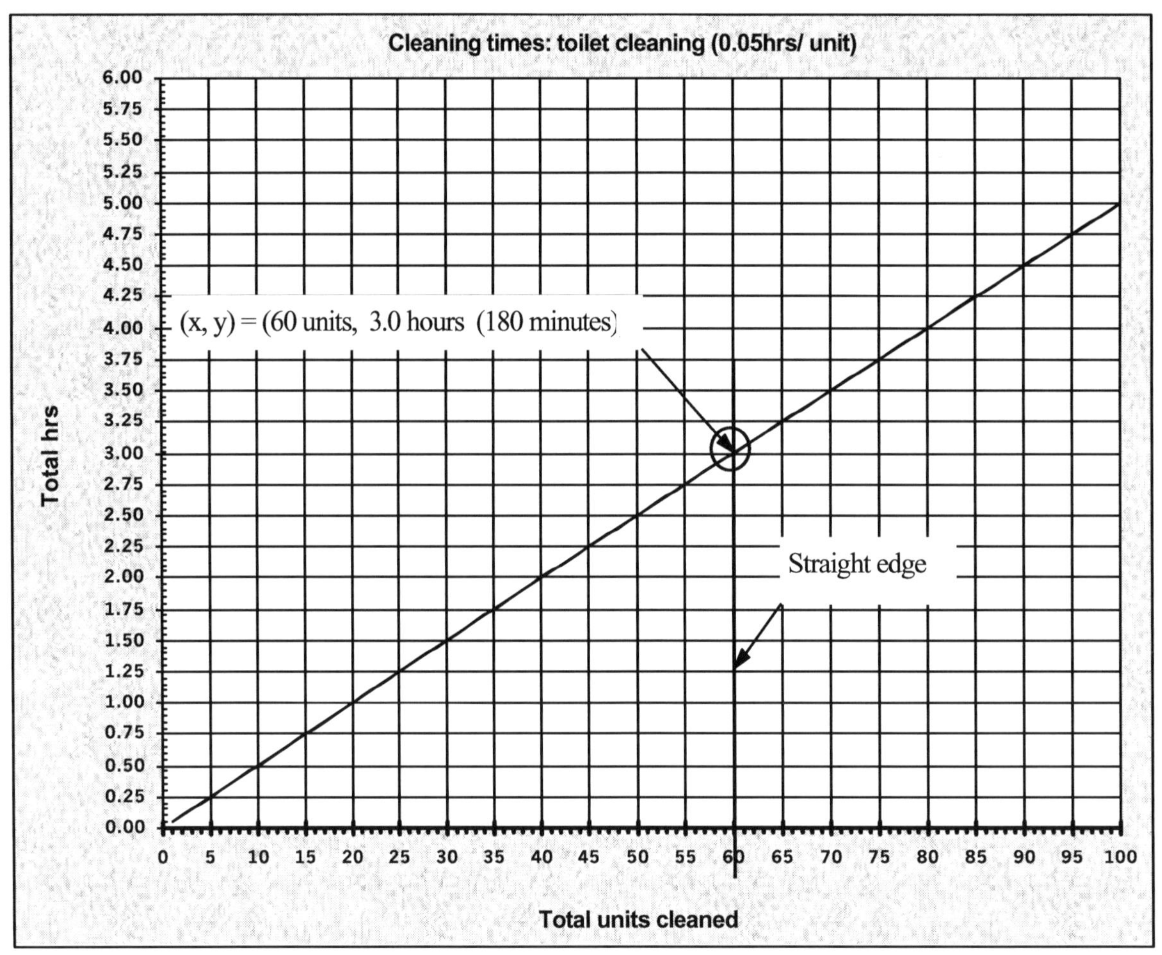

The calculation of an estimate of the cleaning time for a given number of units (e.g., 60 units x 0.05 hrs/ unit = 3.0 hrs), and to the estimation of cleaning times for numbers of units greater than 100, i.e., 100-1,000 units (e.g., for 600 units, find the cleaning time for 60 units and multiply by 10, or 3.0 hrs x 10 = 30 hrs), are determined in the same manner as in the "vacuum" example. Companion charts expressed in minutes, work in the same manner as those expressed in hours.

Some published tables or charts for typical production rates and cleaning times for various tasks, may express production rates differently, then the rates shown in the titles of each of the charts for typical production rates and cleaning times in this guide. For example, many production rates will be expressed in hours or minutes per 1000 sq. ft., . To illustrate, let's take the vacuuming production rate example shown previously.

The rate shown in the title is (0.0005 hrs/ sq. ft.). Other tables might express the production rate as (2000 sq. ft./ hr). This is the inverse of the value expressed as time/ sq. ft. and visa versa, that is, 1/ 2000 sq. ft./ hr = 0.0005 hrs/ sq. ft. and 1/ 0.0005 hrs/ sq. ft. = 2000 sq. ft./ hr,.

It is generally more intuitive to want to multiply by a rate, than to divide by a rate, in order to obtain a result, for that reason, the rates in this section are written, so that all you have to do is to multiply the area or number of units cleaned by the rate provided in the chart title. In the section of this guide containing generic production rates, both ways of expressing production rates (i.e., time/ sq. ft. and sq. ft./ time) are provided in the chart title.

Cleaning times or rates, for cleaning fixtures, such as sinks or commodes, are often expressed as the number of minutes to clean each unit, this guide provides rates expressed in both hours and minutes per unit cleaned. The rates expressed in hours, are especially useful in avoiding an extra conversion from minutes to hours, when calculating the total cleaning time for groups of tasks in a column, where some tasks take less than an hour and some greater than one hour.

Cleaning solution usage

The charts in this section, are useful for determining the amount a chemical or cleaning solution to use for a given cleanable surface area, once a "working" estimate for usage has been established. The charts are expressed in terms of gallons/ sq. ft.,. The range of charts is from 1/30th of a gallon/ 1000 sq. ft. - 1 gallon/ 1000 sq. ft. and a range from 1 gallon/1500 sq. ft. - 1 gallon/ 10,000 sq. ft., in 500 and 2500 sq. ft. increments.

The charts may be used for neat cleaning chemicals (i.e., chemicals used in the undiluted form) and for cleaning solutions made from concentrates. In the latter case, two estimates can be made using the charts, one for usage of the concentrate (i.e., liquid concentrates only) and one for the usage of the corresponding diluted cleaning solution. The charts are also useful for pinpointing total usage (total gallons or quarts) and usage rates (gallons or quarts per area), in cases where the ratio of a cleaning solution concentrate has been adjusted from the manufacturer's recommended ratio, or proportions, in the interest of cost savings or cleaning effectiveness.

Some examples should illustrate a couple of the potential uses for these charts. For example, a gallon of a typical floor finish, as recommended by the manufacturer, provides coverage of 1500 - 2500 sq. ft. (this is typical, but will vary depending on application technique and finish formulation parameters such as % solids, etc.,). To estimate the number of gallons of floor finish that is needed for a single coat over 4, 800 sq. ft. of flooring, at each end of the manufacturer's recommended coverage range, find the appropriate charts and estimate the total usage for the floor finish, in the same manner presented in previous examples, illustrating other applications (e.g., production rate charts).

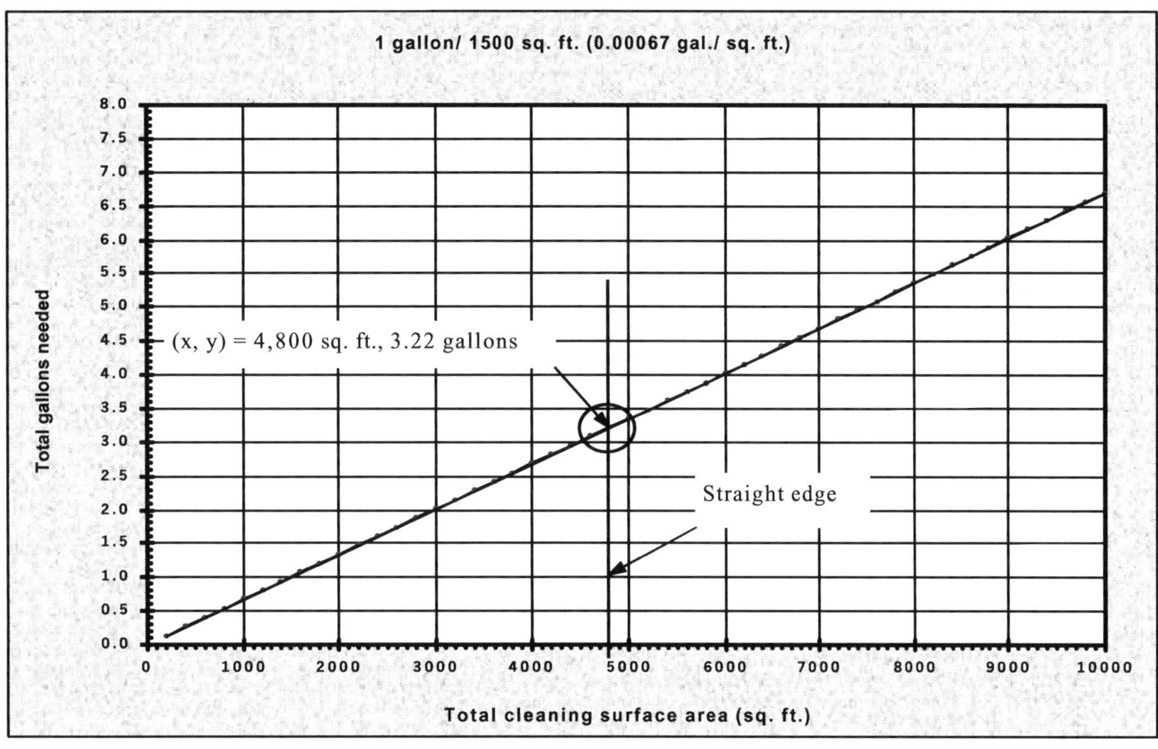

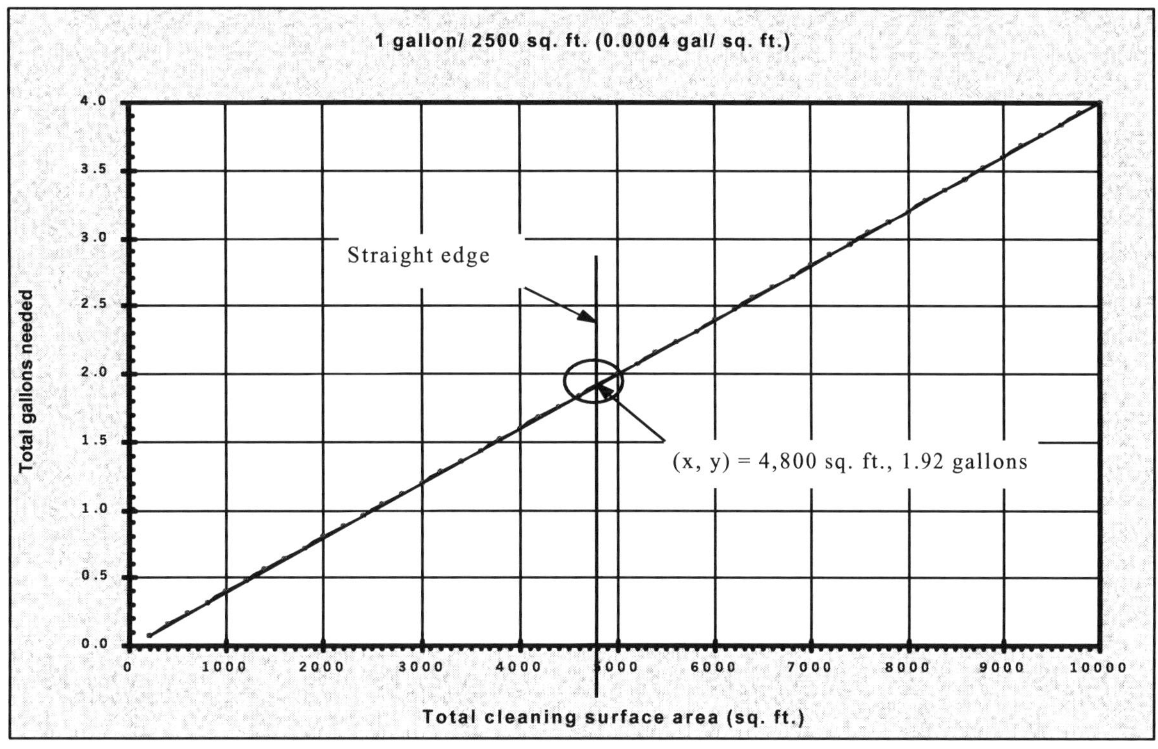

As shown in the illustration, the usage of the floor finish at the high end of the manufacturer's recommended usage for 4,800 sq. ft. of flooring is: (4,800 sq. ft. x 0.00067 gal/ sq. ft.= 3.22 gal). Note that 0.00067 gal/ sq. ft.= 1 gal/ 2,500 sq. ft.,. Similarly, the usage of the floor finish at the low end of the manufacturer's recommendation is (4,800 sq. ft. x 0.0004 gal/ sq. ft.= 1.92 gal).

For cleaning surface areas from 10,000 – 100,000 sq. ft., find the usage for 1/10th of the cleaning area and multiply by 10. For example, the usage for 48,000 sq. ft. at the low and high end of the manufacturer's range would be (1.92 gal x 10= 19.2 and 3.22 gal x 10= 32.2 gal).

In our second example, a floor care services contractor finds that after stripping and waxing a floor surface area of 4,800 sq. ft., at one his accounts several times, the average usage of the floor finish is ~2.5 gallons. He notes further, that the floor finish holds up well to the fairly heavy traffic that is experienced at this client's facility. He decides that the usage of floor finish for this account is representative of most of the most applications he might encounter in the future.

He can find an estimate for the "typical" rate of usage of this floor finish quickly, by finding the cleaning chemicals usage chart which has the <u>closest</u> total usage for 4,800 sq. ft.,. Using a straight edge, he find that the 1 gal/ 2000 sq. ft. or 0.0005 gal/ sq. ft., chart has the closest match of (x, y) = (4,800, 2.4 gal). Going forward, he can quickly find an estimate for the total usage of the floor finish, for <u>any</u> size cleaning area, using that chart.

Another potential use for these charts, might be to estimate the total usage of a cleaning chemical concentrate and the diluted cleaning solution, in which the cleaning chemical concentration has been <u>modified</u> from the manufacturer's <u>recommended</u> mixture or ratio, in order to increase the effectiveness or potency of the cleaning solution, or to reduce costs, without sacrificing the quality of the cleaning service.

For example, an experienced janitorial service supervisor finds that the cleaning maintenance frequency at most of his company's clients, is sufficient to warrant trying a less concentrated wet mopping solution for general office cleaning, in order to reduce cleaning supply costs. The manufacturer recommends that 1 part in 20 to 1 part in 15 (e.g., 1/ 20th or 1/ 15th of a gallon to 1 gallon of water) of its multi-purpose degreaser be used for floor cleaning applications. The manufacturer's literature indicates usage at ~ 1000 sq. ft., of floor per gallon of cleaning solution (i.e., concentrate + water).

The supervisor tries reducing the concentration of the degreaser, on a trial basis in a single facility, with a total hard floor area of 3,300 sq. ft., in order to test the effectiveness of the diluted cleaning solutions. At first, the cleaning solution is reduced in concentration from 1 part in 15 for the degreaser, to 1 part in 20 and then to 1 part in 25. The most dilute solution was shown to be effective, given the aggressive cleaning schedule employed at this account. The supervisor obtains approval to prepare concentrates for all facilities having a comparable cleaning maintenance schedule to the trial facility. The reduction in the amount of degreaser being used represents a savings of ~ 40%.

The usage of the degreaser at the test facility, for a 1 part in 25 concentration (1/25th of a gallon per 1000 sq. ft.) and 1 part in 15 concentration, is illustrated here, to show the ease with which changes in usage for cleaning chemicals can be determined for any size cleaning area. If the cleaning technicians use the same volume of cleaning solution, regardless of the concentration of the degreaser, the usage will be 1 gallon per thousand sq. ft.,. Therefore in the above example, 3.3 gallons of the final diluted cleaning solution will be used for 3,300 sq. ft.,.

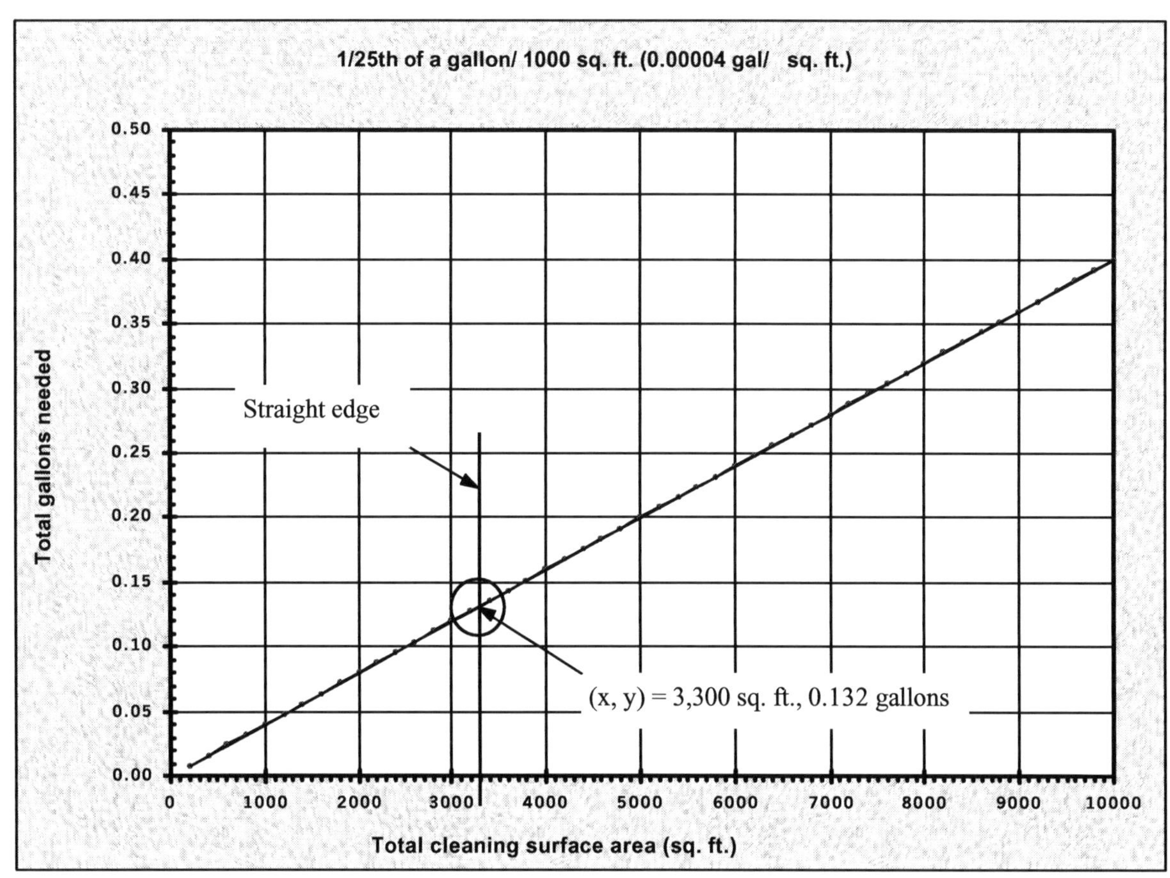
1/25th of a gallon/ 1000 sq. ft. (0.00004 gal/ sq. ft.)
Total gallons needed
0.50
0.45
0.40
0.35
0.30
0.25
0.20
0.15
0.10
0.05
0.00
Straight edge
(x, y) = 3,300 sq. ft., 0.132 gallons
0
1000
2000
3000
4000
5000
6000
7000
8000
9000
10000
Total cleaning surface area (sq. ft.)

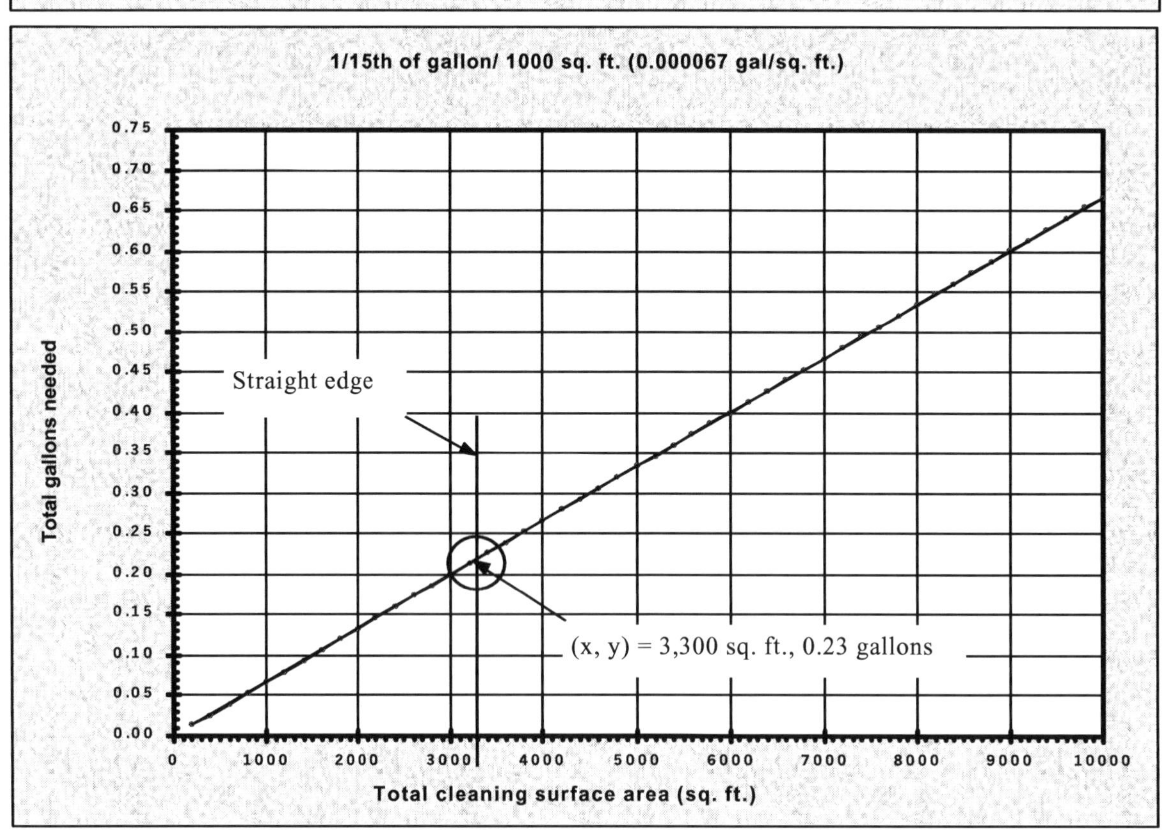
1/15th of gallon/ 1000 sq. ft. (0.000067 gal/sq. ft.)
Total gallons needed
0.75
0.70
0.65
0.60
0.55
0.50
0.45
0.40
0.35
0.30
0.25
0.20
0.15
0.10
0.05
0.00
Straight edge
(x, y) = 3,300 sq. ft., 0.23 gallons
0
1000
2000
3000
4000
5000
6000
7000
8000
9000
10000
Total cleaning surface area (sq. ft.)

To find the total usage, or usage rates, for cleaning areas from 10,000-100,000, as with previous examples, find the values 1/10th the area and multiply by ten (e.g., for 33,000 sq. ft., the total usage for the cleaning solution is 3.3 gal x 10= 33 gal, and the degreaser concentrate usage at 1 part in 25 would be 0.132 x 10= 1.32 gal).

Because the cleaning solution usage charts represent usage expressed as simple ratios (i.e., fractions of a gallon), they may be used with virtually any units of volume. For example, if a cleaning concentrate's instructions are expressed in units of liters instead of gallons, the same charts can be used, by treating the usage units as liters instead of gallons.

If the cleaner is to be diluted 1 to 15 for instance, and the diluted cleaning solution has a coverage or unit usage of 1 liter per 1,000 sq. ft., then the total usage for 3,300 sq. ft. would be 0.23 liters. This is true because the charts are based on ratios of volumes used per 1000 sq. ft.,. The same would be true if the units were expressed in quarts.

A conversion between units is different however. The above example will illustrate the point. For 3,300 sq, ft., the usage of the concentrate, at 1 part in 15, at 1 gallon per 1,000 sq. ft., is 0.23 gal and the total gallons of diluted degreaser is 3.3 gallons. In liters, these volumes are (0.23 gal x 3.79 l/ gal= 0.87 l and 3.3 gal x 3.79 l/ gal= 12.5 l).

If the unit usage area is different than 1,000 sq. ft., it is necessary to make a conversion to use these charts. The above example will illustrate the point. Let's suppose that the recommended unit usage for the diluted degreaser cleaning solution is 1 gallon per 2,000 sq. ft. or 1 gallon per 500 sq. ft., for a degreaser that should be diluted 1 to 15, (i.e., 1/15th gal to 1 gal). The easiest way to make the conversion, is to find the value for total usage of the concentrate and the diluted cleaning solution using the charts, as if the unit usage area is 1,000 sq. ft., and then multiply or divide by the appropriate factor.

For example, for a cleaning area of 3,300 sq. ft., using the charts the total usage of the concentrate is 0.23 gal and 3.3 gal for the diluted cleaning solution (at a unit usage area of 1,000 sq. ft.). If the actual unit usage, recommended by the manufacturer is 2,000 sq. ft., then multiply the total usage as determined from the charts, by the fraction of unit usage area (e.g., 0.23 gal x 1,000/ 2,000 = 0.12 gal and 3.3 gal x 1,000/ 2,000 = 1.65 gal). The same conversion applies for an actual unit usage of 500 sq. ft. (i.e., 1/15th gal per 500 sq. ft.). That is (0.23 gal x 1,000/ 500 = 0.46 gal and 3.3 gal x 1,000/ 500 = 6.6 gal).

Cleaning supplies cost estimation

The charts in chapter 5, can be used for estimating the cost of cleaning supplies or housekeeping materials which can be expressed in terms of dollars/ sq. ft.,. Once a unit cost rate has been determined, the total cost for supplies for any size cleaning area can be quickly found. If the unit cost of supplies should rise (or drops), it is a simple task to refigure your total costs using the charts.

An example will illustrate one of the potential uses of these charts. A floor finish cost $15/ gal and has an approximate unit usage of 2,000 sq. ft. per gallon, (e.g., the midrange of 1,500 - 2,500 sq. ft.). The unit cost rate is simply $15/ 2,000 sq. ft. = $0.0075/ sq. ft., or ~$0.008/ sq. ft.,. Looking at the charts for cleaning supplies cost estimation, the closest match is $0.008/ sq. ft.,. The total cost for finishing 3,300 sq. ft. is $26.40 or ~ $26 as shown in the illustration. For cleaning surface areas from 10,000 - 100,000 sq. ft., calculations are similar to previous applications, presented (i.e., for 33,000 sq. ft., find the cost for 3,300 sq. ft. and multiply by 10, or $26.40 x 10 = $264).

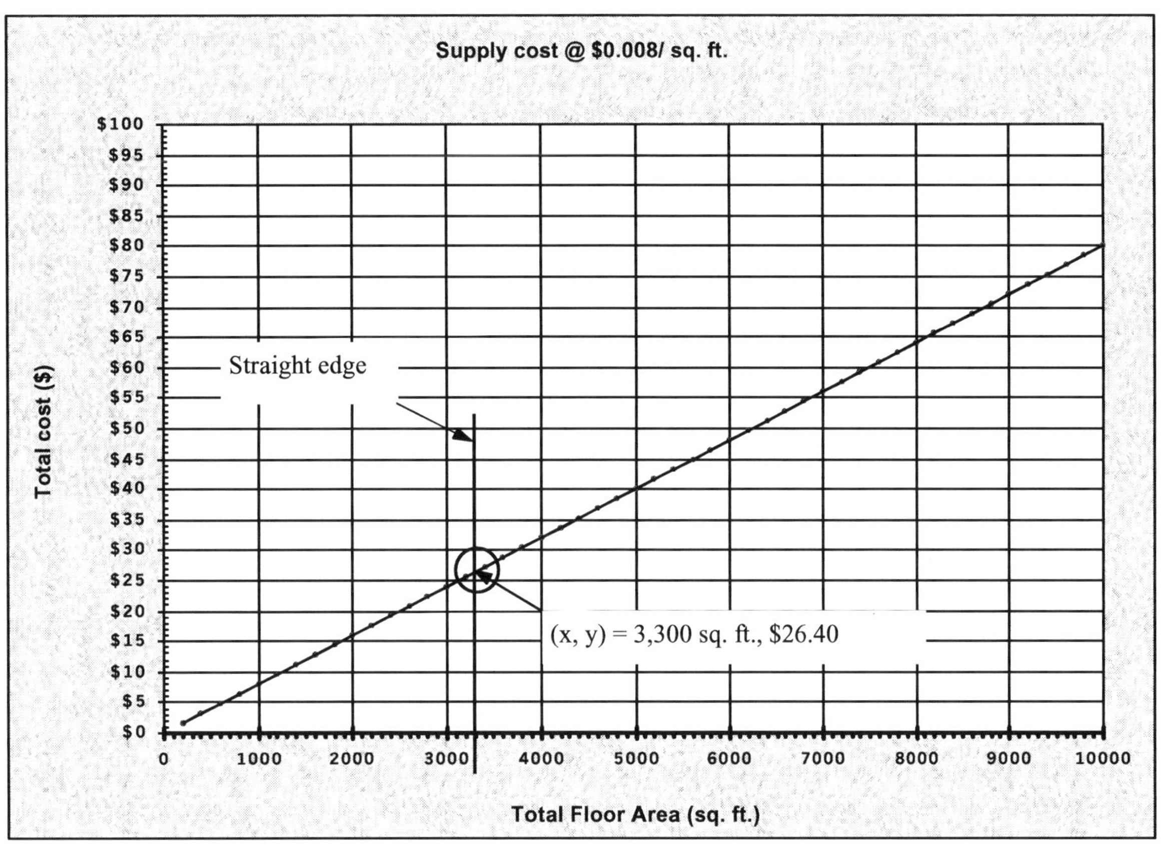

Generic production rate charts

The generic production rate charts in this guide range from 100 sq. ft./ hr (0.01 hr/ sq. ft.) to 25,000 sq. ft./ hr (0.00004 hr/ sq. ft.). Some typical production rate charts for various cleaning tasks, are found in chapter 2, as a reference or starting point. As mentioned in the introduction, estimates for production rates can be derived from published charts and tables, or from data collected in the service of clients, or by careful simulation of each cleaning task.

A table of typical ranges of production rates for some cleaning tasks is found in the table below. In many instances, efficiencies, can be improved greatly through thoughtful repetition, the use of team based cleaning concepts and state of the art equipment, as well as through proper staging and preparation.

Cleaning services production rate ranges*

Cleaning task	Production rate range
Carpet cleaning	**500-1,500 sq. ft./ hr** (varies with process, equipment and carpet type)
Hard floor care Tasks	**275-1,500 sq. ft./ hr** (low speed floor machines, varies with type of task)
Burnishing	**10,000-25,000 sq. ft./ hr** (varies with equipment)
General office cleaning	**2,500-7,000 sq. ft./ hr** (upper range based on use of team cleaning concepts)
School classroom cleaning	**1,000-2,000 sq. ft./ hr**
Individual manual Cleaning tasks	**500-12,000 sq. ft./ hr** (dust mopping, window washing, vacuuming etc.,)

*** note: see the introduction for the various factors affecting production rates**

To use these charts, based on data derived in the service of clients or from careful simulation of cleaning tasks, match the (x, y) coordinates for the total cleaning area and total cleaning time, to the chart with the closet matching production rate (note: the rate may also be calculated directly by dividing y/x (i.e., y hrs ÷ x sq. ft.). From there, you can determine an estimate for the total cleaning time for <u>any</u> task, going forward, based on the working estimate for the production rate and the cleaning surface area in question, using the appropriate chart. This of course, assumes that a comparable level of difficulty is involved for the new cleaning area in question.

For example, a person starting a solo janitorial cleaning services business is trying his hand at various specialty cleaning tasks and decides to incorporate carpet extraction into the services he provides. He finds that for his first carpet care account, which has 4,500 sq. ft. of carpet, it takes him on average 3.75 hrs to clean the carpet.

Looking through the production rate charts, he quickly finds that the closest match for a chart with these coordinates, is the 1,200 sq. ft./ hr production rate chart. Alternatively, he could have calculated the rate directly from the data. He obtains an offer to bid on another account which has 3,700 sq. ft. of carpeting and wants to know what the total cleaning time is, in order to establish labor costs for his bid proposal. As shown in the illustration, he refers to the 1,200 sq. ft./ hr chart and finds a corresponding estimate for cleaning 3,700 sq. ft. of carpet and finds that it will take 3.2 hrs.

As with previous examples, to find the total cleaning time for cleaning areas from 10,000-100,000 sq. ft., find the result for 1/10th the area and multiply by 10 (i.e., for 37,000 sq. ft., 3.2 hrs x 10= 32 hrs). Note that production rates for carpet extraction will vary greatly, depending on the type of equipment and the type of carpet involved, as well as the amount of soiling in the carpet.

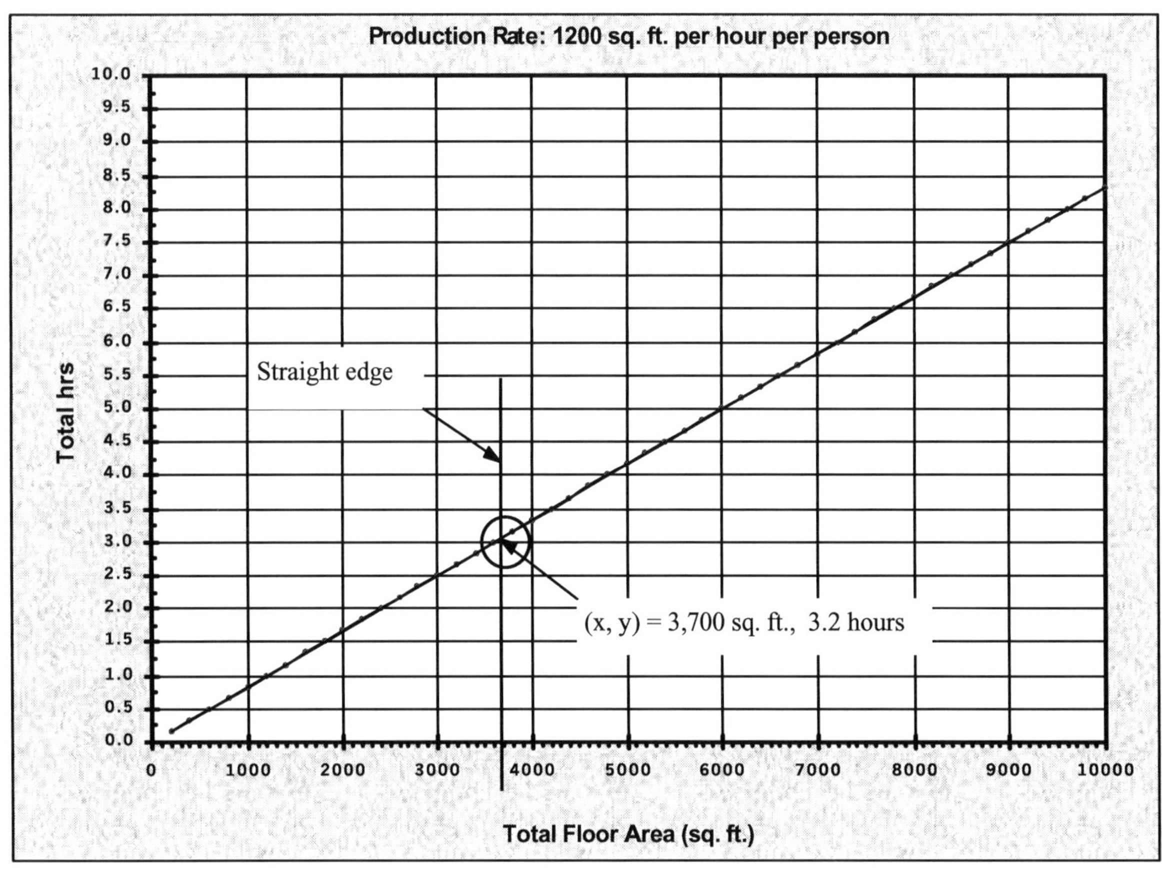

Generic bid pricing charts

The generic bid pricing charts found in chapters 7 and 8, were designed to encompass pricing for a wide range of individual cleaning services or tasks, as well as pricing for comprehensive cleaning services, based on norms in major cleaning services industry sectors and established cleaning services niches. The charts in chapter 7 range from $0.05/ sq. ft.- $0.50/ sq. ft., and are best used to determine estimates for pricing, by the job and by the month. The charts in chapter 8 range from $0.84/ sq. ft.- $6.00/ sq. ft. and are intended for use in determining estimates for annual pricing per sq. ft.,.

One of the most common questions that beginning cleaning services professionals ask industry experts, is "What prices should we charge or bid on prospective jobs or accounts?". There is no single answer.

Cleaning services rates will vary widely with one or more factors, such as the type and frequency of the cleaning services involved, the cost of labor and supplies in the region or market where you provide your services, the type and size of the business or establishment involved, facility personnel density, the level of difficulty or labor intensity involved, as well as the relative level of competition with other businesses that provide the same services as your business. Striking a balance, between what the market will bear for your services at any given time and maintaining competitive pricing to attract business on a consistent basis, is a challenge that most every business faces.

A table is shown here, to provide some reference or guidance for the beginning cleaning services professional. Generally, at the lower end of a pricing range, the more competitive the market is for that particular type of service. Conversely, towards the higher end of each price range, the services offered or required, are more likely to be more costly to provide, difficult in scope, or more labor intensive. A less competitive market environment may also contribute to higher pricing. To ensure that your bid proposals or pricing structures are competitive, it will be necessary to carefully research the markets your company provides services in.

For example, researching your competitor's advertisements and government NOAs (i.e., cleaning services contract notice of award), "cold calling" a few competitors and several potential customers, polling industry professionals (e.g., at local or regional cleaning services supply vendors, cleaning services industry associations and websites, etc.,), can provide your business with invaluable pricing information, that can guide you in preparing bid proposals and setting pricing structures for various services.

Once you have an idea of what the competition is charging for cleaning services, in the markets that you wish to compete in, then it necessary to calculate the cost of providing your services and to determine what your profit margins should be, in order to remain competitive and to grow your business effectively.

Pricing ranges for various cleaning services*

General office cleaning	**monthly:**	**$0.07/ sq. ft. - $0.45/sq. ft.**
Carpet cleaning	**per job:**	**$0.07/ sq. ft. - $0.16/ sq. ft.**
Hard floor care	**per job:**	**$0.12/ sq. ft. - $0.50/ sq. ft.**
Pressure washing	**per job:**	**$0.03/ sq. ft. - $0.05/ sq. ft.**
Window washing	**per job:**	**$0.06/ sq. ft. - $0.42/ sq. ft.**

*** pricing will vary with the various factors as mentioned on page 25**

Chapter 9 contains bid estimation, work loading and cost accounting forms to accomplish these tasks. The examples and explanations that are included with these forms, should provide the cleaning services novice, with insight into how to calculate the cost of providing cleaning services and profit margins, when preparing bid estimates or price structures. The experienced professional will also find these forms useful and convenient in organizing their bidding and bookkeeping processes.

Once the rates for cleaning services have been determined through experience or research, it is a fairly easy task to find the cost per job, monthly price or annual price, for any size facility of <u>comparable</u> labor intensity. Some idealized examples should serve to illustrate some of the uses of the bid estimation tables in chapter 7 & 8.

For example, a janitorial services contractor has several accounts of comparable size and difficulty, that he bills monthly at about the same rate (e.g., facilities ranging from 5,000-7,000 sq. ft. in size, billed an average of $780 month).

Our contractor overhears a conversation at the next table, at lunch one day. One of the participants is a purchasing agent for a medium sized business that is located in the area. He hears the purchasing agent discussing the upcoming deadline for the selection of a new cleaning services contractor. Our contractor introduces himself and presents his business card, asking the purchasing agent for an opportunity to provide an onsite consultation. The purchasing agent indicates that the bidding process is nearing completion, but offers to consider a meeting, if our contractor can provide a rough quote over the phone, based on an annual price per foot, by the end of the day.

He provides our contractor with general information on the number of employees at his facility, the frequency of general cleaning required, the total cleanable surface area, the number of bathrooms and the total square footage and frequency required for hard floor and carpet care.

Our janitorial services contractor has never prepared a bid proposal on the basis of the annual price per sq. ft.,. He makes the assumption based on the information provided by the purchasing agent, that the level of difficulty and labor intensity is comparable to his present accounts. Multiplying the average price per month for his present accounts by 12, he arrives at a total average annual price of $9,360, for his present accounts, that average about 6,000 sq. ft. in cleanable surface area. He then quickly finds the closest matching annual price per sq. ft., using the tables in chapter 8, as illustrated below (i.e., $1.56/ sq. ft. per year, or $0.13/ sq. ft. per month).

The facility he is providing a verbal quote for is 25,000 sq. ft.,. To find the annual price per sq. ft., he finds the value for 1/10th the area

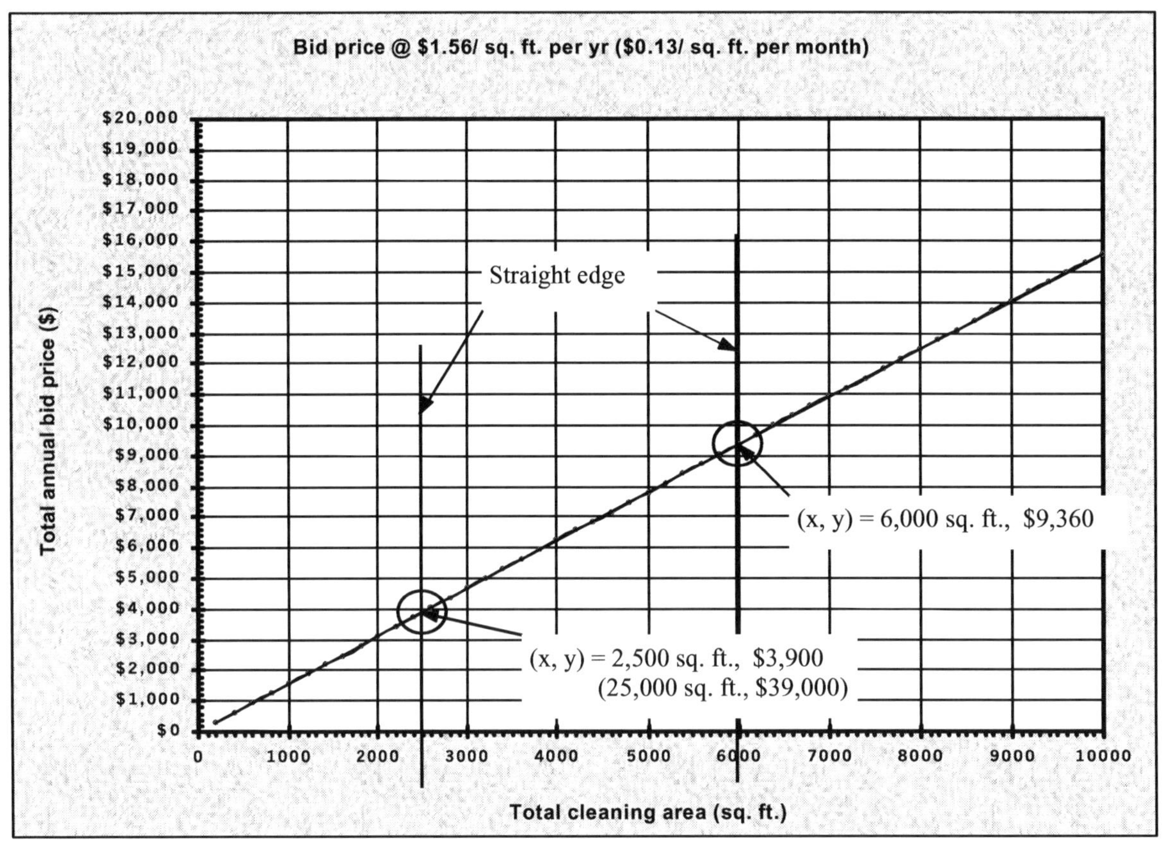

and multiplies by 10 (i.e., for 25,000 sq. ft. he find the price for 2,500 sq. ft. and multiplies by 10, or $3,900 x 10= $39,000). He quickly calls his purchasing contact with a verbal quote, who then extends our contractor an opportunity to provide an onsite consultation and subsequently, to submit a formal bid proposal.

An example of how the generic bid estimation charts in chapter 7 can be used, is in determining cleaning services rates on a per job basis. For instance, a janitorial services contractor is expanding the services he provides, to include residential and commercial exterior pressure washing. After determining his costs in providing the service and researching the market for exterior pressure washing pricing, he arrives at an average rate of $0.04/ sq. ft., based on the size of the cleanable surface area (i.e., living or occupancy area in sq. ft.).

He plans to place a targeted ad in a neighborhood mailer, in order to alert potential residential customers and also to include a flyer with his monthly billing, in order to alert his commercial customers about his expanded services. In his research, he notes that residential pressure washing services are providing discounts based on the size of the home. He decides to set his pricing for residential customers based on typical home dimensions of 1,500 sq. ft.-2,500 sq. ft., 2,500 sq. ft.-3,500 sq. ft., and 3,500 sq. ft. and above. He sets his pricing so that prices goes up with the size of the home, but the rate drops based on the total surface area, in order to compress the range of prices and remain competitive with other pressure washing services in the area. The mid-point of the range for home size in his target market is between 2,500 sq. ft.-3,500 sq. ft., (i.e., 3,000 sq. ft,).

Using the charts in chapter 7, he finds the matching price for a single cleaning at a rate of $0.04/ sq. ft. and a home with 2,500 sq. ft.-3,500 sq. ft. (i.e., $120) as shown in the illustration below. He sees that he can roughly maintain an average $0.04/ sq. ft., over the total range of home sizes by stepping his rates in increments $0.01/ sq. ft., (i.e.,

$0.030 sq. ft. for 3,500 sq. ft. and above, $0.04/ sq. ft. for 2,500-3,500 sq. ft. and , $0.05/ sq. ft. for 1,500-2,500 sq. ft.,).

The fixed price he advertises for each range of home sizes, is easily found using the bid estimation charts in chapter 7 (i.e., $100, $120 and $0.03/ sq. ft., for any home larger than 3,500 sq. ft.). Advertising <u>fixed</u> prices in residential advertisements, makes his cleaning service

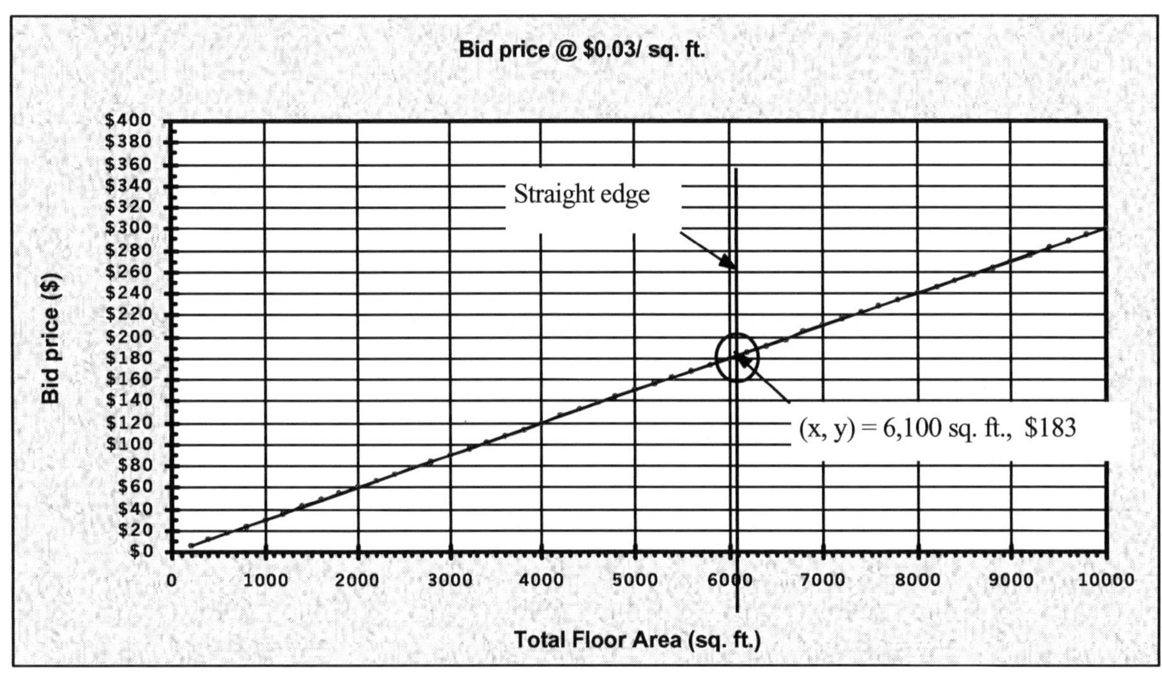

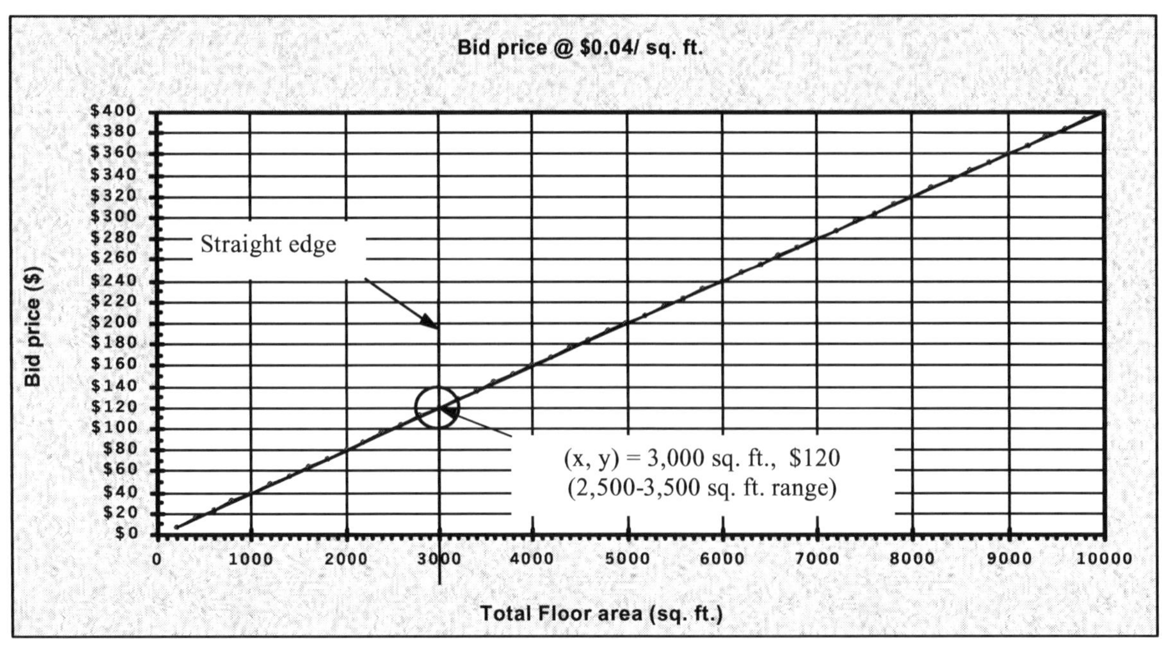

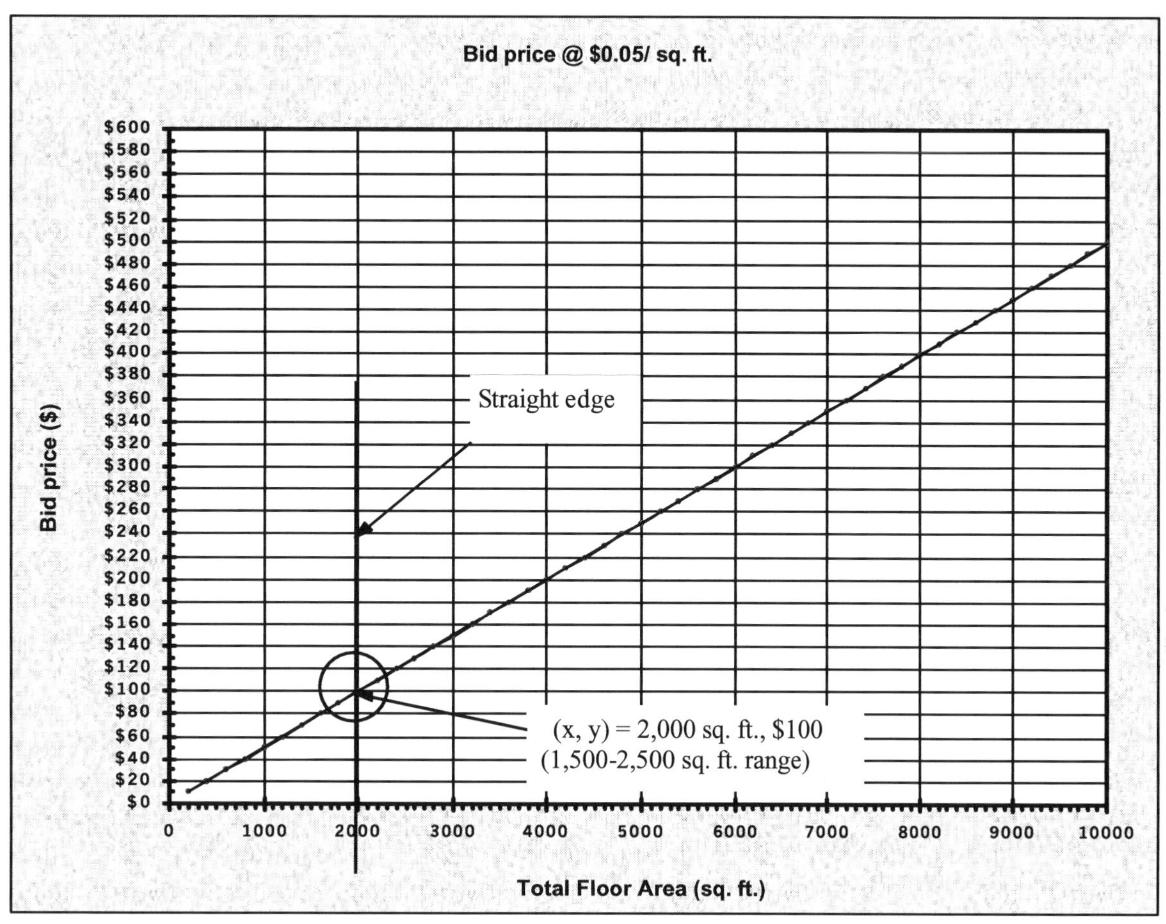

rates easier to understand at a glance, for the typical range of customers. For a larger home of 6,100 sq. ft., our contractor would charge $183 per washing, as shown in the illustration.

For his commercial customers, he offers a flat rate of $0.035/ sq. ft., for facilities ranging from 5,000-10,000 sq. ft. (e.g., $245 for 7,000 sq. ft.) and $0.030/ sq. ft., for buildings ranging from 10,000-100,000 sq. ft.,. To calculate the price to bid or charge on facilities with greater than 10,000 sq. ft., find the price for 1/10th the area and multiply by 10 (e.g., find the price for 8,800 sq. ft.= $245 and then, $245 x 10= $2,450, for 88,000 sq. ft.).

The bid estimation charts in chapter 7, are also designed for determining the total cost of monthly cleaning services, based on a monthly cleaning services rate per sq. ft., for any size cleaning area of comparable difficulty or level of service. Conversely, you can quickly determine a matching monthly rate per sq. ft., from the intersection of the total cleaning area and the corresponding monthly cost (e.g., based on typical or average data derived from existing accounts), for use in preparing future bid proposals, that involve cleaning areas of different size, but requiring a comparable level of service.

For example, a janitorial contractor's clients, ranges from small sole proprietorships to mid-sized businesses. He charges a monthly fee that covers his labor, supplies and overhead costs and an average profit margin of 20% (e.g., 1.20 x $571 average base costs = $685/ mo). He learns in his efforts to solicit business from larger customers, that many government and large corporate institutions require bid proposals be submitted based on a monthly price per square foot.

Our contractor decides to use data from his two largest "full service" customers (i.e., general office cleaning, floor care, window/ window blind care, housekeeping supply services, etc.,), as a model for establishing "full service" cleaning services rates, for use in future solicitations, bid proposals and negotiations. He uses the generic bid pricing charts in order to establish a median "full service" cleaning services rate, by matching the average monthly price of $685, for these two accounts to the corresponding average cleaning surface of 5,700 sq. ft.,. As illustrated below, the best match is $0.12/ sq. ft. per month.

He knows that there will be differences in his costs for any given new account and in the profit margin he will be able to charge and still remain competitive. As a "rough cut", he decides to determine a range of "full service rates", by varying his profit margin from 15%-30%,. He believes that being able to have a range of pricing, "at the ready", for use in counter proposals during negotiations, initial solicitations etc., will be put him at an advantage with prospective customers.

Based on a 20% profit margin at \$0.12/ sq. ft. per month, he calculates estimates of cleaning services rates, for a range of profit margins from 15%, 20%, 25%, 30%, (i.e., \$0.115/ sq. ft.*, \$0.12/ sq. ft., \$0.125/ sq. ft.*, \$0.13/ sq. ft., e.g., (1.15 x 571)/5,700 = \$0.115/ sq. ft.,). Going forward, our contractor can quickly determine the total monthly price at these various rates from the generic bid pricing charts, for <u>any</u> size cleaning area. To a good approximation, he will also know what his profit margin will be. This is provided that the new accounts in question, are comparable in labor intensity and <u>cost</u> of services, to the two accounts that he derived his median "full service" rates from.

*When you are determining total monthly bid prices for a cleaning service rate that is between the rates found in the charts in this guide, e.g., \$0.126/ sq. ft., you have a choice of interpolating or "splitting the difference" between the two closest rates, i.e., \$0.12 sq. ft. and \$0.13 sq. ft. or rounding to the nearest rate in this guide.

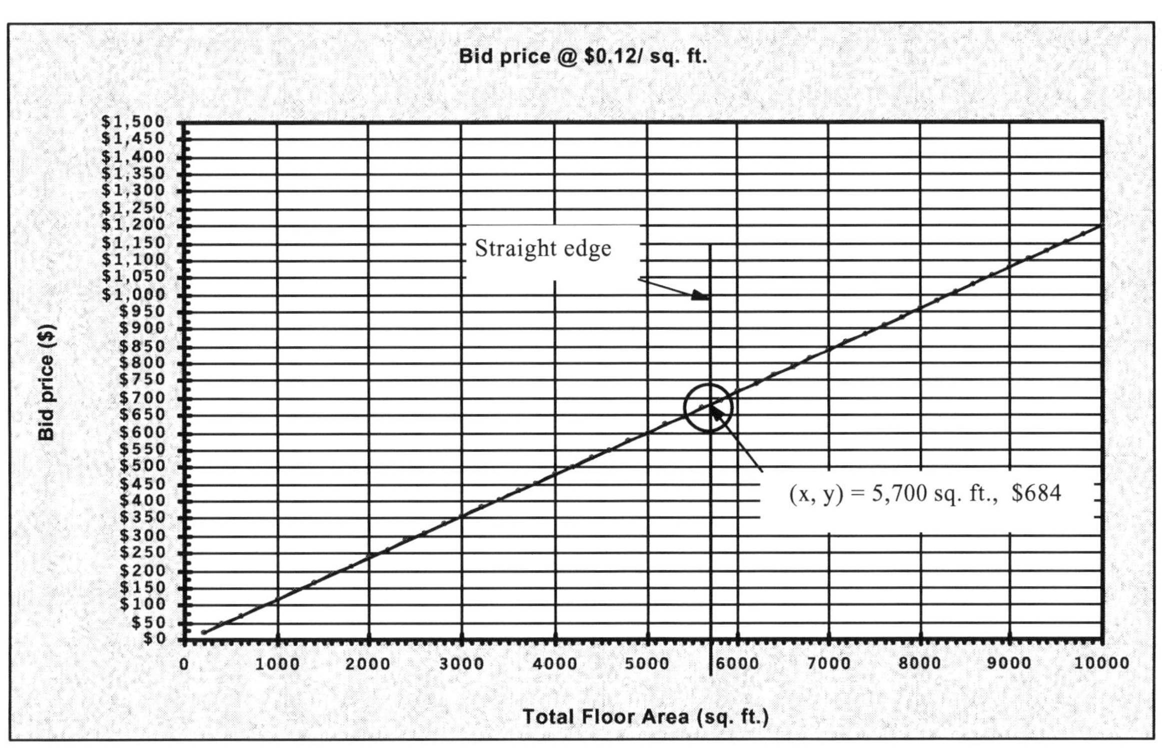

For example, you can find the total monthly price at $0.12/ sq. ft., ($684 for 5,700 sq. ft.) and $0.13/ sq. ft., ($741 for 5,700 sq. ft.) and take the average (($684 + $741)/ 2 = $712/ mo, for 5,700 sq. ft.). Conversely, you can round up (e.g., $0.125-$0.129/ sq. ft.) to $0.13/ sq. ft., or round down (e.g., $0.121-$124/ sq. ft.) to $0.12/ sq. ft.,.

Some of the supporting calculations, assumptions and decision making involved in setting up the examples that are presented in this chapter, are simplified or idealized to an extent, for the purpose of illustrating how the charts and tables may be used in practice. Specifically, many examples state or assume, a requirement for comparable or proportionate equivalence in the level of difficulty, labor intensity or cost of service, for two or more accounts or situations.

While the charts and tables in this guide are convenient and helpful in business planning and in preparation for, or during onsite negotiations, it is important to understand, that a certain amount of experience or research is necessary in many cases, in order to use these charts and tables in the most effective manner possible. Having noted this, readers that either have the requisite experience or skills for bid estimating and work loading, or are willing to work to acquire them, will soon discover on their own, the advantages or utility of using the charts in this guide, over other approaches.

Users may find that the some of the advantages or utility of charts and tables in this guide will be (but are not limited to):

- ***in their convenience and ease of use***; or
- ***in cases where more in depth hand held calculator or PC computations are not possible due to time constraints, or when such devices are unavailable****; or*
- ***in cases where the potential for error, due to time constraints or***

"personal stress", during an onsite meeting, or over the phone, lends itself to the reassuring structure and precision of the guide, rather than relying on a hasty series of hand held calculator computations that can't be carefully verified; *or*

- ***in the advanced preparation of counter offers or proposals, to aid in establishing an advantage in negotiations and solicitations***; or
- ***in "on the spot" determinations of counter offers or proposals, during a phone or onsite consultation;*** *or*
- ***as an aid in preparing detailed bid estimates or workload estimates;*** *or*
- ***at any time, that a quick estimate will suffice in lieu of detailed calculations.***

The worksheet forms for bid estimation, work loading and cost accounting, are discussed in chapter 9. In addition to their obvious utility, the discussion of the worksheet materials presented in chapter 9 that follows, as well as their initial use by the reader, for business planning or in the service of clients, will also help the cleaning services novice, to understand the "how and why" of the supporting calculations, assumptions and decision making, involved in using the generic production rate and bid pricing charts in this guide, in the most effective manner.

Note: in the discussion of **cleaning supplies usage**, some of the end points or results, for volumes, of both cleaning solution concentrates and final diluted cleaning solutions, may appear to some users, to be of an impractical level of accuracy or detail, for dispensing and mixing in actual cleaning situations (e.g., 3.3 gal, 0.132 gal, etc.,). It should be mentioned, that in cases where automated dispensing equipment is in-appropriate or unavailable, inexpensive hand held measuring devices, that have measuring graduations, that divide English units of volume such as gallons and quarts, into "tenths", are inexpensive and are commonly available (e.g., as food preparation utensils, industrial or scientific measuring devices etc.,). Alternatively, it is often possible, to label most common containers, which are uniform in shape (e.g., cylindrical), into graduations of ten equal increments, manually.

Chapter 3

Typical production rates and cleaning times for various tasks

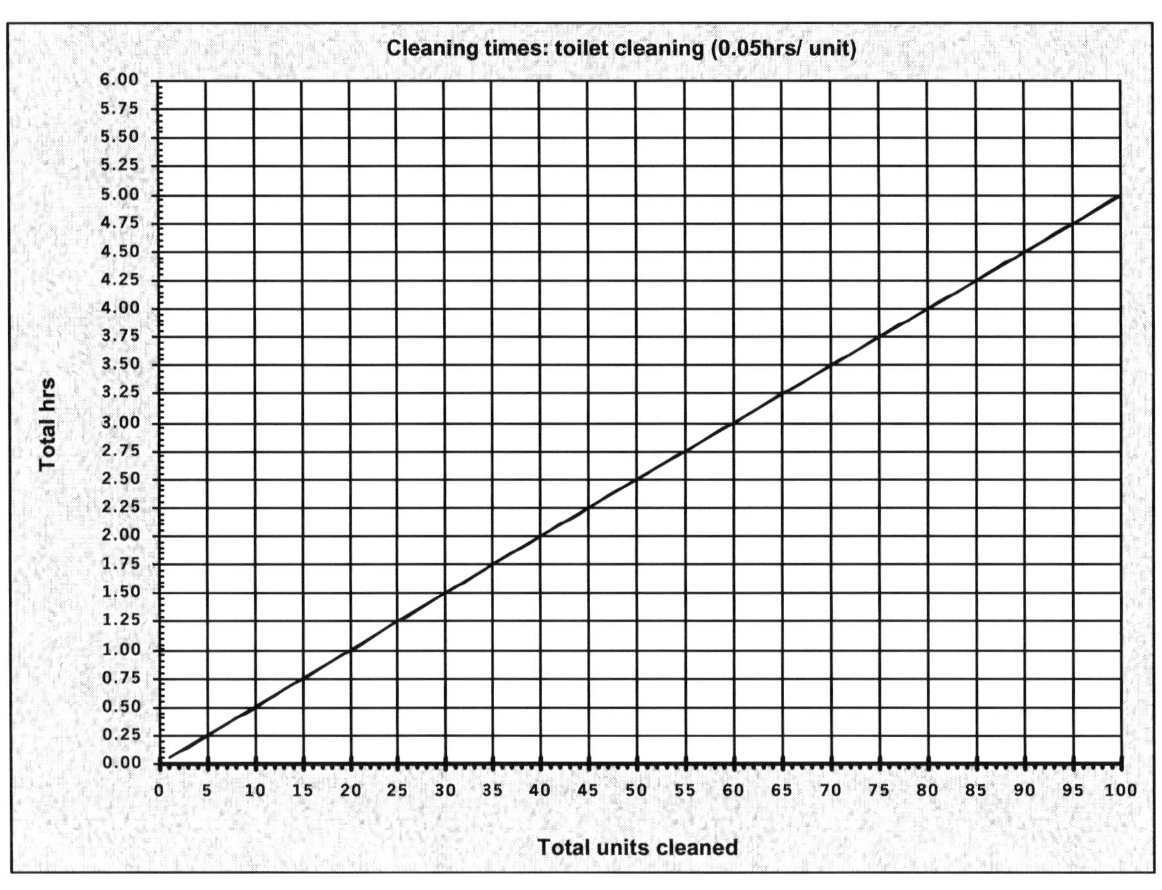

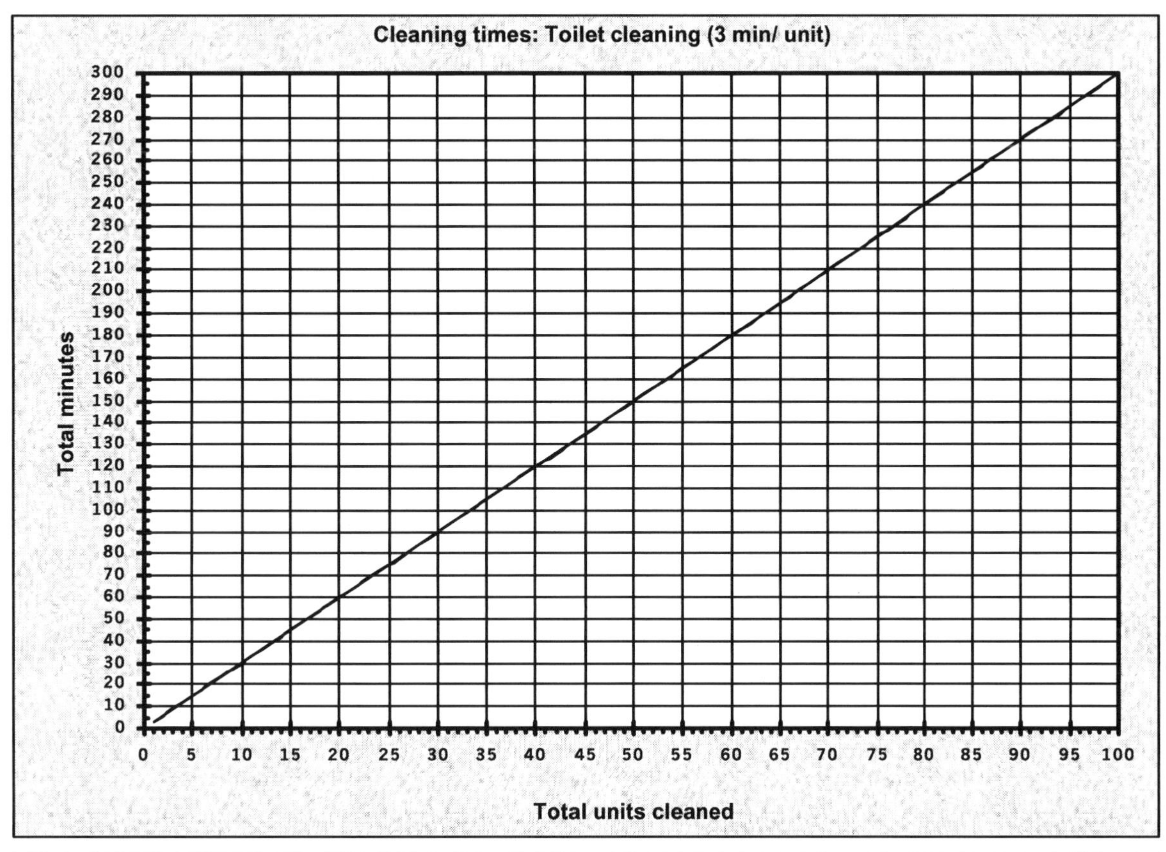
Cleaning times: Toilet cleaning (3 min/ unit)
Total minutes
300
290
280
270
260
250
240
230
220
210
200
190
180
170
160
150
140
130
120
110
100
90
80
70
60
50
40
30
20
10
0
0 5 10 15 20 25 30 35 40 45 50 55 60 65 70 75 80 85 90 95 100
Total units cleaned

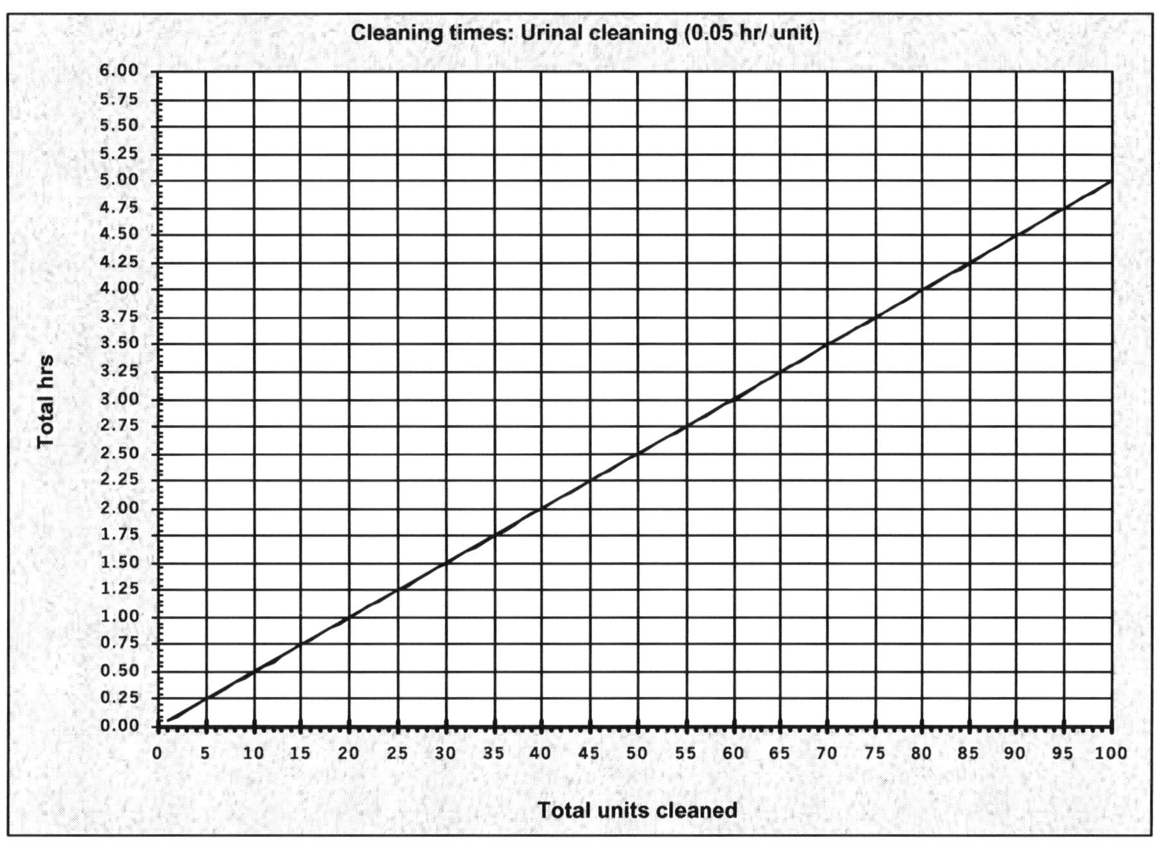
Cleaning times: Urinal cleaning (0.05 hr/ unit)
Total hrs
6.00
5.75
5.50
5.25
5.00
4.75
4.50
4.25
4.00
3.75
3.50
3.25
3.00
2.75
2.50
2.25
2.00
1.75
1.50
1.25
1.00
0.75
0.50
0.25
0.00
0 5 10 15 20 25 30 35 40 45 50 55 60 65 70 75 80 85 90 95 100
Total units cleaned

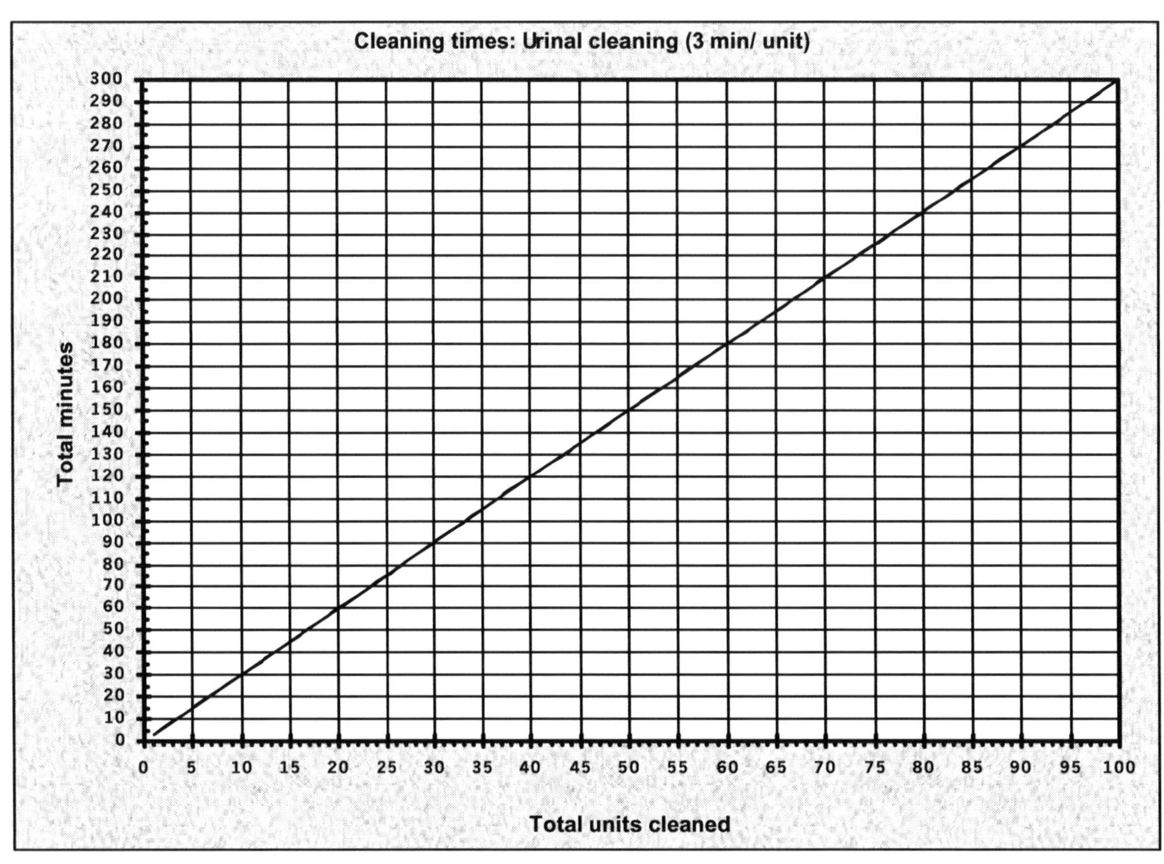
Cleaning times: Urinal cleaning (3 min/ unit)
Total minutes
300
290
280
270
260
250
240
230
220
210
200
190
180
170
160
150
140
130
120
110
100
90
80
70
60
50
40
30
20
10
0
0 5 10 15 20 25 30 35 40 45 50 55 60 65 70 75 80 85 90 95 100
Total units cleaned

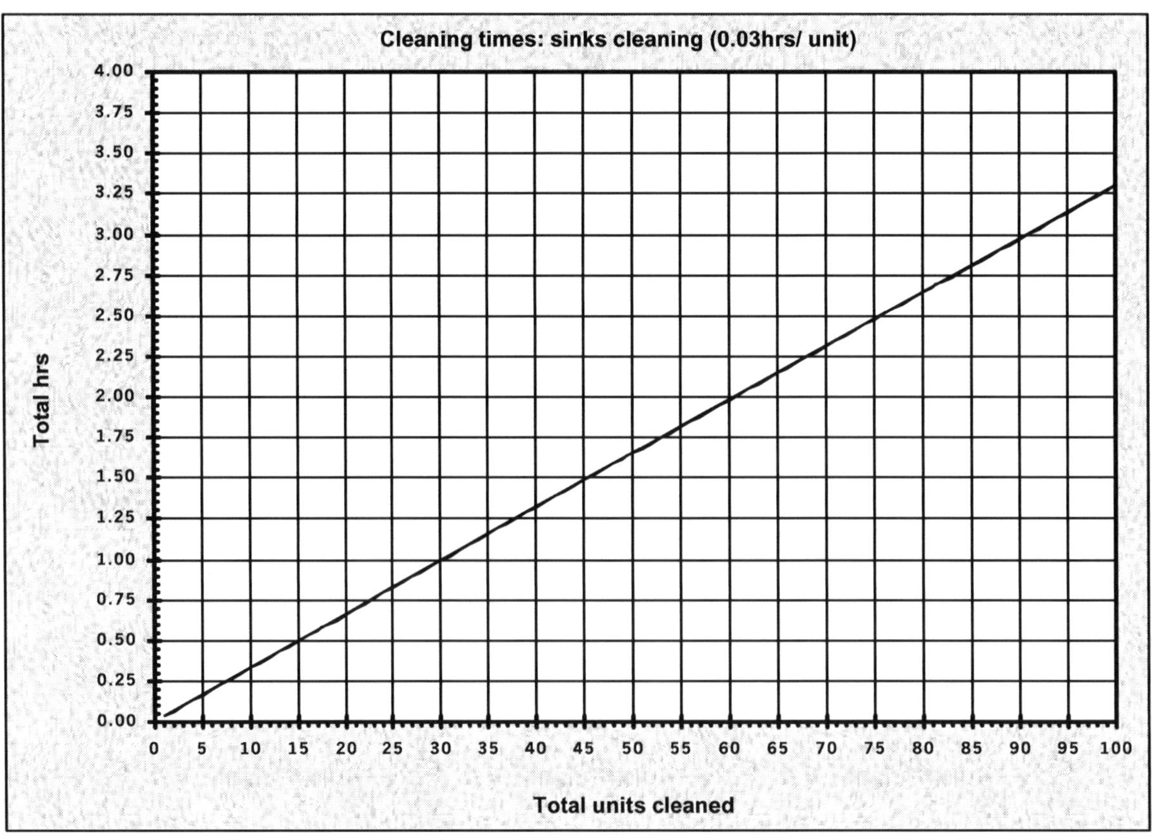
Cleaning times: sinks cleaning (0.03hrs/ unit)
Total hrs
4.00
3.75
3.50
3.25
3.00
2.75
2.50
2.25
2.00
1.75
1.50
1.25
1.00
0.75
0.50
0.25
0.00
0 5 10 15 20 25 30 35 40 45 50 55 60 65 70 75 80 85 90 95 100
Total units cleaned

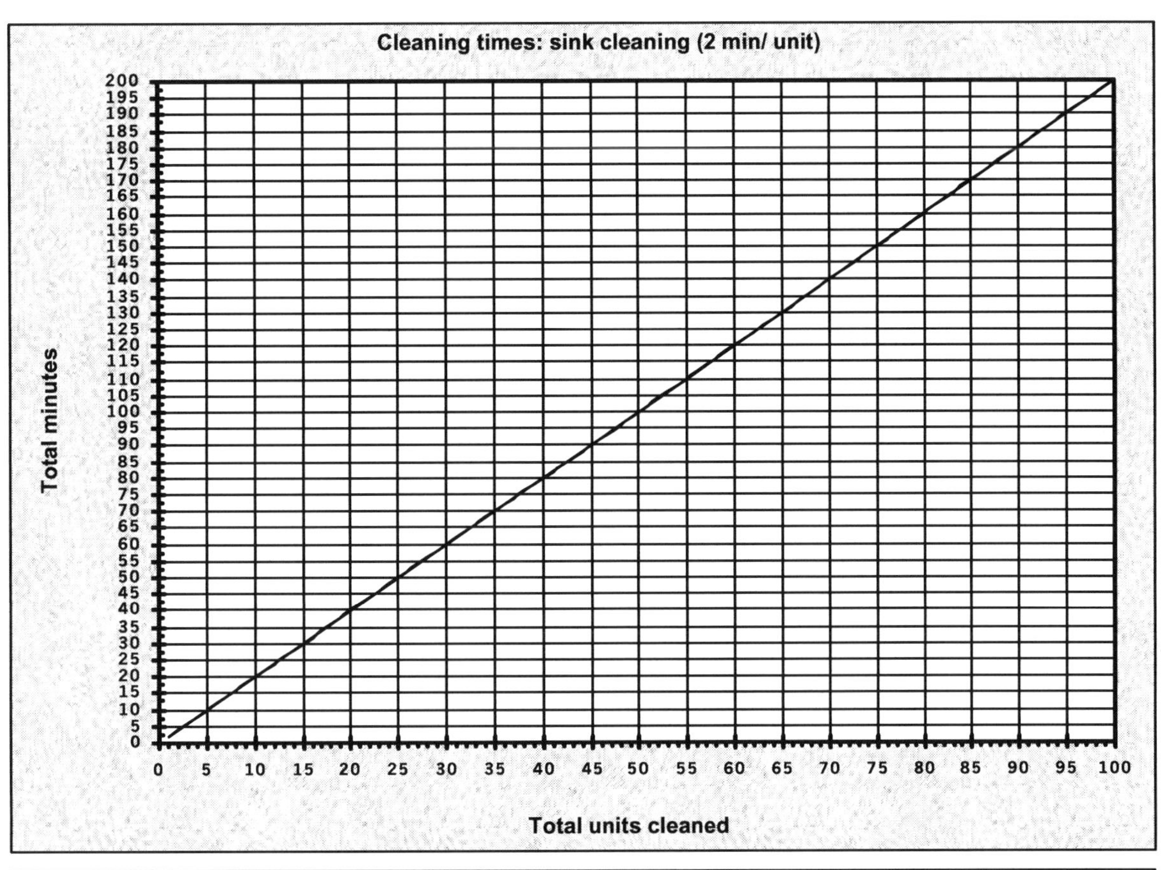
Cleaning times: sink cleaning (2 min/ unit)
Total minutes
Total units cleaned

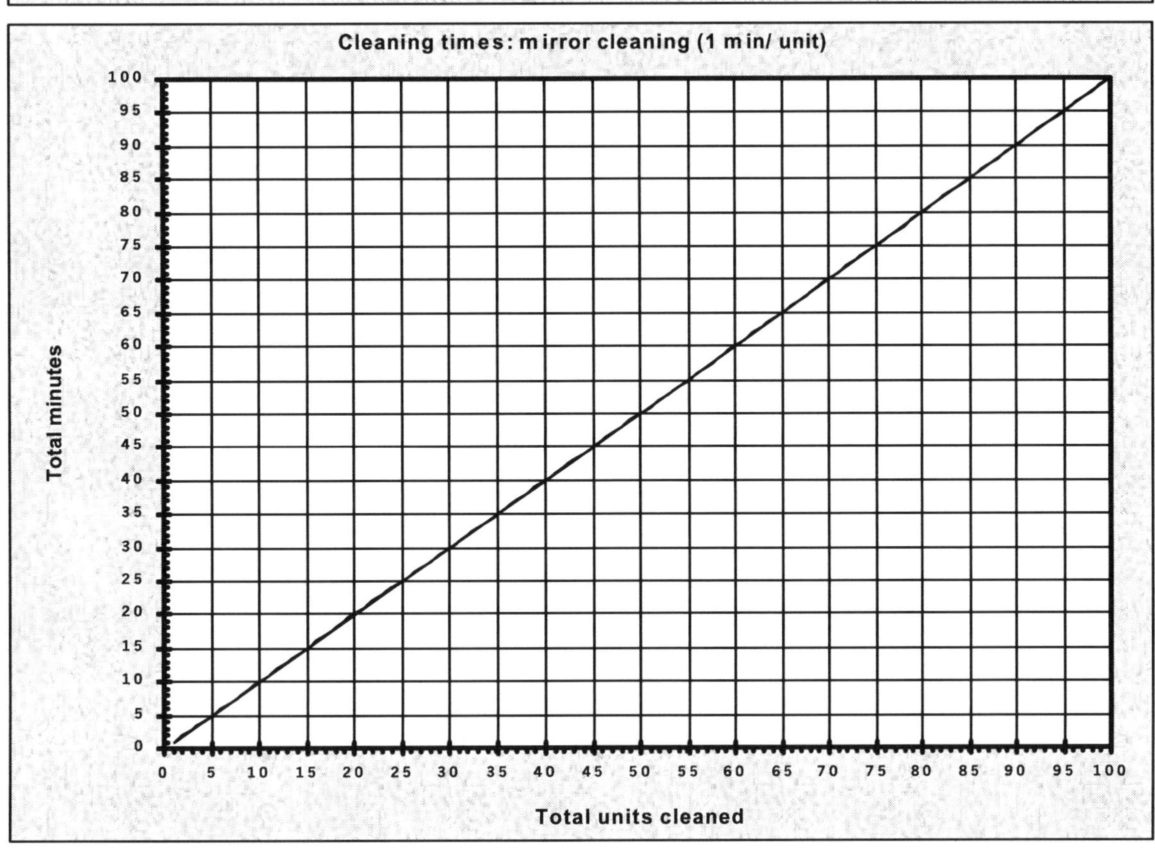
Cleaning times: mirror cleaning (1 min/ unit)
Total minutes
Total units cleaned

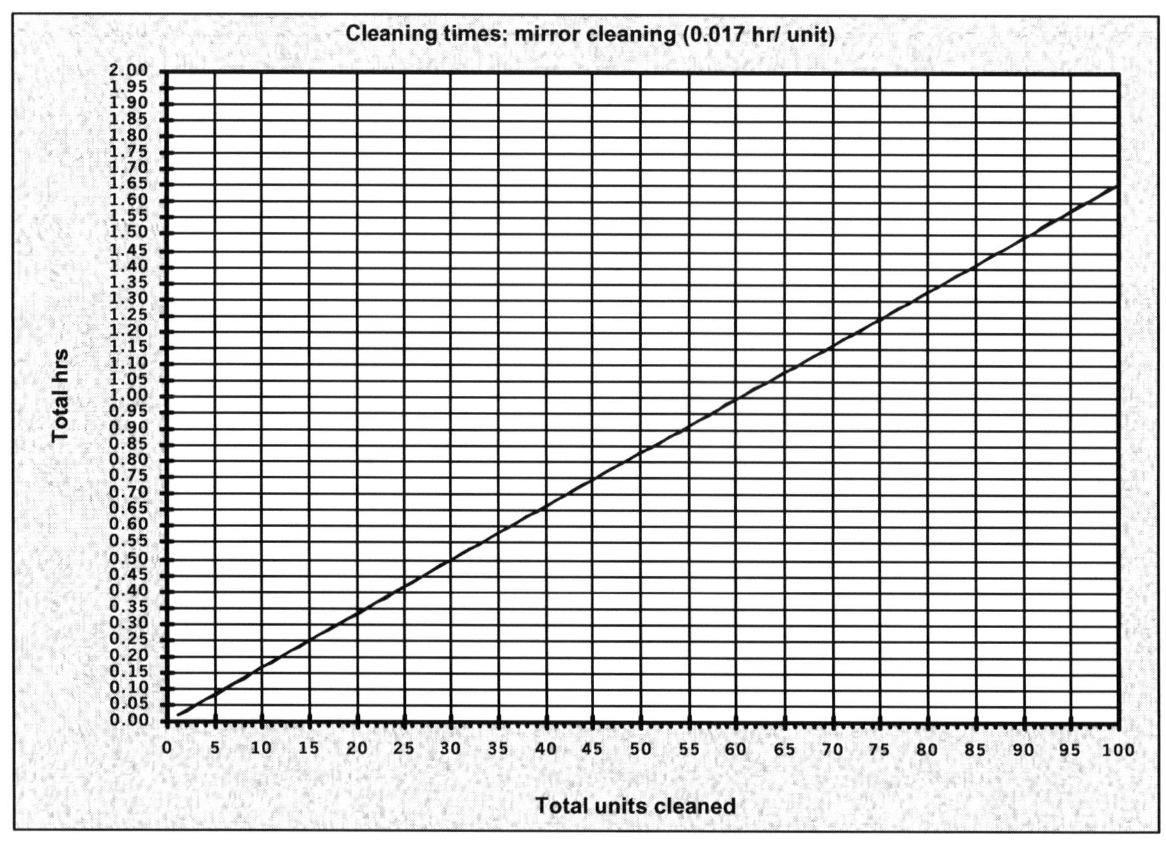
Cleaning times: mirror cleaning (0.017 hr/ unit)
Total hrs
2.00
1.95
1.90
1.85
1.80
1.75
1.70
1.65
1.60
1.55
1.50
1.45
1.40
1.35
1.30
1.25
1.20
1.15
1.10
1.05
1.00
0.95
0.90
0.85
0.80
0.75
0.70
0.65
0.60
0.55
0.50
0.45
0.40
0.35
0.30
0.25
0.20
0.15
0.10
0.05
0.00
0 5 10 15 20 25 30 35 40 45 50 55 60 65 70 75 80 85 90 95 100
Total units cleaned

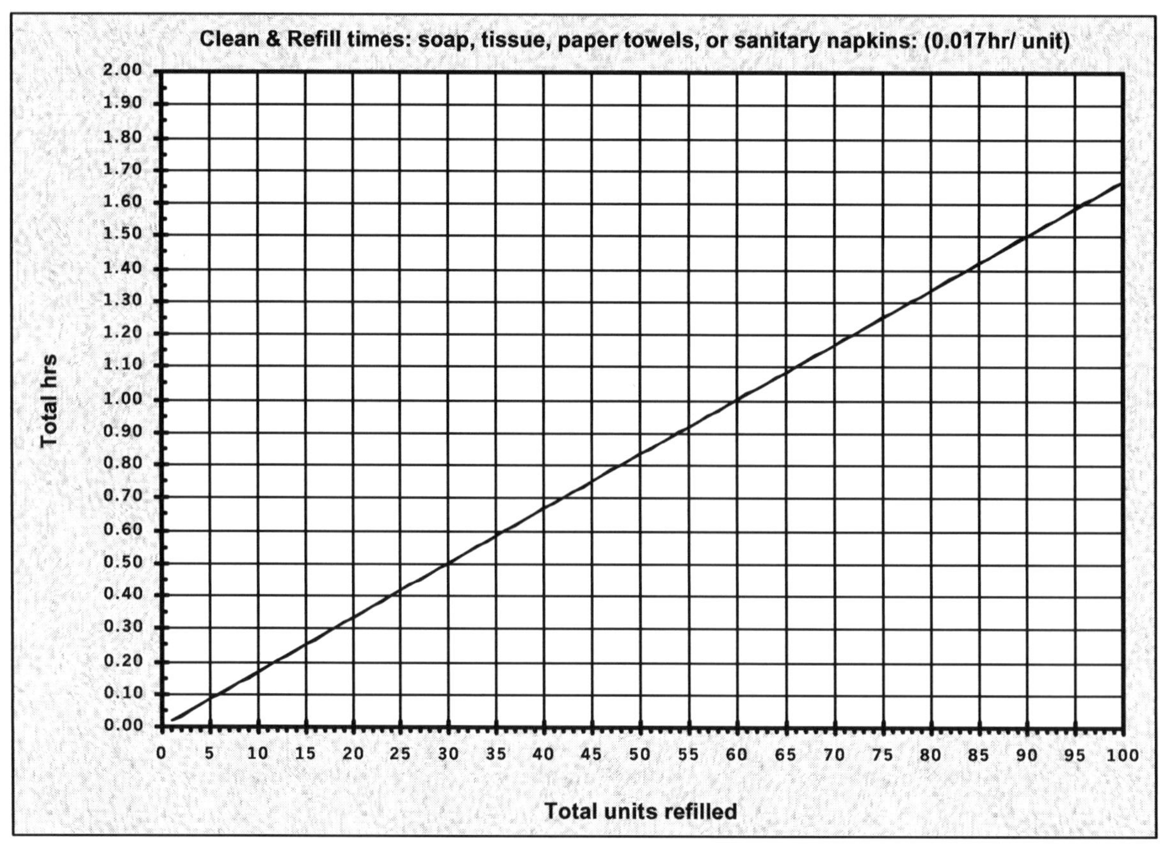
Clean & Refill times: soap, tissue, paper towels, or sanitary napkins: (0.017hr/ unit)
Total hrs
2.00
1.90
1.80
1.70
1.60
1.50
1.40
1.30
1.20
1.10
1.00
0.90
0.80
0.70
0.60
0.50
0.40
0.30
0.20
0.10
0.00
0 5 10 15 20 25 30 35 40 45 50 55 60 65 70 75 80 85 90 95 100
Total units refilled

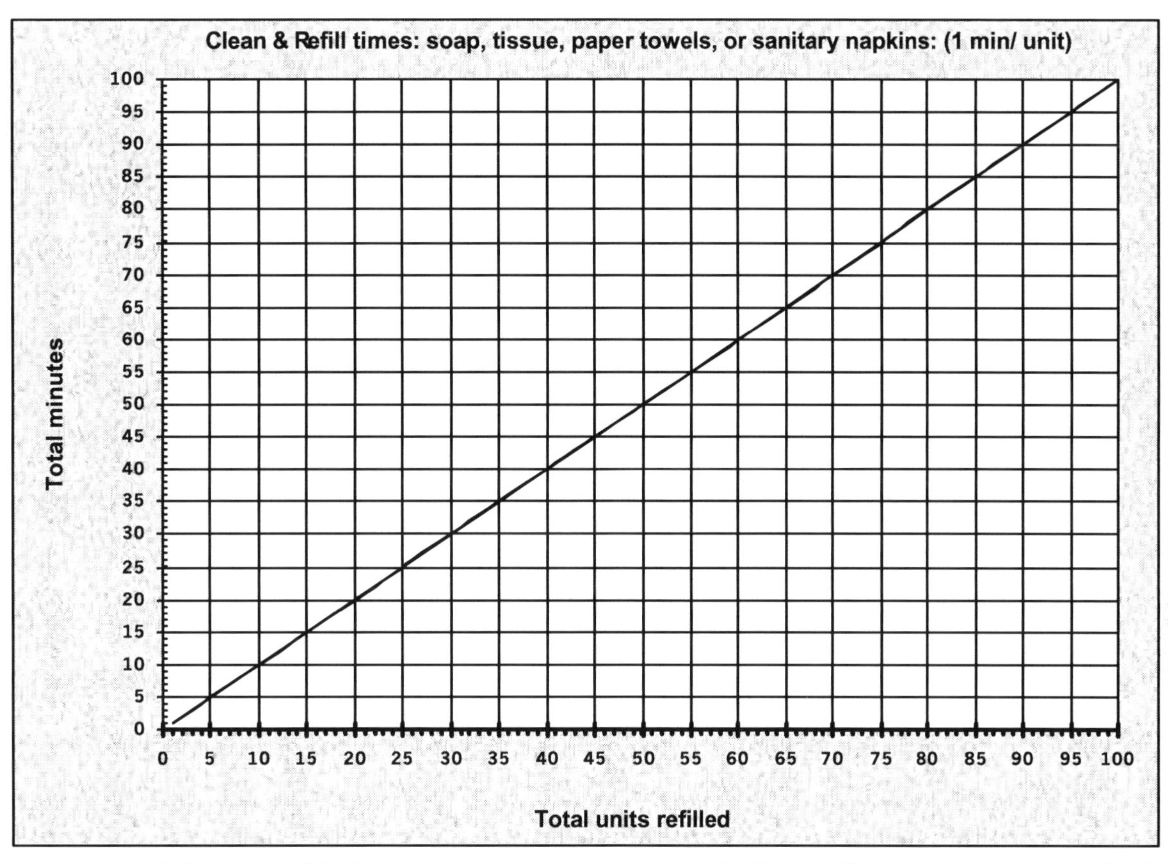
Clean & Refill times: soap, tissue, paper towels, or sanitary napkins: (1 min/ unit)
Total minutes
0
5
10
15
20
25
30
35
40
45
50
55
60
65
70
75
80
85
90
95
100
Total units refilled

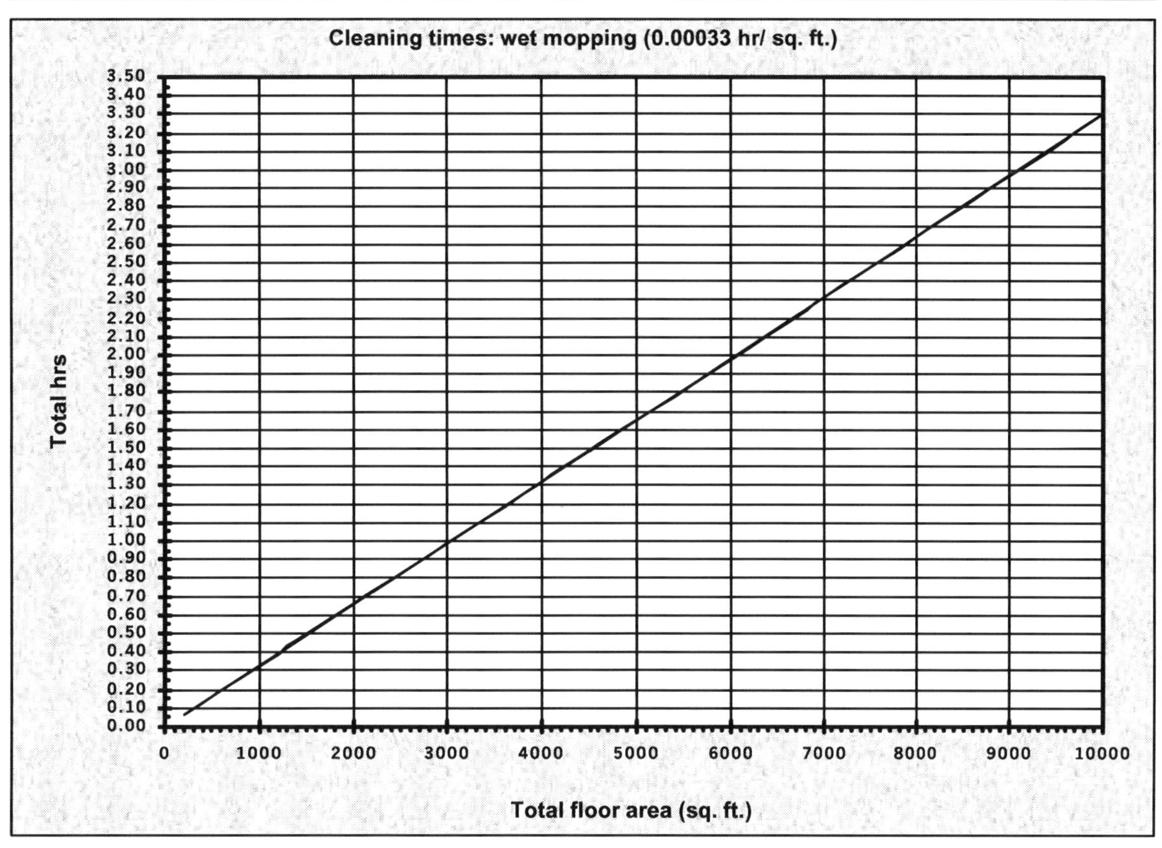
Cleaning times: wet mopping (0.00033 hr/ sq. ft.)
Total hrs
0.00
0.10
0.20
0.30
0.40
0.50
0.60
0.70
0.80
0.90
1.00
1.10
1.20
1.30
1.40
1.50
1.60
1.70
1.80
1.90
2.00
2.10
2.20
2.30
2.40
2.50
2.60
2.70
2.80
2.90
3.00
3.10
3.20
3.30
3.40
3.50
0
1000
2000
3000
4000
5000
6000
7000
8000
9000
10000
Total floor area (sq. ft.)

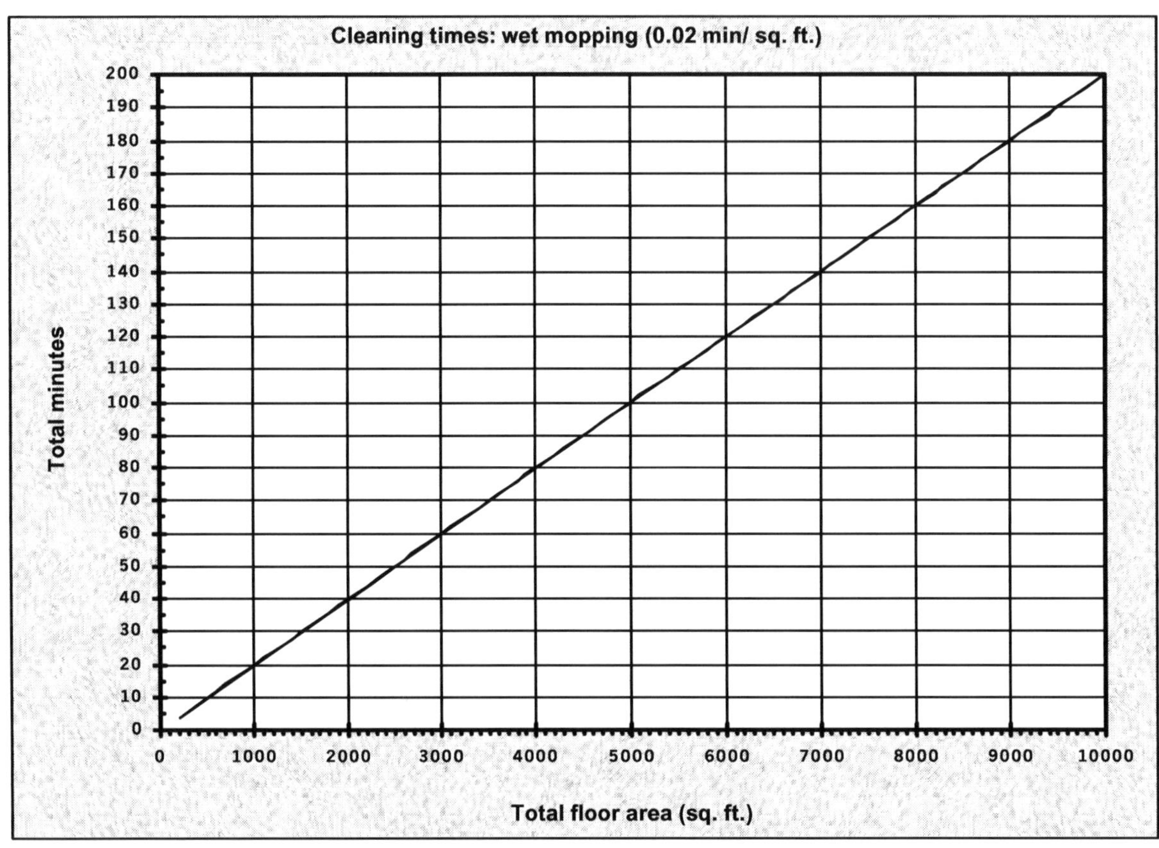
Cleaning times: wet mopping (0.02 min/ sq. ft.)
Total minutes
200
190
180
170
160
150
140
130
120
110
100
90
80
70
60
50
40
30
20
10
0
0
1000
2000
3000
4000
5000
6000
7000
8000
9000
10000
Total floor area (sq. ft.)

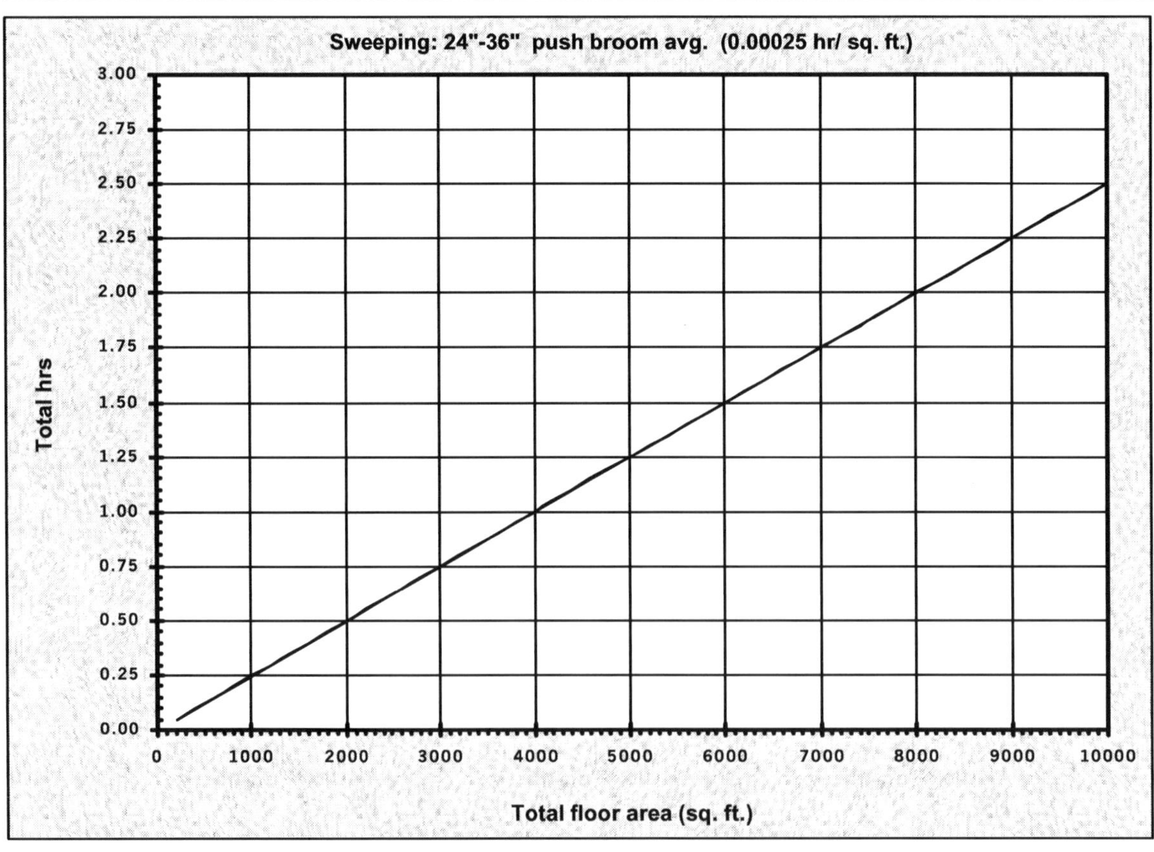
Sweeping: 24"-36" push broom avg. (0.00025 hr/ sq. ft.)
Total hrs
3.00
2.75
2.50
2.25
2.00
1.75
1.50
1.25
1.00
0.75
0.50
0.25
0.00
0
1000
2000
3000
4000
5000
6000
7000
8000
9000
10000
Total floor area (sq. ft.)

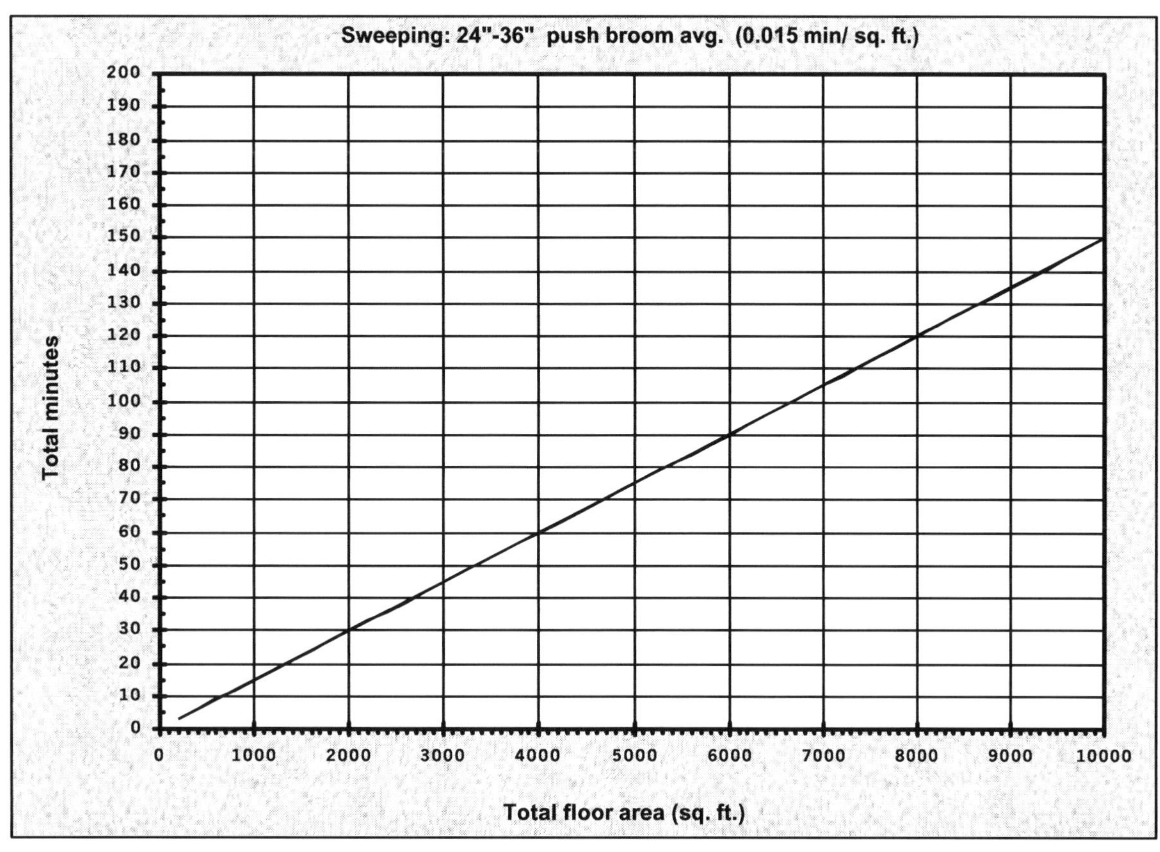
Sweeping: 24"-36" push broom avg. (0.015 min/ sq. ft.)
Total minutes
0
10
20
30
40
50
60
70
80
90
100
110
120
130
140
150
160
170
180
190
200
0
1000
2000
3000
4000
5000
6000
7000
8000
9000
10000
Total floor area (sq. ft.)

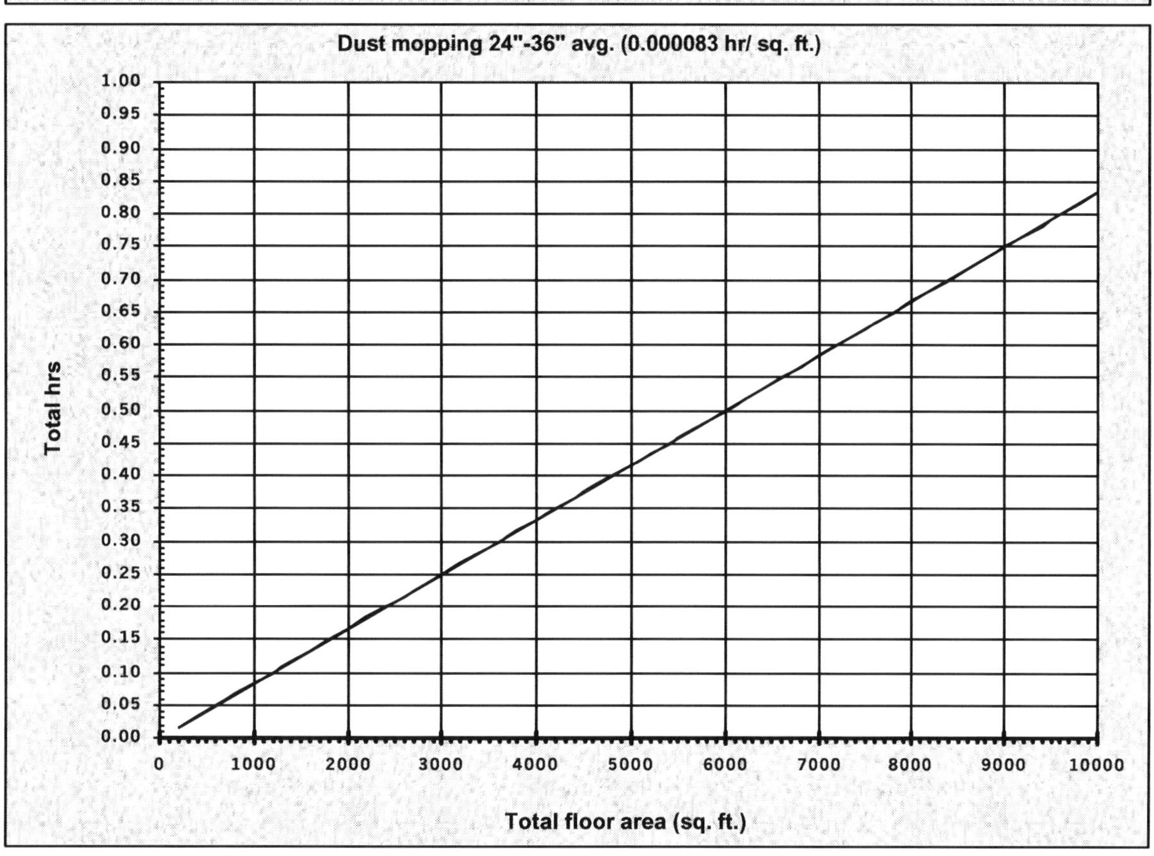
Dust mopping 24"-36" avg. (0.000083 hr/ sq. ft.)
Total hrs
0.00
0.05
0.10
0.15
0.20
0.25
0.30
0.35
0.40
0.45
0.50
0.55
0.60
0.65
0.70
0.75
0.80
0.85
0.90
0.95
1.00
0
1000
2000
3000
4000
5000
6000
7000
8000
9000
10000
Total floor area (sq. ft.)

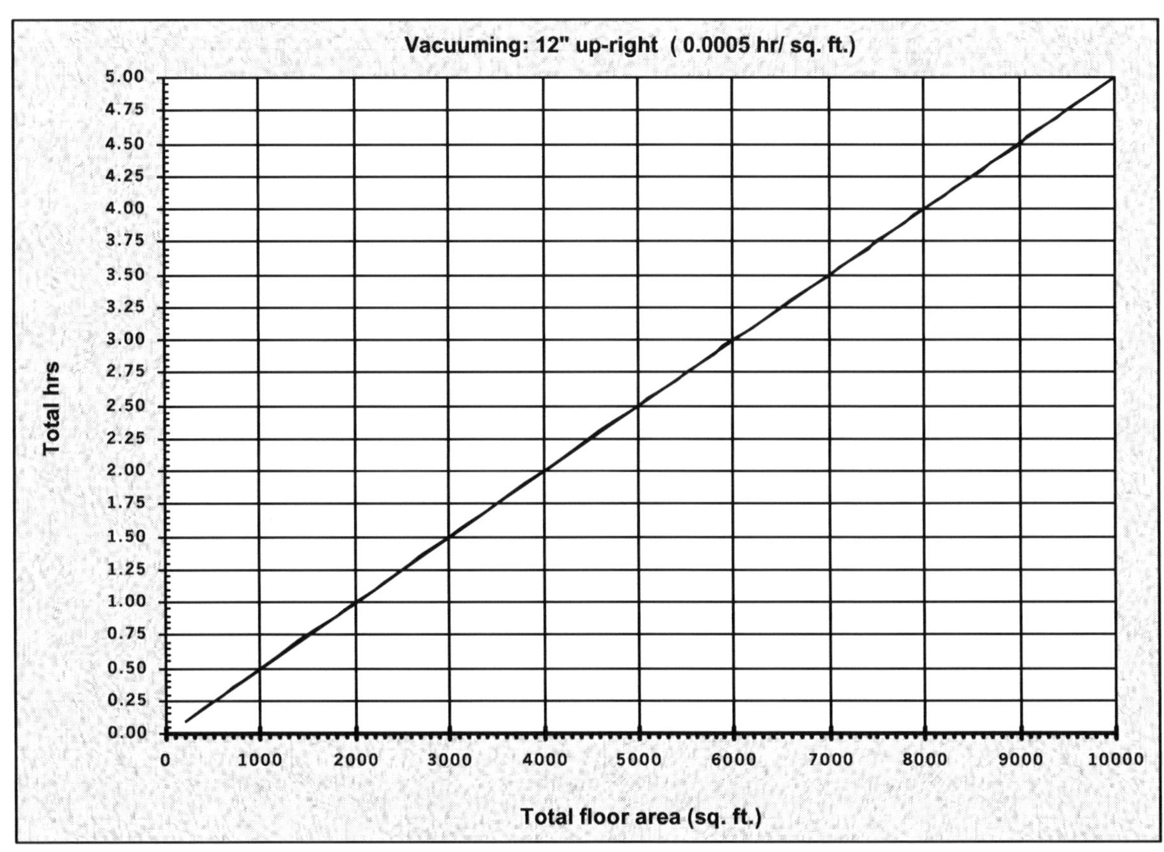
Vacuuming: 12" up-right (0.0005 hr/ sq. ft.)
Total hrs
5.00
4.75
4.50
4.25
4.00
3.75
3.50
3.25
3.00
2.75
2.50
2.25
2.00
1.75
1.50
1.25
1.00
0.75
0.50
0.25
0.00
0
1000
2000
3000
4000
5000
6000
7000
8000
9000
10000
Total floor area (sq. ft.)

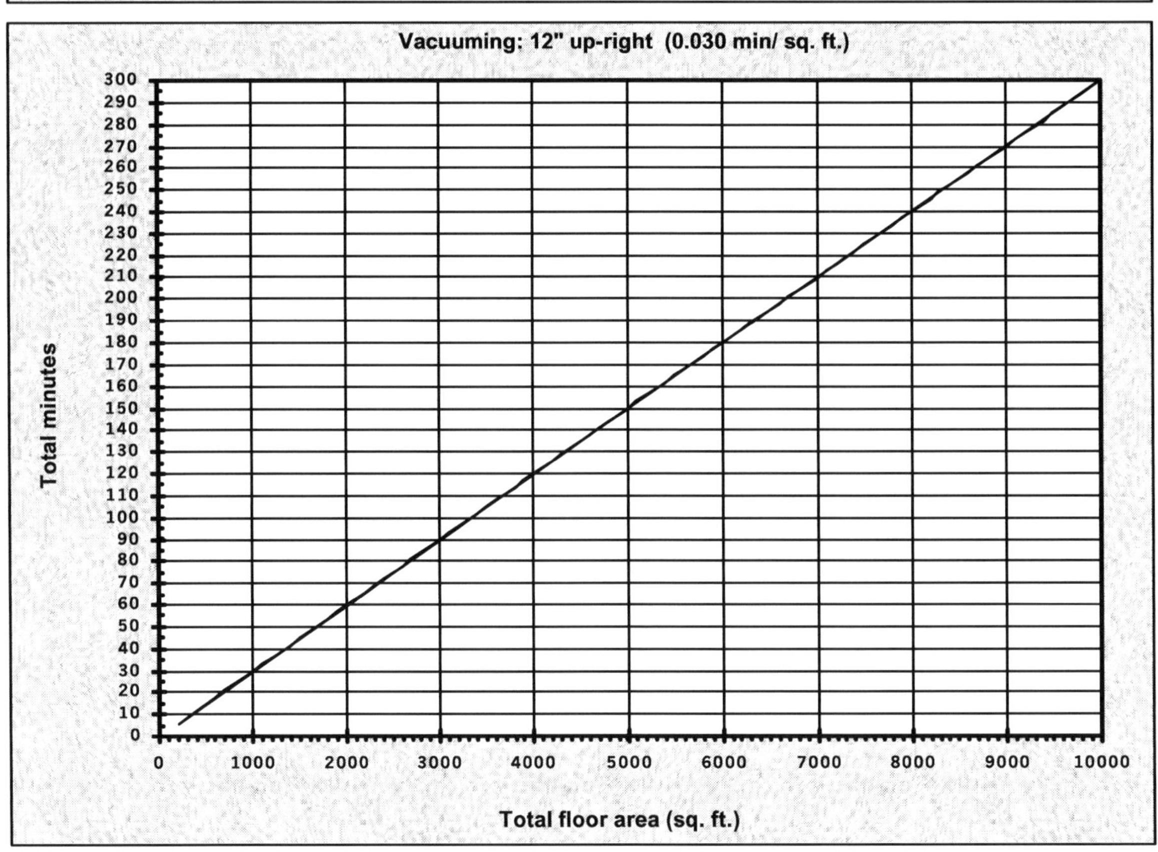
Vacuuming: 12" up-right (0.030 min/ sq. ft.)
Total minutes
300
290
280
270
260
250
240
230
220
210
200
190
180
170
160
150
140
130
120
110
100
90
80
70
60
50
40
30
20
10
0
0
1000
2000
3000
4000
5000
6000
7000
8000
9000
10000
Total floor area (sq. ft.)

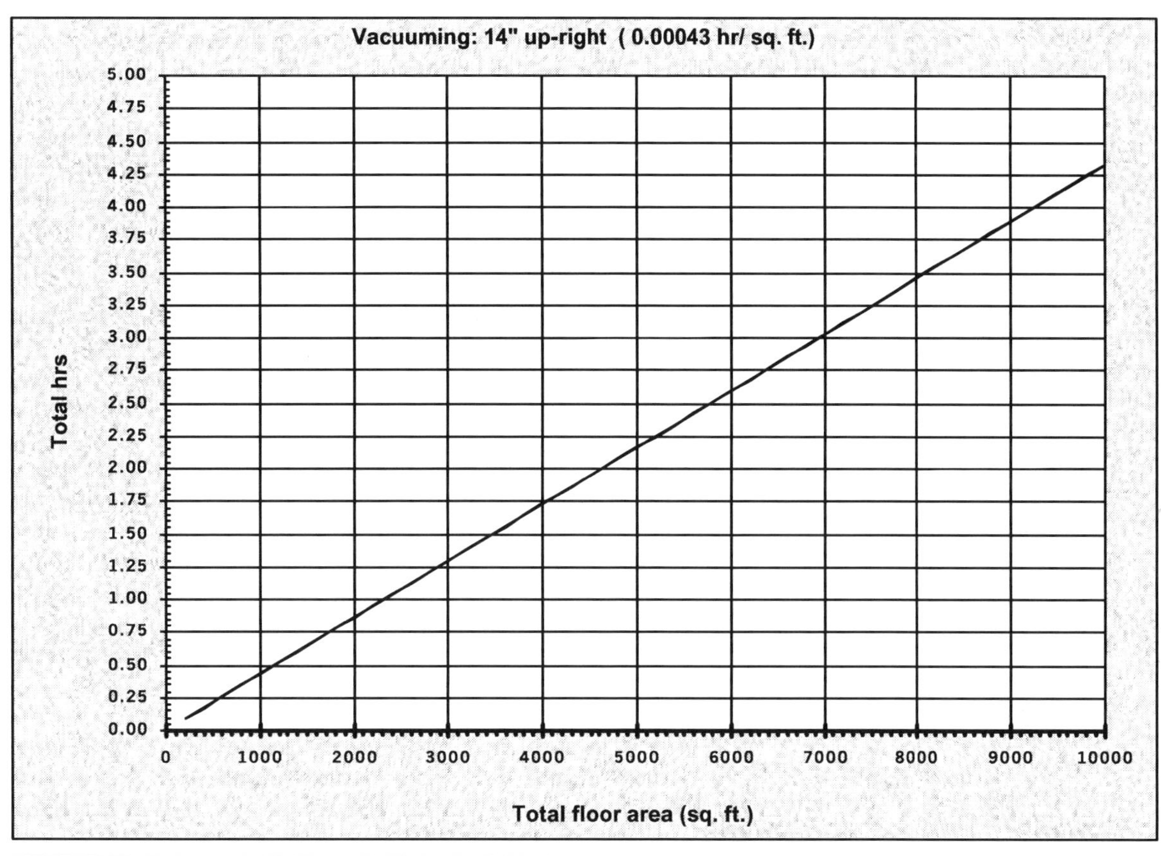
Vacuuming: 14" up-right (0.00043 hr/ sq. ft.)
Total hrs
5.00
4.75
4.50
4.25
4.00
3.75
3.50
3.25
3.00
2.75
2.50
2.25
2.00
1.75
1.50
1.25
1.00
0.75
0.50
0.25
0.00
0
1000
2000
3000
4000
5000
6000
7000
8000
9000
10000
Total floor area (sq. ft.)

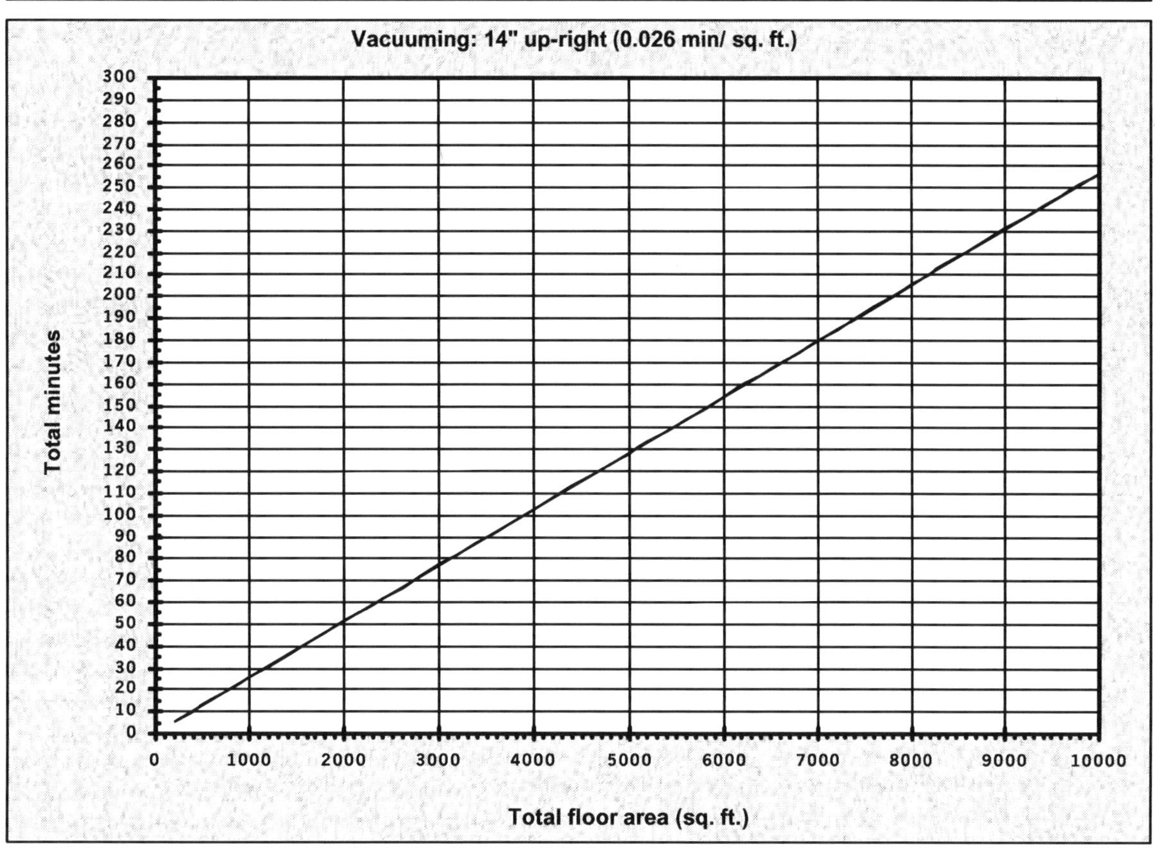
Vacuuming: 14" up-right (0.026 min/ sq. ft.)
Total minutes
300
290
280
270
260
250
240
230
220
210
200
190
180
170
160
150
140
130
120
110
100
90
80
70
60
50
40
30
20
10
0
0
1000
2000
3000
4000
5000
6000
7000
8000
9000
10000
Total floor area (sq. ft.)

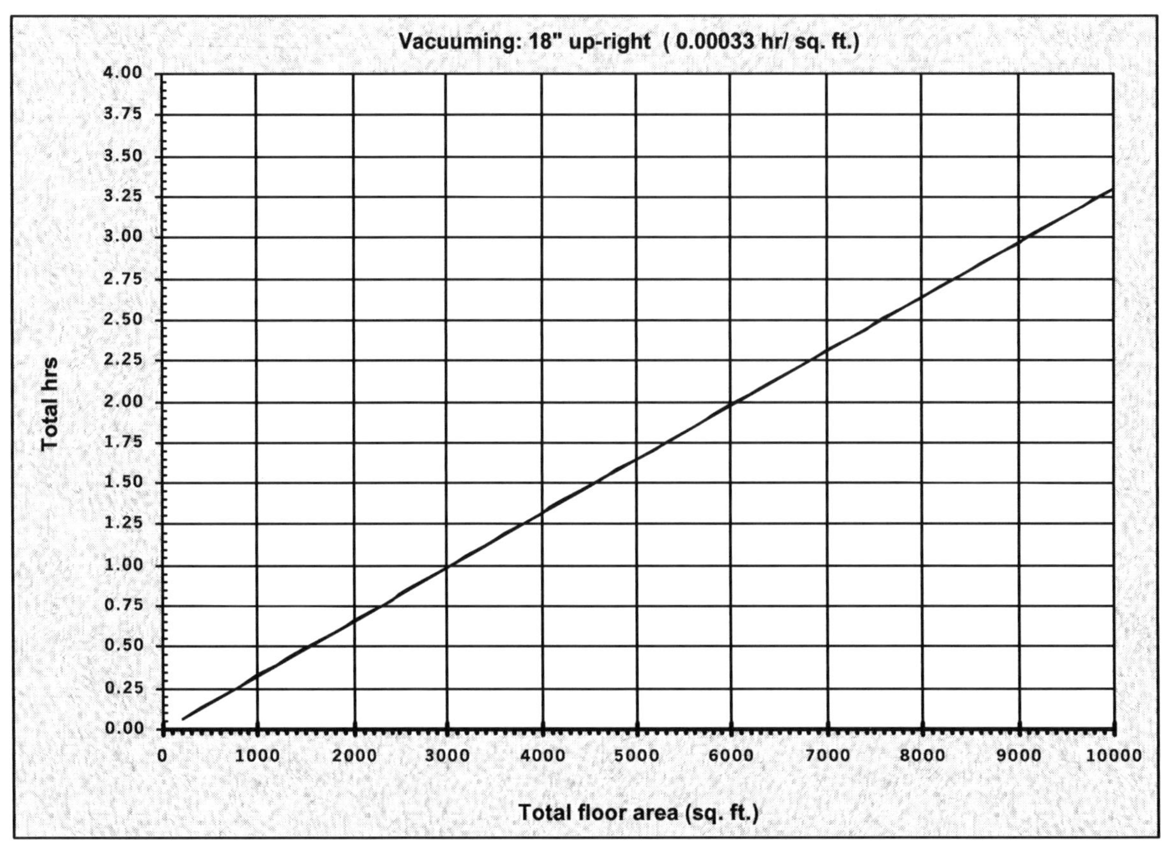
Vacuuming: 18" up-right (0.00033 hr/ sq. ft.)
Total hrs
4.00
3.75
3.50
3.25
3.00
2.75
2.50
2.25
2.00
1.75
1.50
1.25
1.00
0.75
0.50
0.25
0.00
0
1000
2000
3000
4000
5000
6000
7000
8000
9000
10000
Total floor area (sq. ft.)

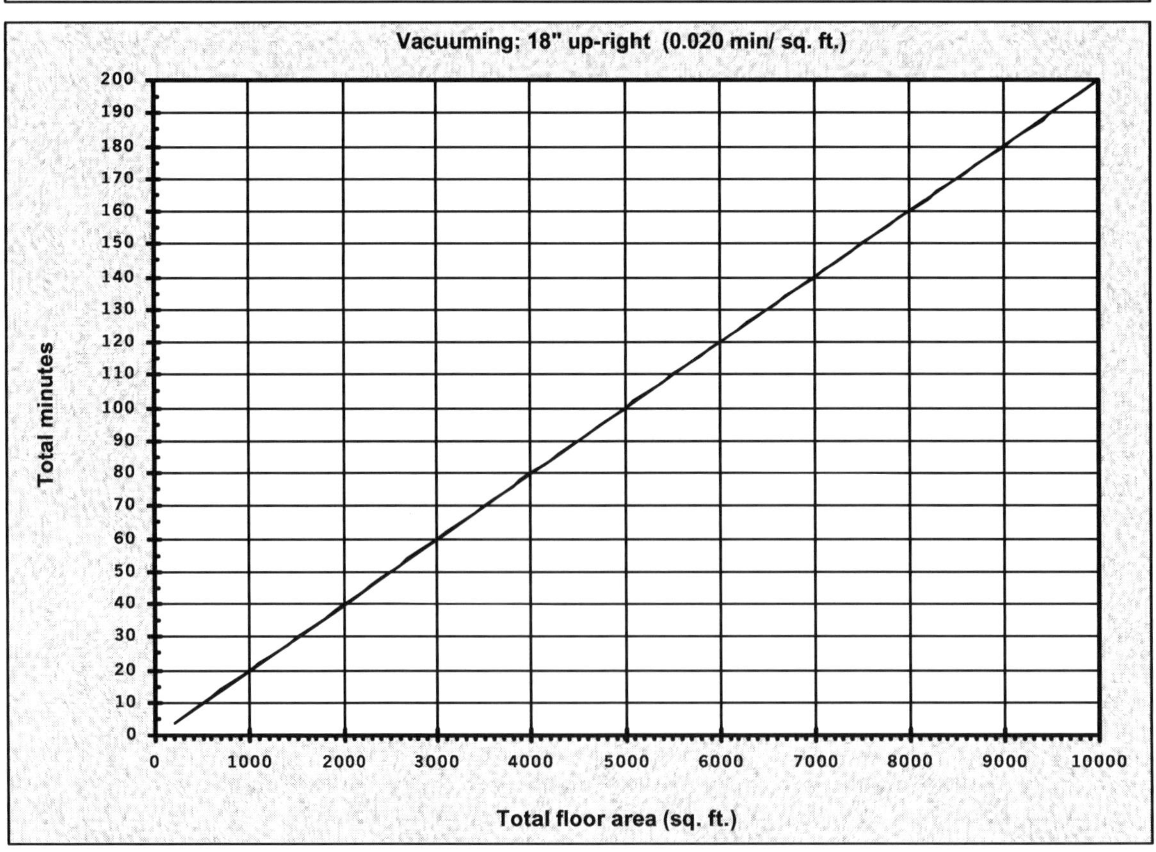
Vacuuming: 18" up-right (0.020 min/ sq. ft.)
Total minutes
200
190
180
170
160
150
140
130
120
110
100
90
80
70
60
50
40
30
20
10
0
0
1000
2000
3000
4000
5000
6000
7000
8000
9000
10000
Total floor area (sq. ft.)

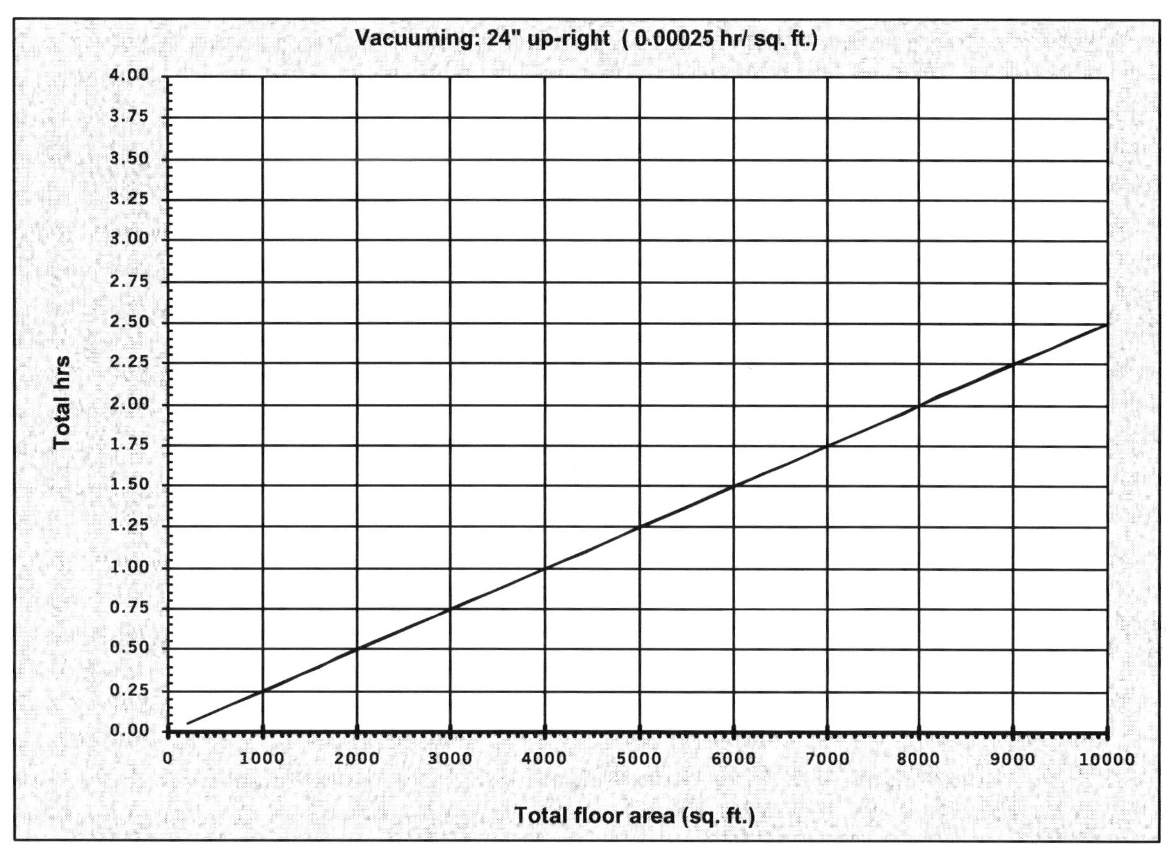
Vacuuming: 24" up-right (0.00025 hr/ sq. ft.)
Total hrs
4.00
3.75
3.50
3.25
3.00
2.75
2.50
2.25
2.00
1.75
1.50
1.25
1.00
0.75
0.50
0.25
0.00
0
1000
2000
3000
4000
5000
6000
7000
8000
9000
10000
Total floor area (sq. ft.)

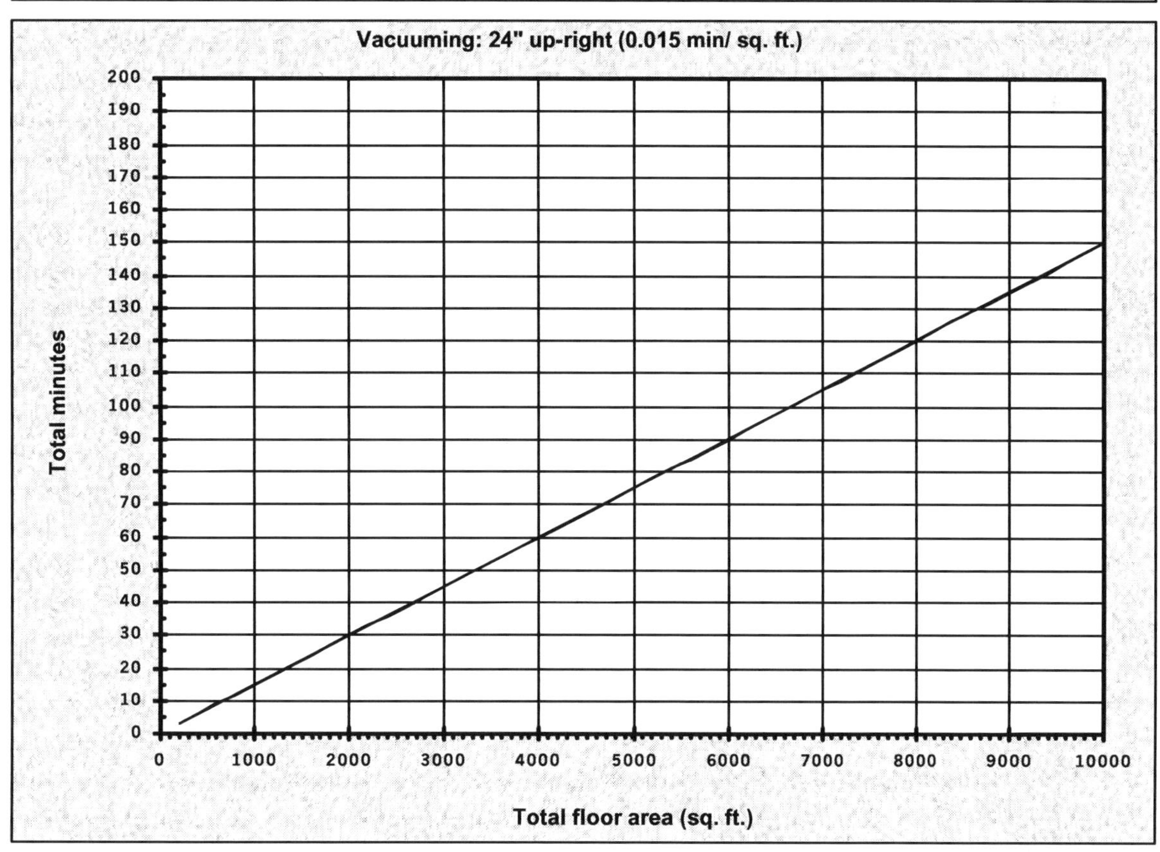
Vacuuming: 24" up-right (0.015 min/ sq. ft.)
Total minutes
200
190
180
170
160
150
140
130
120
110
100
90
80
70
60
50
40
30
20
10
0
0
1000
2000
3000
4000
5000
6000
7000
8000
9000
10000
Total floor area (sq. ft.)

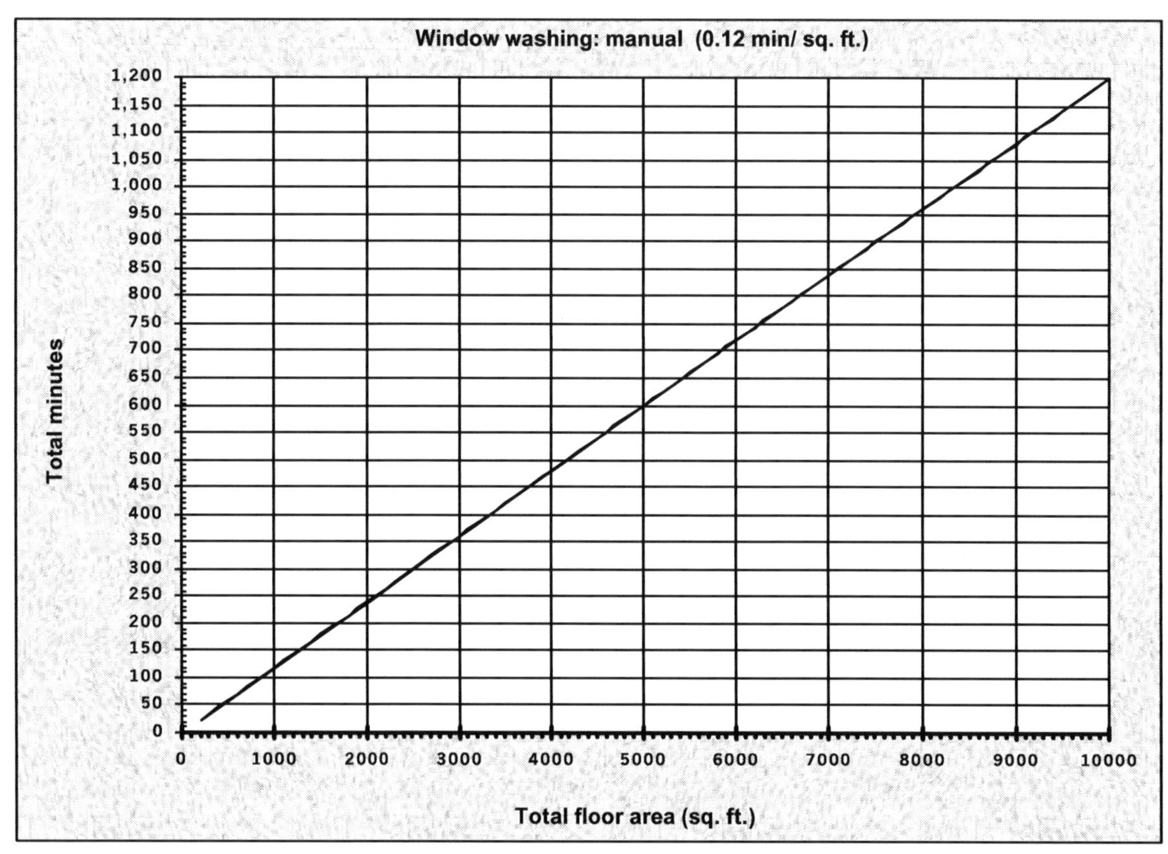
Window washing: manual (0.12 min/ sq. ft.)
Total minutes
1,200
1,150
1,100
1,050
1,000
950
900
850
800
750
700
650
600
550
500
450
400
350
300
250
200
150
100
50
0
0
1000
2000
3000
4000
5000
6000
7000
8000
9000
10000
Total floor area (sq. ft.)

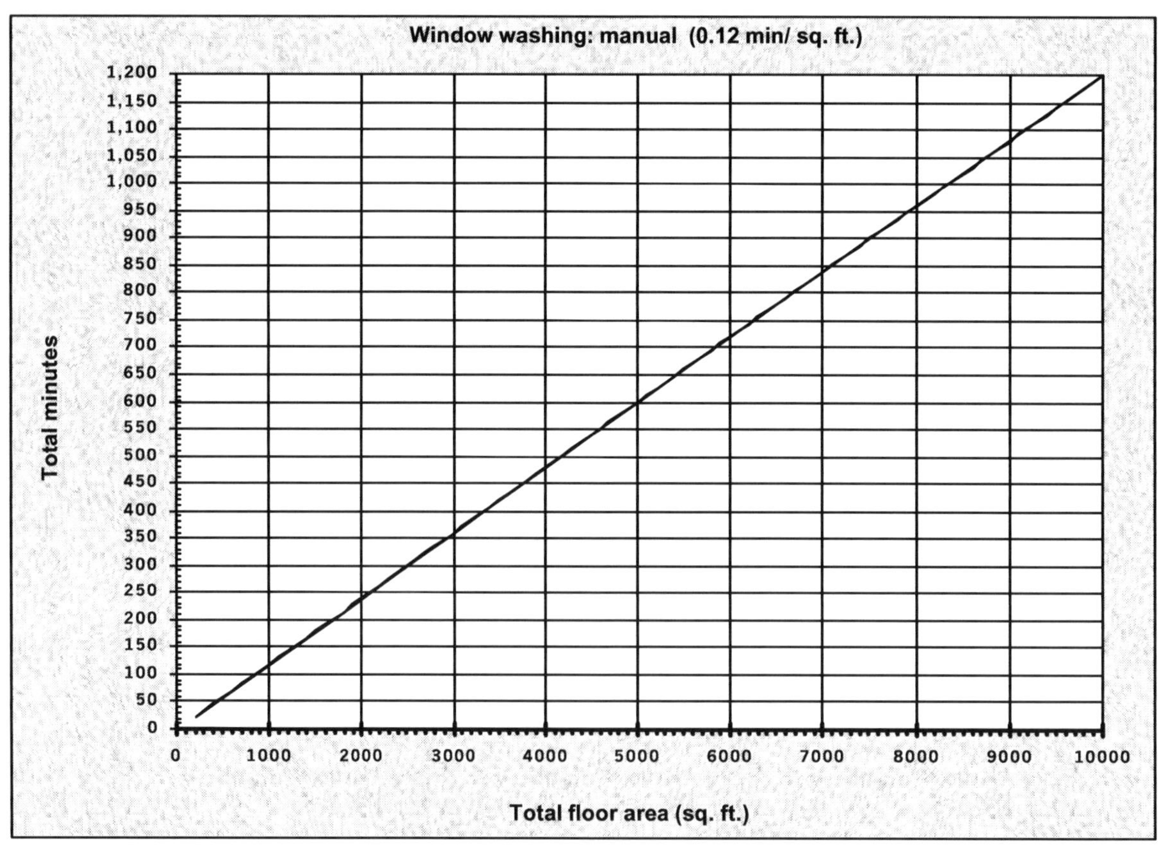
Window washing: manual (0.12 min/ sq. ft.)
Total minutes
1,200
1,150
1,100
1,050
1,000
950
900
850
800
750
700
650
600
550
500
450
400
350
300
250
200
150
100
50
0
0
1000
2000
3000
4000
5000
6000
7000
8000
9000
10000
Total floor area (sq. ft.)

Windows cleaned manually (0.002 hr/ sq. ft.) (various dimensions)

w (ft.)		h (ft.)	area sq. ft.	min/ unit	hrs/ unit	no.units/ hr
2	x	2	4	0.5	0.008	250
2	x	3	6	0.7	0.012	167
2	x	4	8	1.0	0.016	125
2	x	5	10	1.2	0.02	100
2	x	6	12	1.4	0.024	83
2	x	8	16	1.9	0.032	63
2	x	10	20	2.4	0.04	50
2	x	12	24	2.9	0.048	42
3	x	2	6	0.7	0.012	167
3	x	3	9	1.1	0.018	111
3	x	4	12	1.4	0.024	83
3	x	5	15	1.8	0.03	67
3	x	6	18	2.2	0.036	56
3	x	8	24	2.9	0.048	42
3	x	10	30	3.6	0.06	33
3	x	12	36	4.3	0.072	28
4	x	2	8	1.0	0.016	125
4	x	3	12	1.4	0.024	83
4	x	4	16	1.9	0.032	63
4	x	5	20	2.4	0.04	50
4	x	6	24	2.9	0.048	42
4	x	8	32	3.8	0.064	31
4	x	10	40	4.8	0.08	25
4	x	12	48	5.8	0.096	21
6	x	2	12	1.4	0.024	83
6	x	3	18	2.2	0.036	56
6	x	4	24	2.9	0.048	42
6	x	5	30	3.6	0.06	33
6	x	6	36	4.3	0.072	28
6	x	8	48	5.8	0.096	21
6	x	10	60	7.2	0.12	17
6	x	12	72	8.6	0.144	14
8	x	2	16	1.9	0.032	63
8	x	3	24	2.9	0.048	42
8	x	4	32	3.8	0.064	31
8	x	5	40	4.8	0.08	25
8	x	6	48	5.8	0.096	21
8	x	8	64	7.7	0.128	16
8	x	10	80	9.6	0.16	13
8	x	12	96	11.5	0.192	10
10	x	2	20	2.4	0.04	50
10	x	3	30	3.6	0.06	33
10	x	4	40	4.8	0.08	25
10	x	5	50	6.0	0.1	20
10	x	6	60	7.2	0.12	17
10	x	8	80	9.6	0.16	13
10	x	10	100	12.0	0.2	10
10	x	12	120	14.4	0.24	8
12	x	2	24	2.9	0.048	42
12	x	3	36	4.3	0.072	28
12	x	4	48	5.8	0.096	21
12	x	5	60	7.2	0.12	17
12	x	6	72	8.6	0.144	14
12	x	8	96	11.5	0.192	10
12	x	10	120	14.4	0.24	8
12	x	12	144	17.3	0.288	7

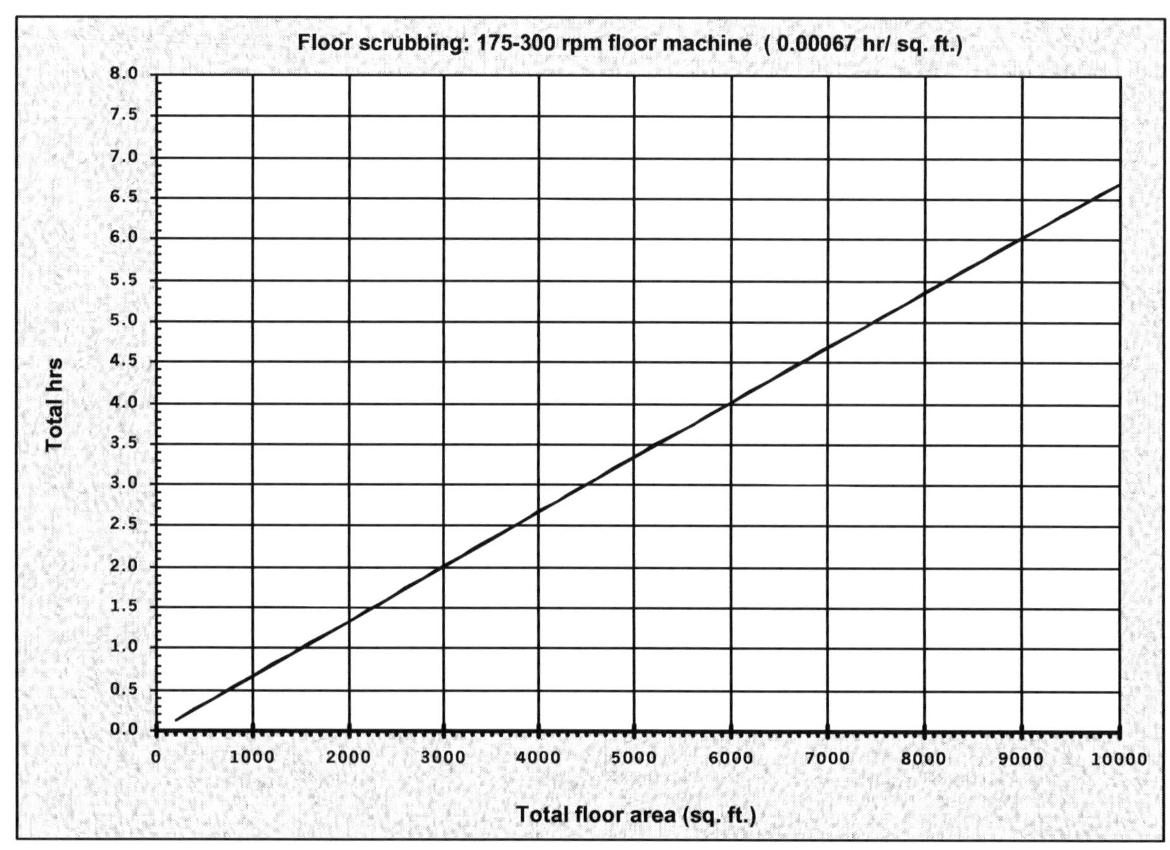
Floor scrubbing: 175-300 rpm floor machine (0.00067 hr/ sq. ft.)
Total hrs
8.0
7.5
7.0
6.5
6.0
5.5
5.0
4.5
4.0
3.5
3.0
2.5
2.0
1.5
1.0
0.5
0.0
0
1000
2000
3000
4000
5000
6000
7000
8000
9000
10000
Total floor area (sq. ft.)

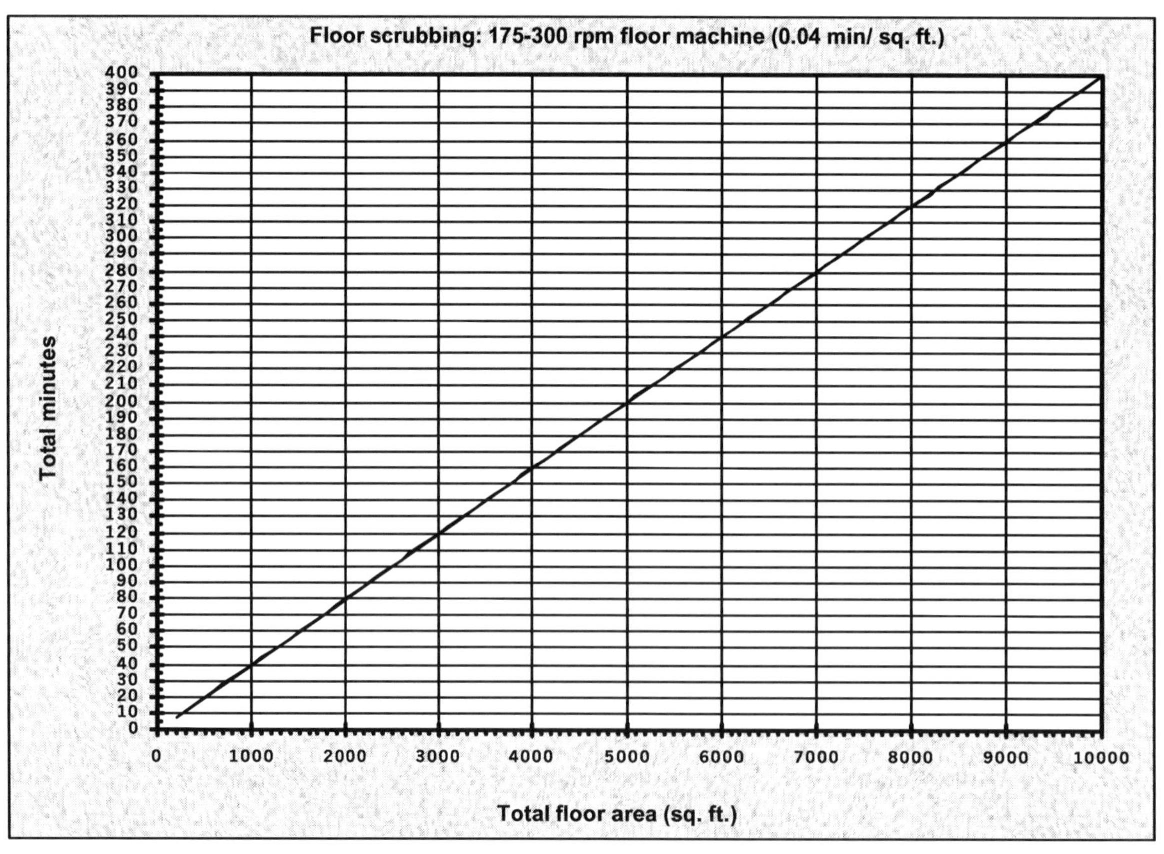
Floor scrubbing: 175-300 rpm floor machine (0.04 min/ sq. ft.)
Total minutes
400
390
380
370
360
350
340
330
320
310
300
290
280
270
260
250
240
230
220
210
200
190
180
170
160
150
140
130
120
110
100
90
80
70
60
50
40
30
20
10
0
0
1000
2000
3000
4000
5000
6000
7000
8000
9000
10000
Total floor area (sq. ft.)

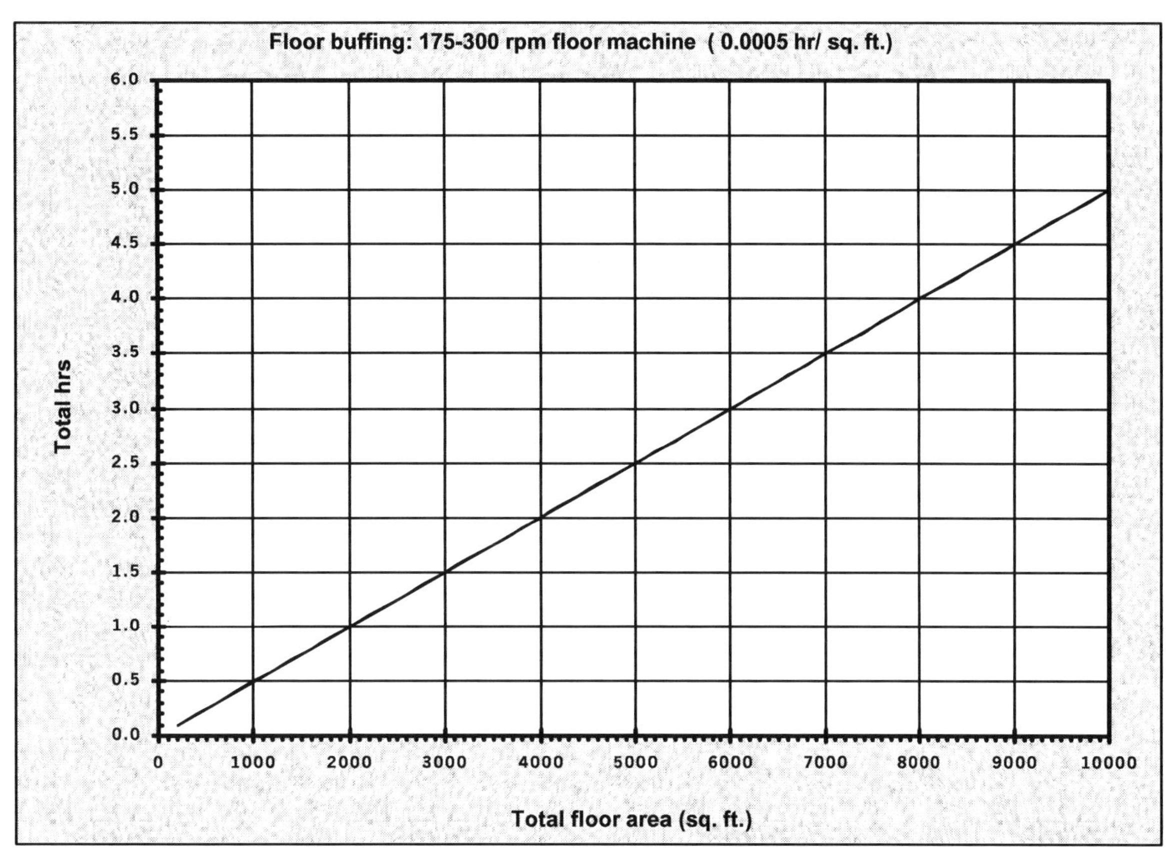
Floor buffing: 175-300 rpm floor machine (0.0005 hr/ sq. ft.)
Total hrs
6.0
5.5
5.0
4.5
4.0
3.5
3.0
2.5
2.0
1.5
1.0
0.5
0.0
0
1000
2000
3000
4000
5000
6000
7000
8000
9000
10000
Total floor area (sq. ft.)

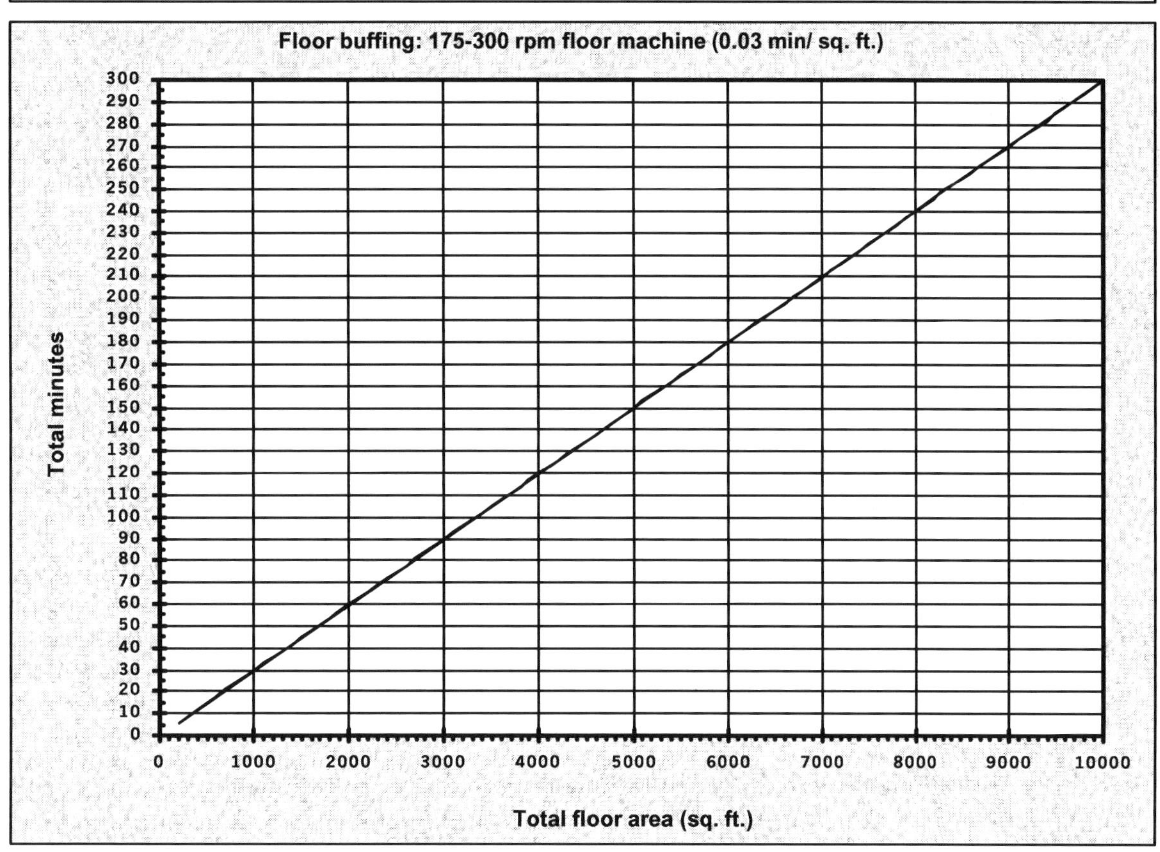
Floor buffing: 175-300 rpm floor machine (0.03 min/ sq. ft.)
Total minutes
300
290
280
270
260
250
240
230
220
210
200
190
180
170
160
150
140
130
120
110
100
90
80
70
60
50
40
30
20
10
0
0
1000
2000
3000
4000
5000
6000
7000
8000
9000
10000
Total floor area (sq. ft.)

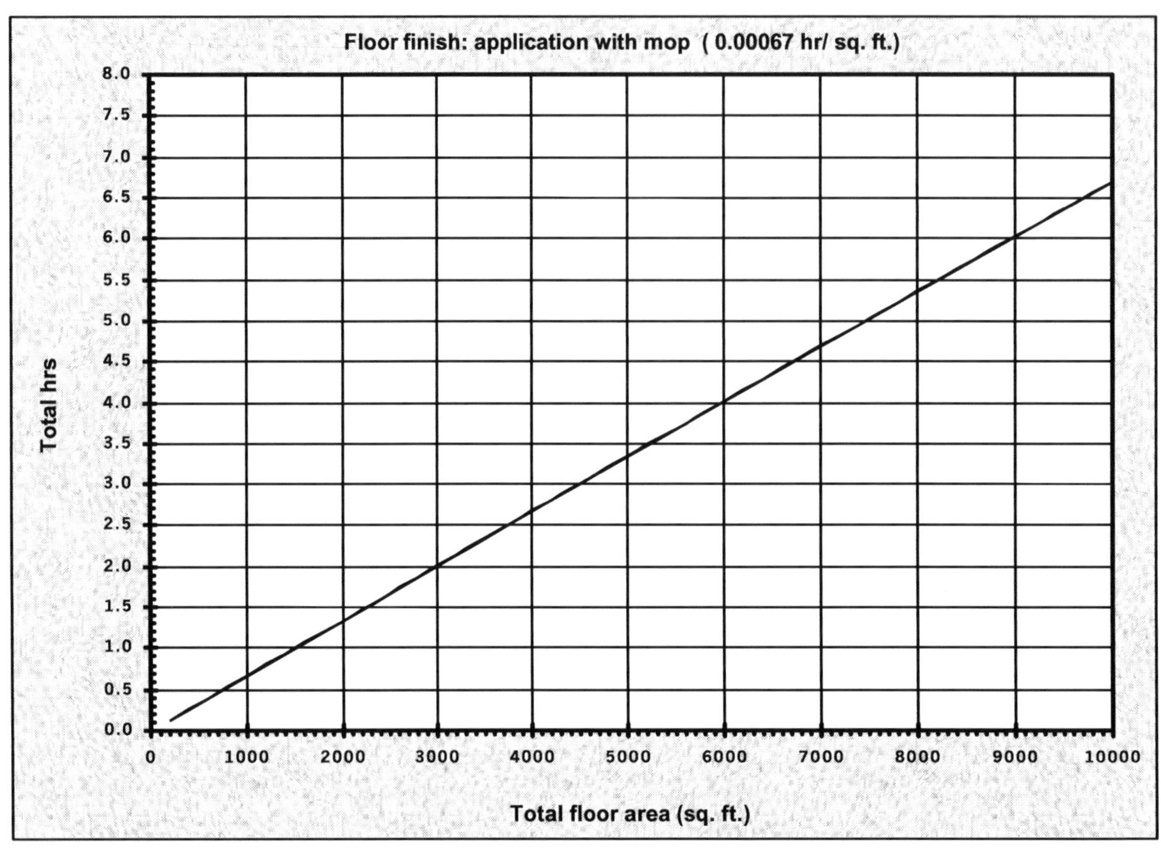
Floor finish: application with mop (0.00067 hr/ sq. ft.)
Total hrs
8.0
7.5
7.0
6.5
6.0
5.5
5.0
4.5
4.0
3.5
3.0
2.5
2.0
1.5
1.0
0.5
0.0
0
1000
2000
3000
4000
5000
6000
7000
8000
9000
10000
Total floor area (sq. ft.)

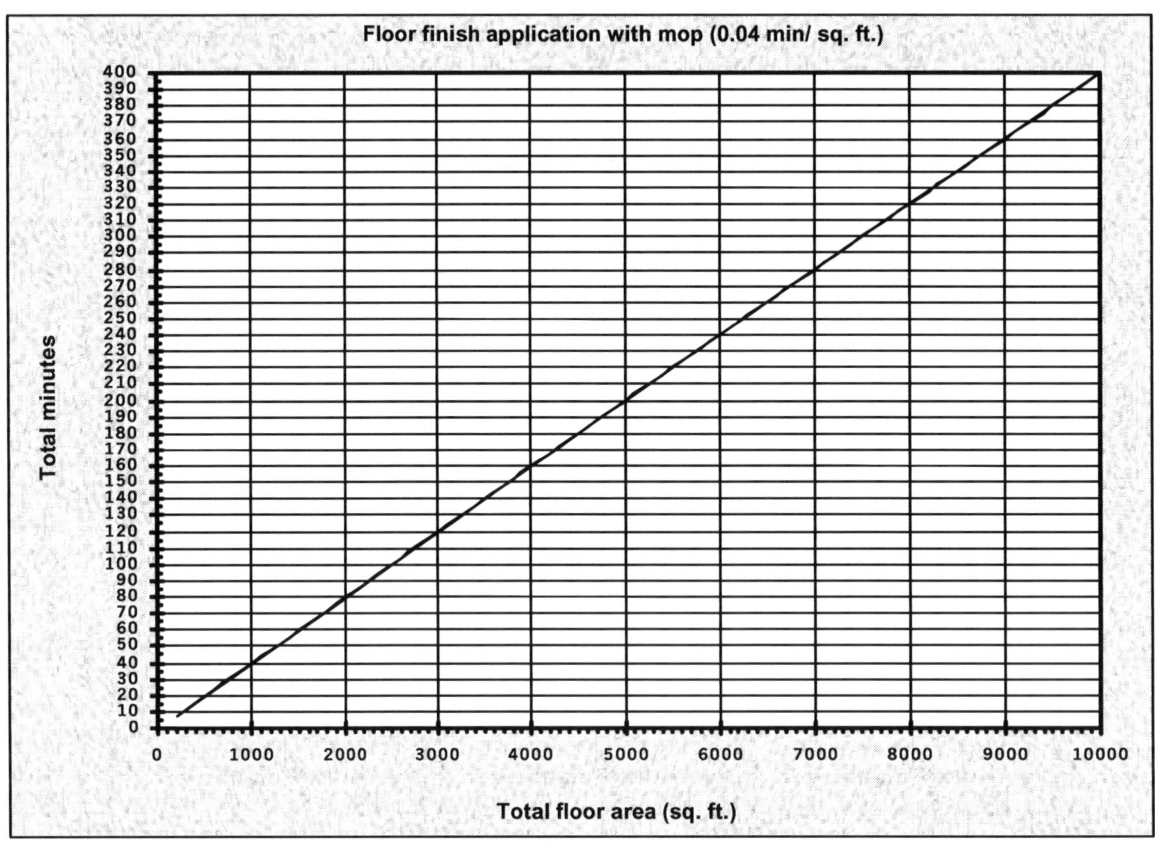
Floor finish application with mop (0.04 min/ sq. ft.)
Total minutes
400
390
380
370
360
350
340
330
320
310
300
290
280
270
260
250
240
230
220
210
200
190
180
170
160
150
140
130
120
110
100
90
80
70
60
50
40
30
20
10
0
0
1000
2000
3000
4000
5000
6000
7000
8000
9000
10000
Total floor area (sq. ft.)

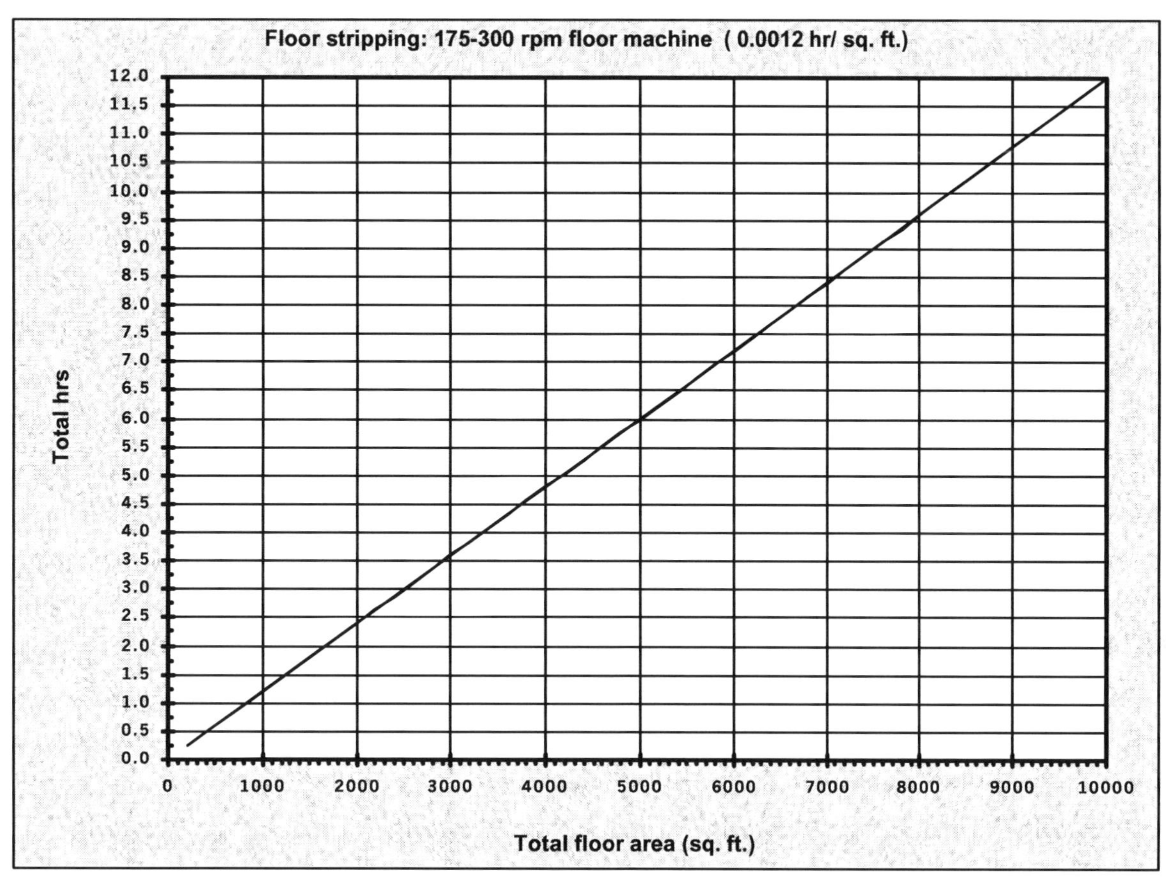
Floor stripping: 175-300 rpm floor machine (0.0012 hr/ sq. ft.)
Total hrs
12.0
11.5
11.0
10.5
10.0
9.5
9.0
8.5
8.0
7.5
7.0
6.5
6.0
5.5
5.0
4.5
4.0
3.5
3.0
2.5
2.0
1.5
1.0
0.5
0.0
0
1000
2000
3000
4000
5000
6000
7000
8000
9000
10000
Total floor area (sq. ft.)

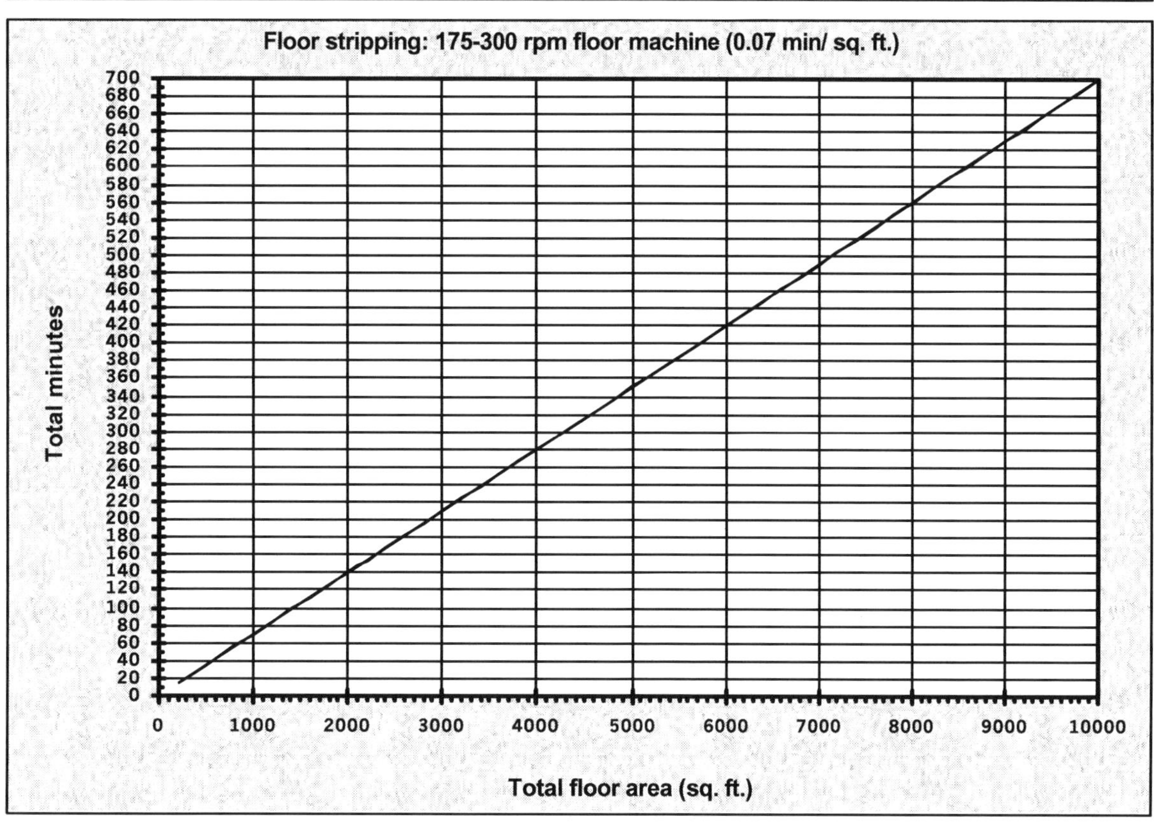
Floor stripping: 175-300 rpm floor machine (0.07 min/ sq. ft.)
Total minutes
700
680
660
640
620
600
580
560
540
520
500
480
460
440
420
400
380
360
340
320
300
280
260
240
220
200
180
160
140
120
100
80
60
40
20
0
0
1000
2000
3000
4000
5000
6000
7000
8000
9000
10000
Total floor area (sq. ft.)

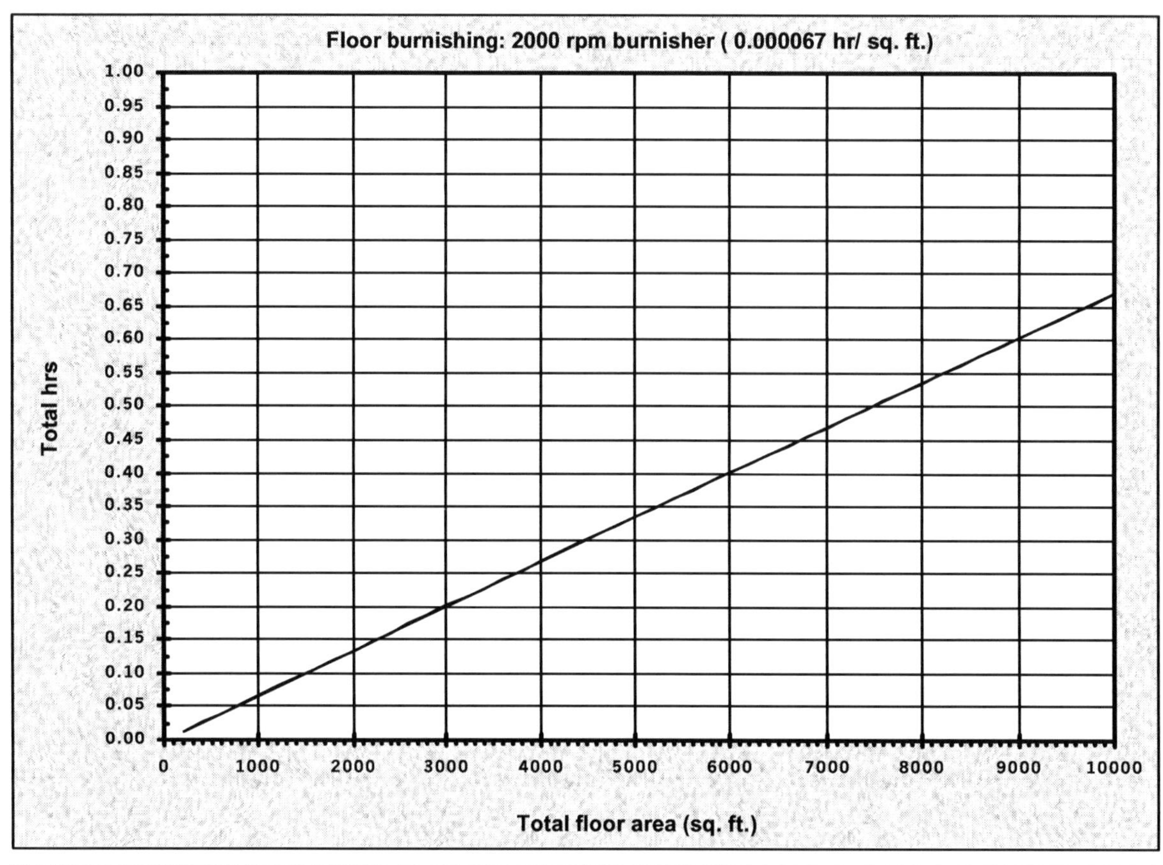
Floor burnishing: 2000 rpm burnisher (0.000067 hr/ sq. ft.)
Total hrs
1.00
0.95
0.90
0.85
0.80
0.75
0.70
0.65
0.60
0.55
0.50
0.45
0.40
0.35
0.30
0.25
0.20
0.15
0.10
0.05
0.00
0
1000
2000
3000
4000
5000
6000
7000
8000
9000
10000
Total floor area (sq. ft.)

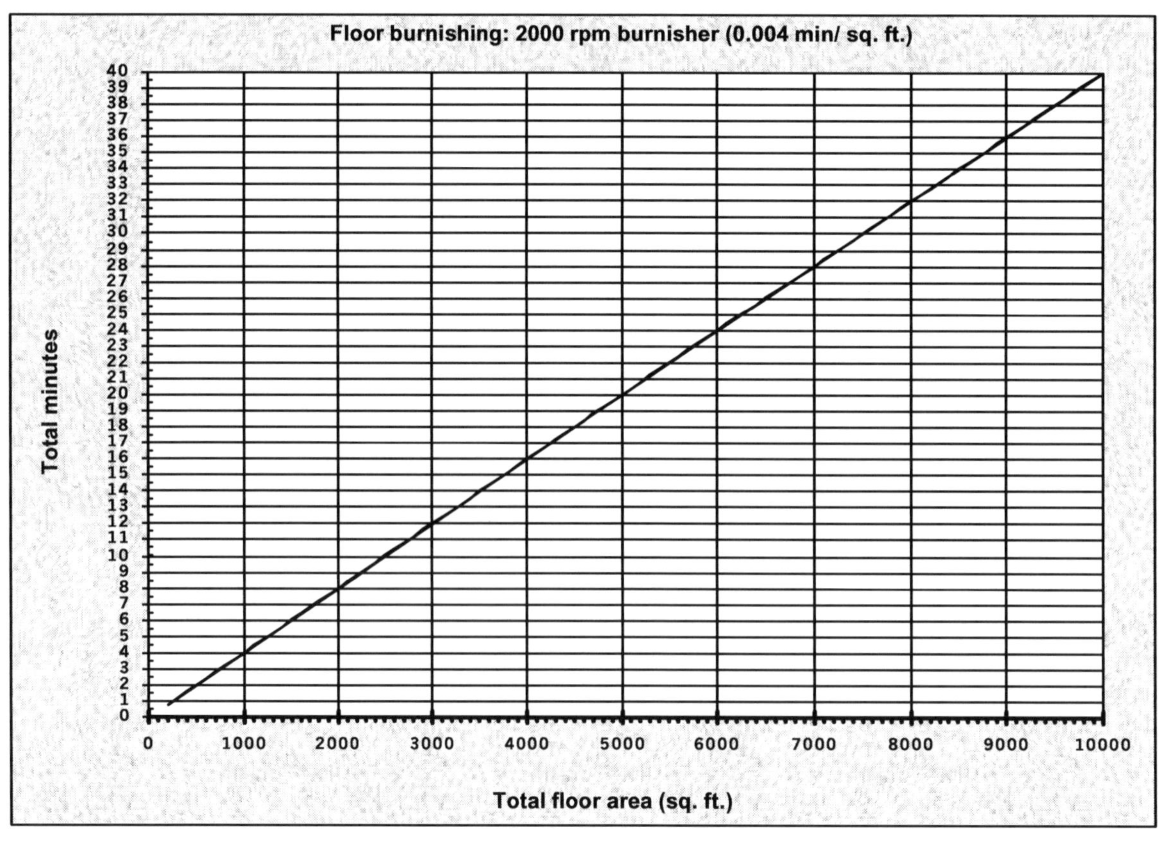
Floor burnishing: 2000 rpm burnisher (0.004 min/ sq. ft.)
Total minutes
40
39
38
37
36
35
34
33
32
31
30
29
28
27
26
25
24
23
22
21
20
19
18
17
16
15
14
13
12
11
10
9
8
7
6
5
4
3
2
1
0
0
1000
2000
3000
4000
5000
6000
7000
8000
9000
10000
Total floor area (sq. ft.)

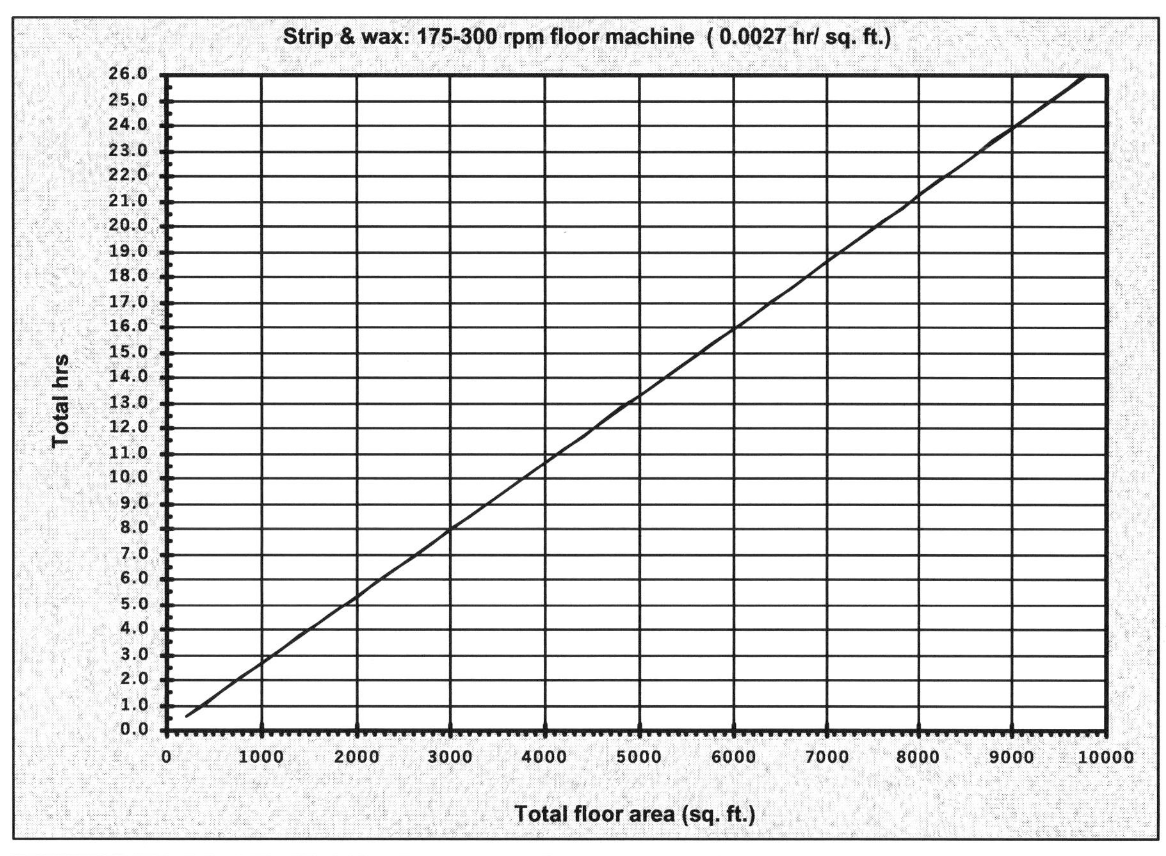
Strip & wax: 175-300 rpm floor machine (0.0027 hr/ sq. ft.)
Total hrs
26.0
25.0
24.0
23.0
22.0
21.0
20.0
19.0
18.0
17.0
16.0
15.0
14.0
13.0
12.0
11.0
10.0
9.0
8.0
7.0
6.0
5.0
4.0
3.0
2.0
1.0
0.0
0
1000
2000
3000
4000
5000
6000
7000
8000
9000
10000
Total floor area (sq. ft.)

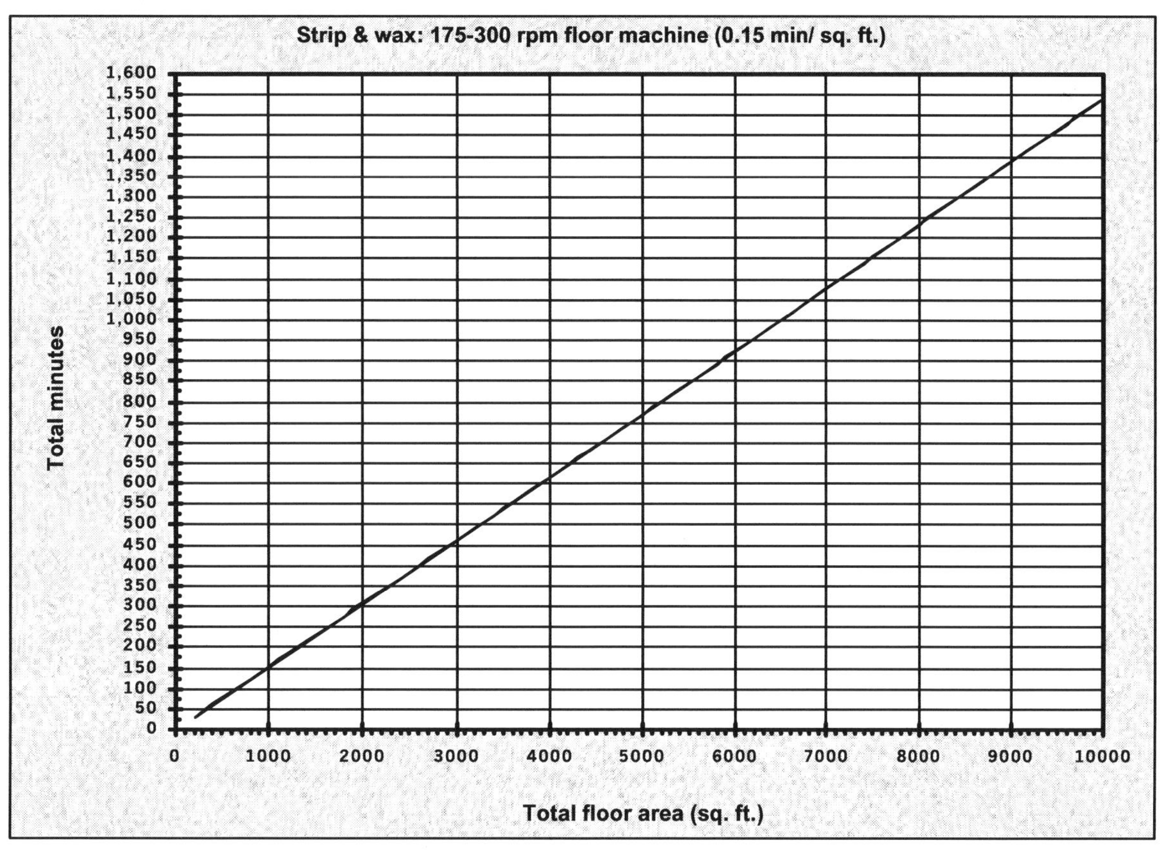
Strip & wax: 175-300 rpm floor machine (0.15 min/ sq. ft.)
Total minutes
1,600
1,550
1,500
1,450
1,400
1,350
1,300
1,250
1,200
1,150
1,100
1,050
1,000
950
900
850
800
750
700
650
600
550
500
450
400
350
300
250
200
150
100
50
0
0
1000
2000
3000
4000
5000
6000
7000
8000
9000
10000
Total floor area (sq. ft.)

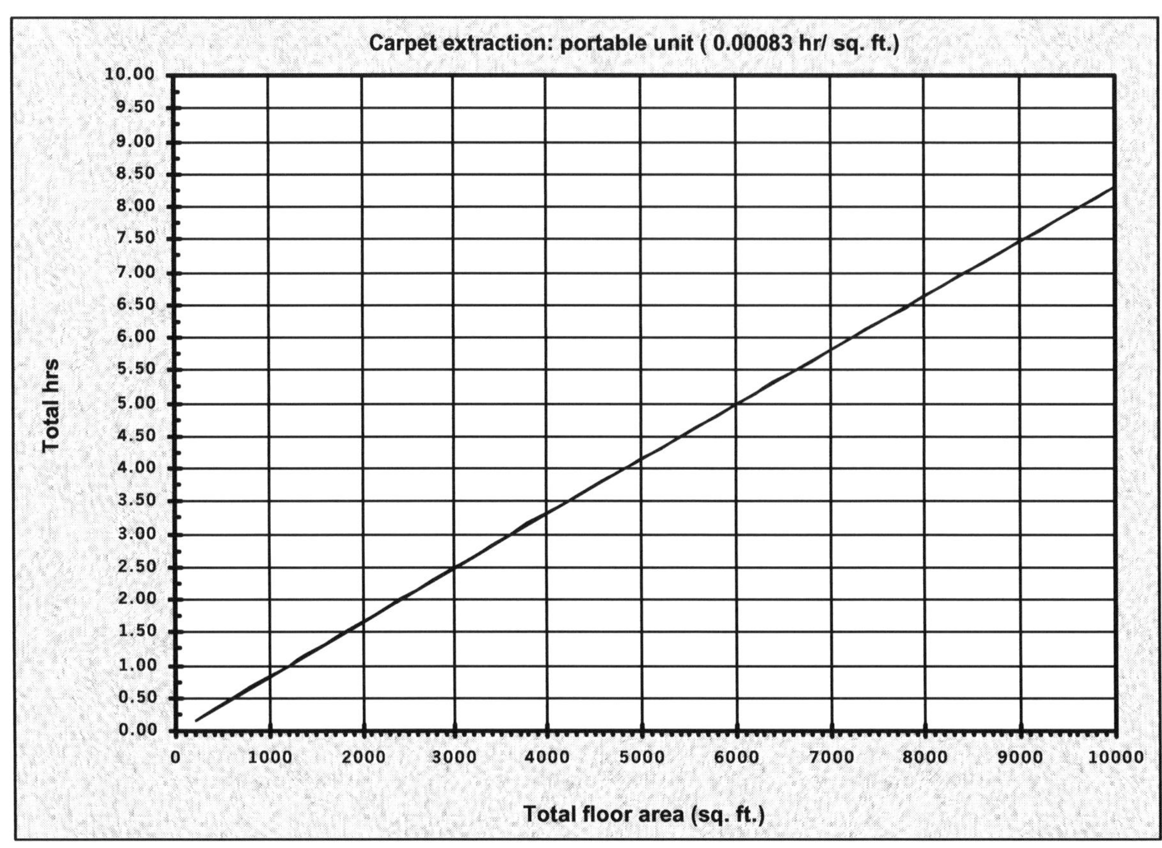
Carpet extraction: portable unit (0.00083 hr/ sq. ft.)
Total hrs
10.00
9.50
9.00
8.50
8.00
7.50
7.00
6.50
6.00
5.50
5.00
4.50
4.00
3.50
3.00
2.50
2.00
1.50
1.00
0.50
0.00
0
1000
2000
3000
4000
5000
6000
7000
8000
9000
10000
Total floor area (sq. ft.)

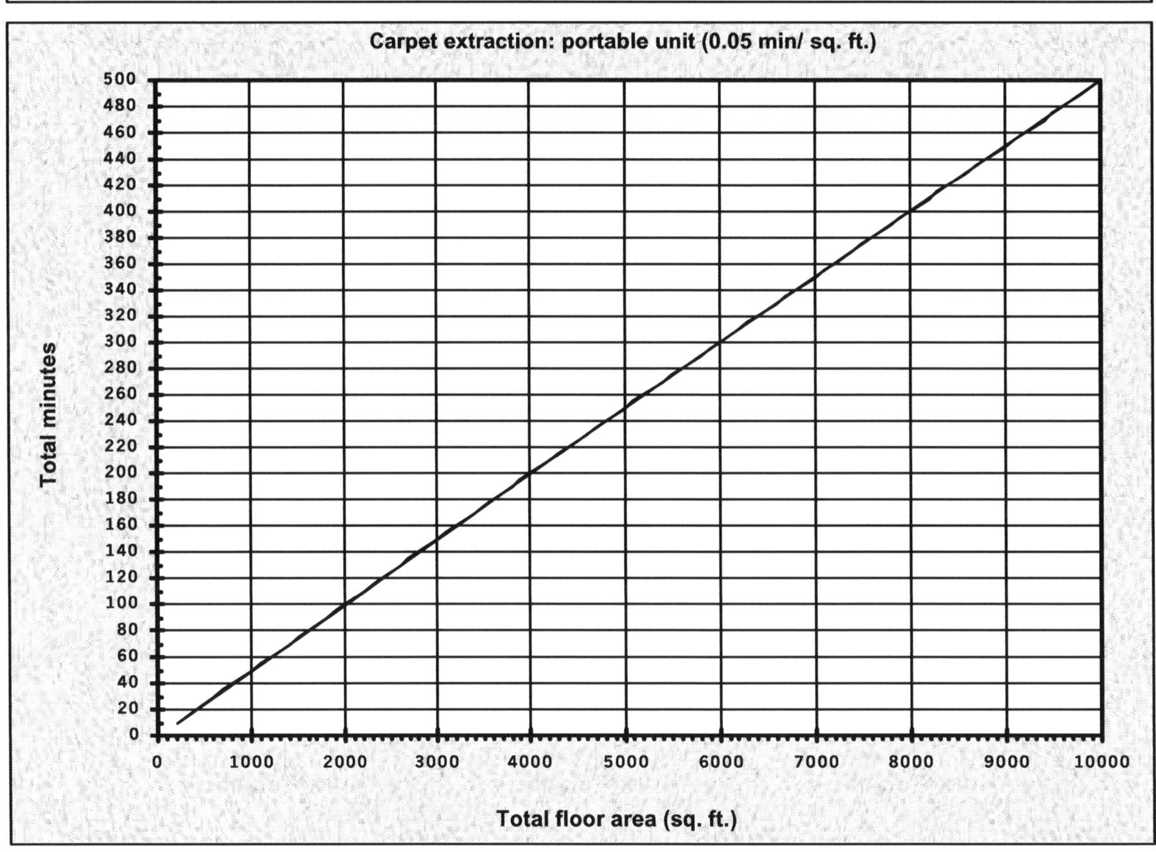
Carpet extraction: portable unit (0.05 min/ sq. ft.)
Total minutes
500
480
460
440
420
400
380
360
340
320
300
280
260
240
220
200
180
160
140
120
100
80
60
40
20
0
0
1000
2000
3000
4000
5000
6000
7000
8000
9000
10000
Total floor area (sq. ft.)

Chapter 4

Generic cleaning solution usage charts

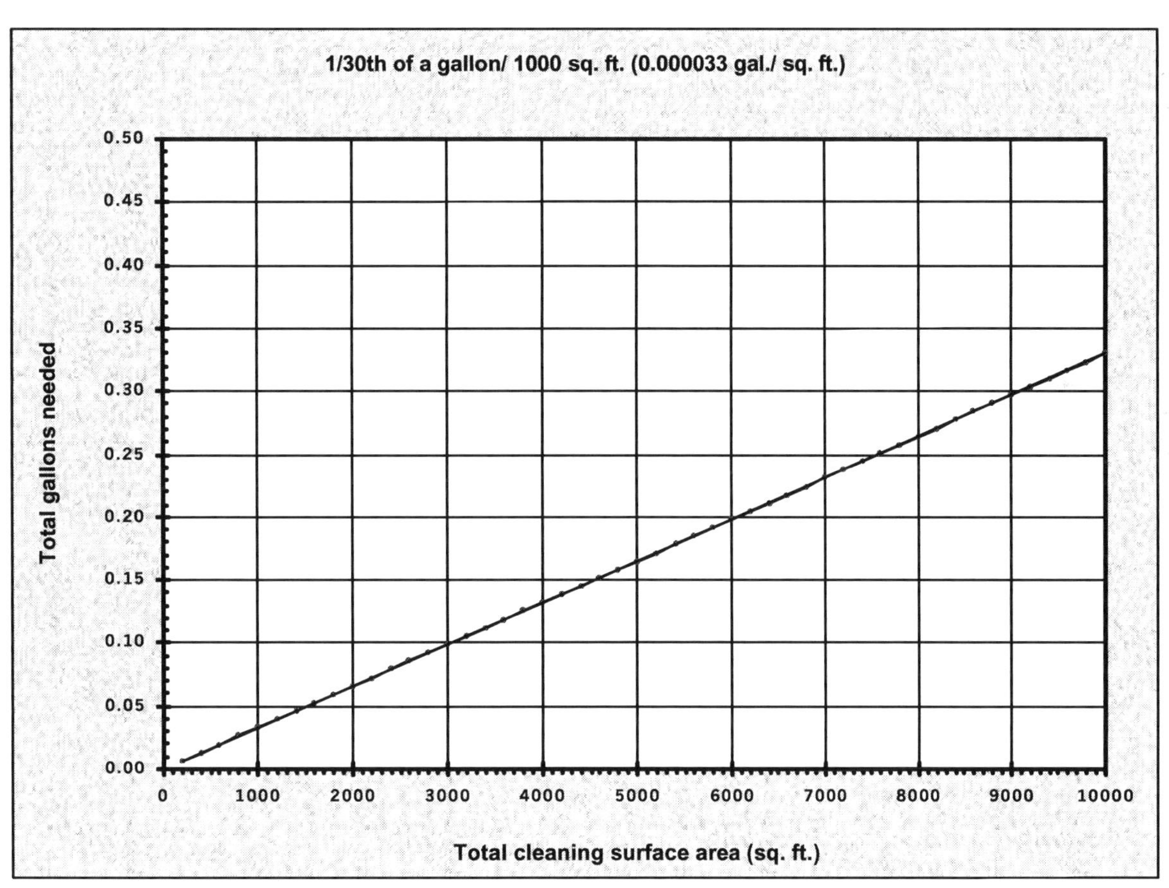

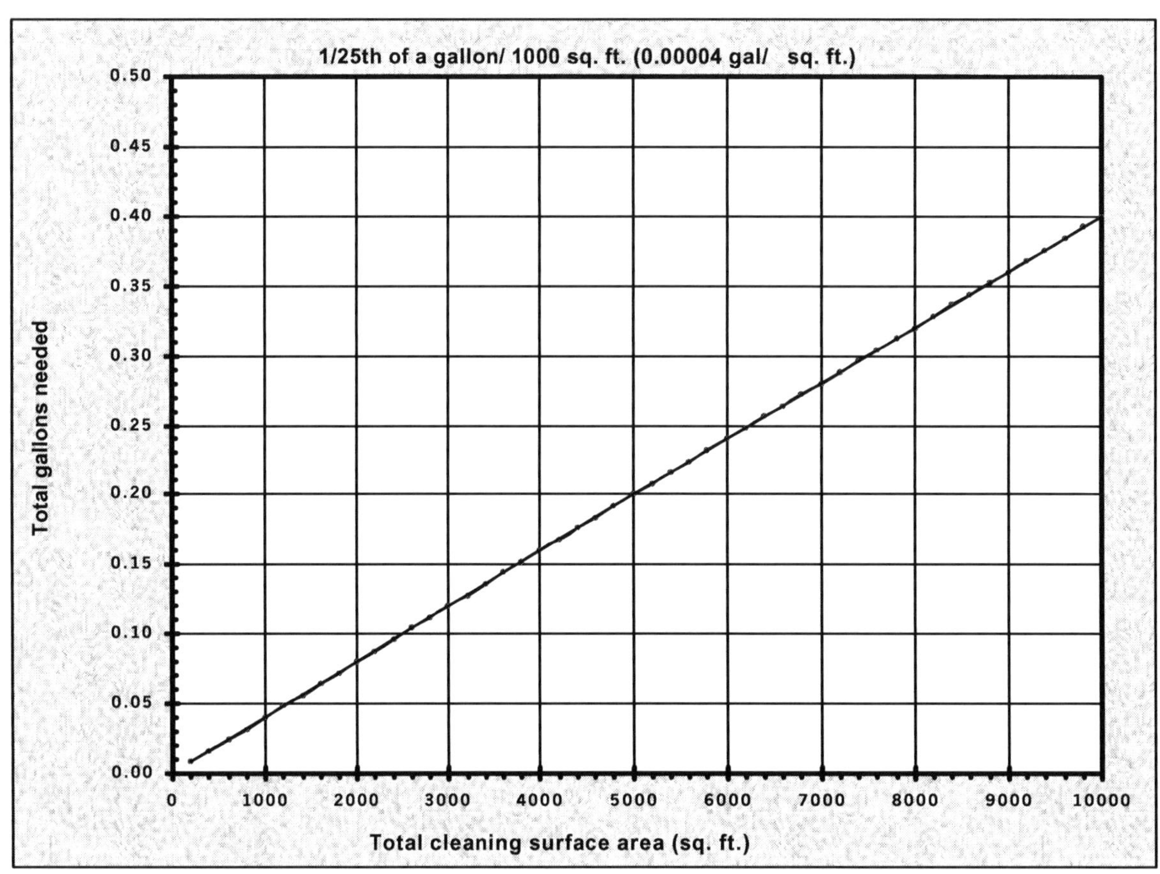
1/25th of a gallon/ 1000 sq. ft. (0.00004 gal/ sq. ft.)
Total gallons needed
0.50
0.45
0.40
0.35
0.30
0.25
0.20
0.15
0.10
0.05
0.00
0
1000
2000
3000
4000
5000
6000
7000
8000
9000
10000
Total cleaning surface area (sq. ft.)

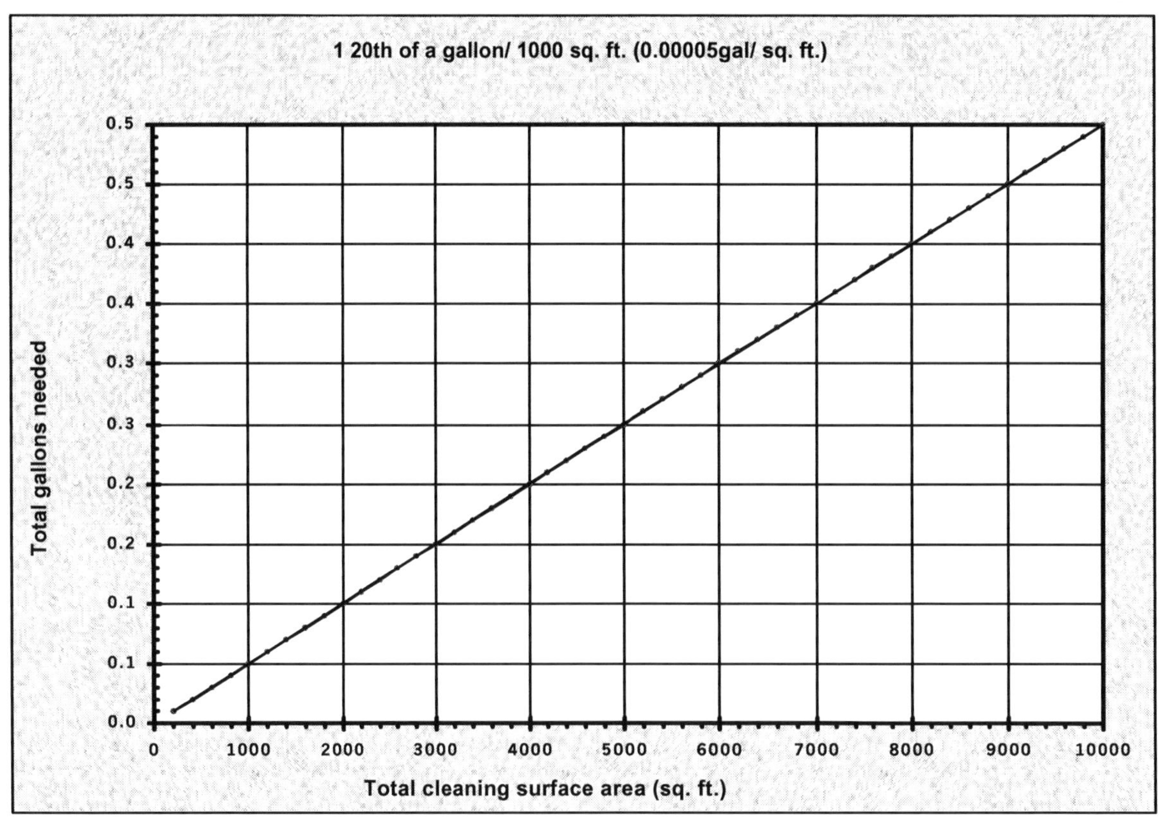
1 20th of a gallon/ 1000 sq. ft. (0.00005gal/ sq. ft.)
Total gallons needed
0.5
0.5
0.4
0.4
0.3
0.3
0.2
0.2
0.1
0.1
0.0
0
1000
2000
3000
4000
5000
6000
7000
8000
9000
10000
Total cleaning surface area (sq. ft.)

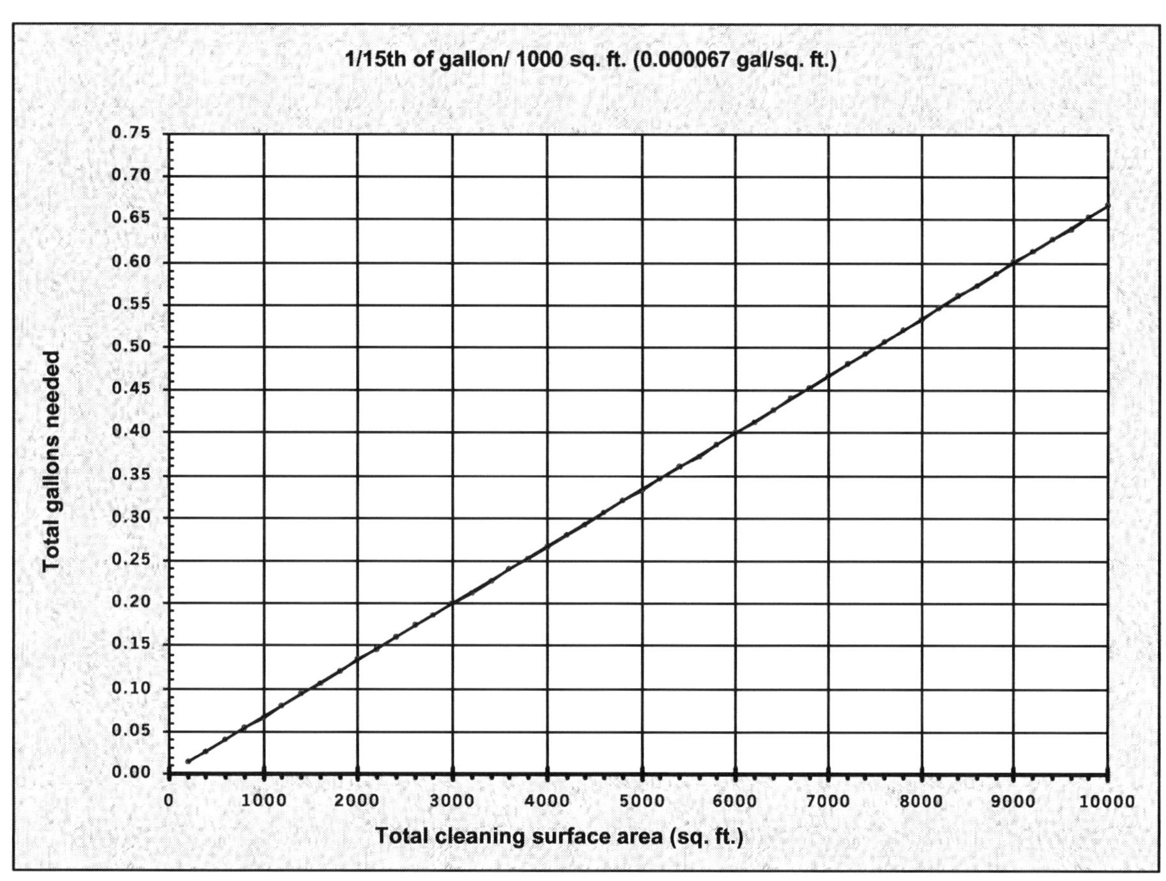
1/15th of gallon/ 1000 sq. ft. (0.000067 gal/sq. ft.)
Total gallons needed
0.75
0.70
0.65
0.60
0.55
0.50
0.45
0.40
0.35
0.30
0.25
0.20
0.15
0.10
0.05
0.00
0
1000
2000
3000
4000
5000
6000
7000
8000
9000
10000
Total cleaning surface area (sq. ft.)

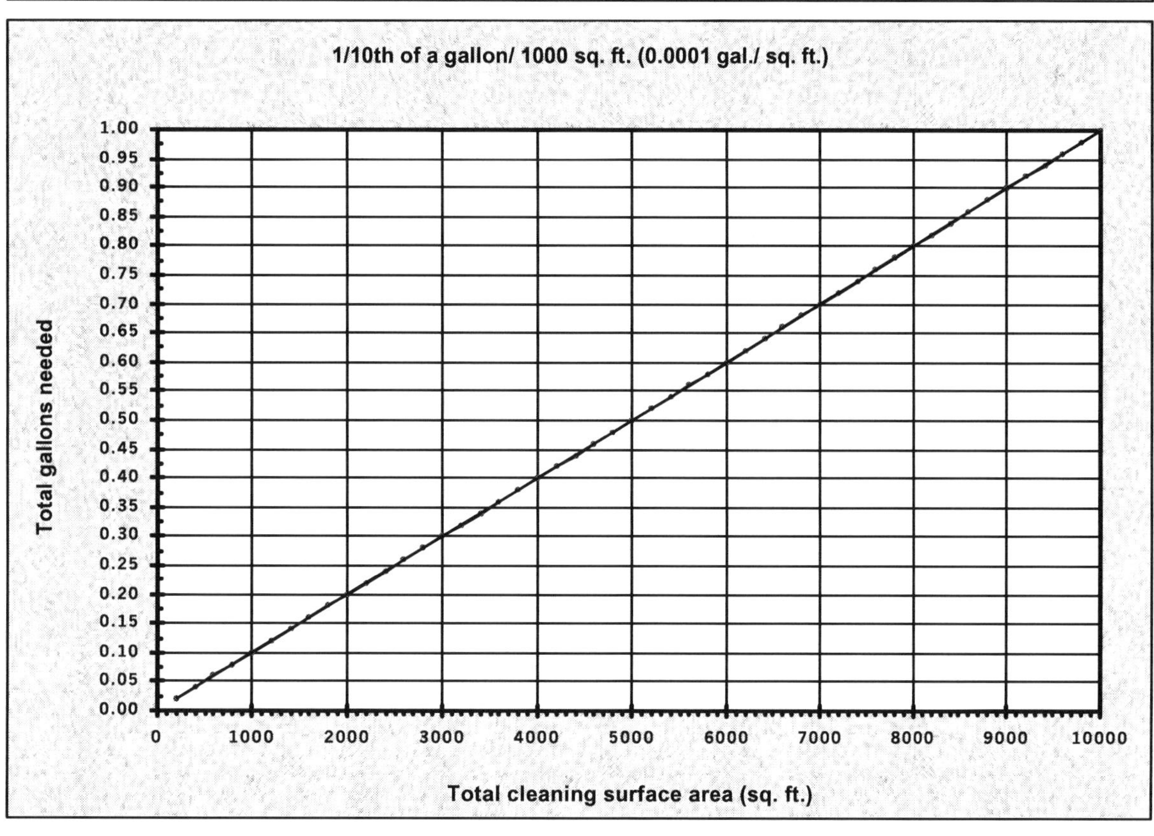
1/10th of a gallon/ 1000 sq. ft. (0.0001 gal./ sq. ft.)
Total gallons needed
1.00
0.95
0.90
0.85
0.80
0.75
0.70
0.65
0.60
0.55
0.50
0.45
0.40
0.35
0.30
0.25
0.20
0.15
0.10
0.05
0.00
0
1000
2000
3000
4000
5000
6000
7000
8000
9000
10000
Total cleaning surface area (sq. ft.)

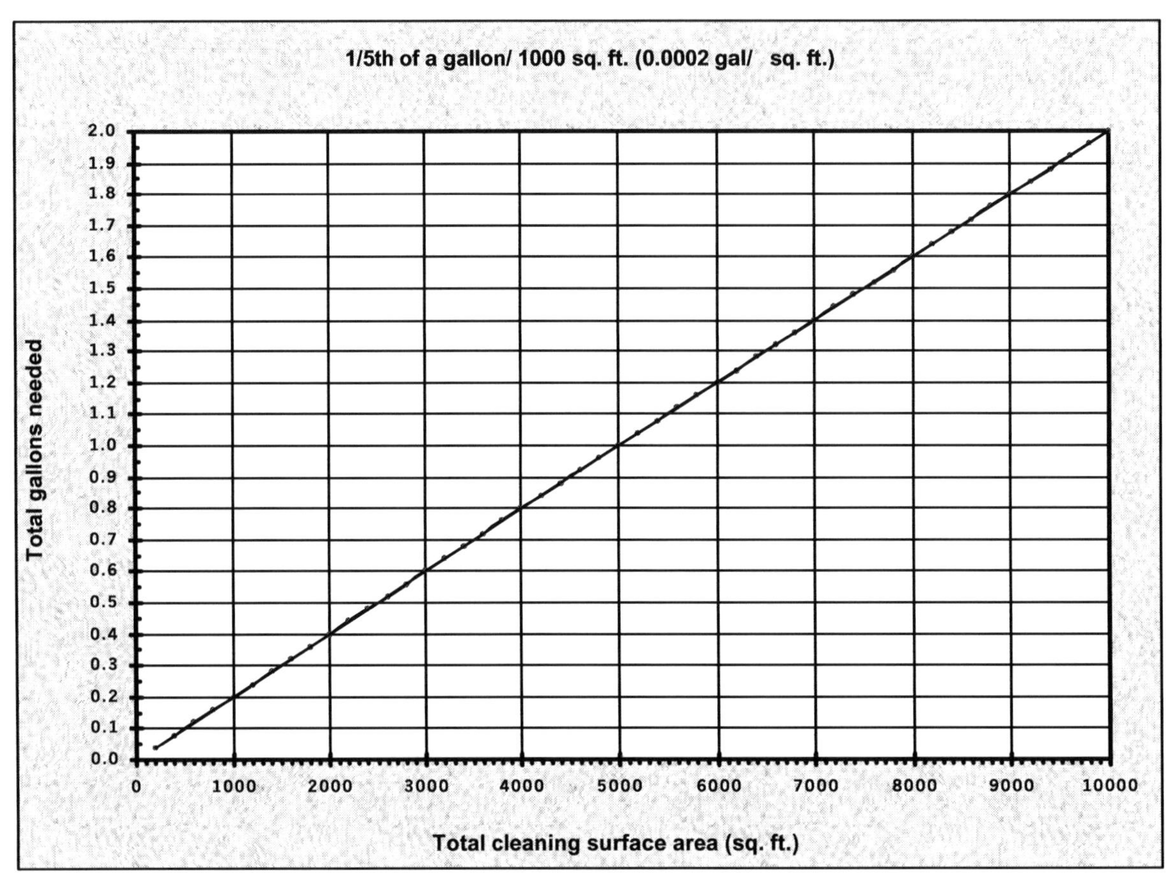
1/5th of a gallon/ 1000 sq. ft. (0.0002 gal/ sq. ft.)
Total gallons needed
2.0
1.9
1.8
1.7
1.6
1.5
1.4
1.3
1.2
1.1
1.0
0.9
0.8
0.7
0.6
0.5
0.4
0.3
0.2
0.1
0.0
0
1000
2000
3000
4000
5000
6000
7000
8000
9000
10000
Total cleaning surface area (sq. ft.)

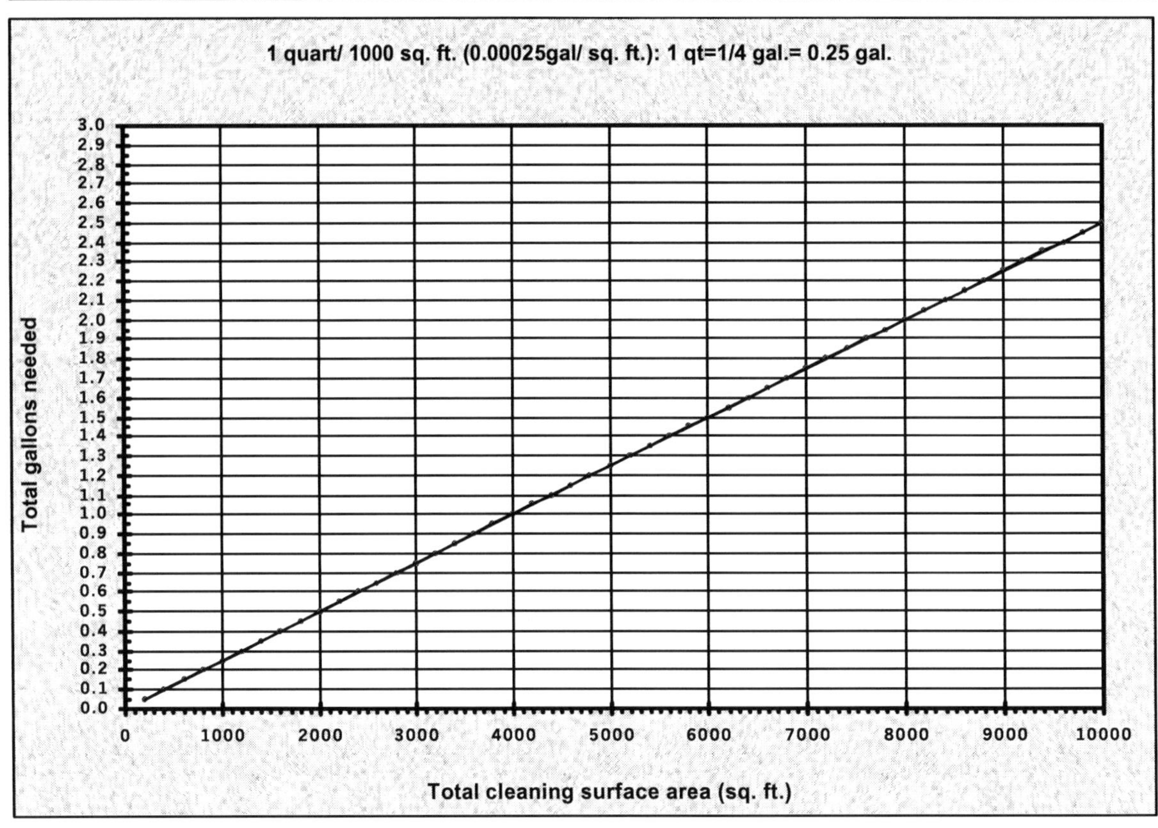
1 quart/ 1000 sq. ft. (0.00025gal/ sq. ft.): 1 qt=1/4 gal.= 0.25 gal.
Total gallons needed
3.0
2.9
2.8
2.7
2.6
2.5
2.4
2.3
2.2
2.1
2.0
1.9
1.8
1.7
1.6
1.5
1.4
1.3
1.2
1.1
1.0
0.9
0.8
0.7
0.6
0.5
0.4
0.3
0.2
0.1
0.0
0
1000
2000
3000
4000
5000
6000
7000
8000
9000
10000
Total cleaning surface area (sq. ft.)

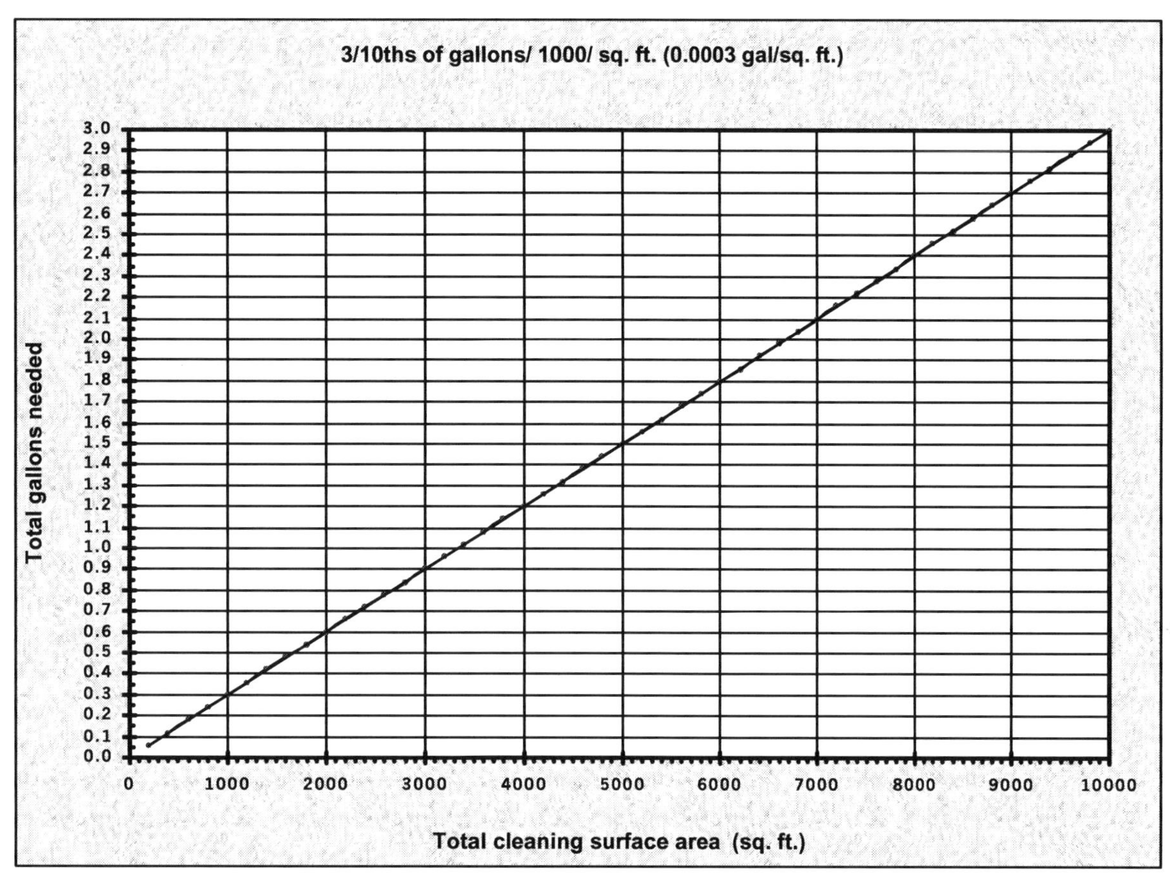
3/10ths of gallons/ 1000/ sq. ft. (0.0003 gal/sq. ft.)
Total gallons needed
3.0
2.9
2.8
2.7
2.6
2.5
2.4
2.3
2.2
2.1
2.0
1.9
1.8
1.7
1.6
1.5
1.4
1.3
1.2
1.1
1.0
0.9
0.8
0.7
0.6
0.5
0.4
0.3
0.2
0.1
0.0
0
1000
2000
3000
4000
5000
6000
7000
8000
9000
10000
Total cleaning surface area (sq. ft.)

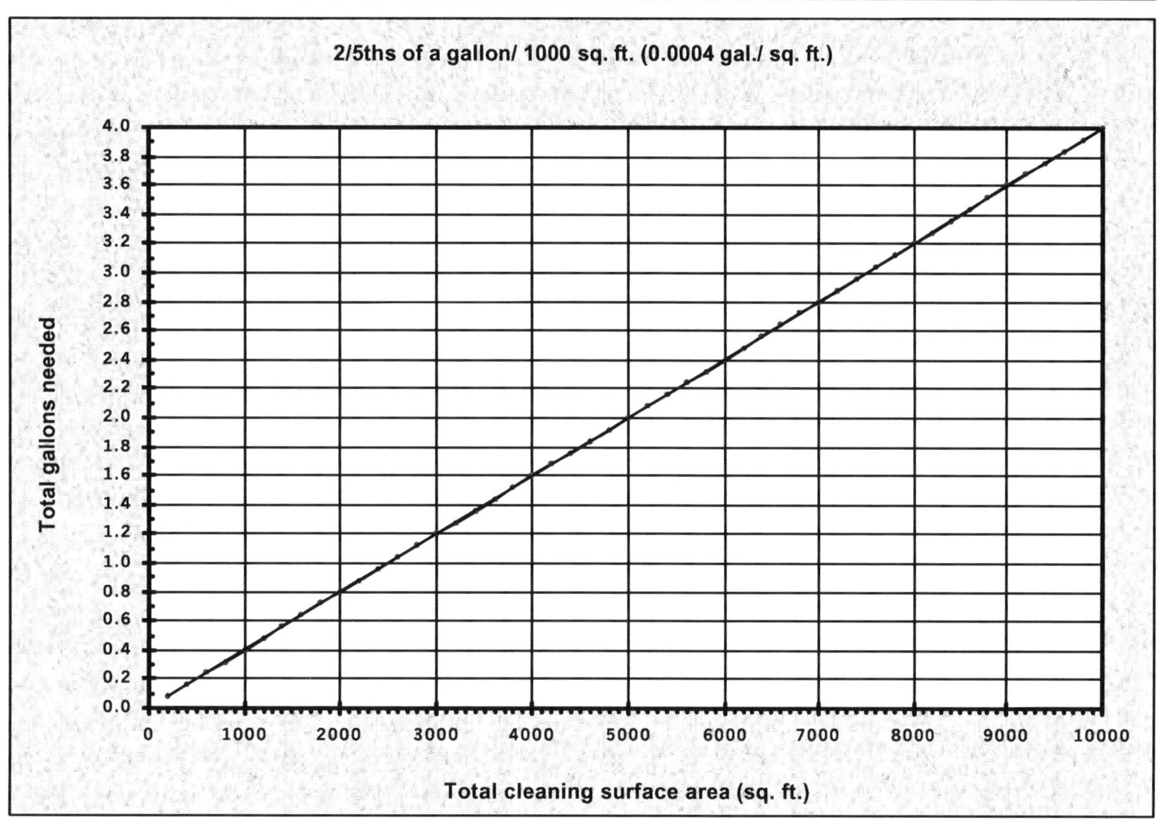
2/5ths of a gallon/ 1000 sq. ft. (0.0004 gal./ sq. ft.)
Total gallons needed
4.0
3.8
3.6
3.4
3.2
3.0
2.8
2.6
2.4
2.2
2.0
1.8
1.6
1.4
1.2
1.0
0.8
0.6
0.4
0.2
0.0
0
1000
2000
3000
4000
5000
6000
7000
8000
9000
10000
Total cleaning surface area (sq. ft.)

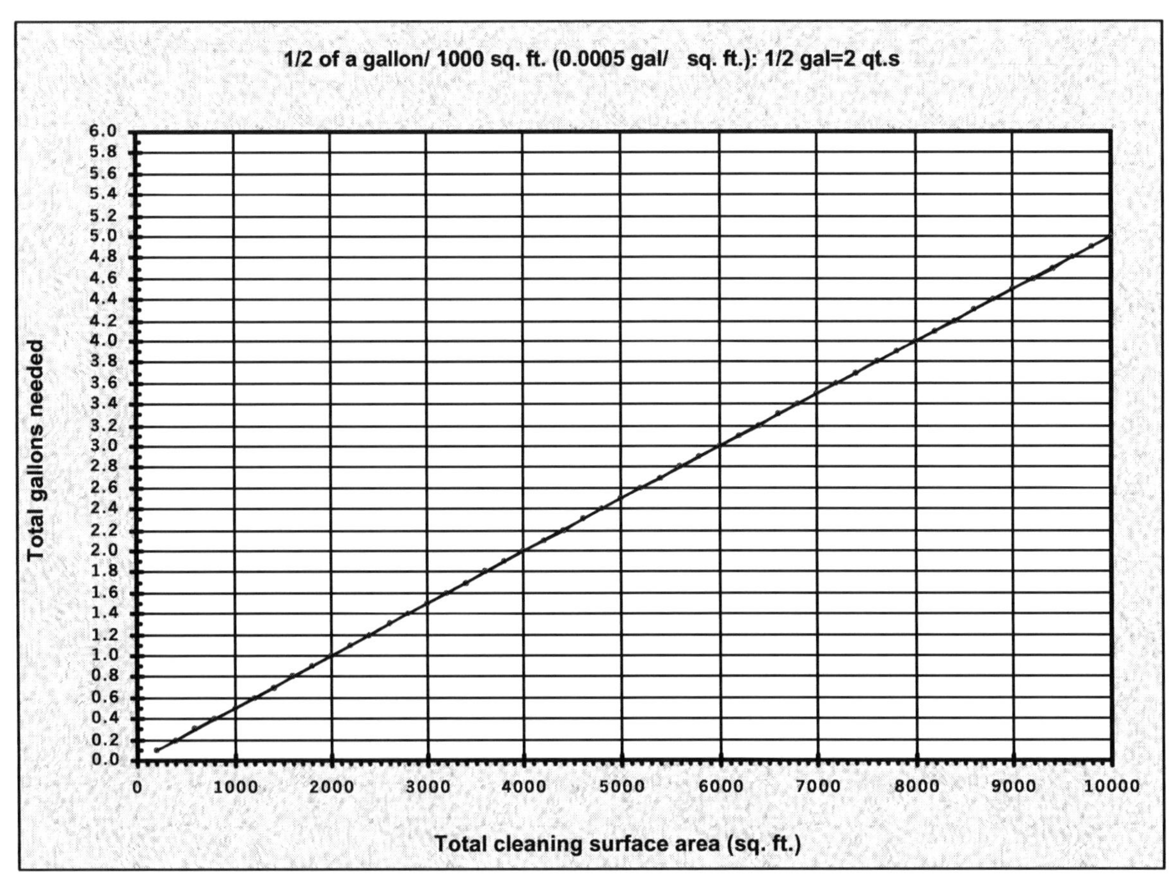
1/2 of a gallon/ 1000 sq. ft. (0.0005 gal/ sq. ft.): 1/2 gal=2 qt.s
Total gallons needed
6.0
5.8
5.6
5.4
5.2
5.0
4.8
4.6
4.4
4.2
4.0
3.8
3.6
3.4
3.2
3.0
2.8
2.6
2.4
2.2
2.0
1.8
1.6
1.4
1.2
1.0
0.8
0.6
0.4
0.2
0.0
0
1000
2000
3000
4000
5000
6000
7000
8000
9000
10000
Total cleaning surface area (sq. ft.)

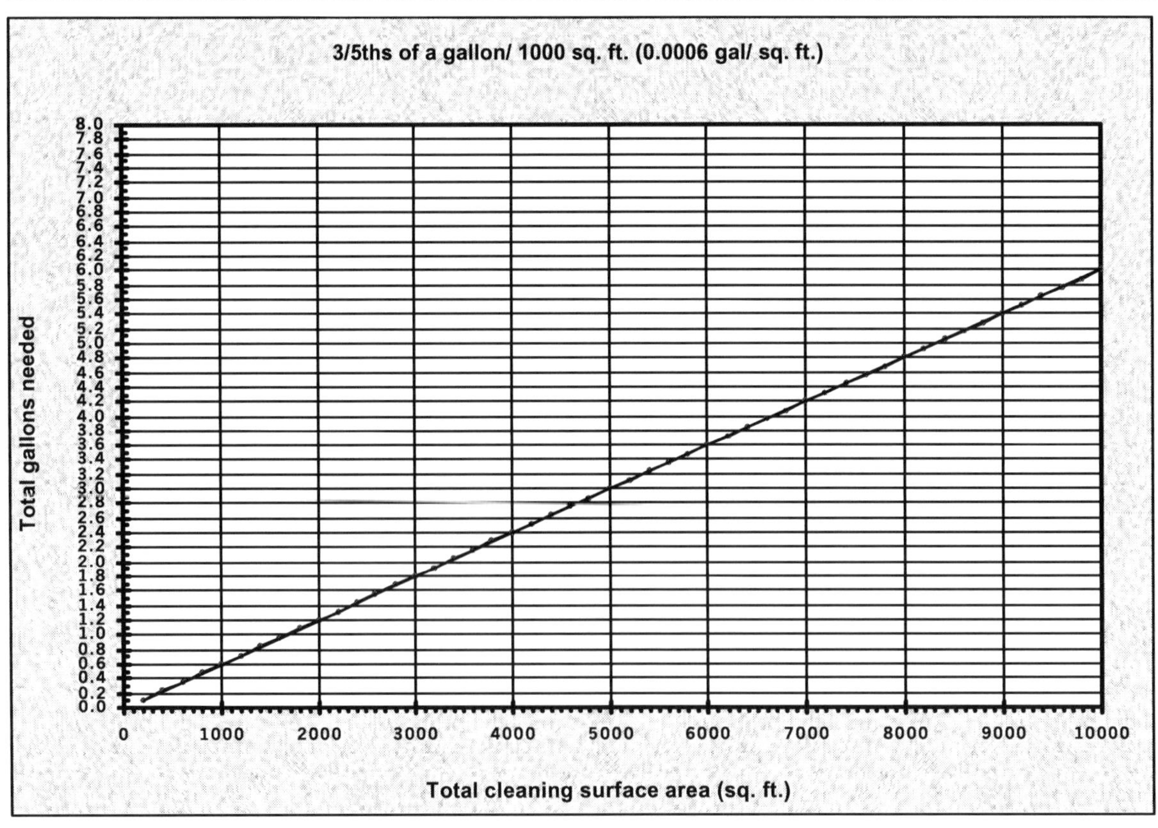
3/5ths of a gallon/ 1000 sq. ft. (0.0006 gal/ sq. ft.)
Total gallons needed
8.0
7.8
7.6
7.4
7.2
7.0
6.8
6.6
6.4
6.2
6.0
5.8
5.6
5.4
5.2
5.0
4.8
4.6
4.4
4.2
4.0
3.8
3.6
3.4
3.2
3.0
2.8
2.6
2.4
2.2
2.0
1.8
1.6
1.4
1.2
1.0
0.8
0.6
0.4
0.2
0.0
0
1000
2000
3000
4000
5000
6000
7000
8000
9000
10000
Total cleaning surface area (sq. ft.)

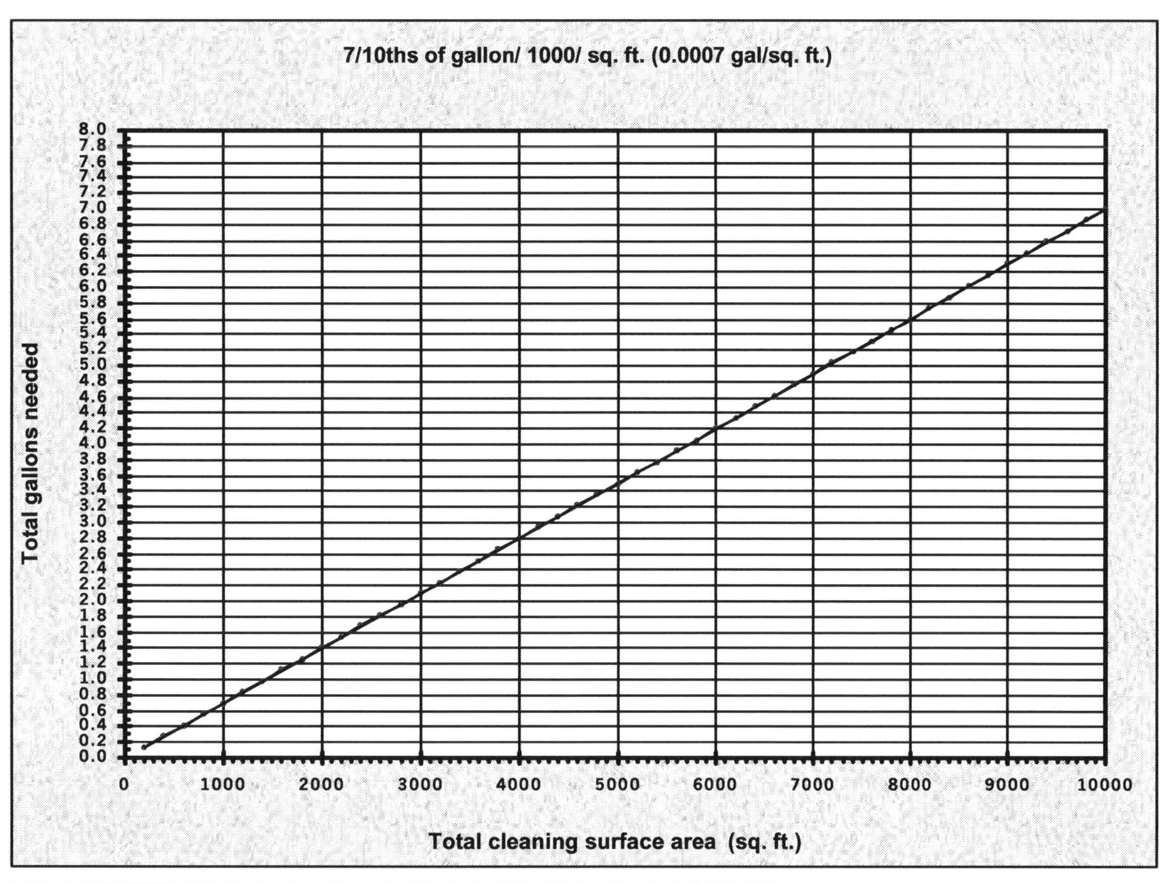
7/10ths of gallon/ 1000/ sq. ft. (0.0007 gal/sq. ft.)
Total gallons needed
8.0
7.8
7.6
7.4
7.2
7.0
6.8
6.6
6.4
6.2
6.0
5.8
5.6
5.4
5.2
5.0
4.8
4.6
4.4
4.2
4.0
3.8
3.6
3.4
3.2
3.0
2.8
2.6
2.4
2.2
2.0
1.8
1.6
1.4
1.2
1.0
0.8
0.6
0.4
0.2
0.0
0
1000
2000
3000
4000
5000
6000
7000
8000
9000
10000
Total cleaning surface area (sq. ft.)

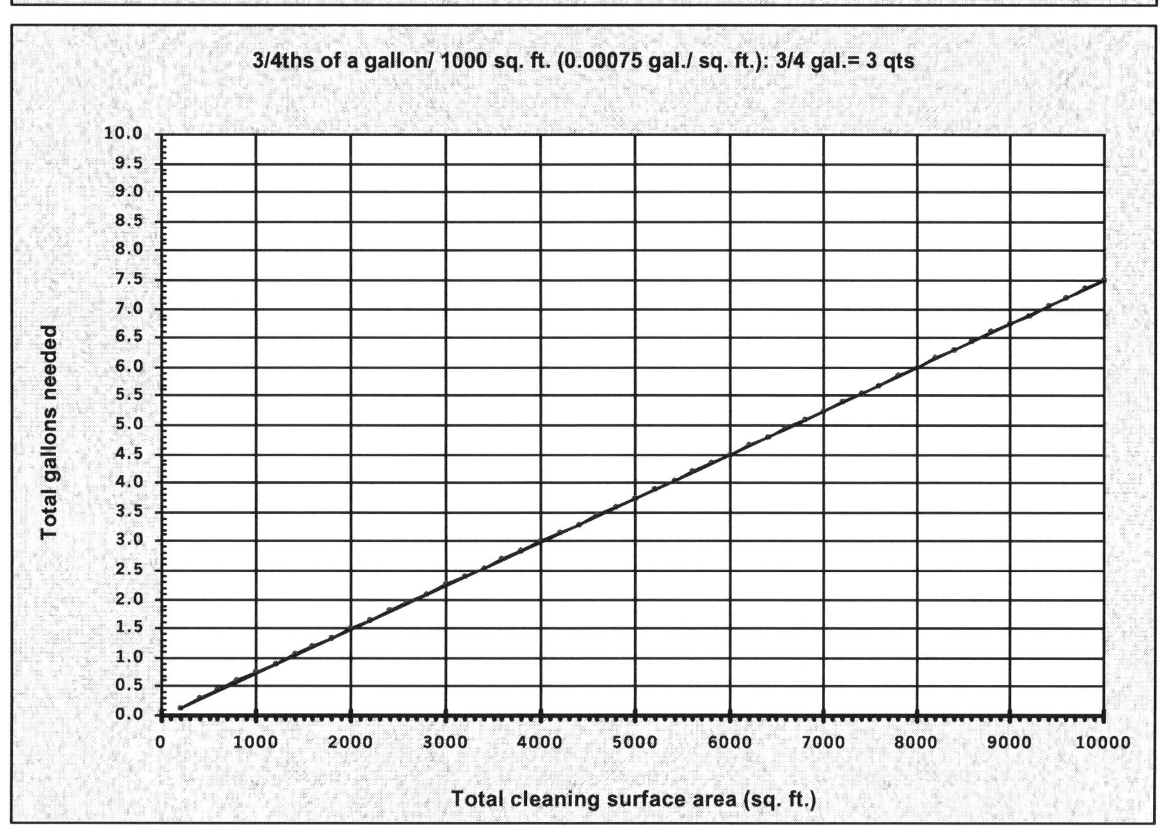
3/4ths of a gallon/ 1000 sq. ft. (0.00075 gal./ sq. ft.): 3/4 gal.= 3 qts
Total gallons needed
10.0
9.5
9.0
8.5
8.0
7.5
7.0
6.5
6.0
5.5
5.0
4.5
4.0
3.5
3.0
2.5
2.0
1.5
1.0
0.5
0.0
0
1000
2000
3000
4000
5000
6000
7000
8000
9000
10000
Total cleaning surface area (sq. ft.)

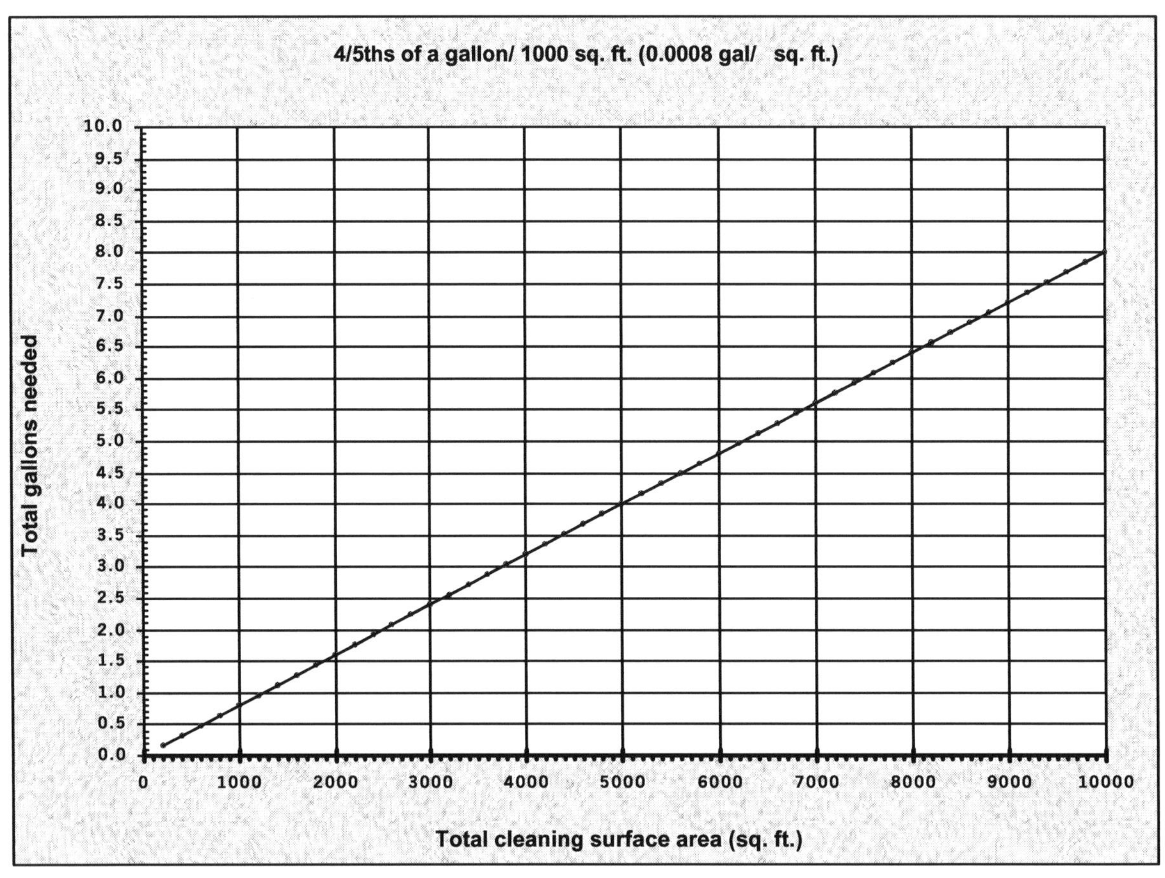
4/5ths of a gallon/ 1000 sq. ft. (0.0008 gal/ sq. ft.)
Total gallons needed
10.0
9.5
9.0
8.5
8.0
7.5
7.0
6.5
6.0
5.5
5.0
4.5
4.0
3.5
3.0
2.5
2.0
1.5
1.0
0.5
0.0
0
1000
2000
3000
4000
5000
6000
7000
8000
9000
10000
Total cleaning surface area (sq. ft.)

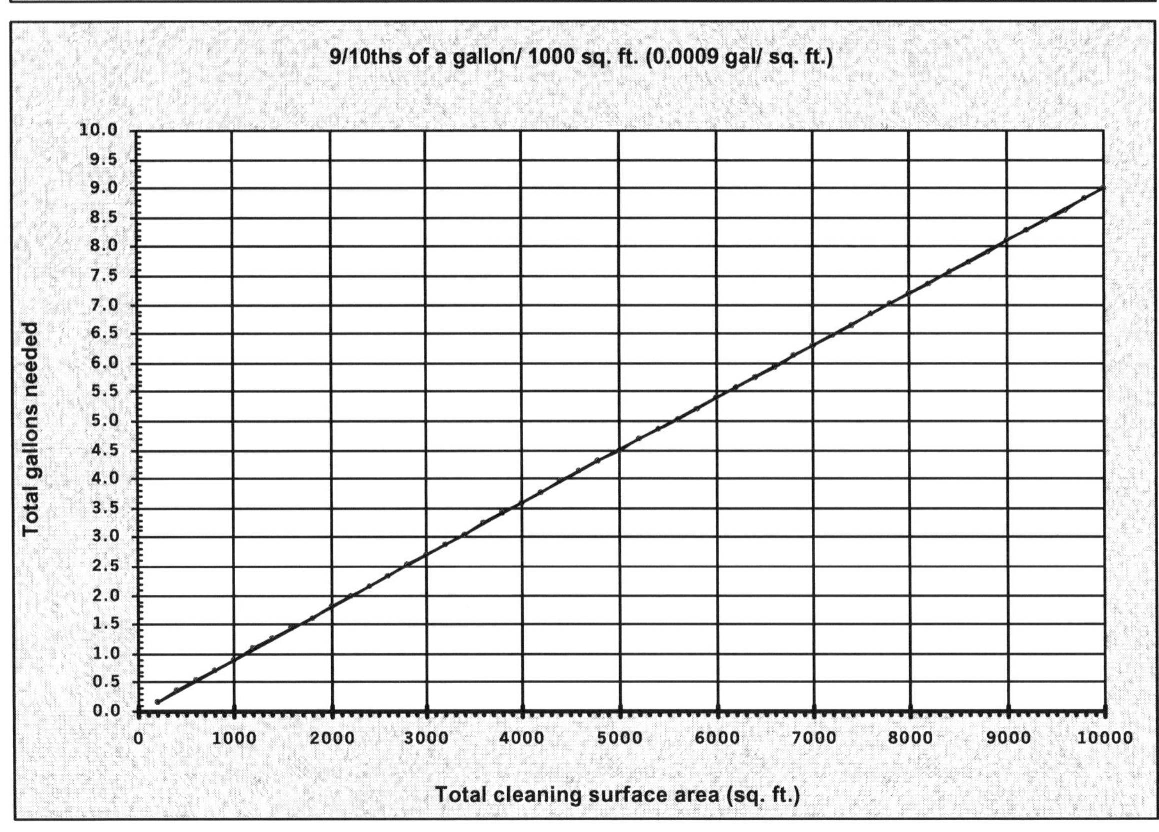
9/10ths of a gallon/ 1000 sq. ft. (0.0009 gal/ sq. ft.)
Total gallons needed
10.0
9.5
9.0
8.5
8.0
7.5
7.0
6.5
6.0
5.5
5.0
4.5
4.0
3.5
3.0
2.5
2.0
1.5
1.0
0.5
0.0
0
1000
2000
3000
4000
5000
6000
7000
8000
9000
10000
Total cleaning surface area (sq. ft.)

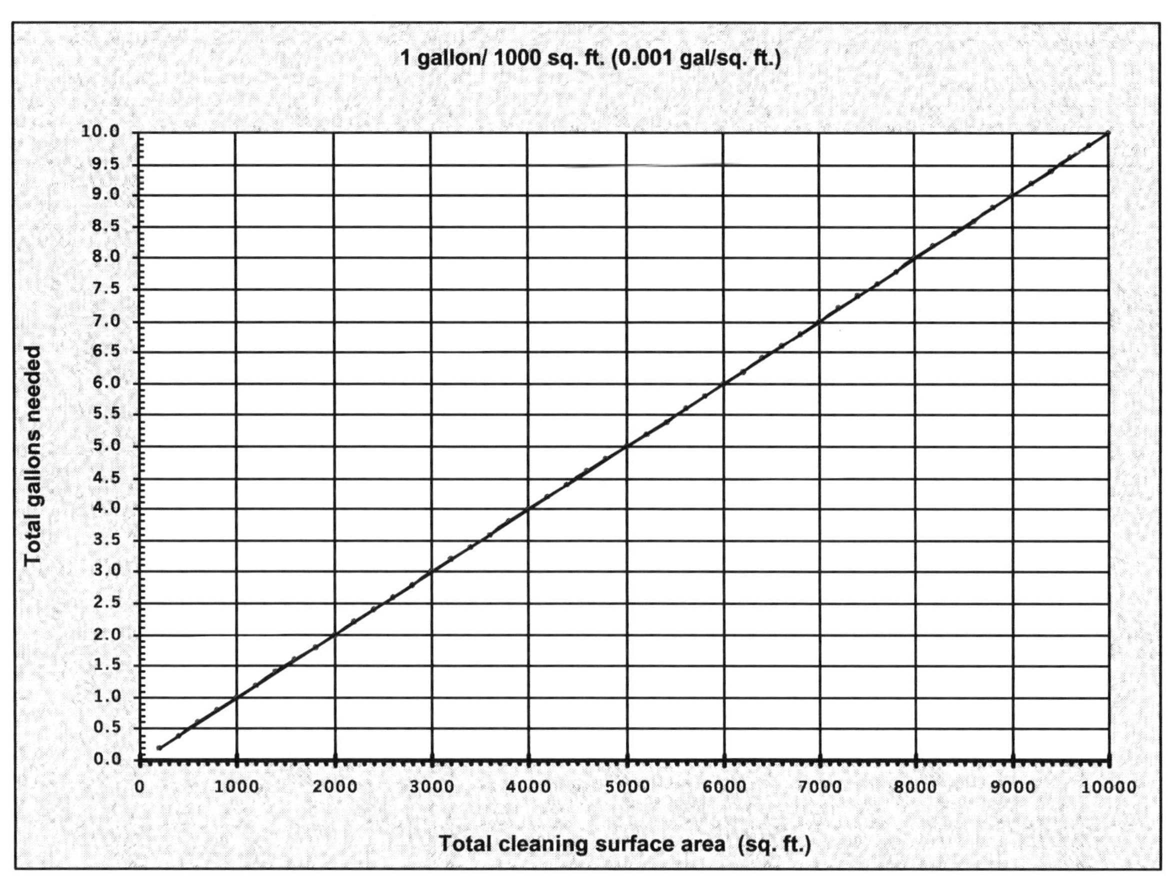
1 gallon/ 1000 sq. ft. (0.001 gal/sq. ft.)
Total gallons needed
10.0
9.5
9.0
8.5
8.0
7.5
7.0
6.5
6.0
5.5
5.0
4.5
4.0
3.5
3.0
2.5
2.0
1.5
1.0
0.5
0.0
0
1000
2000
3000
4000
5000
6000
7000
8000
9000
10000
Total cleaning surface area (sq. ft.)

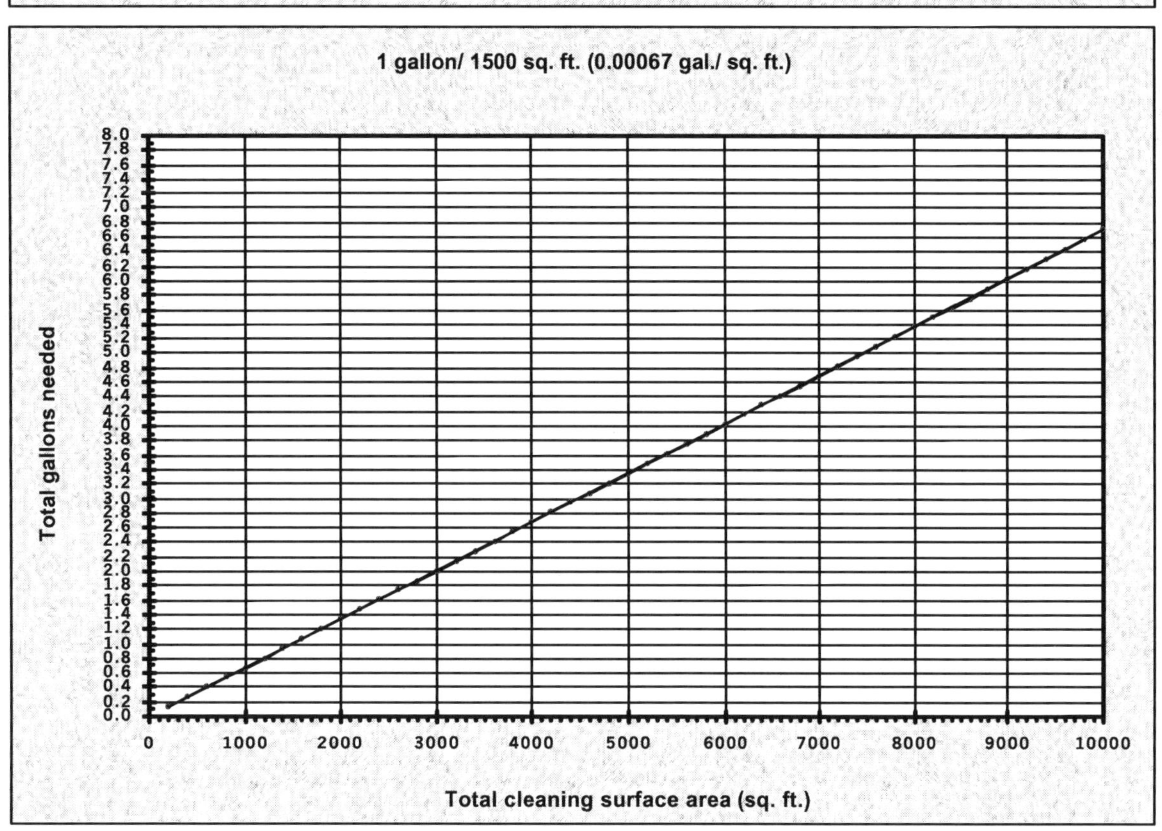
1 gallon/ 1500 sq. ft. (0.00067 gal./ sq. ft.)
Total gallons needed
8.0
7.8
7.6
7.4
7.2
7.0
6.8
6.6
6.4
6.2
6.0
5.8
5.6
5.4
5.2
5.0
4.8
4.6
4.4
4.2
4.0
3.8
3.6
3.4
3.2
3.0
2.8
2.6
2.4
2.2
2.0
1.8
1.6
1.4
1.2
1.0
0.8
0.6
0.4
0.2
0.0
0
1000
2000
3000
4000
5000
6000
7000
8000
9000
10000
Total cleaning surface area (sq. ft.)

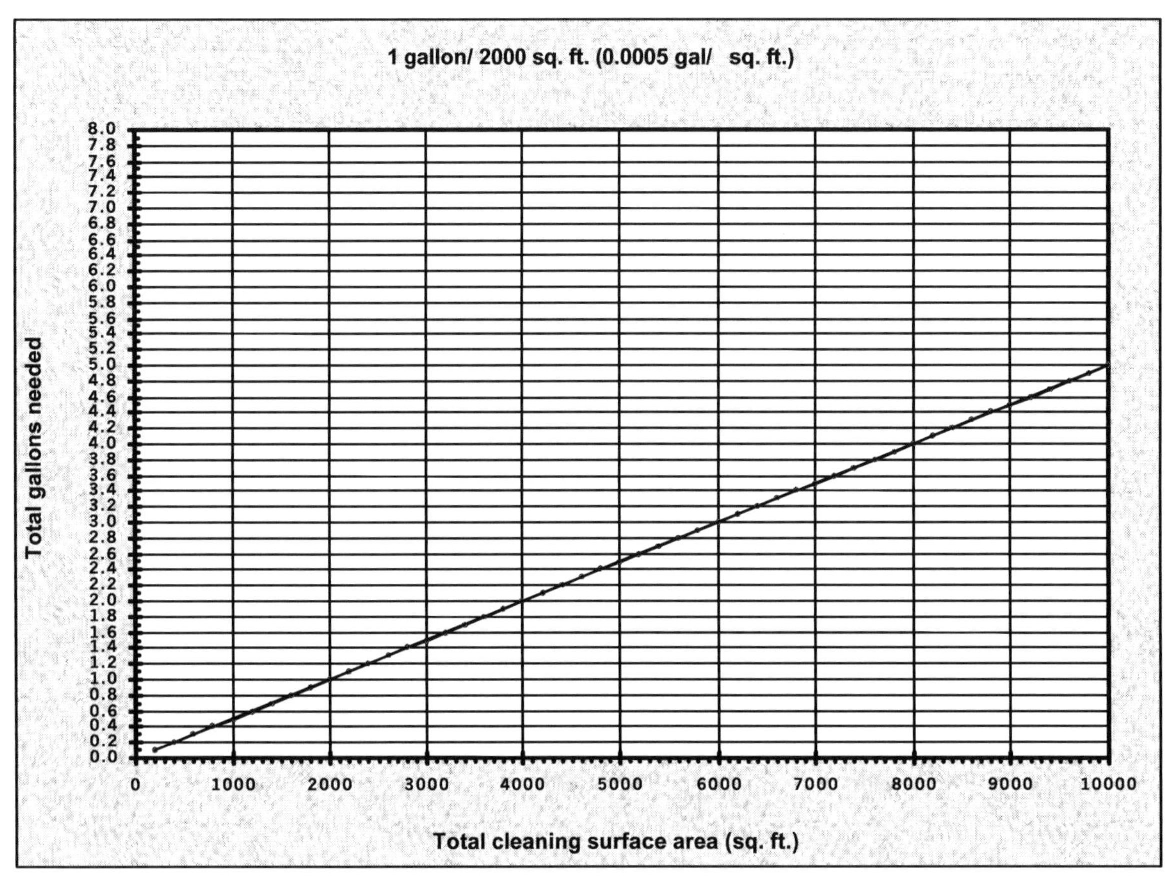
1 gallon/ 2000 sq. ft. (0.0005 gal/ sq. ft.)
Total gallons needed
Total cleaning surface area (sq. ft.)
0
1000
2000
3000
4000
5000
6000
7000
8000
9000
10000

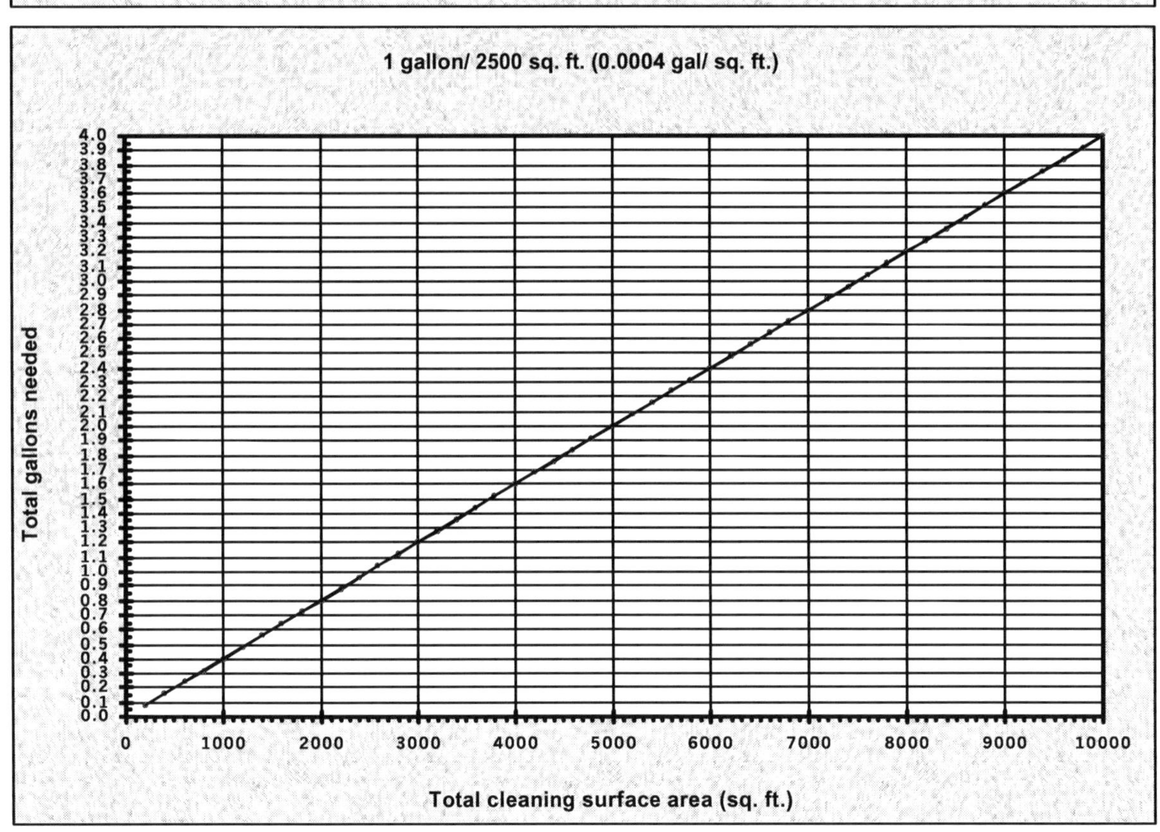
1 gallon/ 2500 sq. ft. (0.0004 gal/ sq. ft.)
Total gallons needed
Total cleaning surface area (sq. ft.)
0
1000
2000
3000
4000
5000
6000
7000
8000
9000
10000

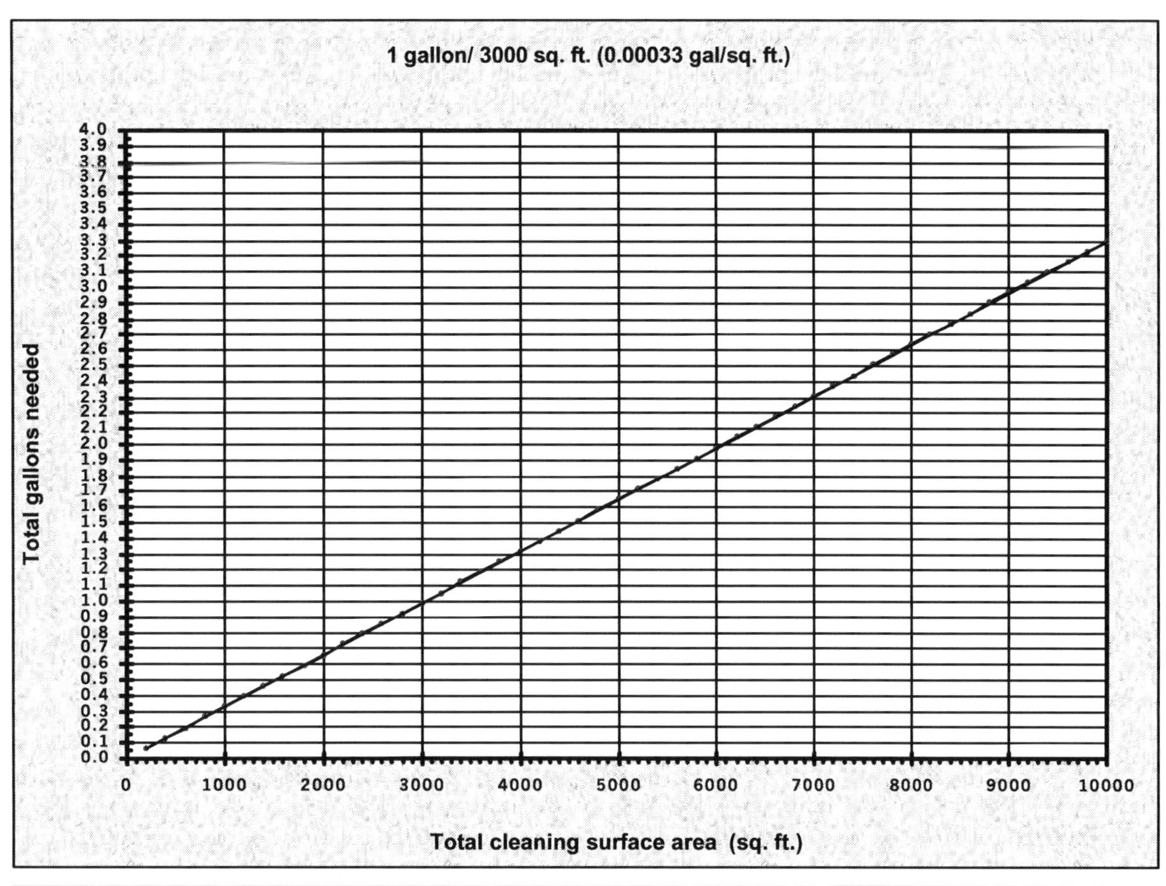
1 gallon/ 3000 sq. ft. (0.00033 gal/sq. ft.)
Total gallons needed
4.0 3.9 3.8 3.7 3.6 3.5 3.4 3.3 3.2 3.1 3.0 2.9 2.8 2.7 2.6 2.5 2.4 2.3 2.2 2.1 2.0 1.9 1.8 1.7 1.6 1.5 1.4 1.3 1.2 1.1 1.0 0.9 0.8 0.7 0.6 0.5 0.4 0.3 0.2 0.1 0.0
0 1000 2000 3000 4000 5000 6000 7000 8000 9000 10000
Total cleaning surface area (sq. ft.)

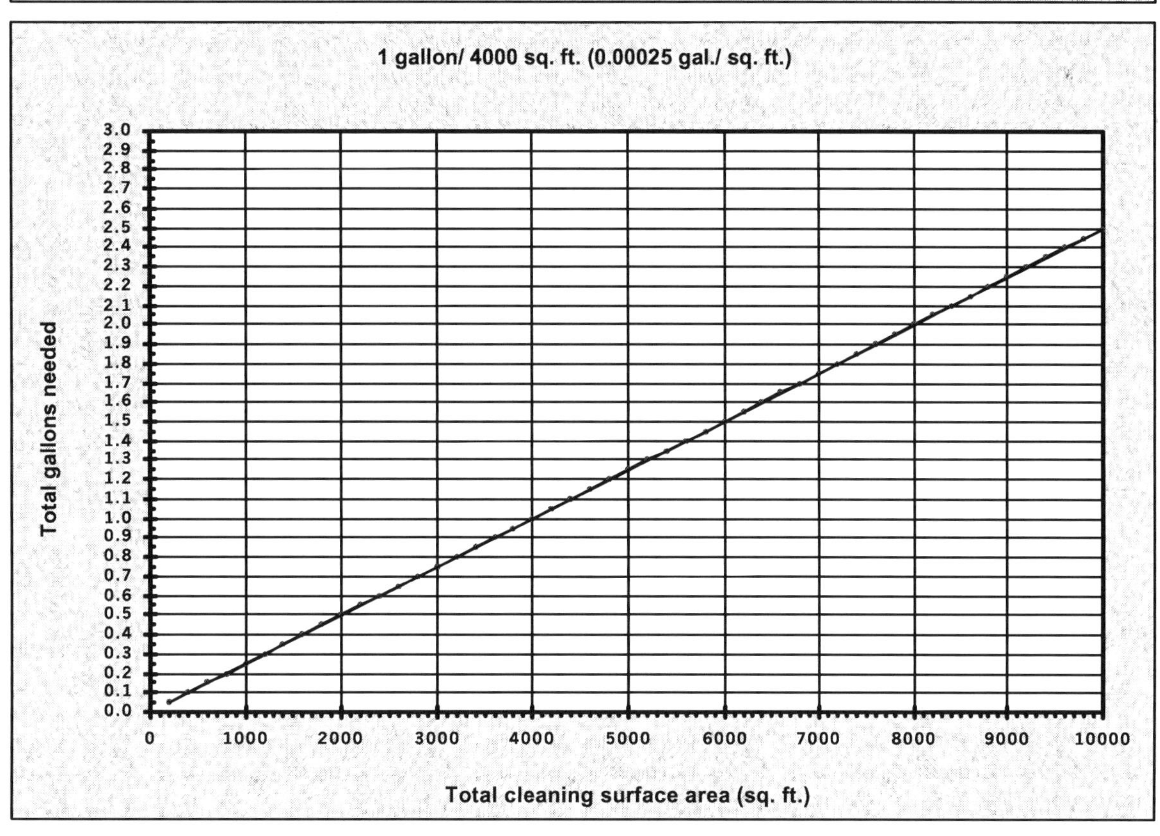
1 gallon/ 4000 sq. ft. (0.00025 gal./ sq. ft.)
Total gallons needed
3.0 2.9 2.8 2.7 2.6 2.5 2.4 2.3 2.2 2.1 2.0 1.9 1.8 1.7 1.6 1.5 1.4 1.3 1.2 1.1 1.0 0.9 0.8 0.7 0.6 0.5 0.4 0.3 0.2 0.1 0.0
0 1000 2000 3000 4000 5000 6000 7000 8000 9000 10000
Total cleaning surface area (sq. ft.)

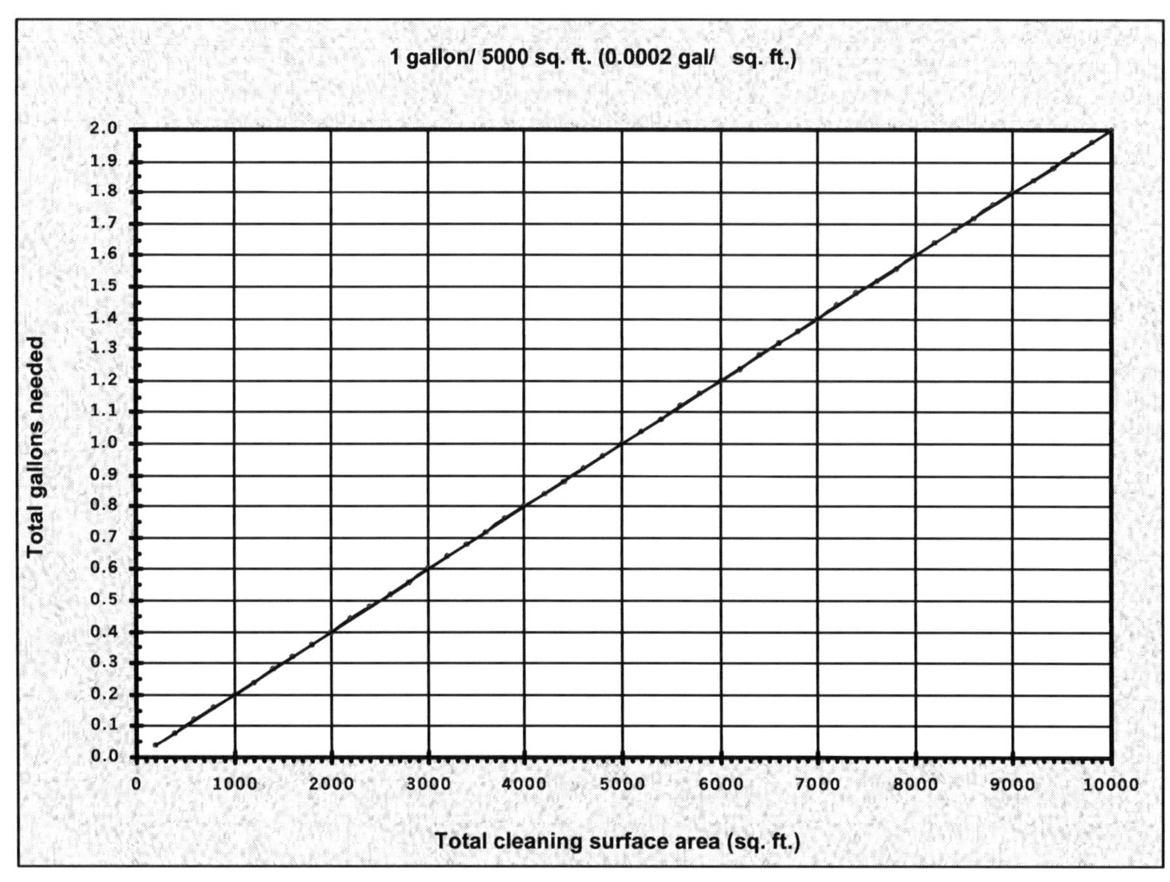
1 gallon/ 5000 sq. ft. (0.0002 gal/ sq. ft.)
Total gallons needed
2.0
1.9
1.8
1.7
1.6
1.5
1.4
1.3
1.2
1.1
1.0
0.9
0.8
0.7
0.6
0.5
0.4
0.3
0.2
0.1
0.0
0
1000
2000
3000
4000
5000
6000
7000
8000
9000
10000
Total cleaning surface area (sq. ft.)

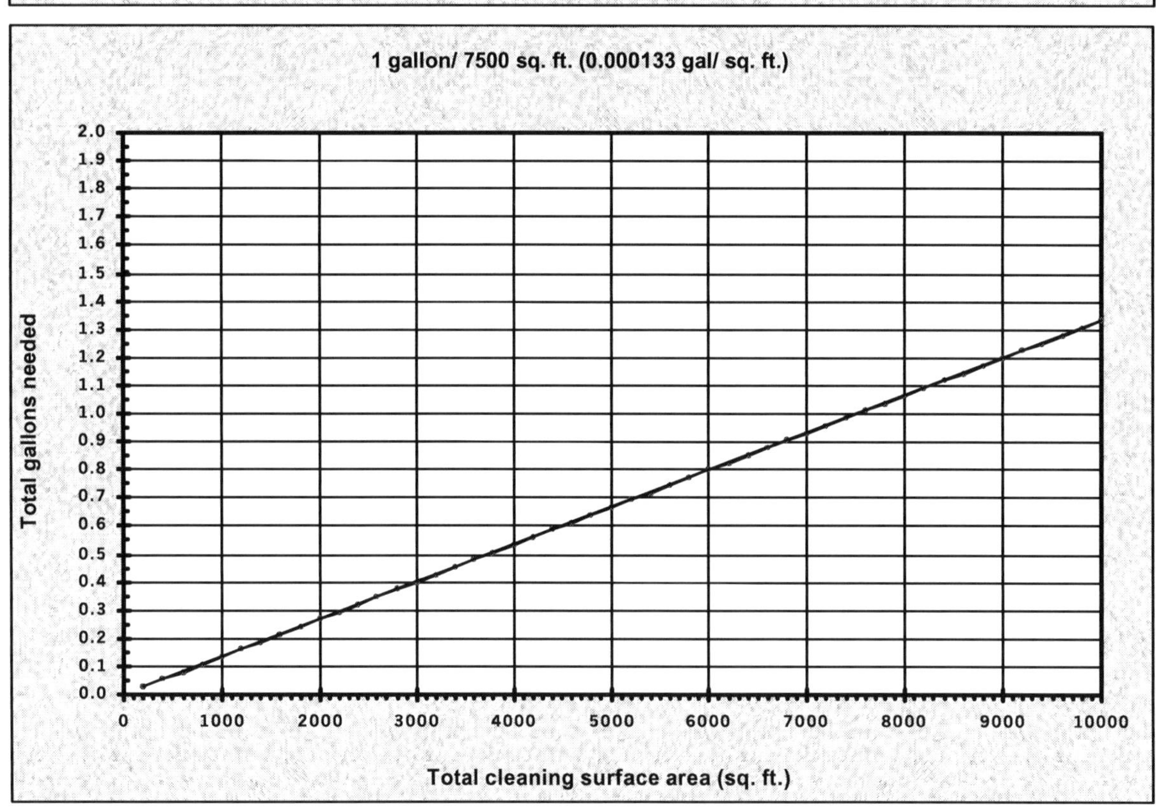
1 gallon/ 7500 sq. ft. (0.000133 gal/ sq. ft.)
Total gallons needed
2.0
1.9
1.8
1.7
1.6
1.5
1.4
1.3
1.2
1.1
1.0
0.9
0.8
0.7
0.6
0.5
0.4
0.3
0.2
0.1
0.0
0
1000
2000
3000
4000
5000
6000
7000
8000
9000
10000
Total cleaning surface area (sq. ft.)

Chapter 5

Generic cleaning supplies cost estimation charts

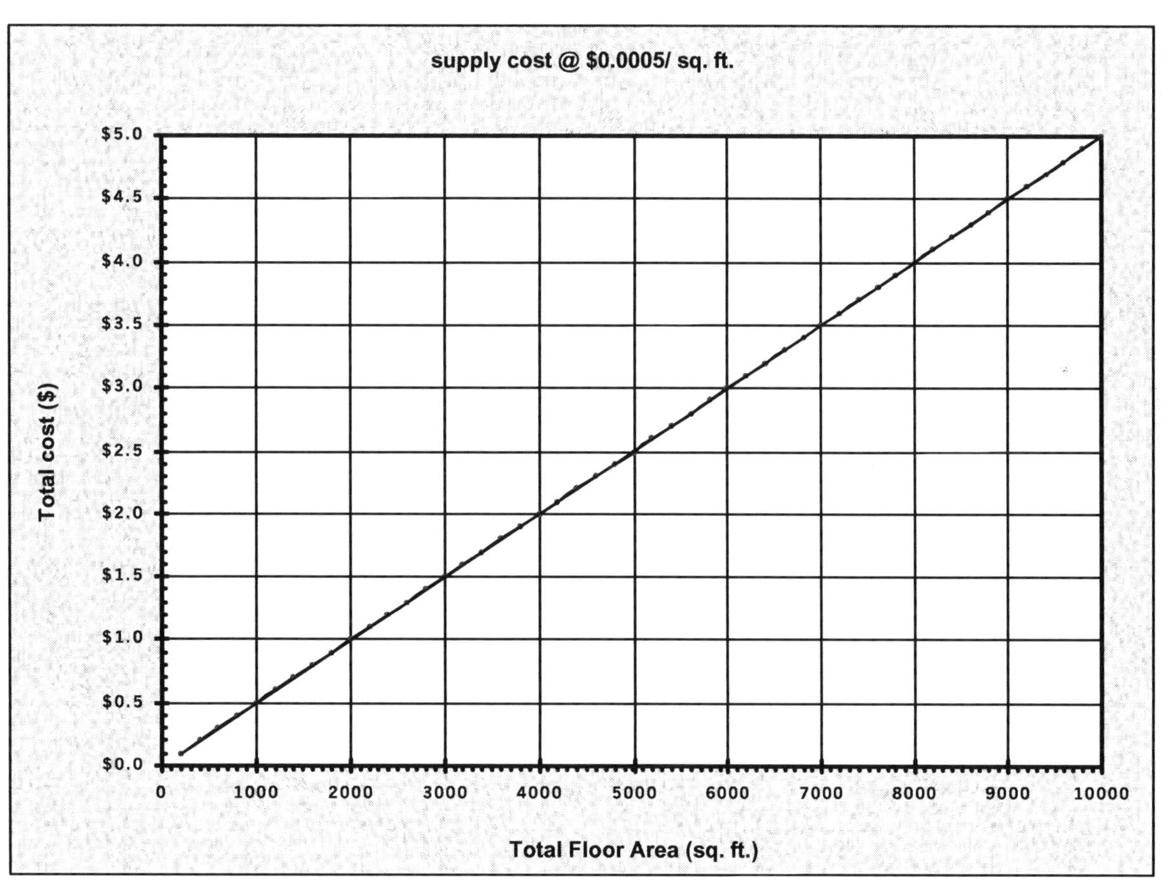

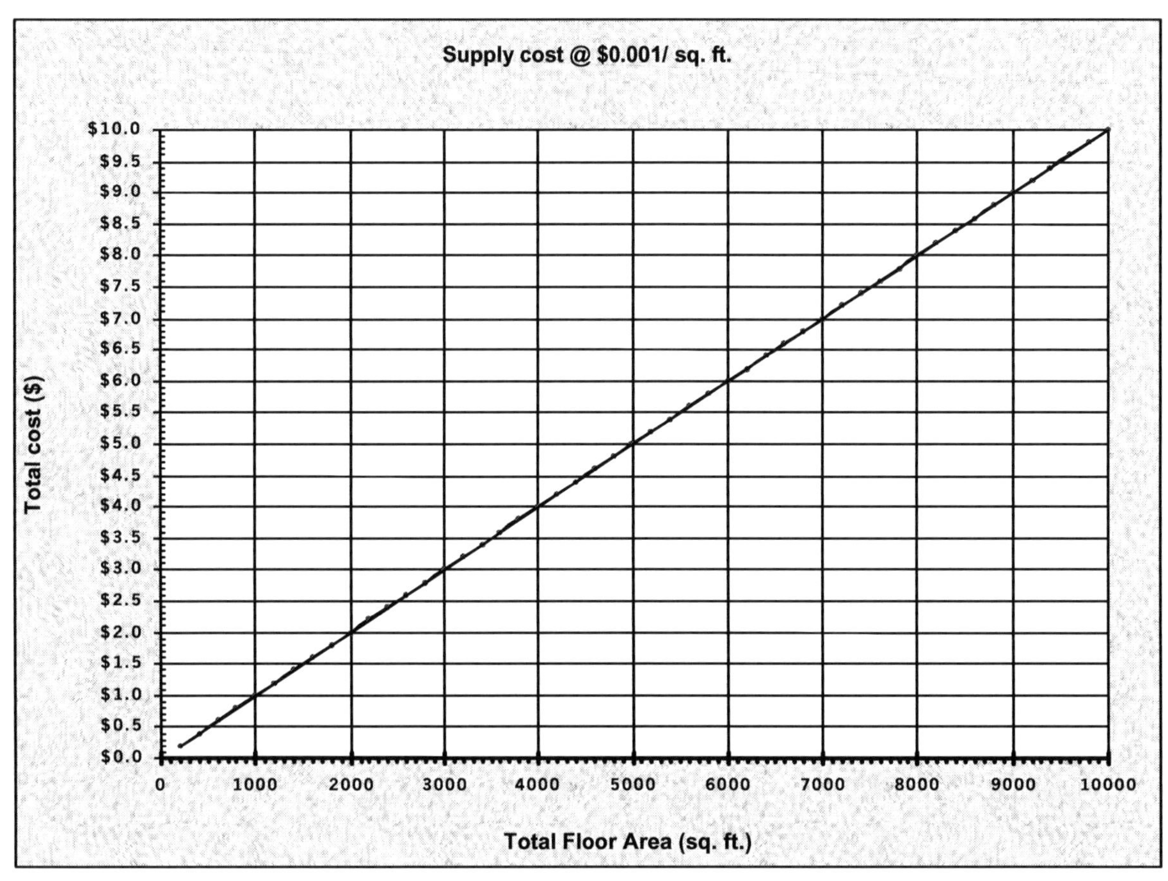
Supply cost @ $0.001/ sq. ft.
Total cost ($)
$10.0
$9.5
$9.0
$8.5
$8.0
$7.5
$7.0
$6.5
$6.0
$5.5
$5.0
$4.5
$4.0
$3.5
$3.0
$2.5
$2.0
$1.5
$1.0
$0.5
$0.0
0
1000
2000
3000
4000
5000
6000
7000
8000
9000
10000
Total Floor Area (sq. ft.)

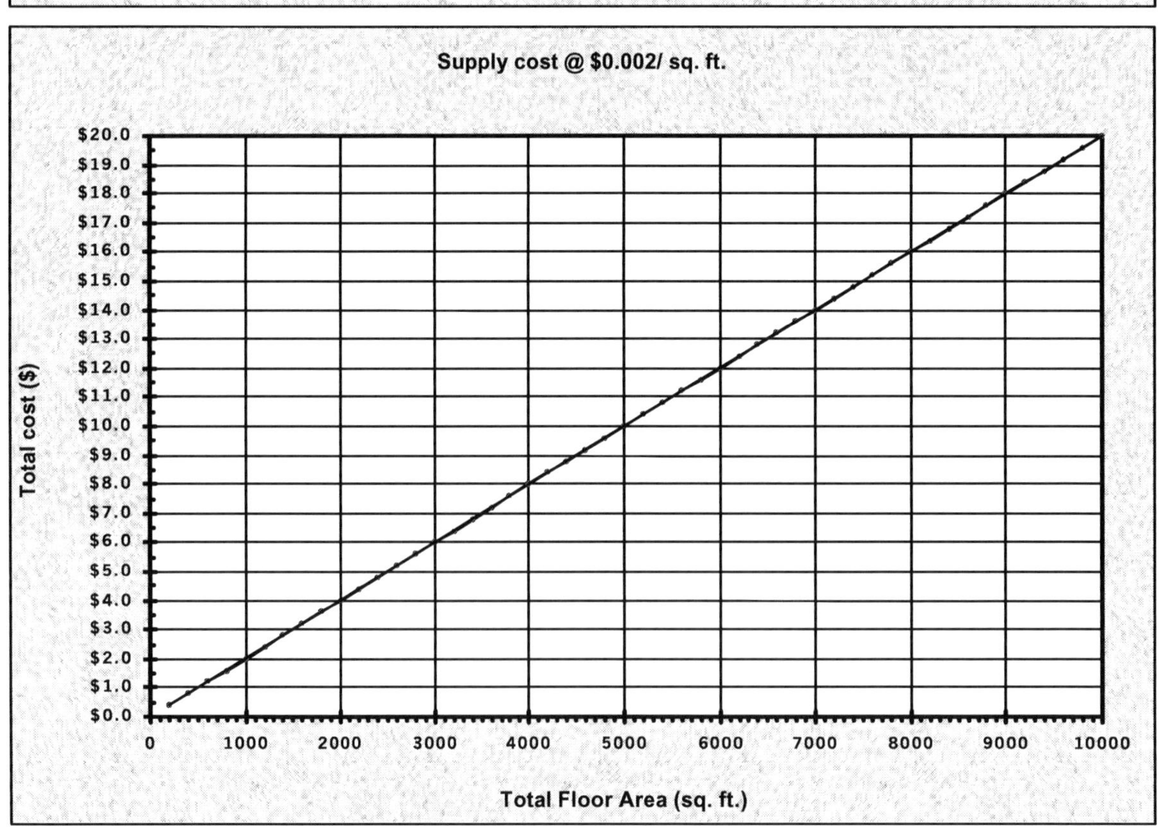
Supply cost @ $0.002/ sq. ft.
Total cost ($)
$20.0
$19.0
$18.0
$17.0
$16.0
$15.0
$14.0
$13.0
$12.0
$11.0
$10.0
$9.0
$8.0
$7.0
$6.0
$5.0
$4.0
$3.0
$2.0
$1.0
$0.0
0
1000
2000
3000
4000
5000
6000
7000
8000
9000
10000
Total Floor Area (sq. ft.)

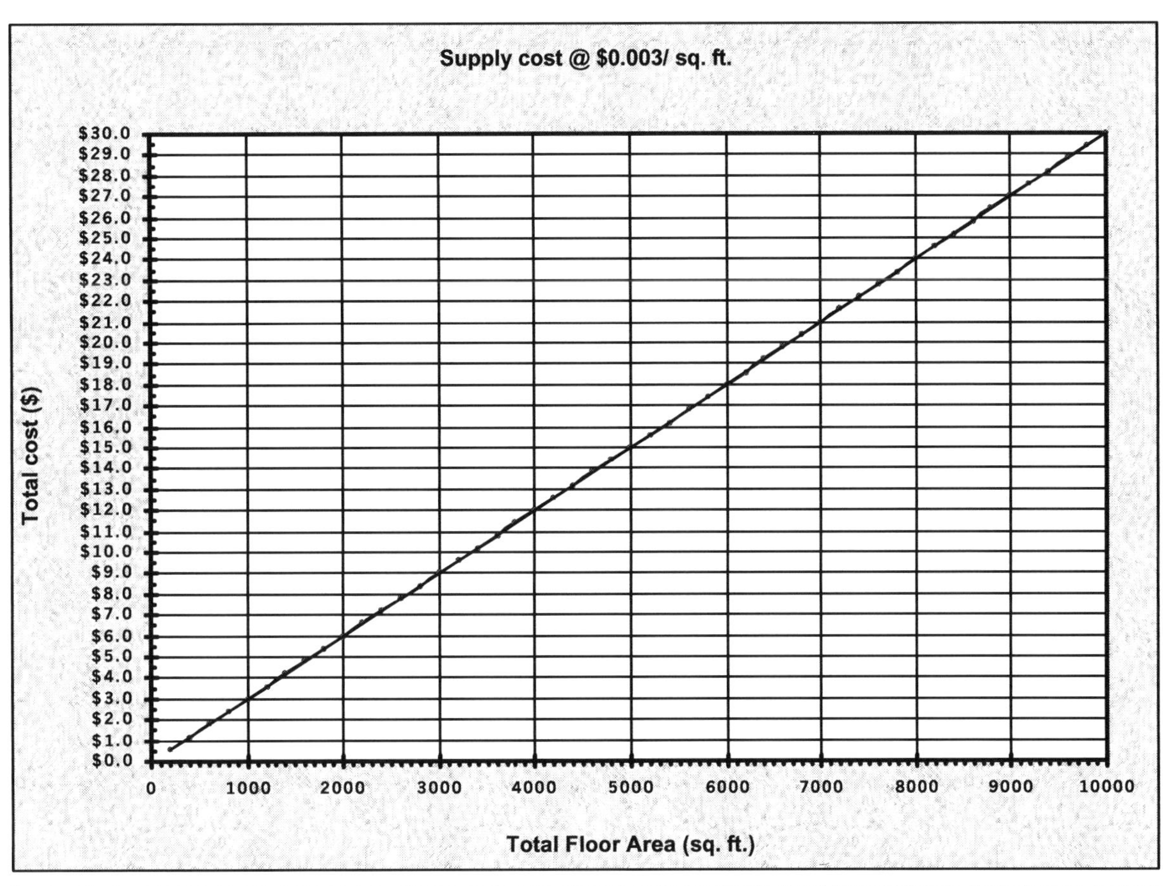
Supply cost @ $0.003/ sq. ft.
Total cost ($)
$30.0
$29.0
$28.0
$27.0
$26.0
$25.0
$24.0
$23.0
$22.0
$21.0
$20.0
$19.0
$18.0
$17.0
$16.0
$15.0
$14.0
$13.0
$12.0
$11.0
$10.0
$9.0
$8.0
$7.0
$6.0
$5.0
$4.0
$3.0
$2.0
$1.0
$0.0
0 1000 2000 3000 4000 5000 6000 7000 8000 9000 10000
Total Floor Area (sq. ft.)

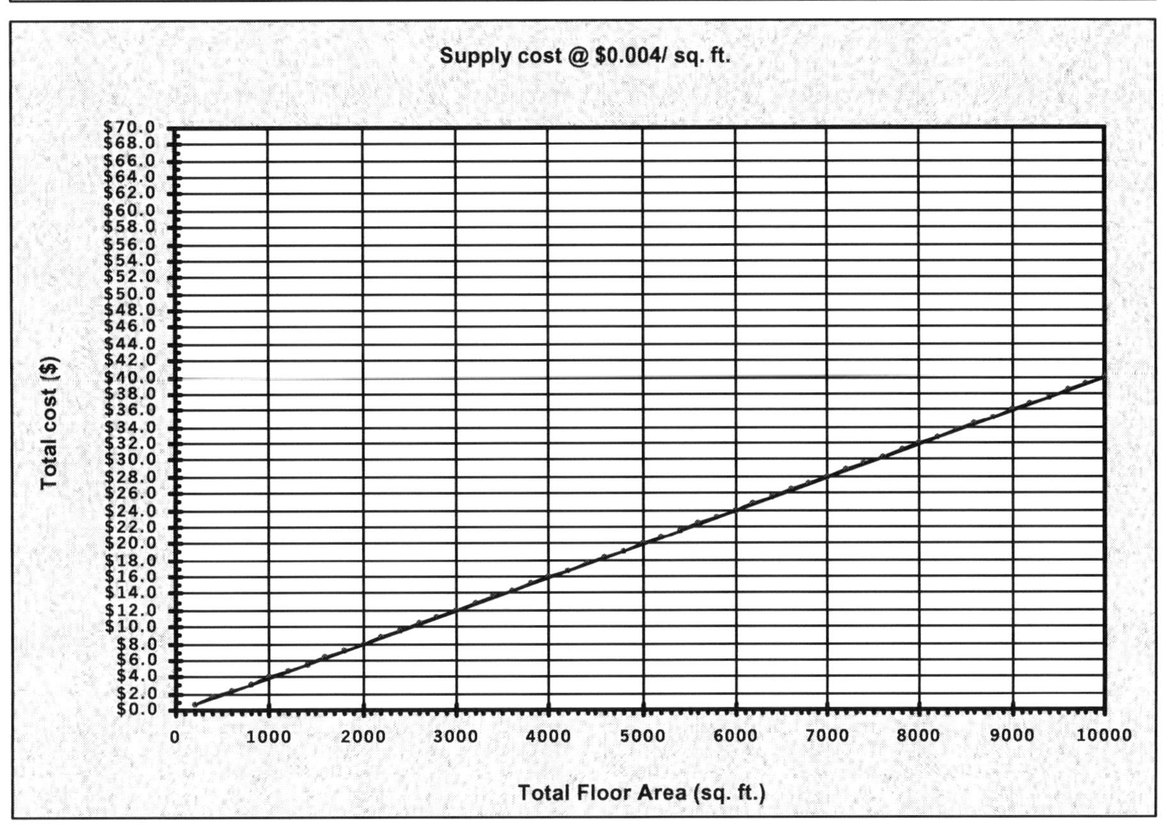
Supply cost @ $0.004/ sq. ft.
Total cost ($)
$70.0
$68.0
$66.0
$64.0
$62.0
$60.0
$58.0
$56.0
$54.0
$52.0
$50.0
$48.0
$46.0
$44.0
$42.0
$40.0
$38.0
$36.0
$34.0
$32.0
$30.0
$28.0
$26.0
$24.0
$22.0
$20.0
$18.0
$16.0
$14.0
$12.0
$10.0
$8.0
$6.0
$4.0
$2.0
$0.0
0 1000 2000 3000 4000 5000 6000 7000 8000 9000 10000
Total Floor Area (sq. ft.)

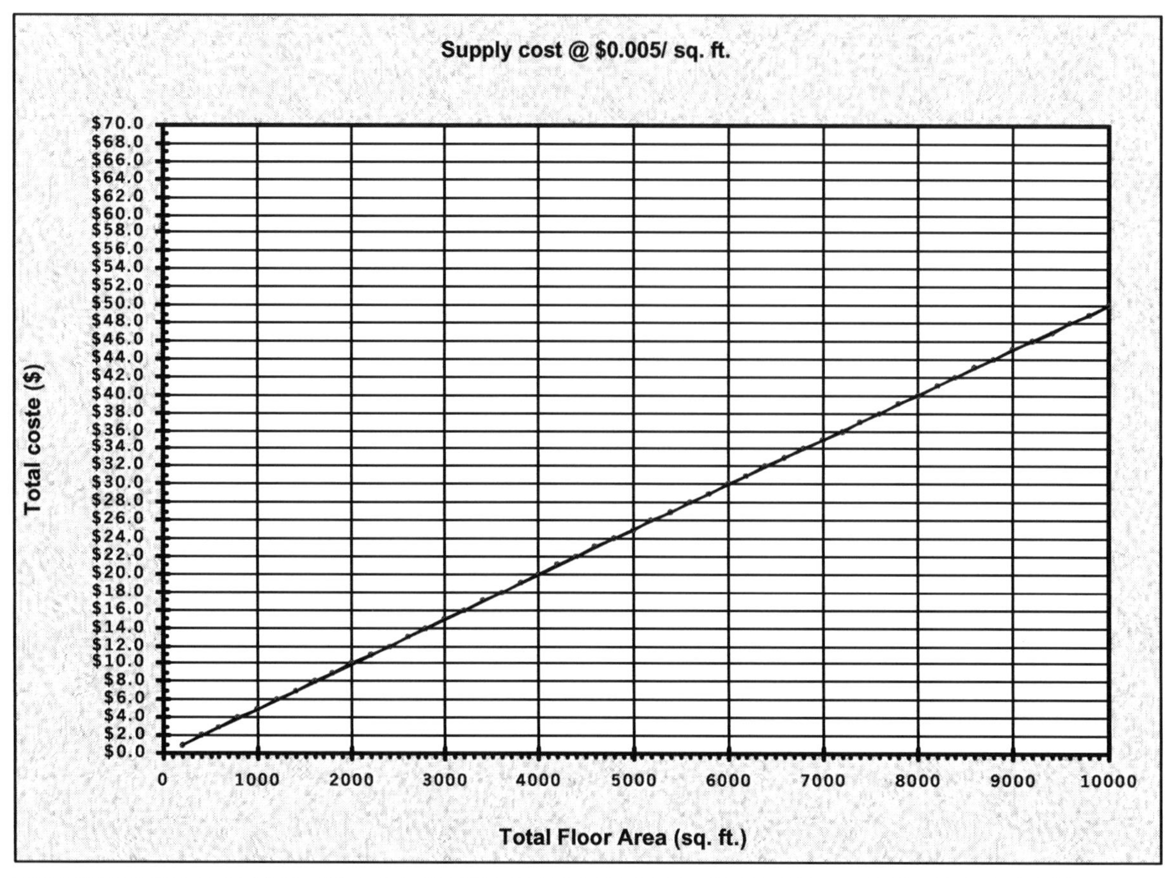
Supply cost @ $0.005/ sq. ft.
Total coste ($)
$70.0
$68.0
$66.0
$64.0
$62.0
$60.0
$58.0
$56.0
$54.0
$52.0
$50.0
$48.0
$46.0
$44.0
$42.0
$40.0
$38.0
$36.0
$34.0
$32.0
$30.0
$28.0
$26.0
$24.0
$22.0
$20.0
$18.0
$16.0
$14.0
$12.0
$10.0
$8.0
$6.0
$4.0
$2.0
$0.0
0
1000
2000
3000
4000
5000
6000
7000
8000
9000
10000
Total Floor Area (sq. ft.)

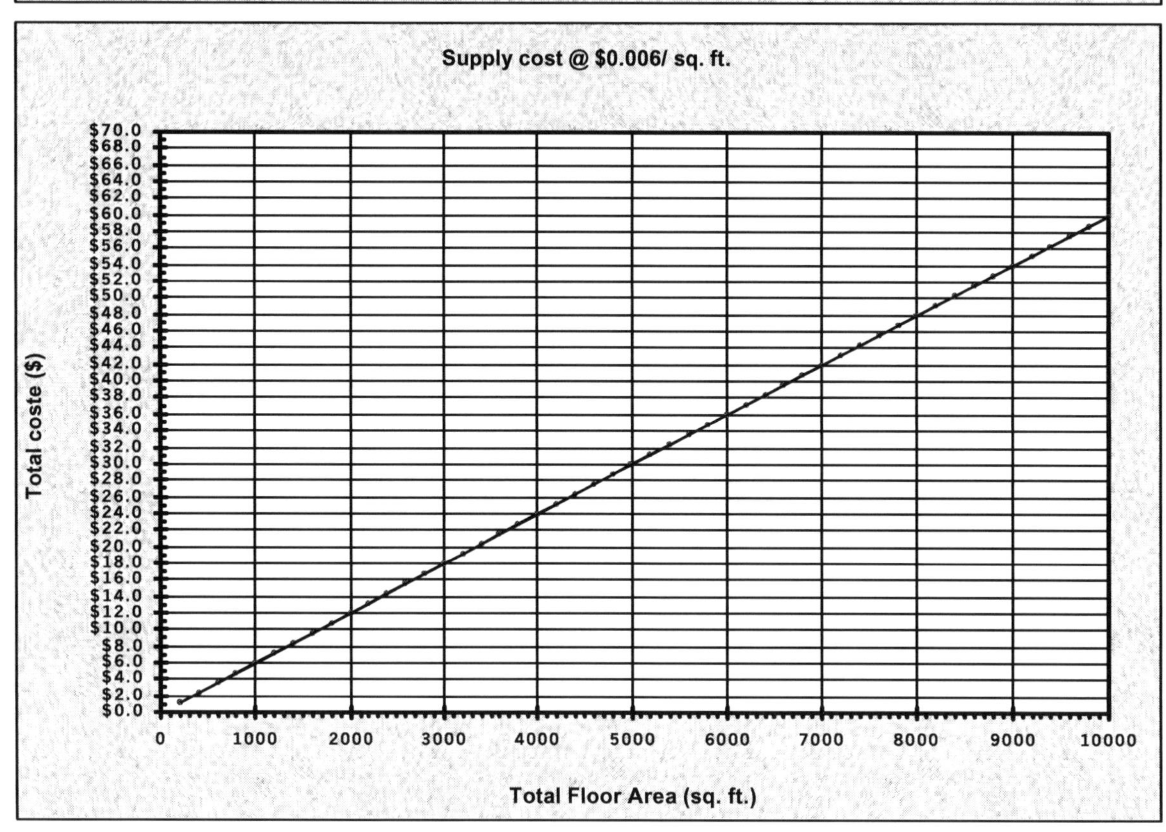
Supply cost @ $0.006/ sq. ft.
Total coste ($)
$70.0
$68.0
$66.0
$64.0
$62.0
$60.0
$58.0
$56.0
$54.0
$52.0
$50.0
$48.0
$46.0
$44.0
$42.0
$40.0
$38.0
$36.0
$34.0
$32.0
$30.0
$28.0
$26.0
$24.0
$22.0
$20.0
$18.0
$16.0
$14.0
$12.0
$10.0
$8.0
$6.0
$4.0
$2.0
$0.0
0
1000
2000
3000
4000
5000
6000
7000
8000
9000
10000
Total Floor Area (sq. ft.)

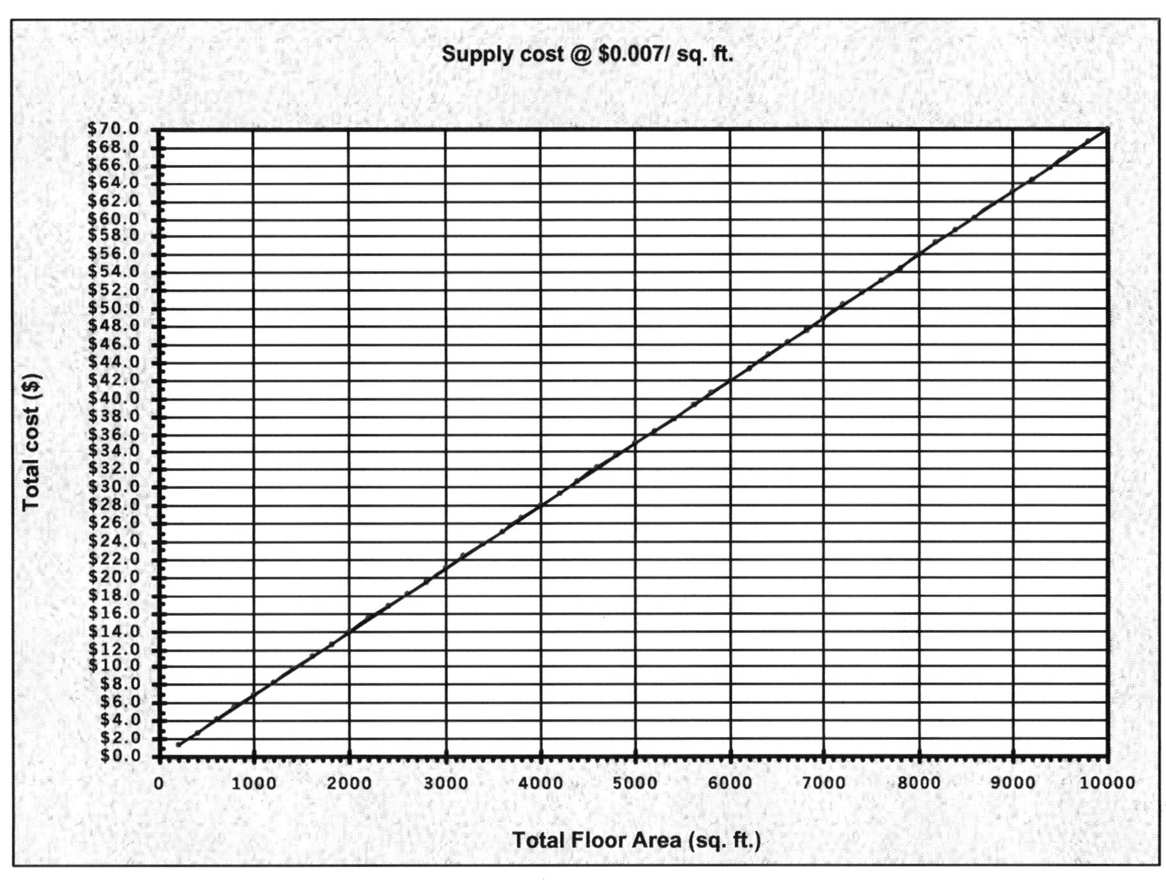

Supply cost @ $0.007/ sq. ft.
Total cost ($)
$70.0
$68.0
$66.0
$64.0
$62.0
$60.0
$58.0
$56.0
$54.0
$52.0
$50.0
$48.0
$46.0
$44.0
$42.0
$40.0
$38.0
$36.0
$34.0
$32.0
$30.0
$28.0
$26.0
$24.0
$22.0
$20.0
$18.0
$16.0
$14.0
$12.0
$10.0
$8.0
$6.0
$4.0
$2.0
$0.0
0
1000
2000
3000
4000
5000
6000
7000
8000
9000
10000
Total Floor Area (sq. ft.)

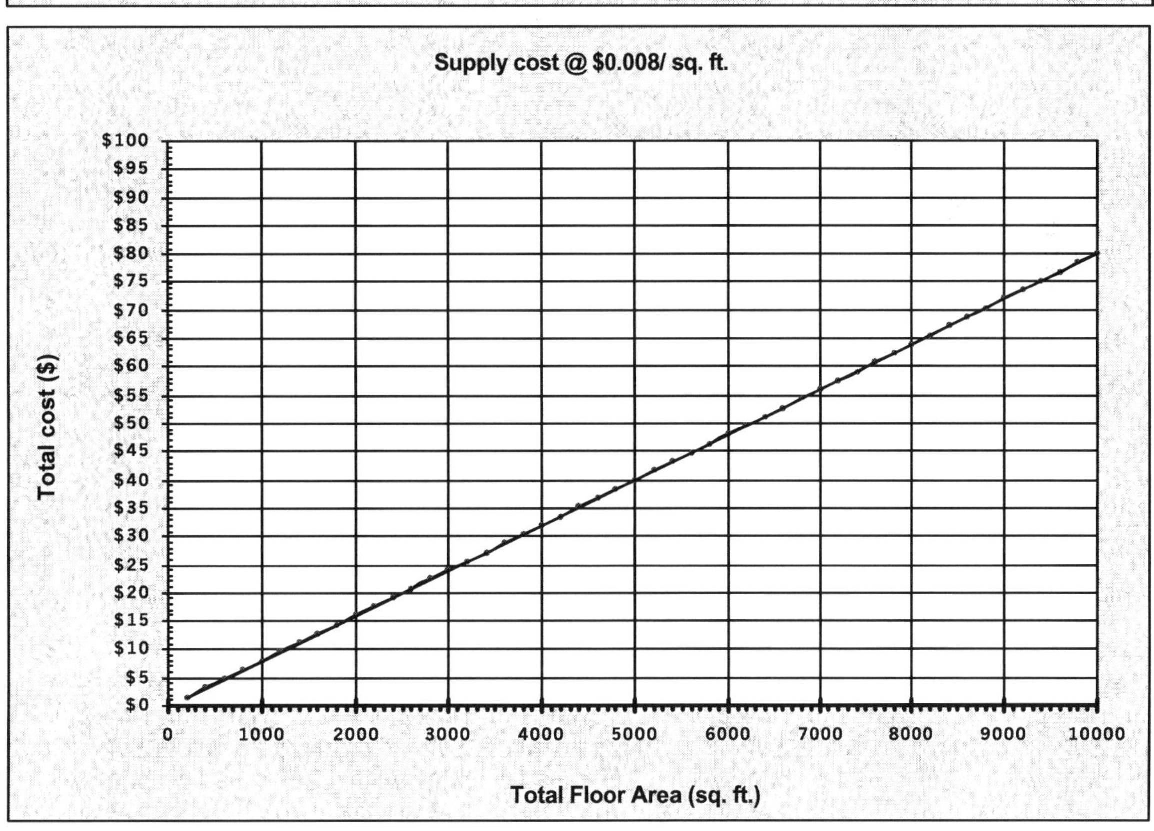

Supply cost @ $0.008/ sq. ft.
Total cost ($)
$100
$95
$90
$85
$80
$75
$70
$65
$60
$55
$50
$45
$40
$35
$30
$25
$20
$15
$10
$5
$0
0
1000
2000
3000
4000
5000
6000
7000
8000
9000
10000
Total Floor Area (sq. ft.)

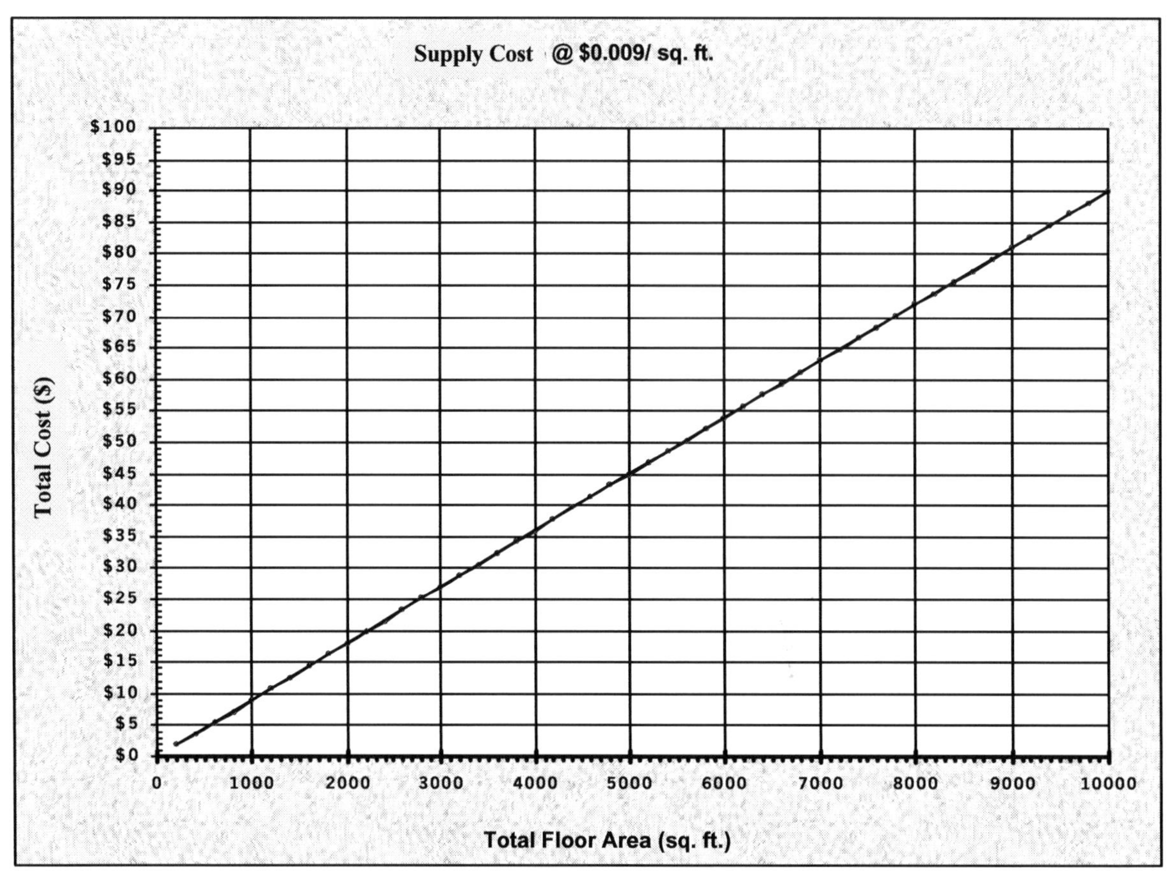
Supply Cost @ $0.009/ sq. ft.
Total Cost ($)
$100
$95
$90
$85
$80
$75
$70
$65
$60
$55
$50
$45
$40
$35
$30
$25
$20
$15
$10
$5
$0
0
1000
2000
3000
4000
5000
6000
7000
8000
9000
10000
Total Floor Area (sq. ft.)

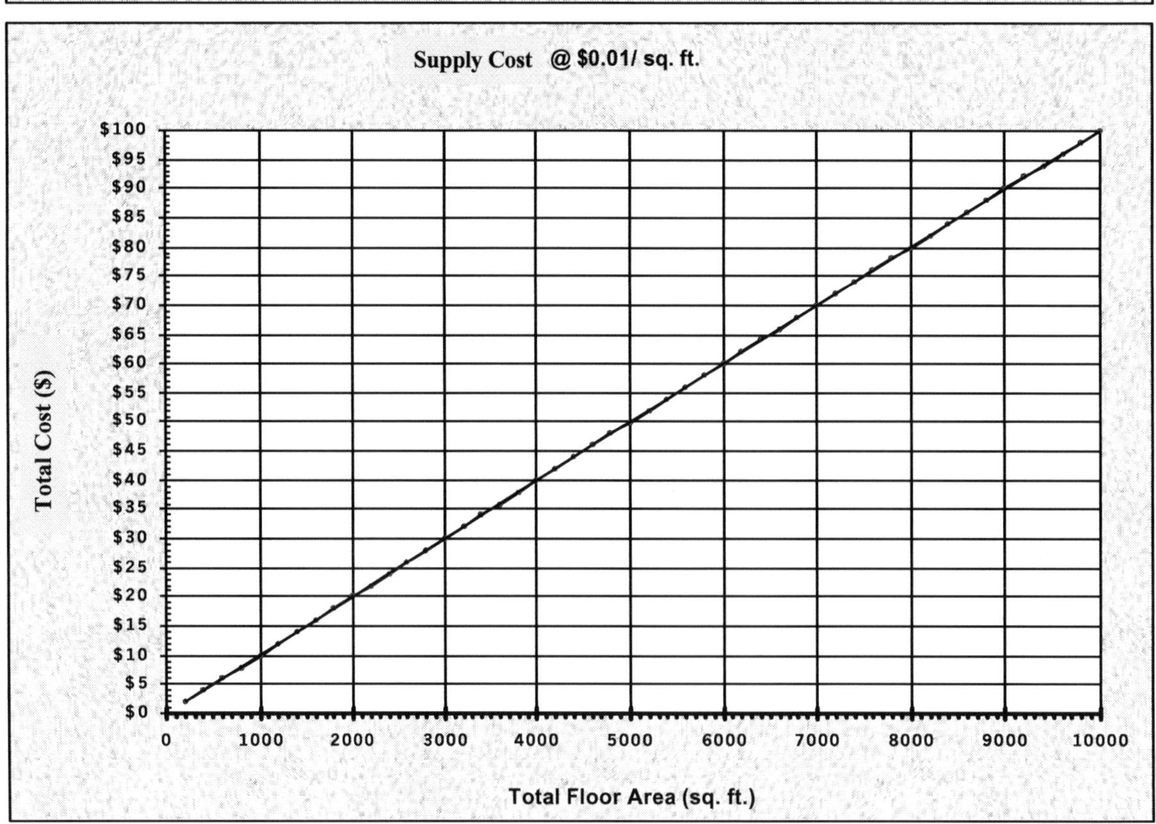
Supply Cost @ $0.01/ sq. ft.
Total Cost ($)
$100
$95
$90
$85
$80
$75
$70
$65
$60
$55
$50
$45
$40
$35
$30
$25
$20
$15
$10
$5
$0
0
1000
2000
3000
4000
5000
6000
7000
8000
9000
10000
Total Floor Area (sq. ft.)

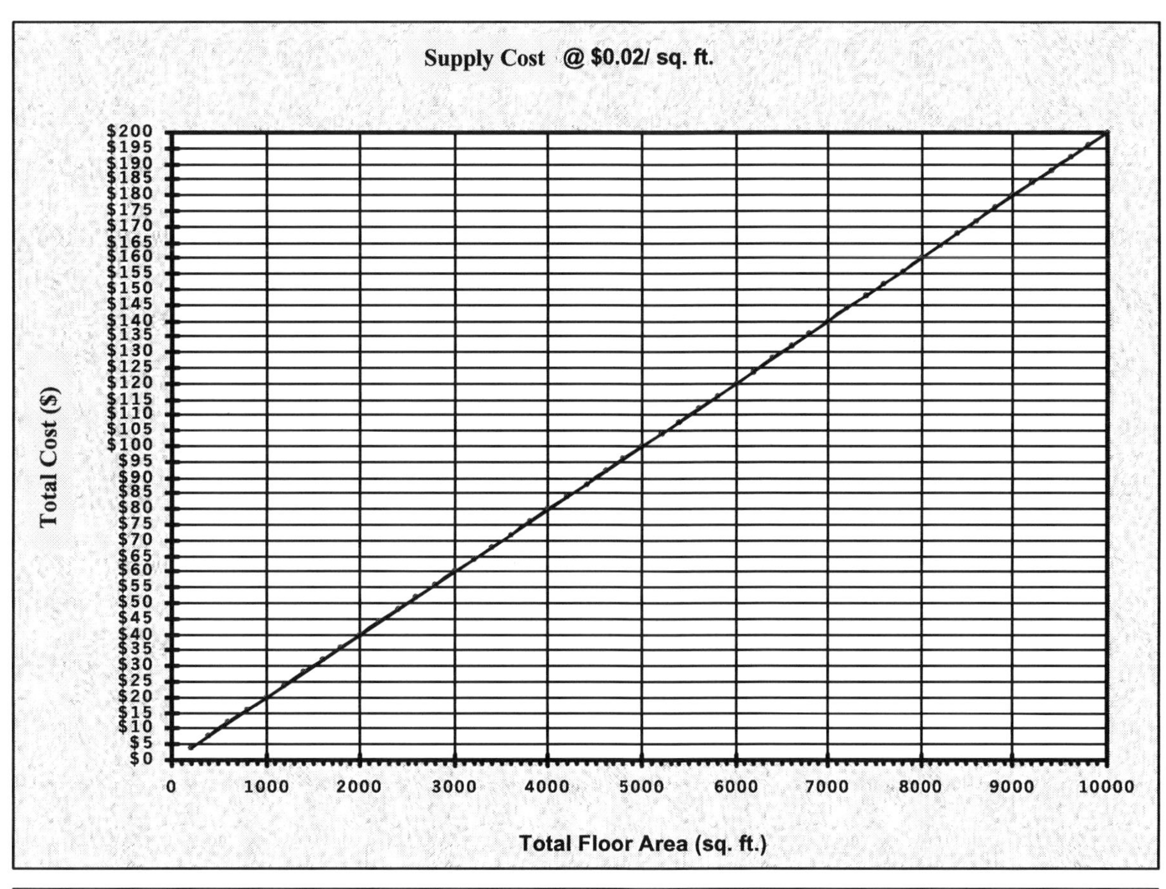
Supply Cost @ $0.02/ sq. ft.
Total Cost ($)
$200
$195
$190
$185
$180
$175
$170
$165
$160
$155
$150
$145
$140
$135
$130
$125
$120
$115
$110
$105
$100
$95
$90
$85
$80
$75
$70
$65
$60
$55
$50
$45
$40
$35
$30
$25
$20
$15
$10
$5
$0
0
1000
2000
3000
4000
5000
6000
7000
8000
9000
10000
Total Floor Area (sq. ft.)

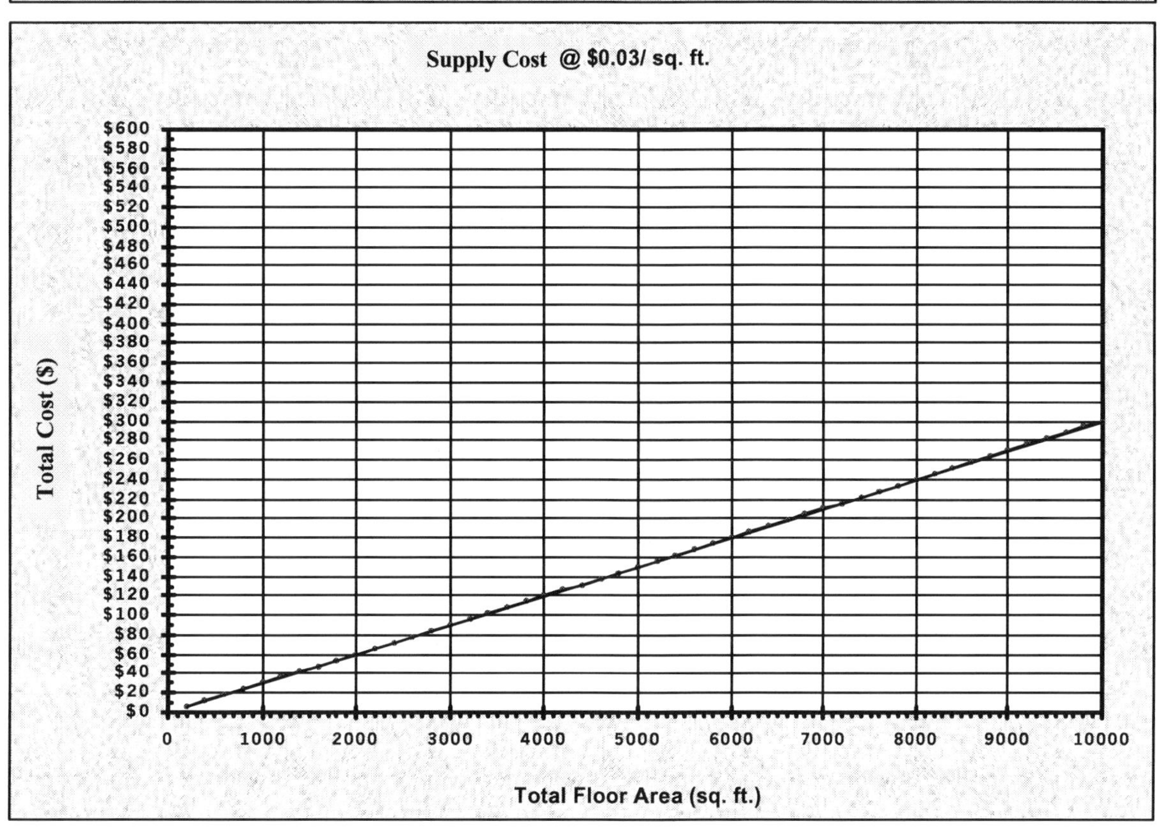
Supply Cost @ $0.03/ sq. ft.
Total Cost ($)
$600
$580
$560
$540
$520
$500
$480
$460
$440
$420
$400
$380
$360
$340
$320
$300
$280
$260
$240
$220
$200
$180
$160
$140
$120
$100
$80
$60
$40
$20
$0
0
1000
2000
3000
4000
5000
6000
7000
8000
9000
10000
Total Floor Area (sq. ft.)

Chapter 6

Generic production rate charts

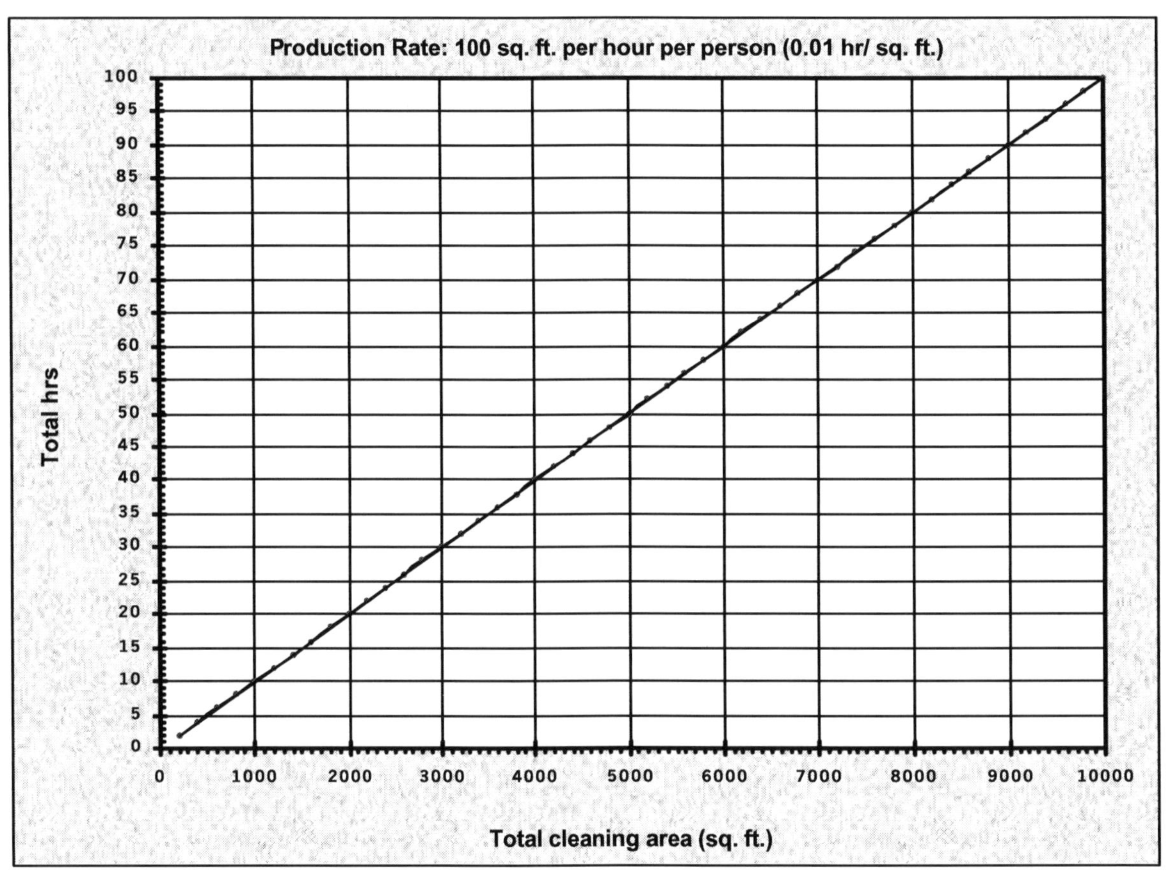

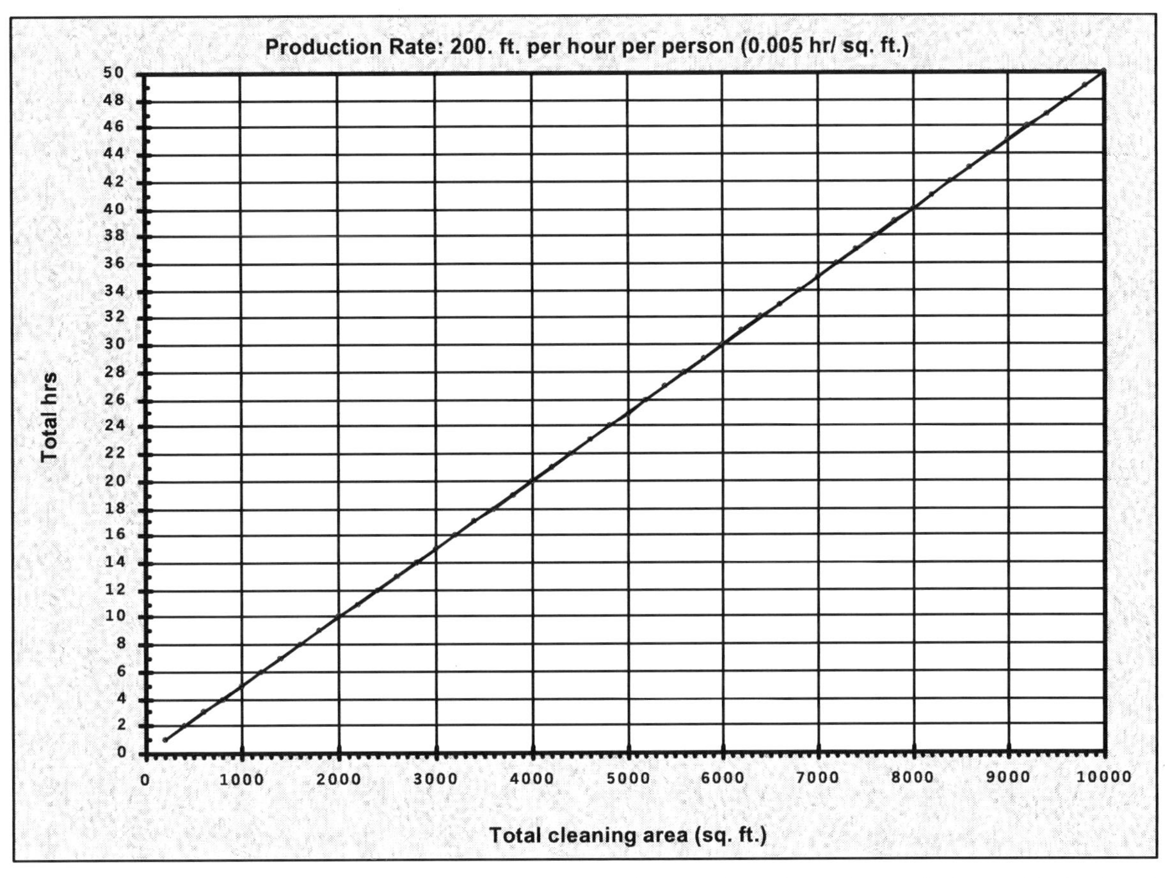
Production Rate: 200. ft. per hour per person (0.005 hr/ sq. ft.)
Total hrs
50
48
46
44
42
40
38
36
34
32
30
28
26
24
22
20
18
16
14
12
10
8
6
4
2
0
0
1000
2000
3000
4000
5000
6000
7000
8000
9000
10000
Total cleaning area (sq. ft.)

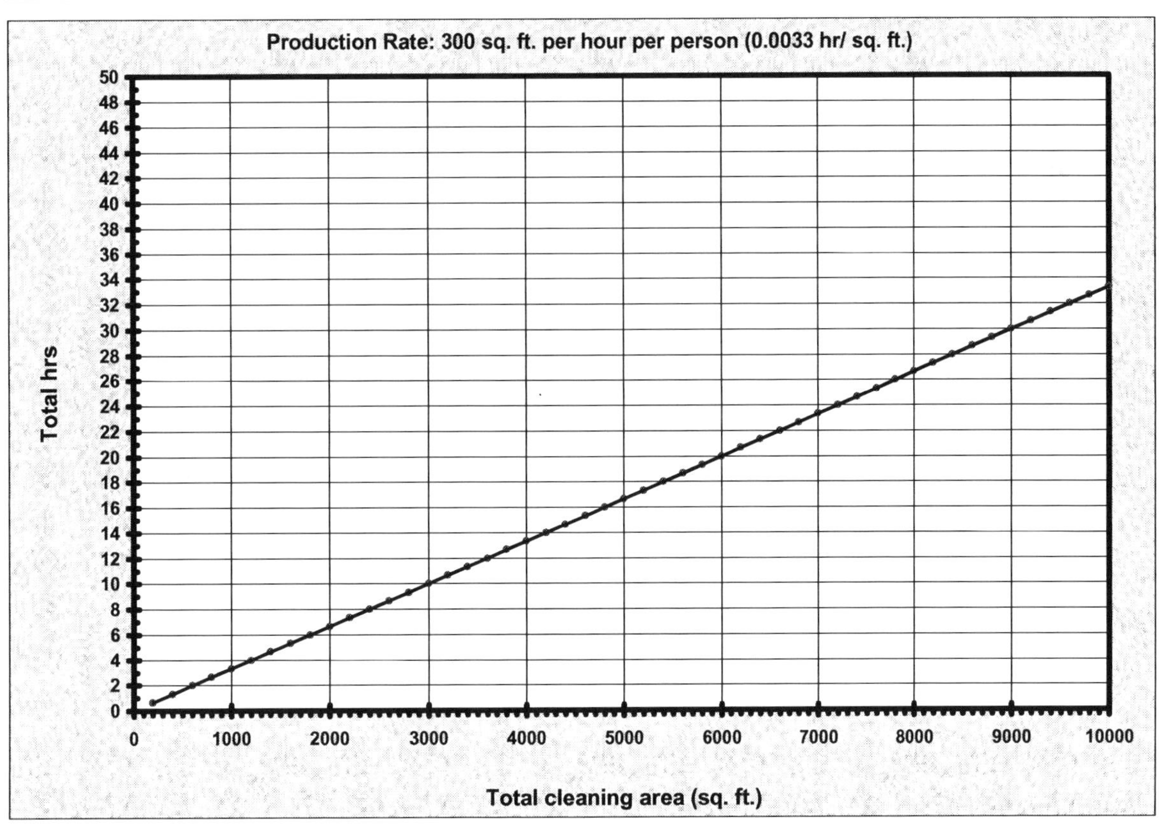
Production Rate: 300 sq. ft. per hour per person (0.0033 hr/ sq. ft.)
Total hrs
50
48
46
44
42
40
38
36
34
32
30
28
26
24
22
20
18
16
14
12
10
8
6
4
2
0
0
1000
2000
3000
4000
5000
6000
7000
8000
9000
10000
Total cleaning area (sq. ft.)

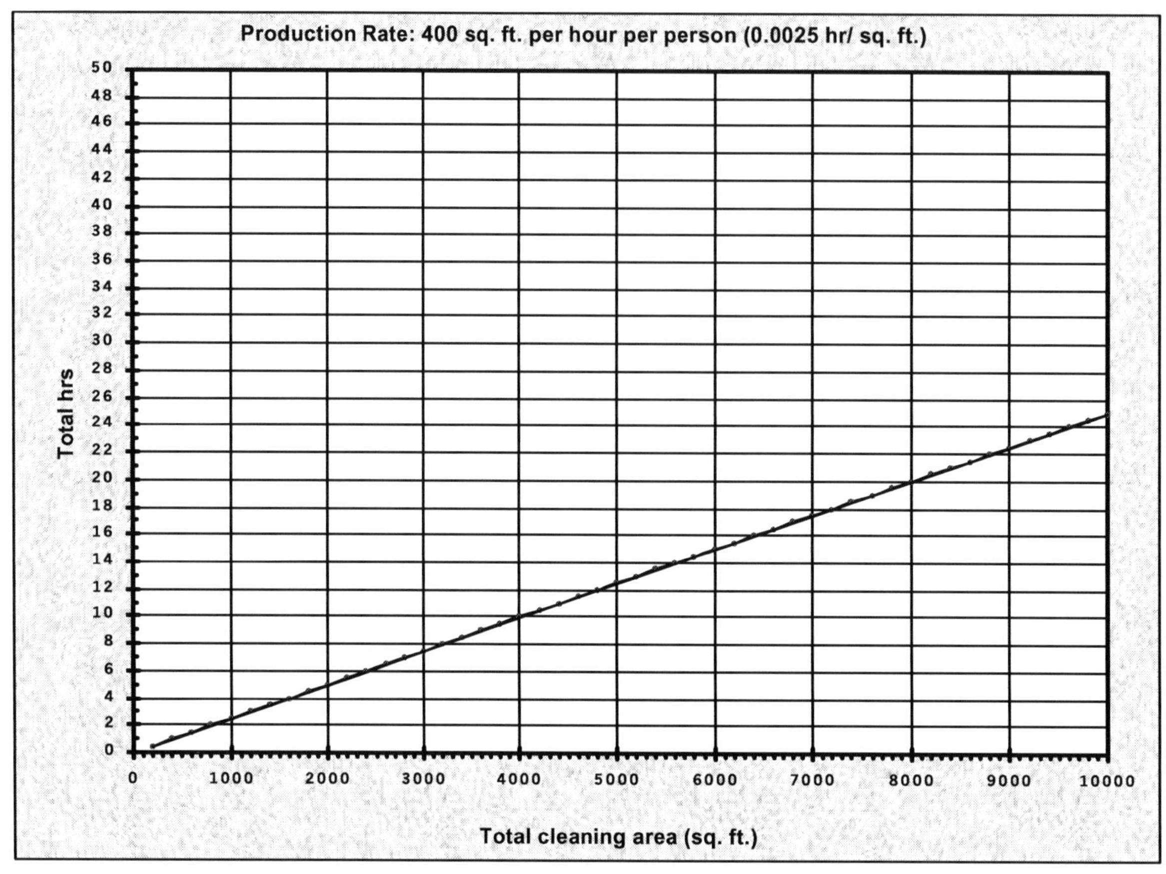
Production Rate: 400 sq. ft. per hour per person (0.0025 hr/ sq. ft.)
Total hrs
0
2
4
6
8
10
12
14
16
18
20
22
24
26
28
30
32
34
36
38
40
42
44
46
48
50
0
1000
2000
3000
4000
5000
6000
7000
8000
9000
10000
Total cleaning area (sq. ft.)

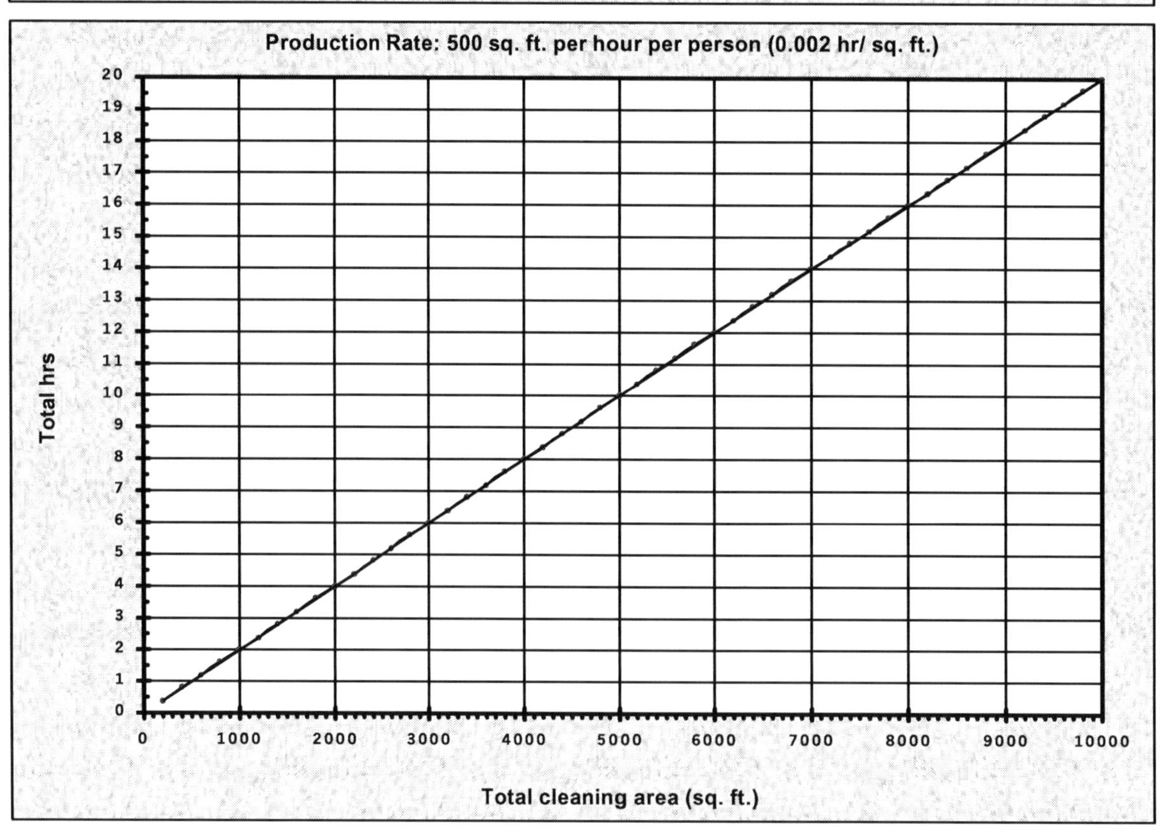
Production Rate: 500 sq. ft. per hour per person (0.002 hr/ sq. ft.)
Total hrs
0
1
2
3
4
5
6
7
8
9
10
11
12
13
14
15
16
17
18
19
20
0
1000
2000
3000
4000
5000
6000
7000
8000
9000
10000
Total cleaning area (sq. ft.)

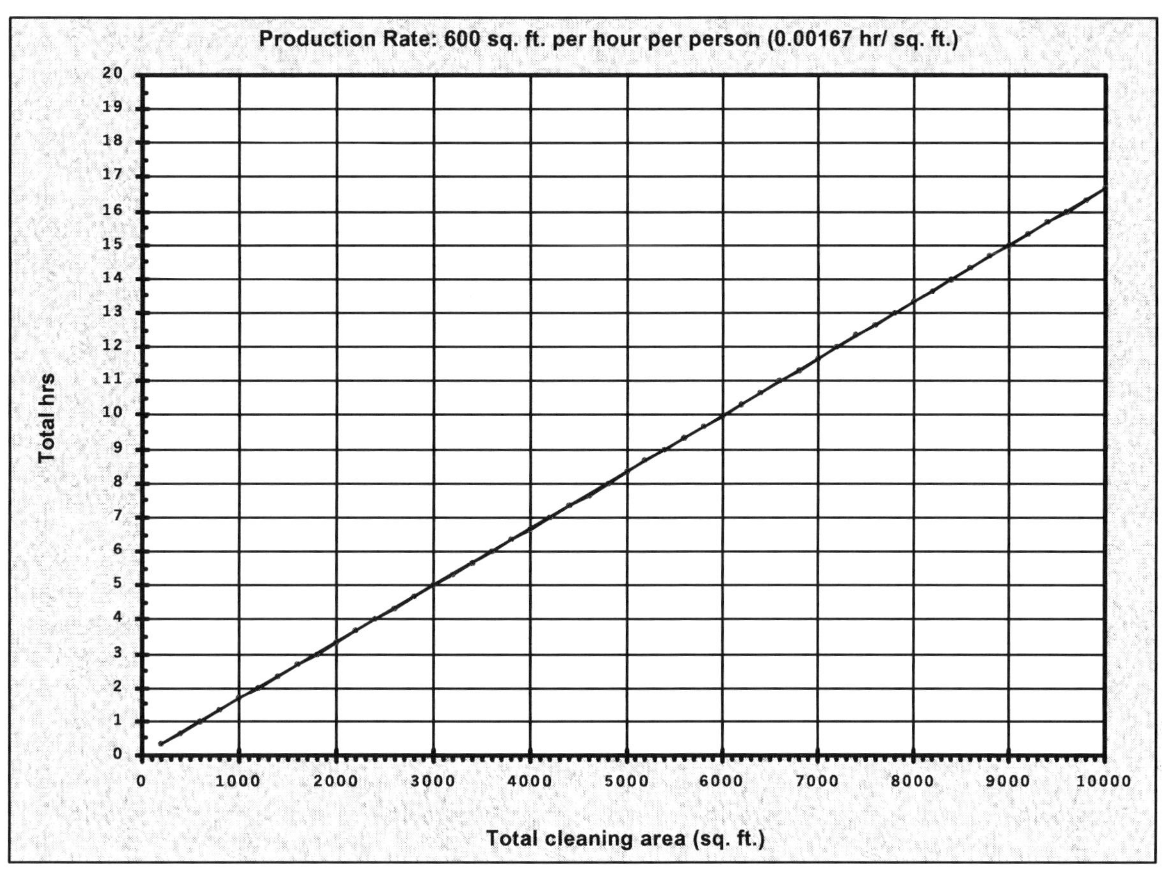
Production Rate: 600 sq. ft. per hour per person (0.00167 hr/ sq. ft.)
Total hrs
0
1
2
3
4
5
6
7
8
9
10
11
12
13
14
15
16
17
18
19
20
0
1000
2000
3000
4000
5000
6000
7000
8000
9000
10000
Total cleaning area (sq. ft.)

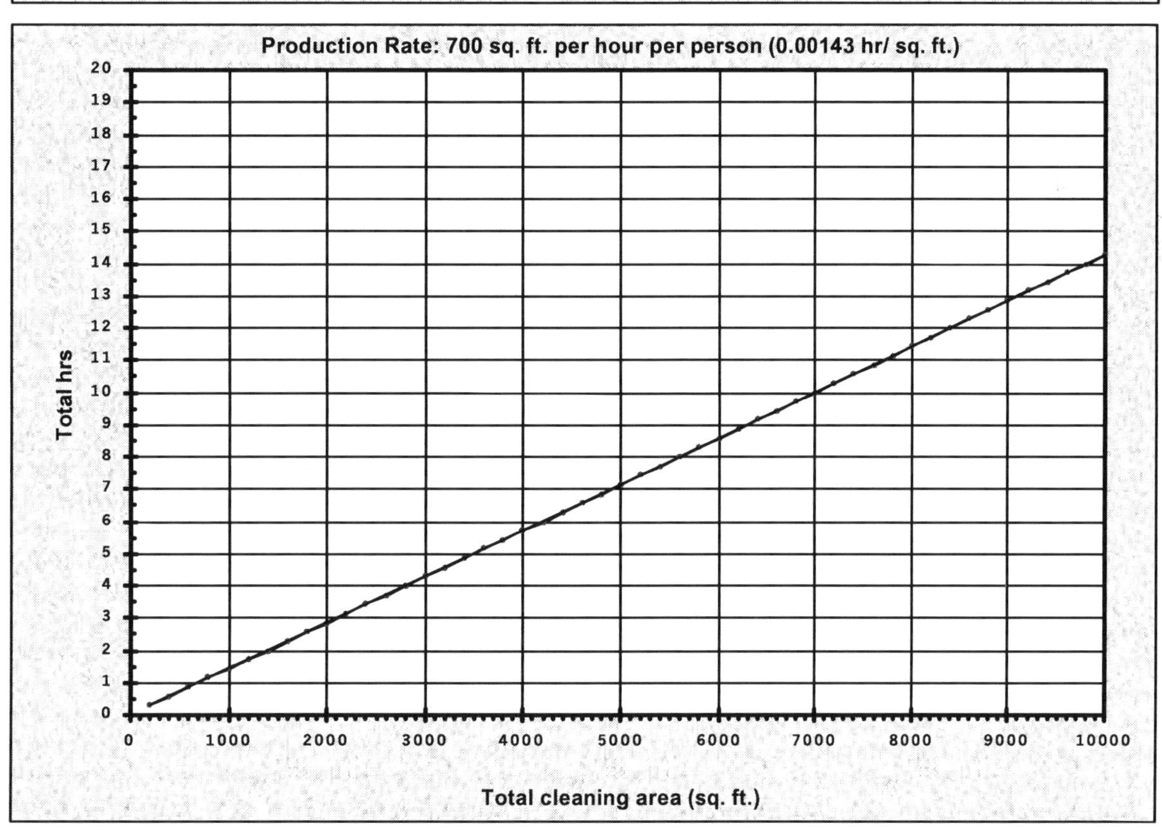
Production Rate: 700 sq. ft. per hour per person (0.00143 hr/ sq. ft.)
Total hrs
0
1
2
3
4
5
6
7
8
9
10
11
12
13
14
15
16
17
18
19
20
0
1000
2000
3000
4000
5000
6000
7000
8000
9000
10000
Total cleaning area (sq. ft.)

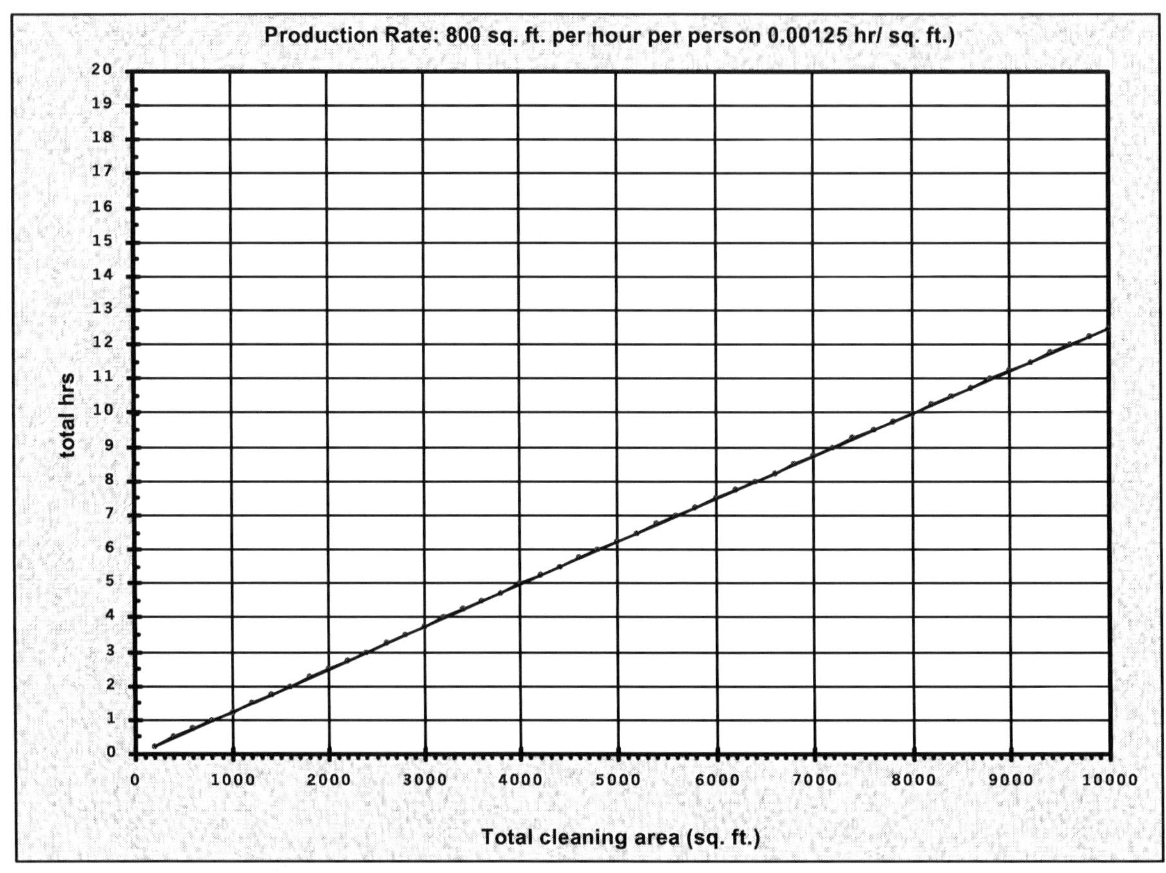
Production Rate: 800 sq. ft. per hour per person 0.00125 hr/ sq. ft.)
total hrs
0
1
2
3
4
5
6
7
8
9
10
11
12
13
14
15
16
17
18
19
20
0
1000
2000
3000
4000
5000
6000
7000
8000
9000
10000
Total cleaning area (sq. ft.)

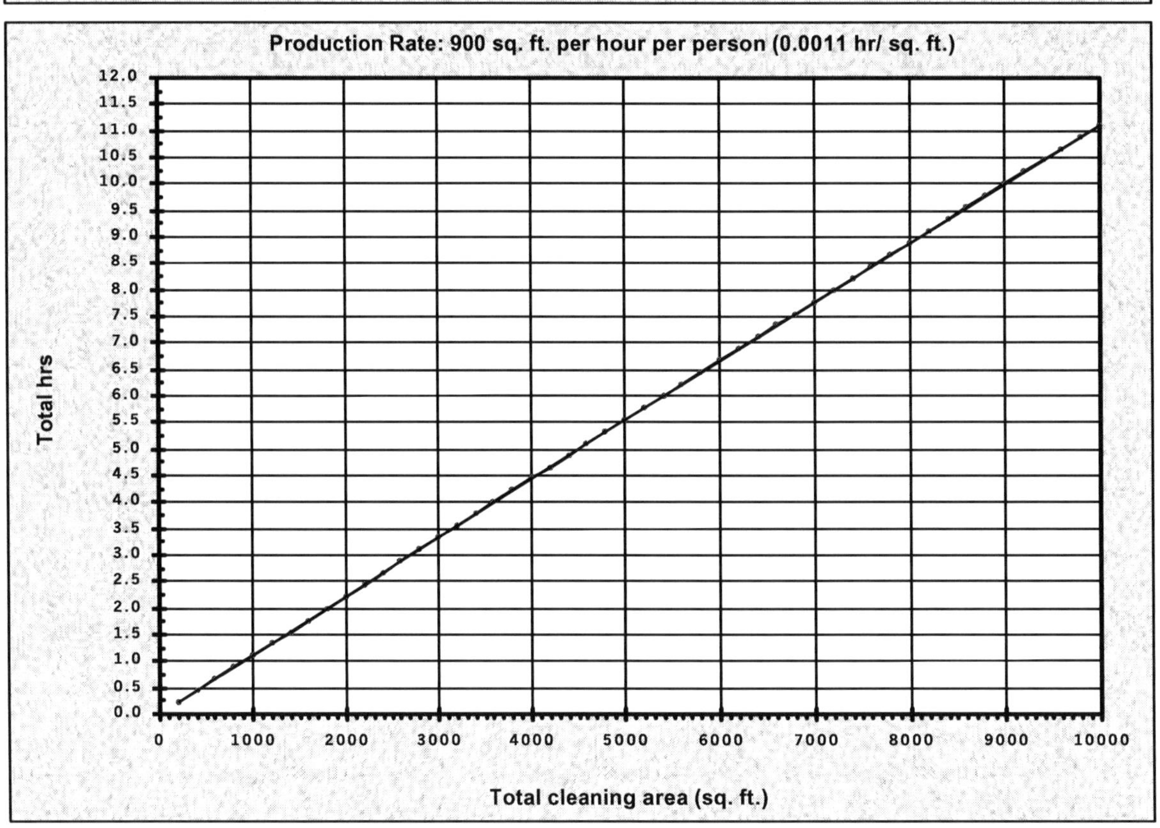
Production Rate: 900 sq. ft. per hour per person (0.0011 hr/ sq. ft.)
Total hrs
0.0
0.5
1.0
1.5
2.0
2.5
3.0
3.5
4.0
4.5
5.0
5.5
6.0
6.5
7.0
7.5
8.0
8.5
9.0
9.5
10.0
10.5
11.0
11.5
12.0
0
1000
2000
3000
4000
5000
6000
7000
8000
9000
10000
Total cleaning area (sq. ft.)

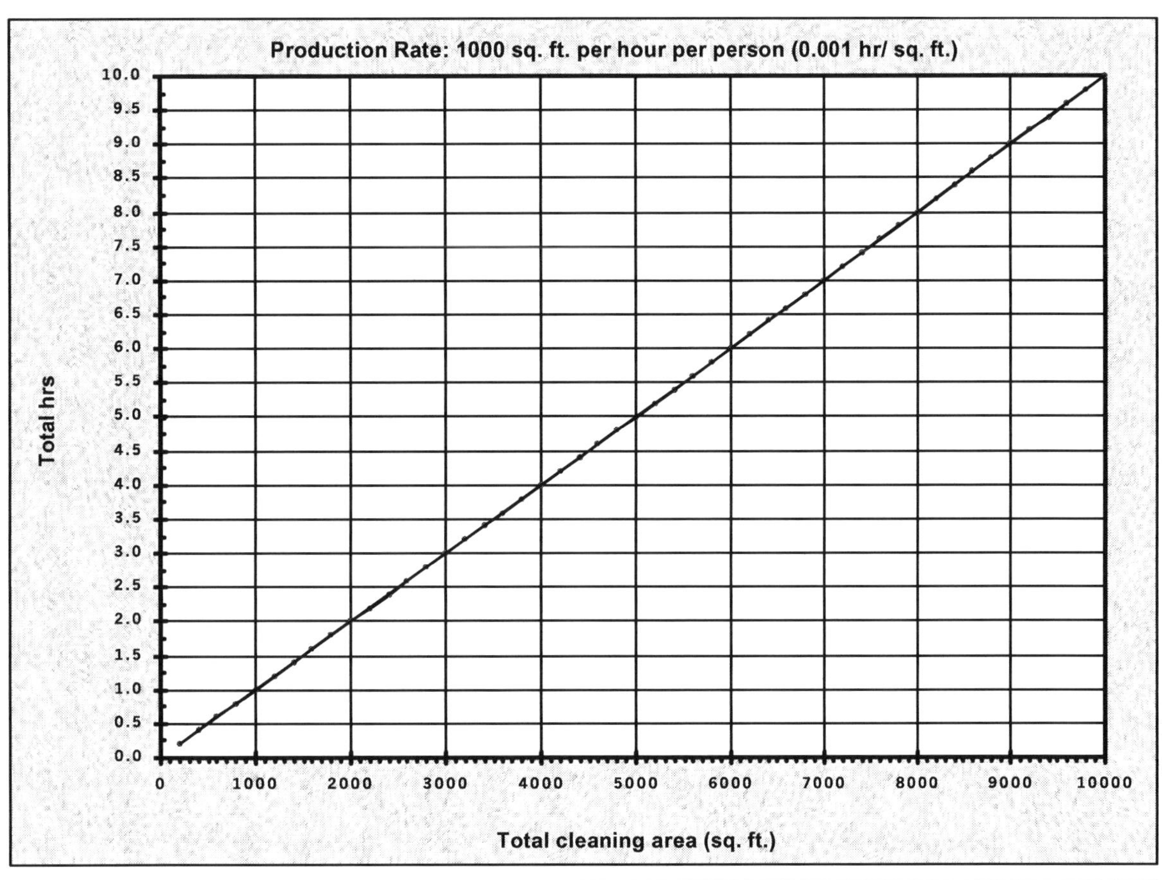
Production Rate: 1000 sq. ft. per hour per person (0.001 hr/ sq. ft.)
Total hrs
10.0
9.5
9.0
8.5
8.0
7.5
7.0
6.5
6.0
5.5
5.0
4.5
4.0
3.5
3.0
2.5
2.0
1.5
1.0
0.5
0.0
0
1000
2000
3000
4000
5000
6000
7000
8000
9000
10000
Total cleaning area (sq. ft.)

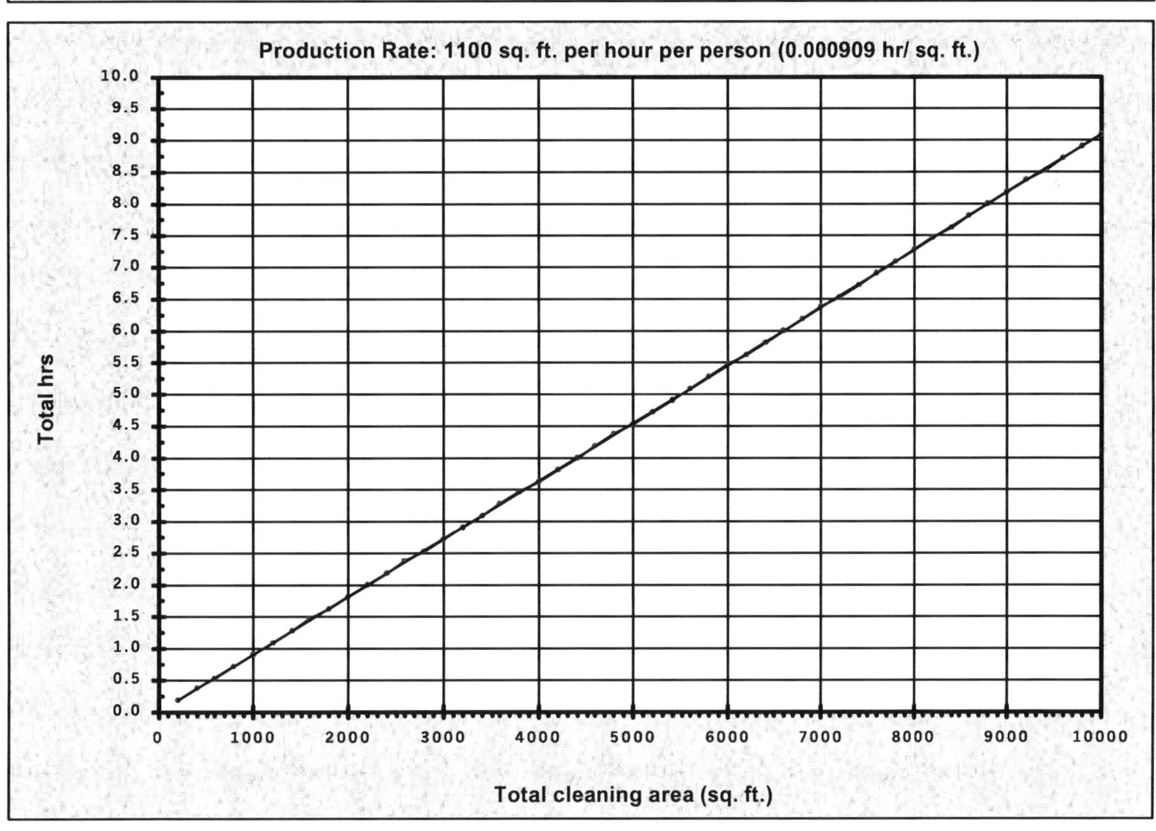
Production Rate: 1100 sq. ft. per hour per person (0.000909 hr/ sq. ft.)
Total hrs
10.0
9.5
9.0
8.5
8.0
7.5
7.0
6.5
6.0
5.5
5.0
4.5
4.0
3.5
3.0
2.5
2.0
1.5
1.0
0.5
0.0
0
1000
2000
3000
4000
5000
6000
7000
8000
9000
10000
Total cleaning area (sq. ft.)

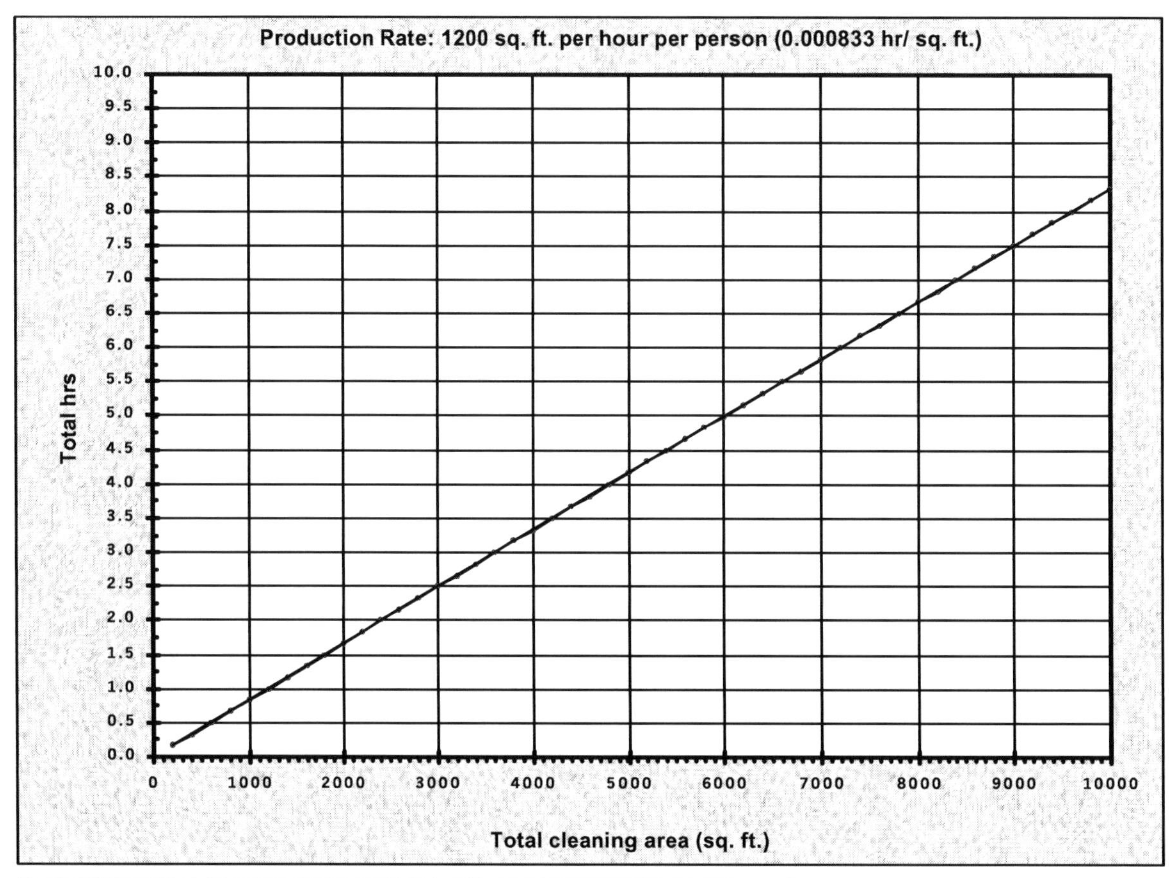
Production Rate: 1200 sq. ft. per hour per person (0.000833 hr/ sq. ft.)
Total hrs
10.0
9.5
9.0
8.5
8.0
7.5
7.0
6.5
6.0
5.5
5.0
4.5
4.0
3.5
3.0
2.5
2.0
1.5
1.0
0.5
0.0
0
1000
2000
3000
4000
5000
6000
7000
8000
9000
10000
Total cleaning area (sq. ft.)

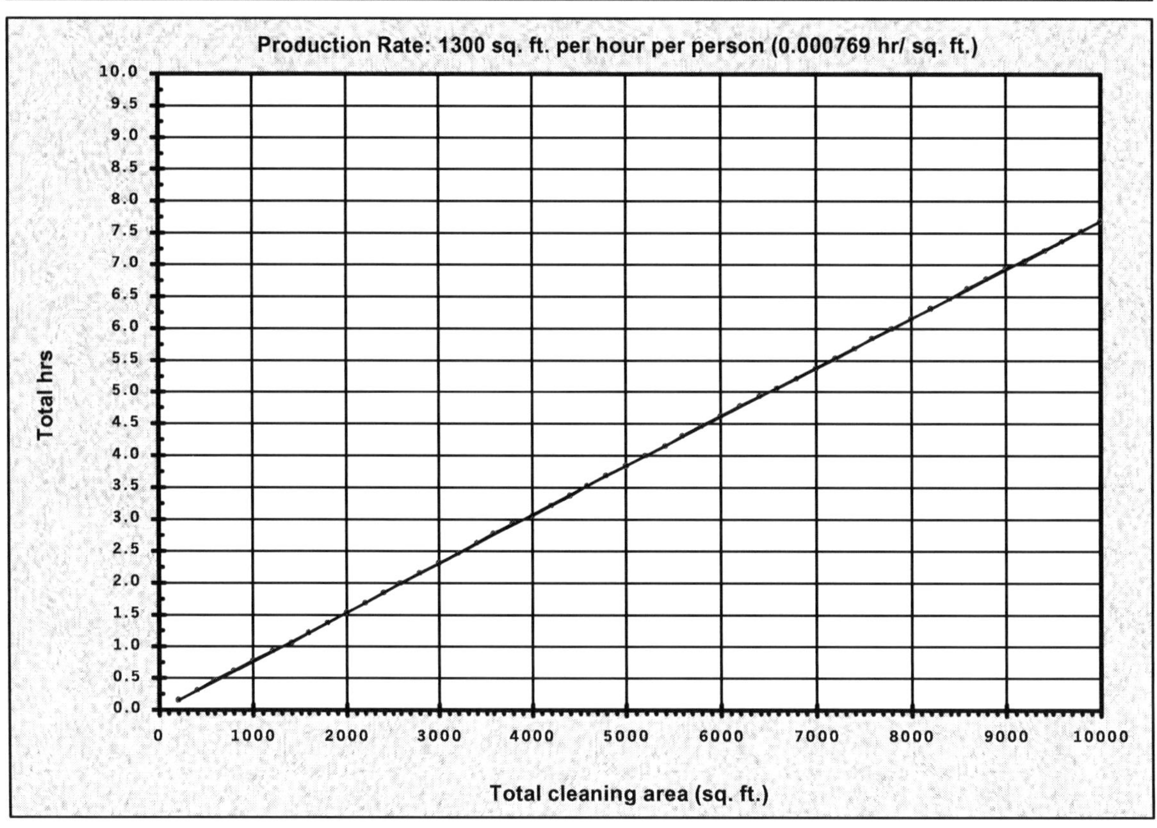
Production Rate: 1300 sq. ft. per hour per person (0.000769 hr/ sq. ft.)
Total hrs
10.0
9.5
9.0
8.5
8.0
7.5
7.0
6.5
6.0
5.5
5.0
4.5
4.0
3.5
3.0
2.5
2.0
1.5
1.0
0.5
0.0
0
1000
2000
3000
4000
5000
6000
7000
8000
9000
10000
Total cleaning area (sq. ft.)

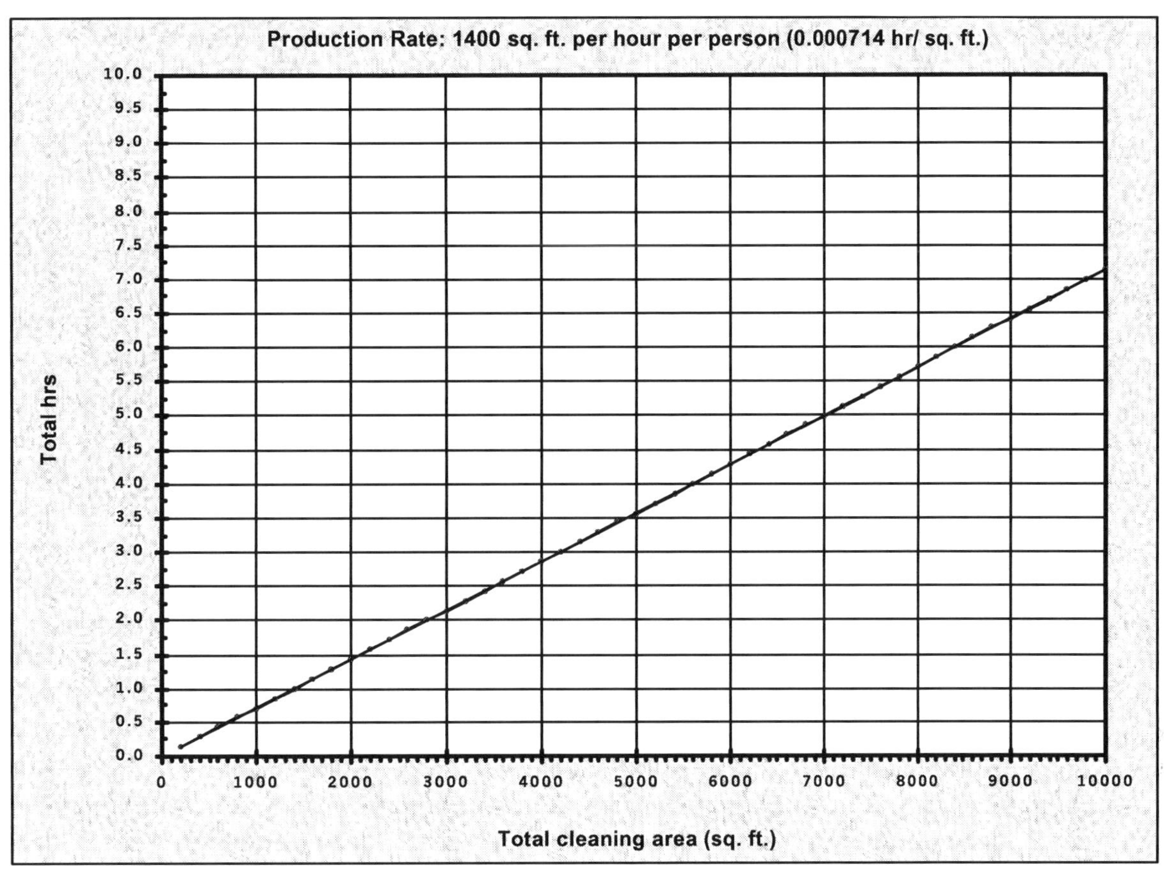
Production Rate: 1400 sq. ft. per hour per person (0.000714 hr/ sq. ft.)
Total hrs
10.0
9.5
9.0
8.5
8.0
7.5
7.0
6.5
6.0
5.5
5.0
4.5
4.0
3.5
3.0
2.5
2.0
1.5
1.0
0.5
0.0
0
1000
2000
3000
4000
5000
6000
7000
8000
9000
10000
Total cleaning area (sq. ft.)

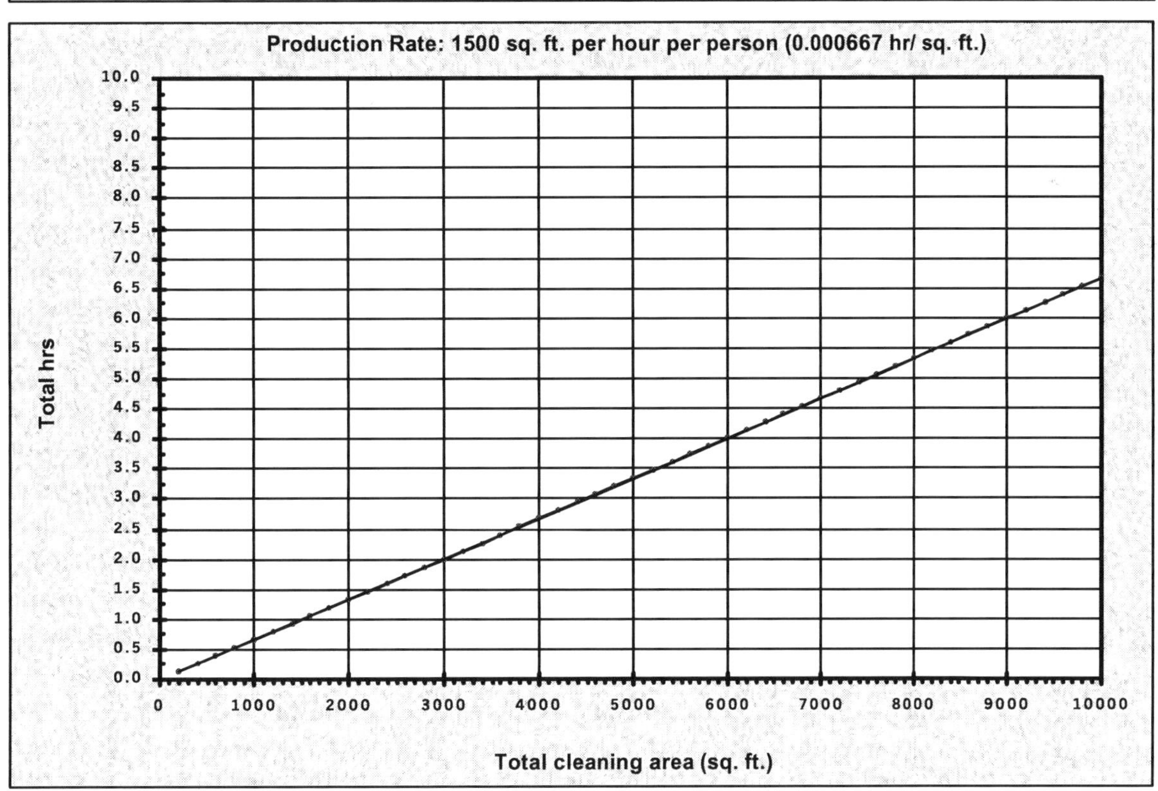
Production Rate: 1500 sq. ft. per hour per person (0.000667 hr/ sq. ft.)
Total hrs
10.0
9.5
9.0
8.5
8.0
7.5
7.0
6.5
6.0
5.5
5.0
4.5
4.0
3.5
3.0
2.5
2.0
1.5
1.0
0.5
0.0
0
1000
2000
3000
4000
5000
6000
7000
8000
9000
10000
Total cleaning area (sq. ft.)

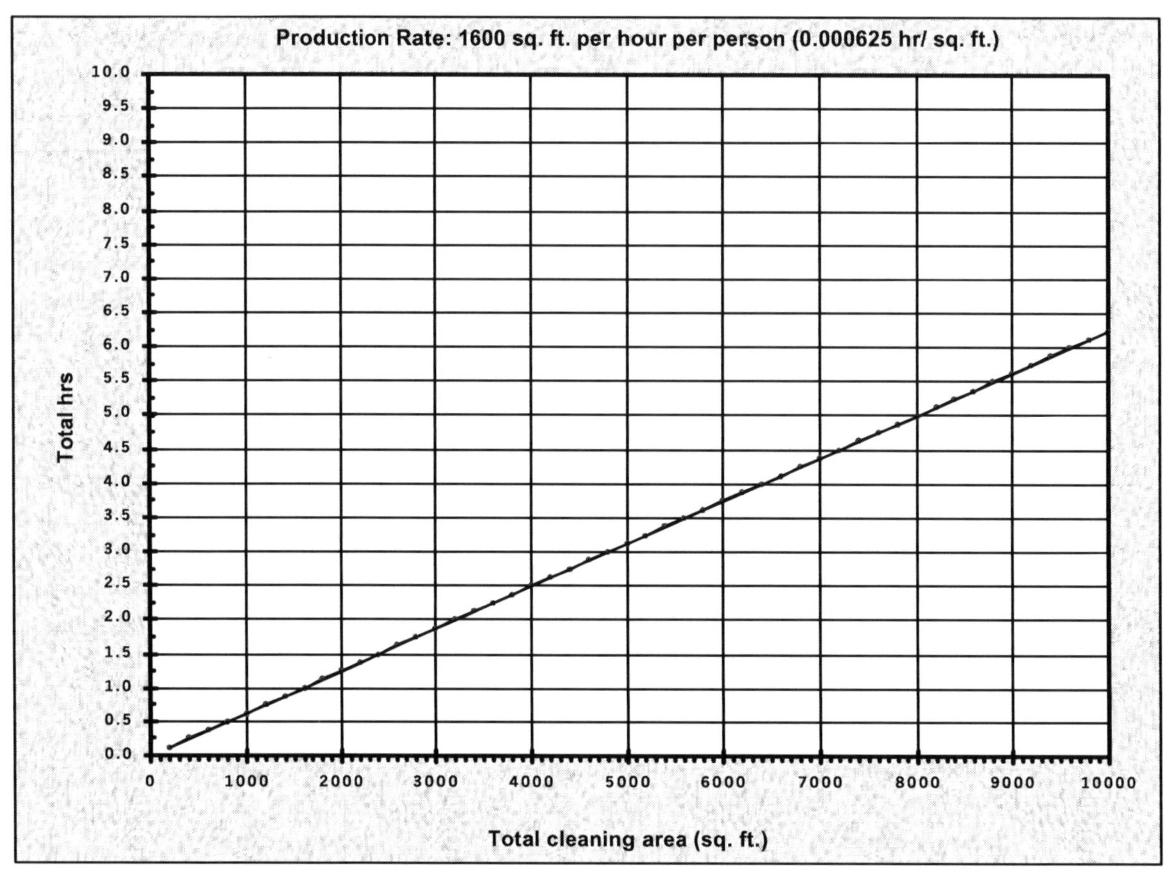
Production Rate: 1600 sq. ft. per hour per person (0.000625 hr/ sq. ft.)
Total hrs
10.0
9.5
9.0
8.5
8.0
7.5
7.0
6.5
6.0
5.5
5.0
4.5
4.0
3.5
3.0
2.5
2.0
1.5
1.0
0.5
0.0
0
1000
2000
3000
4000
5000
6000
7000
8000
9000
10000
Total cleaning area (sq. ft.)

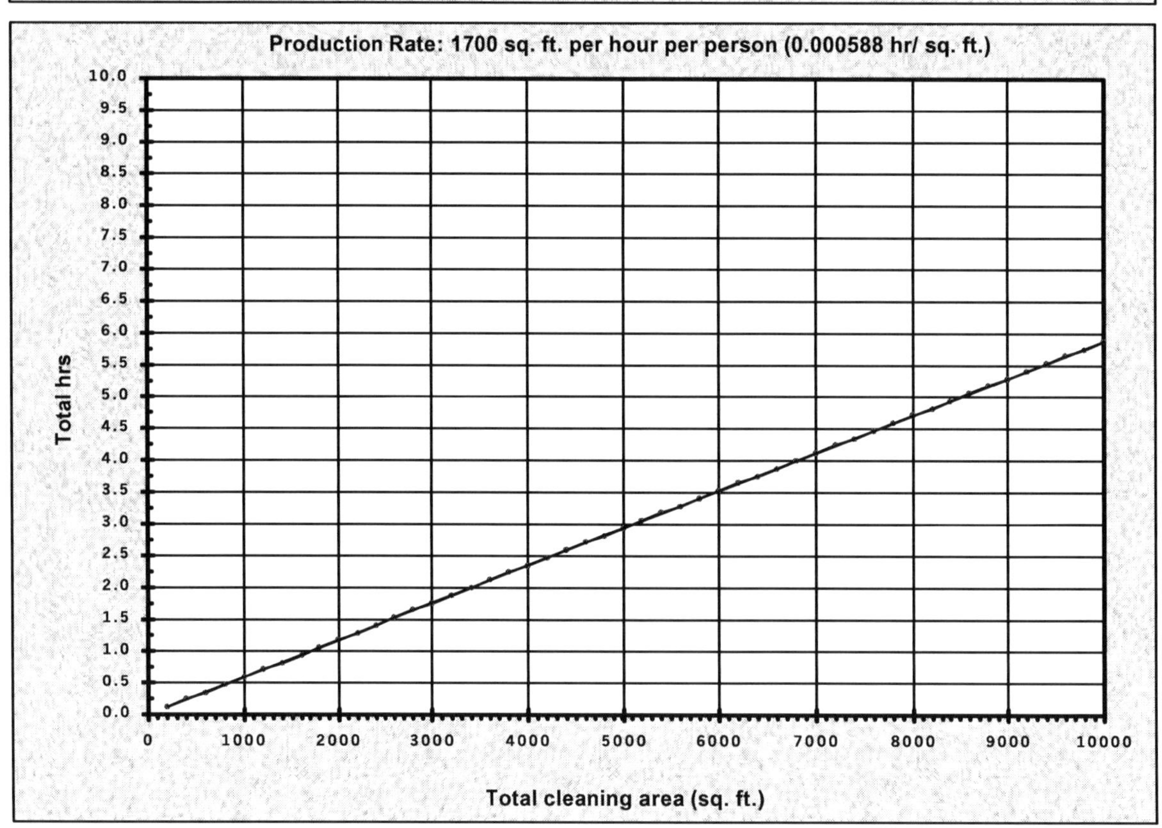
Production Rate: 1700 sq. ft. per hour per person (0.000588 hr/ sq. ft.)
Total hrs
10.0
9.5
9.0
8.5
8.0
7.5
7.0
6.5
6.0
5.5
5.0
4.5
4.0
3.5
3.0
2.5
2.0
1.5
1.0
0.5
0.0
0
1000
2000
3000
4000
5000
6000
7000
8000
9000
10000
Total cleaning area (sq. ft.)

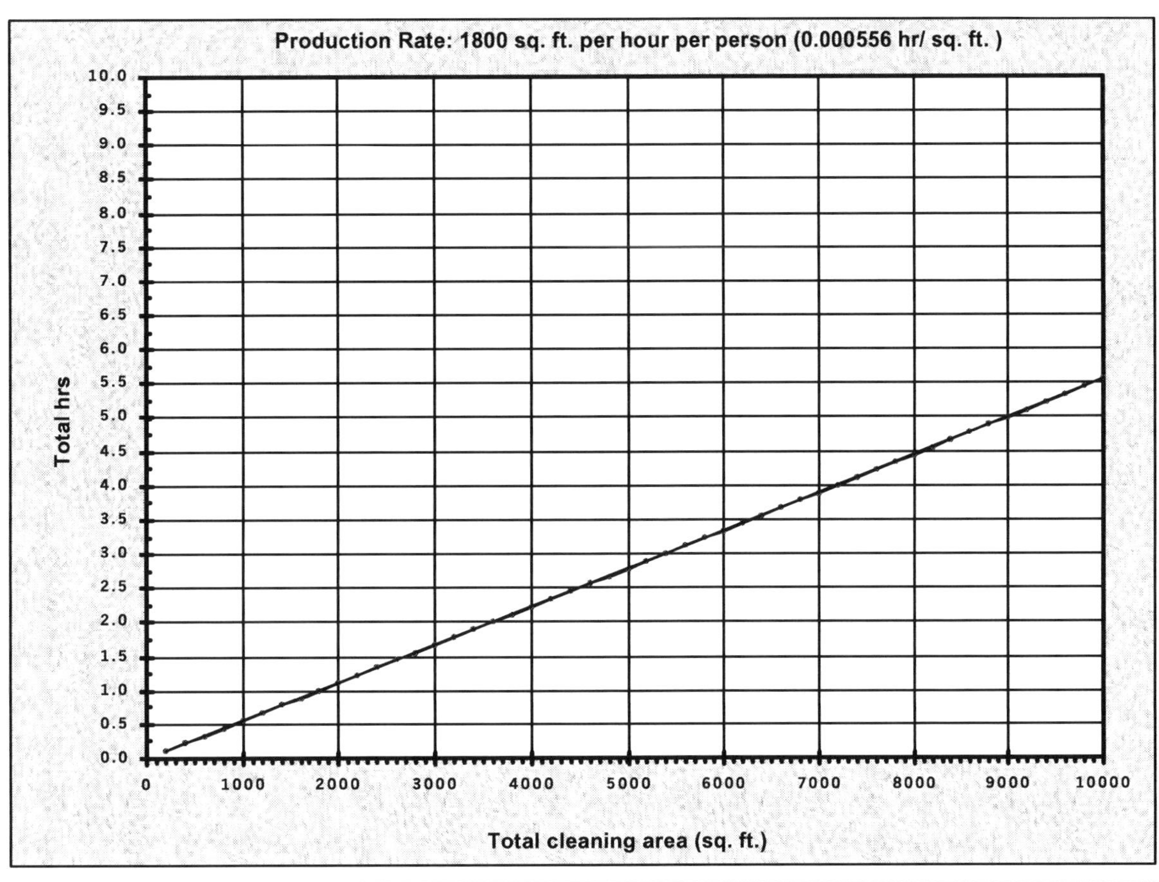
Production Rate: 1800 sq. ft. per hour per person (0.000556 hr/ sq. ft.)
Total hrs
10.0
9.5
9.0
8.5
8.0
7.5
7.0
6.5
6.0
5.5
5.0
4.5
4.0
3.5
3.0
2.5
2.0
1.5
1.0
0.5
0.0
0
1000
2000
3000
4000
5000
6000
7000
8000
9000
10000
Total cleaning area (sq. ft.)

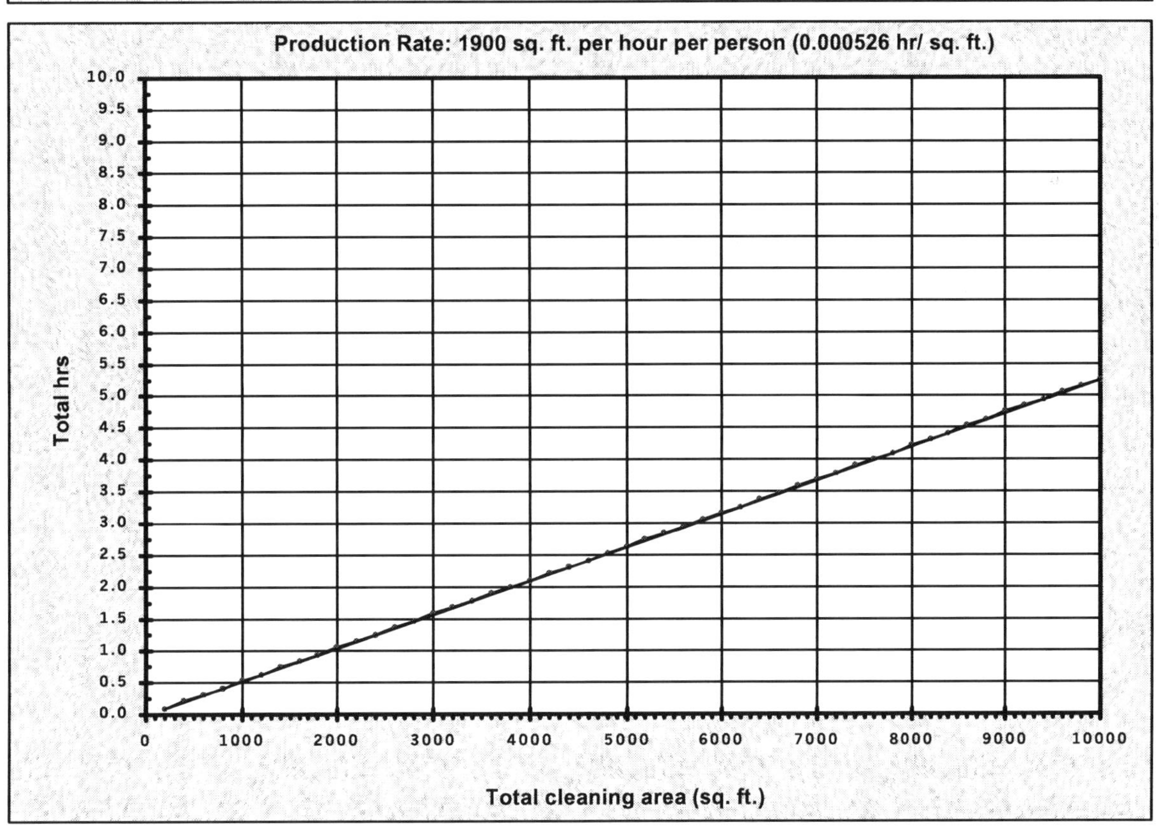
Production Rate: 1900 sq. ft. per hour per person (0.000526 hr/ sq. ft.)
Total hrs
10.0
9.5
9.0
8.5
8.0
7.5
7.0
6.5
6.0
5.5
5.0
4.5
4.0
3.5
3.0
2.5
2.0
1.5
1.0
0.5
0.0
0
1000
2000
3000
4000
5000
6000
7000
8000
9000
10000
Total cleaning area (sq. ft.)

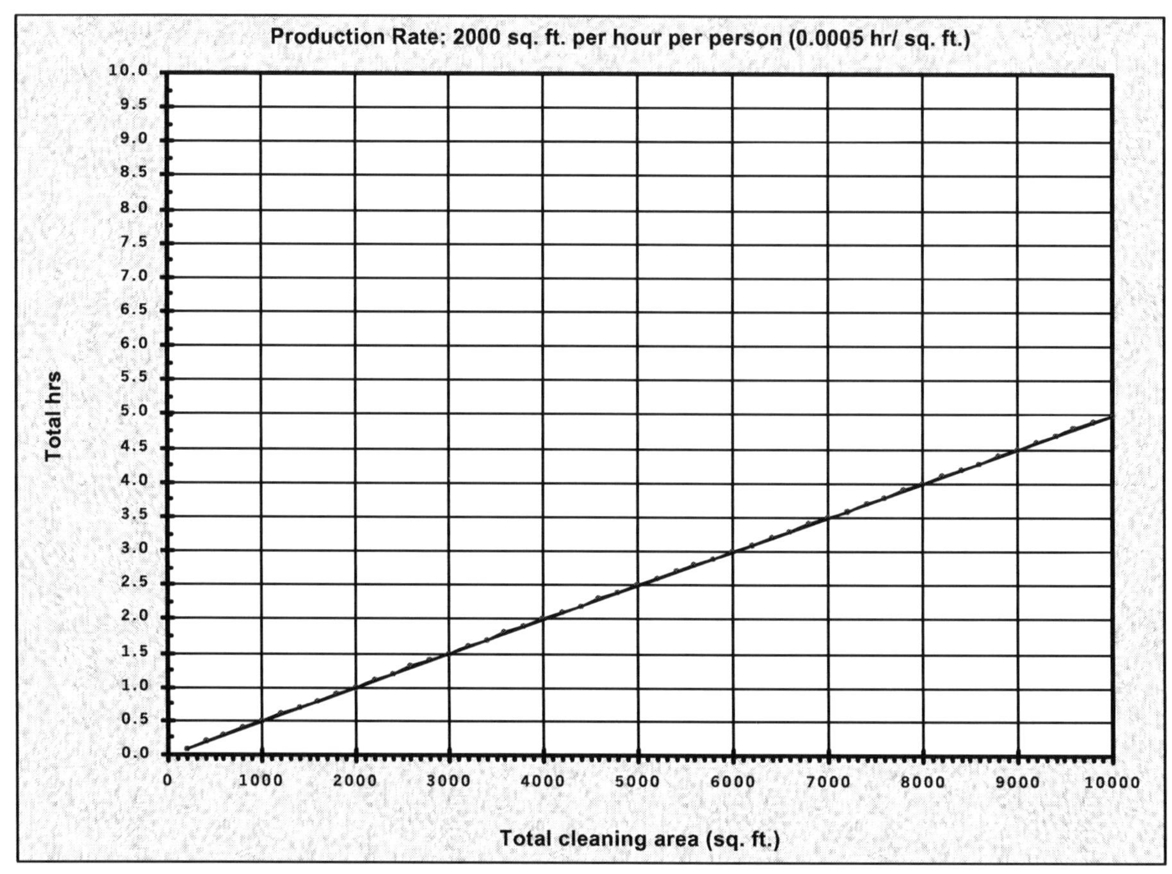
Production Rate: 2000 sq. ft. per hour per person (0.0005 hr/ sq. ft.)
Total hrs
10.0
9.5
9.0
8.5
8.0
7.5
7.0
6.5
6.0
5.5
5.0
4.5
4.0
3.5
3.0
2.5
2.0
1.5
1.0
0.5
0.0
0
1000
2000
3000
4000
5000
6000
7000
8000
9000
10000
Total cleaning area (sq. ft.)

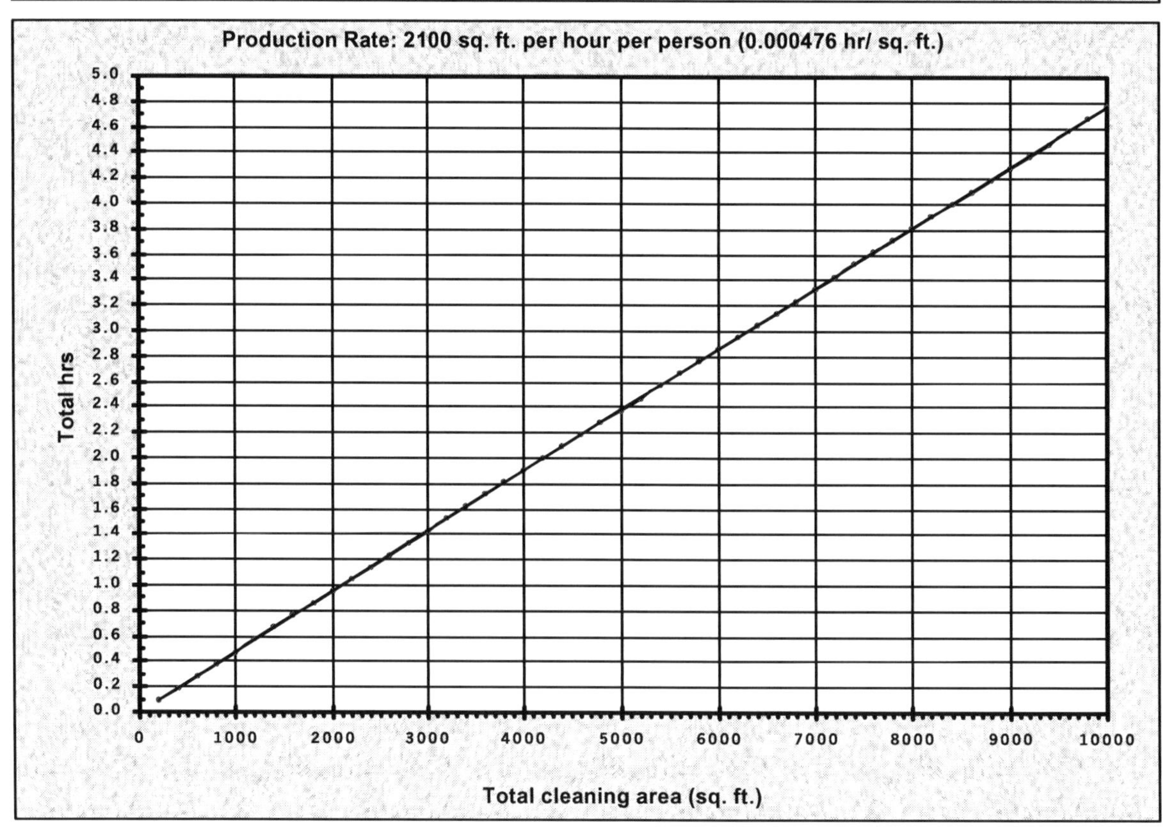
Production Rate: 2100 sq. ft. per hour per person (0.000476 hr/ sq. ft.)
Total hrs
5.0
4.8
4.6
4.4
4.2
4.0
3.8
3.6
3.4
3.2
3.0
2.8
2.6
2.4
2.2
2.0
1.8
1.6
1.4
1.2
1.0
0.8
0.6
0.4
0.2
0.0
0
1000
2000
3000
4000
5000
6000
7000
8000
9000
10000
Total cleaning area (sq. ft.)

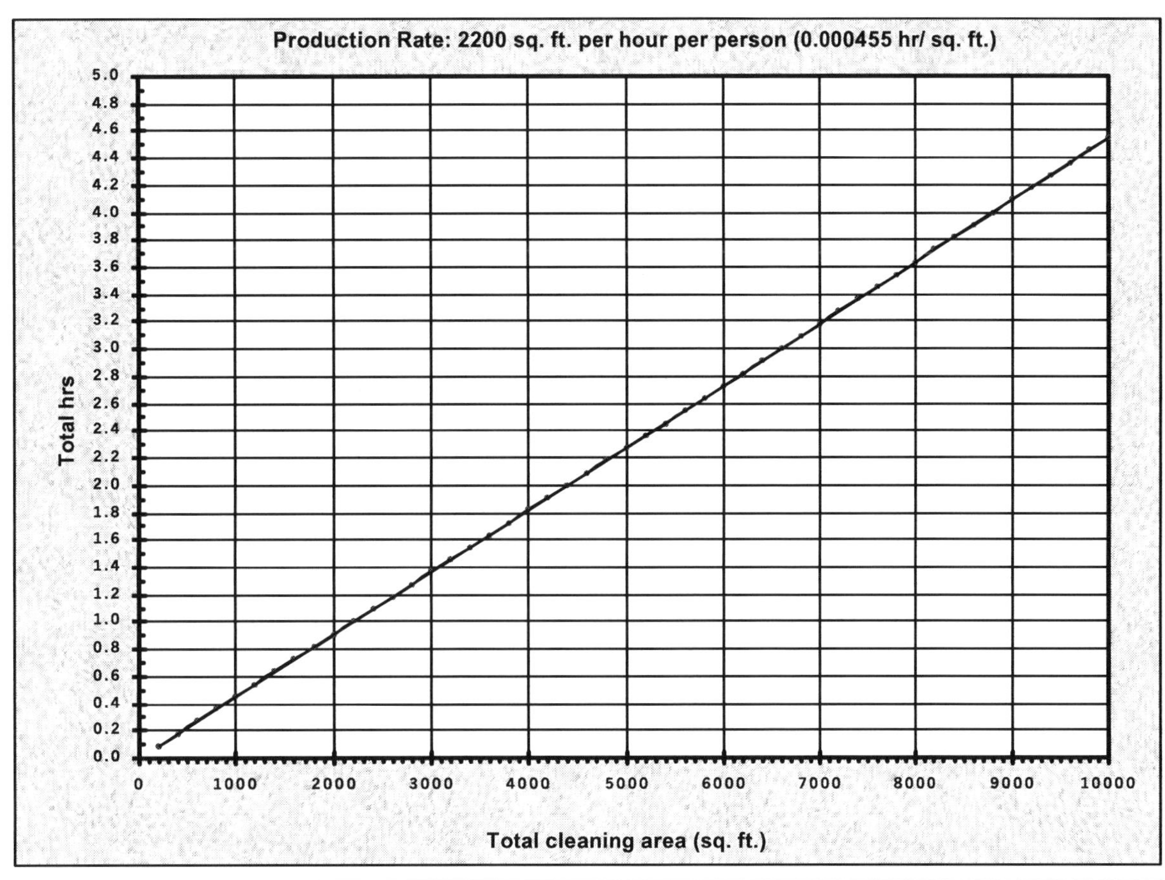
Production Rate: 2200 sq. ft. per hour per person (0.000455 hr/ sq. ft.)
Total hrs
5.0
4.8
4.6
4.4
4.2
4.0
3.8
3.6
3.4
3.2
3.0
2.8
2.6
2.4
2.2
2.0
1.8
1.6
1.4
1.2
1.0
0.8
0.6
0.4
0.2
0.0
0
1000
2000
3000
4000
5000
6000
7000
8000
9000
10000
Total cleaning area (sq. ft.)

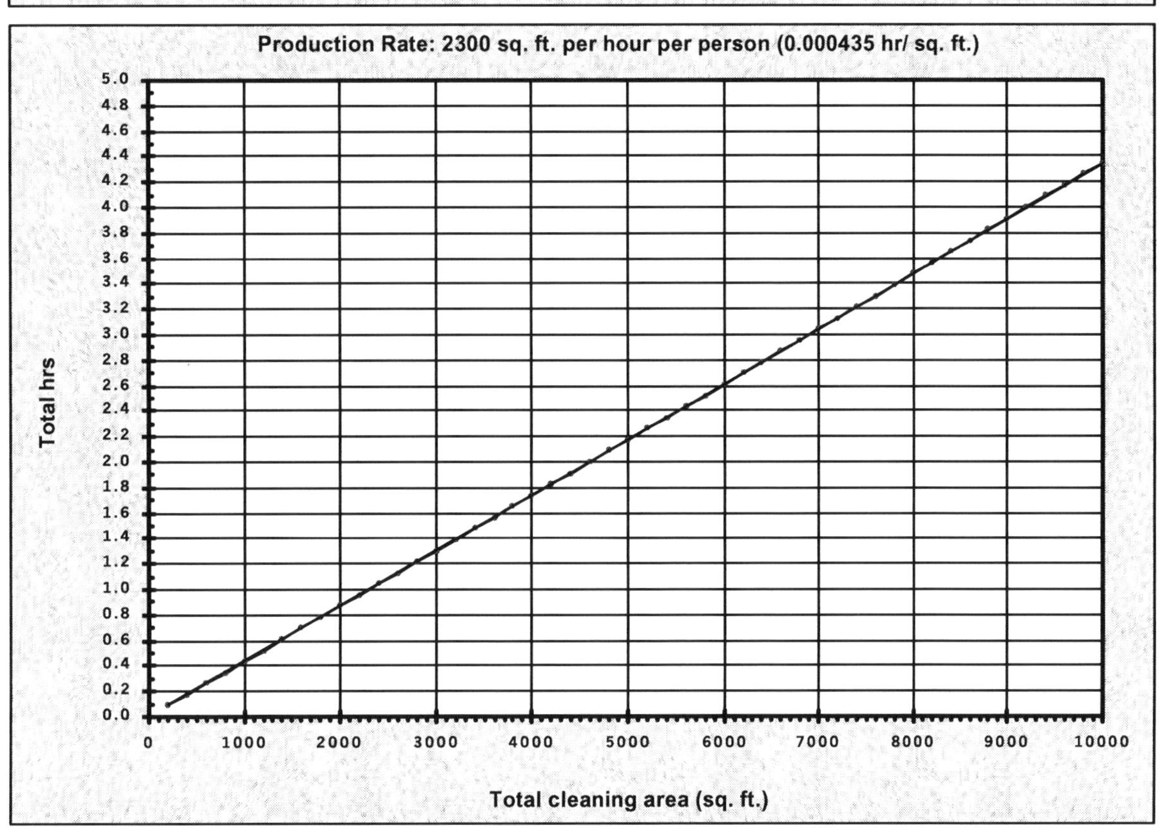
Production Rate: 2300 sq. ft. per hour per person (0.000435 hr/ sq. ft.)
Total hrs
5.0
4.8
4.6
4.4
4.2
4.0
3.8
3.6
3.4
3.2
3.0
2.8
2.6
2.4
2.2
2.0
1.8
1.6
1.4
1.2
1.0
0.8
0.6
0.4
0.2
0.0
0
1000
2000
3000
4000
5000
6000
7000
8000
9000
10000
Total cleaning area (sq. ft.)

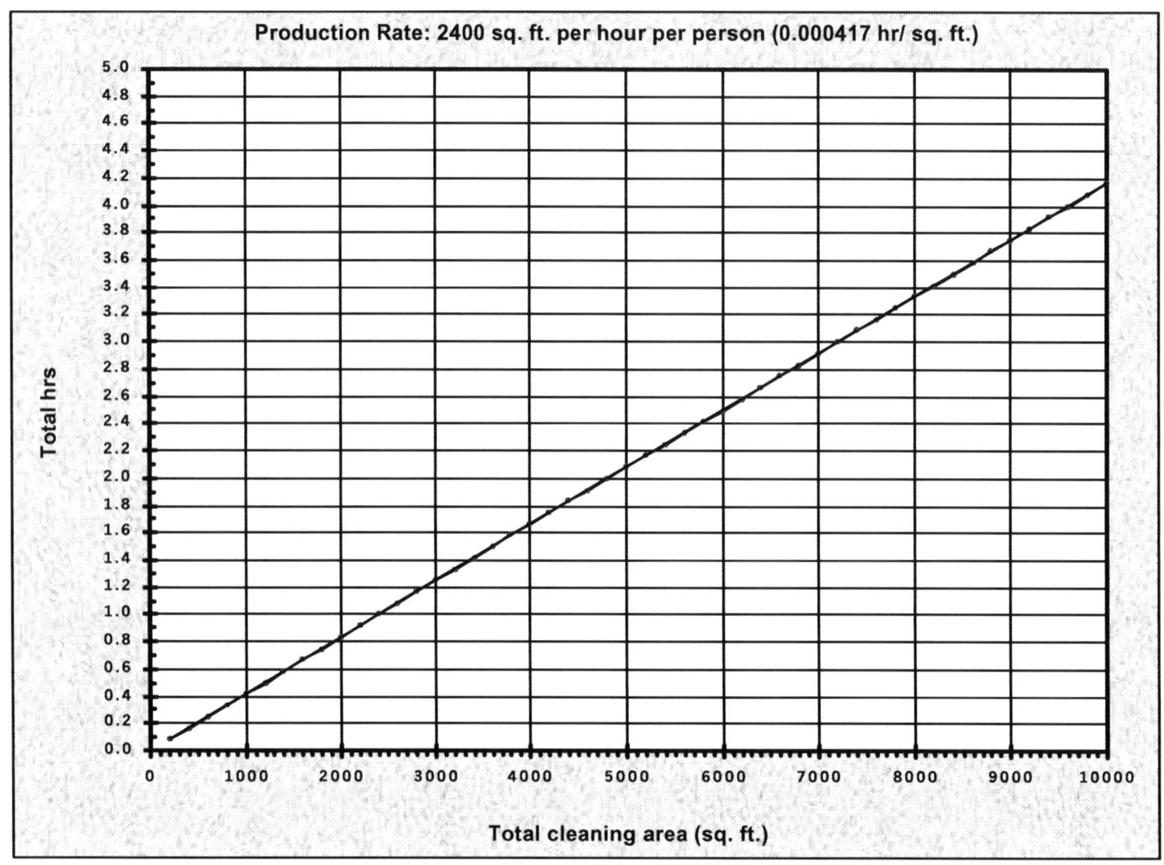
Production Rate: 2400 sq. ft. per hour per person (0.000417 hr/ sq. ft.)
Total hrs
5.0
4.8
4.6
4.4
4.2
4.0
3.8
3.6
3.4
3.2
3.0
2.8
2.6
2.4
2.2
2.0
1.8
1.6
1.4
1.2
1.0
0.8
0.6
0.4
0.2
0.0
0
1000
2000
3000
4000
5000
6000
7000
8000
9000
10000
Total cleaning area (sq. ft.)

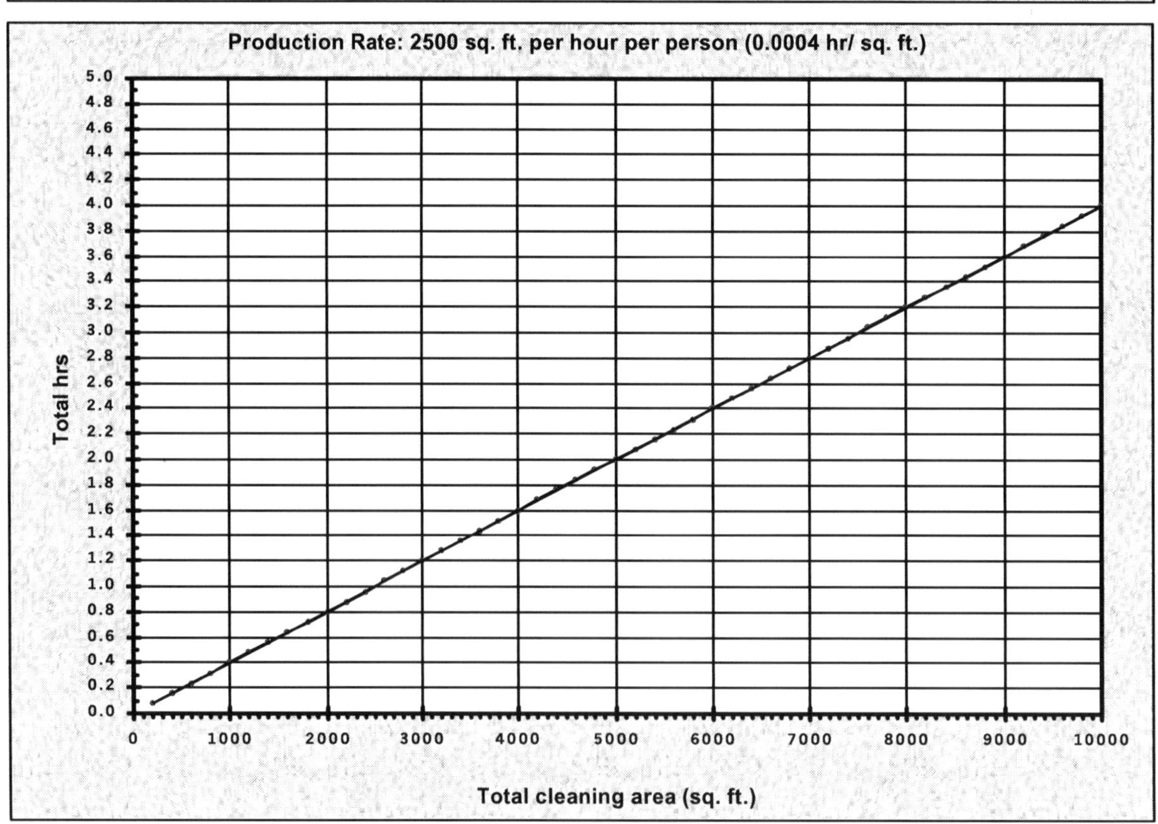
Production Rate: 2500 sq. ft. per hour per person (0.0004 hr/ sq. ft.)
Total hrs
5.0
4.8
4.6
4.4
4.2
4.0
3.8
3.6
3.4
3.2
3.0
2.8
2.6
2.4
2.2
2.0
1.8
1.6
1.4
1.2
1.0
0.8
0.6
0.4
0.2
0.0
0
1000
2000
3000
4000
5000
6000
7000
8000
9000
10000
Total cleaning area (sq. ft.)

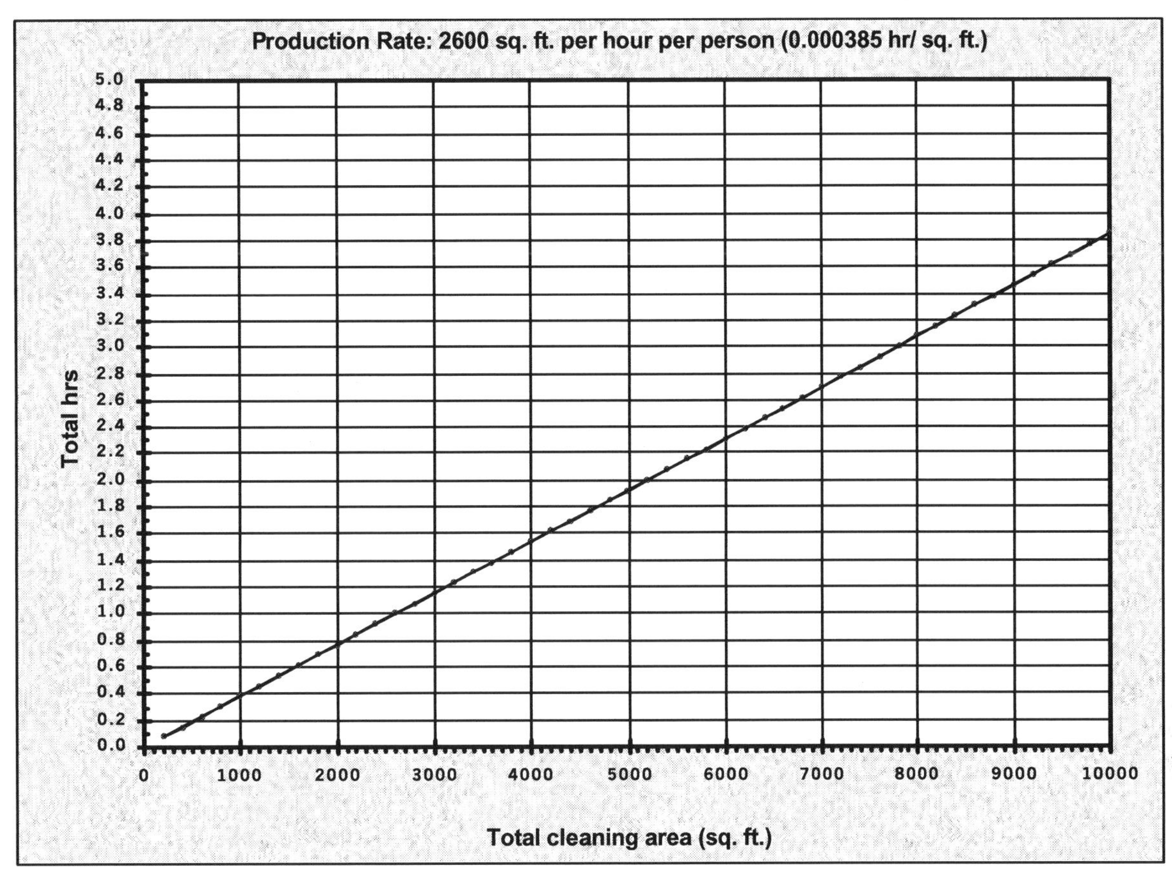
Production Rate: 2600 sq. ft. per hour per person (0.000385 hr/ sq. ft.)
Total hrs
5.0
4.8
4.6
4.4
4.2
4.0
3.8
3.6
3.4
3.2
3.0
2.8
2.6
2.4
2.2
2.0
1.8
1.6
1.4
1.2
1.0
0.8
0.6
0.4
0.2
0.0
0
1000
2000
3000
4000
5000
6000
7000
8000
9000
10000
Total cleaning area (sq. ft.)

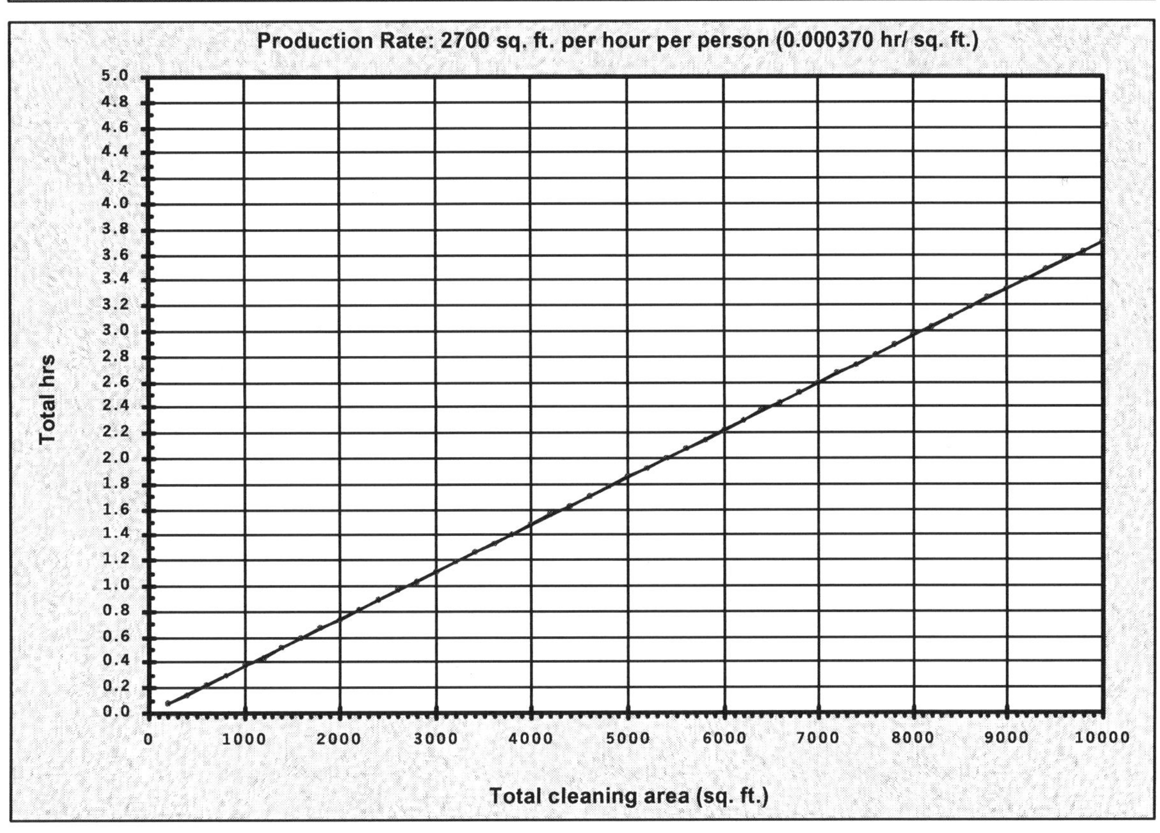
Production Rate: 2700 sq. ft. per hour per person (0.000370 hr/ sq. ft.)
Total hrs
5.0
4.8
4.6
4.4
4.2
4.0
3.8
3.6
3.4
3.2
3.0
2.8
2.6
2.4
2.2
2.0
1.8
1.6
1.4
1.2
1.0
0.8
0.6
0.4
0.2
0.0
0
1000
2000
3000
4000
5000
6000
7000
8000
9000
10000
Total cleaning area (sq. ft.)

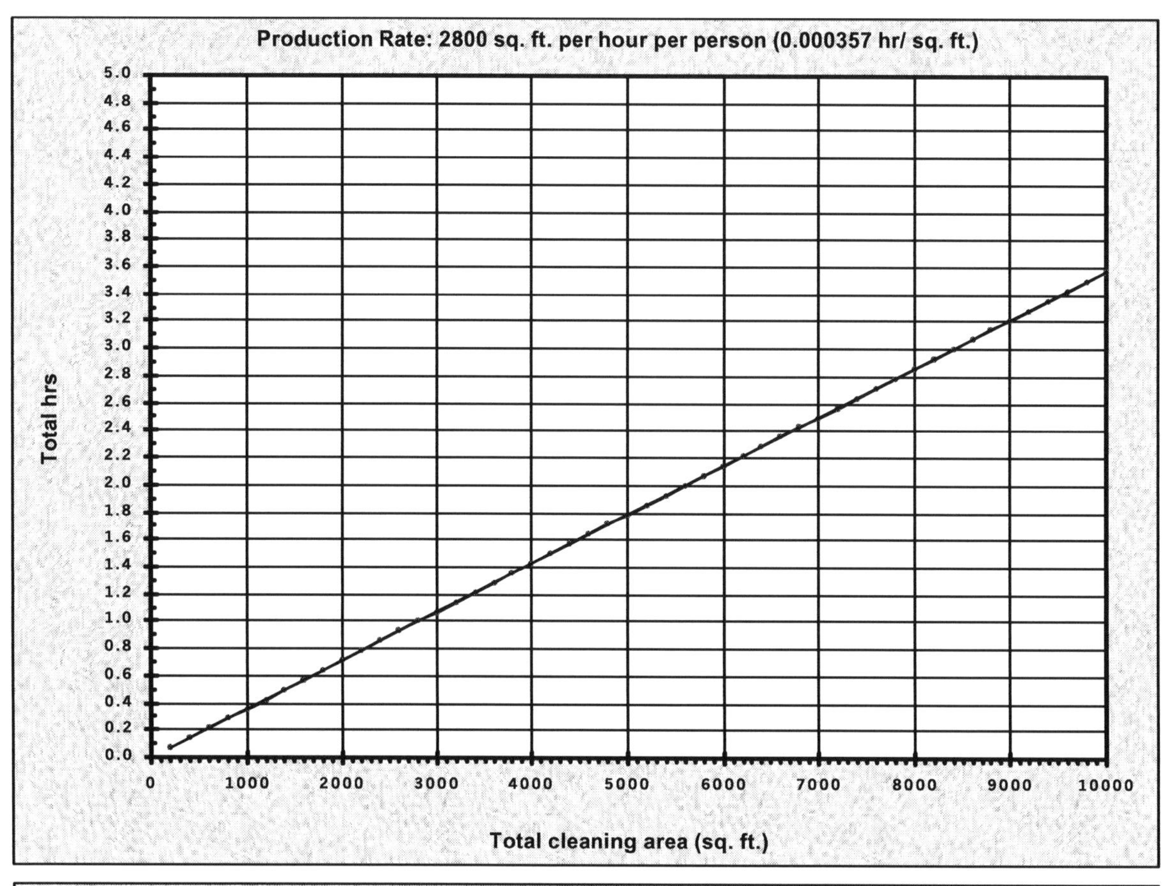
Production Rate: 2800 sq. ft. per hour per person (0.000357 hr/ sq. ft.)
Total hrs
5.0
4.8
4.6
4.4
4.2
4.0
3.8
3.6
3.4
3.2
3.0
2.8
2.6
2.4
2.2
2.0
1.8
1.6
1.4
1.2
1.0
0.8
0.6
0.4
0.2
0.0
0
1000
2000
3000
4000
5000
6000
7000
8000
9000
10000
Total cleaning area (sq. ft.)

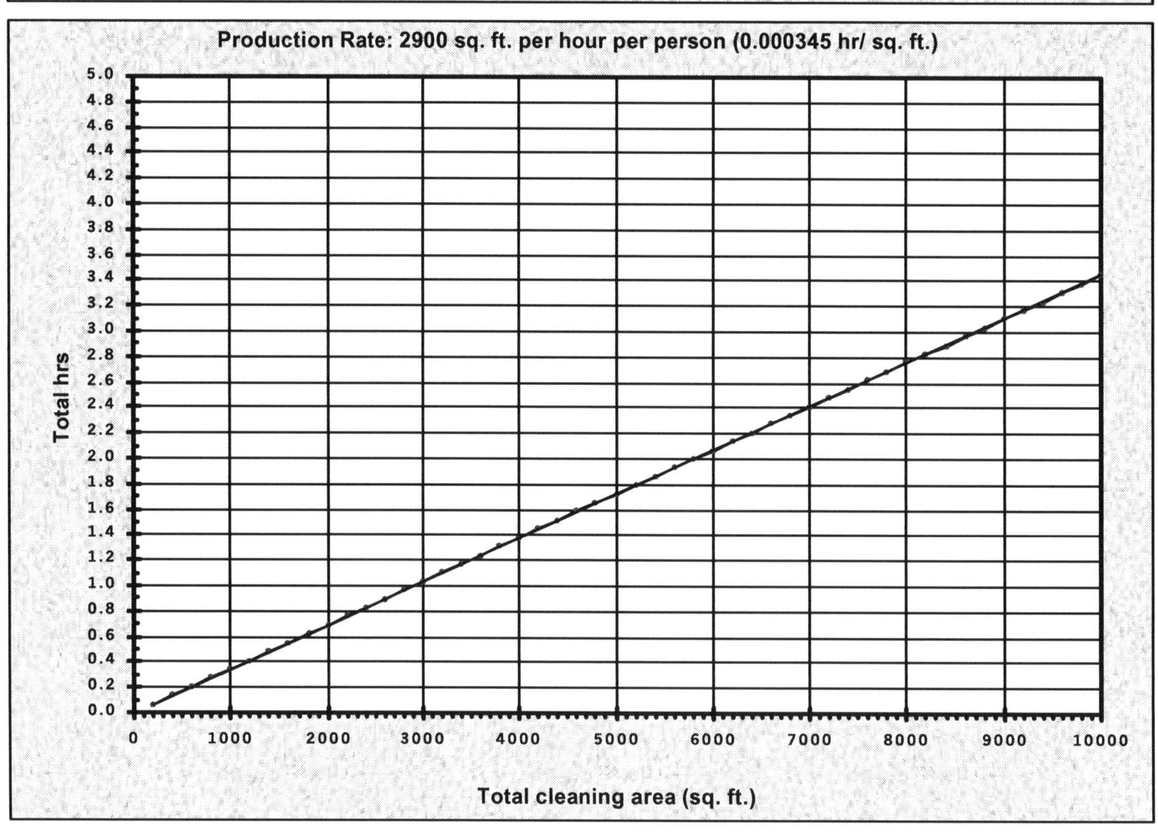
Production Rate: 2900 sq. ft. per hour per person (0.000345 hr/ sq. ft.)
Total hrs
5.0
4.8
4.6
4.4
4.2
4.0
3.8
3.6
3.4
3.2
3.0
2.8
2.6
2.4
2.2
2.0
1.8
1.6
1.4
1.2
1.0
0.8
0.6
0.4
0.2
0.0
0
1000
2000
3000
4000
5000
6000
7000
8000
9000
10000
Total cleaning area (sq. ft.)

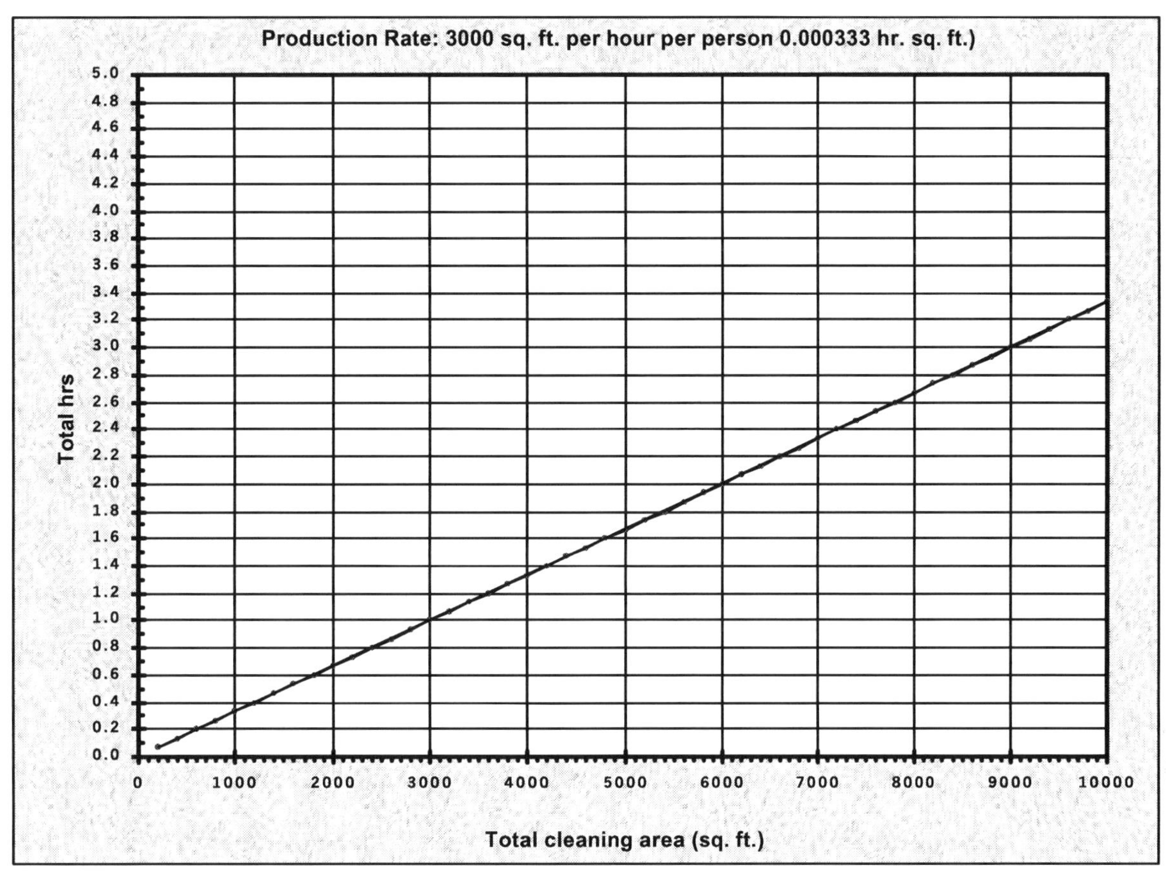
Production Rate: 3000 sq. ft. per hour per person 0.000333 hr. sq. ft.)
Total hrs
5.0
4.8
4.6
4.4
4.2
4.0
3.8
3.6
3.4
3.2
3.0
2.8
2.6
2.4
2.2
2.0
1.8
1.6
1.4
1.2
1.0
0.8
0.6
0.4
0.2
0.0
0
1000
2000
3000
4000
5000
6000
7000
8000
9000
10000
Total cleaning area (sq. ft.)

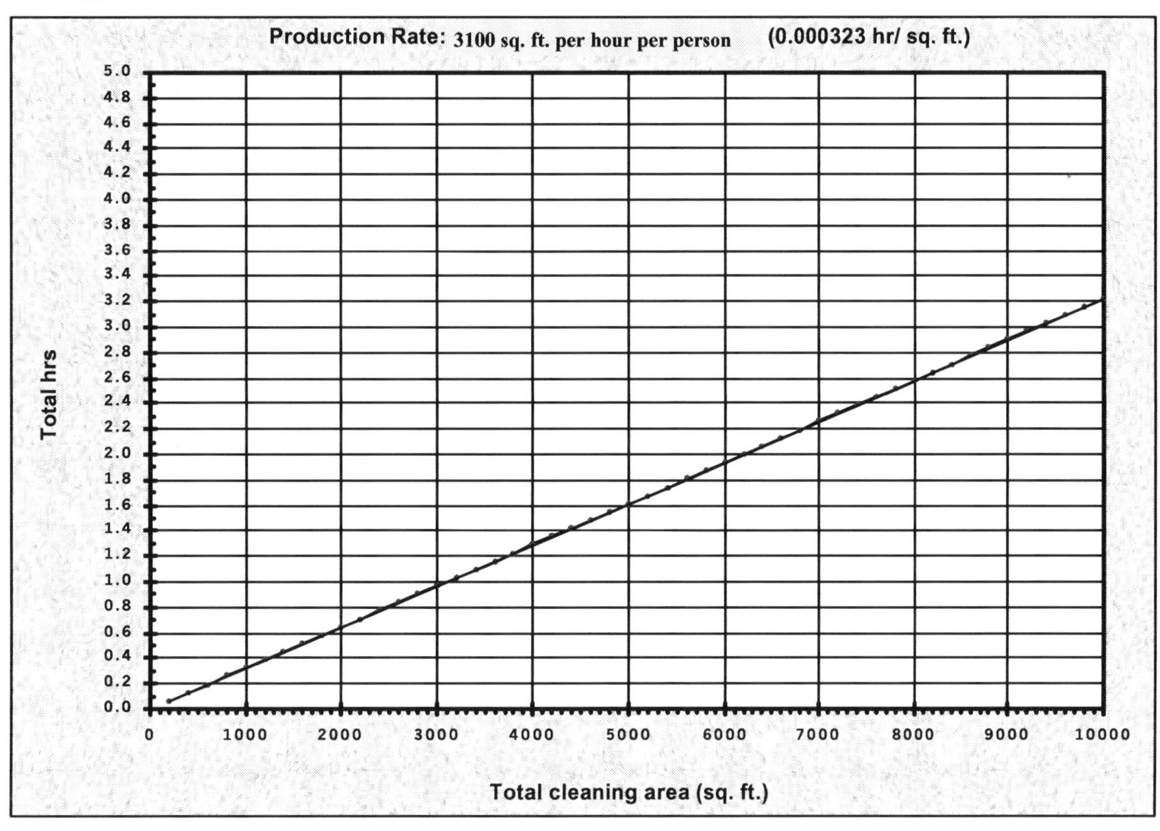
Production Rate: 3100 sq. ft. per hour per person (0.000323 hr/ sq. ft.)
Total hrs
5.0
4.8
4.6
4.4
4.2
4.0
3.8
3.6
3.4
3.2
3.0
2.8
2.6
2.4
2.2
2.0
1.8
1.6
1.4
1.2
1.0
0.8
0.6
0.4
0.2
0.0
0
1000
2000
3000
4000
5000
6000
7000
8000
9000
10000
Total cleaning area (sq. ft.)

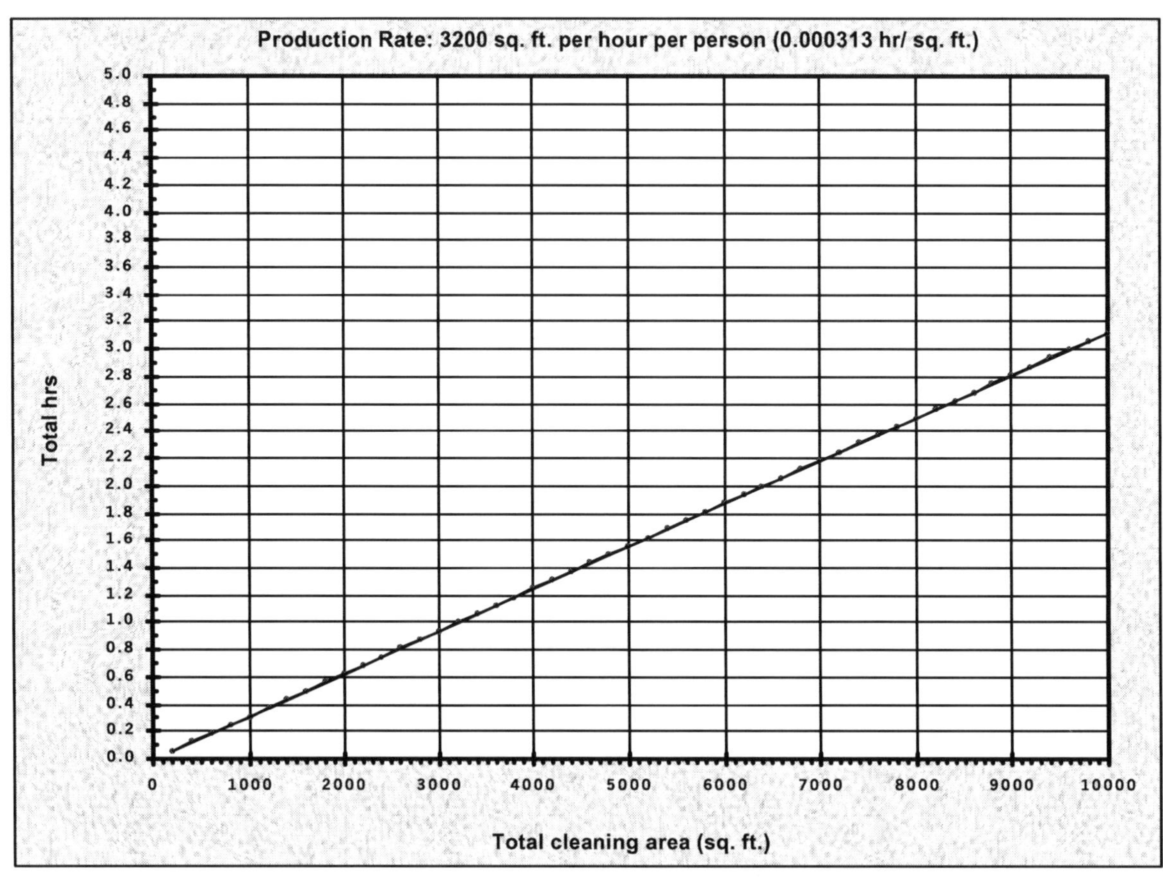
Production Rate: 3200 sq. ft. per hour per person (0.000313 hr/ sq. ft.)
Total hrs
5.0
4.8
4.6
4.4
4.2
4.0
3.8
3.6
3.4
3.2
3.0
2.8
2.6
2.4
2.2
2.0
1.8
1.6
1.4
1.2
1.0
0.8
0.6
0.4
0.2
0.0
0
1000
2000
3000
4000
5000
6000
7000
8000
9000
10000
Total cleaning area (sq. ft.)

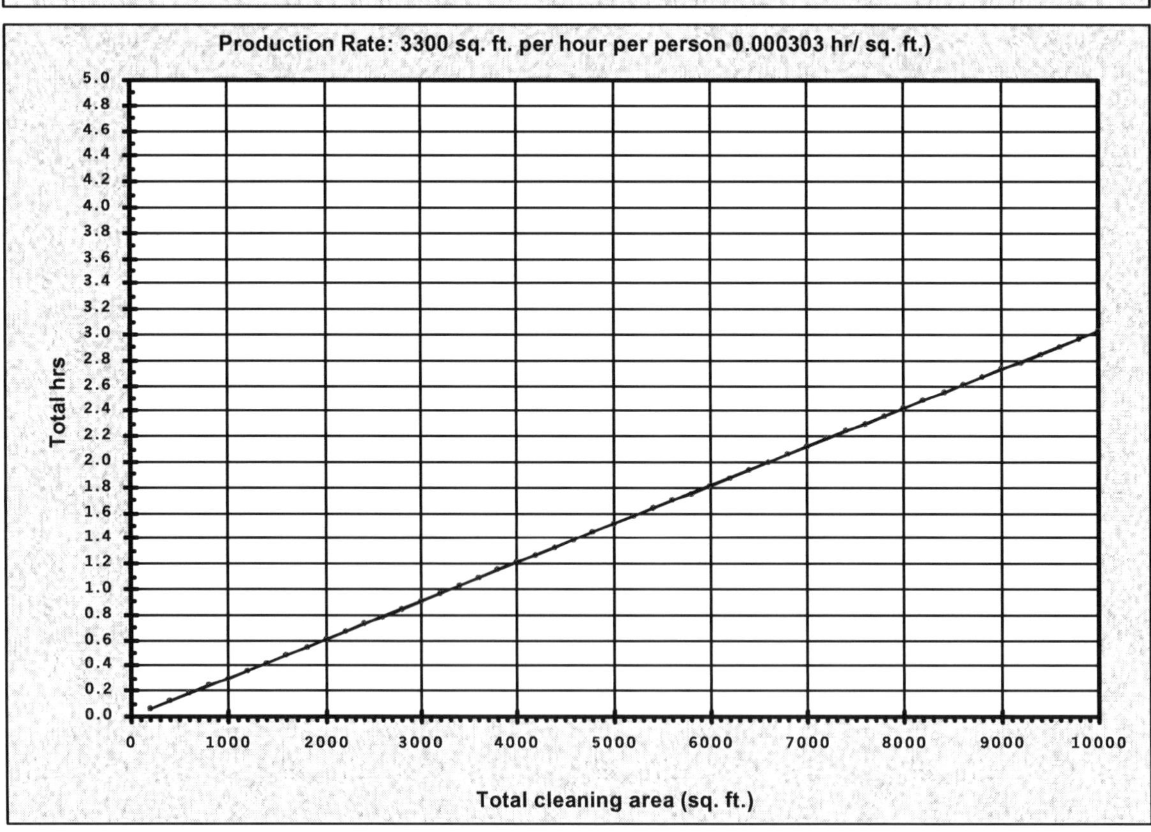
Production Rate: 3300 sq. ft. per hour per person 0.000303 hr/ sq. ft.)
Total hrs
5.0
4.8
4.6
4.4
4.2
4.0
3.8
3.6
3.4
3.2
3.0
2.8
2.6
2.4
2.2
2.0
1.8
1.6
1.4
1.2
1.0
0.8
0.6
0.4
0.2
0.0
0
1000
2000
3000
4000
5000
6000
7000
8000
9000
10000
Total cleaning area (sq. ft.)

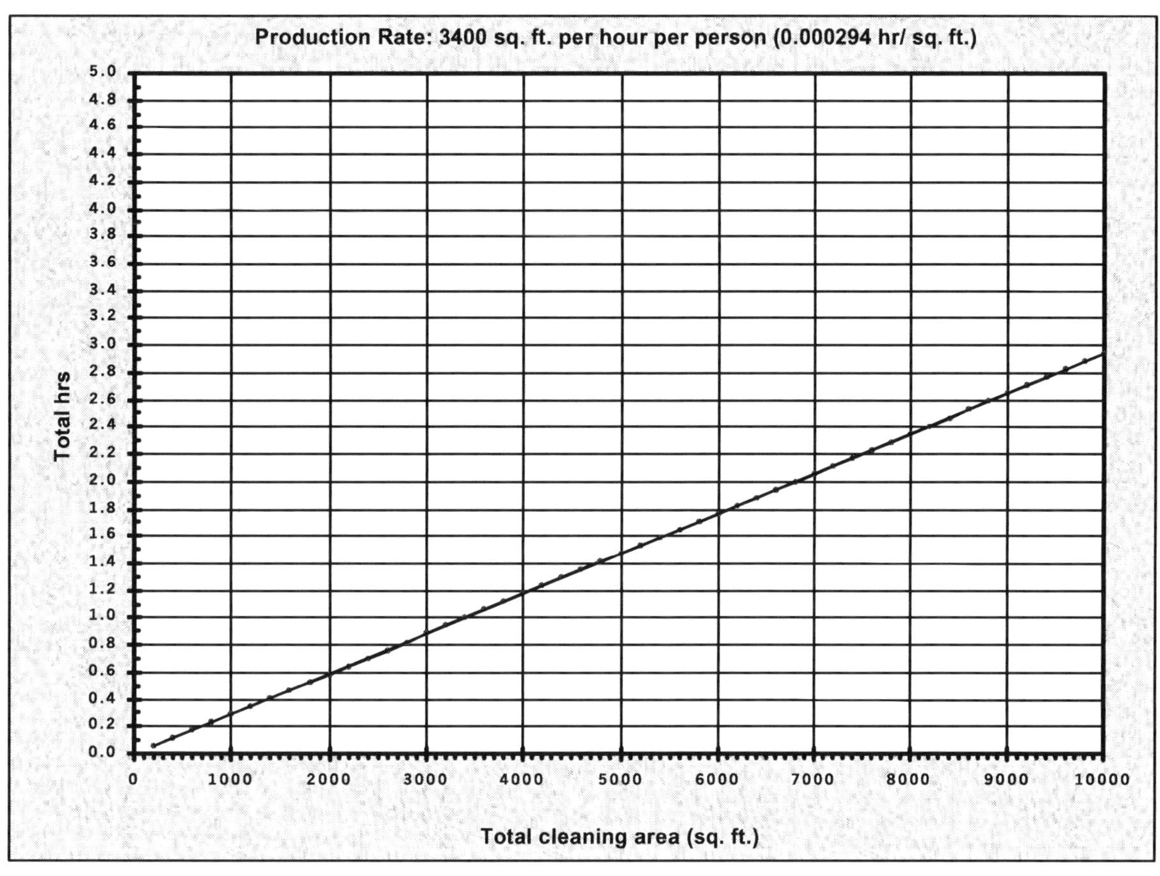
Production Rate: 3400 sq. ft. per hour per person (0.000294 hr/ sq. ft.)
Total hrs
5.0
4.8
4.6
4.4
4.2
4.0
3.8
3.6
3.4
3.2
3.0
2.8
2.6
2.4
2.2
2.0
1.8
1.6
1.4
1.2
1.0
0.8
0.6
0.4
0.2
0.0
0
1000
2000
3000
4000
5000
6000
7000
8000
9000
10000
Total cleaning area (sq. ft.)

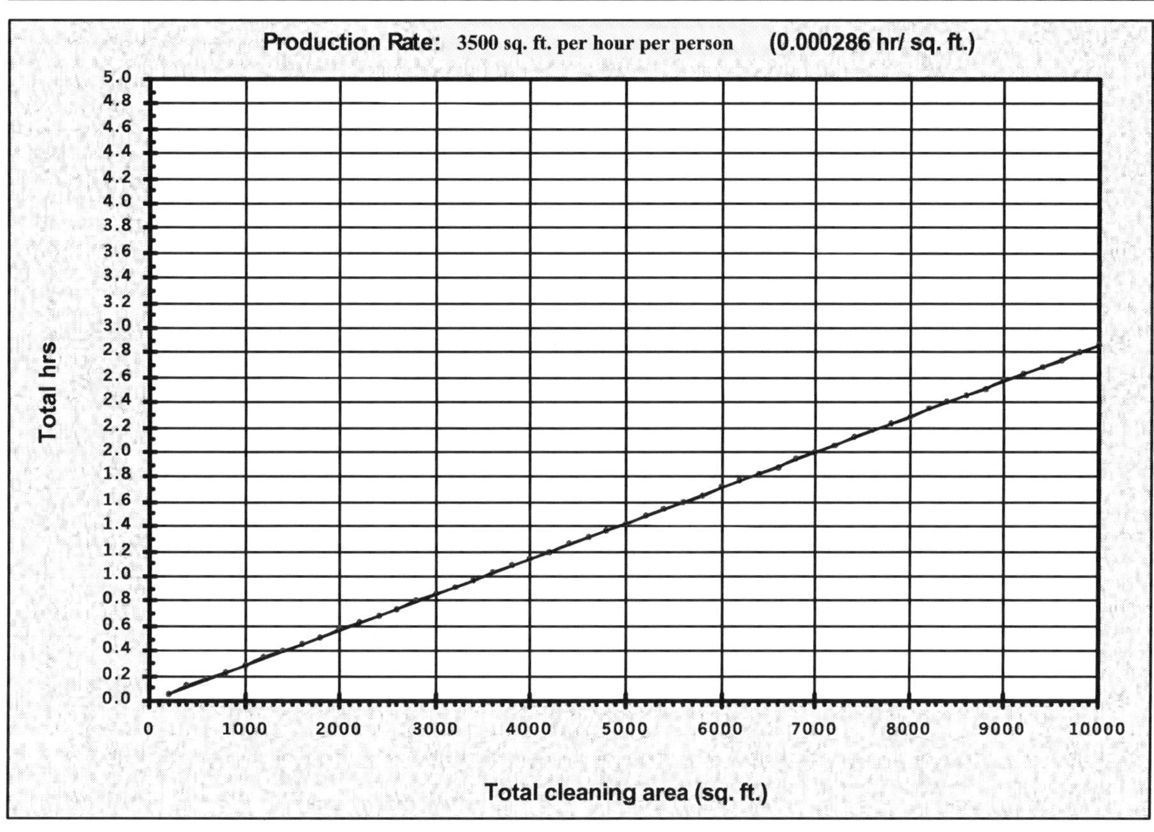
Production Rate: 3500 sq. ft. per hour per person (0.000286 hr/ sq. ft.)
Total hrs
5.0
4.8
4.6
4.4
4.2
4.0
3.8
3.6
3.4
3.2
3.0
2.8
2.6
2.4
2.2
2.0
1.8
1.6
1.4
1.2
1.0
0.8
0.6
0.4
0.2
0.0
0
1000
2000
3000
4000
5000
6000
7000
8000
9000
10000
Total cleaning area (sq. ft.)

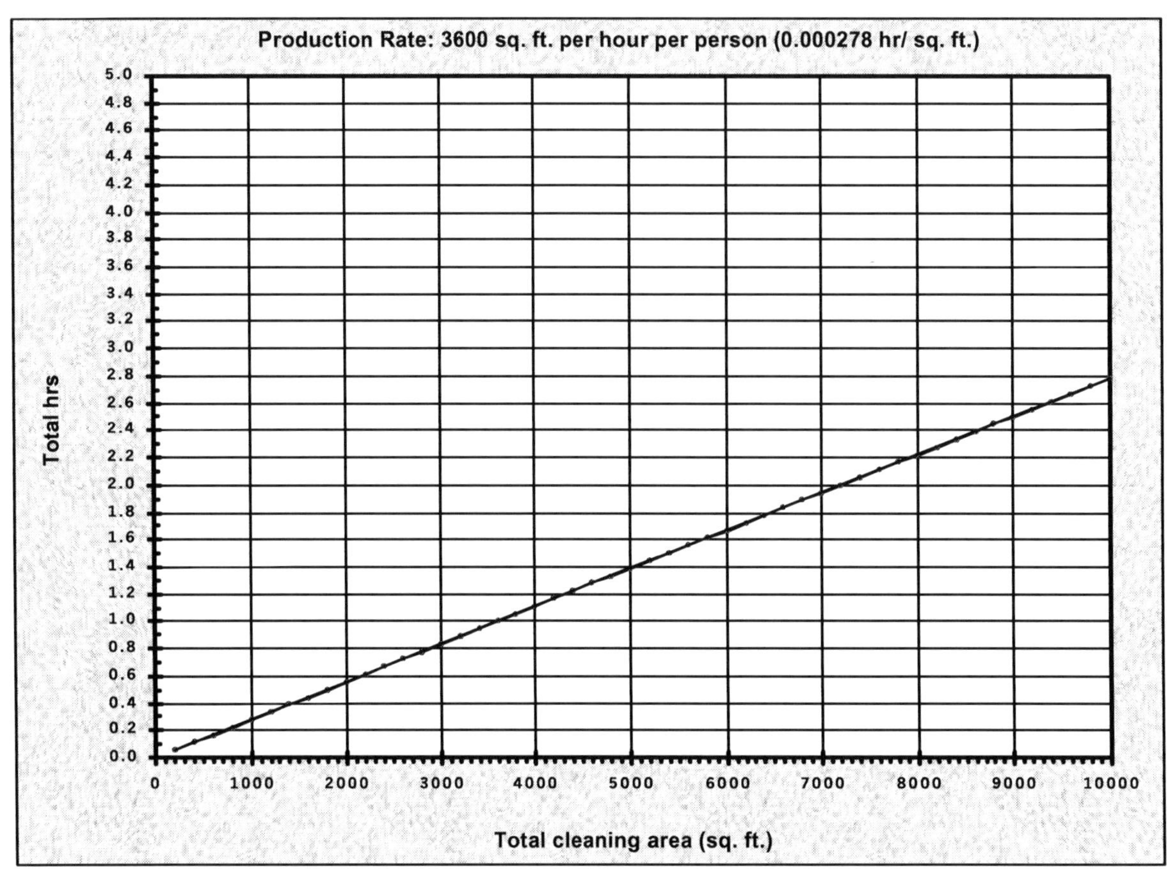
Production Rate: 3600 sq. ft. per hour per person (0.000278 hr/ sq. ft.)
Total hrs
5.0
4.8
4.6
4.4
4.2
4.0
3.8
3.6
3.4
3.2
3.0
2.8
2.6
2.4
2.2
2.0
1.8
1.6
1.4
1.2
1.0
0.8
0.6
0.4
0.2
0.0
0
1000
2000
3000
4000
5000
6000
7000
8000
9000
10000
Total cleaning area (sq. ft.)

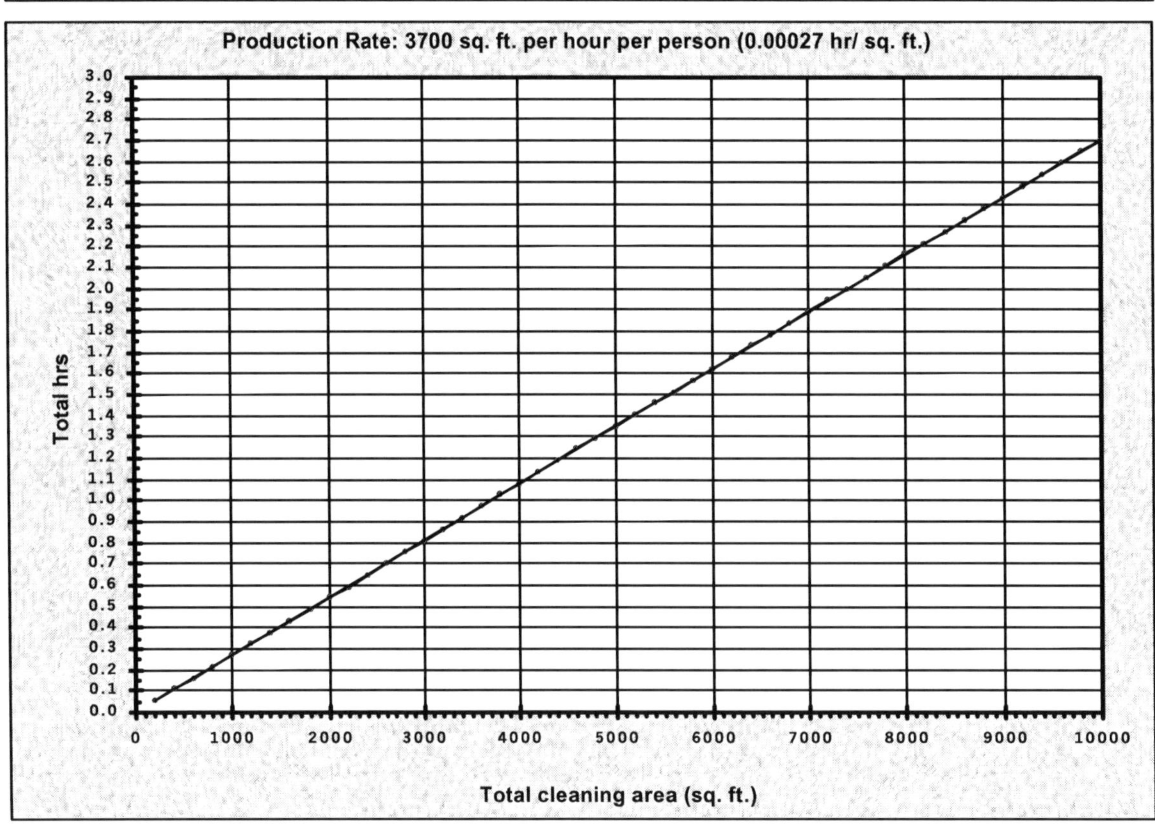
Production Rate: 3700 sq. ft. per hour per person (0.00027 hr/ sq. ft.)
Total hrs
3.0
2.9
2.8
2.7
2.6
2.5
2.4
2.3
2.2
2.1
2.0
1.9
1.8
1.7
1.6
1.5
1.4
1.3
1.2
1.1
1.0
0.9
0.8
0.7
0.6
0.5
0.4
0.3
0.2
0.1
0.0
0
1000
2000
3000
4000
5000
6000
7000
8000
9000
10000
Total cleaning area (sq. ft.)

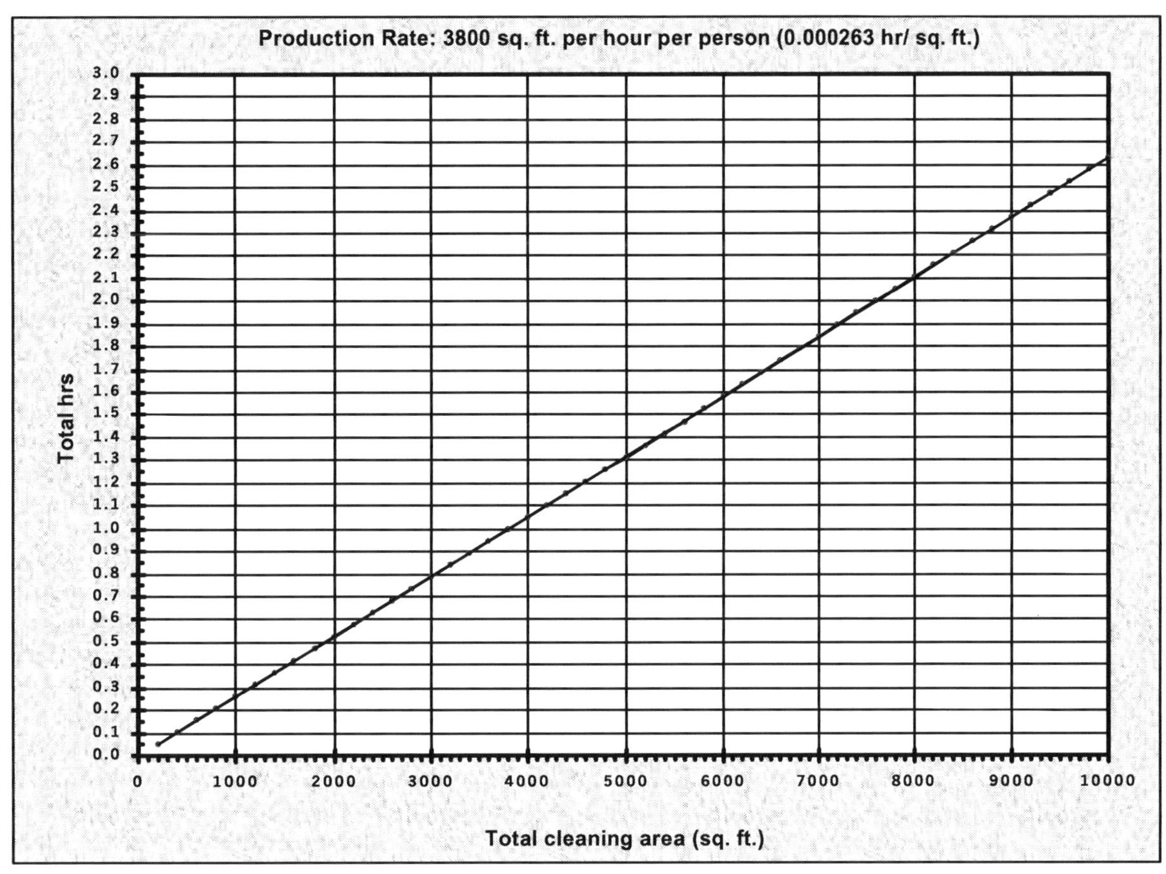
Production Rate: 3800 sq. ft. per hour per person (0.000263 hr/ sq. ft.)
Total hrs
3.0
2.9
2.8
2.7
2.6
2.5
2.4
2.3
2.2
2.1
2.0
1.9
1.8
1.7
1.6
1.5
1.4
1.3
1.2
1.1
1.0
0.9
0.8
0.7
0.6
0.5
0.4
0.3
0.2
0.1
0.0
0
1000
2000
3000
4000
5000
6000
7000
8000
9000
10000
Total cleaning area (sq. ft.)

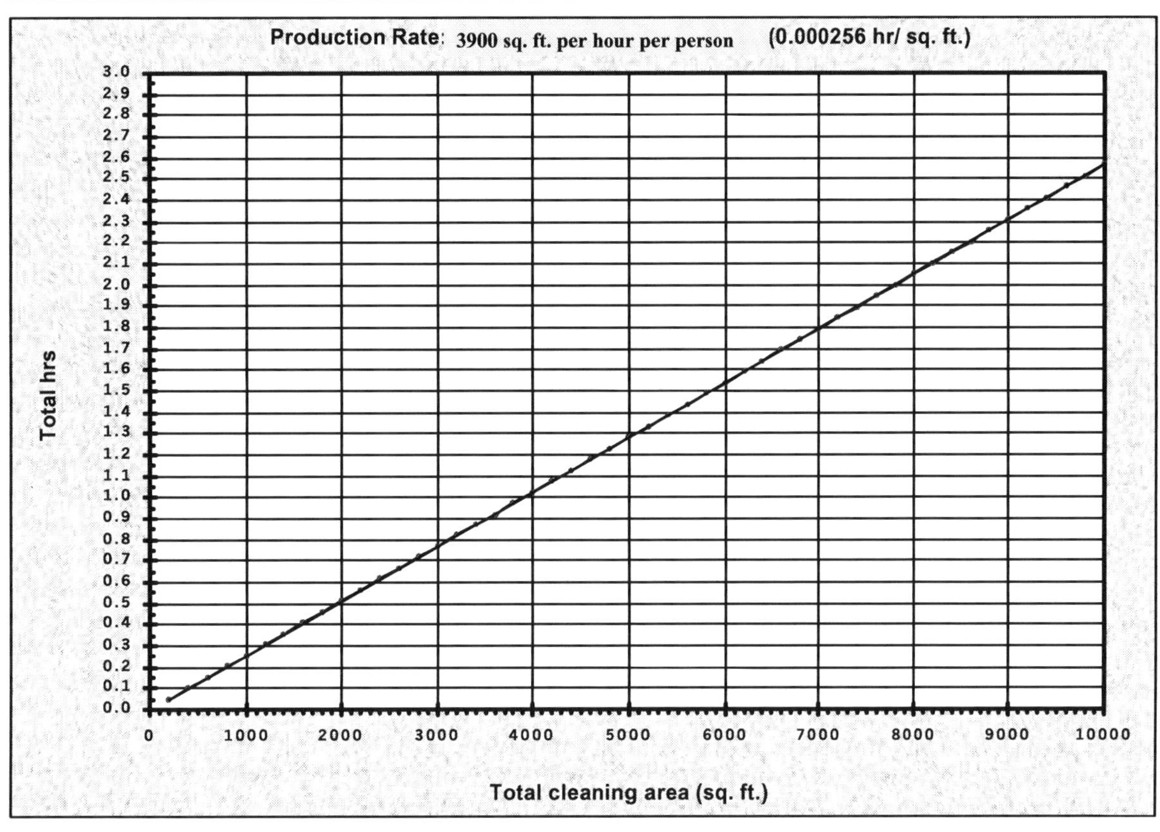
Production Rate: 3900 sq. ft. per hour per person (0.000256 hr/ sq. ft.)
Total hrs
3.0
2.9
2.8
2.7
2.6
2.5
2.4
2.3
2.2
2.1
2.0
1.9
1.8
1.7
1.6
1.5
1.4
1.3
1.2
1.1
1.0
0.9
0.8
0.7
0.6
0.5
0.4
0.3
0.2
0.1
0.0
0
1000
2000
3000
4000
5000
6000
7000
8000
9000
10000
Total cleaning area (sq. ft.)

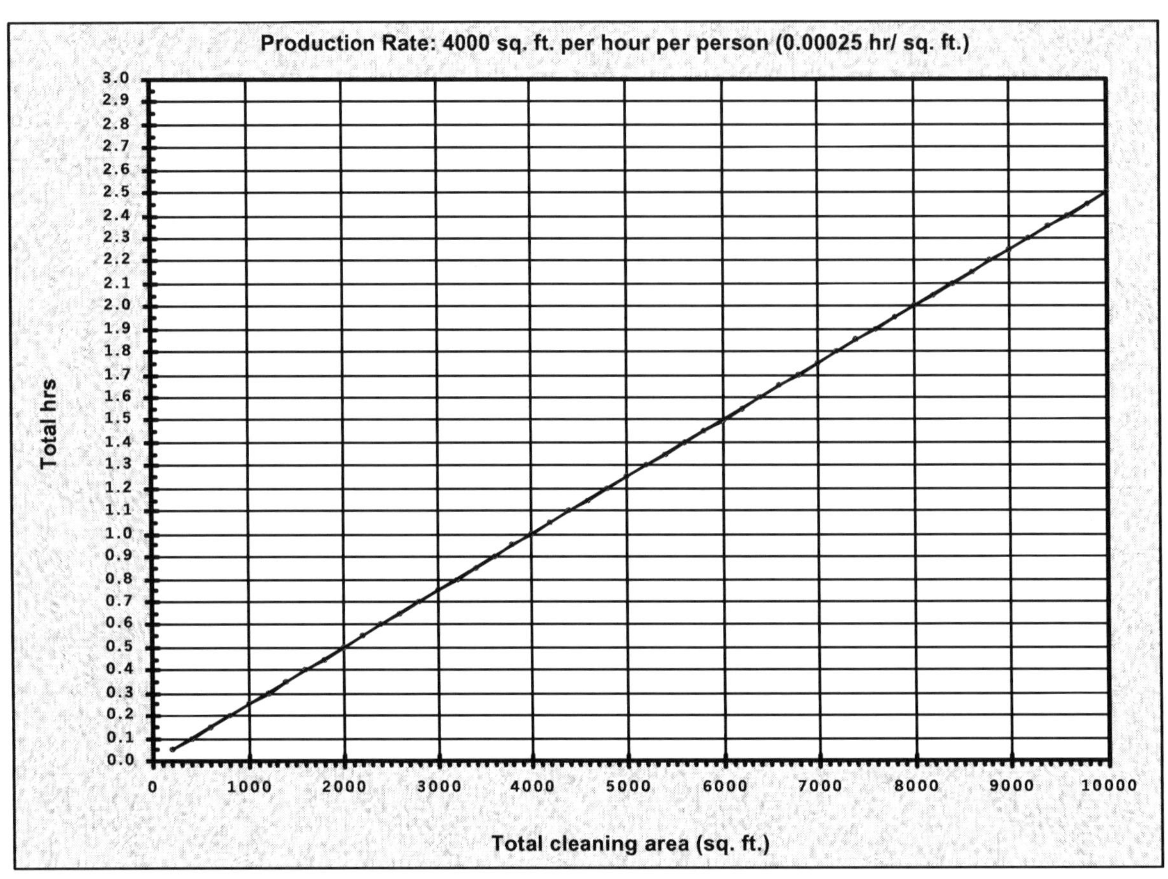
Production Rate: 4000 sq. ft. per hour per person (0.00025 hr/ sq. ft.)
Total hrs
3.0
2.9
2.8
2.7
2.6
2.5
2.4
2.3
2.2
2.1
2.0
1.9
1.8
1.7
1.6
1.5
1.4
1.3
1.2
1.1
1.0
0.9
0.8
0.7
0.6
0.5
0.4
0.3
0.2
0.1
0.0
0
1000
2000
3000
4000
5000
6000
7000
8000
9000
10000
Total cleaning area (sq. ft.)

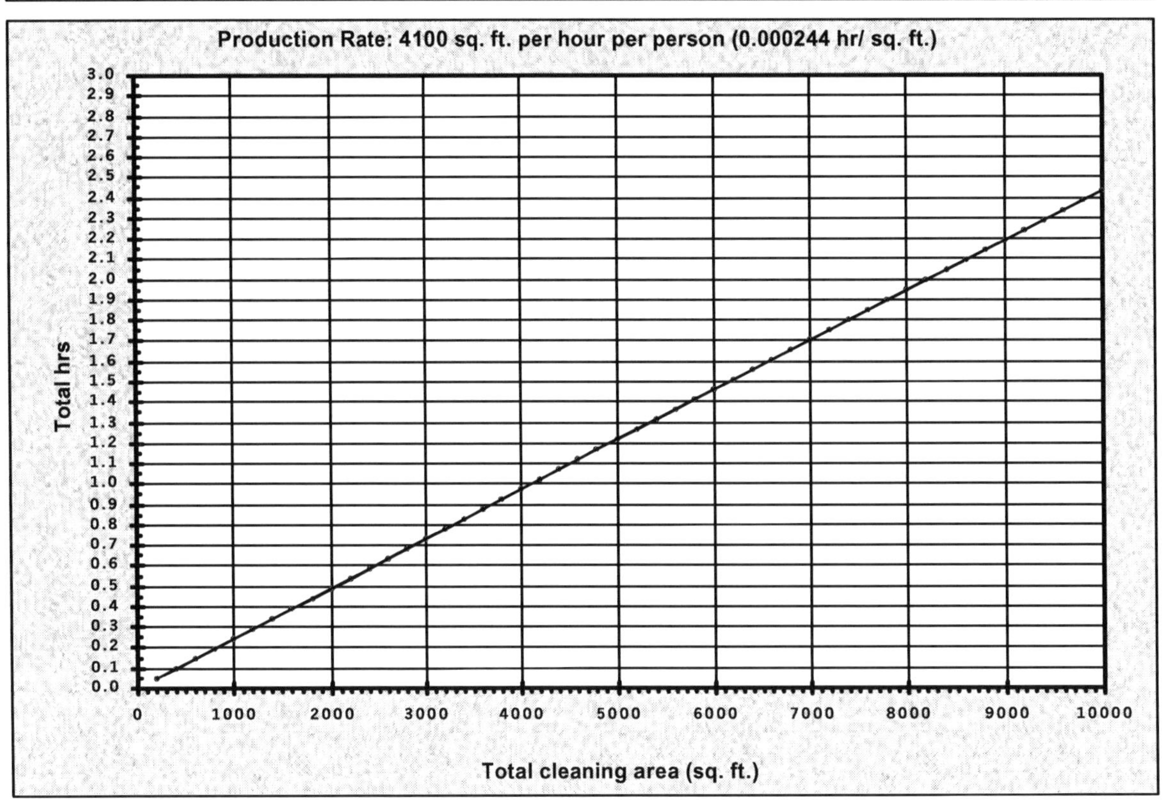
Production Rate: 4100 sq. ft. per hour per person (0.000244 hr/ sq. ft.)
Total hrs
3.0
2.9
2.8
2.7
2.6
2.5
2.4
2.3
2.2
2.1
2.0
1.9
1.8
1.7
1.6
1.5
1.4
1.3
1.2
1.1
1.0
0.9
0.8
0.7
0.6
0.5
0.4
0.3
0.2
0.1
0.0
0
1000
2000
3000
4000
5000
6000
7000
8000
9000
10000
Total cleaning area (sq. ft.)

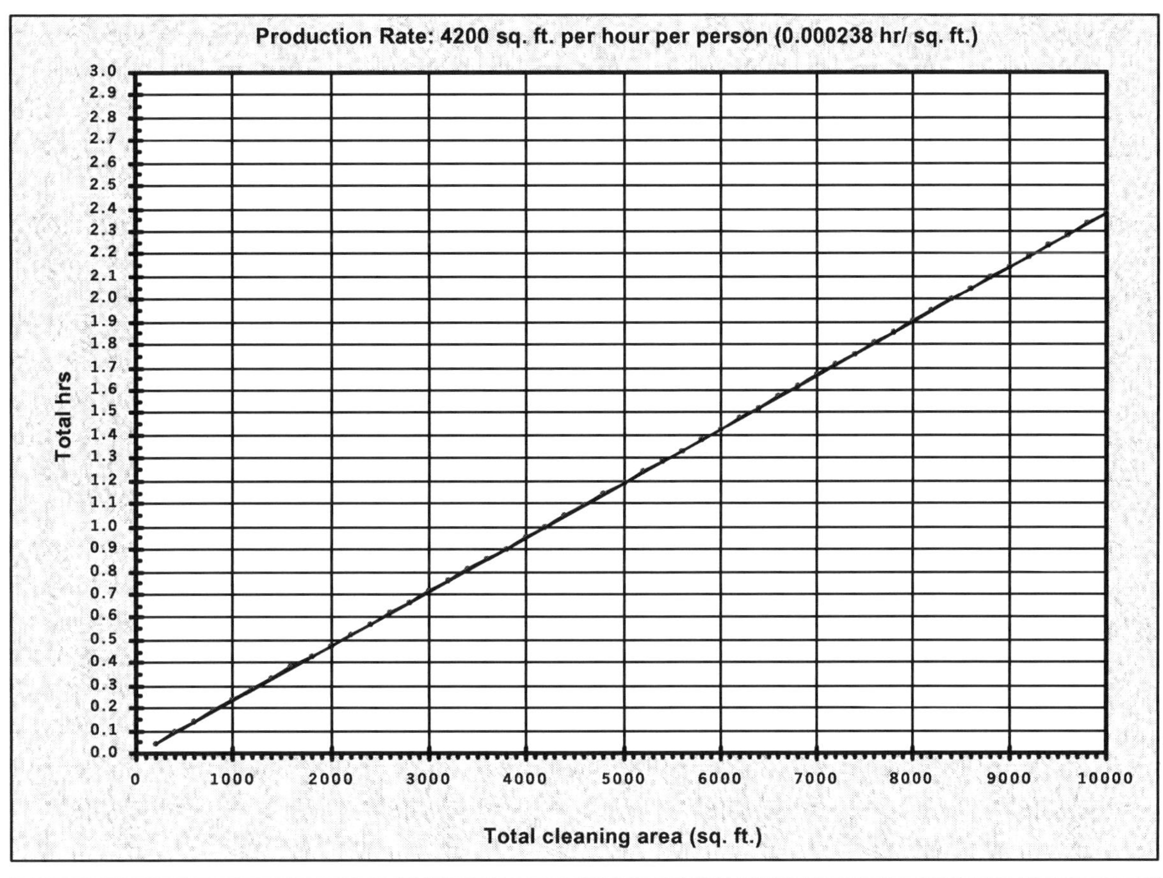
Production Rate: 4200 sq. ft. per hour per person (0.000238 hr/ sq. ft.)
Total hrs
3.0
2.9
2.8
2.7
2.6
2.5
2.4
2.3
2.2
2.1
2.0
1.9
1.8
1.7
1.6
1.5
1.4
1.3
1.2
1.1
1.0
0.9
0.8
0.7
0.6
0.5
0.4
0.3
0.2
0.1
0.0
0
1000
2000
3000
4000
5000
6000
7000
8000
9000
10000
Total cleaning area (sq. ft.)

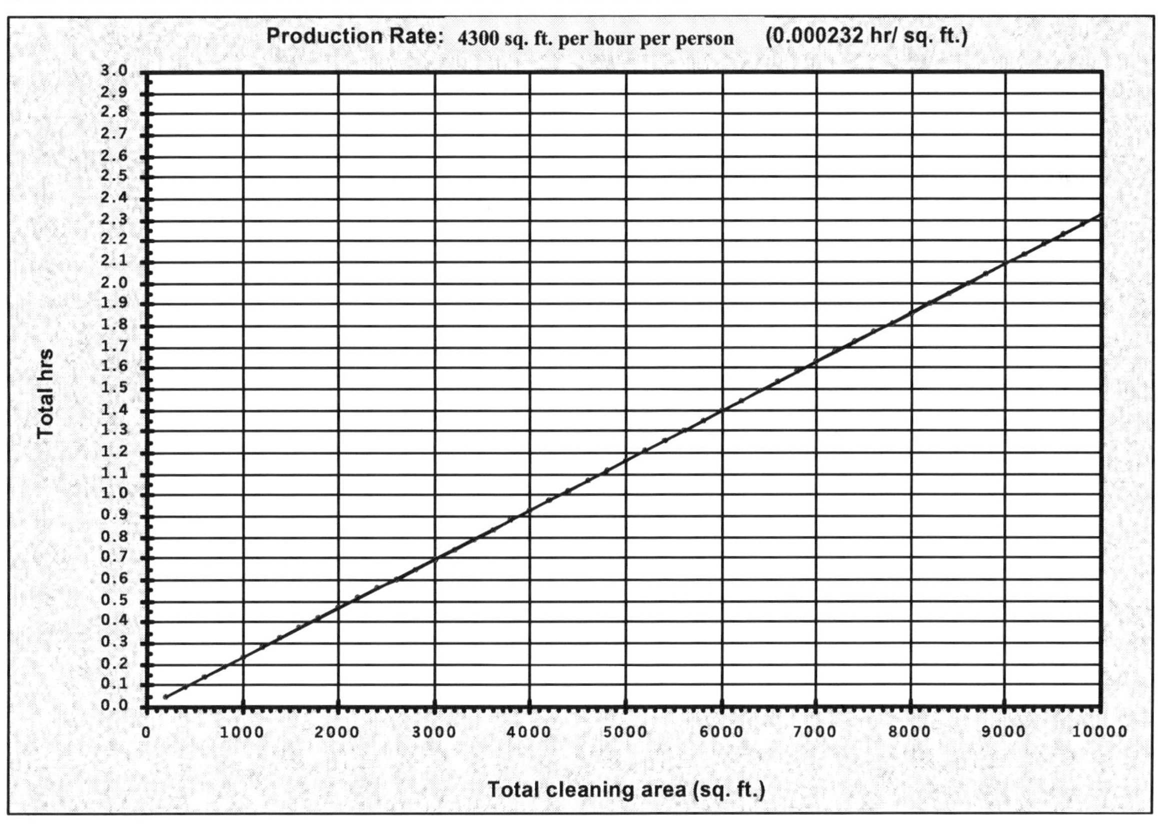
Production Rate: 4300 sq. ft. per hour per person (0.000232 hr/ sq. ft.)
Total hrs
3.0
2.9
2.8
2.7
2.6
2.5
2.4
2.3
2.2
2.1
2.0
1.9
1.8
1.7
1.6
1.5
1.4
1.3
1.2
1.1
1.0
0.9
0.8
0.7
0.6
0.5
0.4
0.3
0.2
0.1
0.0
0
1000
2000
3000
4000
5000
6000
7000
8000
9000
10000
Total cleaning area (sq. ft.)

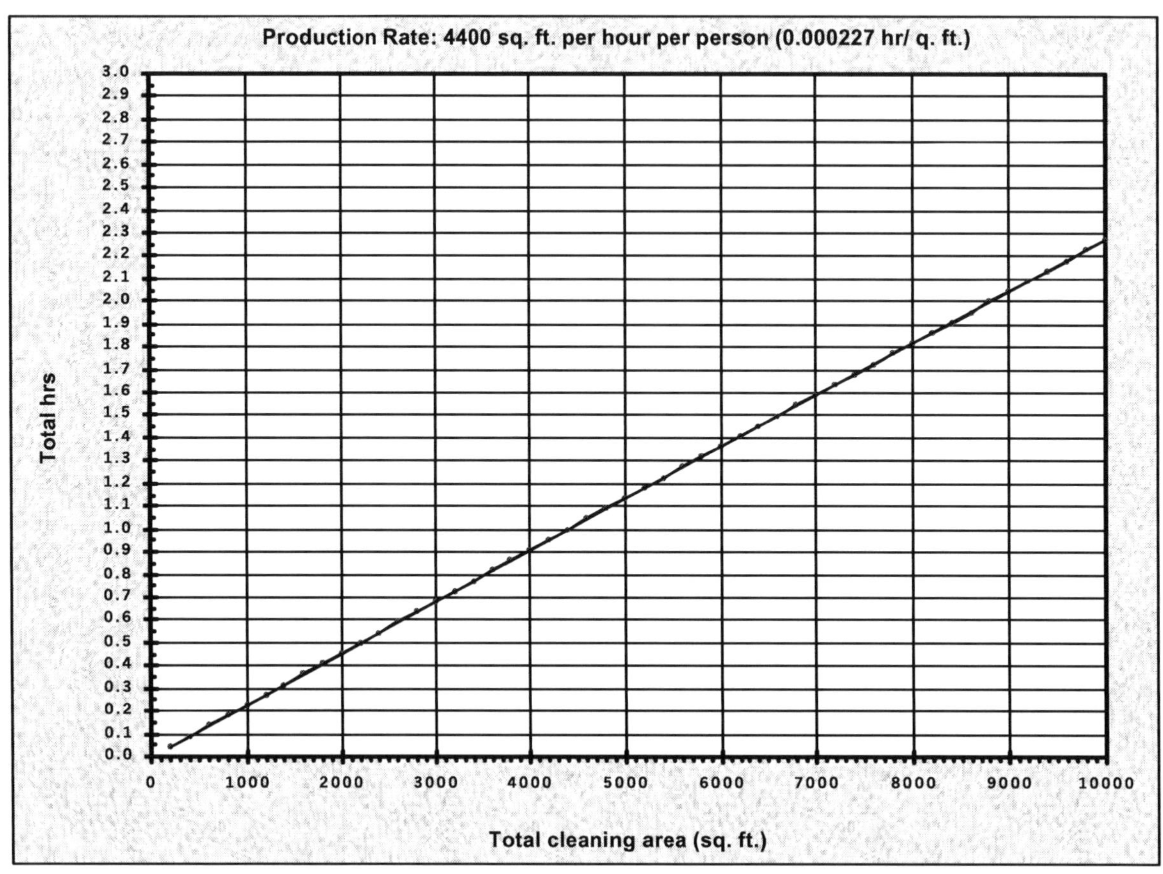
Production Rate: 4400 sq. ft. per hour per person (0.000227 hr/ q. ft.)
Total hrs
3.0
2.9
2.8
2.7
2.6
2.5
2.4
2.3
2.2
2.1
2.0
1.9
1.8
1.7
1.6
1.5
1.4
1.3
1.2
1.1
1.0
0.9
0.8
0.7
0.6
0.5
0.4
0.3
0.2
0.1
0.0
0
1000
2000
3000
4000
5000
6000
7000
8000
9000
10000
Total cleaning area (sq. ft.)

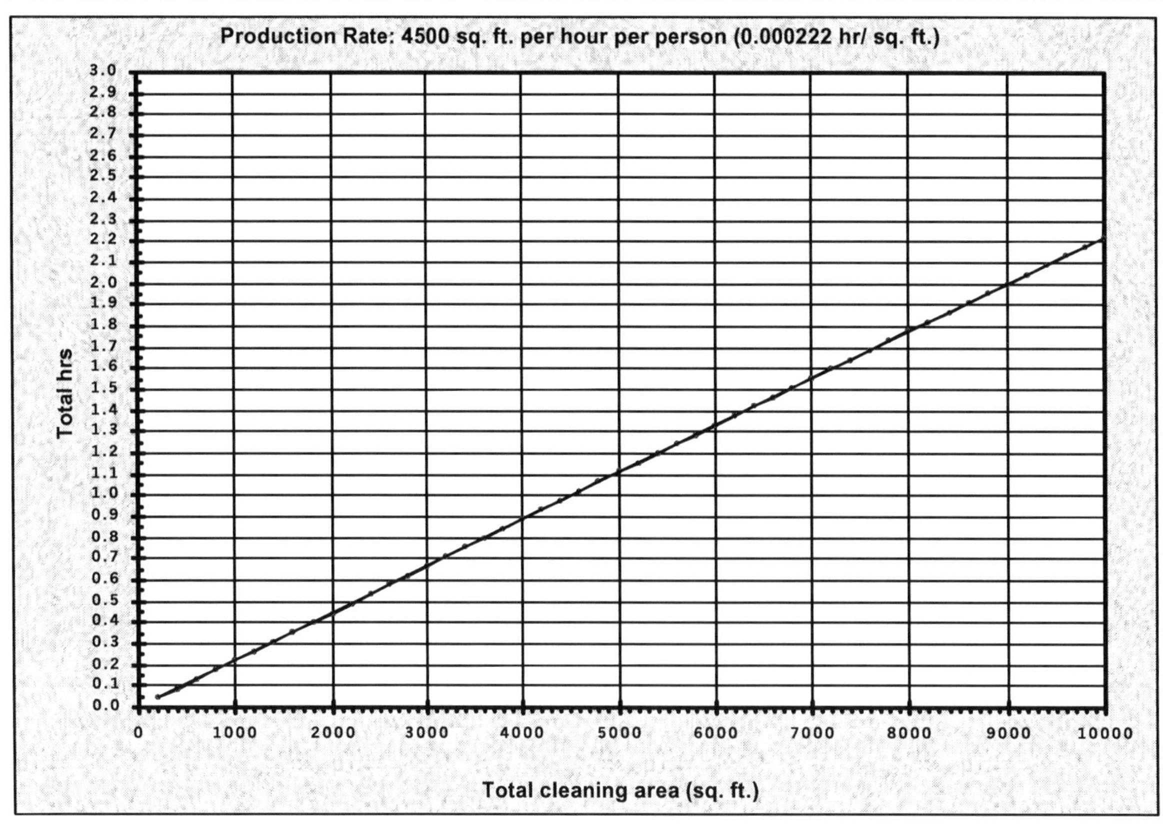
Production Rate: 4500 sq. ft. per hour per person (0.000222 hr/ sq. ft.)
Total hrs
3.0
2.9
2.8
2.7
2.6
2.5
2.4
2.3
2.2
2.1
2.0
1.9
1.8
1.7
1.6
1.5
1.4
1.3
1.2
1.1
1.0
0.9
0.8
0.7
0.6
0.5
0.4
0.3
0.2
0.1
0.0
0
1000
2000
3000
4000
5000
6000
7000
8000
9000
10000
Total cleaning area (sq. ft.)

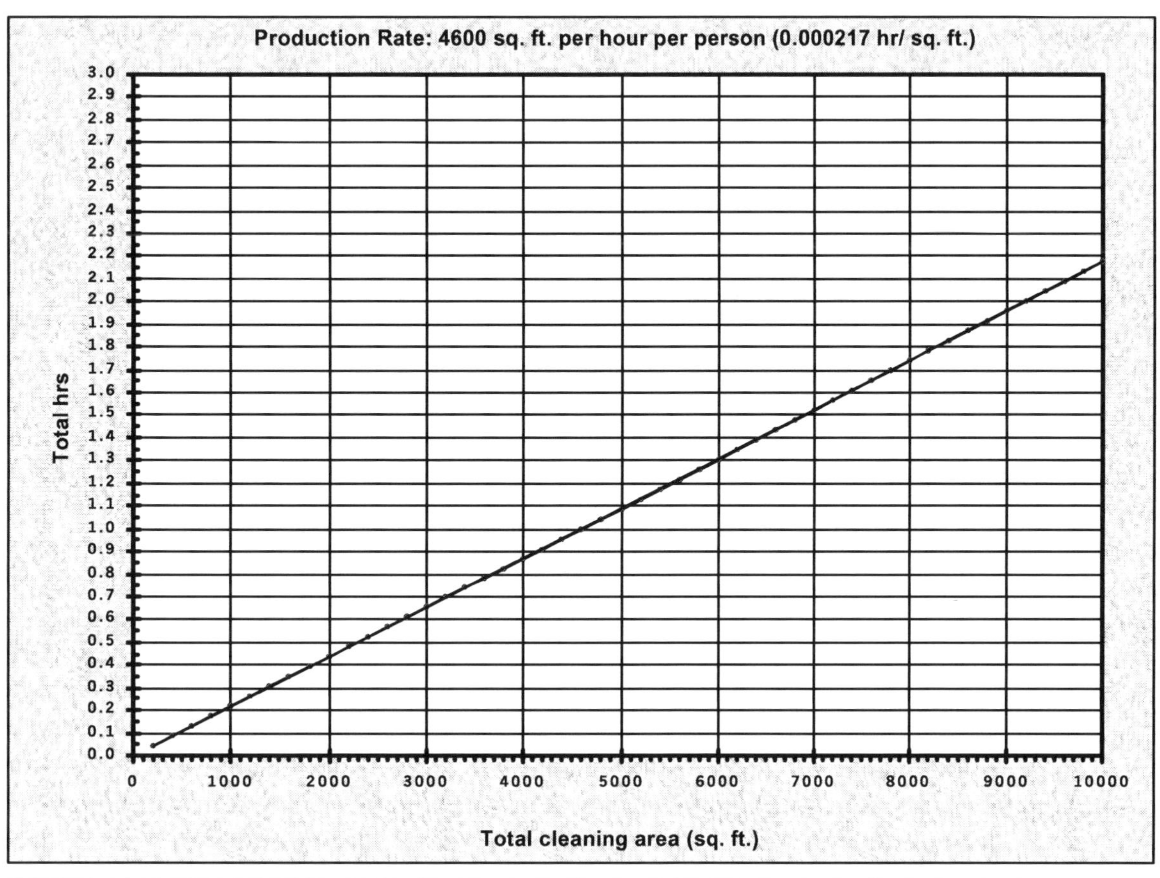
Production Rate: 4600 sq. ft. per hour per person (0.000217 hr/ sq. ft.)
Total hrs
3.0
2.9
2.8
2.7
2.6
2.5
2.4
2.3
2.2
2.1
2.0
1.9
1.8
1.7
1.6
1.5
1.4
1.3
1.2
1.1
1.0
0.9
0.8
0.7
0.6
0.5
0.4
0.3
0.2
0.1
0.0
0
1000
2000
3000
4000
5000
6000
7000
8000
9000
10000
Total cleaning area (sq. ft.)

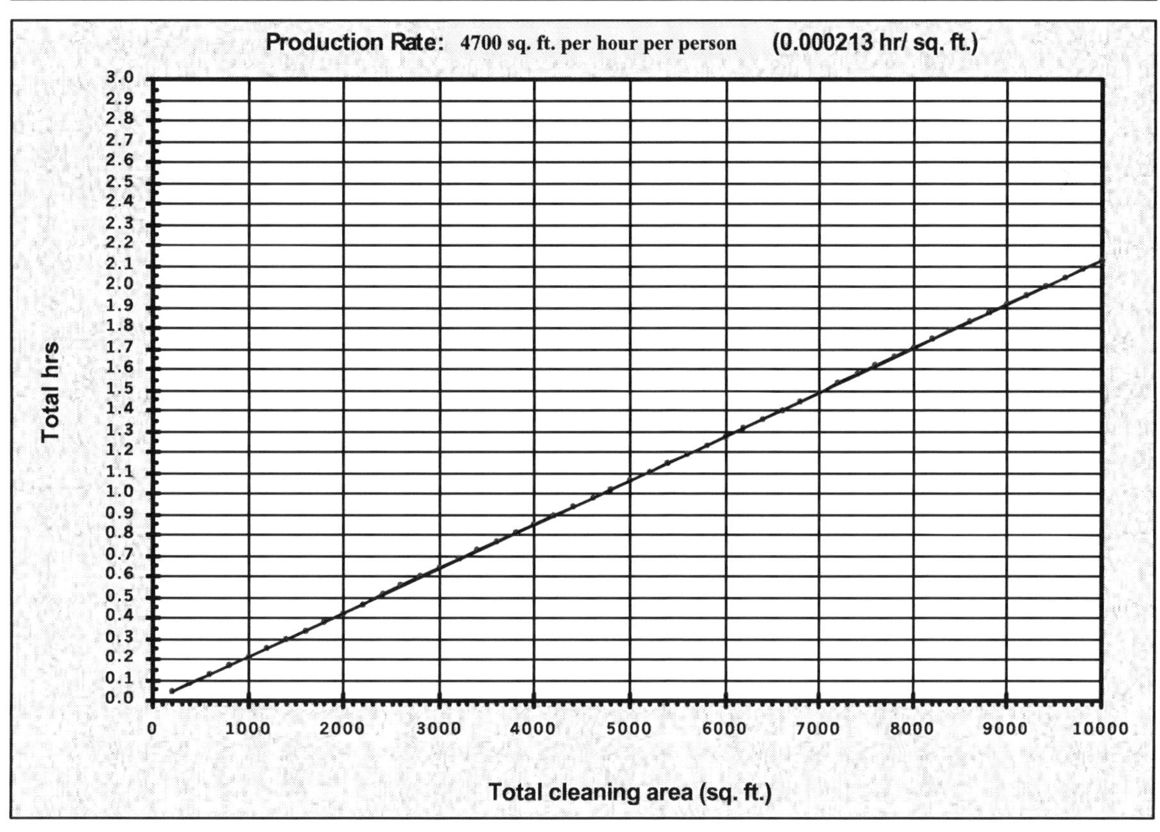
Production Rate: 4700 sq. ft. per hour per person (0.000213 hr/ sq. ft.)
Total hrs
3.0
2.9
2.8
2.7
2.6
2.5
2.4
2.3
2.2
2.1
2.0
1.9
1.8
1.7
1.6
1.5
1.4
1.3
1.2
1.1
1.0
0.9
0.8
0.7
0.6
0.5
0.4
0.3
0.2
0.1
0.0
0
1000
2000
3000
4000
5000
6000
7000
8000
9000
10000
Total cleaning area (sq. ft.)

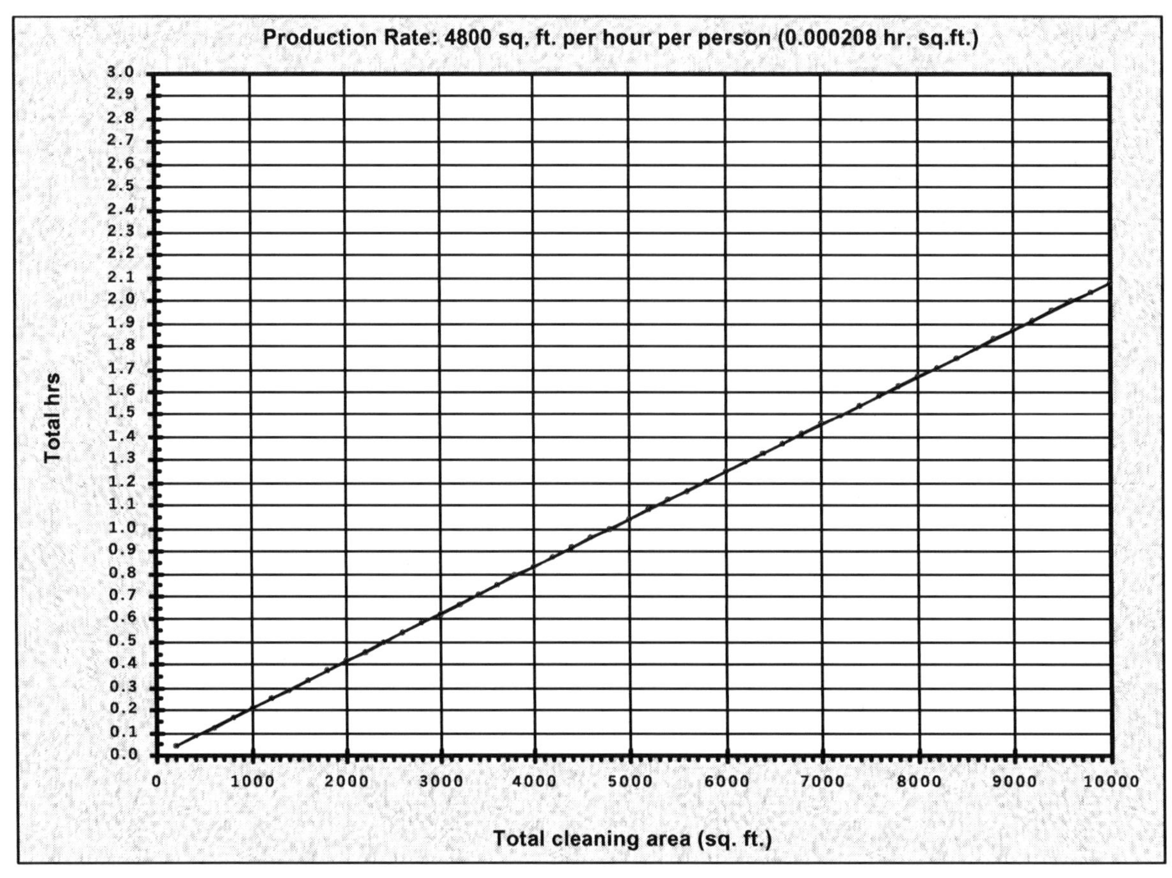

Production Rate: 4800 sq. ft. per hour per person (0.000208 hr. sq.ft.)
Total hrs
3.0
2.9
2.8
2.7
2.6
2.5
2.4
2.3
2.2
2.1
2.0
1.9
1.8
1.7
1.6
1.5
1.4
1.3
1.2
1.1
1.0
0.9
0.8
0.7
0.6
0.5
0.4
0.3
0.2
0.1
0.0
0
1000
2000
3000
4000
5000
6000
7000
8000
9000
10000
Total cleaning area (sq. ft.)

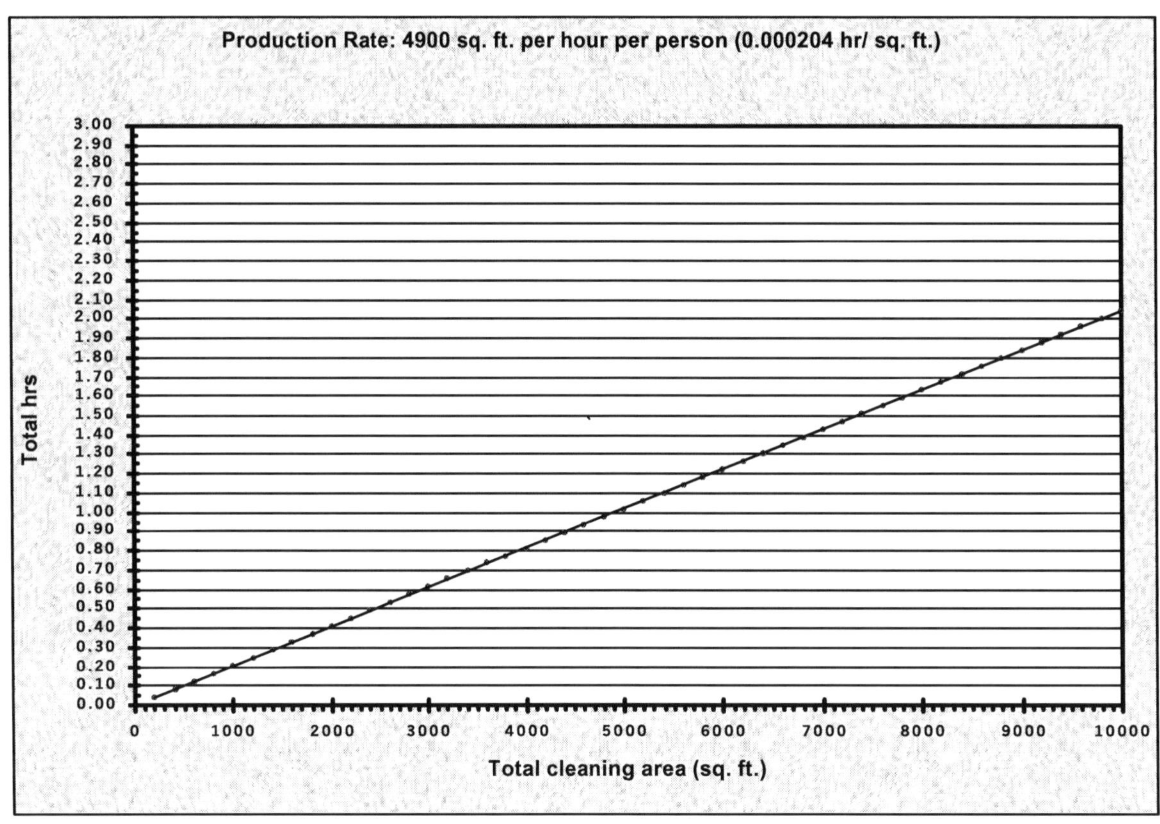

Production Rate: 4900 sq. ft. per hour per person (0.000204 hr/ sq. ft.)
Total hrs
3.00
2.90
2.80
2.70
2.60
2.50
2.40
2.30
2.20
2.10
2.00
1.90
1.80
1.70
1.60
1.50
1.40
1.30
1.20
1.10
1.00
0.90
0.80
0.70
0.60
0.50
0.40
0.30
0.20
0.10
0.00
0
1000
2000
3000
4000
5000
6000
7000
8000
9000
10000
Total cleaning area (sq. ft.)

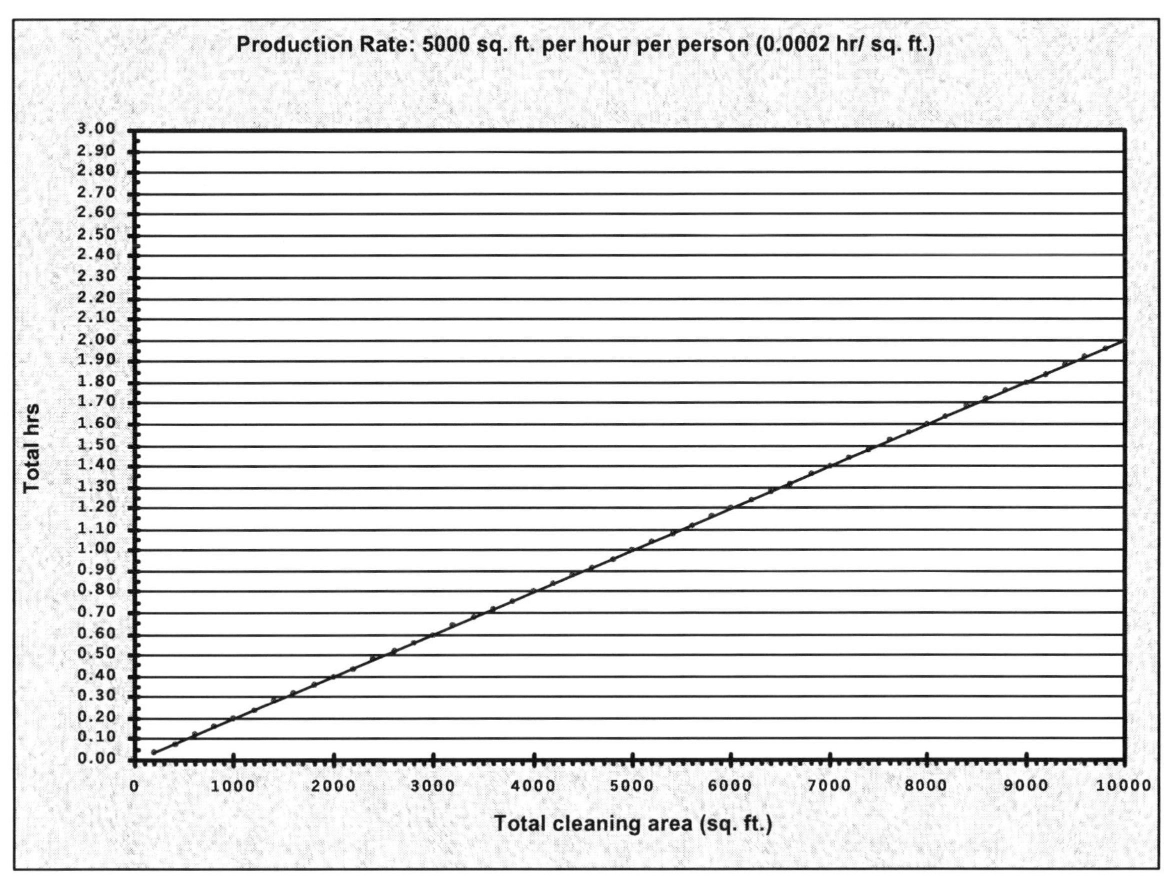
Production Rate: 5000 sq. ft. per hour per person (0.0002 hr/ sq. ft.)
Total hrs
3.00
2.90
2.80
2.70
2.60
2.50
2.40
2.30
2.20
2.10
2.00
1.90
1.80
1.70
1.60
1.50
1.40
1.30
1.20
1.10
1.00
0.90
0.80
0.70
0.60
0.50
0.40
0.30
0.20
0.10
0.00
0
1000
2000
3000
4000
5000
6000
7000
8000
9000
10000
Total cleaning area (sq. ft.)

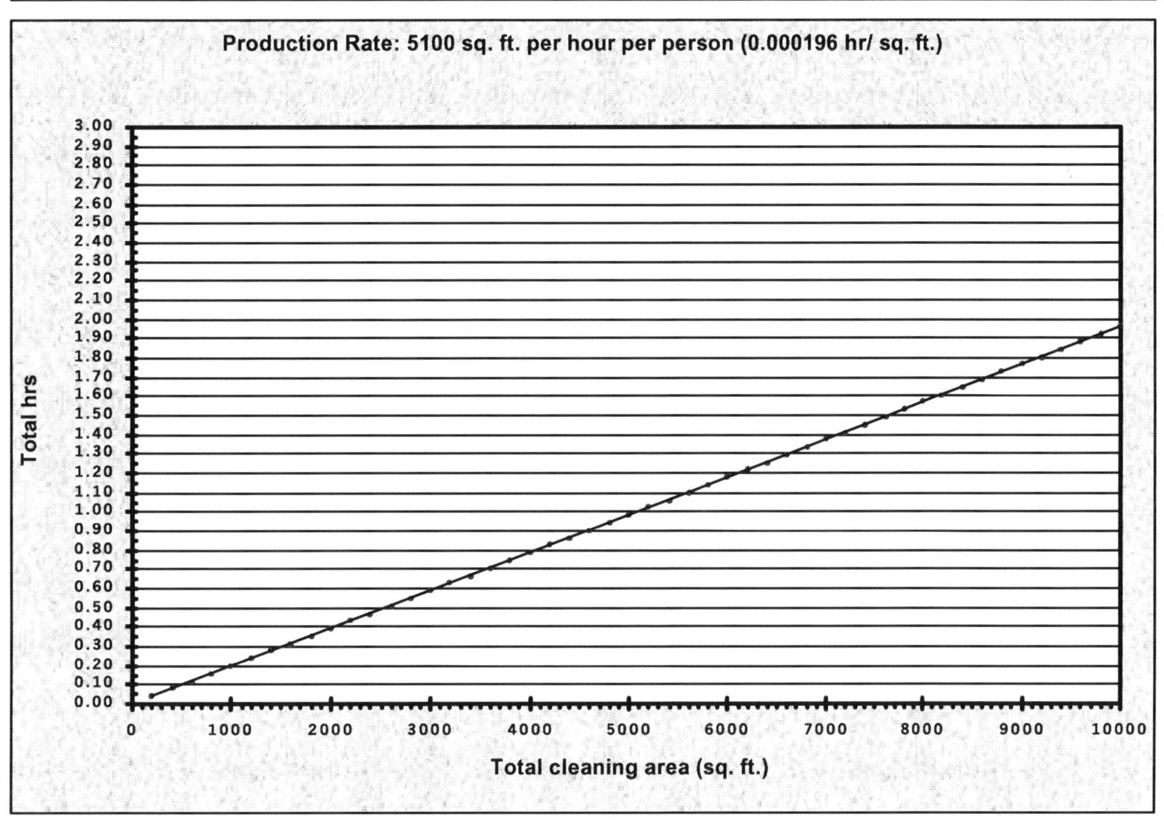
Production Rate: 5100 sq. ft. per hour per person (0.000196 hr/ sq. ft.)
Total hrs
3.00
2.90
2.80
2.70
2.60
2.50
2.40
2.30
2.20
2.10
2.00
1.90
1.80
1.70
1.60
1.50
1.40
1.30
1.20
1.10
1.00
0.90
0.80
0.70
0.60
0.50
0.40
0.30
0.20
0.10
0.00
0
1000
2000
3000
4000
5000
6000
7000
8000
9000
10000
Total cleaning area (sq. ft.)

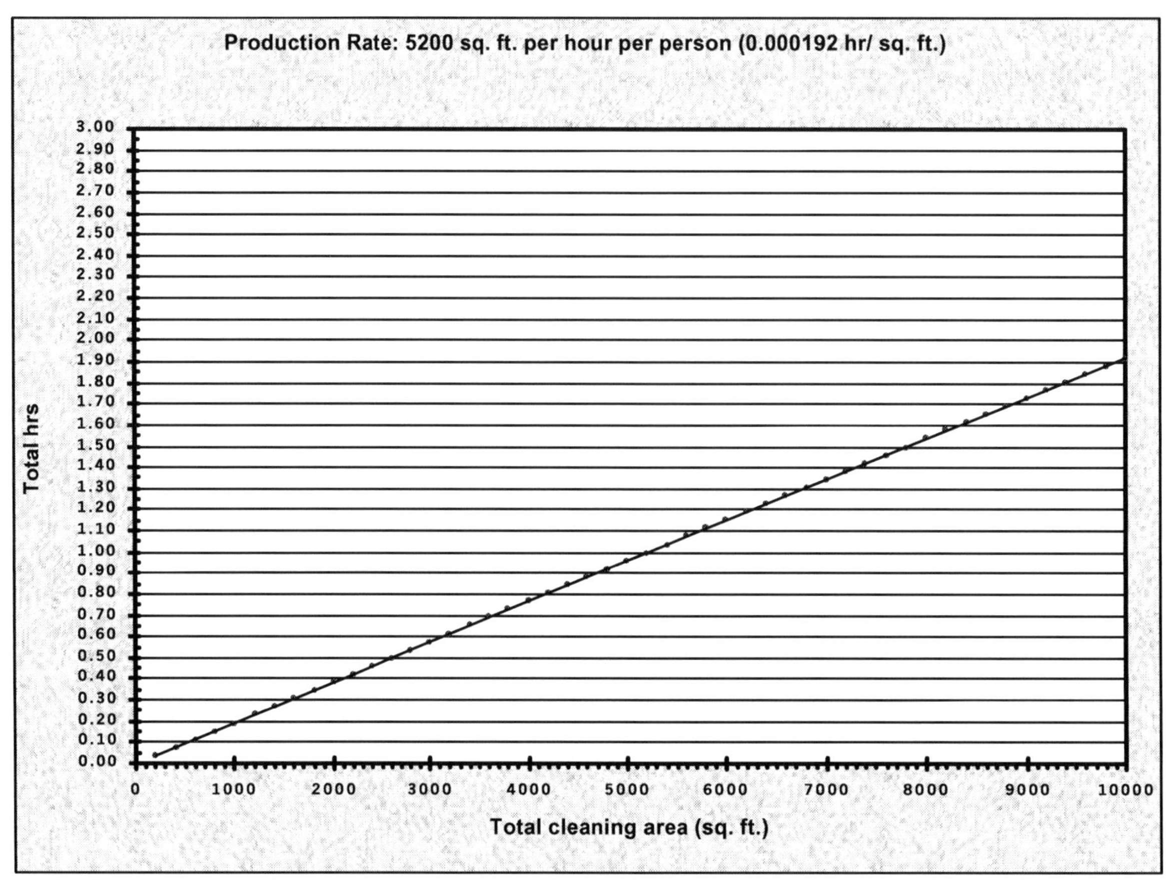

Production Rate: 5200 sq. ft. per hour per person (0.000192 hr/ sq. ft.)
Total hrs
3.00
2.90
2.80
2.70
2.60
2.50
2.40
2.30
2.20
2.10
2.00
1.90
1.80
1.70
1.60
1.50
1.40
1.30
1.20
1.10
1.00
0.90
0.80
0.70
0.60
0.50
0.40
0.30
0.20
0.10
0.00
0
1000
2000
3000
4000
5000
6000
7000
8000
9000
10000
Total cleaning area (sq. ft.)

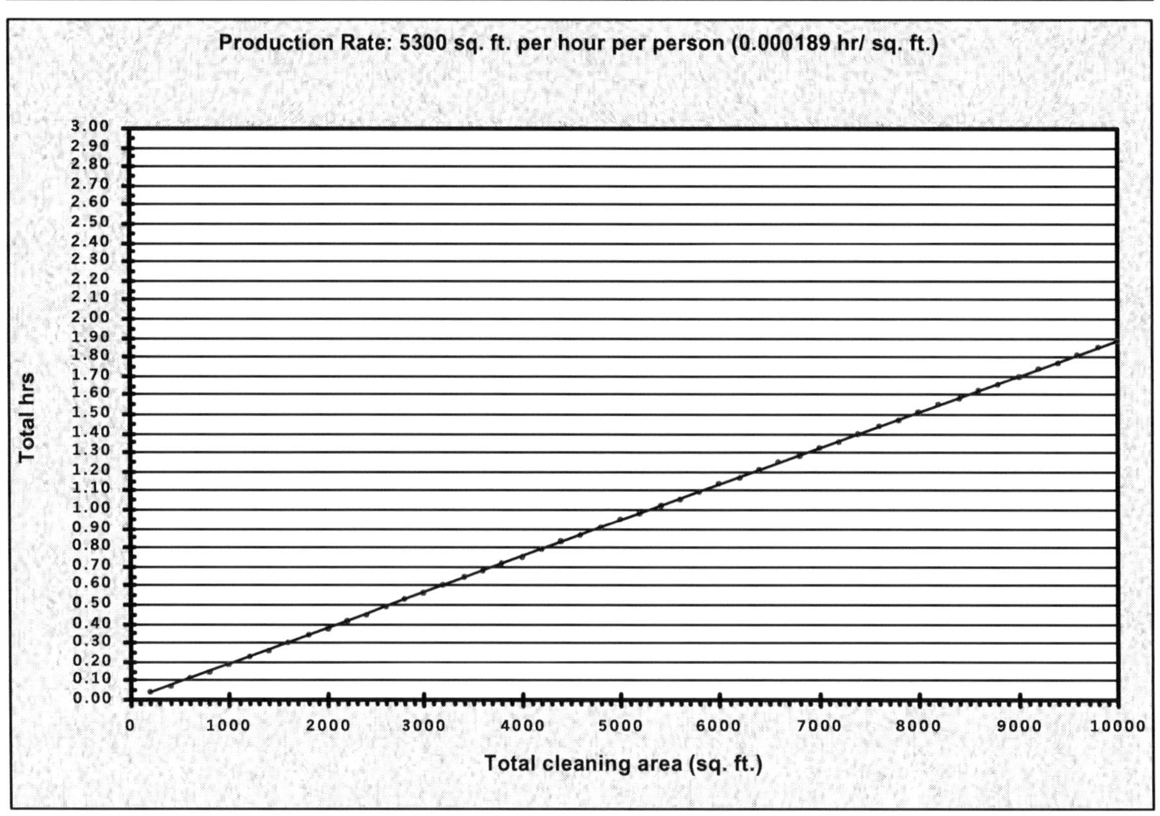

Production Rate: 5300 sq. ft. per hour per person (0.000189 hr/ sq. ft.)
Total hrs
3.00
2.90
2.80
2.70
2.60
2.50
2.40
2.30
2.20
2.10
2.00
1.90
1.80
1.70
1.60
1.50
1.40
1.30
1.20
1.10
1.00
0.90
0.80
0.70
0.60
0.50
0.40
0.30
0.20
0.10
0.00
0
1000
2000
3000
4000
5000
6000
7000
8000
9000
10000
Total cleaning area (sq. ft.)

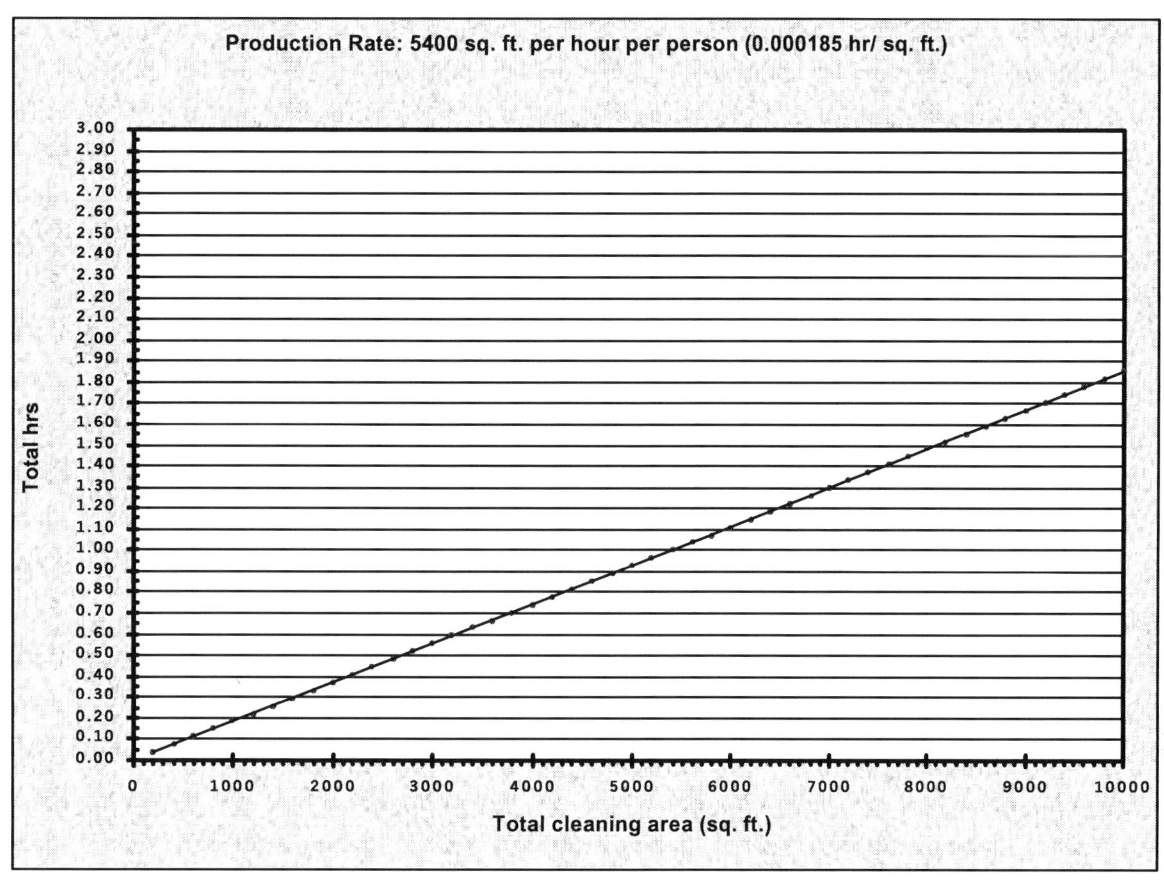
Production Rate: 5400 sq. ft. per hour per person (0.000185 hr/ sq. ft.)
Total hrs
3.00
2.90
2.80
2.70
2.60
2.50
2.40
2.30
2.20
2.10
2.00
1.90
1.80
1.70
1.60
1.50
1.40
1.30
1.20
1.10
1.00
0.90
0.80
0.70
0.60
0.50
0.40
0.30
0.20
0.10
0.00
0
1000
2000
3000
4000
5000
6000
7000
8000
9000
10000
Total cleaning area (sq. ft.)

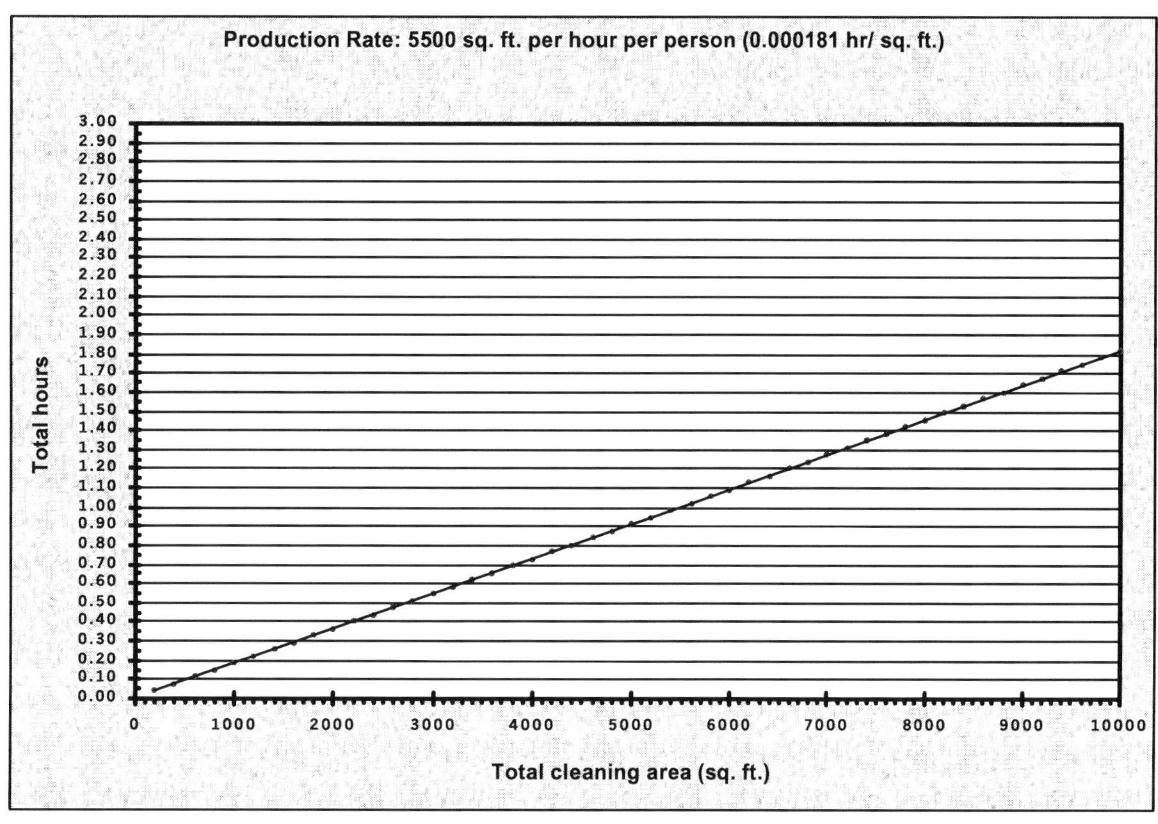
Production Rate: 5500 sq. ft. per hour per person (0.000181 hr/ sq. ft.)
Total hours
3.00
2.90
2.80
2.70
2.60
2.50
2.40
2.30
2.20
2.10
2.00
1.90
1.80
1.70
1.60
1.50
1.40
1.30
1.20
1.10
1.00
0.90
0.80
0.70
0.60
0.50
0.40
0.30
0.20
0.10
0.00
0
1000
2000
3000
4000
5000
6000
7000
8000
9000
10000
Total cleaning area (sq. ft.)

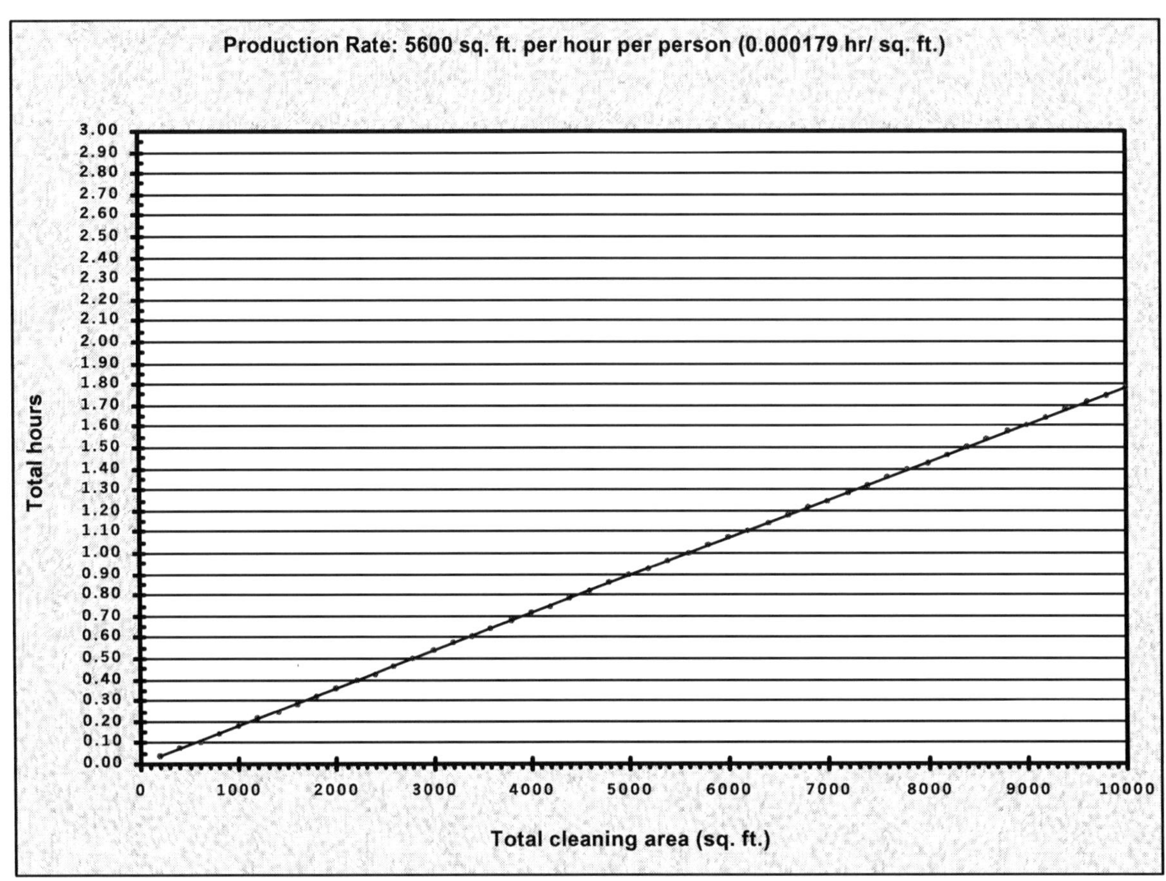
Production Rate: 5600 sq. ft. per hour per person (0.000179 hr/ sq. ft.)
Total hours
3.00
2.90
2.80
2.70
2.60
2.50
2.40
2.30
2.20
2.10
2.00
1.90
1.80
1.70
1.60
1.50
1.40
1.30
1.20
1.10
1.00
0.90
0.80
0.70
0.60
0.50
0.40
0.30
0.20
0.10
0.00
0
1000
2000
3000
4000
5000
6000
7000
8000
9000
10000
Total cleaning area (sq. ft.)

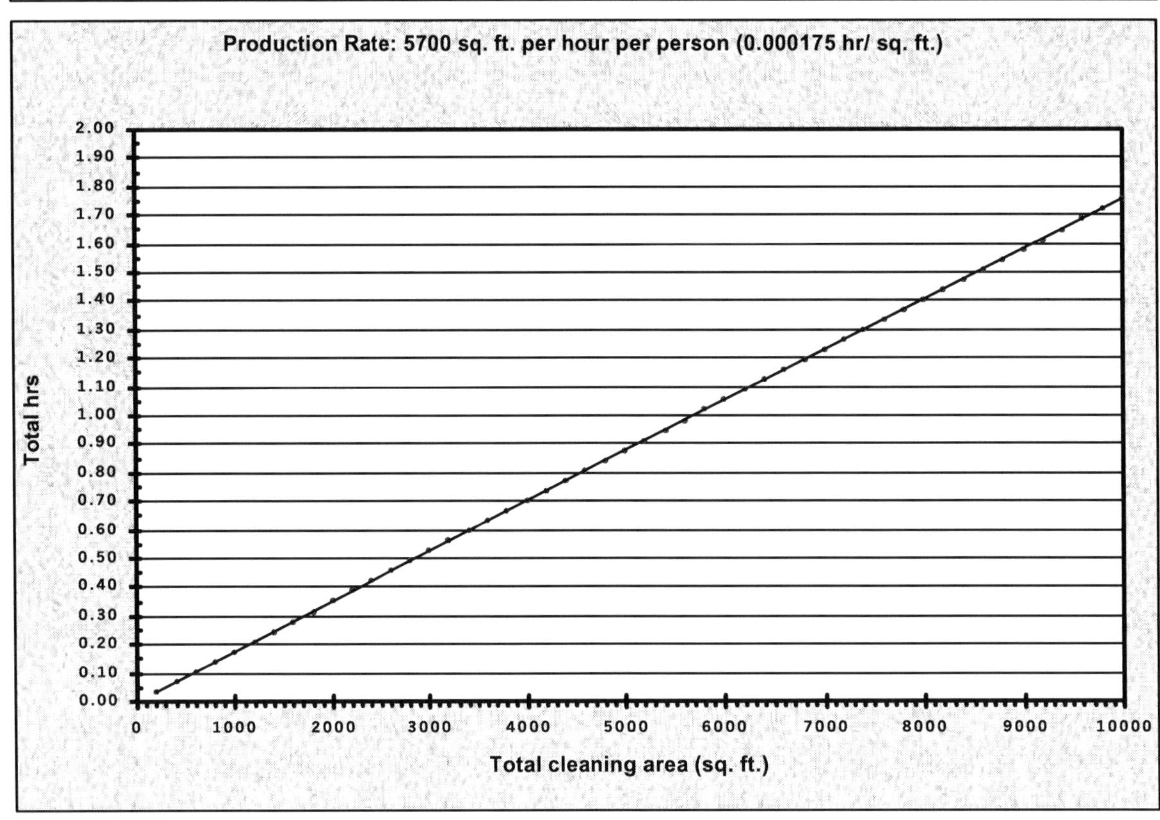
Production Rate: 5700 sq. ft. per hour per person (0.000175 hr/ sq. ft.)
Total hrs
2.00
1.90
1.80
1.70
1.60
1.50
1.40
1.30
1.20
1.10
1.00
0.90
0.80
0.70
0.60
0.50
0.40
0.30
0.20
0.10
0.00
0
1000
2000
3000
4000
5000
6000
7000
8000
9000
10000
Total cleaning area (sq. ft.)

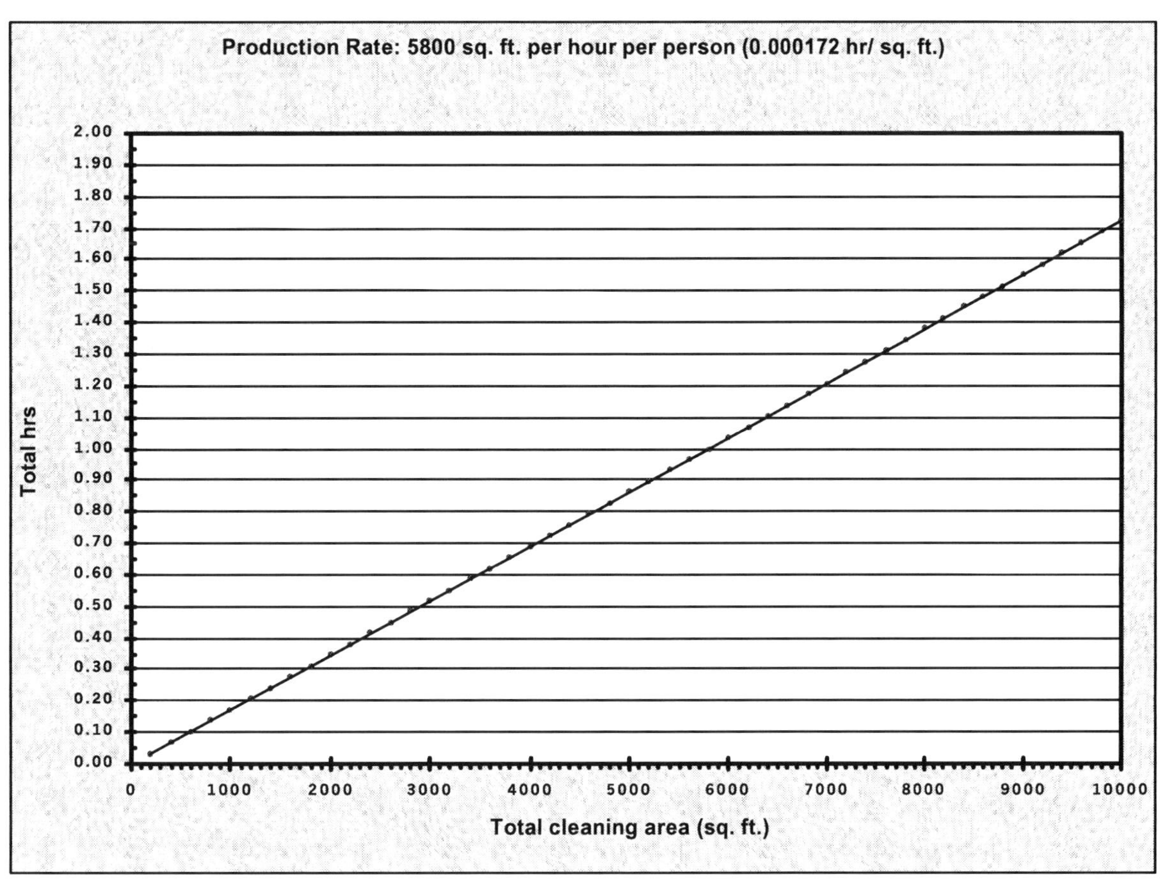
Production Rate: 5800 sq. ft. per hour per person (0.000172 hr/ sq. ft.)
Total hrs
2.00
1.90
1.80
1.70
1.60
1.50
1.40
1.30
1.20
1.10
1.00
0.90
0.80
0.70
0.60
0.50
0.40
0.30
0.20
0.10
0.00
0
1000
2000
3000
4000
5000
6000
7000
8000
9000
10000
Total cleaning area (sq. ft.)

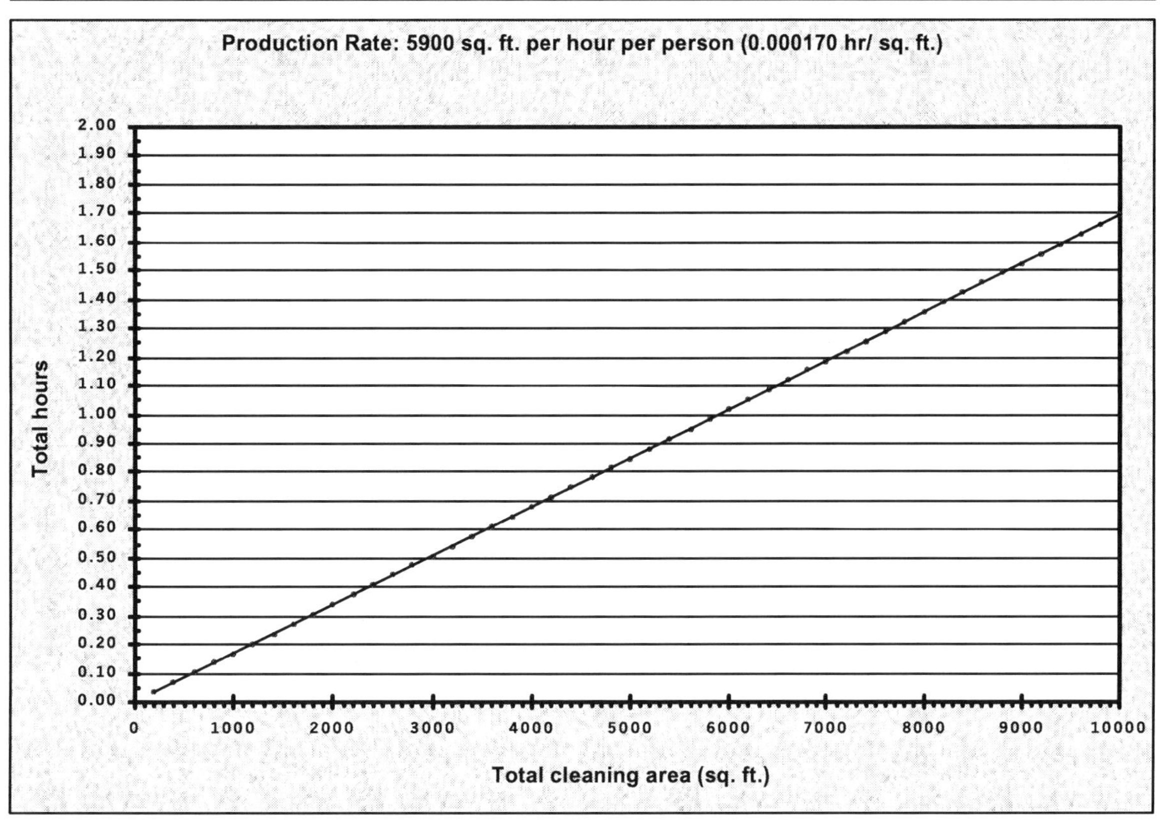
Production Rate: 5900 sq. ft. per hour per person (0.000170 hr/ sq. ft.)
Total hours
2.00
1.90
1.80
1.70
1.60
1.50
1.40
1.30
1.20
1.10
1.00
0.90
0.80
0.70
0.60
0.50
0.40
0.30
0.20
0.10
0.00
0
1000
2000
3000
4000
5000
6000
7000
8000
9000
10000
Total cleaning area (sq. ft.)

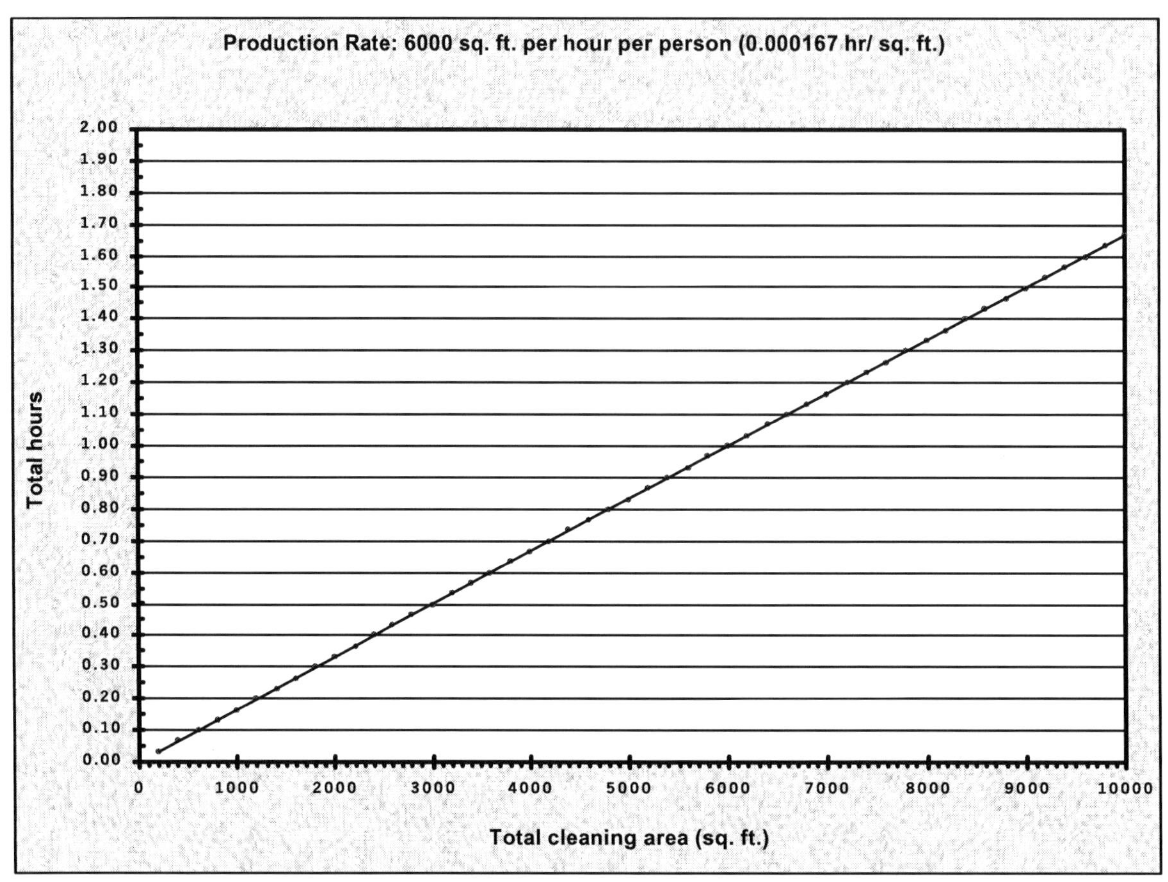
Production Rate: 6000 sq. ft. per hour per person (0.000167 hr/ sq. ft.)
Total hours
2.00
1.90
1.80
1.70
1.60
1.50
1.40
1.30
1.20
1.10
1.00
0.90
0.80
0.70
0.60
0.50
0.40
0.30
0.20
0.10
0.00
0
1000
2000
3000
4000
5000
6000
7000
8000
9000
10000
Total cleaning area (sq. ft.)

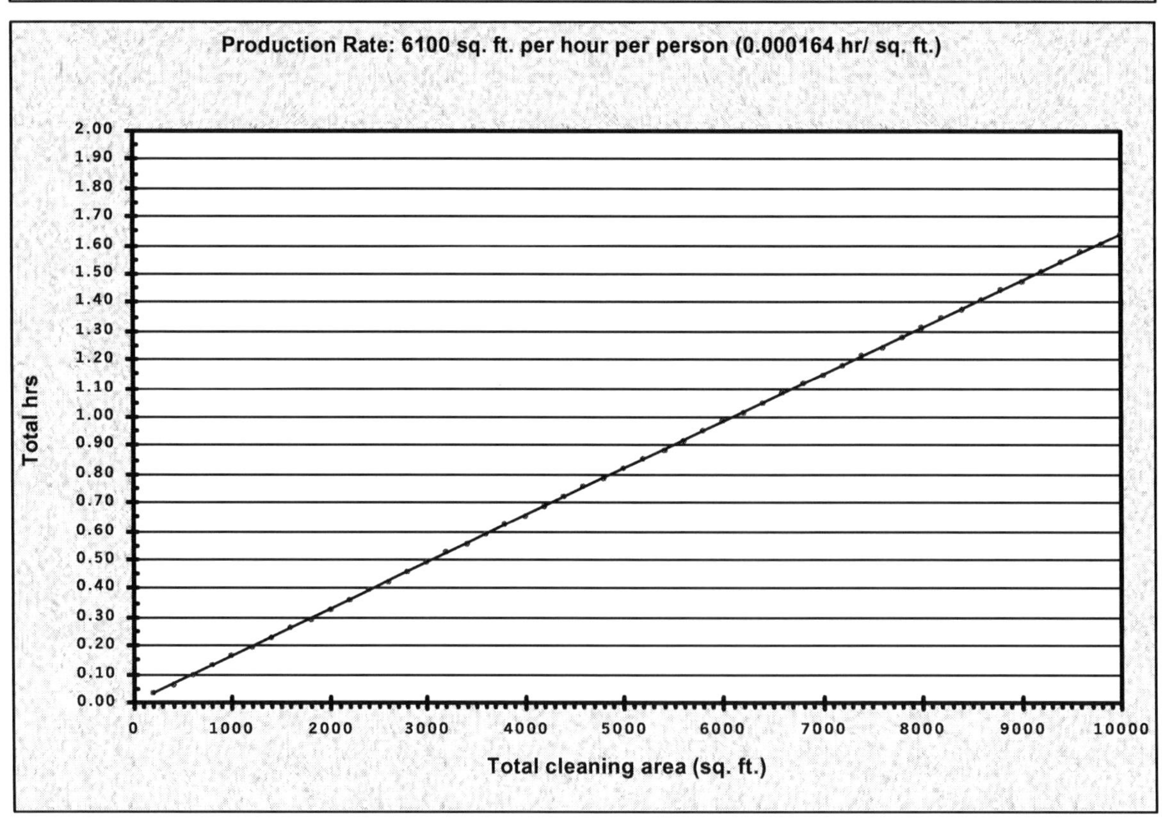
Production Rate: 6100 sq. ft. per hour per person (0.000164 hr/ sq. ft.)
Total hrs
2.00
1.90
1.80
1.70
1.60
1.50
1.40
1.30
1.20
1.10
1.00
0.90
0.80
0.70
0.60
0.50
0.40
0.30
0.20
0.10
0.00
0
1000
2000
3000
4000
5000
6000
7000
8000
9000
10000
Total cleaning area (sq. ft.)

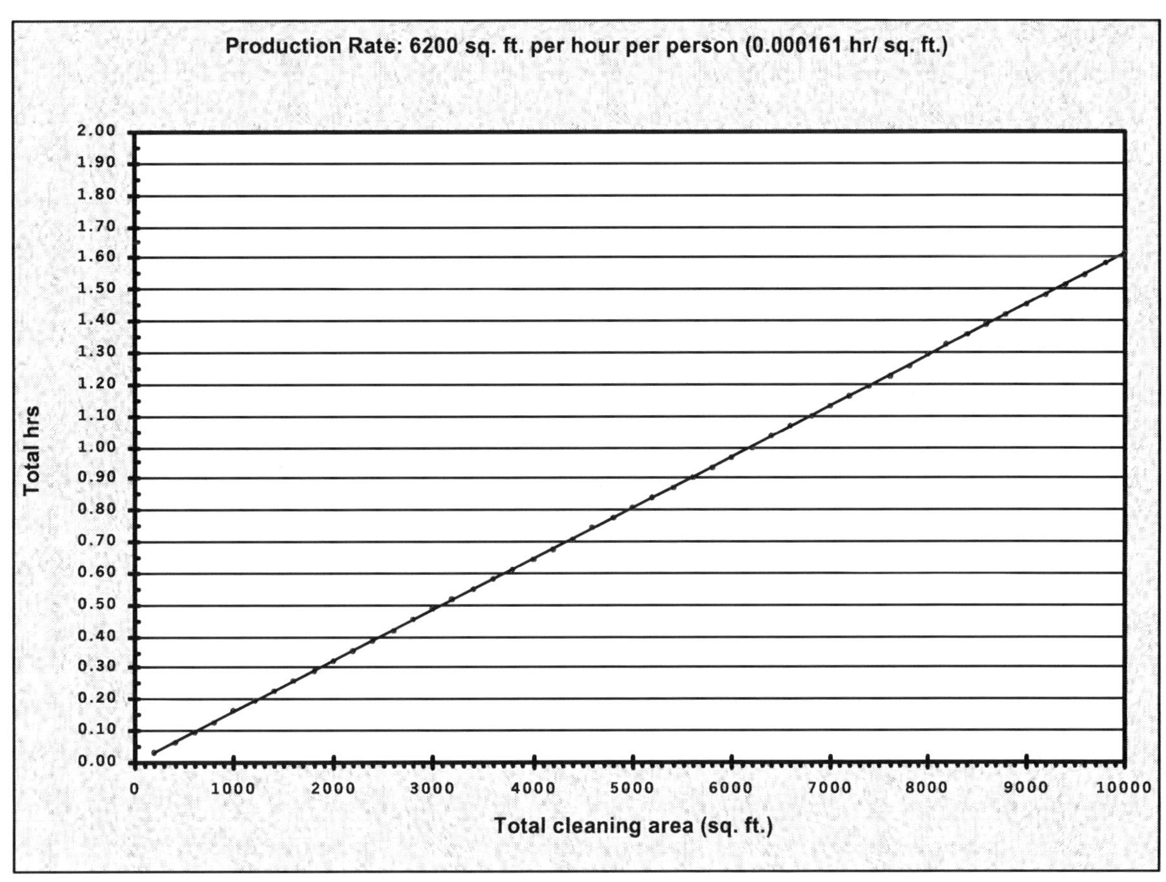
Production Rate: 6200 sq. ft. per hour per person (0.000161 hr/ sq. ft.)
Total hrs
2.00
1.90
1.80
1.70
1.60
1.50
1.40
1.30
1.20
1.10
1.00
0.90
0.80
0.70
0.60
0.50
0.40
0.30
0.20
0.10
0.00
0
1000
2000
3000
4000
5000
6000
7000
8000
9000
10000
Total cleaning area (sq. ft.)

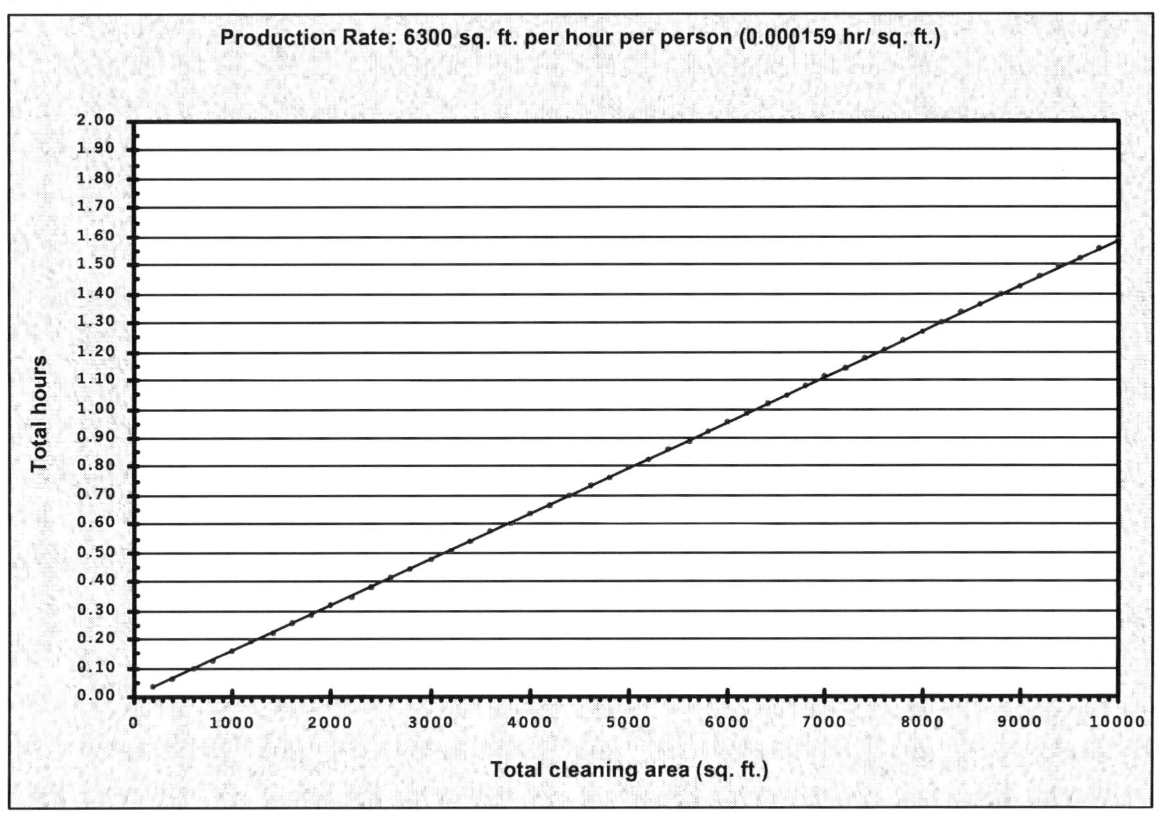
Production Rate: 6300 sq. ft. per hour per person (0.000159 hr/ sq. ft.)
Total hours
2.00
1.90
1.80
1.70
1.60
1.50
1.40
1.30
1.20
1.10
1.00
0.90
0.80
0.70
0.60
0.50
0.40
0.30
0.20
0.10
0.00
0
1000
2000
3000
4000
5000
6000
7000
8000
9000
10000
Total cleaning area (sq. ft.)

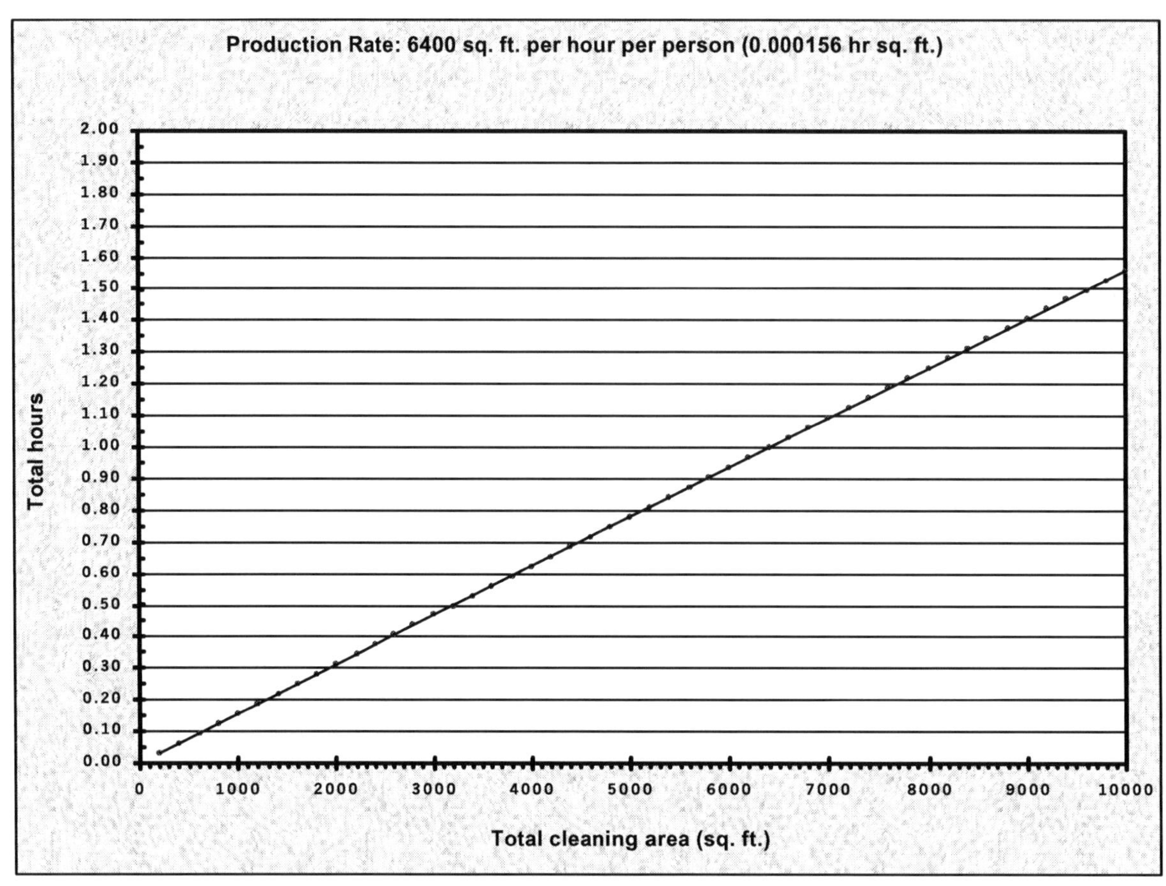
Production Rate: 6400 sq. ft. per hour per person (0.000156 hr sq. ft.)
Total hours
2.00
1.90
1.80
1.70
1.60
1.50
1.40
1.30
1.20
1.10
1.00
0.90
0.80
0.70
0.60
0.50
0.40
0.30
0.20
0.10
0.00
0
1000
2000
3000
4000
5000
6000
7000
8000
9000
10000
Total cleaning area (sq. ft.)

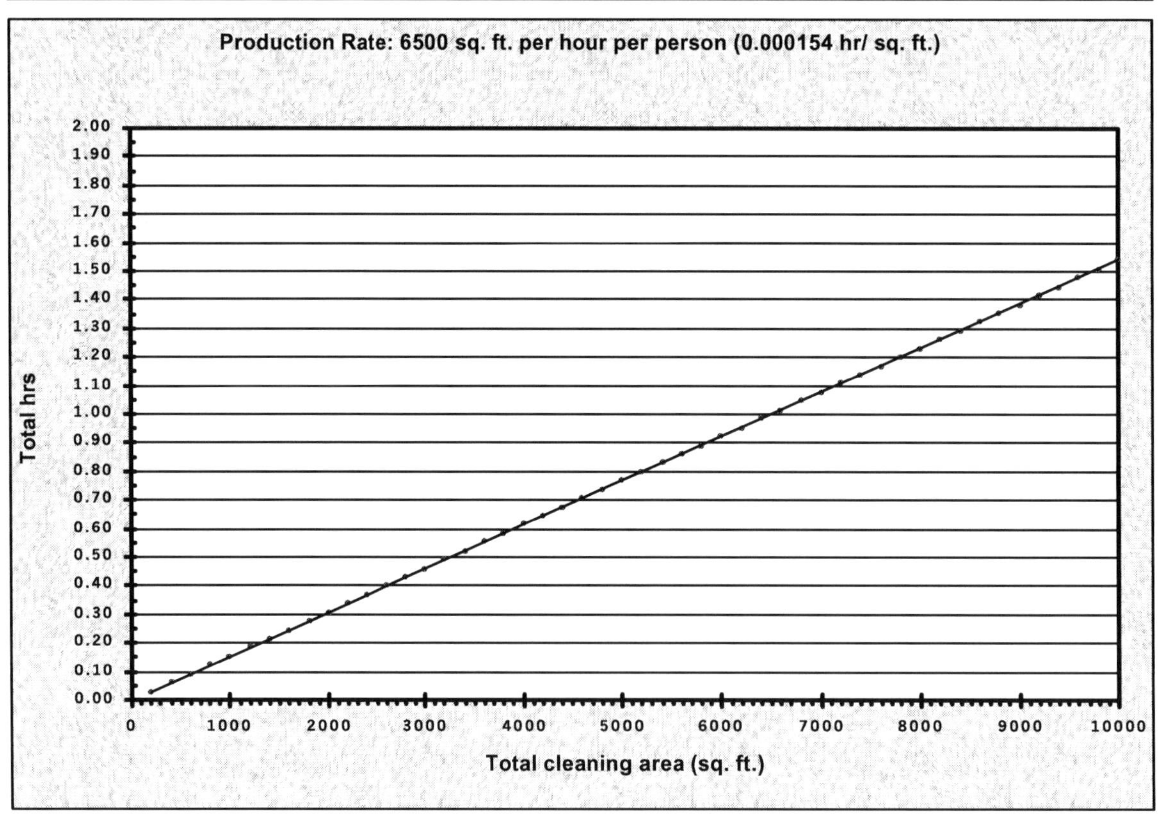
Production Rate: 6500 sq. ft. per hour per person (0.000154 hr/ sq. ft.)
Total hrs
2.00
1.90
1.80
1.70
1.60
1.50
1.40
1.30
1.20
1.10
1.00
0.90
0.80
0.70
0.60
0.50
0.40
0.30
0.20
0.10
0.00
0
1000
2000
3000
4000
5000
6000
7000
8000
9000
10000
Total cleaning area (sq. ft.)

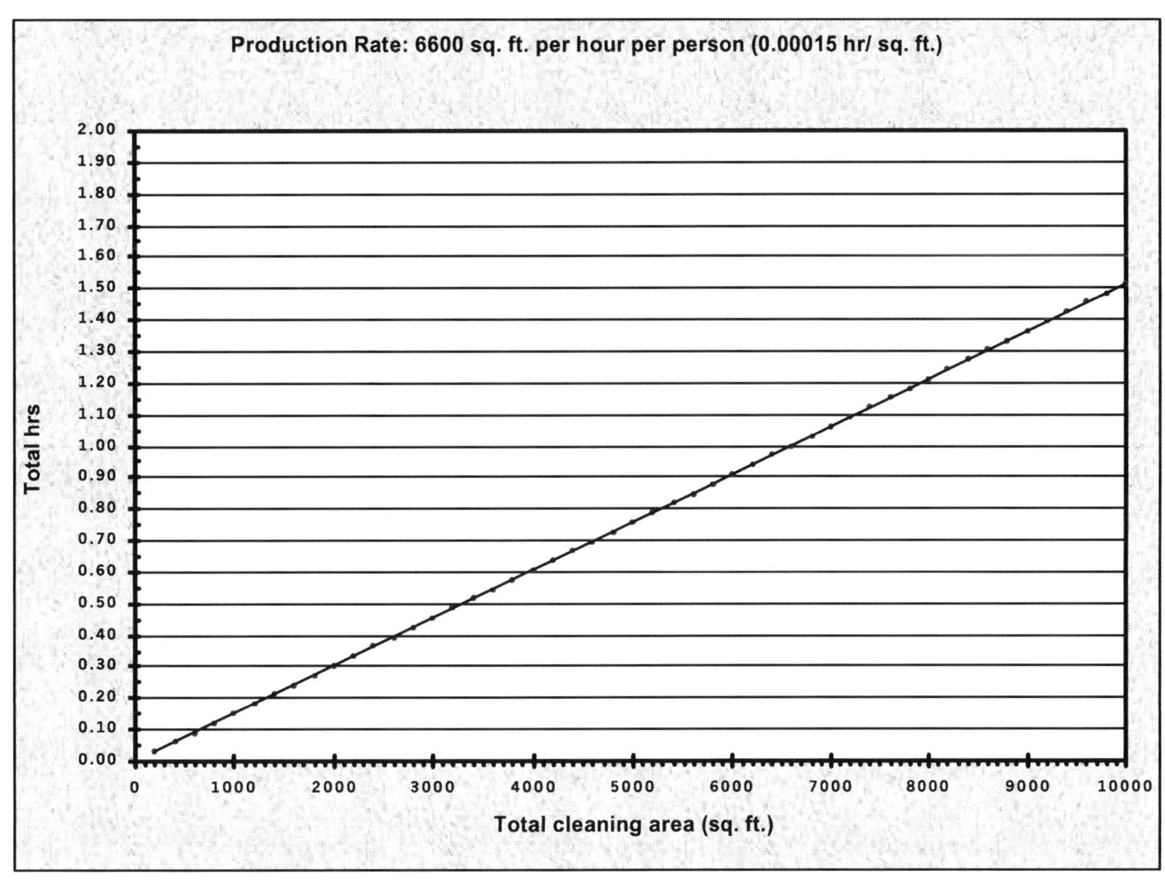
Production Rate: 6600 sq. ft. per hour per person (0.00015 hr/ sq. ft.)
Total hrs
2.00
1.90
1.80
1.70
1.60
1.50
1.40
1.30
1.20
1.10
1.00
0.90
0.80
0.70
0.60
0.50
0.40
0.30
0.20
0.10
0.00
0
1000
2000
3000
4000
5000
6000
7000
8000
9000
10000
Total cleaning area (sq. ft.)

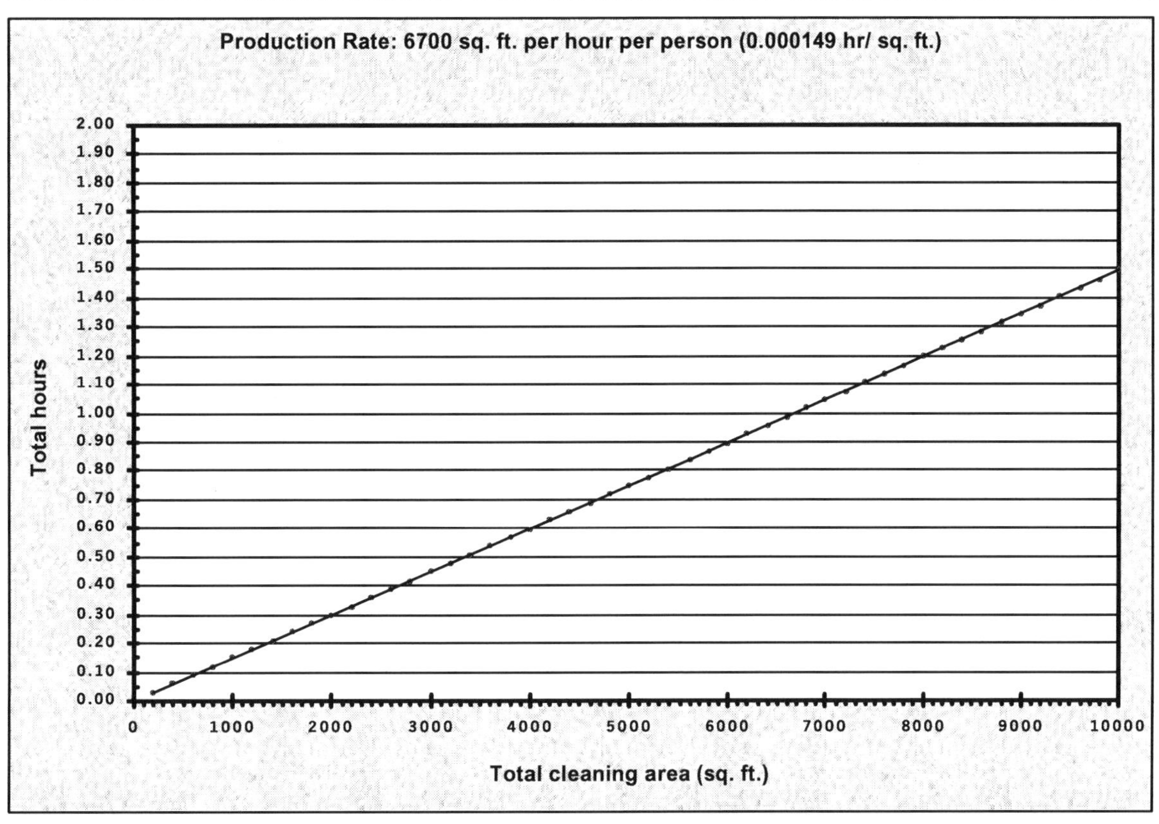
Production Rate: 6700 sq. ft. per hour per person (0.000149 hr/ sq. ft.)
Total hours
2.00
1.90
1.80
1.70
1.60
1.50
1.40
1.30
1.20
1.10
1.00
0.90
0.80
0.70
0.60
0.50
0.40
0.30
0.20
0.10
0.00
0
1000
2000
3000
4000
5000
6000
7000
8000
9000
10000
Total cleaning area (sq. ft.)

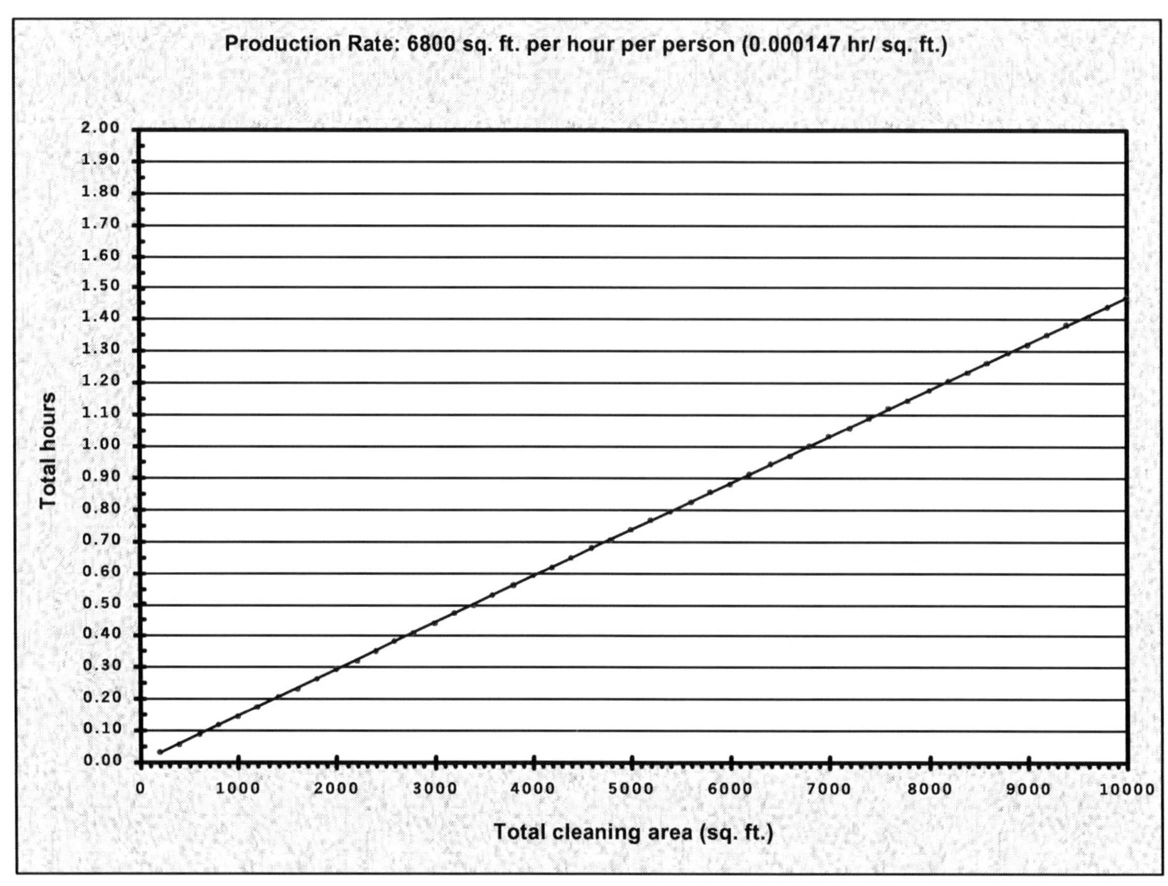
Production Rate: 6800 sq. ft. per hour per person (0.000147 hr/ sq. ft.)
Total hours
2.00
1.90
1.80
1.70
1.60
1.50
1.40
1.30
1.20
1.10
1.00
0.90
0.80
0.70
0.60
0.50
0.40
0.30
0.20
0.10
0.00
0
1000
2000
3000
4000
5000
6000
7000
8000
9000
10000
Total cleaning area (sq. ft.)

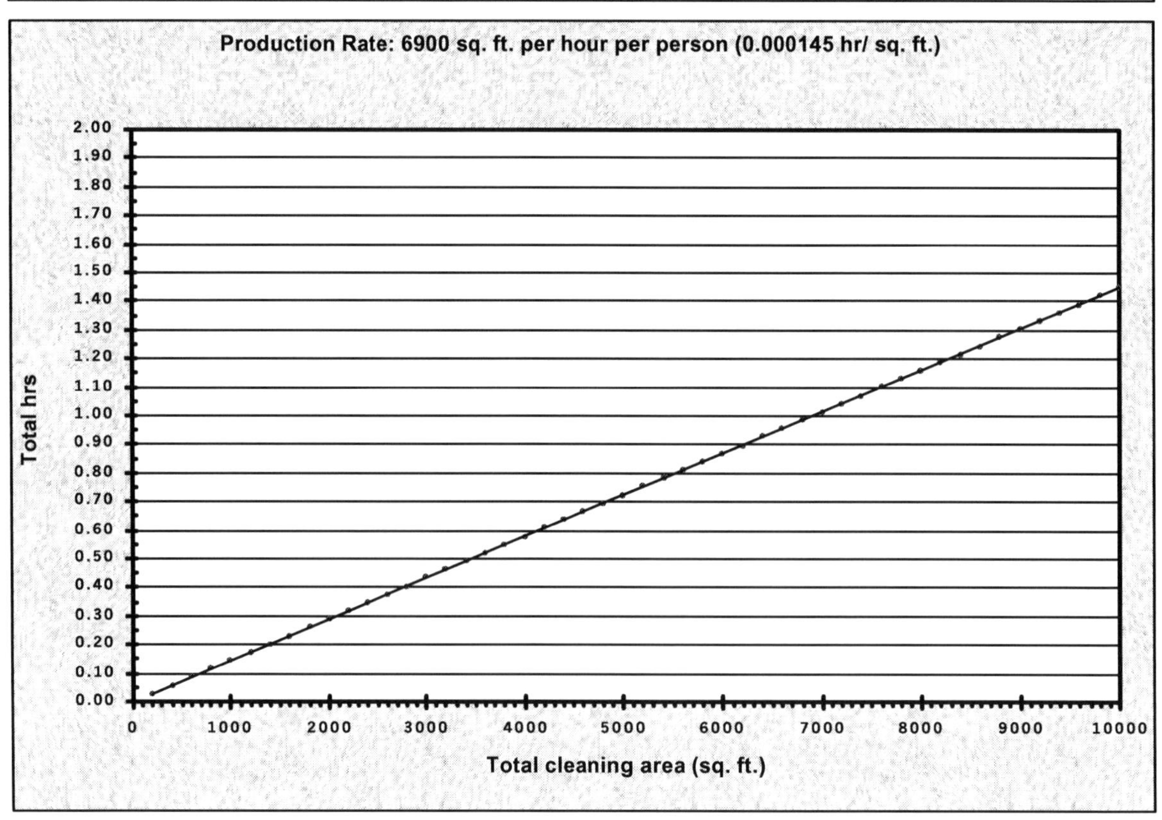
Production Rate: 6900 sq. ft. per hour per person (0.000145 hr/ sq. ft.)
Total hrs
2.00
1.90
1.80
1.70
1.60
1.50
1.40
1.30
1.20
1.10
1.00
0.90
0.80
0.70
0.60
0.50
0.40
0.30
0.20
0.10
0.00
0
1000
2000
3000
4000
5000
6000
7000
8000
9000
10000
Total cleaning area (sq. ft.)

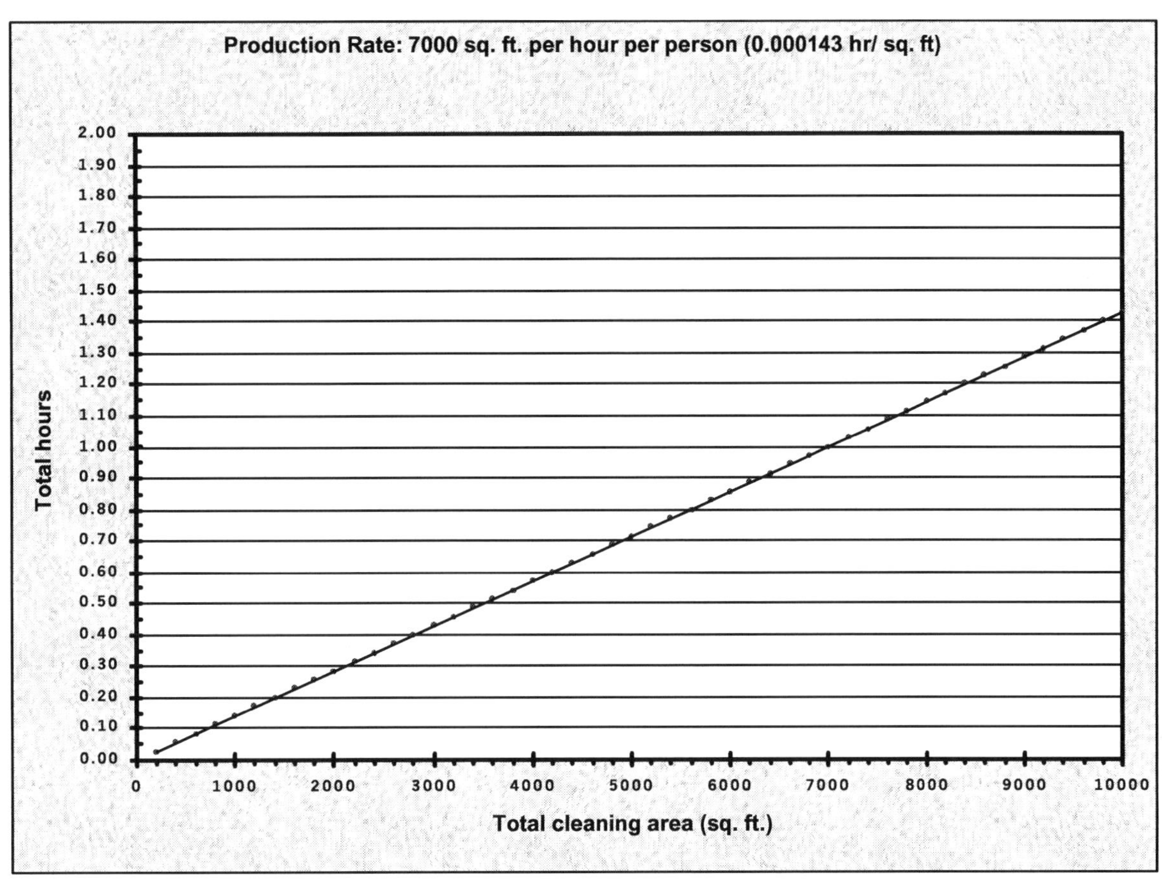
Production Rate: 7000 sq. ft. per hour per person (0.000143 hr/ sq. ft)
Total hours
2.00
1.90
1.80
1.70
1.60
1.50
1.40
1.30
1.20
1.10
1.00
0.90
0.80
0.70
0.60
0.50
0.40
0.30
0.20
0.10
0.00
0
1000
2000
3000
4000
5000
6000
7000
8000
9000
10000
Total cleaning area (sq. ft.)

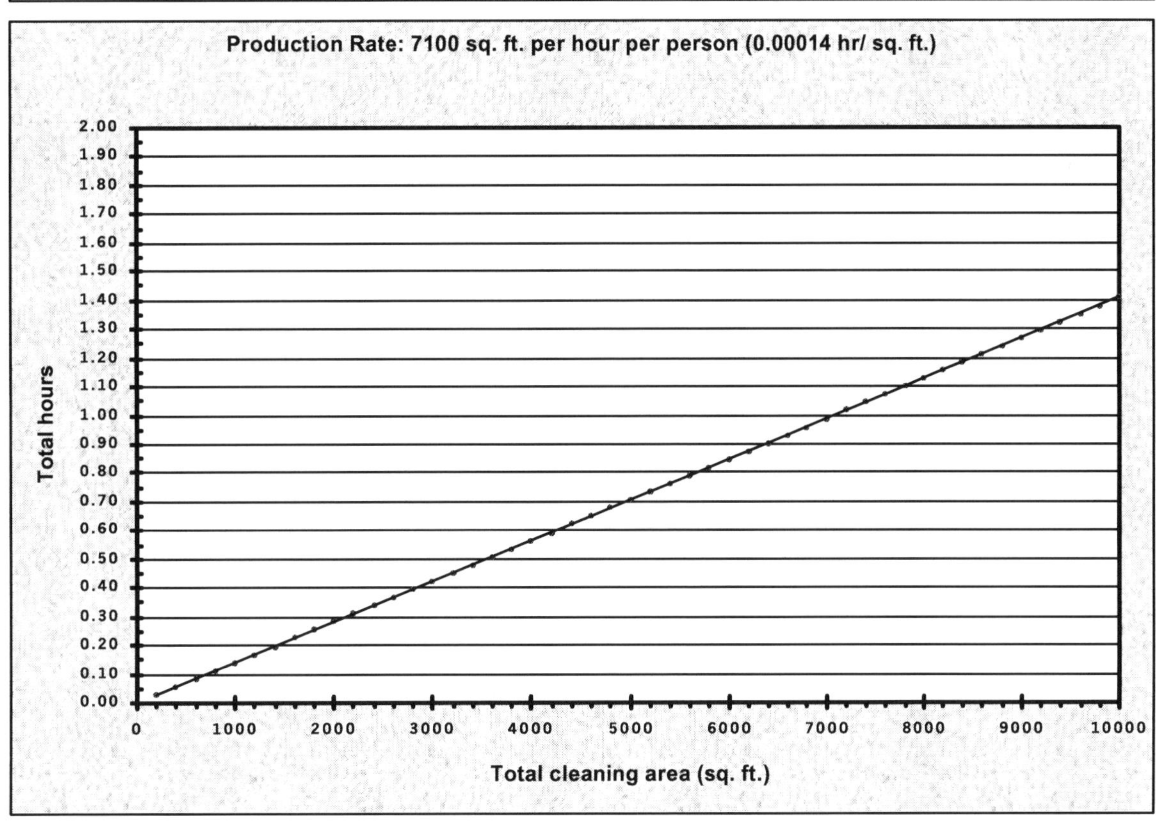
Production Rate: 7100 sq. ft. per hour per person (0.00014 hr/ sq. ft.)
Total hours
2.00
1.90
1.80
1.70
1.60
1.50
1.40
1.30
1.20
1.10
1.00
0.90
0.80
0.70
0.60
0.50
0.40
0.30
0.20
0.10
0.00
0
1000
2000
3000
4000
5000
6000
7000
8000
9000
10000
Total cleaning area (sq. ft.)

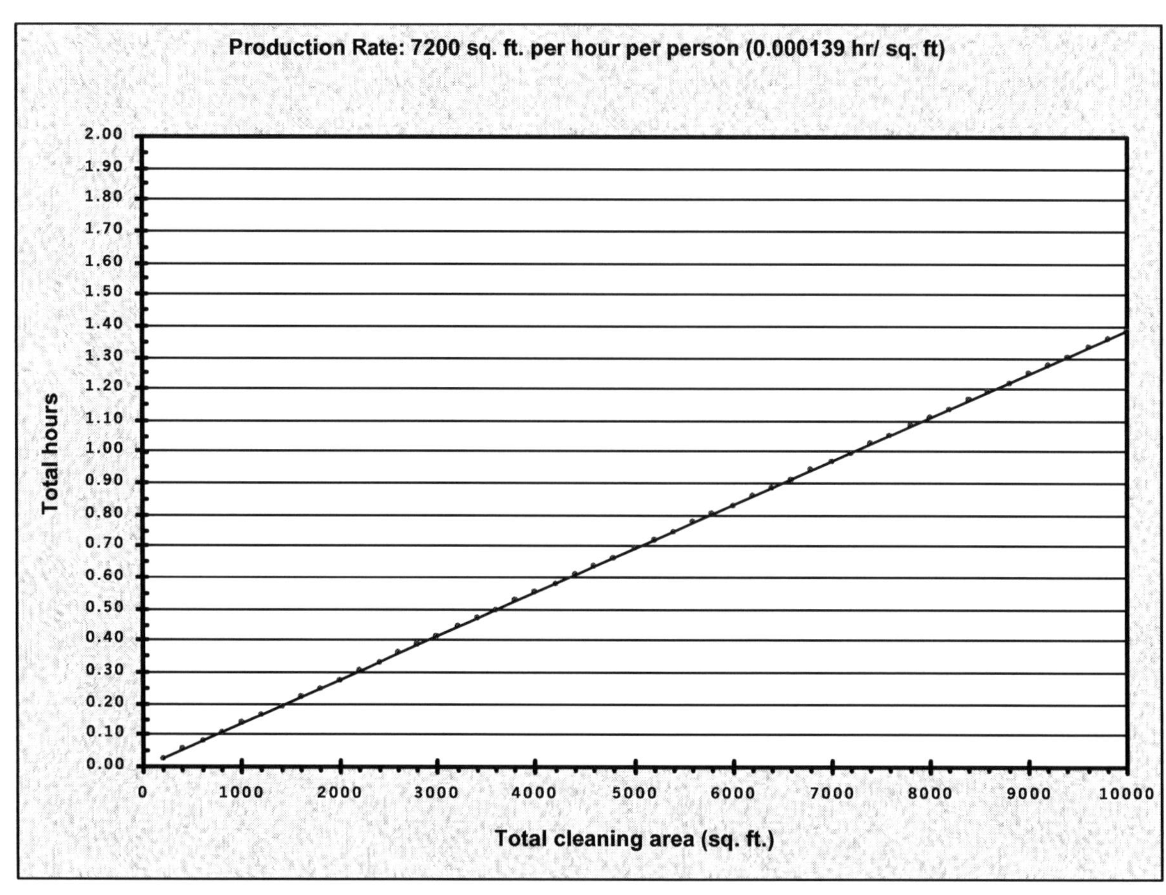
Production Rate: 7200 sq. ft. per hour per person (0.000139 hr/ sq. ft)
Total hours
2.00
1.90
1.80
1.70
1.60
1.50
1.40
1.30
1.20
1.10
1.00
0.90
0.80
0.70
0.60
0.50
0.40
0.30
0.20
0.10
0.00
0
1000
2000
3000
4000
5000
6000
7000
8000
9000
10000
Total cleaning area (sq. ft.)

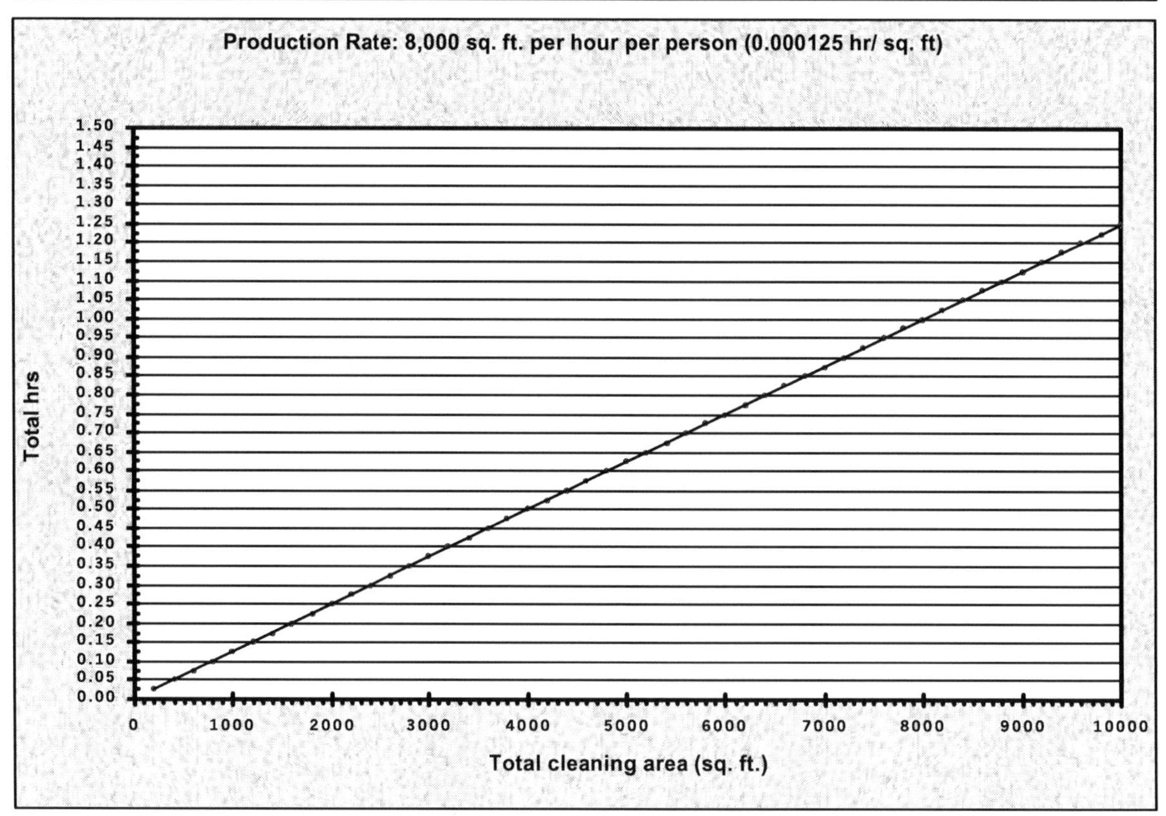
Production Rate: 8,000 sq. ft. per hour per person (0.000125 hr/ sq. ft)
Total hrs
1.50
1.45
1.40
1.35
1.30
1.25
1.20
1.15
1.10
1.05
1.00
0.95
0.90
0.85
0.80
0.75
0.70
0.65
0.60
0.55
0.50
0.45
0.40
0.35
0.30
0.25
0.20
0.15
0.10
0.05
0.00
0
1000
2000
3000
4000
5000
6000
7000
8000
9000
10000
Total cleaning area (sq. ft.)

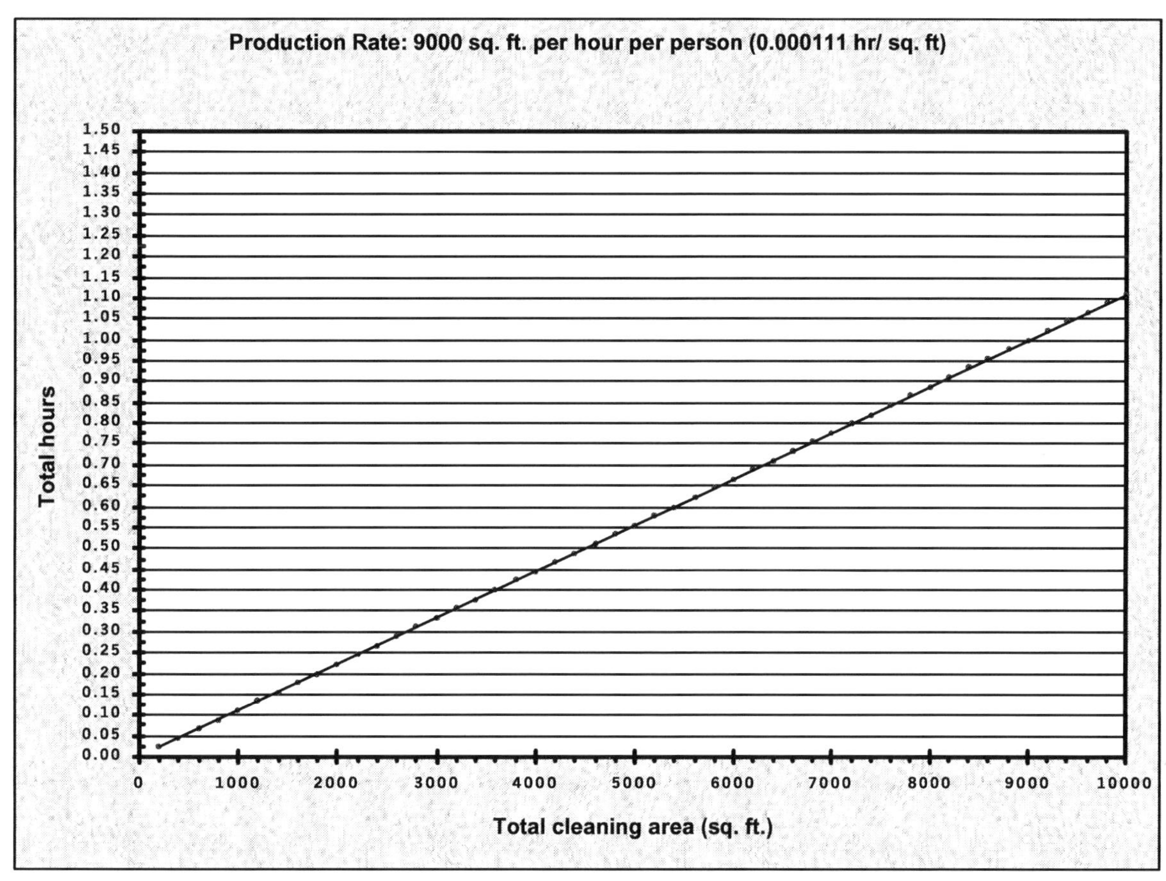
Production Rate: 9000 sq. ft. per hour per person (0.000111 hr/ sq. ft)
Total hours
1.50
1.45
1.40
1.35
1.30
1.25
1.20
1.15
1.10
1.05
1.00
0.95
0.90
0.85
0.80
0.75
0.70
0.65
0.60
0.55
0.50
0.45
0.40
0.35
0.30
0.25
0.20
0.15
0.10
0.05
0.00
0
1000
2000
3000
4000
5000
6000
7000
8000
9000
10000
Total cleaning area (sq. ft.)

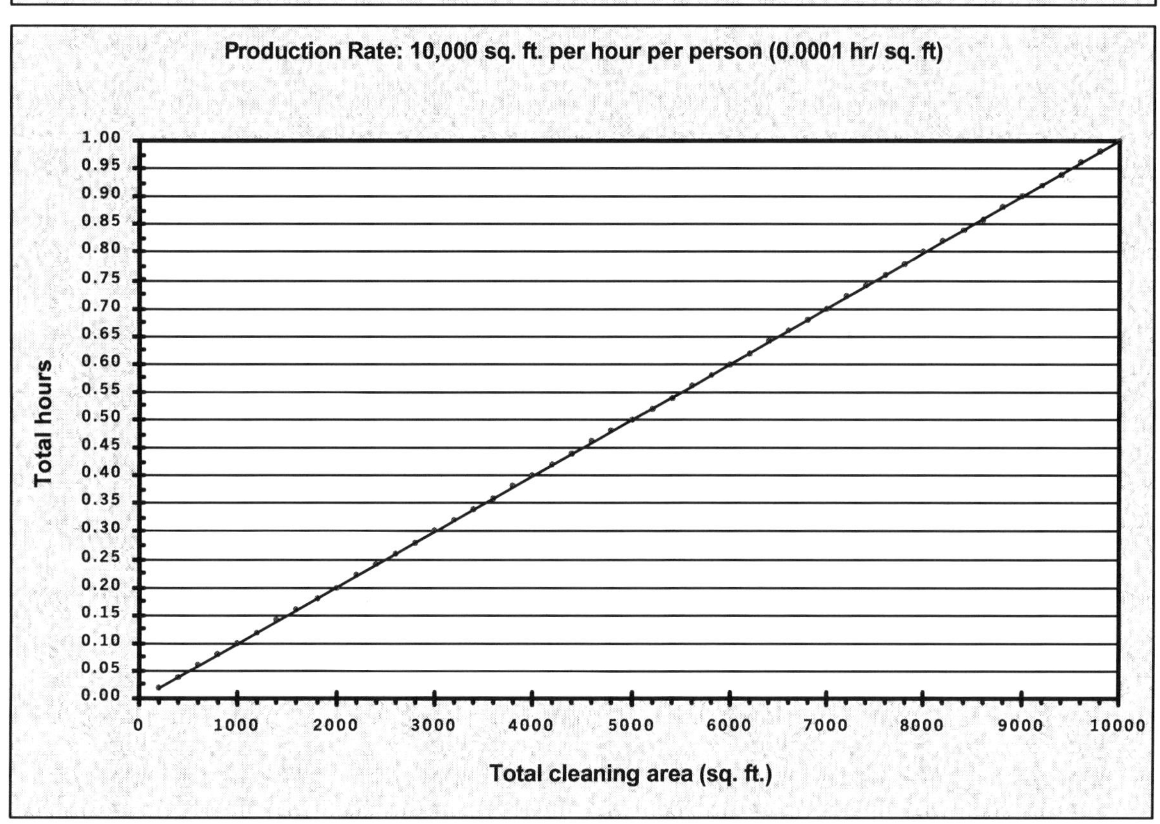
Production Rate: 10,000 sq. ft. per hour per person (0.0001 hr/ sq. ft)
Total hours
1.00
0.95
0.90
0.85
0.80
0.75
0.70
0.65
0.60
0.55
0.50
0.45
0.40
0.35
0.30
0.25
0.20
0.15
0.10
0.05
0.00
0
1000
2000
3000
4000
5000
6000
7000
8000
9000
10000
Total cleaning area (sq. ft.)

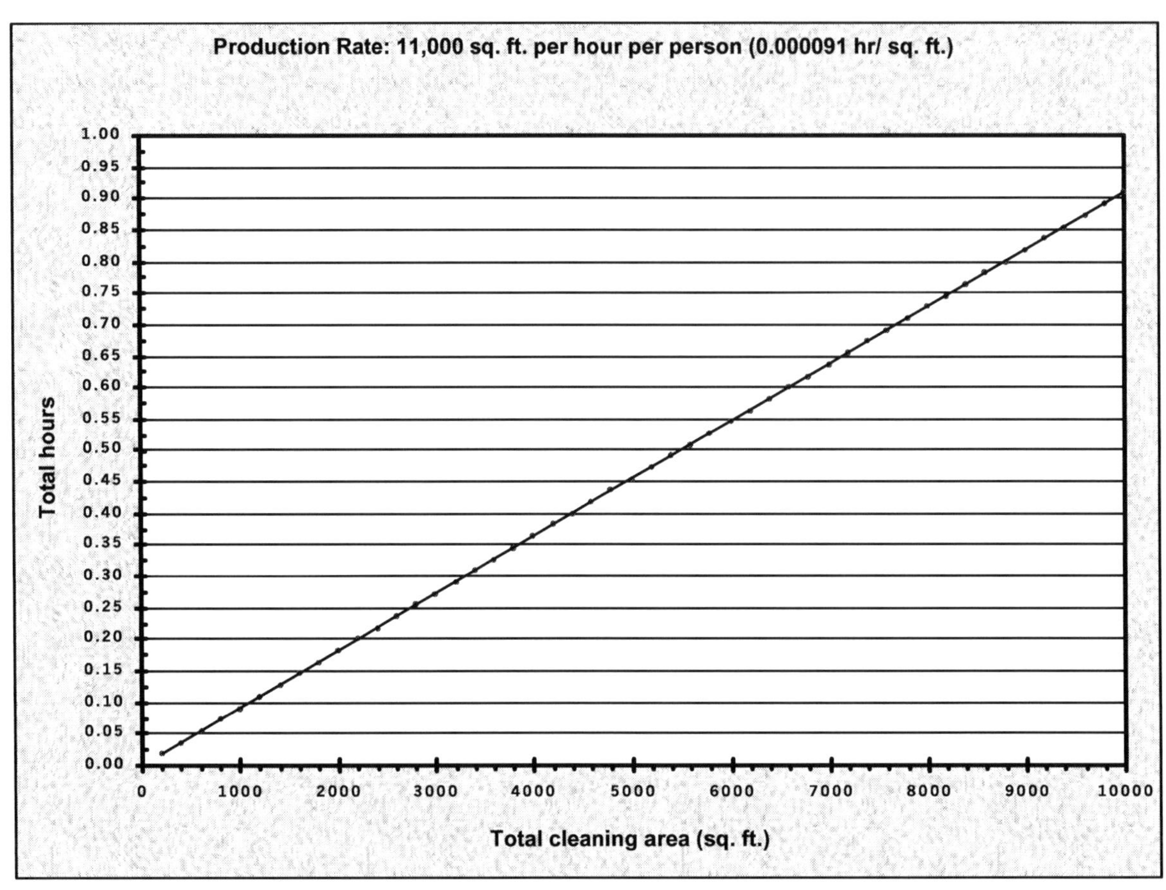
Production Rate: 11,000 sq. ft. per hour per person (0.000091 hr/ sq. ft.)
Total hours
1.00
0.95
0.90
0.85
0.80
0.75
0.70
0.65
0.60
0.55
0.50
0.45
0.40
0.35
0.30
0.25
0.20
0.15
0.10
0.05
0.00
0
1000
2000
3000
4000
5000
6000
7000
8000
9000
10000
Total cleaning area (sq. ft.)

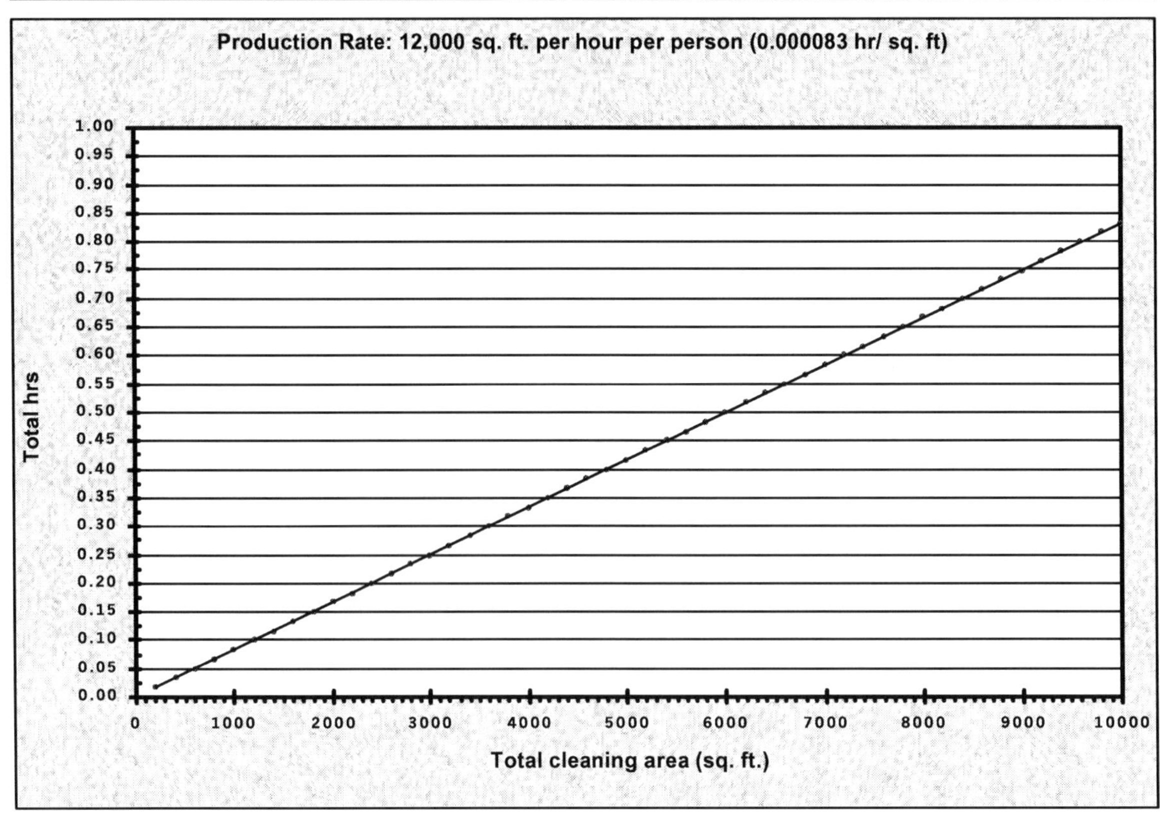
Production Rate: 12,000 sq. ft. per hour per person (0.000083 hr/ sq. ft)
Total hrs
1.00
0.95
0.90
0.85
0.80
0.75
0.70
0.65
0.60
0.55
0.50
0.45
0.40
0.35
0.30
0.25
0.20
0.15
0.10
0.05
0.00
0
1000
2000
3000
4000
5000
6000
7000
8000
9000
10000
Total cleaning area (sq. ft.)

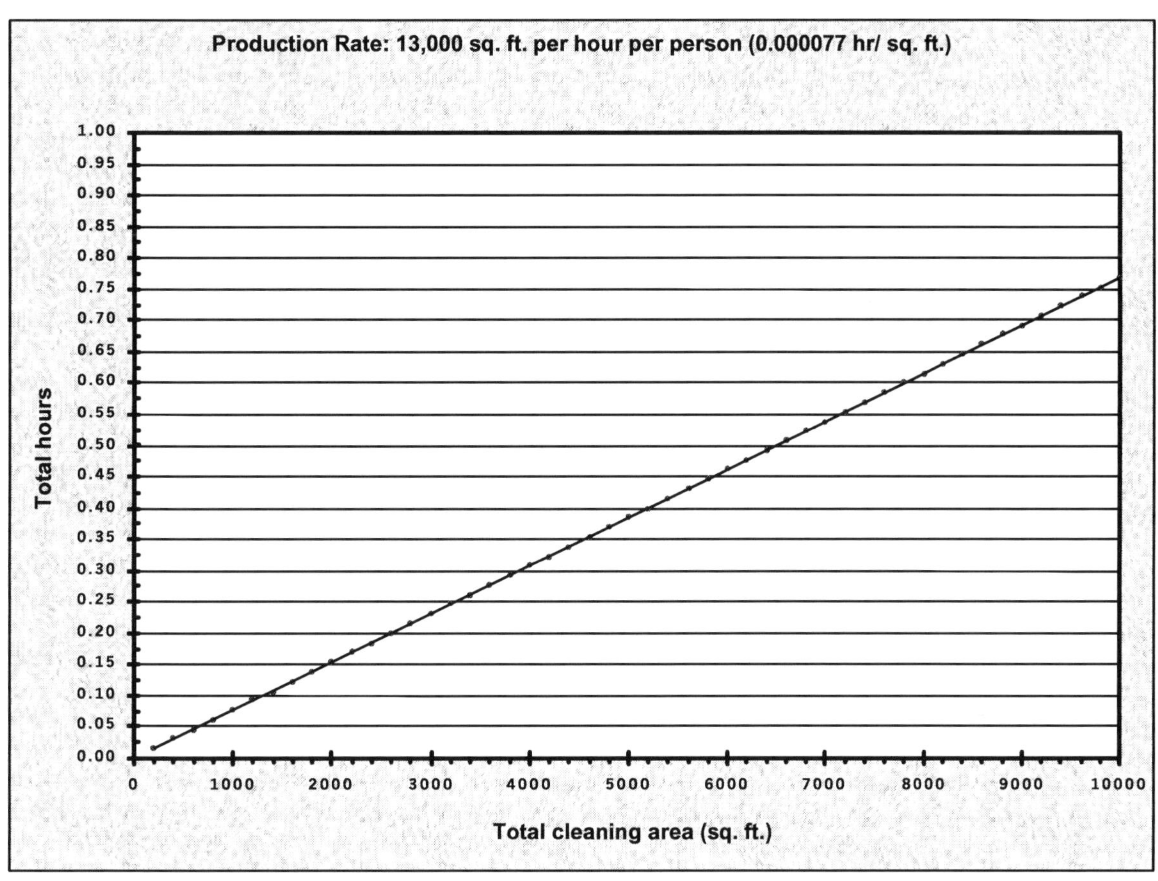
Production Rate: 13,000 sq. ft. per hour per person (0.000077 hr/ sq. ft.)
Total hours
1.00
0.95
0.90
0.85
0.80
0.75
0.70
0.65
0.60
0.55
0.50
0.45
0.40
0.35
0.30
0.25
0.20
0.15
0.10
0.05
0.00
0
1000
2000
3000
4000
5000
6000
7000
8000
9000
10000
Total cleaning area (sq. ft.)

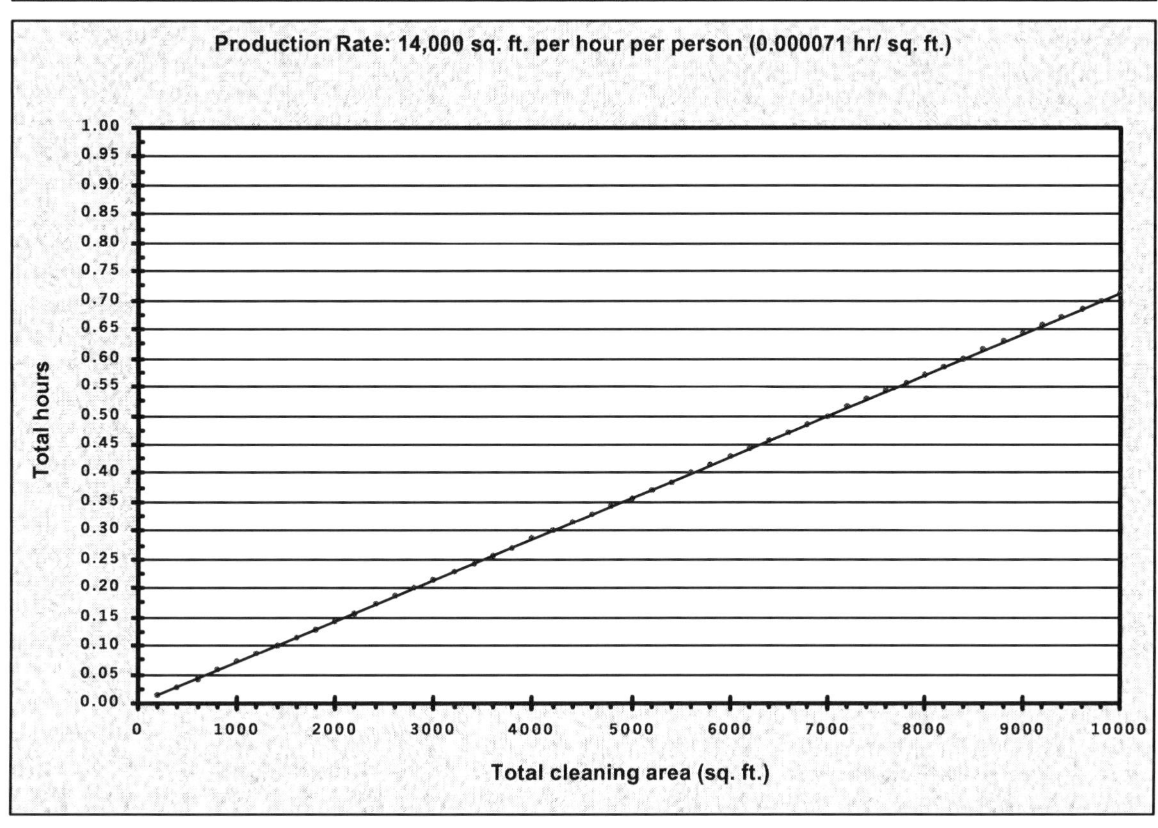
Production Rate: 14,000 sq. ft. per hour per person (0.000071 hr/ sq. ft.)
Total hours
1.00
0.95
0.90
0.85
0.80
0.75
0.70
0.65
0.60
0.55
0.50
0.45
0.40
0.35
0.30
0.25
0.20
0.15
0.10
0.05
0.00
0
1000
2000
3000
4000
5000
6000
7000
8000
9000
10000
Total cleaning area (sq. ft.)

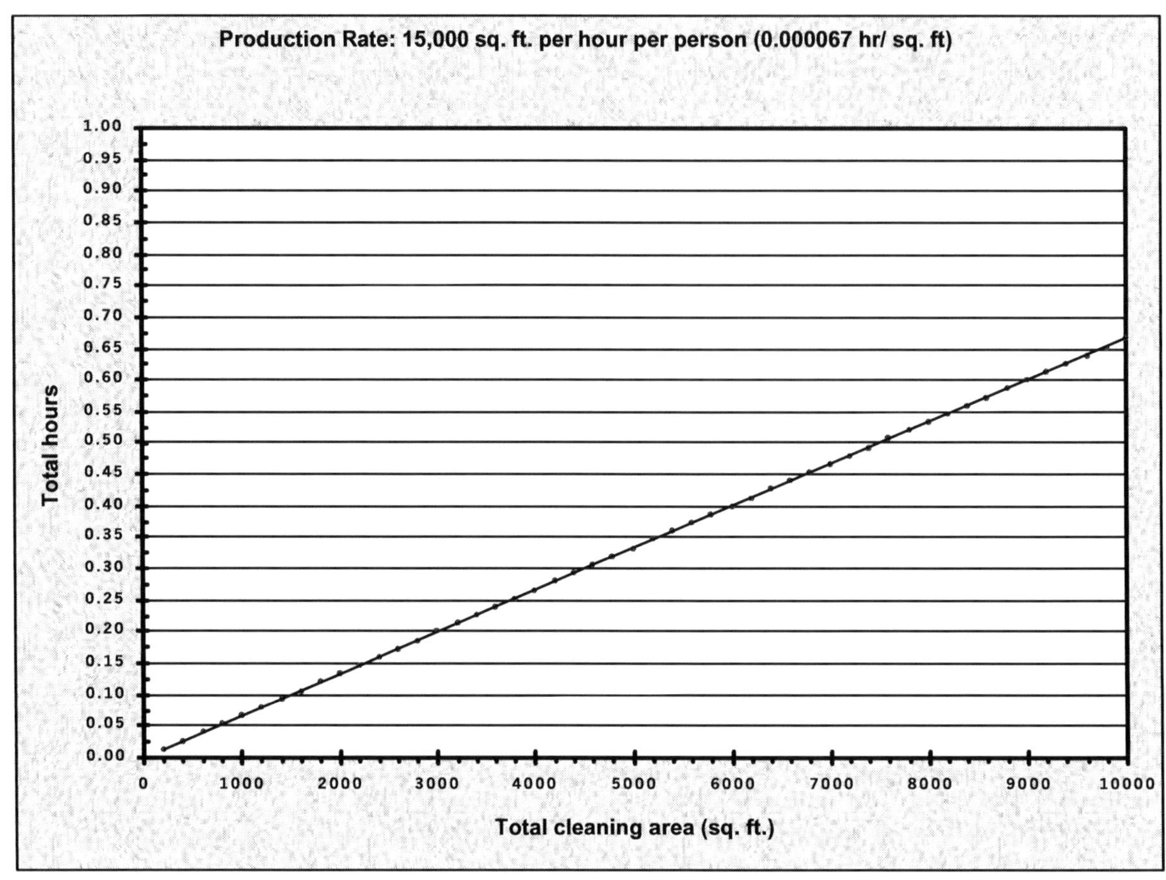
Production Rate: 15,000 sq. ft. per hour per person (0.000067 hr/ sq. ft)
Total hours
1.00
0.95
0.90
0.85
0.80
0.75
0.70
0.65
0.60
0.55
0.50
0.45
0.40
0.35
0.30
0.25
0.20
0.15
0.10
0.05
0.00
0
1000
2000
3000
4000
5000
6000
7000
8000
9000
10000
Total cleaning area (sq. ft.)

Chapter 7

Generic bid pricing: By the job or monthly

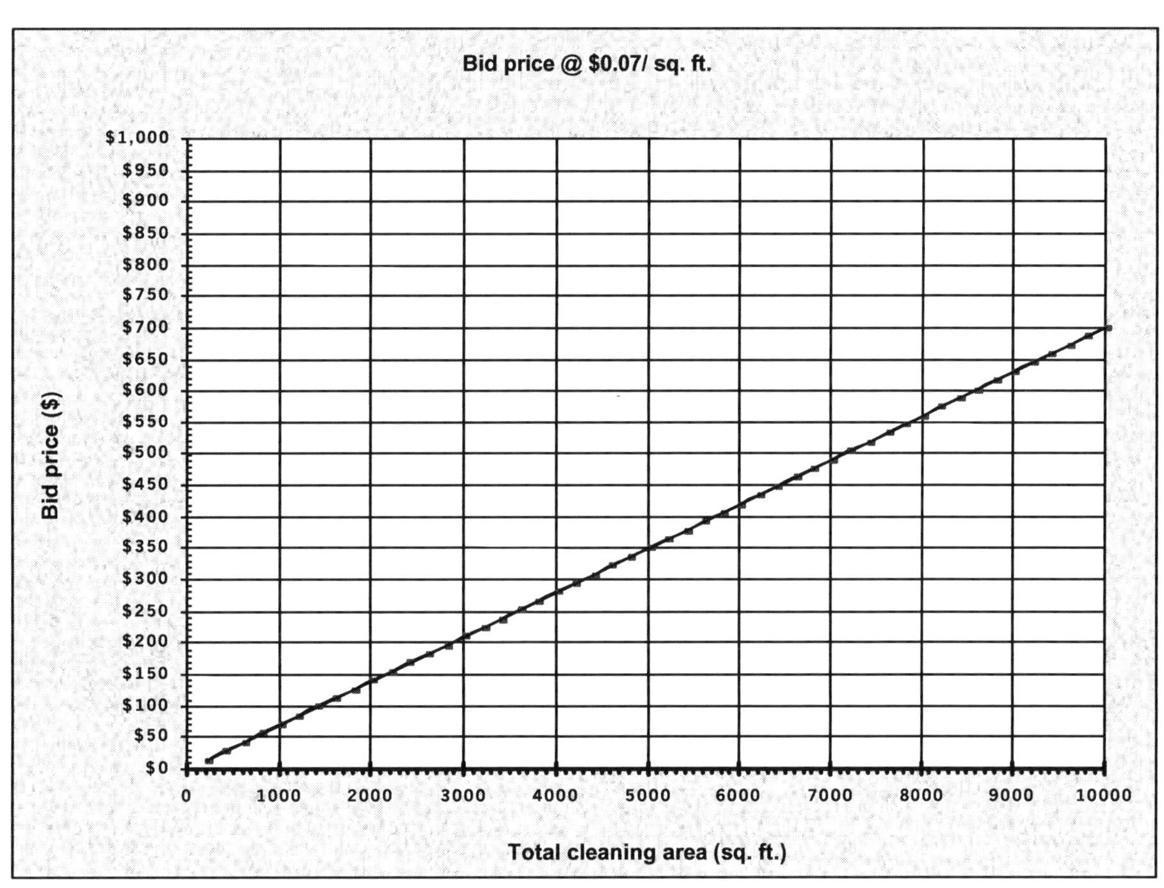

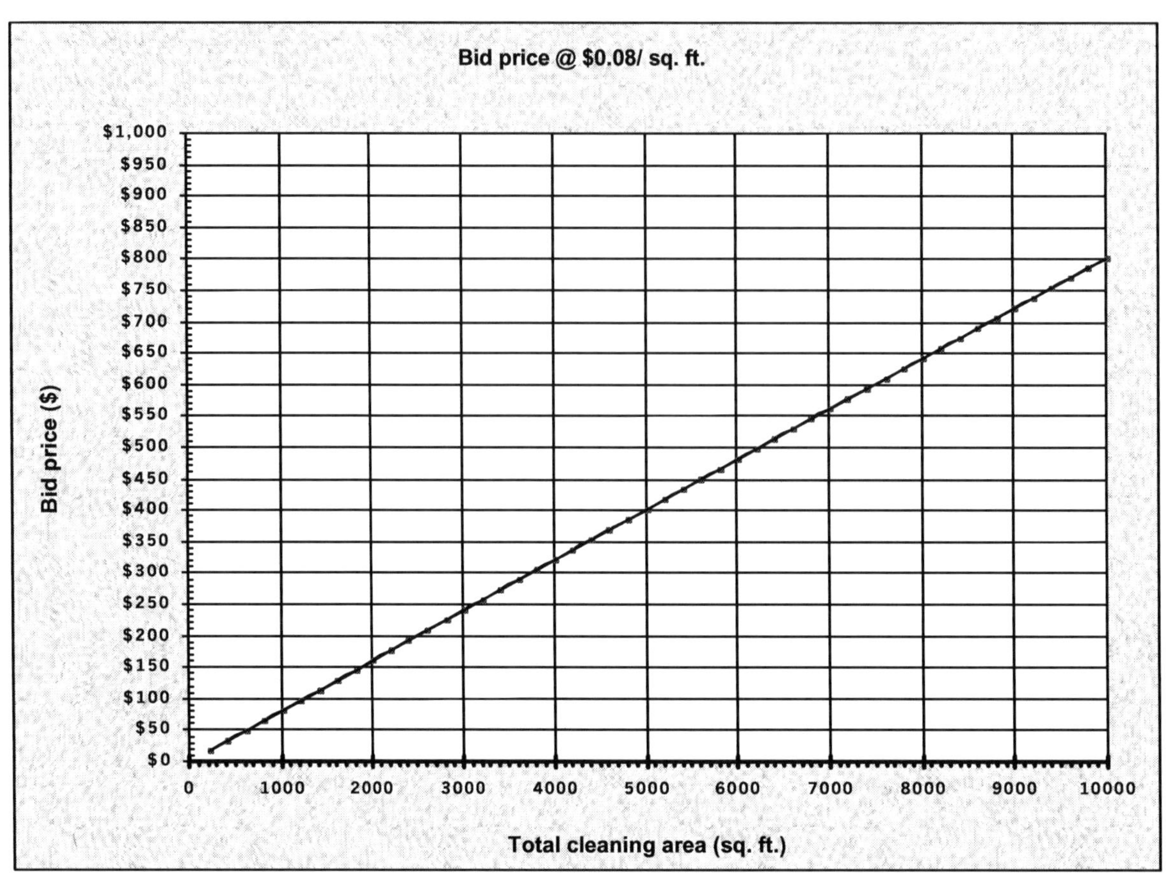
Bid price @ $0.08/ sq. ft.
Bid price ($)
$1,000
$950
$900
$850
$800
$750
$700
$650
$600
$550
$500
$450
$400
$350
$300
$250
$200
$150
$100
$50
$0
0
1000
2000
3000
4000
5000
6000
7000
8000
9000
10000
Total cleaning area (sq. ft.)

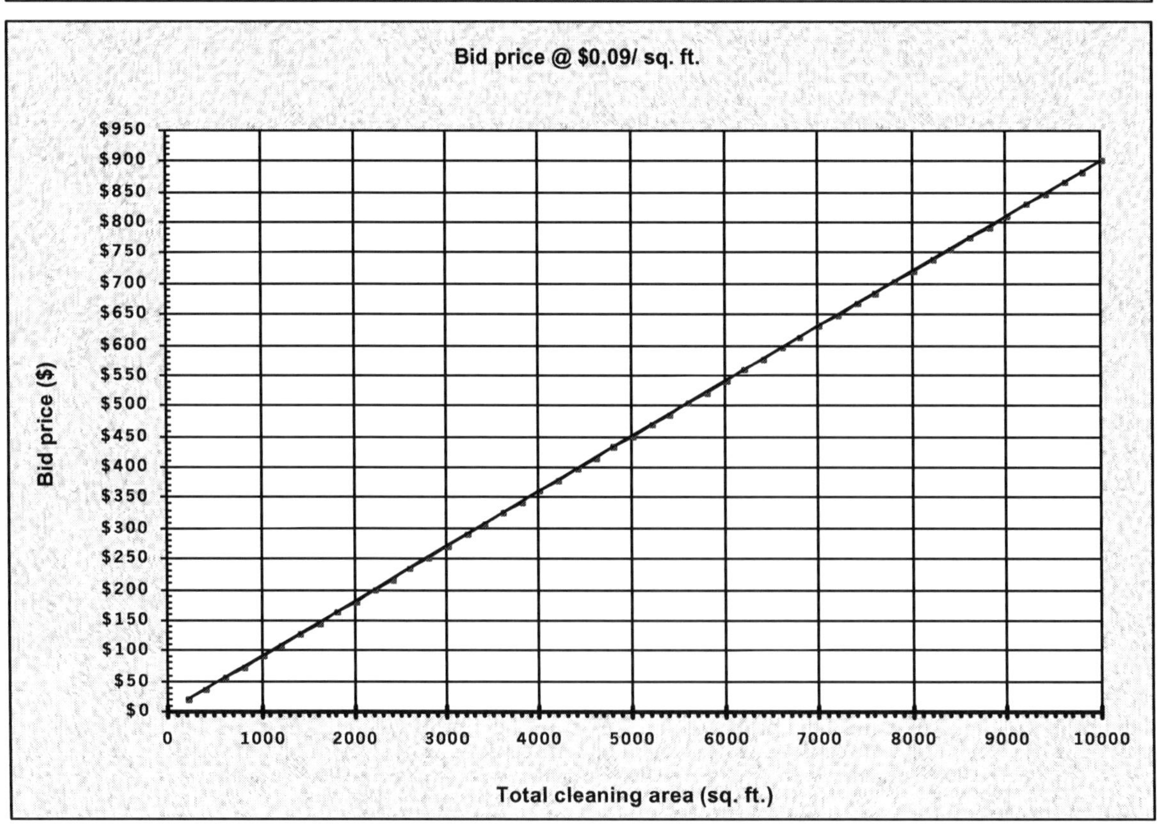
Bid price @ $0.09/ sq. ft.
Bid price ($)
$950
$900
$850
$800
$750
$700
$650
$600
$550
$500
$450
$400
$350
$300
$250
$200
$150
$100
$50
$0
0
1000
2000
3000
4000
5000
6000
7000
8000
9000
10000
Total cleaning area (sq. ft.)

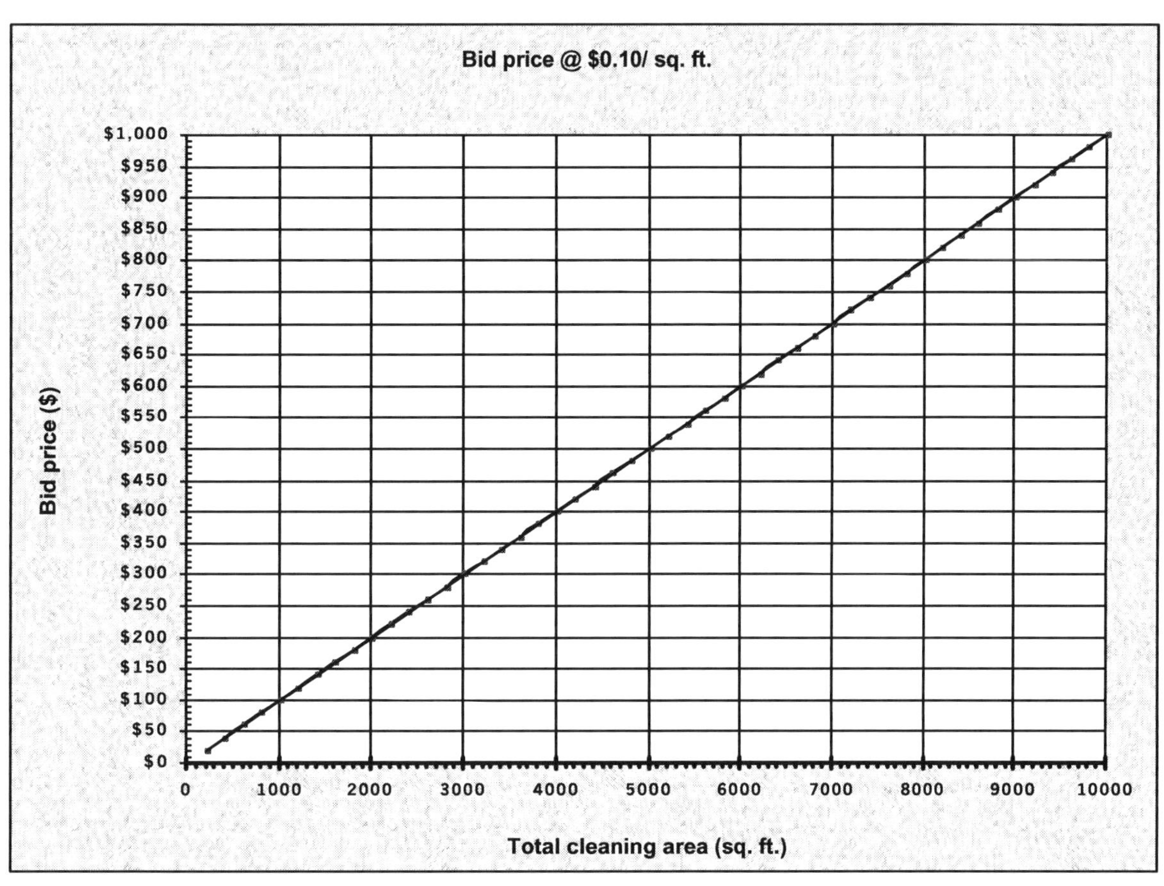
Bid price @ $0.10/ sq. ft.
Bid price ($)
$1,000
$950
$900
$850
$800
$750
$700
$650
$600
$550
$500
$450
$400
$350
$300
$250
$200
$150
$100
$50
$0
0
1000
2000
3000
4000
5000
6000
7000
8000
9000
10000
Total cleaning area (sq. ft.)

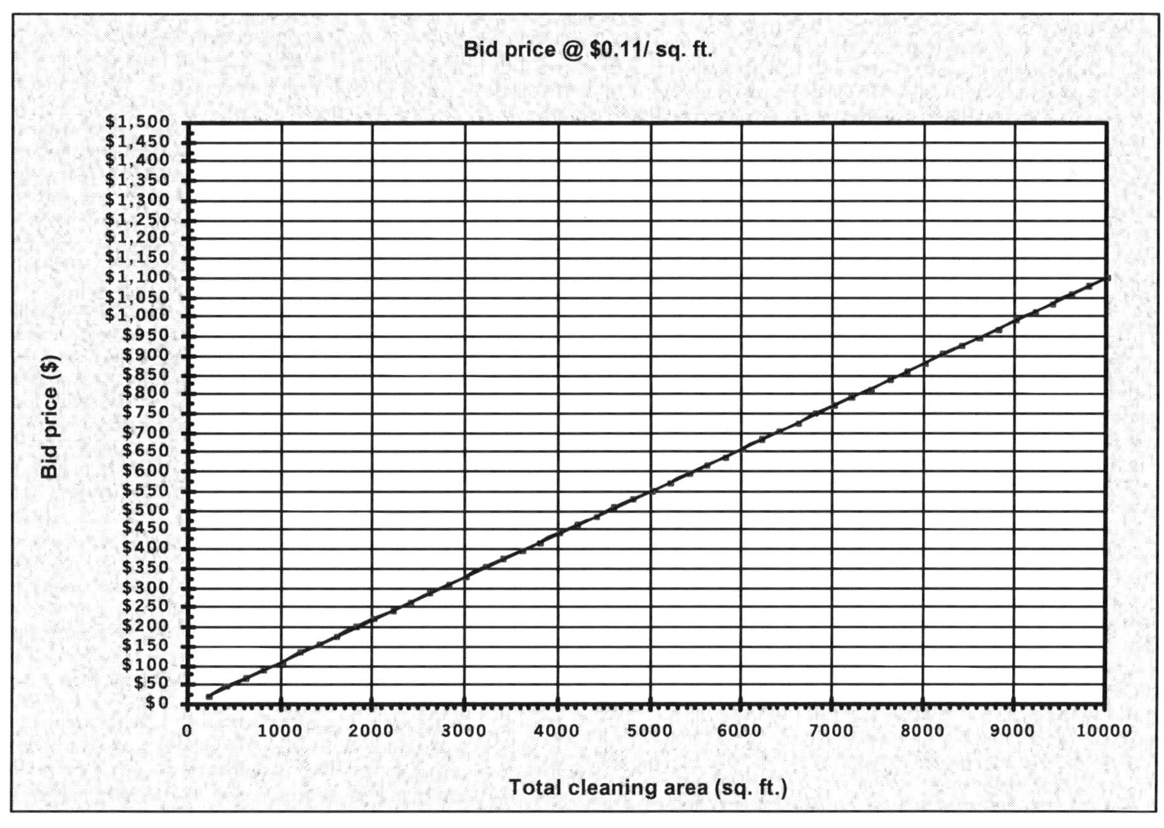
Bid price @ $0.11/ sq. ft.
Bid price ($)
$1,500
$1,450
$1,400
$1,350
$1,300
$1,250
$1,200
$1,150
$1,100
$1,050
$1,000
$950
$900
$850
$800
$750
$700
$650
$600
$550
$500
$450
$400
$350
$300
$250
$200
$150
$100
$50
$0
0
1000
2000
3000
4000
5000
6000
7000
8000
9000
10000
Total cleaning area (sq. ft.)

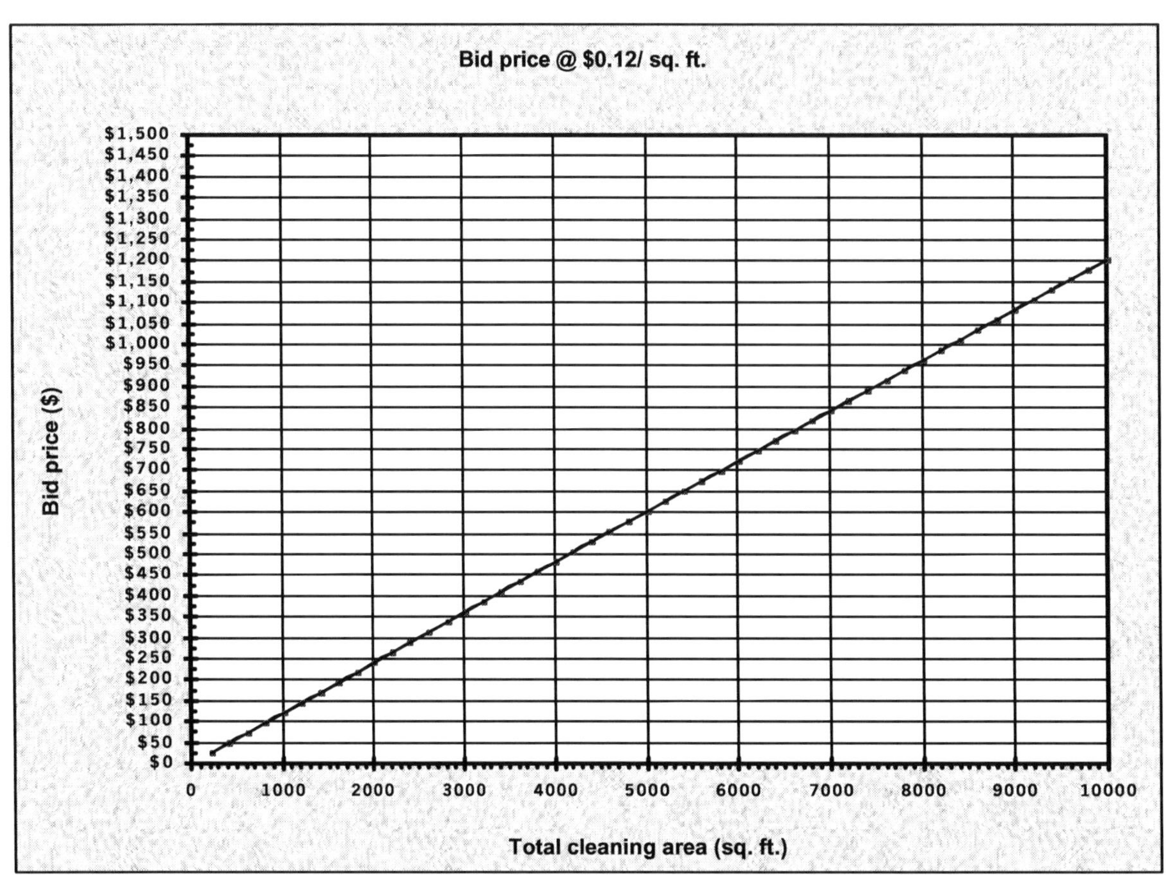
Bid price @ $0.12/ sq. ft.
Bid price ($)
$1,500
$1,450
$1,400
$1,350
$1,300
$1,250
$1,200
$1,150
$1,100
$1,050
$1,000
$950
$900
$850
$800
$750
$700
$650
$600
$550
$500
$450
$400
$350
$300
$250
$200
$150
$100
$50
$0
0
1000
2000
3000
4000
5000
6000
7000
8000
9000
10000
Total cleaning area (sq. ft.)

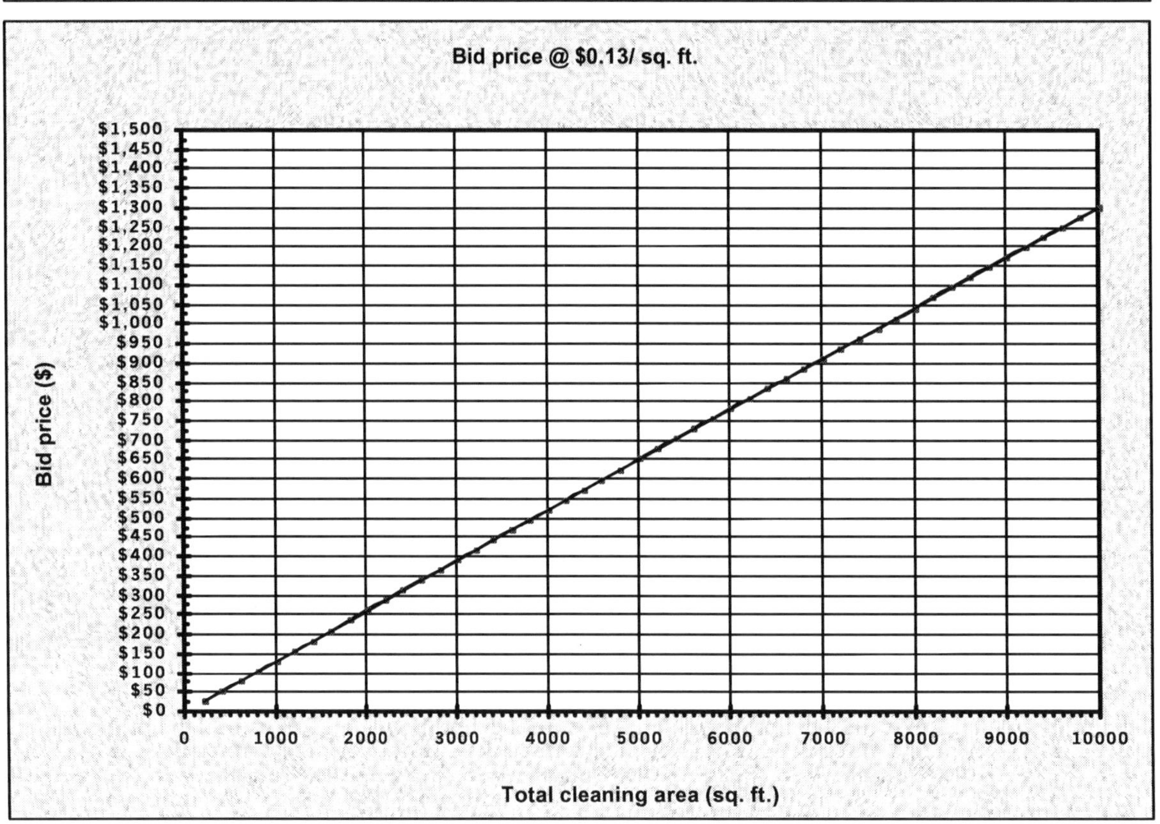
Bid price @ $0.13/ sq. ft.
Bid price ($)
$1,500
$1,450
$1,400
$1,350
$1,300
$1,250
$1,200
$1,150
$1,100
$1,050
$1,000
$950
$900
$850
$800
$750
$700
$650
$600
$550
$500
$450
$400
$350
$300
$250
$200
$150
$100
$50
$0
0
1000
2000
3000
4000
5000
6000
7000
8000
9000
10000
Total cleaning area (sq. ft.)

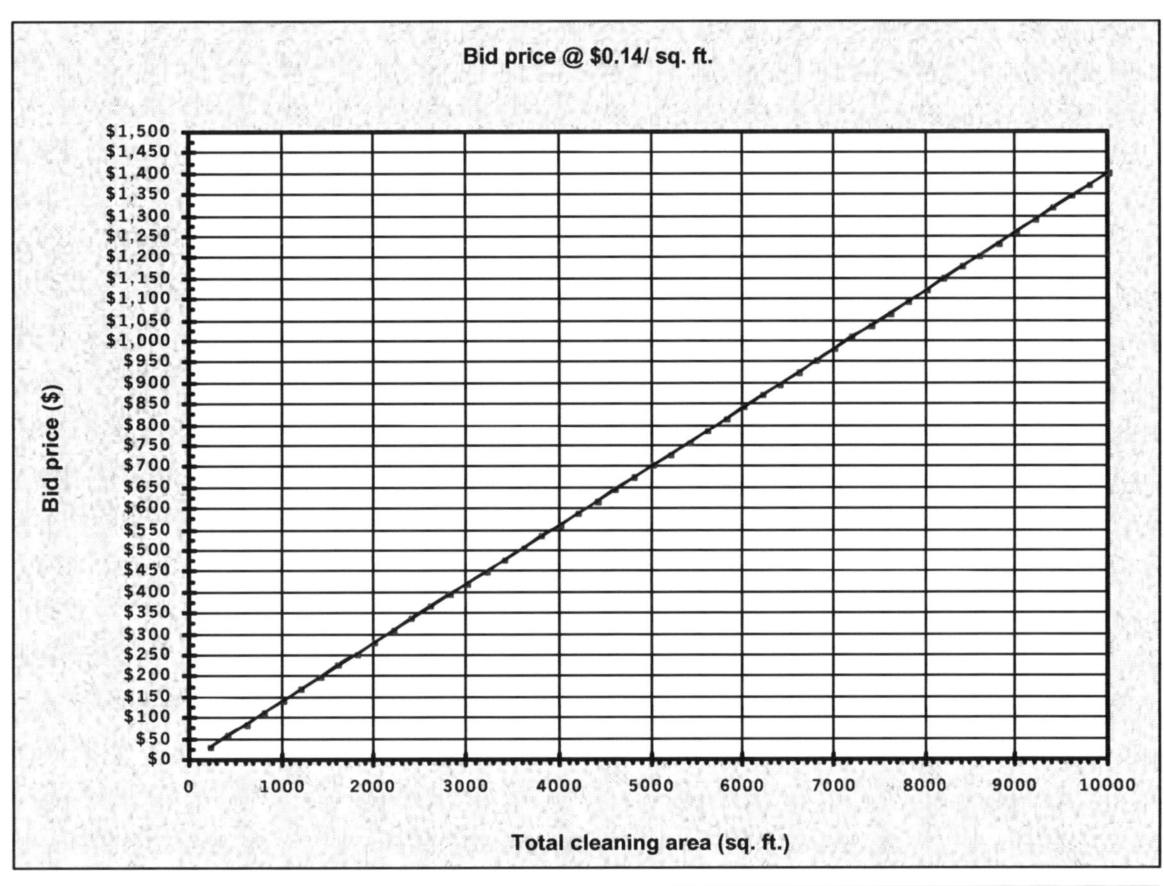
Bid price @ $0.14/ sq. ft.
Bid price ($)
$1,500
$1,450
$1,400
$1,350
$1,300
$1,250
$1,200
$1,150
$1,100
$1,050
$1,000
$950
$900
$850
$800
$750
$700
$650
$600
$550
$500
$450
$400
$350
$300
$250
$200
$150
$100
$50
$0
0
1000
2000
3000
4000
5000
6000
7000
8000
9000
10000
Total cleaning area (sq. ft.)

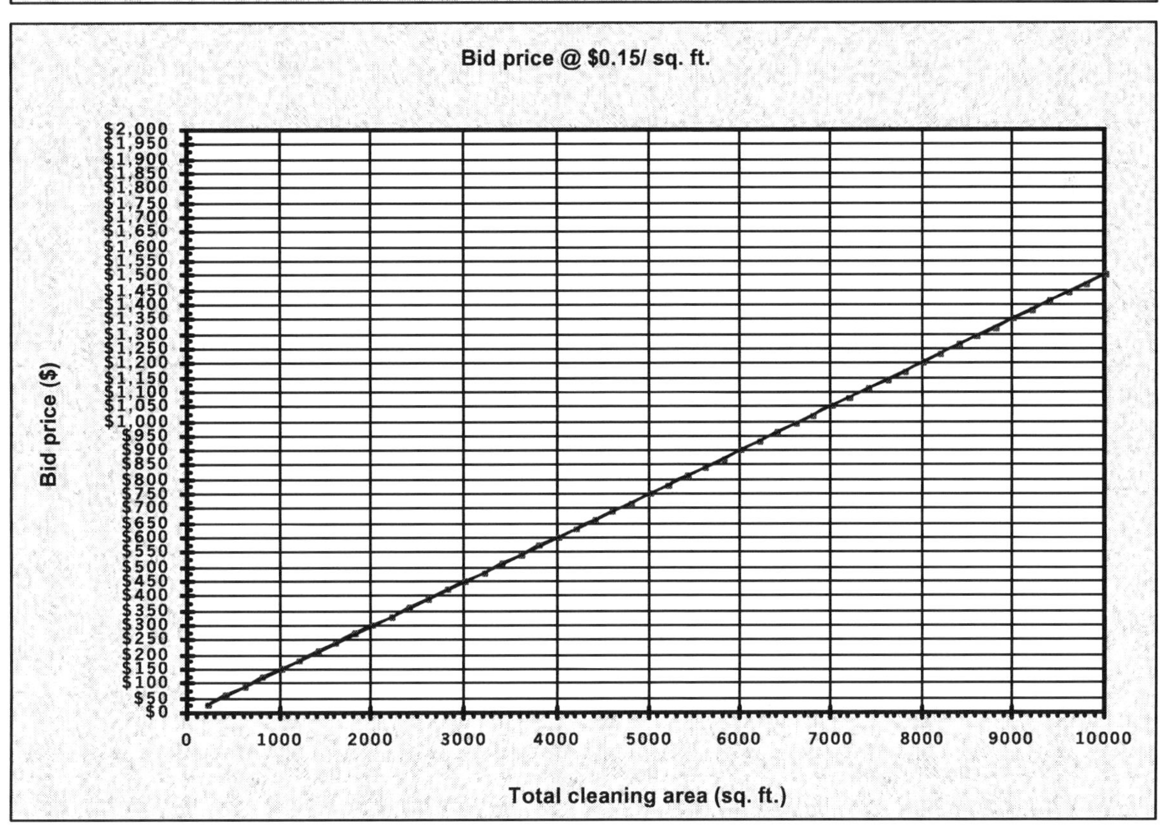
Bid price @ $0.15/ sq. ft.
Bid price ($)
$2,000
$1,500
$1,000
$500
$0
0
1000
2000
3000
4000
5000
6000
7000
8000
9000
10000
Total cleaning area (sq. ft.)

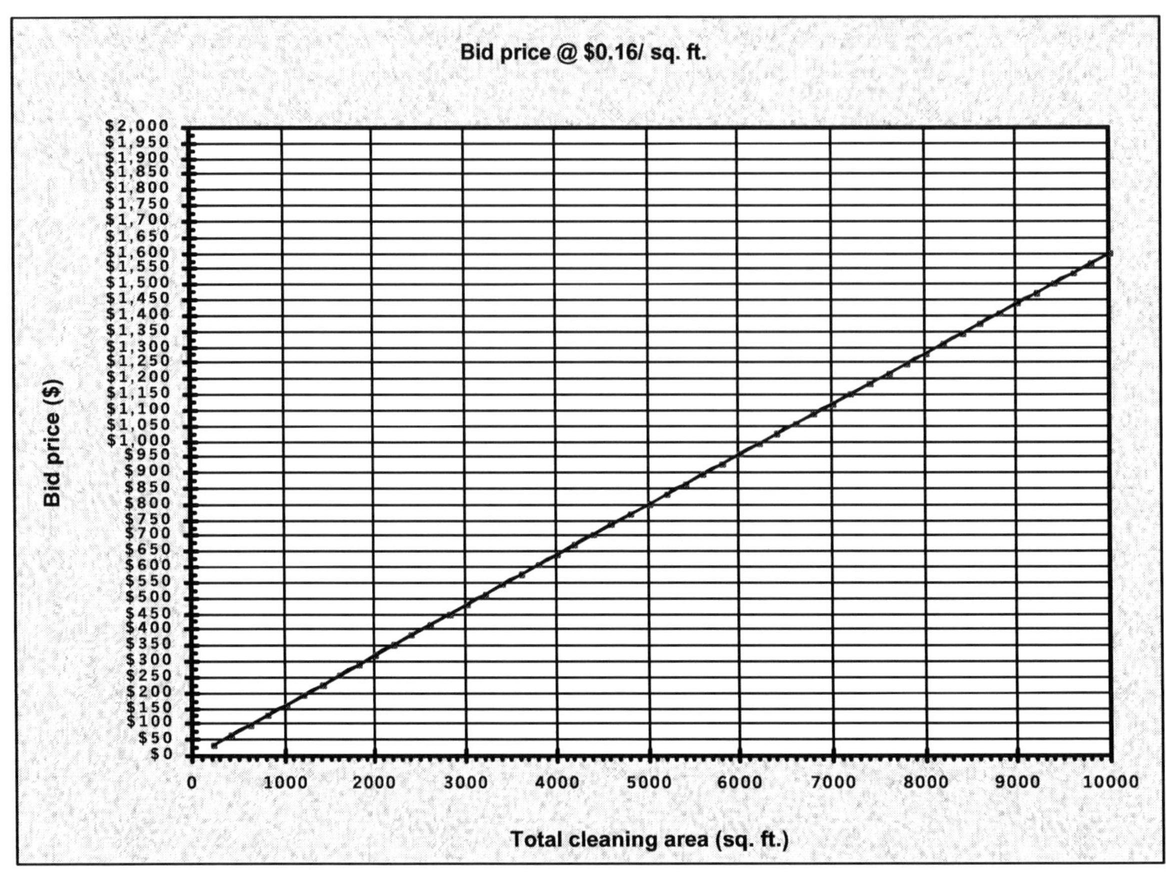
Bid price @ $0.16/ sq. ft.
Bid price ($)
$2,000
$1,950
$1,900
$1,850
$1,800
$1,750
$1,700
$1,650
$1,600
$1,550
$1,500
$1,450
$1,400
$1,350
$1,300
$1,250
$1,200
$1,150
$1,100
$1,050
$1,000
$950
$900
$850
$800
$750
$700
$650
$600
$550
$500
$450
$400
$350
$300
$250
$200
$150
$100
$50
$0
0
1000
2000
3000
4000
5000
6000
7000
8000
9000
10000
Total cleaning area (sq. ft.)

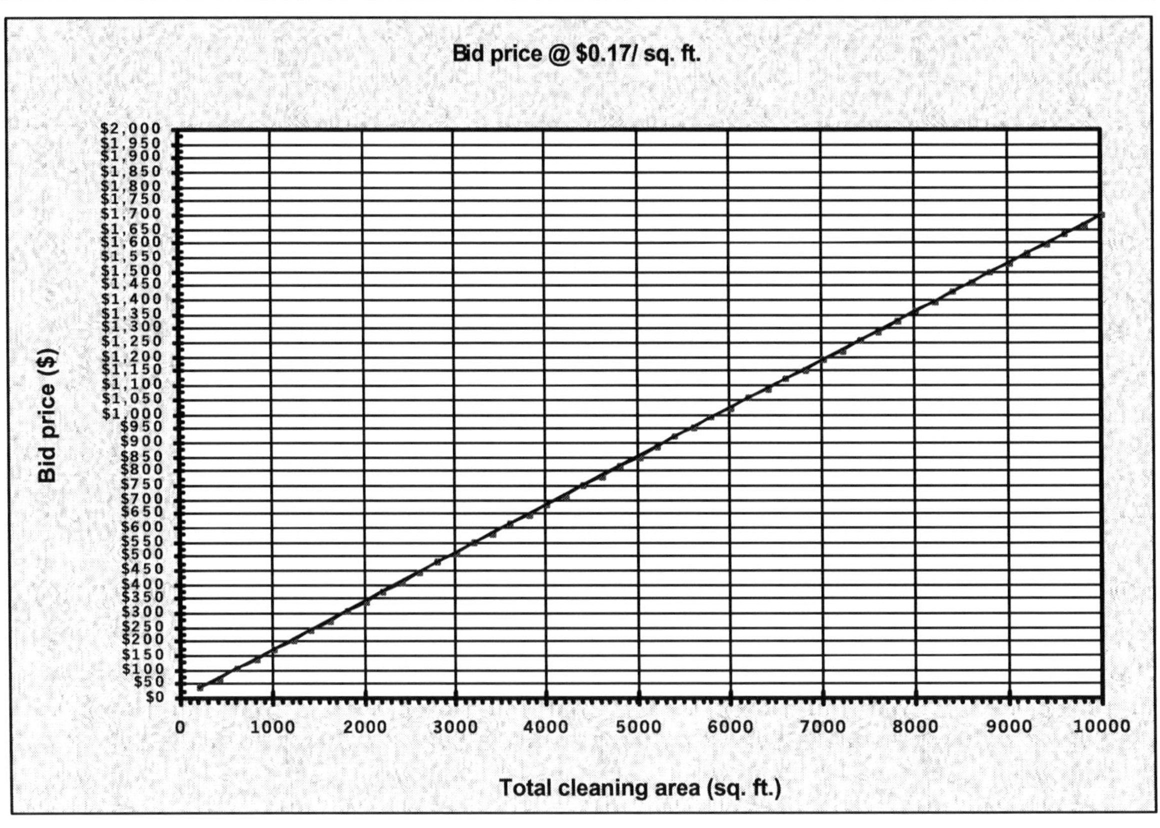
Bid price @ $0.17/ sq. ft.
Bid price ($)
$2,000
$1,950
$1,900
$1,850
$1,800
$1,750
$1,700
$1,650
$1,600
$1,550
$1,500
$1,450
$1,400
$1,350
$1,300
$1,250
$1,200
$1,150
$1,100
$1,050
$1,000
$950
$900
$850
$800
$750
$700
$650
$600
$550
$500
$450
$400
$350
$300
$250
$200
$150
$100
$50
$0
0
1000
2000
3000
4000
5000
6000
7000
8000
9000
10000
Total cleaning area (sq. ft.)

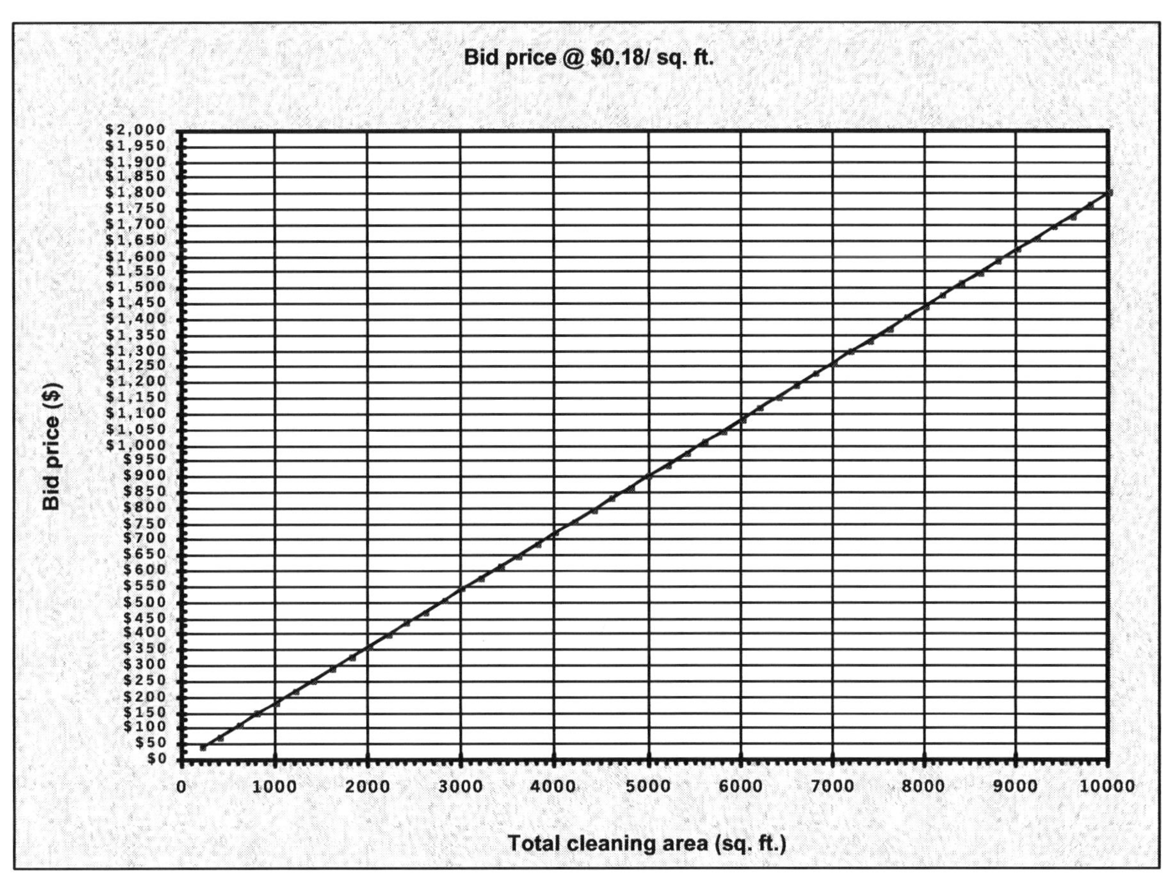
Bid price @ $0.18/ sq. ft.
Bid price ($)
$2,000
$1,950
$1,900
$1,850
$1,800
$1,750
$1,700
$1,650
$1,600
$1,550
$1,500
$1,450
$1,400
$1,350
$1,300
$1,250
$1,200
$1,150
$1,100
$1,050
$1,000
$950
$900
$850
$800
$750
$700
$650
$600
$550
$500
$450
$400
$350
$300
$250
$200
$150
$100
$50
$0
0
1000
2000
3000
4000
5000
6000
7000
8000
9000
10000
Total cleaning area (sq. ft.)

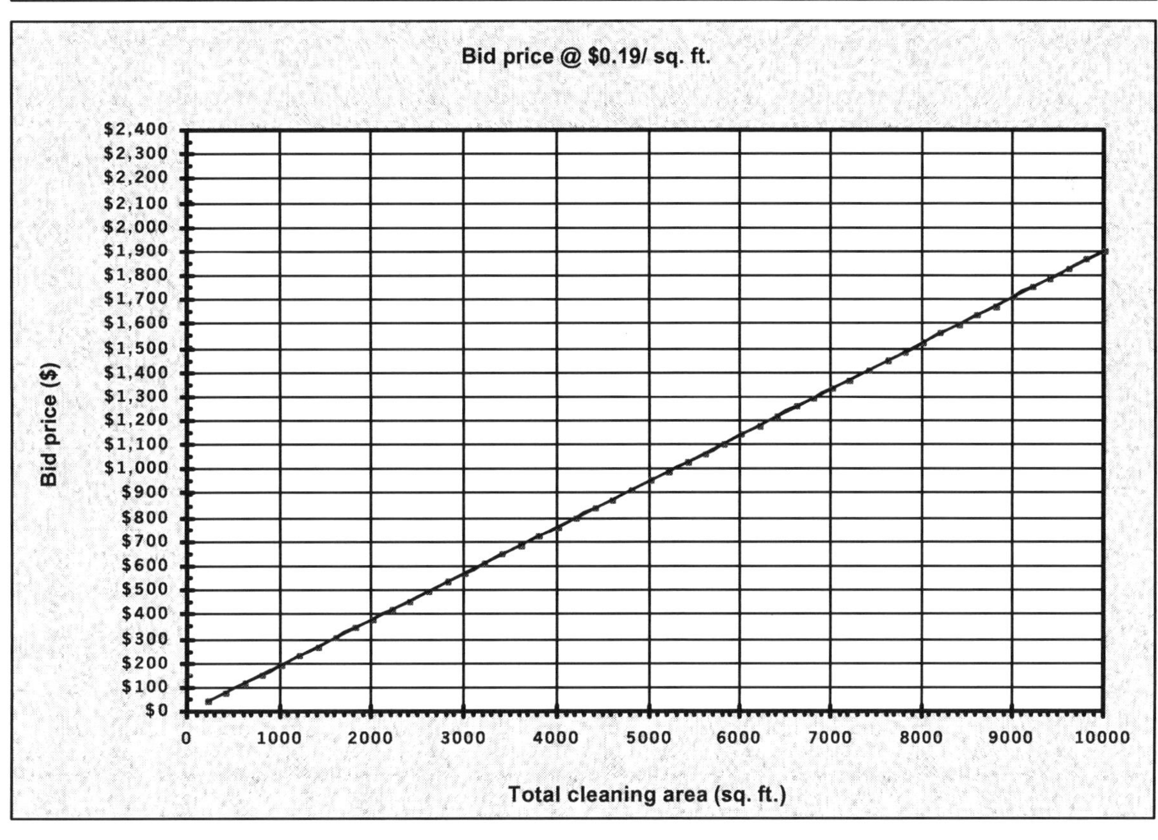
Bid price @ $0.19/ sq. ft.
Bid price ($)
$2,400
$2,300
$2,200
$2,100
$2,000
$1,900
$1,800
$1,700
$1,600
$1,500
$1,400
$1,300
$1,200
$1,100
$1,000
$900
$800
$700
$600
$500
$400
$300
$200
$100
$0
0
1000
2000
3000
4000
5000
6000
7000
8000
9000
10000
Total cleaning area (sq. ft.)

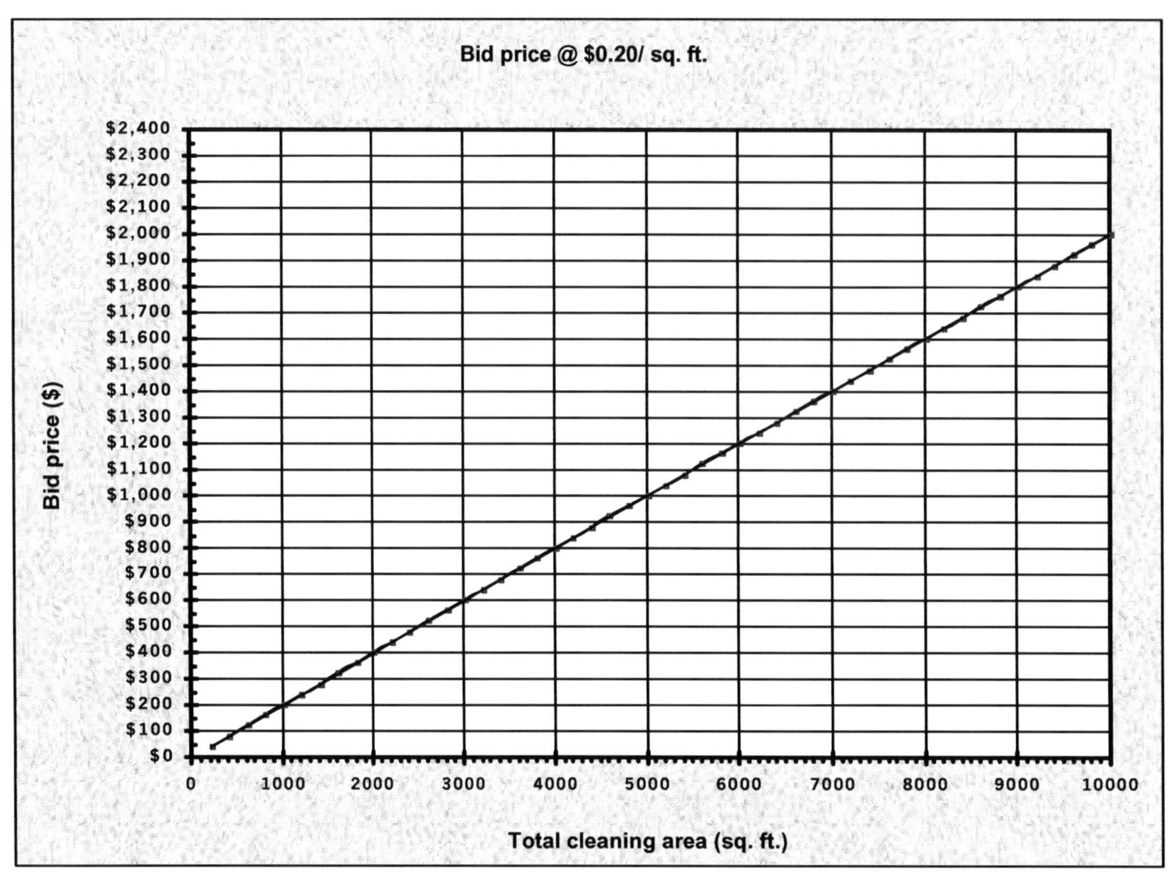
Bid price @ $0.20/ sq. ft.
Bid price ($)
$2,400
$2,300
$2,200
$2,100
$2,000
$1,900
$1,800
$1,700
$1,600
$1,500
$1,400
$1,300
$1,200
$1,100
$1,000
$900
$800
$700
$600
$500
$400
$300
$200
$100
$0
0
1000
2000
3000
4000
5000
6000
7000
8000
9000
10000
Total cleaning area (sq. ft.)

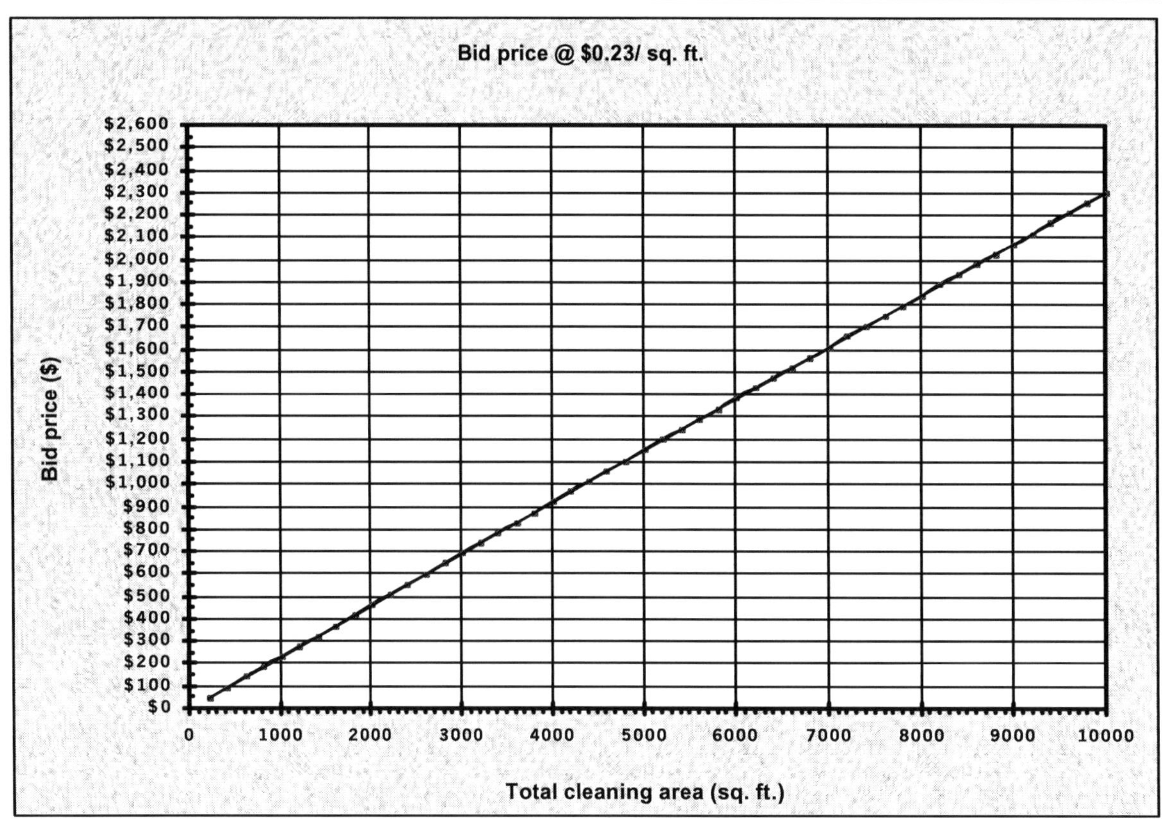
Bid price @ $0.23/ sq. ft.
Bid price ($)
$2,600
$2,500
$2,400
$2,300
$2,200
$2,100
$2,000
$1,900
$1,800
$1,700
$1,600
$1,500
$1,400
$1,300
$1,200
$1,100
$1,000
$900
$800
$700
$600
$500
$400
$300
$200
$100
$0
0
1000
2000
3000
4000
5000
6000
7000
8000
9000
10000
Total cleaning area (sq. ft.)

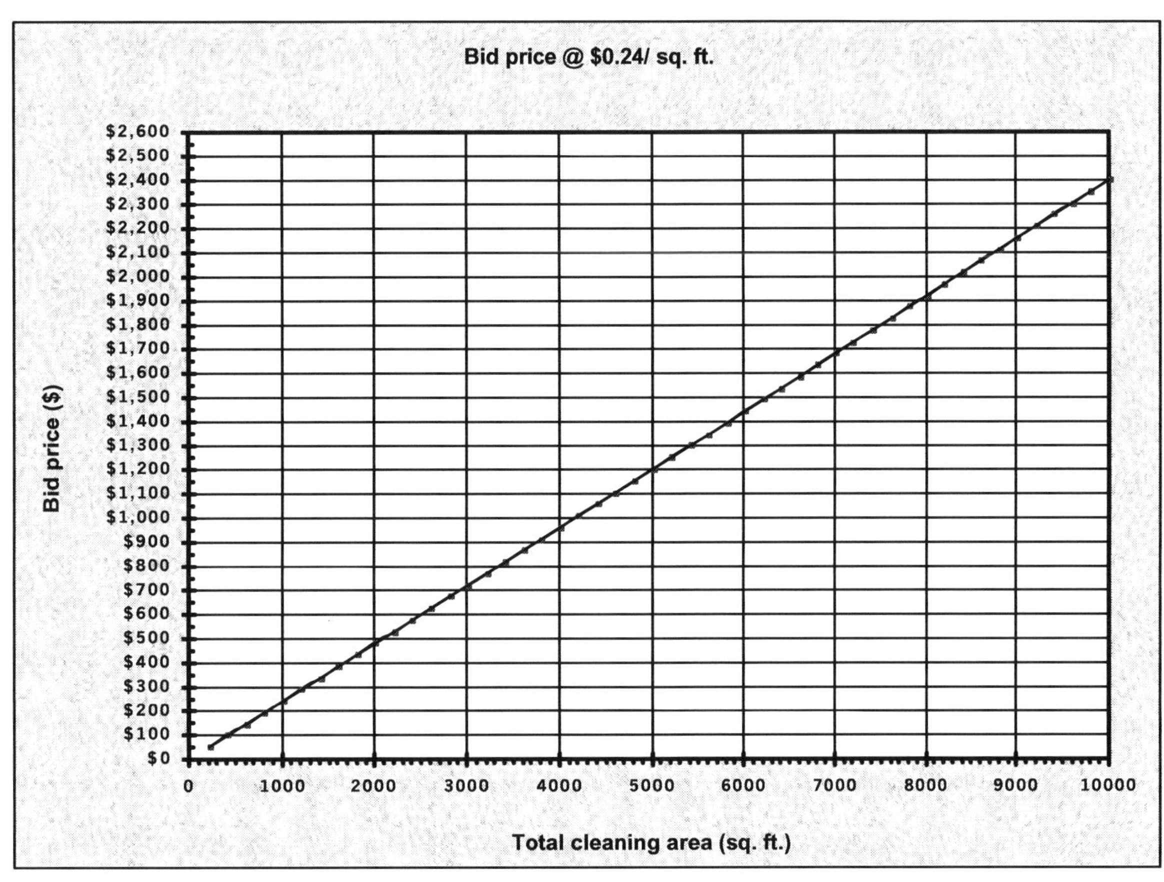
Bid price @ $0.24/ sq. ft.
Bid price ($)
$2,600
$2,500
$2,400
$2,300
$2,200
$2,100
$2,000
$1,900
$1,800
$1,700
$1,600
$1,500
$1,400
$1,300
$1,200
$1,100
$1,000
$900
$800
$700
$600
$500
$400
$300
$200
$100
$0
0
1000
2000
3000
4000
5000
6000
7000
8000
9000
10000
Total cleaning area (sq. ft.)

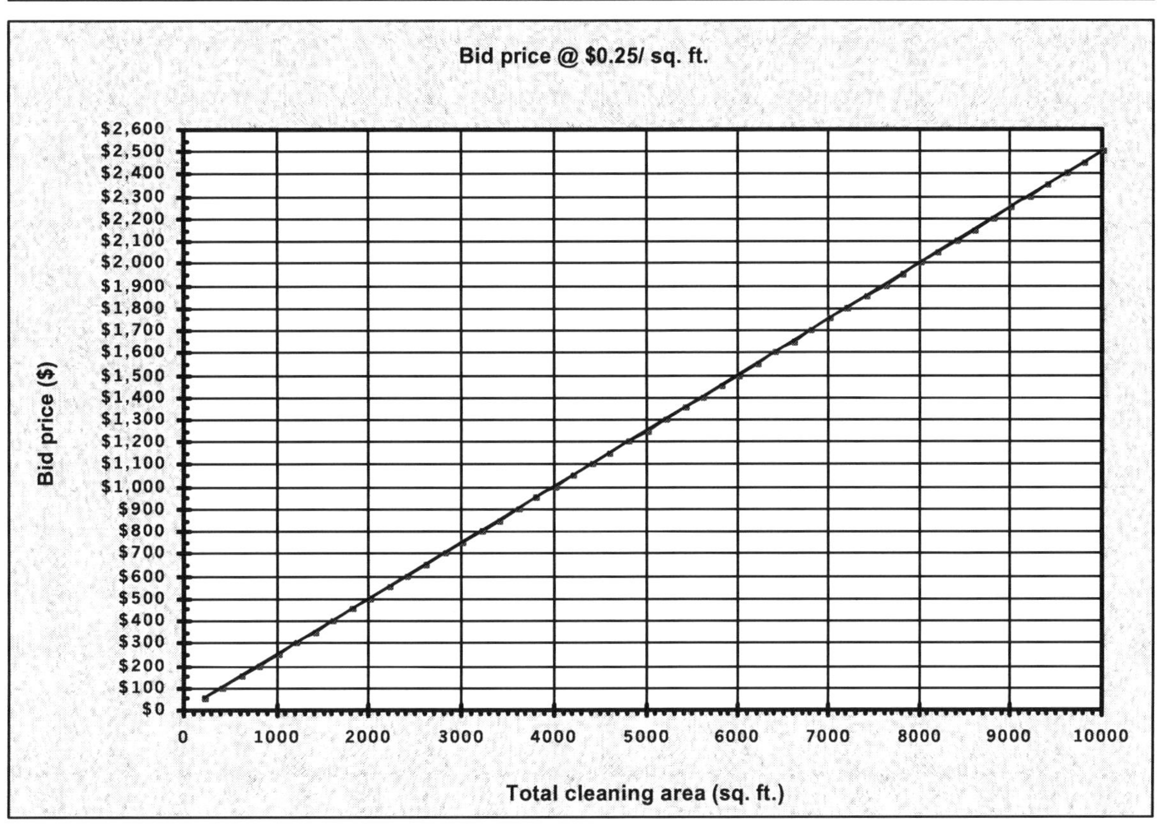
Bid price @ $0.25/ sq. ft.
Bid price ($)
$2,600
$2,500
$2,400
$2,300
$2,200
$2,100
$2,000
$1,900
$1,800
$1,700
$1,600
$1,500
$1,400
$1,300
$1,200
$1,100
$1,000
$900
$800
$700
$600
$500
$400
$300
$200
$100
$0
0
1000
2000
3000
4000
5000
6000
7000
8000
9000
10000
Total cleaning area (sq. ft.)

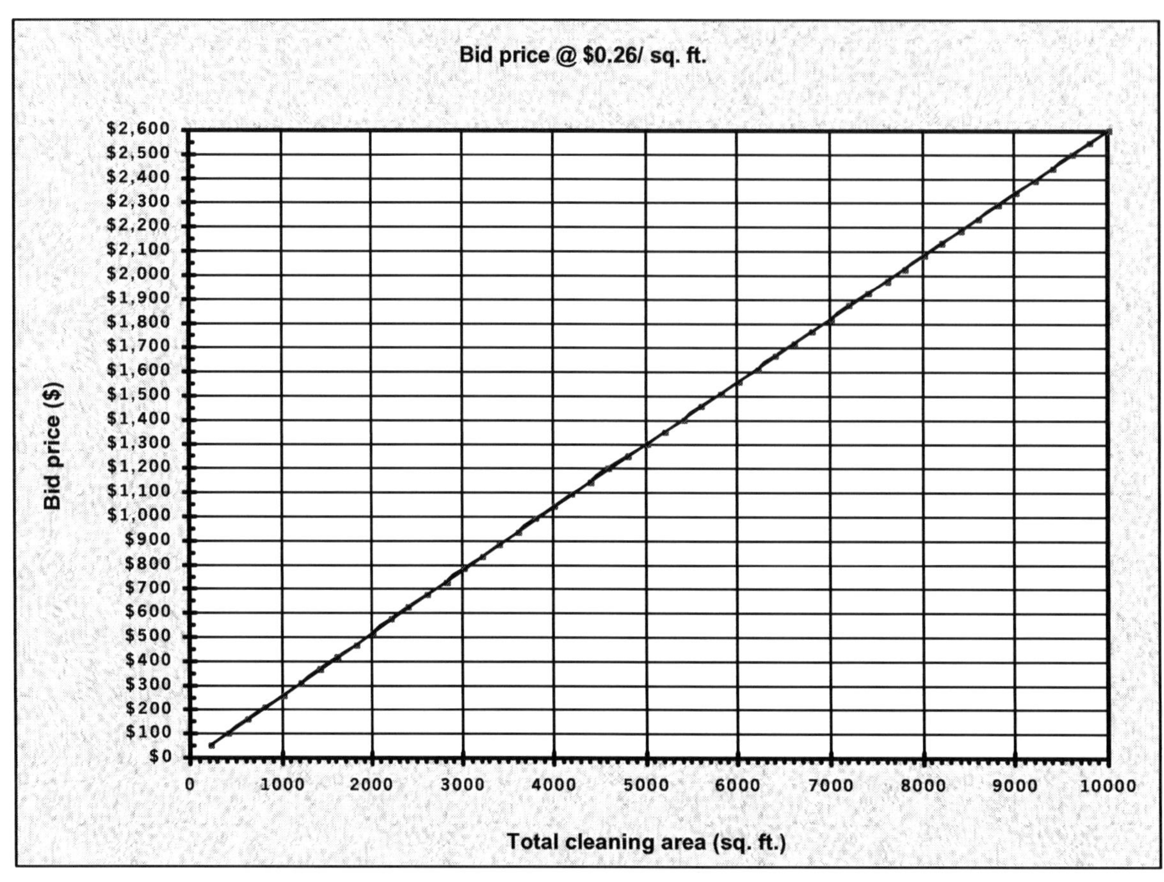
Bid price @ $0.26/ sq. ft.
Bid price ($)
$2,600
$2,500
$2,400
$2,300
$2,200
$2,100
$2,000
$1,900
$1,800
$1,700
$1,600
$1,500
$1,400
$1,300
$1,200
$1,100
$1,000
$900
$800
$700
$600
$500
$400
$300
$200
$100
$0
0
1000
2000
3000
4000
5000
6000
7000
8000
9000
10000
Total cleaning area (sq. ft.)

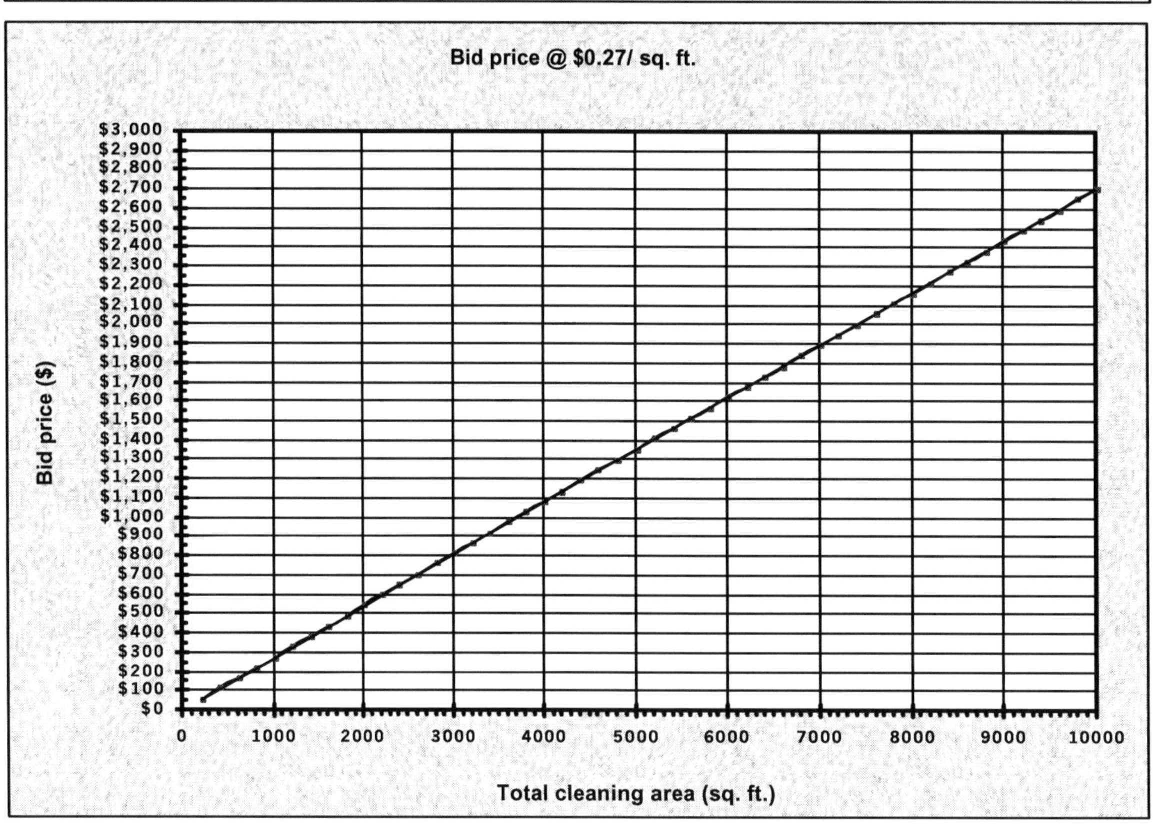
Bid price @ $0.27/ sq. ft.
Bid price ($)
$3,000
$2,900
$2,800
$2,700
$2,600
$2,500
$2,400
$2,300
$2,200
$2,100
$2,000
$1,900
$1,800
$1,700
$1,600
$1,500
$1,400
$1,300
$1,200
$1,100
$1,000
$900
$800
$700
$600
$500
$400
$300
$200
$100
$0
0
1000
2000
3000
4000
5000
6000
7000
8000
9000
10000
Total cleaning area (sq. ft.)

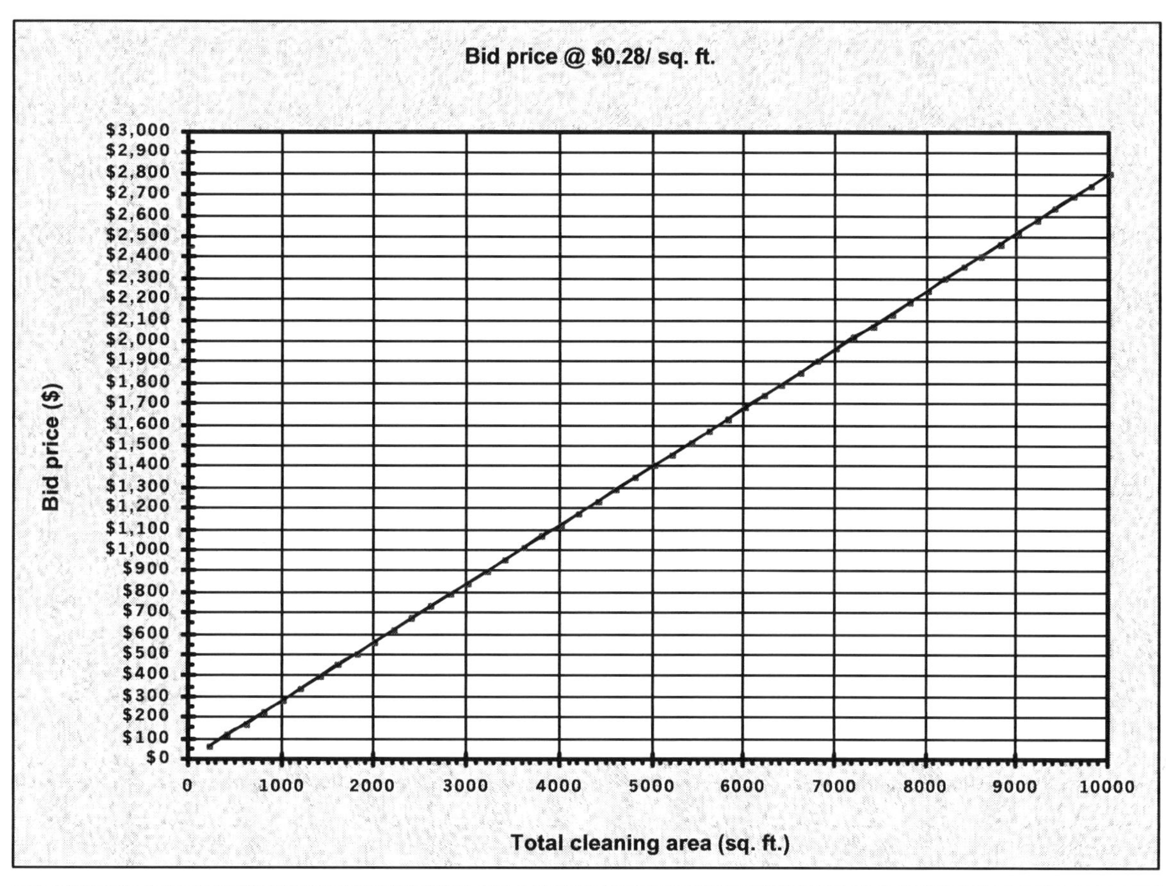
Bid price @ $0.28/ sq. ft.
Bid price ($)
$3,000
$2,900
$2,800
$2,700
$2,600
$2,500
$2,400
$2,300
$2,200
$2,100
$2,000
$1,900
$1,800
$1,700
$1,600
$1,500
$1,400
$1,300
$1,200
$1,100
$1,000
$900
$800
$700
$600
$500
$400
$300
$200
$100
$0
0
1000
2000
3000
4000
5000
6000
7000
8000
9000
10000
Total cleaning area (sq. ft.)

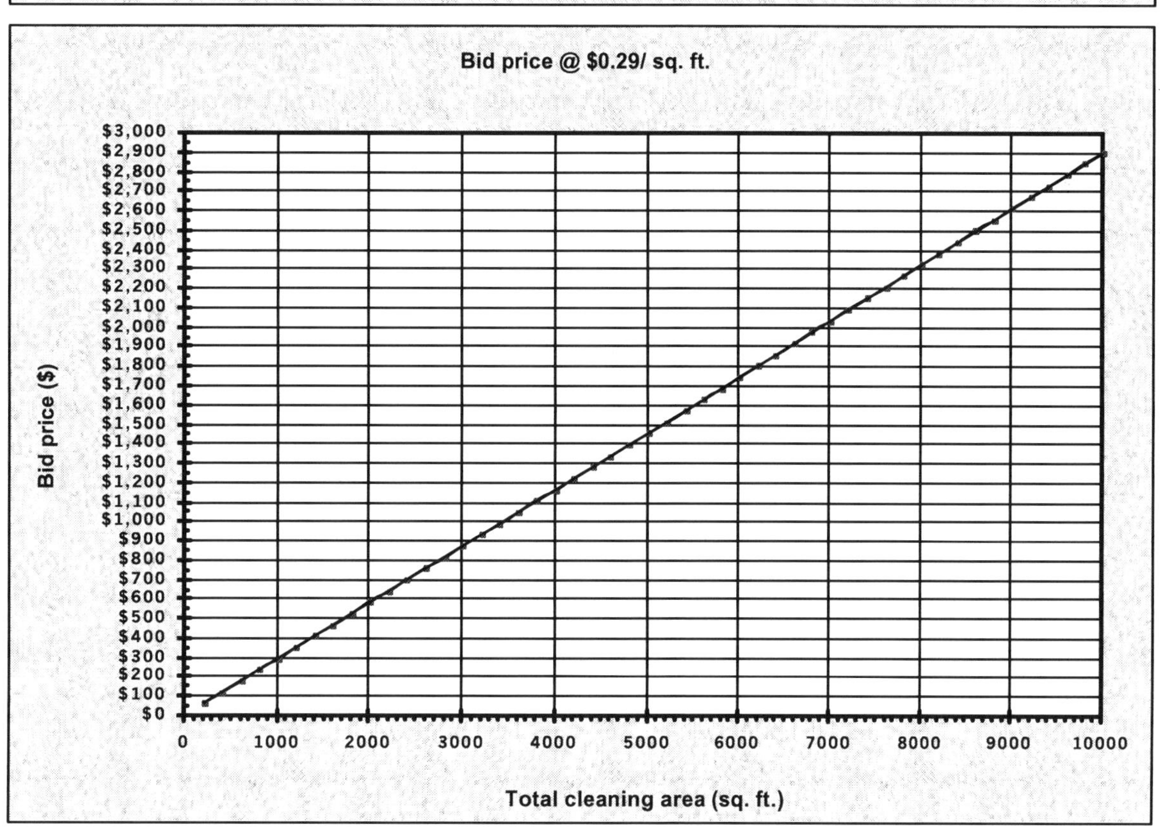
Bid price @ $0.29/ sq. ft.
Bid price ($)
$3,000
$2,900
$2,800
$2,700
$2,600
$2,500
$2,400
$2,300
$2,200
$2,100
$2,000
$1,900
$1,800
$1,700
$1,600
$1,500
$1,400
$1,300
$1,200
$1,100
$1,000
$900
$800
$700
$600
$500
$400
$300
$200
$100
$0
0
1000
2000
3000
4000
5000
6000
7000
8000
9000
10000
Total cleaning area (sq. ft.)

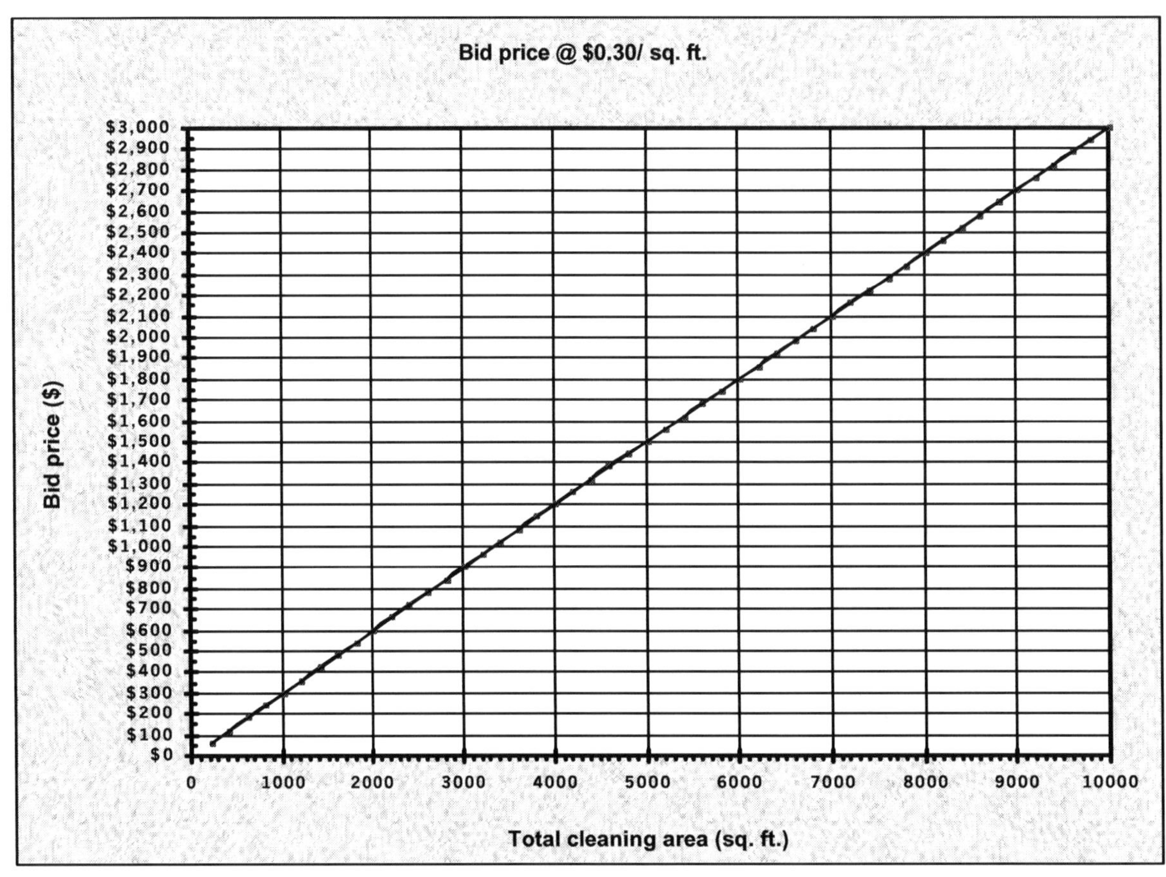
Bid price @ $0.30/ sq. ft.
Bid price ($)
$3,000
$2,900
$2,800
$2,700
$2,600
$2,500
$2,400
$2,300
$2,200
$2,100
$2,000
$1,900
$1,800
$1,700
$1,600
$1,500
$1,400
$1,300
$1,200
$1,100
$1,000
$900
$800
$700
$600
$500
$400
$300
$200
$100
$0
0
1000
2000
3000
4000
5000
6000
7000
8000
9000
10000
Total cleaning area (sq. ft.)

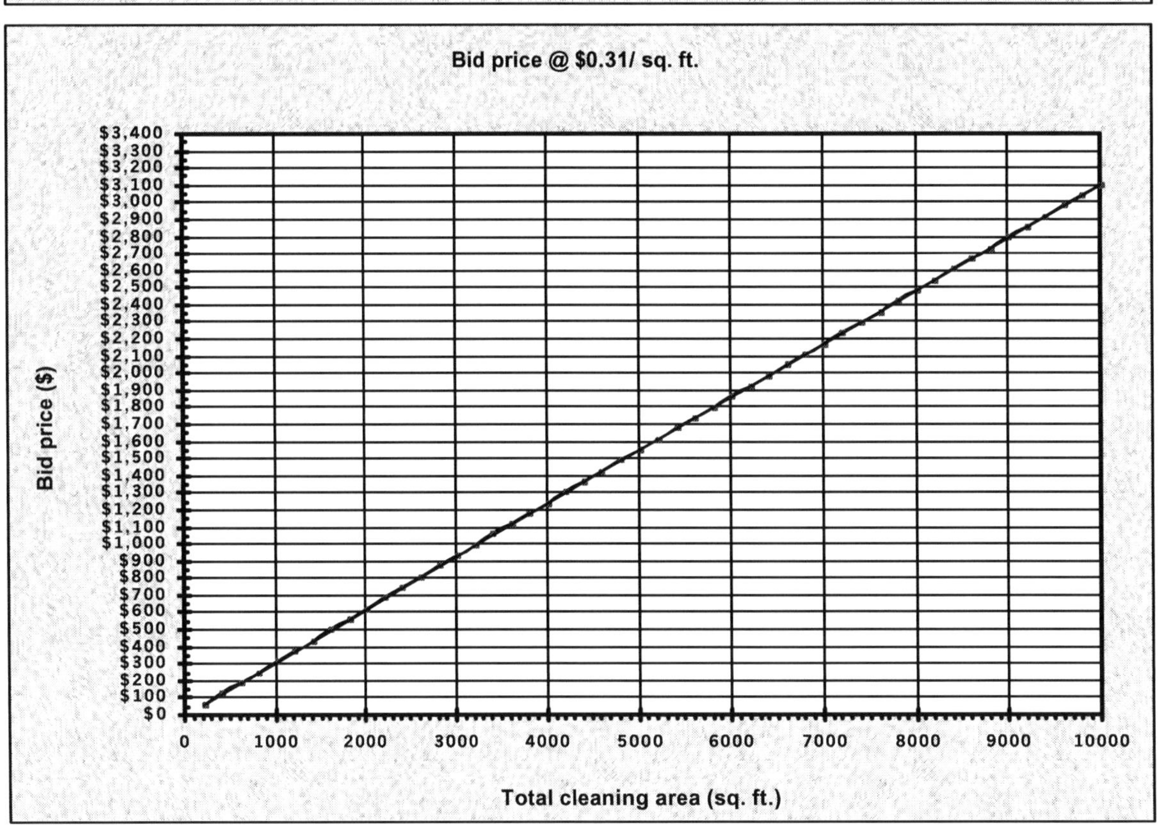
Bid price @ $0.31/ sq. ft.
Bid price ($)
$3,400
$3,300
$3,200
$3,100
$3,000
$2,900
$2,800
$2,700
$2,600
$2,500
$2,400
$2,300
$2,200
$2,100
$2,000
$1,900
$1,800
$1,700
$1,600
$1,500
$1,400
$1,300
$1,200
$1,100
$1,000
$900
$800
$700
$600
$500
$400
$300
$200
$100
$0
0
1000
2000
3000
4000
5000
6000
7000
8000
9000
10000
Total cleaning area (sq. ft.)

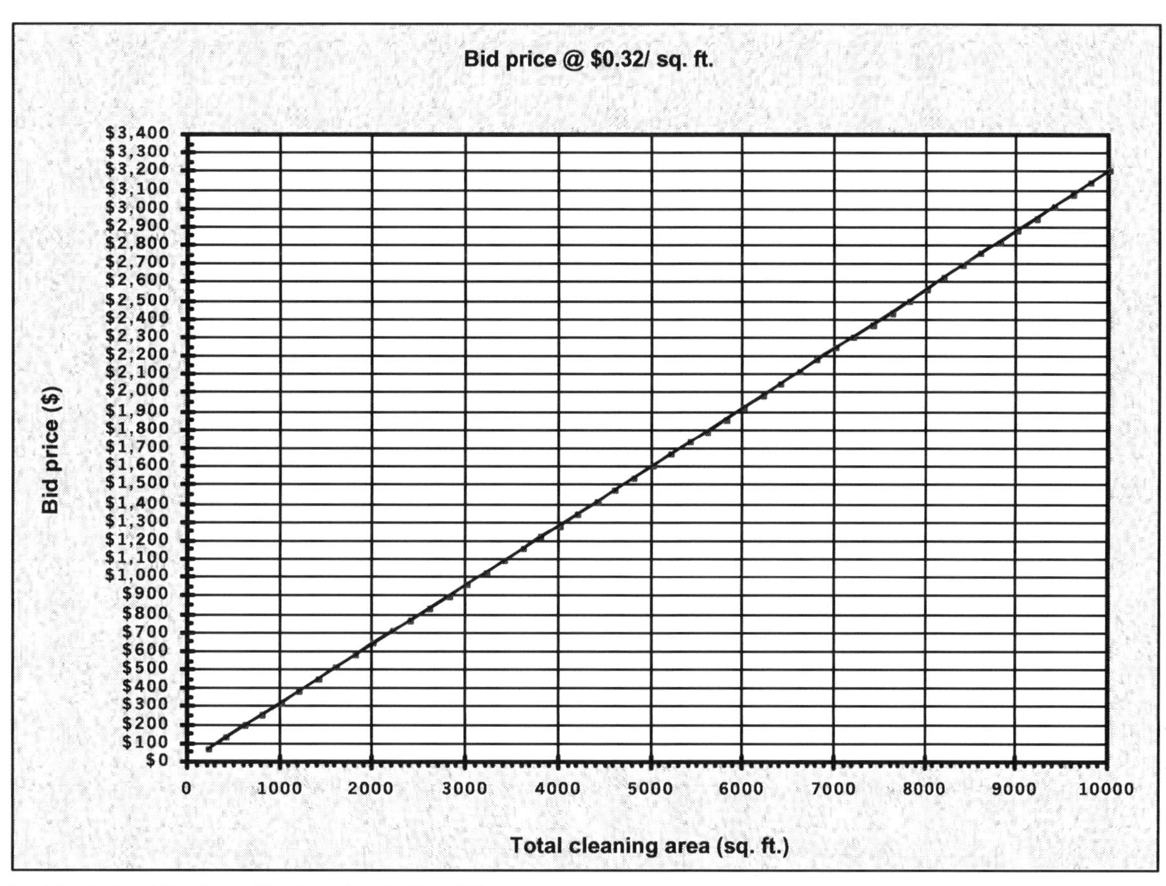
Bid price @ $0.32/ sq. ft.
Bid price ($)
$3,400
$3,300
$3,200
$3,100
$3,000
$2,900
$2,800
$2,700
$2,600
$2,500
$2,400
$2,300
$2,200
$2,100
$2,000
$1,900
$1,800
$1,700
$1,600
$1,500
$1,400
$1,300
$1,200
$1,100
$1,000
$900
$800
$700
$600
$500
$400
$300
$200
$100
$0
0
1000
2000
3000
4000
5000
6000
7000
8000
9000
10000
Total cleaning area (sq. ft.)

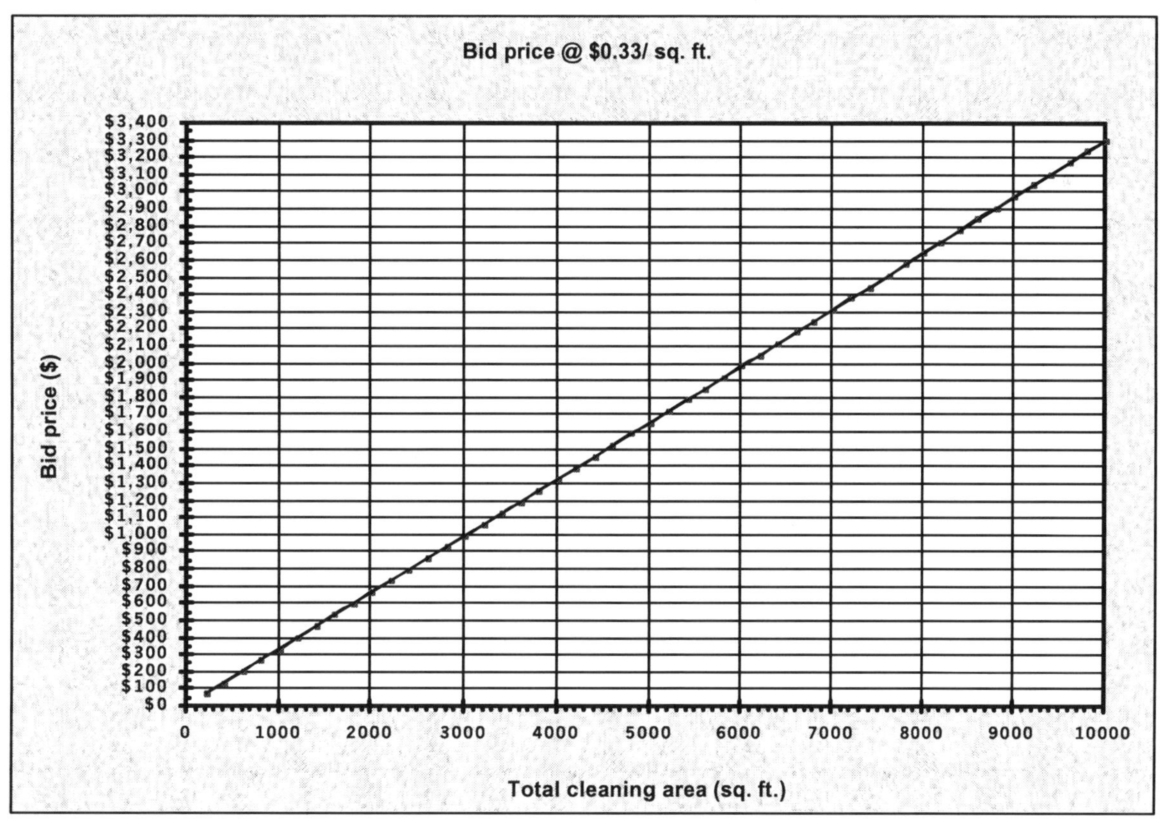
Bid price @ $0.33/ sq. ft.
Bid price ($)
$3,400
$3,300
$3,200
$3,100
$3,000
$2,900
$2,800
$2,700
$2,600
$2,500
$2,400
$2,300
$2,200
$2,100
$2,000
$1,900
$1,800
$1,700
$1,600
$1,500
$1,400
$1,300
$1,200
$1,100
$1,000
$900
$800
$700
$600
$500
$400
$300
$200
$100
$0
0
1000
2000
3000
4000
5000
6000
7000
8000
9000
10000
Total cleaning area (sq. ft.)

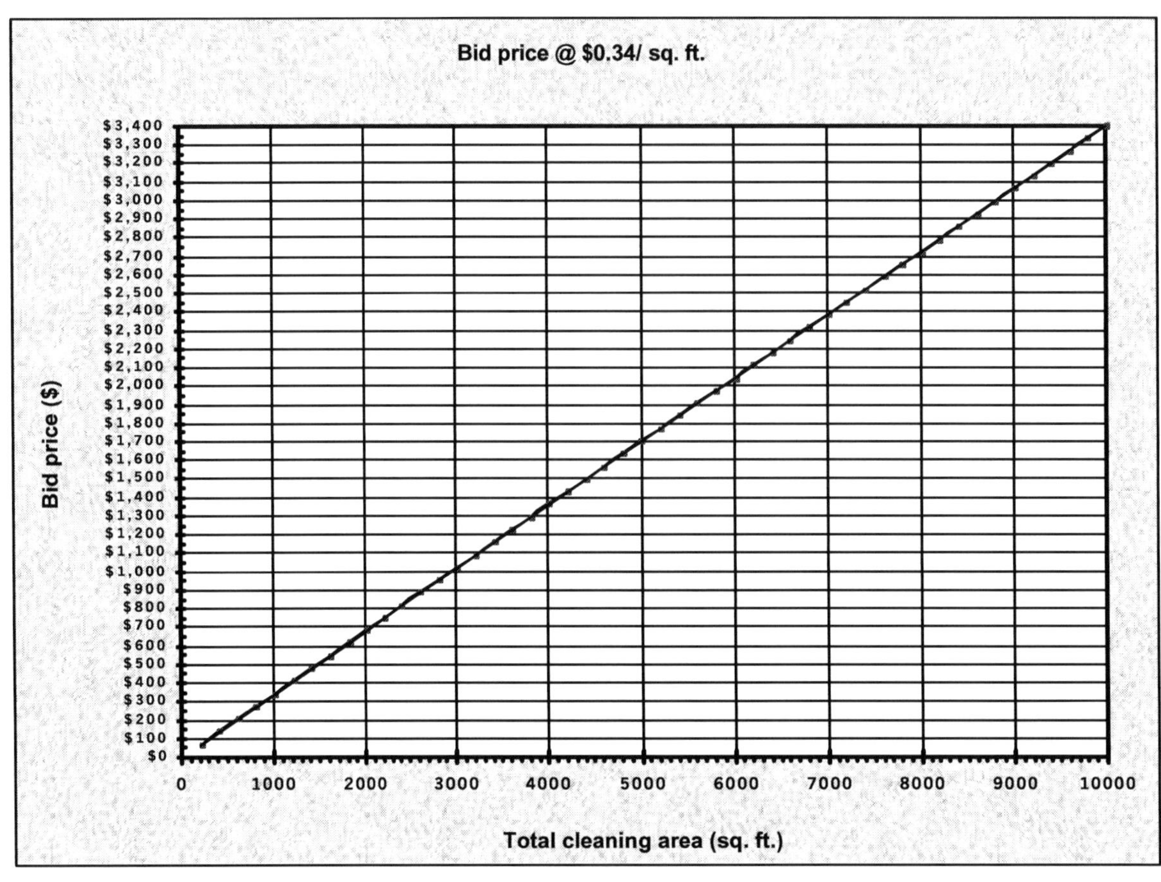
Bid price @ $0.34/ sq. ft.
Bid price ($)
$3,400
$3,300
$3,200
$3,100
$3,000
$2,900
$2,800
$2,700
$2,600
$2,500
$2,400
$2,300
$2,200
$2,100
$2,000
$1,900
$1,800
$1,700
$1,600
$1,500
$1,400
$1,300
$1,200
$1,100
$1,000
$900
$800
$700
$600
$500
$400
$300
$200
$100
$0
0
1000
2000
3000
4000
5000
6000
7000
8000
9000
10000
Total cleaning area (sq. ft.)

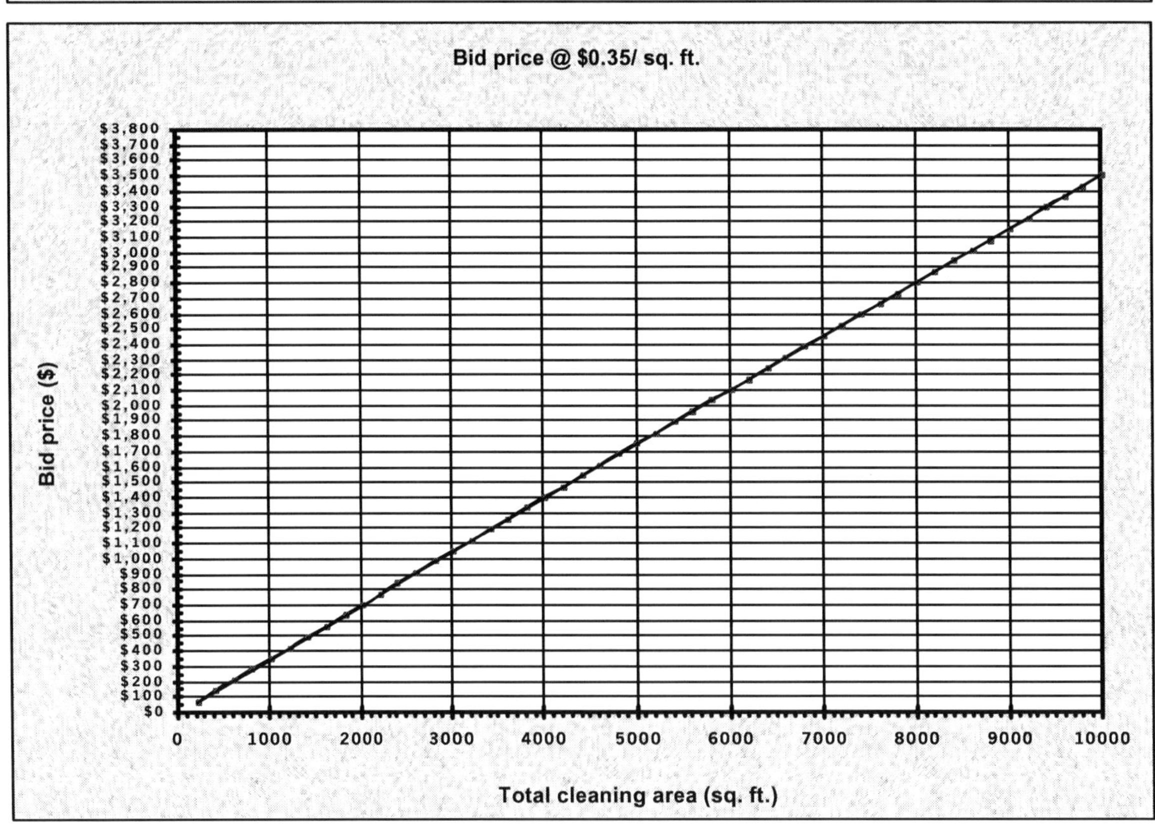
Bid price @ $0.35/ sq. ft.
Bid price ($)
$3,800
$3,700
$3,600
$3,500
$3,400
$3,300
$3,200
$3,100
$3,000
$2,900
$2,800
$2,700
$2,600
$2,500
$2,400
$2,300
$2,200
$2,100
$2,000
$1,900
$1,800
$1,700
$1,600
$1,500
$1,400
$1,300
$1,200
$1,100
$1,000
$900
$800
$700
$600
$500
$400
$300
$200
$100
$0
0
1000
2000
3000
4000
5000
6000
7000
8000
9000
10000
Total cleaning area (sq. ft.)

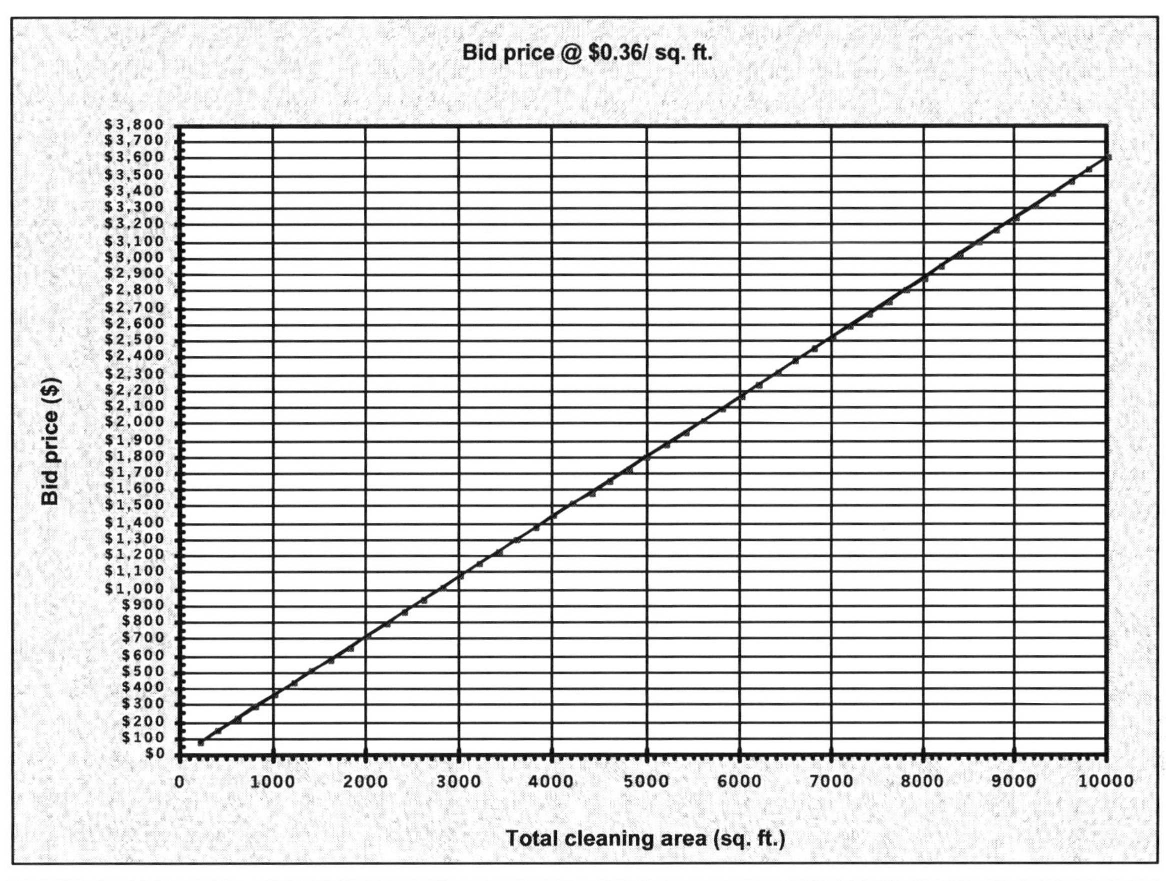
Bid price @ $0.36/ sq. ft.
Bid price ($)
$3,800
$3,700
$3,600
$3,500
$3,400
$3,300
$3,200
$3,100
$3,000
$2,900
$2,800
$2,700
$2,600
$2,500
$2,400
$2,300
$2,200
$2,100
$2,000
$1,900
$1,800
$1,700
$1,600
$1,500
$1,400
$1,300
$1,200
$1,100
$1,000
$900
$800
$700
$600
$500
$400
$300
$200
$100
$0
0
1000
2000
3000
4000
5000
6000
7000
8000
9000
10000
Total cleaning area (sq. ft.)

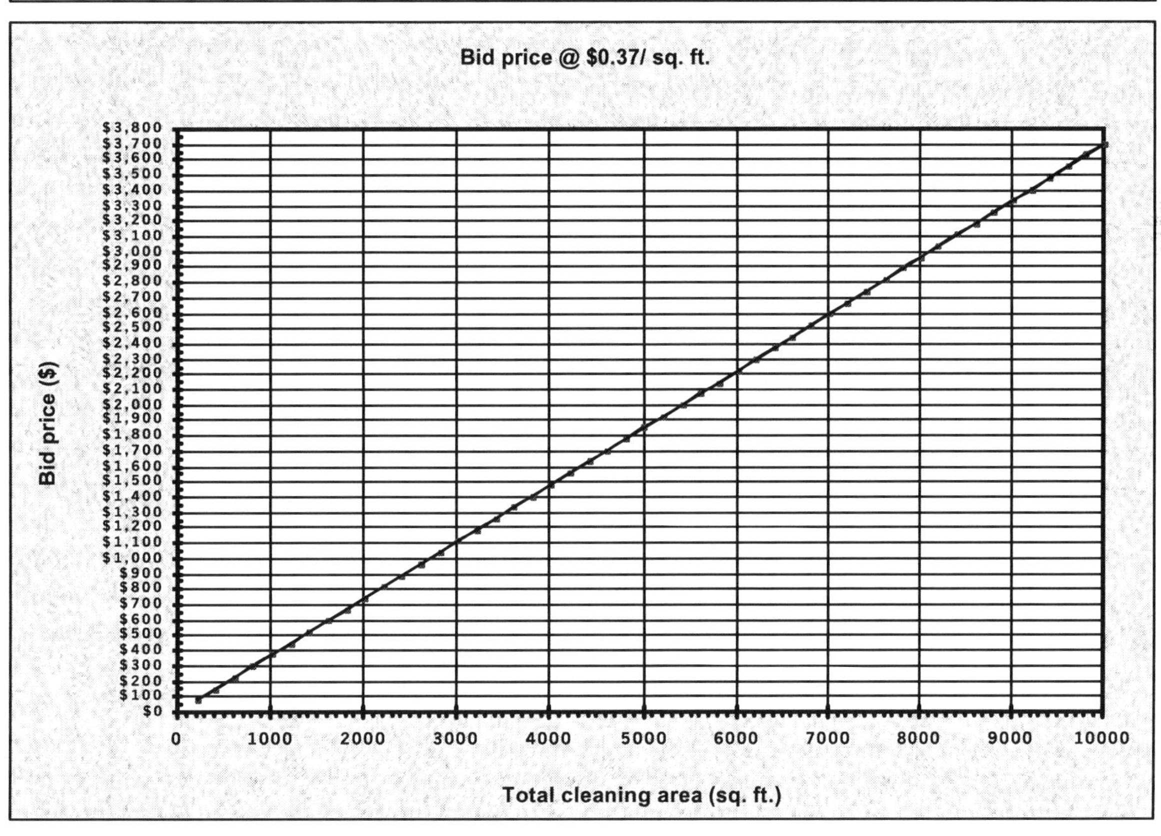
Bid price @ $0.37/ sq. ft.
Bid price ($)
$3,800
$3,700
$3,600
$3,500
$3,400
$3,300
$3,200
$3,100
$3,000
$2,900
$2,800
$2,700
$2,600
$2,500
$2,400
$2,300
$2,200
$2,100
$2,000
$1,900
$1,800
$1,700
$1,600
$1,500
$1,400
$1,300
$1,200
$1,100
$1,000
$900
$800
$700
$600
$500
$400
$300
$200
$100
$0
0
1000
2000
3000
4000
5000
6000
7000
8000
9000
10000
Total cleaning area (sq. ft.)

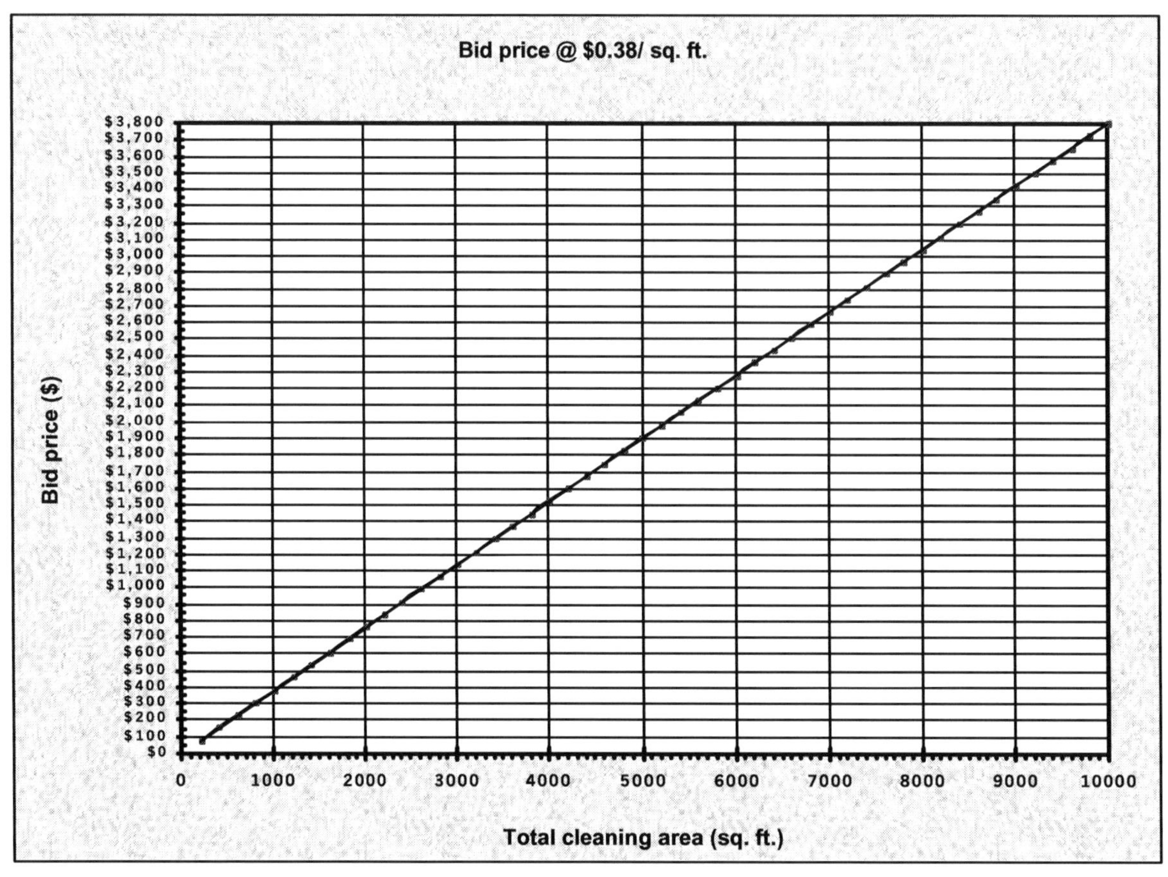
Bid price @ $0.38/ sq. ft.
Bid price ($)
$3,800
$3,700
$3,600
$3,500
$3,400
$3,300
$3,200
$3,100
$3,000
$2,900
$2,800
$2,700
$2,600
$2,500
$2,400
$2,300
$2,200
$2,100
$2,000
$1,900
$1,800
$1,700
$1,600
$1,500
$1,400
$1,300
$1,200
$1,100
$1,000
$900
$800
$700
$600
$500
$400
$300
$200
$100
$0
0
1000
2000
3000
4000
5000
6000
7000
8000
9000
10000
Total cleaning area (sq. ft.)

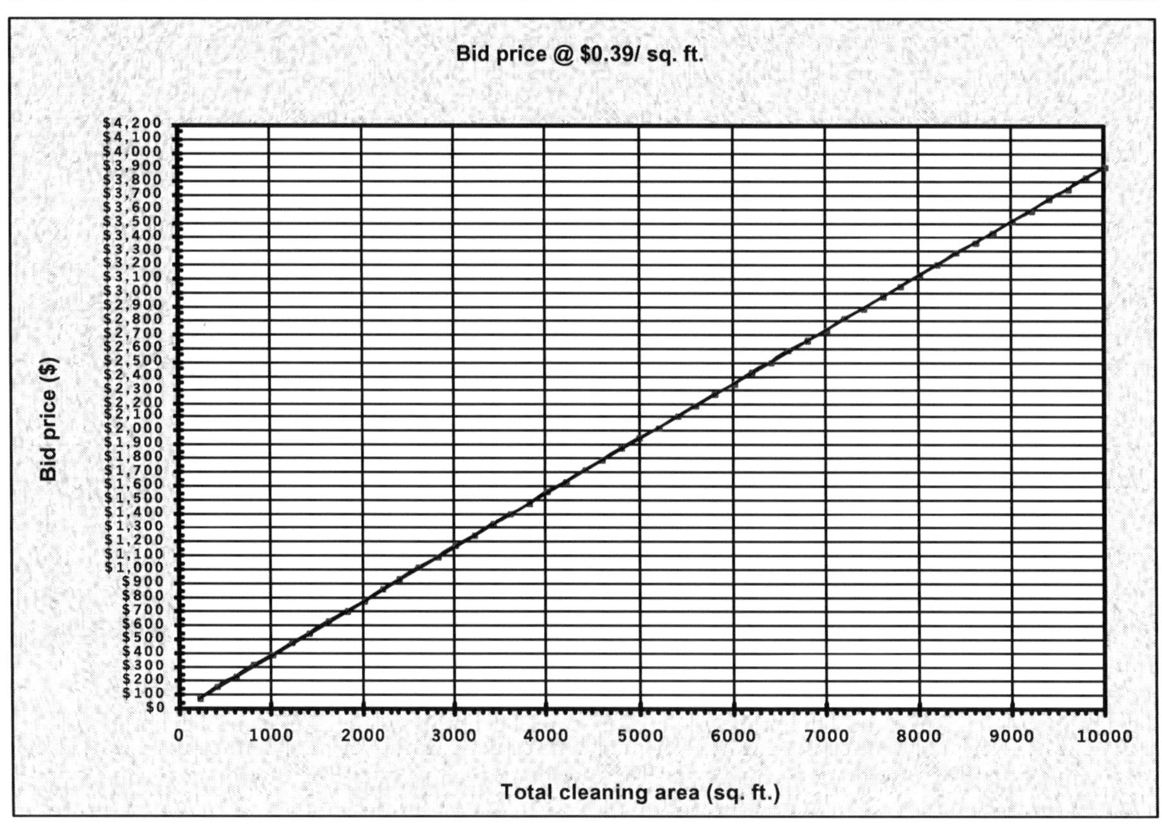
Bid price @ $0.39/ sq. ft.
Bid price ($)
$4,200
$4,100
$4,000
$3,900
$3,800
$3,700
$3,600
$3,500
$3,400
$3,300
$3,200
$3,100
$3,000
$2,900
$2,800
$2,700
$2,600
$2,500
$2,400
$2,300
$2,200
$2,100
$2,000
$1,900
$1,800
$1,700
$1,600
$1,500
$1,400
$1,300
$1,200
$1,100
$1,000
$900
$800
$700
$600
$500
$400
$300
$200
$100
$0
0
1000
2000
3000
4000
5000
6000
7000
8000
9000
10000
Total cleaning area (sq. ft.)

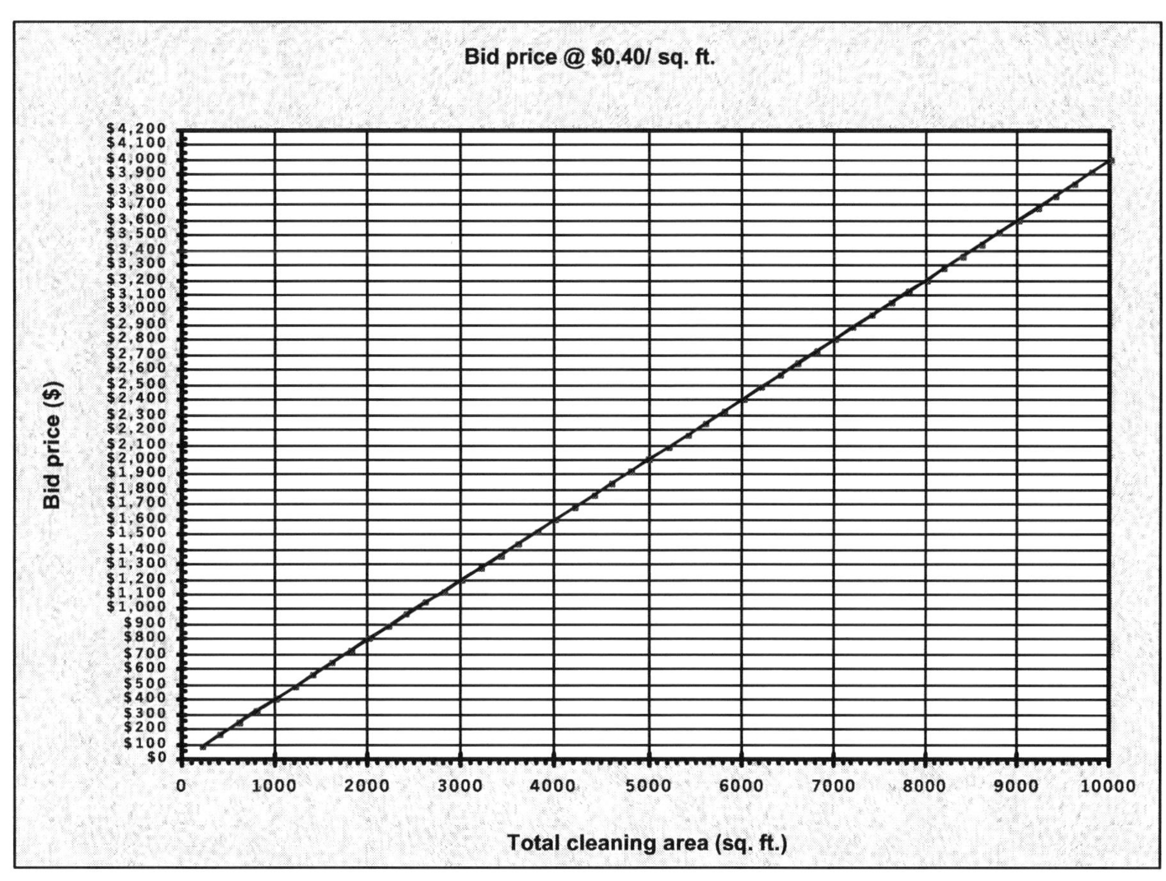
Bid price @ $0.40/ sq. ft.
Bid price ($)
$4,200
$4,100
$4,000
$3,900
$3,800
$3,700
$3,600
$3,500
$3,400
$3,300
$3,200
$3,100
$3,000
$2,900
$2,800
$2,700
$2,600
$2,500
$2,400
$2,300
$2,200
$2,100
$2,000
$1,900
$1,800
$1,700
$1,600
$1,500
$1,400
$1,300
$1,200
$1,100
$1,000
$900
$800
$700
$600
$500
$400
$300
$200
$100
$0
0
1000
2000
3000
4000
5000
6000
7000
8000
9000
10000
Total cleaning area (sq. ft.)

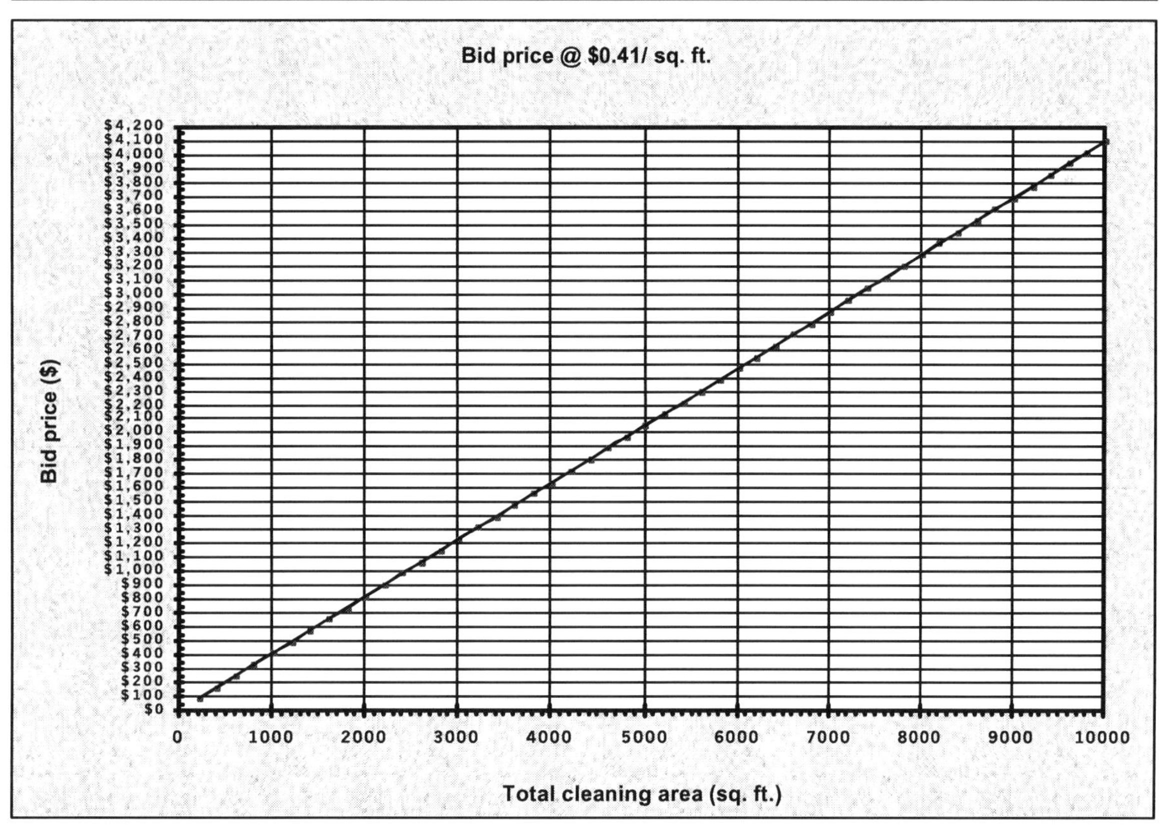
Bid price @ $0.41/ sq. ft.
Bid price ($)
$4,200
$4,100
$4,000
$3,900
$3,800
$3,700
$3,600
$3,500
$3,400
$3,300
$3,200
$3,100
$3,000
$2,900
$2,800
$2,700
$2,600
$2,500
$2,400
$2,300
$2,200
$2,100
$2,000
$1,900
$1,800
$1,700
$1,600
$1,500
$1,400
$1,300
$1,200
$1,100
$1,000
$900
$800
$700
$600
$500
$400
$300
$200
$100
$0
0
1000
2000
3000
4000
5000
6000
7000
8000
9000
10000
Total cleaning area (sq. ft.)

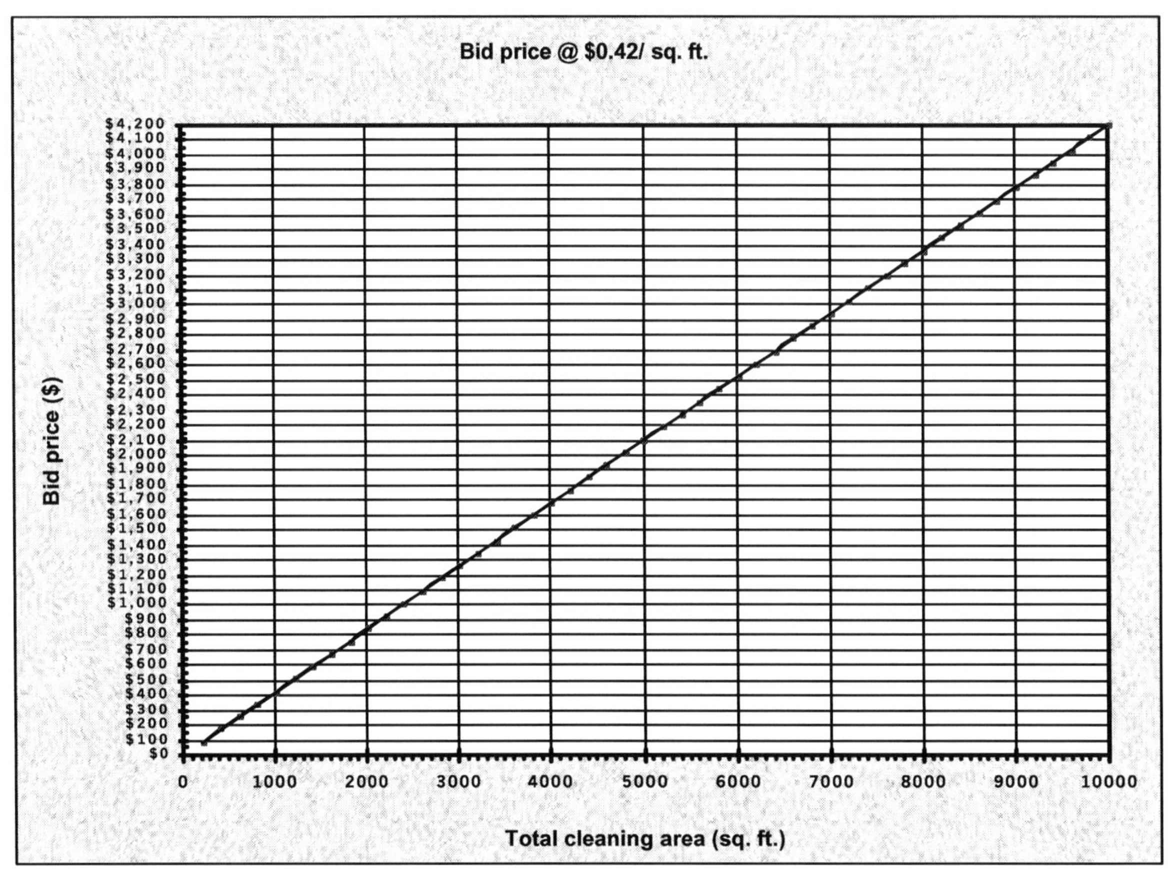
Bid price @ $0.42/ sq. ft.
Bid price ($)
$4,200
$4,100
$4,000
$3,900
$3,800
$3,700
$3,600
$3,500
$3,400
$3,300
$3,200
$3,100
$3,000
$2,900
$2,800
$2,700
$2,600
$2,500
$2,400
$2,300
$2,200
$2,100
$2,000
$1,900
$1,800
$1,700
$1,600
$1,500
$1,400
$1,300
$1,200
$1,100
$1,000
$900
$800
$700
$600
$500
$400
$300
$200
$100
$0
0
1000
2000
3000
4000
5000
6000
7000
8000
9000
10000
Total cleaning area (sq. ft.)

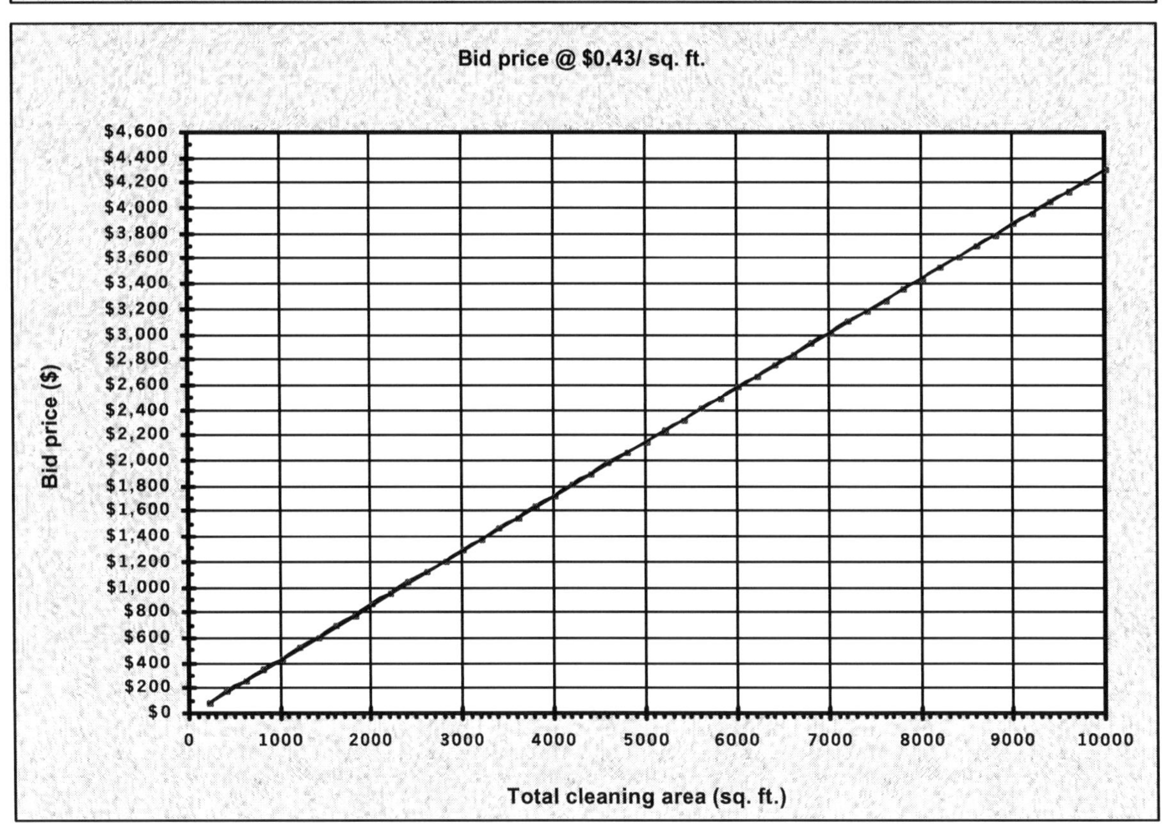
Bid price @ $0.43/ sq. ft.
Bid price ($)
$4,600
$4,400
$4,200
$4,000
$3,800
$3,600
$3,400
$3,200
$3,000
$2,800
$2,600
$2,400
$2,200
$2,000
$1,800
$1,600
$1,400
$1,200
$1,000
$800
$600
$400
$200
$0
0
1000
2000
3000
4000
5000
6000
7000
8000
9000
10000
Total cleaning area (sq. ft.)

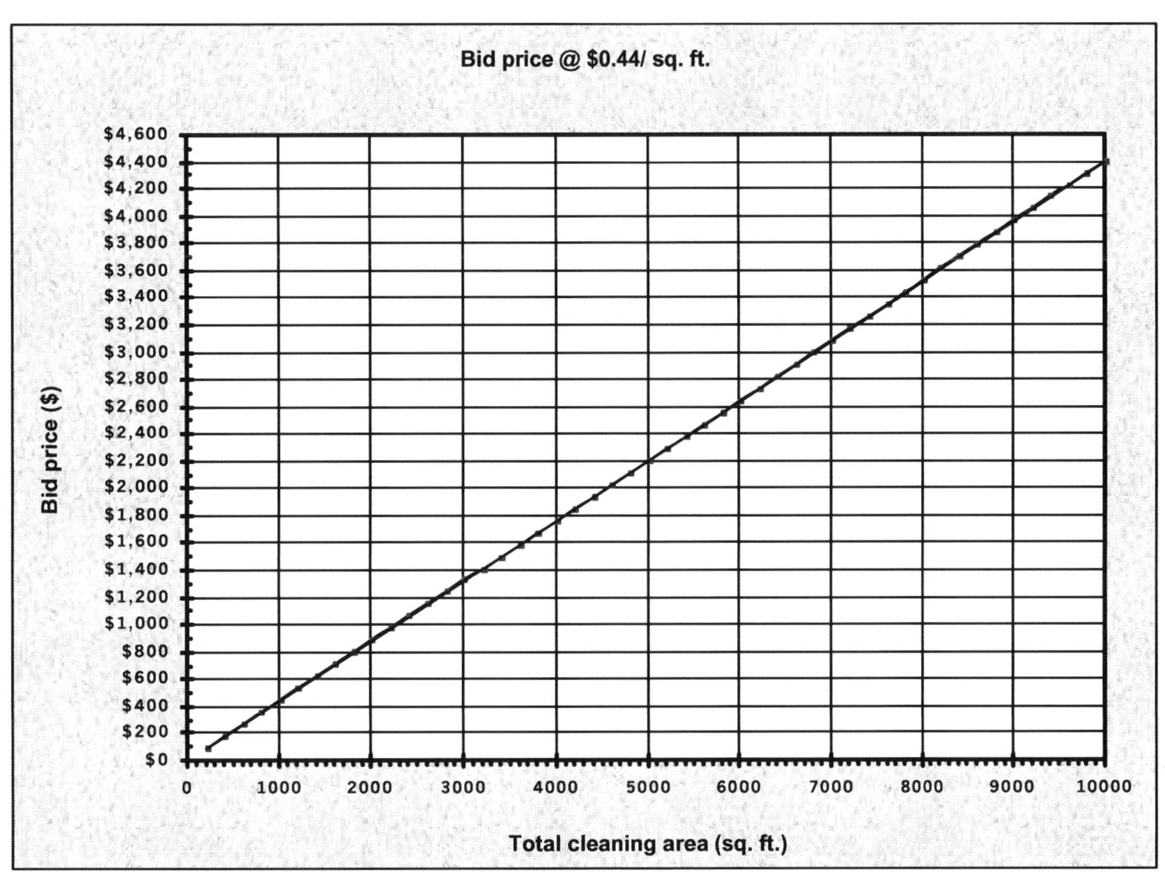
Bid price @ $0.44/ sq. ft.
Bid price ($)
$4,600
$4,400
$4,200
$4,000
$3,800
$3,600
$3,400
$3,200
$3,000
$2,800
$2,600
$2,400
$2,200
$2,000
$1,800
$1,600
$1,400
$1,200
$1,000
$800
$600
$400
$200
$0
0
1000
2000
3000
4000
5000
6000
7000
8000
9000
10000
Total cleaning area (sq. ft.)

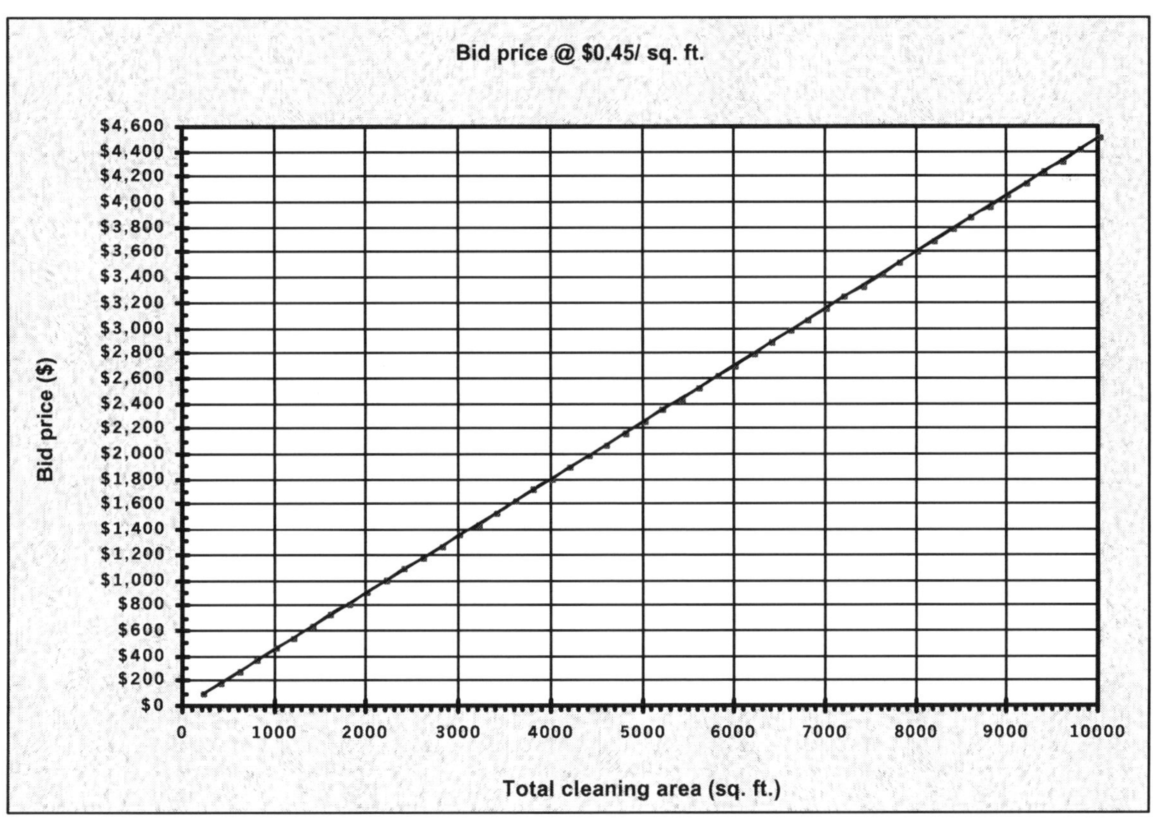
Bid price @ $0.45/ sq. ft.
Bid price ($)
$4,600
$4,400
$4,200
$4,000
$3,800
$3,600
$3,400
$3,200
$3,000
$2,800
$2,600
$2,400
$2,200
$2,000
$1,800
$1,600
$1,400
$1,200
$1,000
$800
$600
$400
$200
$0
0
1000
2000
3000
4000
5000
6000
7000
8000
9000
10000
Total cleaning area (sq. ft.)

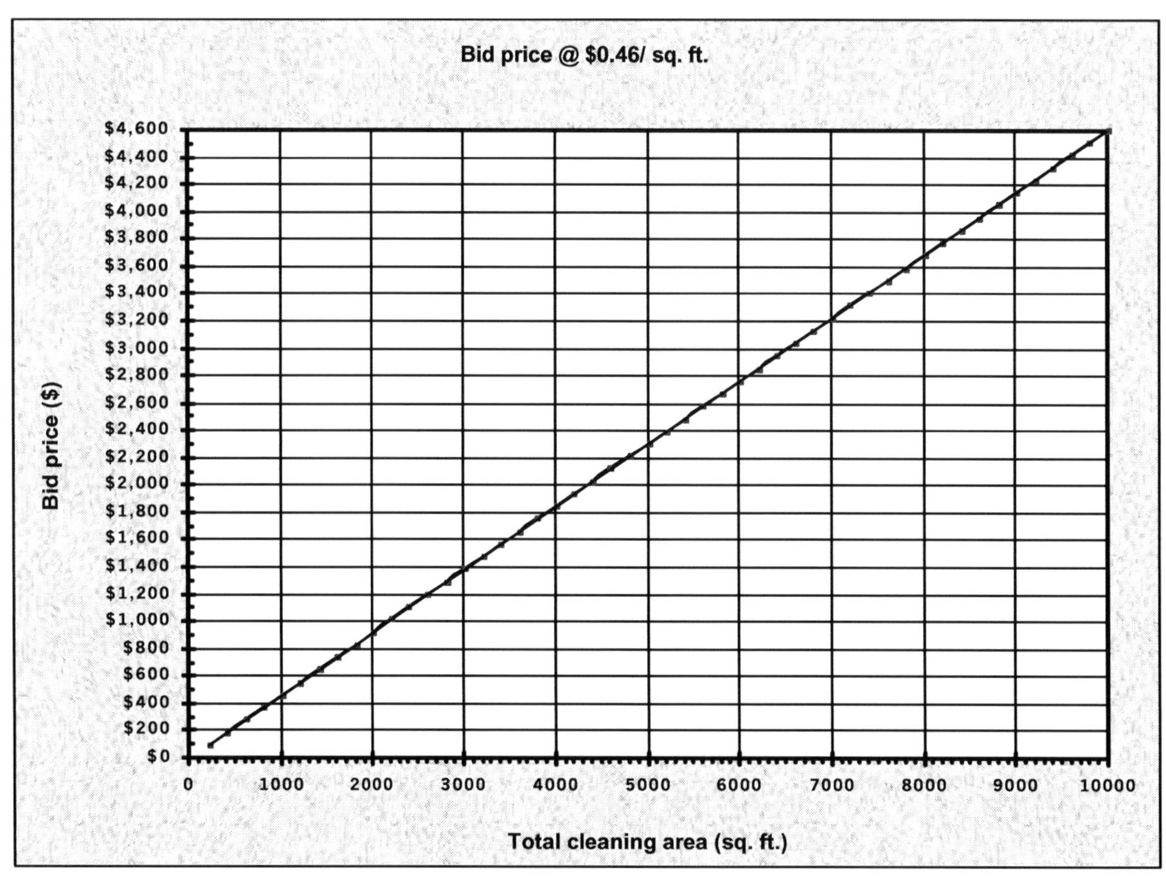

Bid price @ $0.46/ sq. ft.
Bid price ($)
$4,600
$4,400
$4,200
$4,000
$3,800
$3,600
$3,400
$3,200
$3,000
$2,800
$2,600
$2,400
$2,200
$2,000
$1,800
$1,600
$1,400
$1,200
$1,000
$800
$600
$400
$200
$0
0
1000
2000
3000
4000
5000
6000
7000
8000
9000
10000
Total cleaning area (sq. ft.)

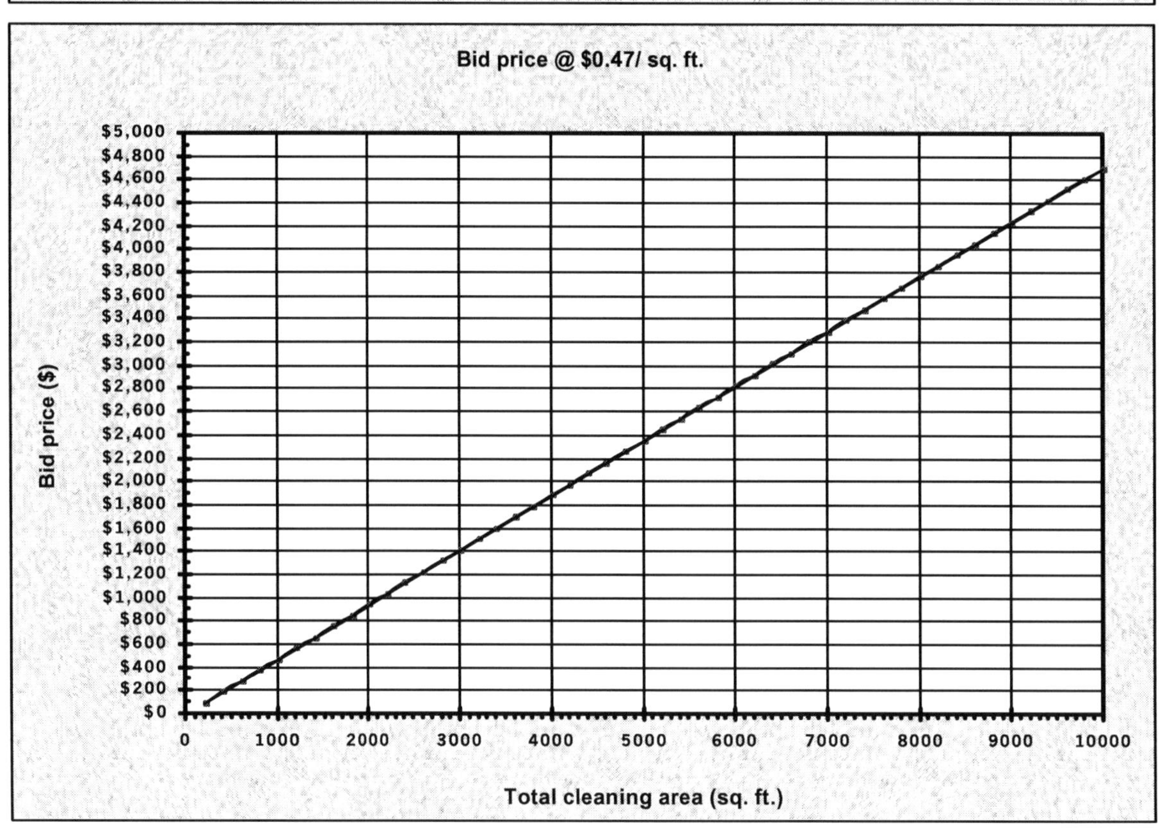

Bid price @ $0.47/ sq. ft.
Bid price ($)
$5,000
$4,800
$4,600
$4,400
$4,200
$4,000
$3,800
$3,600
$3,400
$3,200
$3,000
$2,800
$2,600
$2,400
$2,200
$2,000
$1,800
$1,600
$1,400
$1,200
$1,000
$800
$600
$400
$200
$0
0
1000
2000
3000
4000
5000
6000
7000
8000
9000
10000
Total cleaning area (sq. ft.)

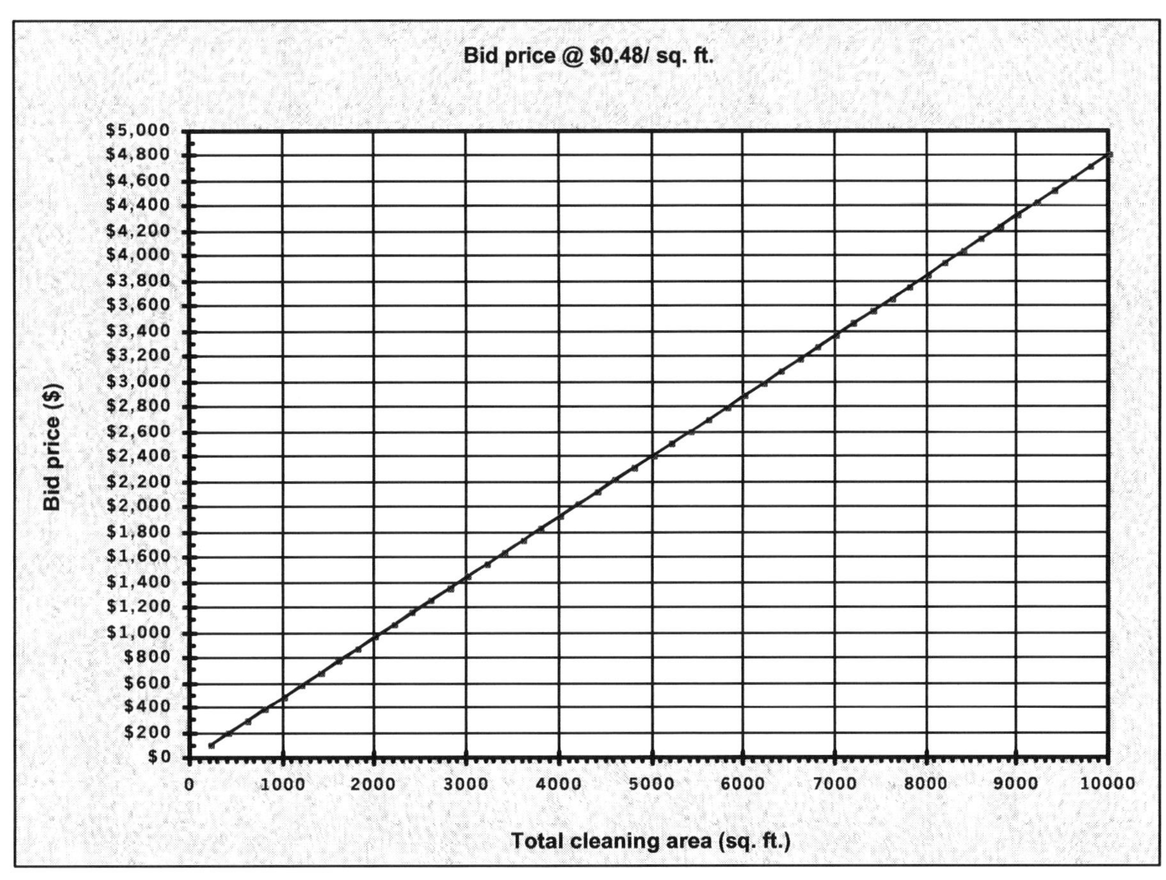
Bid price @ $0.48/ sq. ft.
Bid price ($)
$5,000
$4,800
$4,600
$4,400
$4,200
$4,000
$3,800
$3,600
$3,400
$3,200
$3,000
$2,800
$2,600
$2,400
$2,200
$2,000
$1,800
$1,600
$1,400
$1,200
$1,000
$800
$600
$400
$200
$0
0
1000
2000
3000
4000
5000
6000
7000
8000
9000
10000
Total cleaning area (sq. ft.)

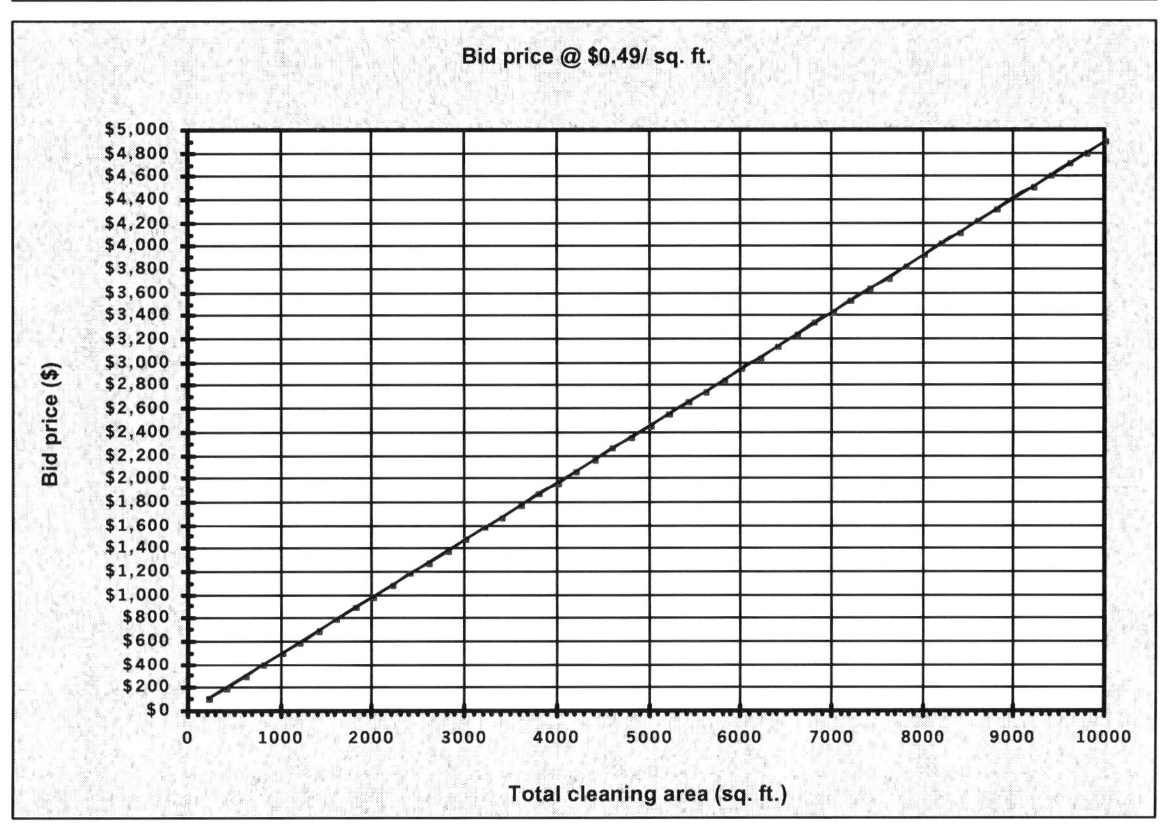
Bid price @ $0.49/ sq. ft.
Bid price ($)
$5,000
$4,800
$4,600
$4,400
$4,200
$4,000
$3,800
$3,600
$3,400
$3,200
$3,000
$2,800
$2,600
$2,400
$2,200
$2,000
$1,800
$1,600
$1,400
$1,200
$1,000
$800
$600
$400
$200
$0
0
1000
2000
3000
4000
5000
6000
7000
8000
9000
10000
Total cleaning area (sq. ft.)

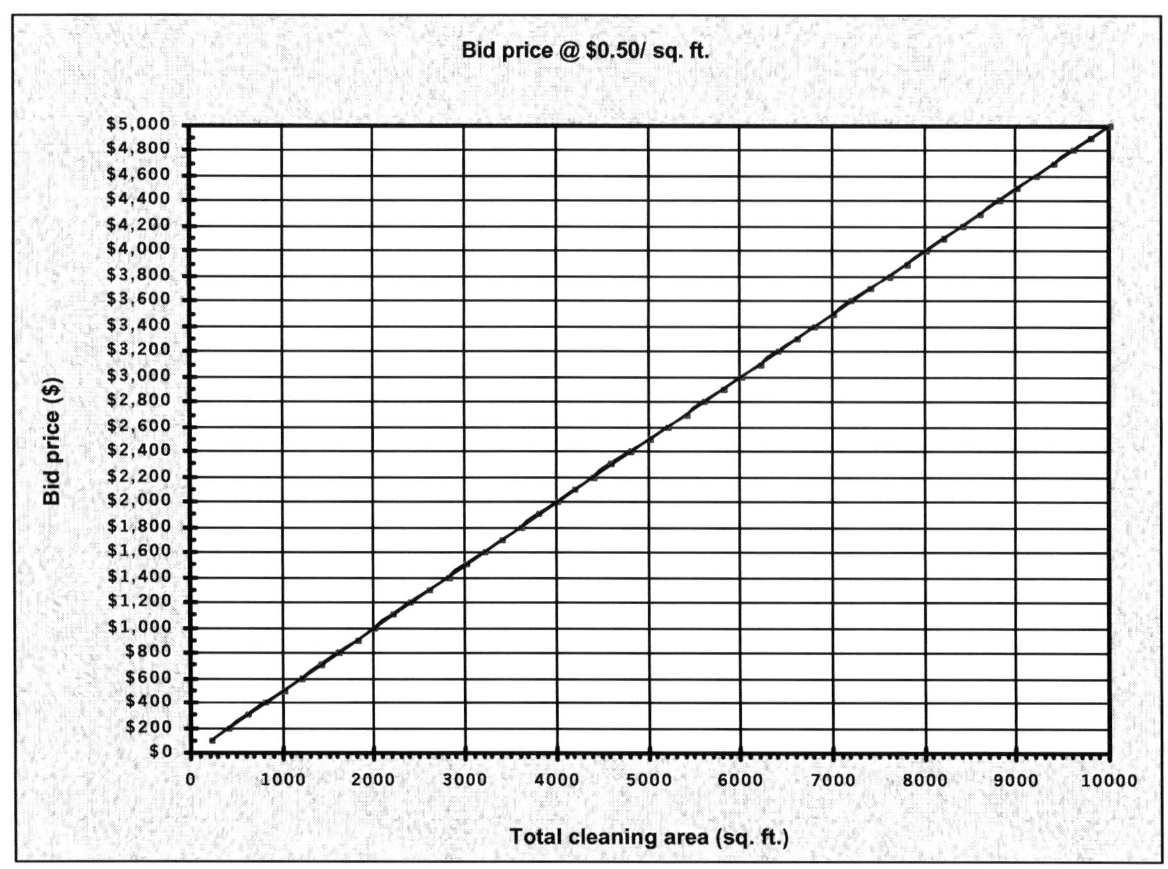
Bid price @ $0.50/ sq. ft.
Bid price ($)
$5,000
$4,800
$4,600
$4,400
$4,200
$4,000
$3,800
$3,600
$3,400
$3,200
$3,000
$2,800
$2,600
$2,400
$2,200
$2,000
$1,800
$1,600
$1,400
$1,200
$1,000
$800
$600
$400
$200
$0
0
1000
2000
3000
4000
5000
6000
7000
8000
9000
10000
Total cleaning area (sq. ft.)

Chapter 8
Bid pricing charts:
Annual price per square foot

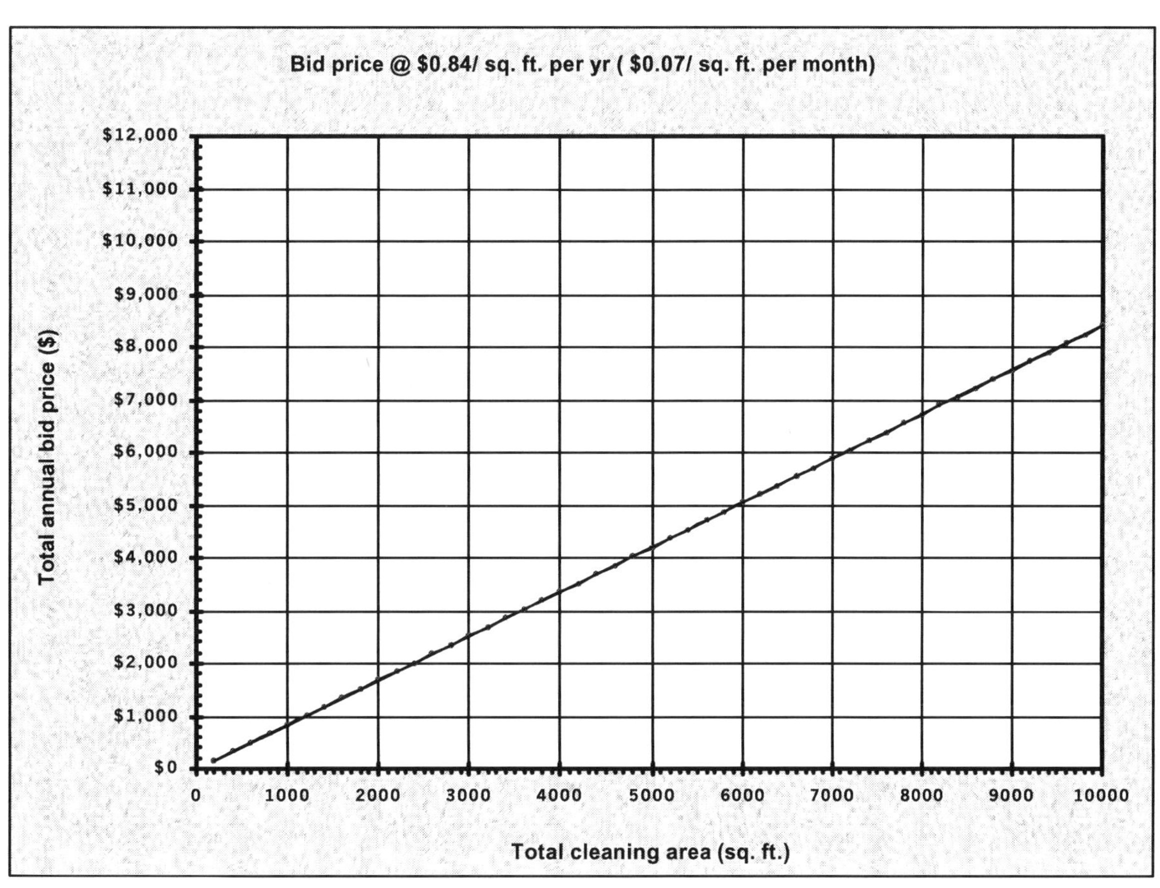

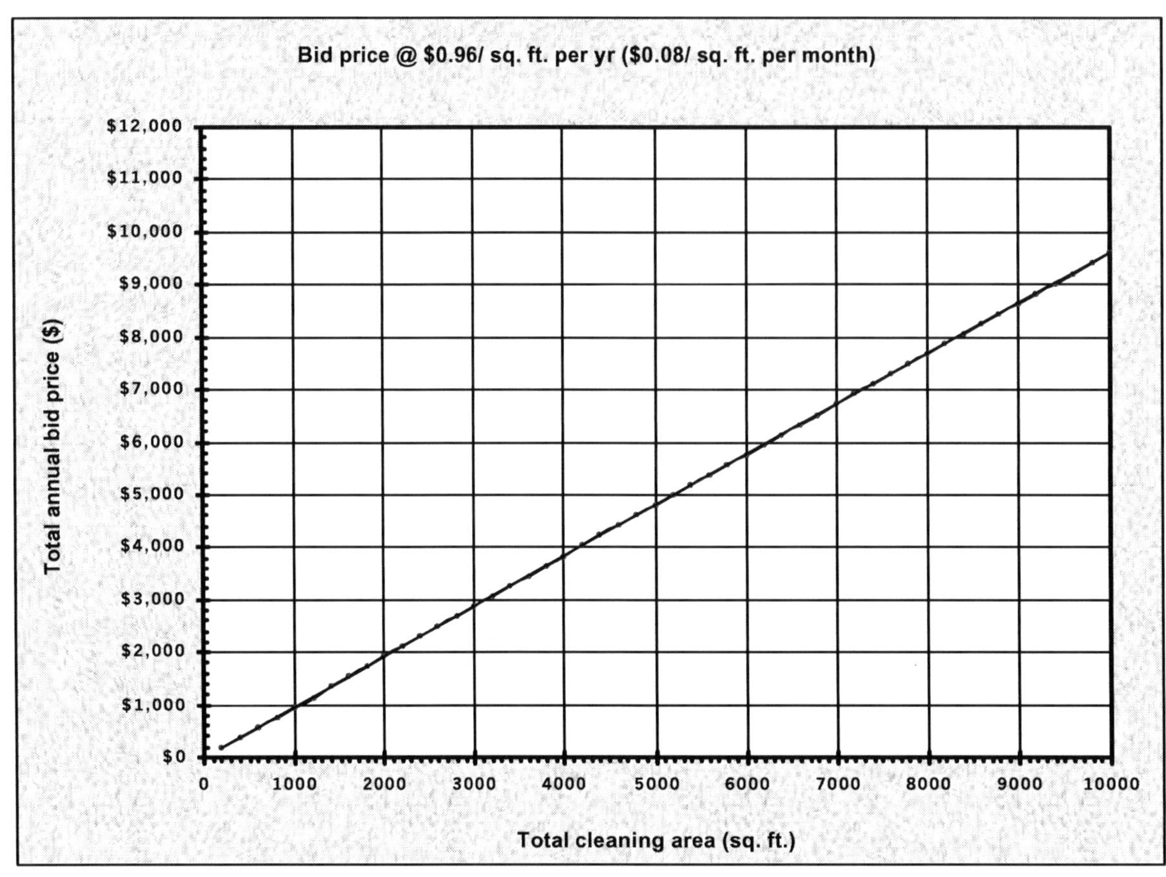
Bid price @ $0.96/ sq. ft. per yr ($0.08/ sq. ft. per month)
Total annual bid price ($)
$12,000
$11,000
$10,000
$9,000
$8,000
$7,000
$6,000
$5,000
$4,000
$3,000
$2,000
$1,000
$0
0
1000
2000
3000
4000
5000
6000
7000
8000
9000
10000
Total cleaning area (sq. ft.)

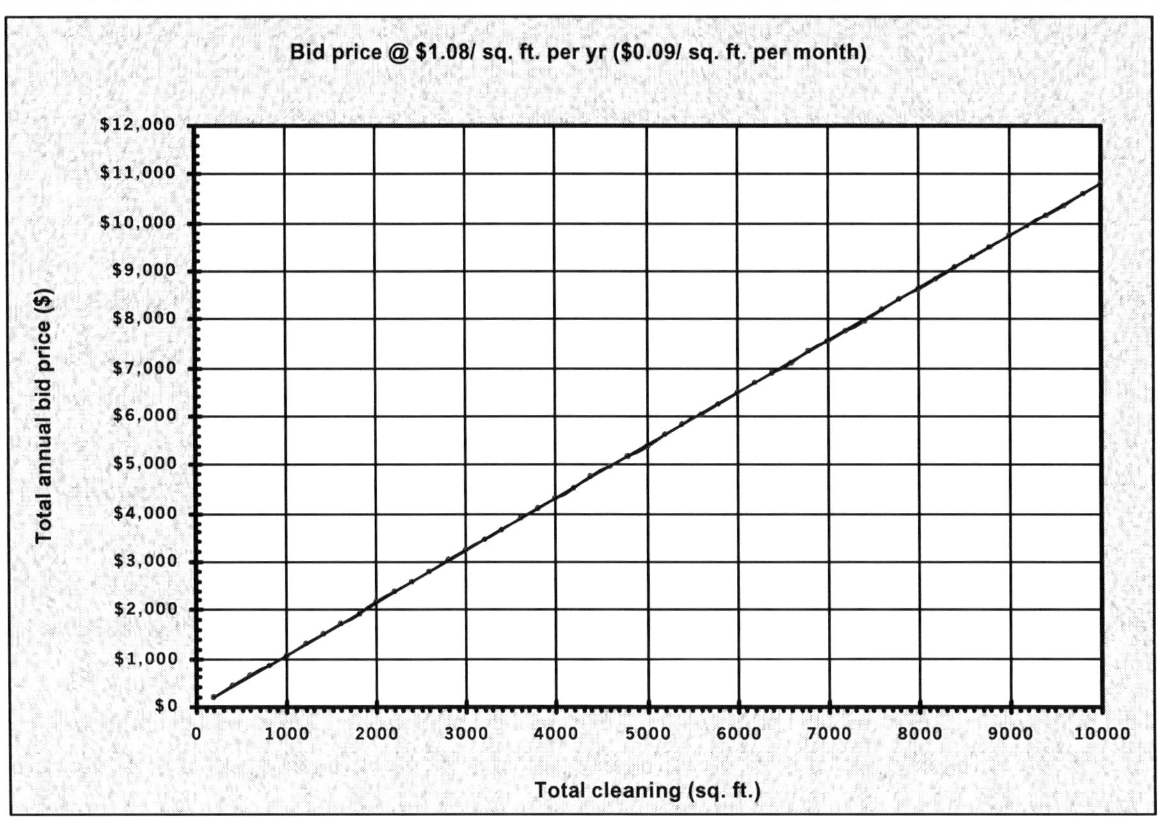
Bid price @ $1.08/ sq. ft. per yr ($0.09/ sq. ft. per month)
Total annual bid price ($)
$12,000
$11,000
$10,000
$9,000
$8,000
$7,000
$6,000
$5,000
$4,000
$3,000
$2,000
$1,000
$0
0
1000
2000
3000
4000
5000
6000
7000
8000
9000
10000
Total cleaning (sq. ft.)

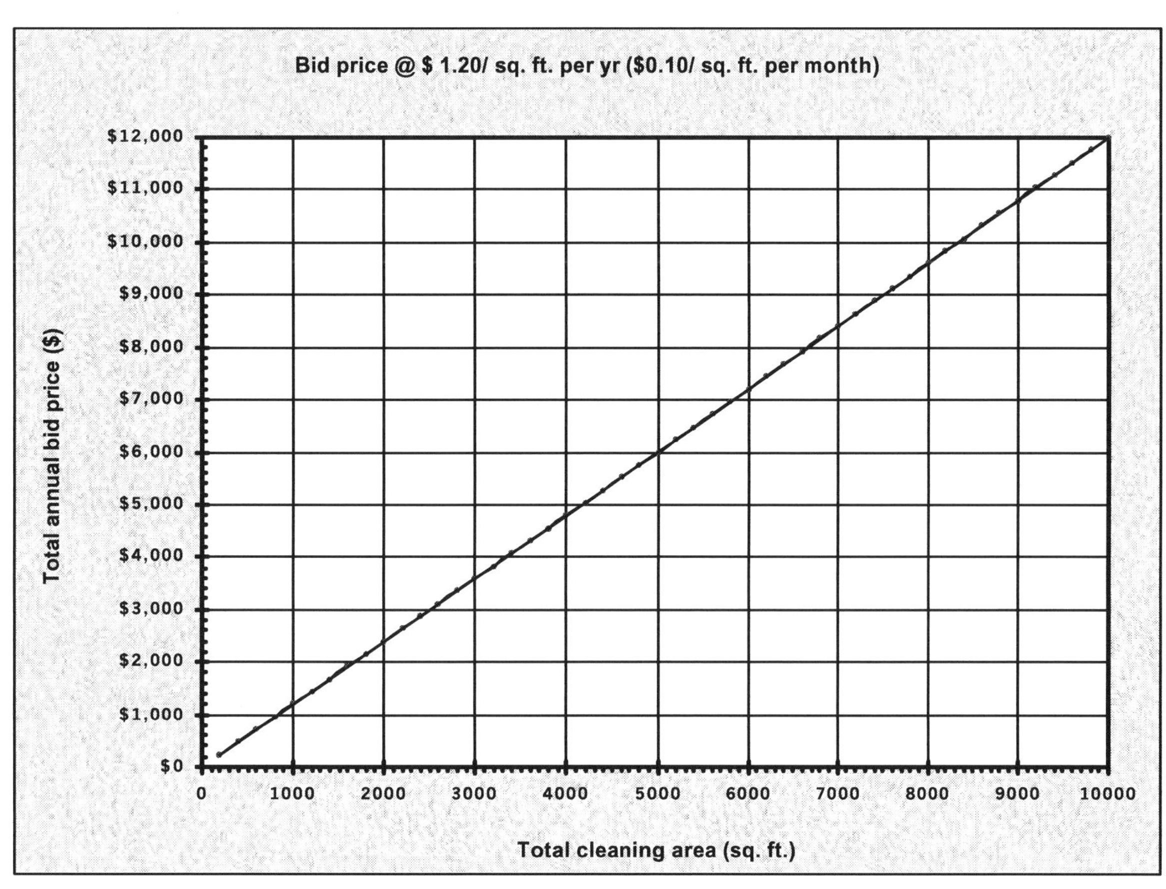
Bid price @ $ 1.20/ sq. ft. per yr ($0.10/ sq. ft. per month)
Total annual bid price ($)
$12,000
$11,000
$10,000
$9,000
$8,000
$7,000
$6,000
$5,000
$4,000
$3,000
$2,000
$1,000
$0
0
1000
2000
3000
4000
5000
6000
7000
8000
9000
10000
Total cleaning area (sq. ft.)

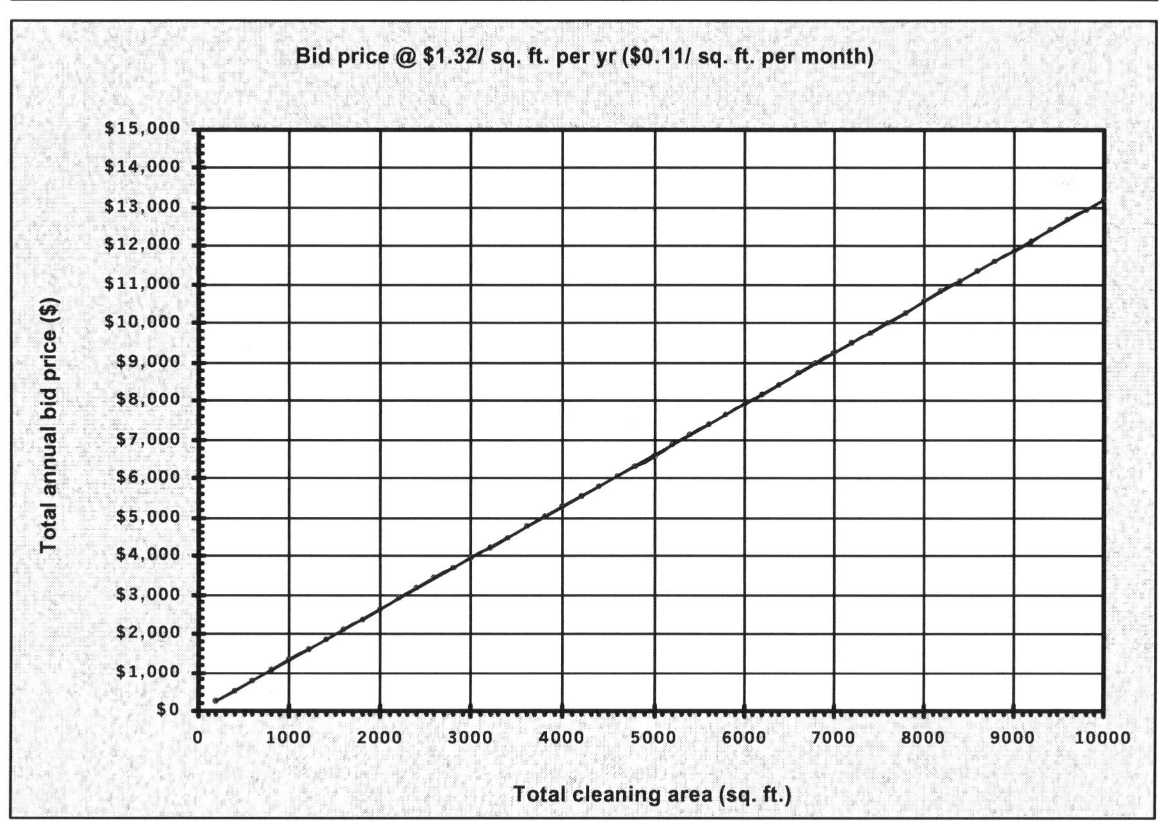
Bid price @ $1.32/ sq. ft. per yr ($0.11/ sq. ft. per month)
Total annual bid price ($)
$15,000
$14,000
$13,000
$12,000
$11,000
$10,000
$9,000
$8,000
$7,000
$6,000
$5,000
$4,000
$3,000
$2,000
$1,000
$0
0
1000
2000
3000
4000
5000
6000
7000
8000
9000
10000
Total cleaning area (sq. ft.)

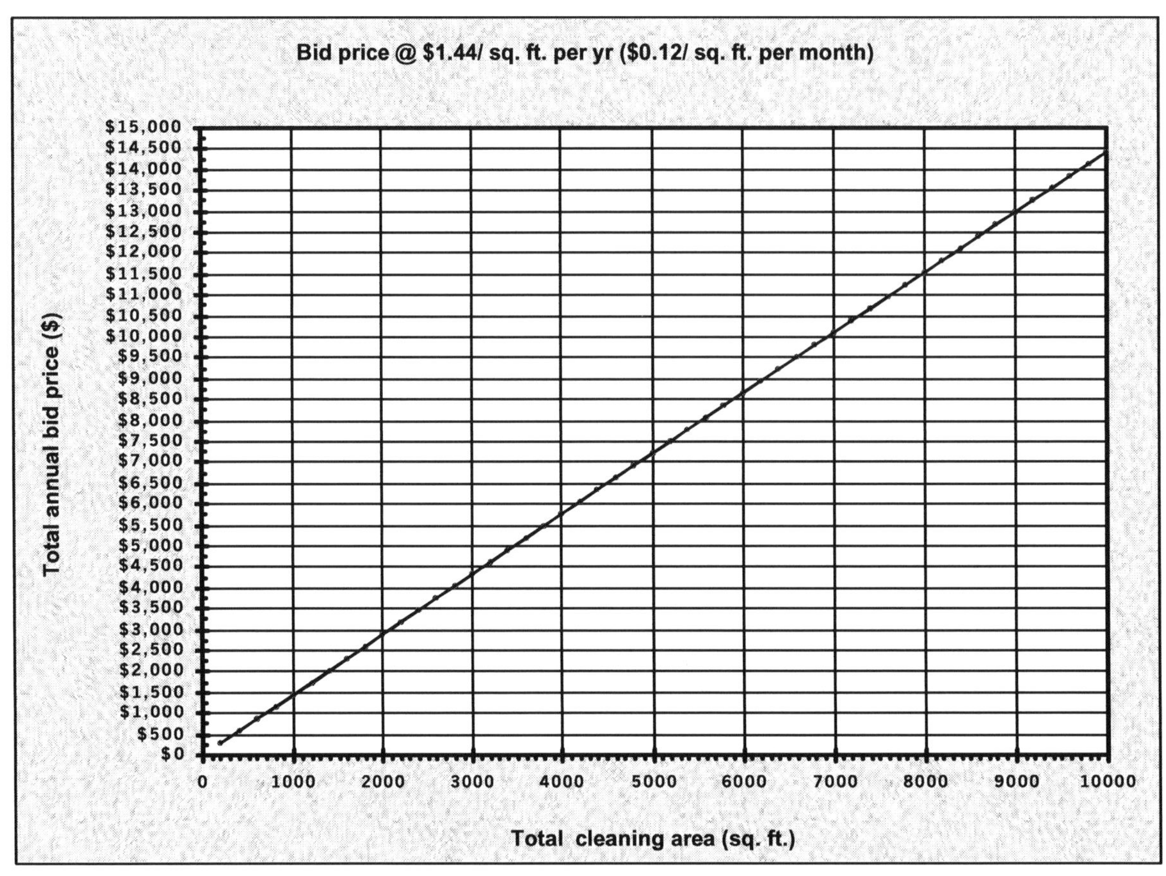
Bid price @ $1.44/ sq. ft. per yr ($0.12/ sq. ft. per month)
Total annual bid price ($)
$15,000
$14,500
$14,000
$13,500
$13,000
$12,500
$12,000
$11,500
$11,000
$10,500
$10,000
$9,500
$9,000
$8,500
$8,000
$7,500
$7,000
$6,500
$6,000
$5,500
$5,000
$4,500
$4,000
$3,500
$3,000
$2,500
$2,000
$1,500
$1,000
$500
$0
0
1000
2000
3000
4000
5000
6000
7000
8000
9000
10000
Total cleaning area (sq. ft.)

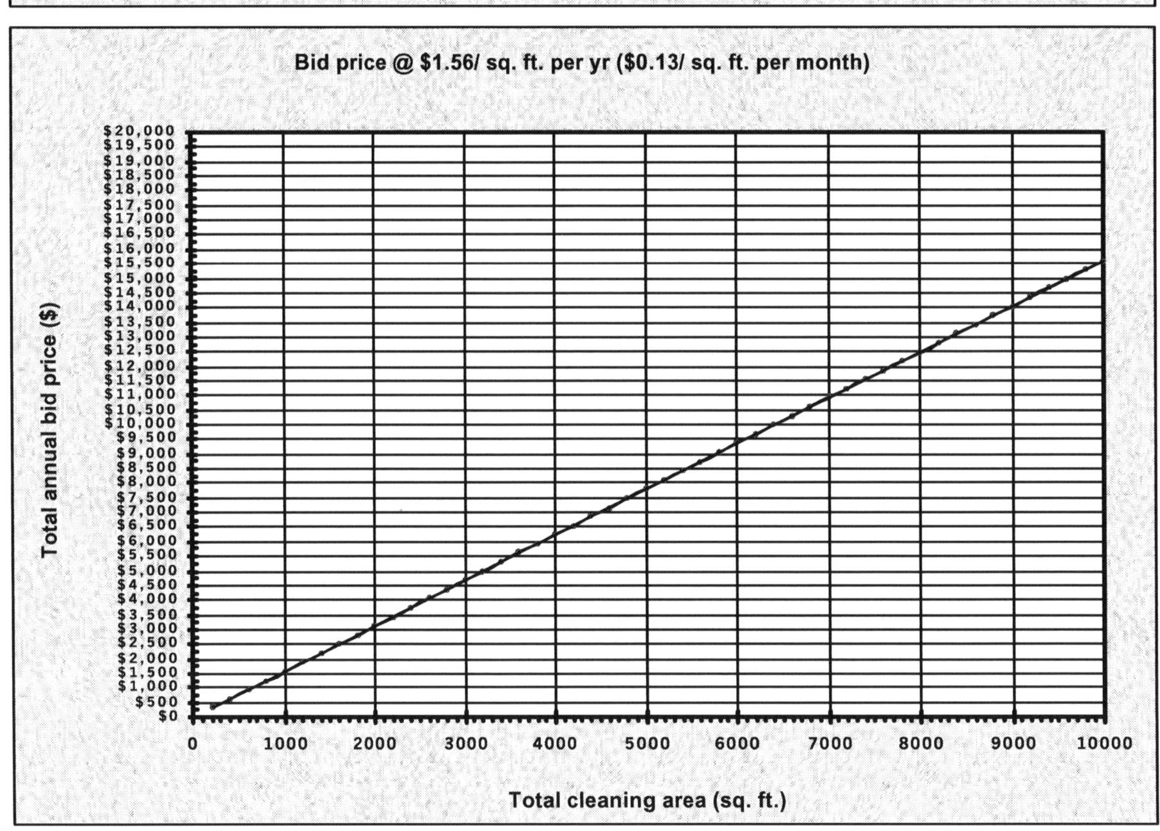
Bid price @ $1.56/ sq. ft. per yr ($0.13/ sq. ft. per month)
Total annual bid price ($)
$20,000
$19,500
$19,000
$18,500
$18,000
$17,500
$17,000
$16,500
$16,000
$15,500
$15,000
$14,500
$14,000
$13,500
$13,000
$12,500
$12,000
$11,500
$11,000
$10,500
$10,000
$9,500
$9,000
$8,500
$8,000
$7,500
$7,000
$6,500
$6,000
$5,500
$5,000
$4,500
$4,000
$3,500
$3,000
$2,500
$2,000
$1,500
$1,000
$500
$0
0
1000
2000
3000
4000
5000
6000
7000
8000
9000
10000
Total cleaning area (sq. ft.)

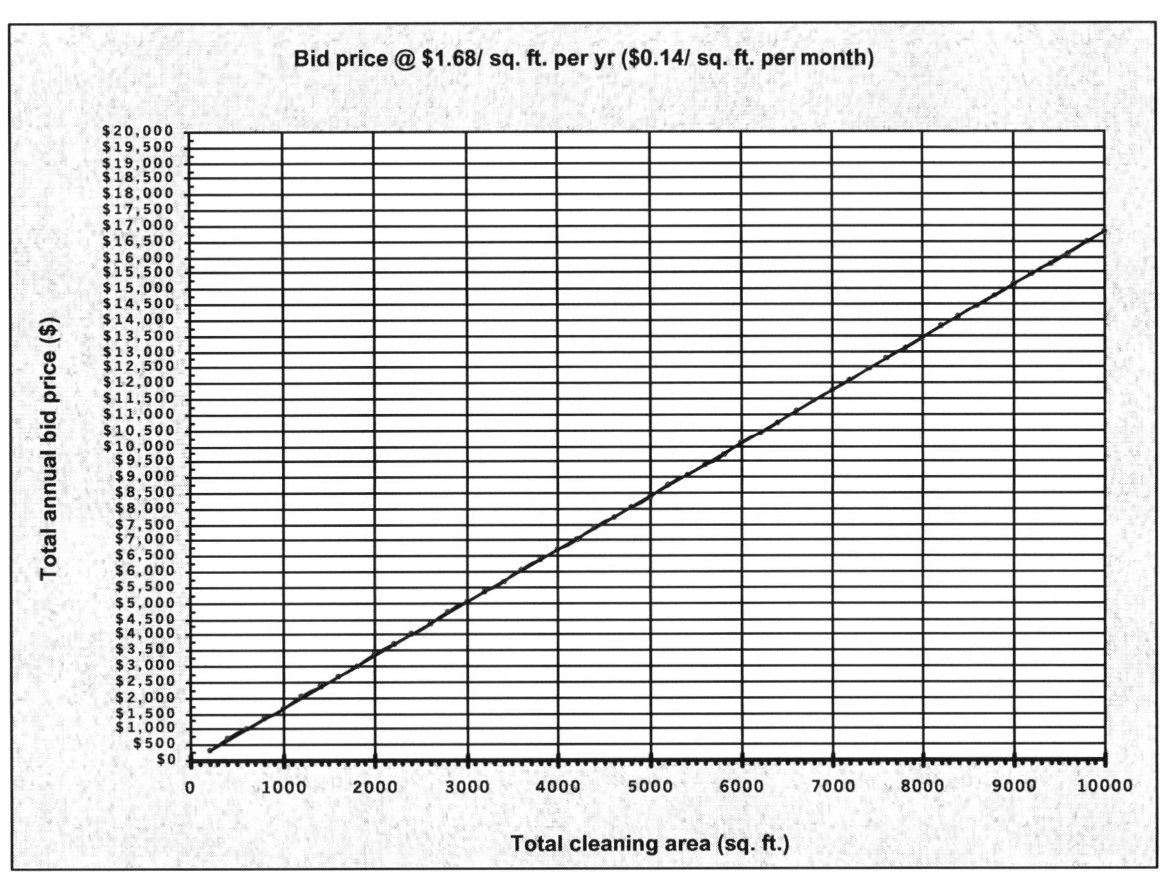
Bid price @ $1.68/ sq. ft. per yr ($0.14/ sq. ft. per month)
Total annual bid price ($)
$20,000
$19,500
$19,000
$18,500
$18,000
$17,500
$17,000
$16,500
$16,000
$15,500
$15,000
$14,500
$14,000
$13,500
$13,000
$12,500
$12,000
$11,500
$11,000
$10,500
$10,000
$9,500
$9,000
$8,500
$8,000
$7,500
$7,000
$6,500
$6,000
$5,500
$5,000
$4,500
$4,000
$3,500
$3,000
$2,500
$2,000
$1,500
$1,000
$500
$0
0
1000
2000
3000
4000
5000
6000
7000
8000
9000
10000
Total cleaning area (sq. ft.)

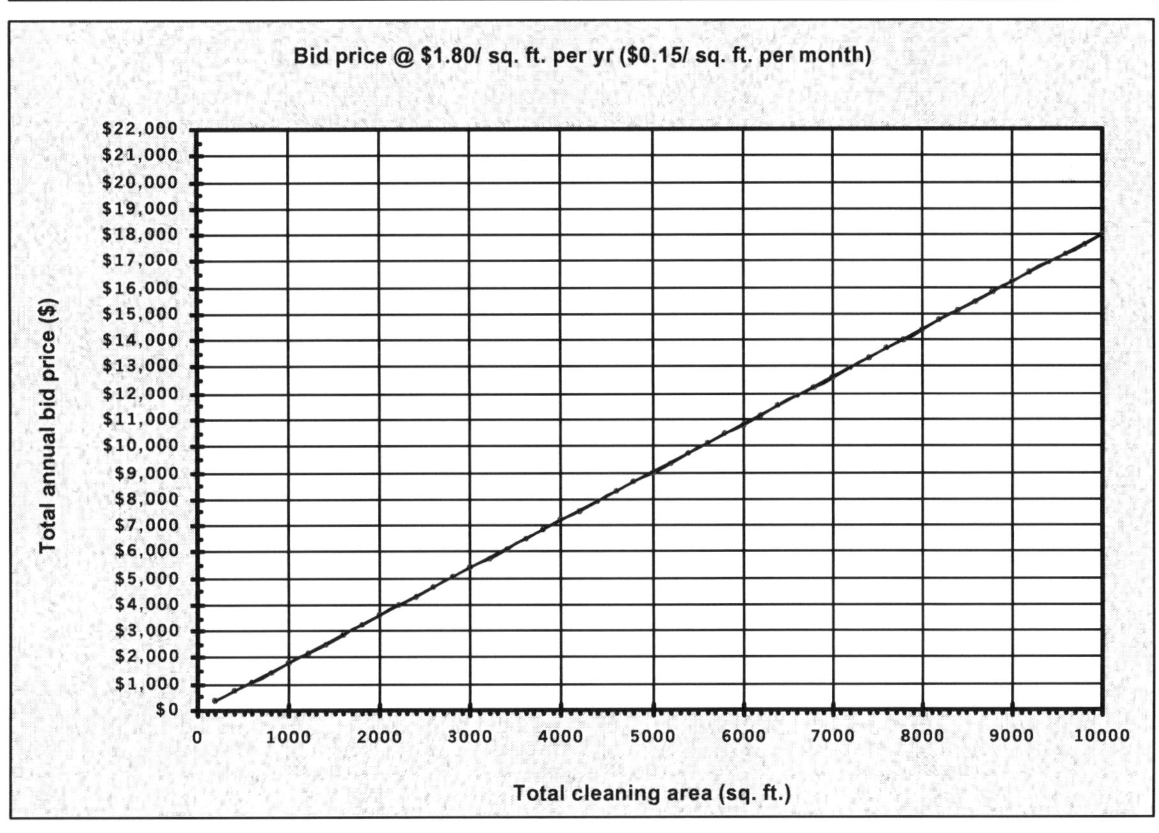
Bid price @ $1.80/ sq. ft. per yr ($0.15/ sq. ft. per month)
Total annual bid price ($)
$22,000
$21,000
$20,000
$19,000
$18,000
$17,000
$16,000
$15,000
$14,000
$13,000
$12,000
$11,000
$10,000
$9,000
$8,000
$7,000
$6,000
$5,000
$4,000
$3,000
$2,000
$1,000
$0
0
1000
2000
3000
4000
5000
6000
7000
8000
9000
10000
Total cleaning area (sq. ft.)

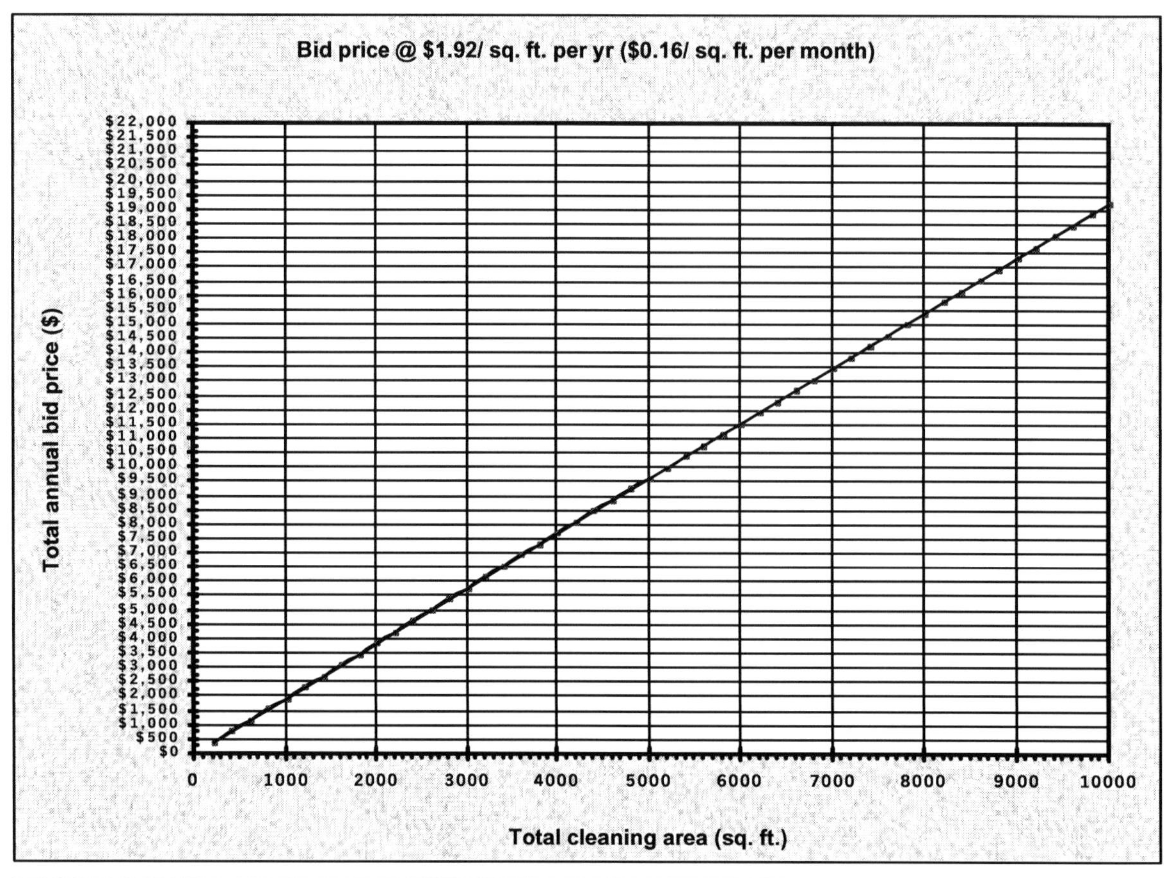
Bid price @ $1.92/ sq. ft. per yr ($0.16/ sq. ft. per month)
Total annual bid price ($)
$22,000
$21,500
$21,000
$20,500
$20,000
$19,500
$19,000
$18,500
$18,000
$17,500
$17,000
$16,500
$16,000
$15,500
$15,000
$14,500
$14,000
$13,500
$13,000
$12,500
$12,000
$11,500
$11,000
$10,500
$10,000
$9,500
$9,000
$8,500
$8,000
$7,500
$7,000
$6,500
$6,000
$5,500
$5,000
$4,500
$4,000
$3,500
$3,000
$2,500
$2,000
$1,500
$1,000
$500
$0
0
1000
2000
3000
4000
5000
6000
7000
8000
9000
10000
Total cleaning area (sq. ft.)

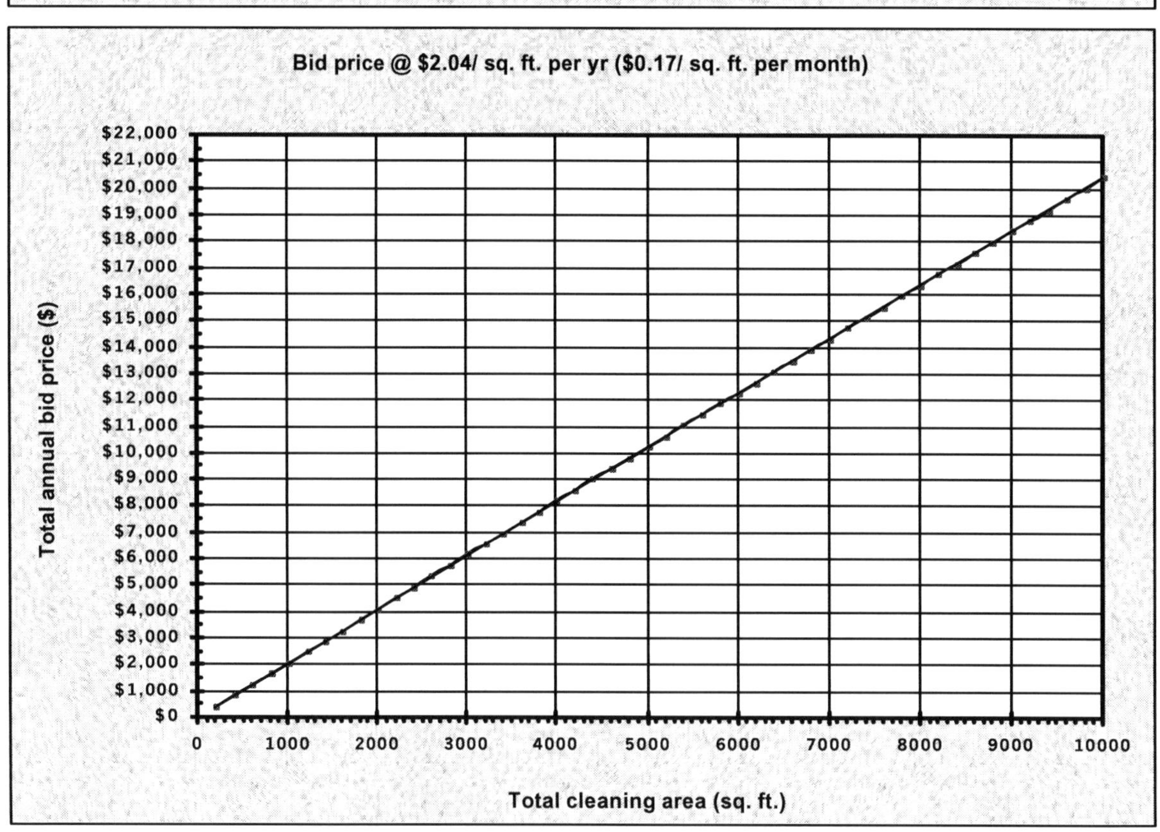
Bid price @ $2.04/ sq. ft. per yr ($0.17/ sq. ft. per month)
Total annual bid price ($)
$22,000
$21,000
$20,000
$19,000
$18,000
$17,000
$16,000
$15,000
$14,000
$13,000
$12,000
$11,000
$10,000
$9,000
$8,000
$7,000
$6,000
$5,000
$4,000
$3,000
$2,000
$1,000
$0
0
1000
2000
3000
4000
5000
6000
7000
8000
9000
10000
Total cleaning area (sq. ft.)

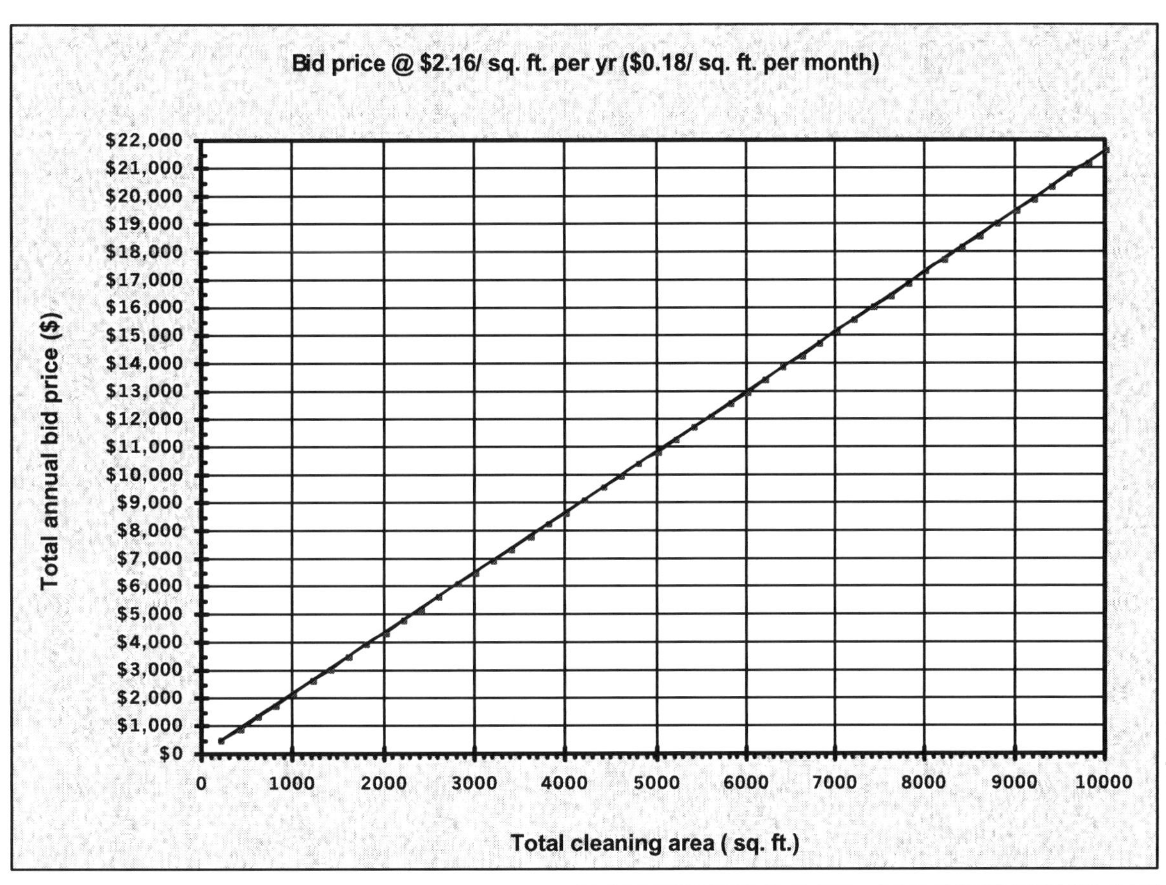
Bid price @ $2.16/ sq. ft. per yr ($0.18/ sq. ft. per month)
Total annual bid price ($)
$22,000
$21,000
$20,000
$19,000
$18,000
$17,000
$16,000
$15,000
$14,000
$13,000
$12,000
$11,000
$10,000
$9,000
$8,000
$7,000
$6,000
$5,000
$4,000
$3,000
$2,000
$1,000
$0
0
1000
2000
3000
4000
5000
6000
7000
8000
9000
10000
Total cleaning area (sq. ft.)

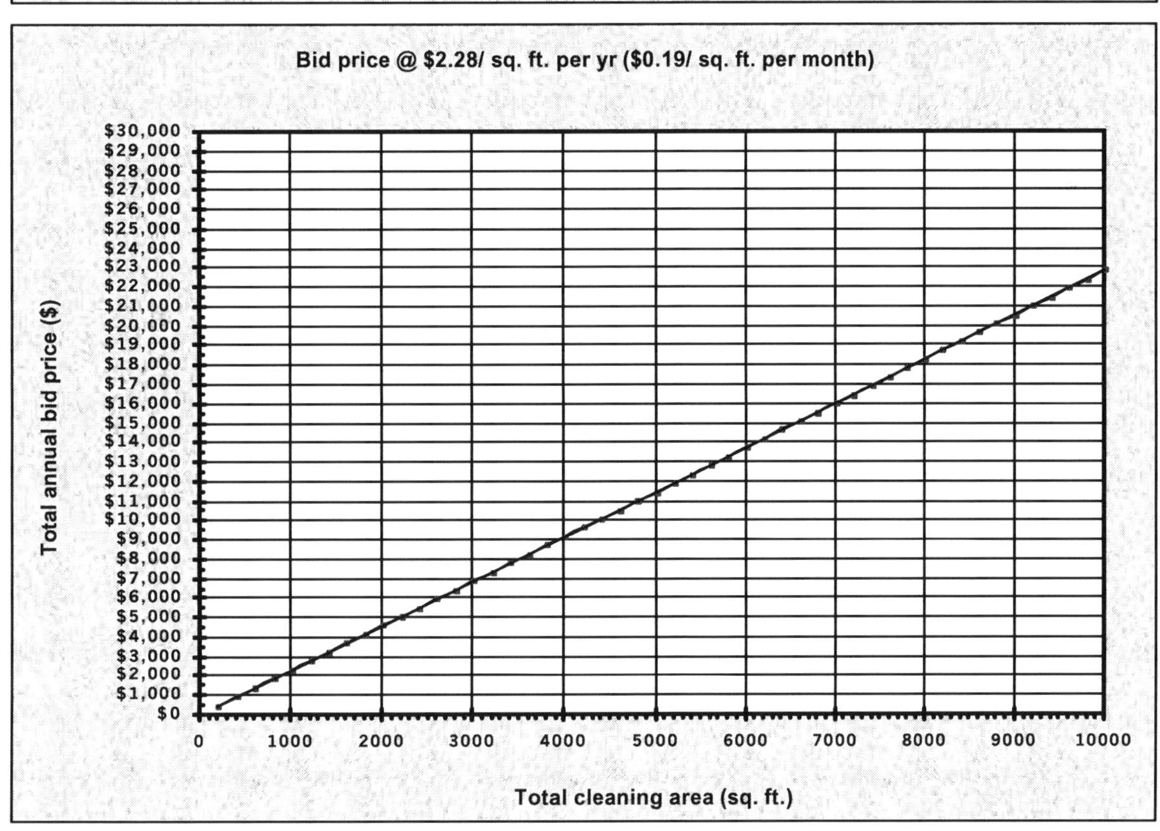
Bid price @ $2.28/ sq. ft. per yr ($0.19/ sq. ft. per month)
Total annual bid price ($)
$30,000
$29,000
$28,000
$27,000
$26,000
$25,000
$24,000
$23,000
$22,000
$21,000
$20,000
$19,000
$18,000
$17,000
$16,000
$15,000
$14,000
$13,000
$12,000
$11,000
$10,000
$9,000
$8,000
$7,000
$6,000
$5,000
$4,000
$3,000
$2,000
$1,000
$0
0
1000
2000
3000
4000
5000
6000
7000
8000
9000
10000
Total cleaning area (sq. ft.)

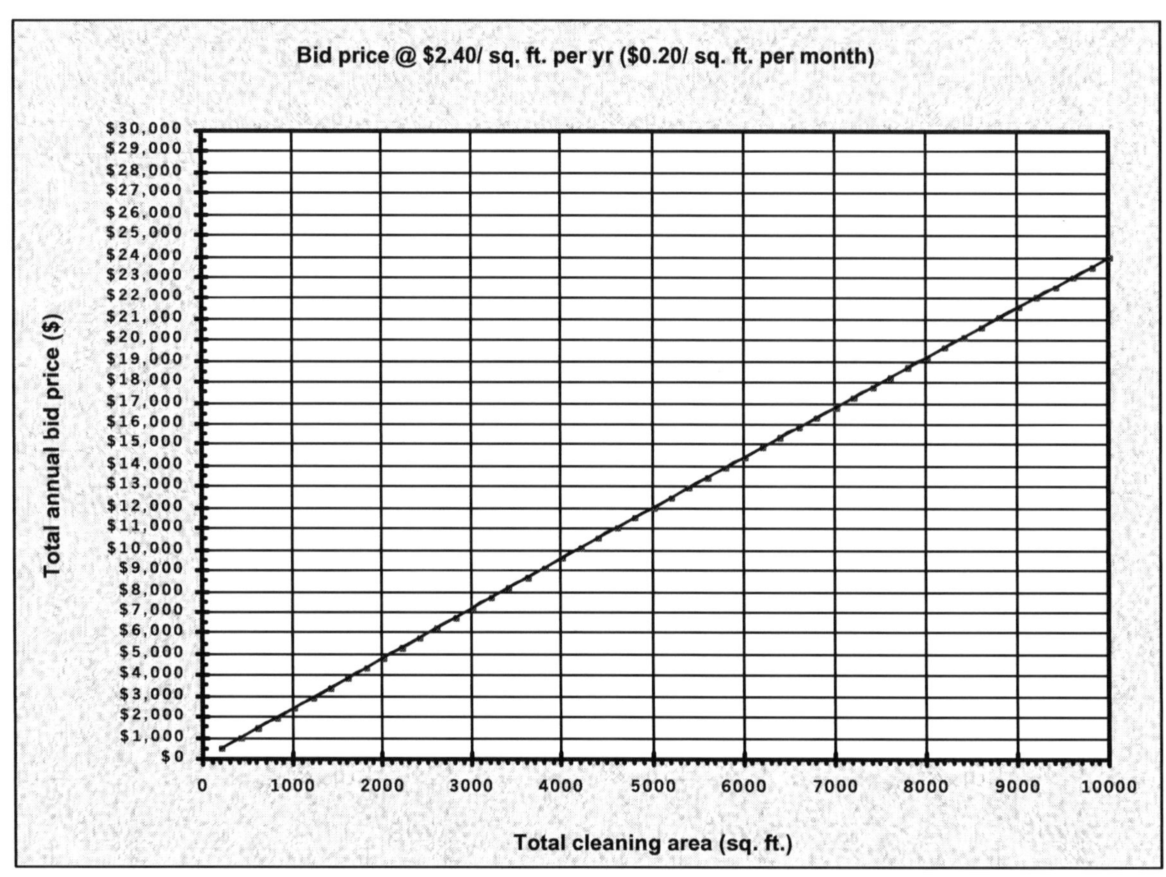
Bid price @ $2.40/ sq. ft. per yr ($0.20/ sq. ft. per month)
Total annual bid price ($)
$30,000
$29,000
$28,000
$27,000
$26,000
$25,000
$24,000
$23,000
$22,000
$21,000
$20,000
$19,000
$18,000
$17,000
$16,000
$15,000
$14,000
$13,000
$12,000
$11,000
$10,000
$9,000
$8,000
$7,000
$6,000
$5,000
$4,000
$3,000
$2,000
$1,000
$0
0
1000
2000
3000
4000
5000
6000
7000
8000
9000
10000
Total cleaning area (sq. ft.)

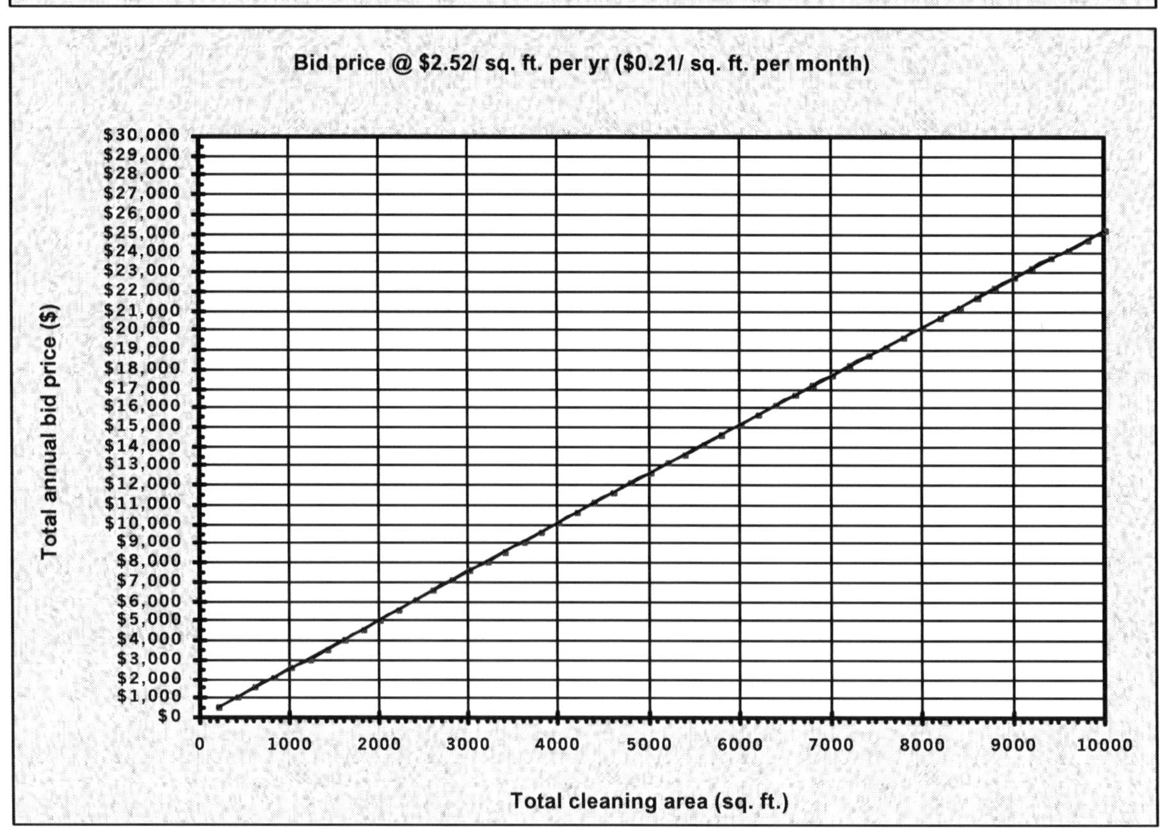
Bid price @ $2.52/ sq. ft. per yr ($0.21/ sq. ft. per month)
Total annual bid price ($)
$30,000
$29,000
$28,000
$27,000
$26,000
$25,000
$24,000
$23,000
$22,000
$21,000
$20,000
$19,000
$18,000
$17,000
$16,000
$15,000
$14,000
$13,000
$12,000
$11,000
$10,000
$9,000
$8,000
$7,000
$6,000
$5,000
$4,000
$3,000
$2,000
$1,000
$0
0
1000
2000
3000
4000
5000
6000
7000
8000
9000
10000
Total cleaning area (sq. ft.)

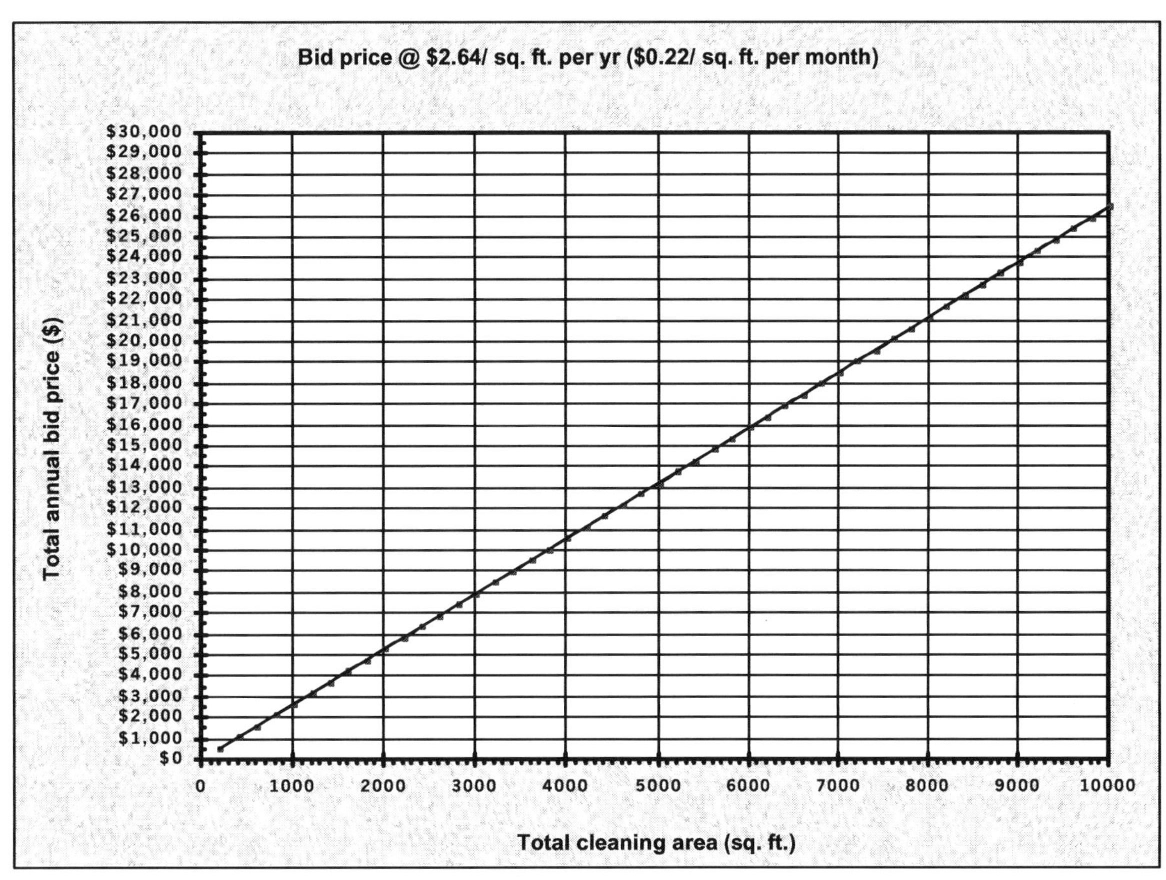
Bid price @ $2.64/ sq. ft. per yr ($0.22/ sq. ft. per month)
Total annual bid price ($)
$30,000
$29,000
$28,000
$27,000
$26,000
$25,000
$24,000
$23,000
$22,000
$21,000
$20,000
$19,000
$18,000
$17,000
$16,000
$15,000
$14,000
$13,000
$12,000
$11,000
$10,000
$9,000
$8,000
$7,000
$6,000
$5,000
$4,000
$3,000
$2,000
$1,000
$0
0
1000
2000
3000
4000
5000
6000
7000
8000
9000
10000
Total cleaning area (sq. ft.)

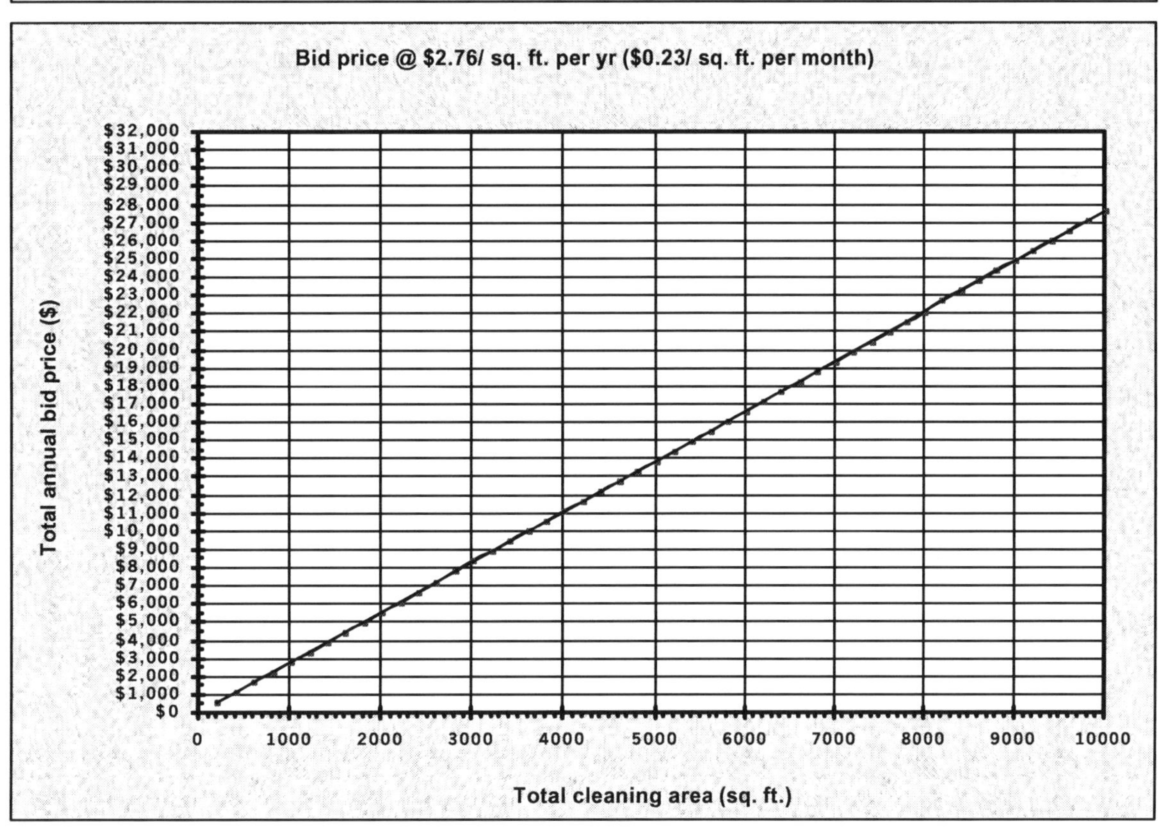
Bid price @ $2.76/ sq. ft. per yr ($0.23/ sq. ft. per month)
Total annual bid price ($)
$32,000
$31,000
$30,000
$29,000
$28,000
$27,000
$26,000
$25,000
$24,000
$23,000
$22,000
$21,000
$20,000
$19,000
$18,000
$17,000
$16,000
$15,000
$14,000
$13,000
$12,000
$11,000
$10,000
$9,000
$8,000
$7,000
$6,000
$5,000
$4,000
$3,000
$2,000
$1,000
$0
0
1000
2000
3000
4000
5000
6000
7000
8000
9000
10000
Total cleaning area (sq. ft.)

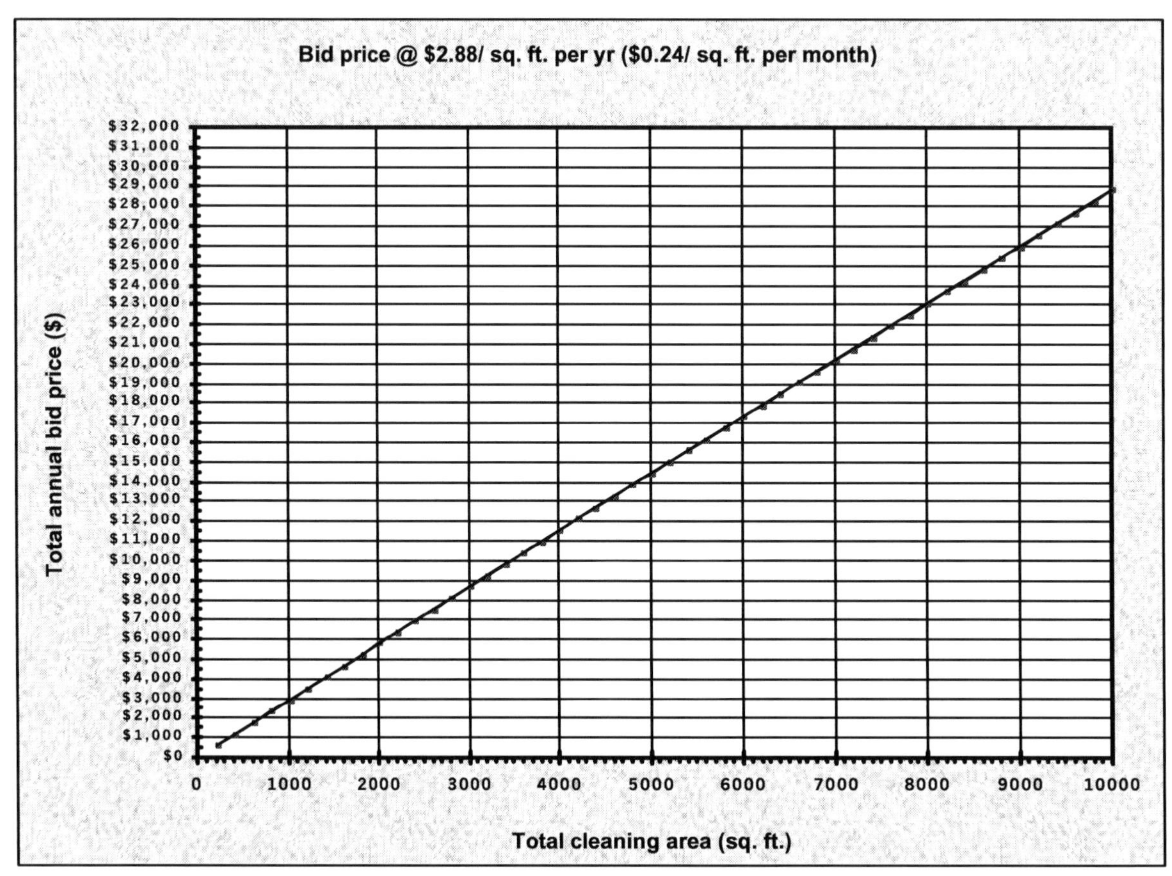
Bid price @ $2.88/ sq. ft. per yr ($0.24/ sq. ft. per month)
Total annual bid price ($)
$32,000
$31,000
$30,000
$29,000
$28,000
$27,000
$26,000
$25,000
$24,000
$23,000
$22,000
$21,000
$20,000
$19,000
$18,000
$17,000
$16,000
$15,000
$14,000
$13,000
$12,000
$11,000
$10,000
$9,000
$8,000
$7,000
$6,000
$5,000
$4,000
$3,000
$2,000
$1,000
$0
0
1000
2000
3000
4000
5000
6000
7000
8000
9000
10000
Total cleaning area (sq. ft.)

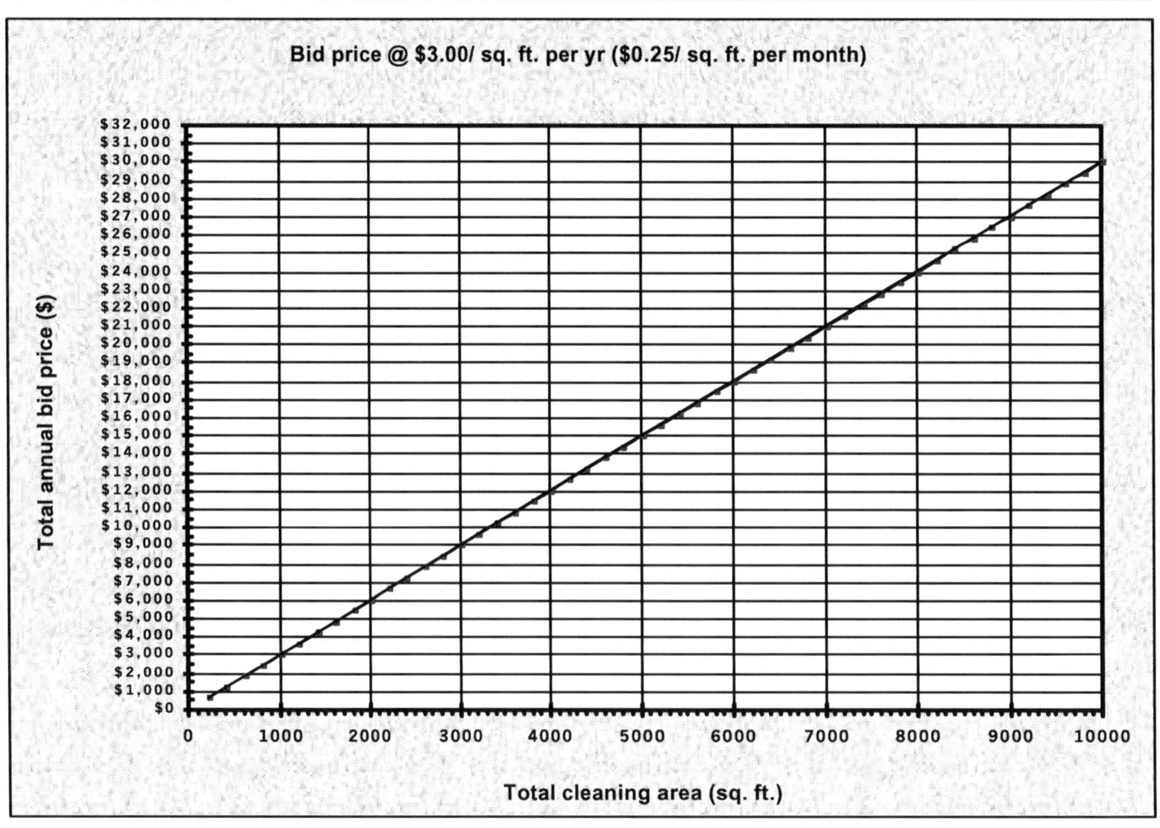
Bid price @ $3.00/ sq. ft. per yr ($0.25/ sq. ft. per month)
Total annual bid price ($)
$32,000
$31,000
$30,000
$29,000
$28,000
$27,000
$26,000
$25,000
$24,000
$23,000
$22,000
$21,000
$20,000
$19,000
$18,000
$17,000
$16,000
$15,000
$14,000
$13,000
$12,000
$11,000
$10,000
$9,000
$8,000
$7,000
$6,000
$5,000
$4,000
$3,000
$2,000
$1,000
$0
0
1000
2000
3000
4000
5000
6000
7000
8000
9000
10000
Total cleaning area (sq. ft.)

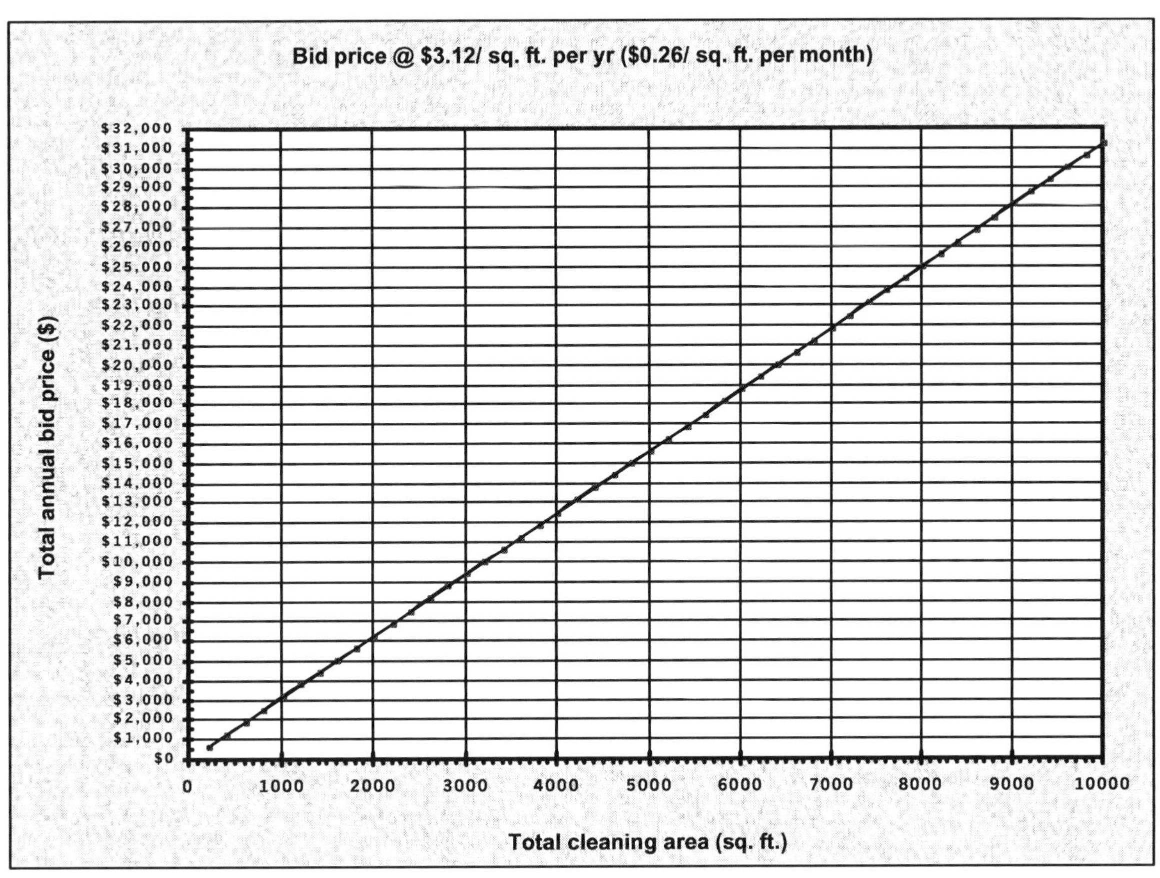
Bid price @ $3.12/ sq. ft. per yr ($0.26/ sq. ft. per month)
Total annual bid price ($)
$32,000
$31,000
$30,000
$29,000
$28,000
$27,000
$26,000
$25,000
$24,000
$23,000
$22,000
$21,000
$20,000
$19,000
$18,000
$17,000
$16,000
$15,000
$14,000
$13,000
$12,000
$11,000
$10,000
$9,000
$8,000
$7,000
$6,000
$5,000
$4,000
$3,000
$2,000
$1,000
$0
0
1000
2000
3000
4000
5000
6000
7000
8000
9000
10000
Total cleaning area (sq. ft.)

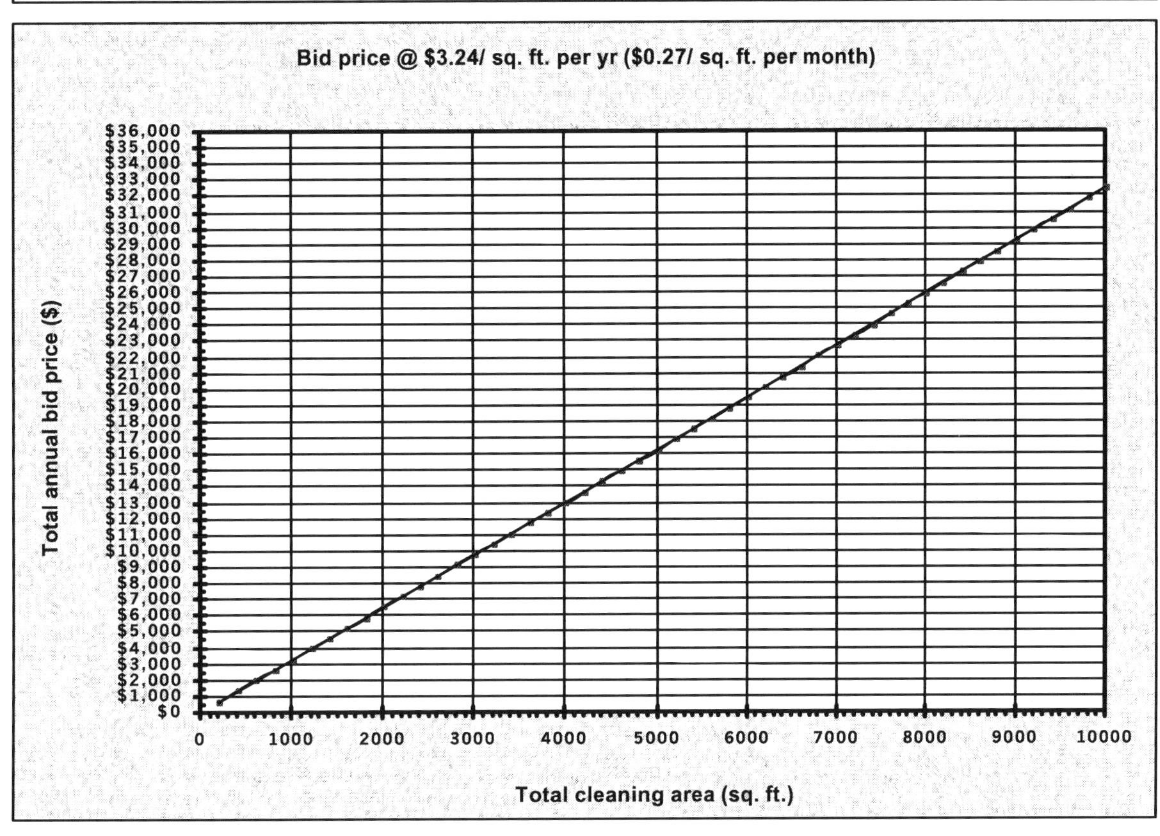
Bid price @ $3.24/ sq. ft. per yr ($0.27/ sq. ft. per month)
Total annual bid price ($)
$36,000
$35,000
$34,000
$33,000
$32,000
$31,000
$30,000
$29,000
$28,000
$27,000
$26,000
$25,000
$24,000
$23,000
$22,000
$21,000
$20,000
$19,000
$18,000
$17,000
$16,000
$15,000
$14,000
$13,000
$12,000
$11,000
$10,000
$9,000
$8,000
$7,000
$6,000
$5,000
$4,000
$3,000
$2,000
$1,000
$0
0
1000
2000
3000
4000
5000
6000
7000
8000
9000
10000
Total cleaning area (sq. ft.)

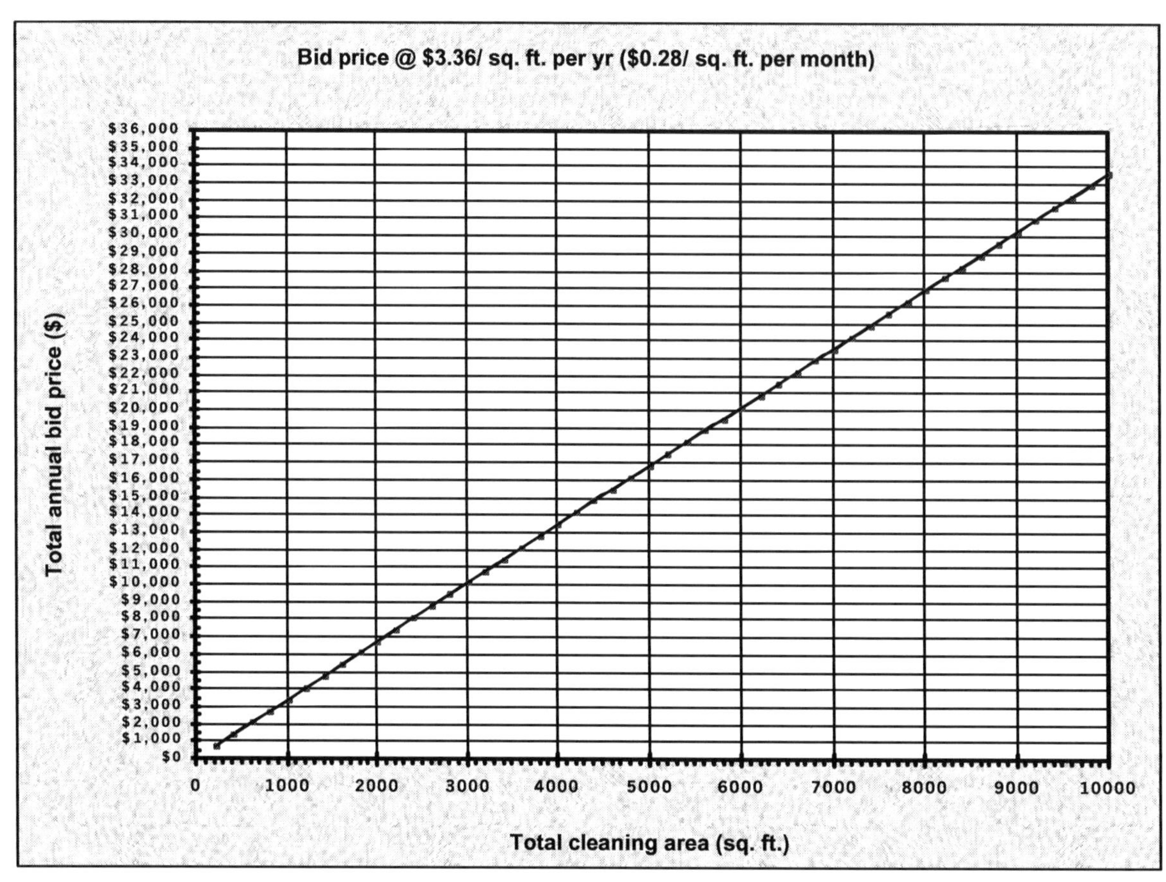
Bid price @ $3.36/ sq. ft. per yr ($0.28/ sq. ft. per month)
Total annual bid price ($)
$36,000
$35,000
$34,000
$33,000
$32,000
$31,000
$30,000
$29,000
$28,000
$27,000
$26,000
$25,000
$24,000
$23,000
$22,000
$21,000
$20,000
$19,000
$18,000
$17,000
$16,000
$15,000
$14,000
$13,000
$12,000
$11,000
$10,000
$9,000
$8,000
$7,000
$6,000
$5,000
$4,000
$3,000
$2,000
$1,000
$0
0
1000
2000
3000
4000
5000
6000
7000
8000
9000
10000
Total cleaning area (sq. ft.)

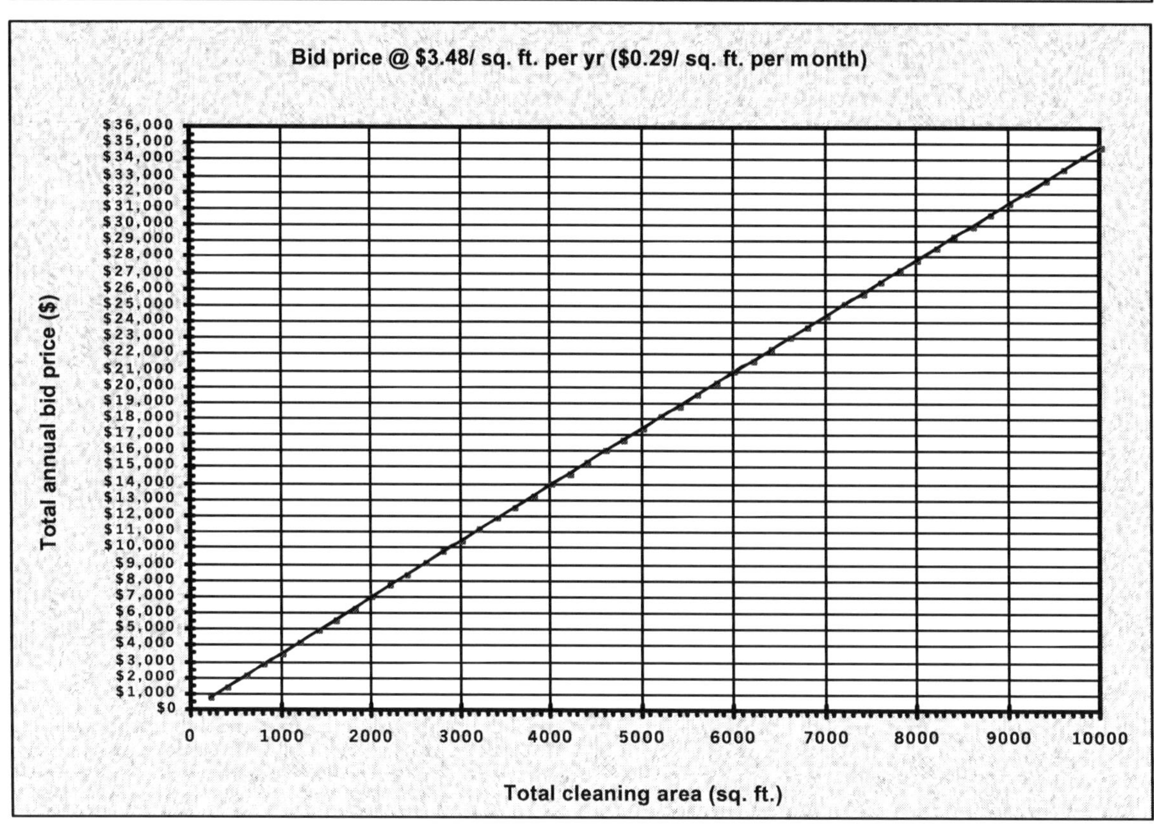
Bid price @ $3.48/ sq. ft. per yr ($0.29/ sq. ft. per month)
Total annual bid price ($)
$36,000
$35,000
$34,000
$33,000
$32,000
$31,000
$30,000
$29,000
$28,000
$27,000
$26,000
$25,000
$24,000
$23,000
$22,000
$21,000
$20,000
$19,000
$18,000
$17,000
$16,000
$15,000
$14,000
$13,000
$12,000
$11,000
$10,000
$9,000
$8,000
$7,000
$6,000
$5,000
$4,000
$3,000
$2,000
$1,000
$0
0
1000
2000
3000
4000
5000
6000
7000
8000
9000
10000
Total cleaning area (sq. ft.)

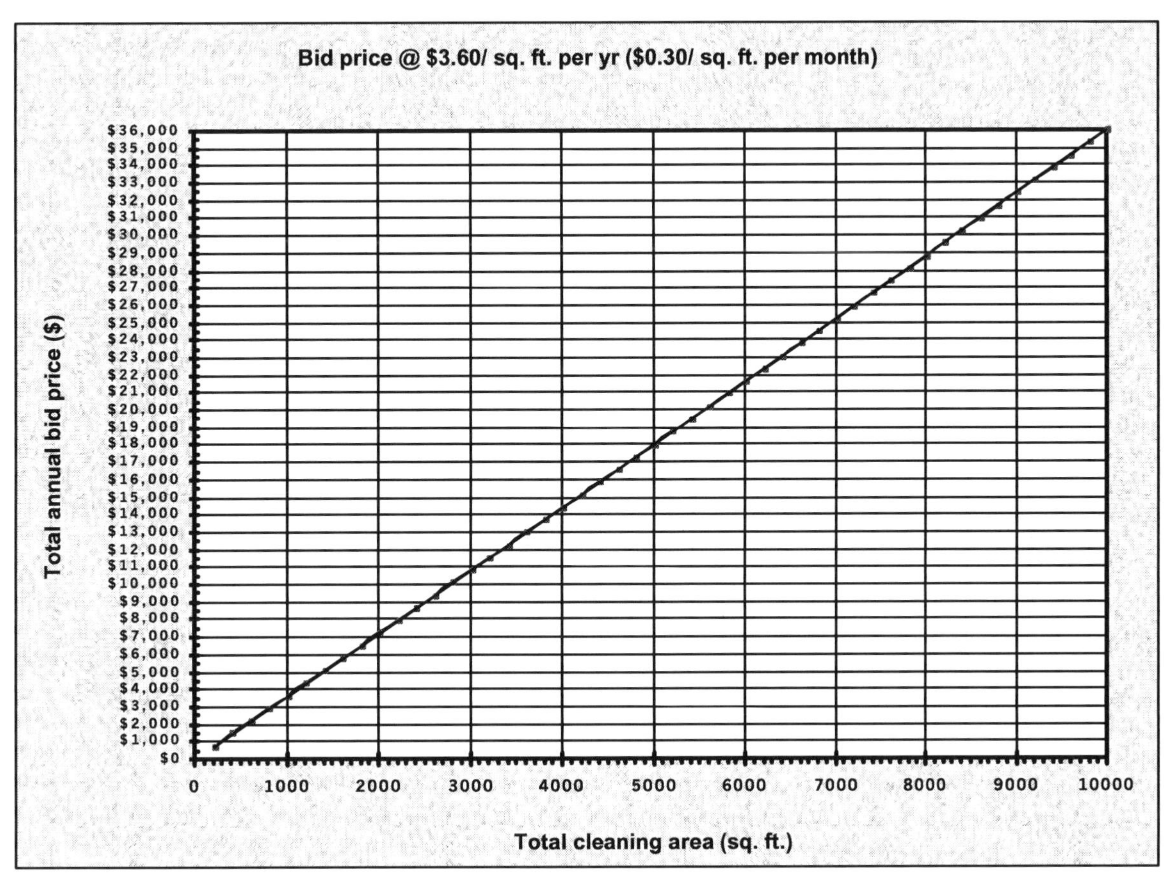
Bid price @ $3.60/ sq. ft. per yr ($0.30/ sq. ft. per month)
Total annual bid price ($)
$36,000
$35,000
$34,000
$33,000
$32,000
$31,000
$30,000
$29,000
$28,000
$27,000
$26,000
$25,000
$24,000
$23,000
$22,000
$21,000
$20,000
$19,000
$18,000
$17,000
$16,000
$15,000
$14,000
$13,000
$12,000
$11,000
$10,000
$9,000
$8,000
$7,000
$6,000
$5,000
$4,000
$3,000
$2,000
$1,000
$0
0
1000
2000
3000
4000
5000
6000
7000
8000
9000
10000
Total cleaning area (sq. ft.)

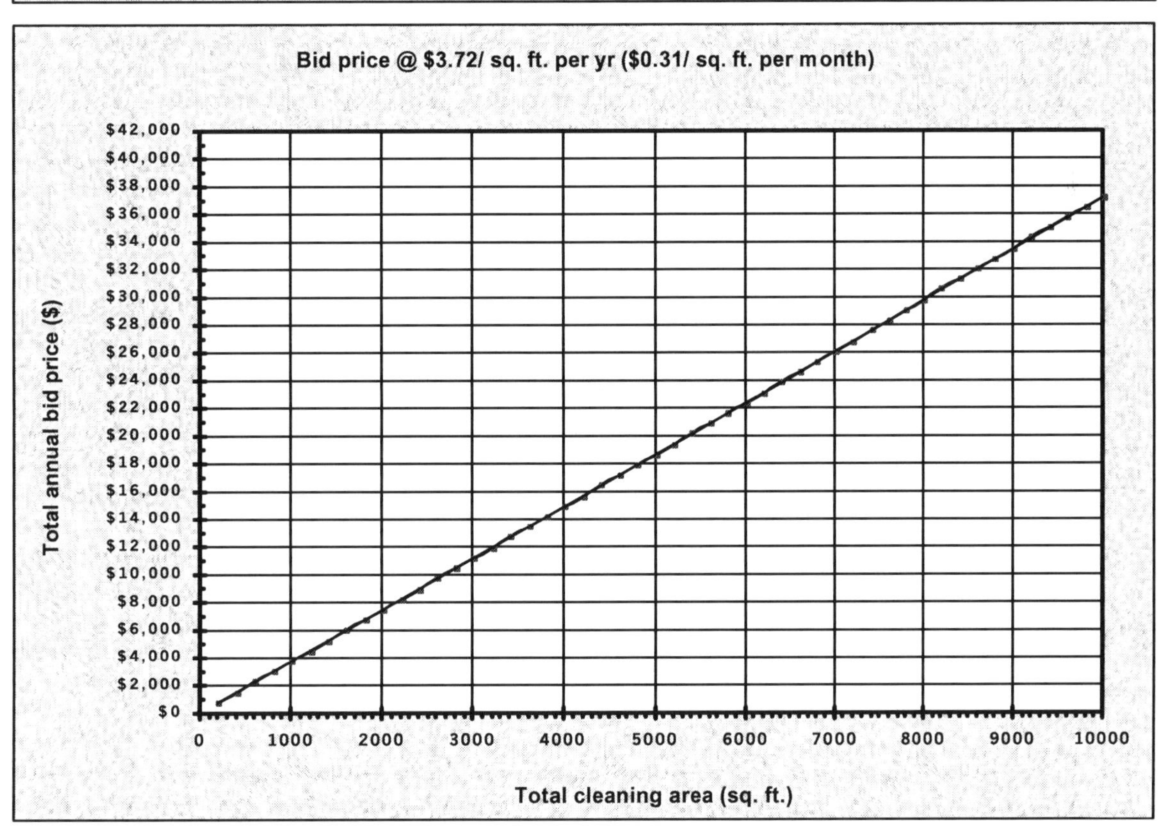
Bid price @ $3.72/ sq. ft. per yr ($0.31/ sq. ft. per month)
Total annual bid price ($)
$42,000
$40,000
$38,000
$36,000
$34,000
$32,000
$30,000
$28,000
$26,000
$24,000
$22,000
$20,000
$18,000
$16,000
$14,000
$12,000
$10,000
$8,000
$6,000
$4,000
$2,000
$0
0
1000
2000
3000
4000
5000
6000
7000
8000
9000
10000
Total cleaning area (sq. ft.)

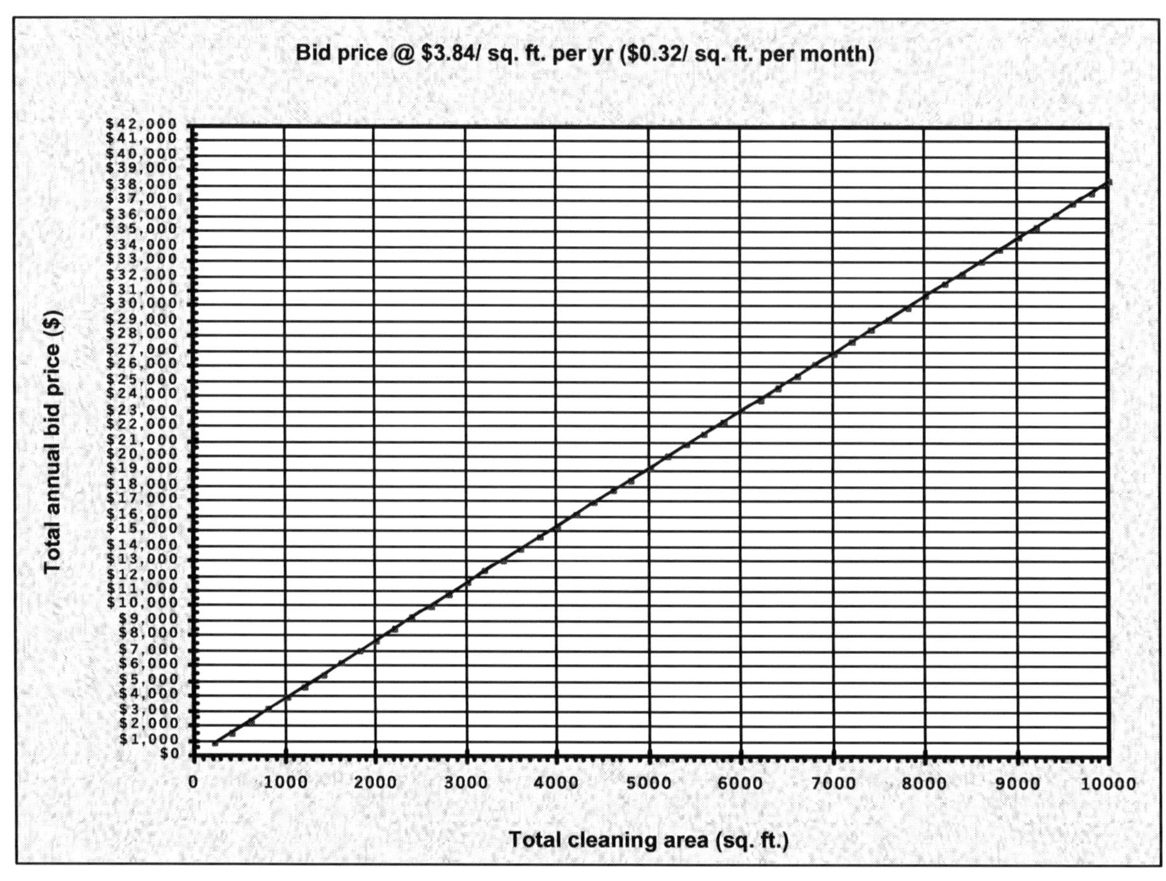
Bid price @ $3.84/ sq. ft. per yr ($0.32/ sq. ft. per month)
Total annual bid price ($)
$42,000
$41,000
$40,000
$39,000
$38,000
$37,000
$36,000
$35,000
$34,000
$33,000
$32,000
$31,000
$30,000
$29,000
$28,000
$27,000
$26,000
$25,000
$24,000
$23,000
$22,000
$21,000
$20,000
$19,000
$18,000
$17,000
$16,000
$15,000
$14,000
$13,000
$12,000
$11,000
$10,000
$9,000
$8,000
$7,000
$6,000
$5,000
$4,000
$3,000
$2,000
$1,000
$0
0
1000
2000
3000
4000
5000
6000
7000
8000
9000
10000
Total cleaning area (sq. ft.)

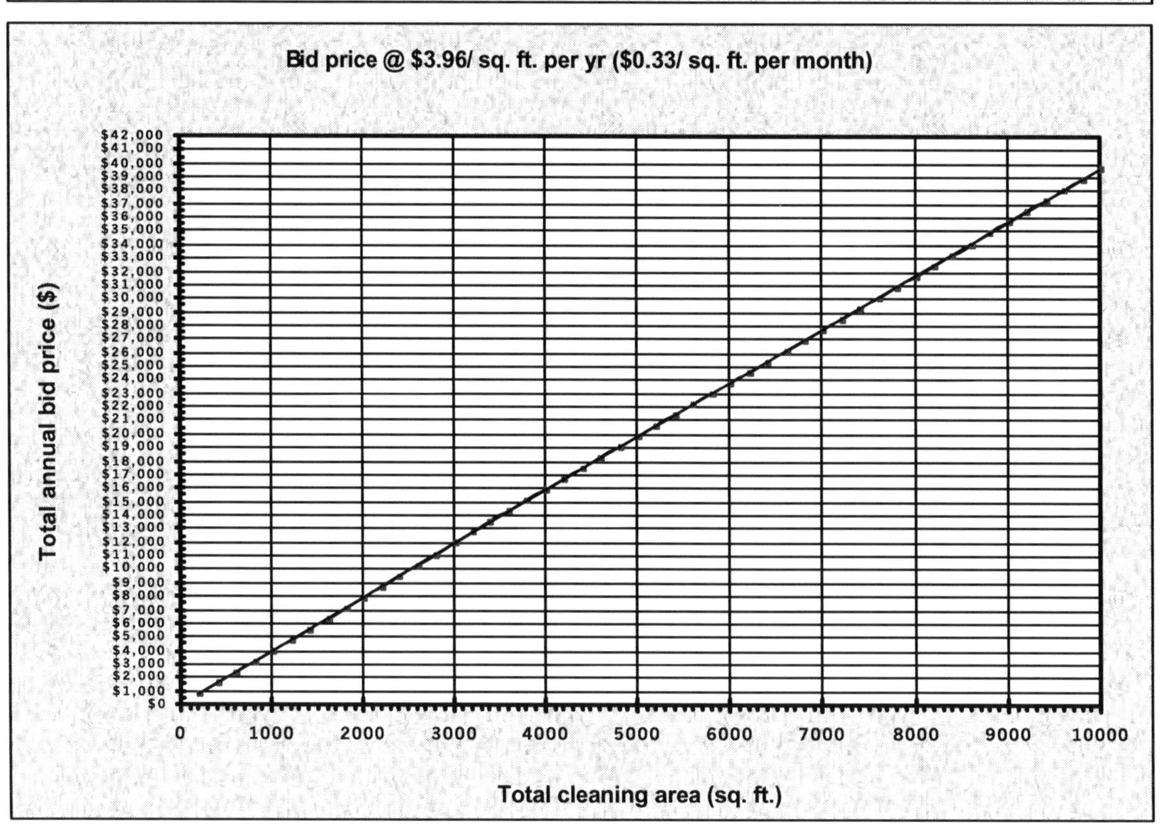
Bid price @ $3.96/ sq. ft. per yr ($0.33/ sq. ft. per month)
Total annual bid price ($)
$42,000
$41,000
$40,000
$39,000
$38,000
$37,000
$36,000
$35,000
$34,000
$33,000
$32,000
$31,000
$30,000
$29,000
$28,000
$27,000
$26,000
$25,000
$24,000
$23,000
$22,000
$21,000
$20,000
$19,000
$18,000
$17,000
$16,000
$15,000
$14,000
$13,000
$12,000
$11,000
$10,000
$9,000
$8,000
$7,000
$6,000
$5,000
$4,000
$3,000
$2,000
$1,000
$0
0
1000
2000
3000
4000
5000
6000
7000
8000
9000
10000
Total cleaning area (sq. ft.)

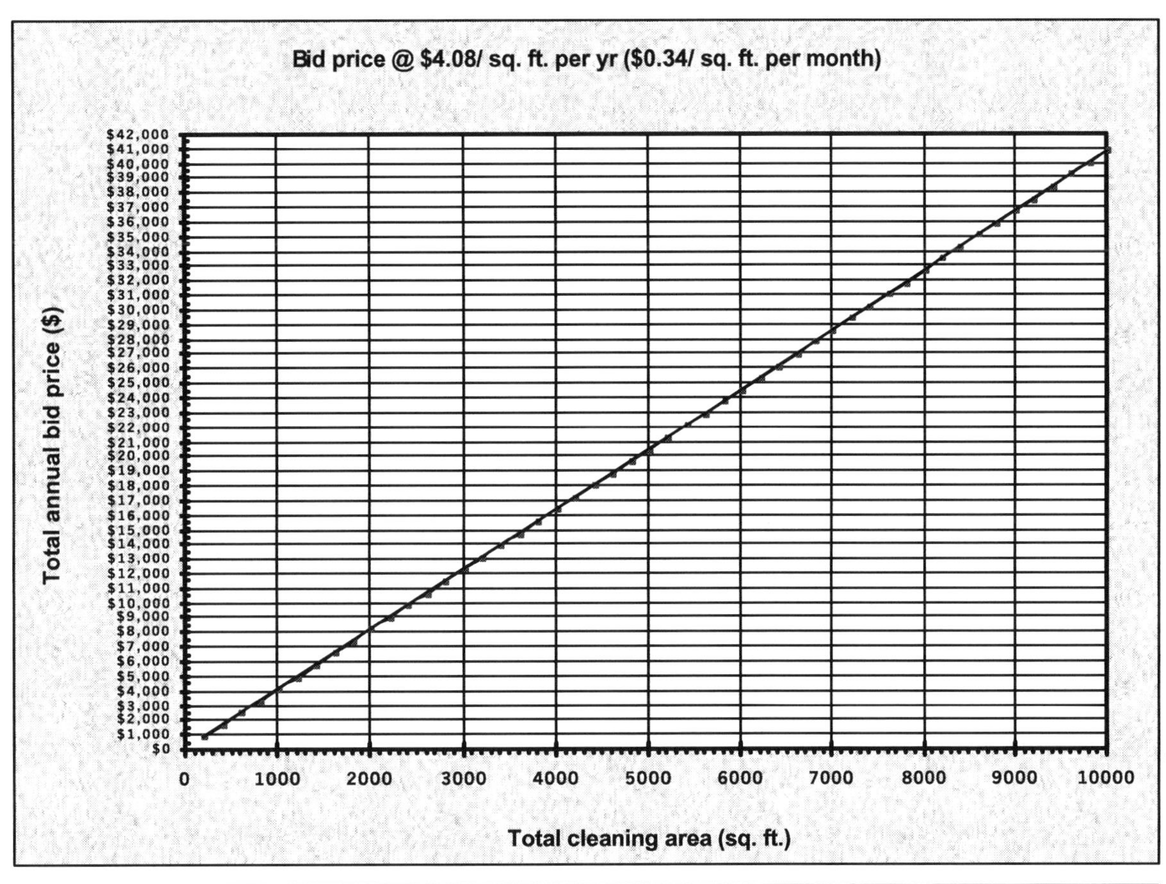
Bid price @ $4.08/ sq. ft. per yr ($0.34/ sq. ft. per month)
Total annual bid price ($)
$42,000
$41,000
$40,000
$39,000
$38,000
$37,000
$36,000
$35,000
$34,000
$33,000
$32,000
$31,000
$30,000
$29,000
$28,000
$27,000
$26,000
$25,000
$24,000
$23,000
$22,000
$21,000
$20,000
$19,000
$18,000
$17,000
$16,000
$15,000
$14,000
$13,000
$12,000
$11,000
$10,000
$9,000
$8,000
$7,000
$6,000
$5,000
$4,000
$3,000
$2,000
$1,000
$0
0
1000
2000
3000
4000
5000
6000
7000
8000
9000
10000
Total cleaning area (sq. ft.)

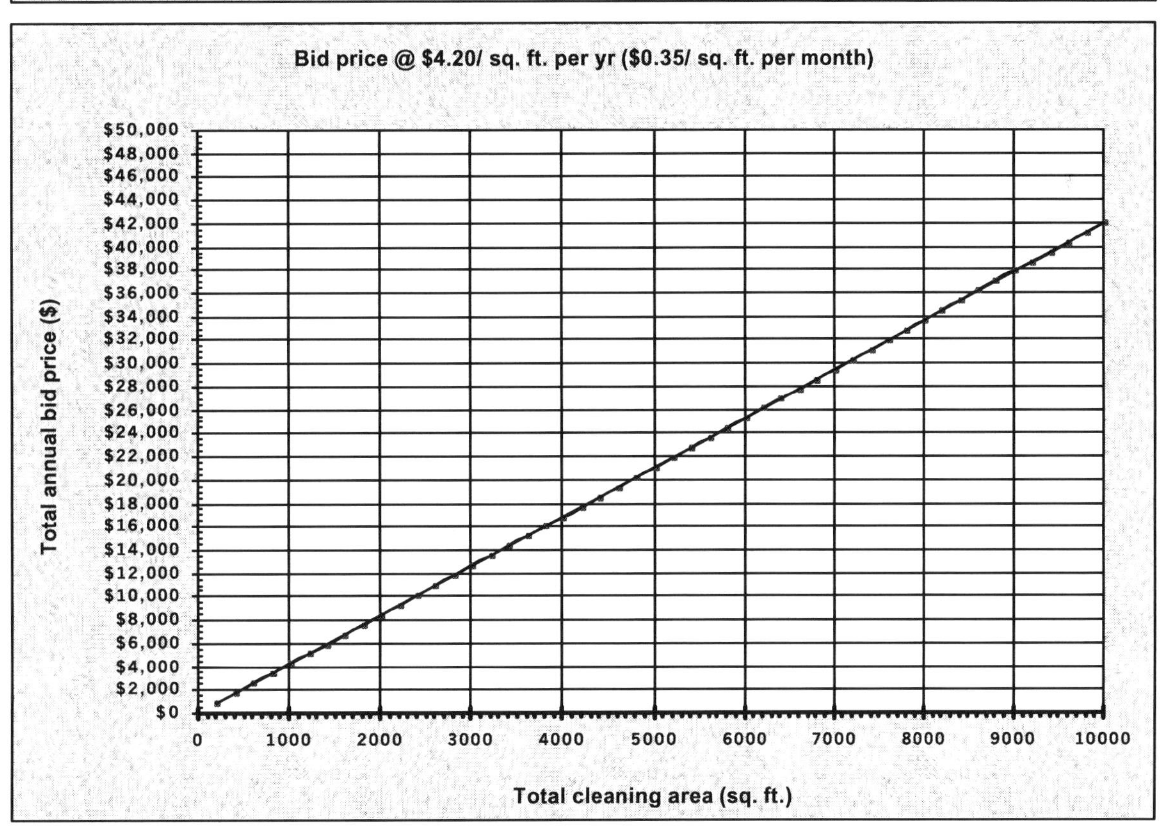
Bid price @ $4.20/ sq. ft. per yr ($0.35/ sq. ft. per month)
Total annual bid price ($)
$50,000
$48,000
$46,000
$44,000
$42,000
$40,000
$38,000
$36,000
$34,000
$32,000
$30,000
$28,000
$26,000
$24,000
$22,000
$20,000
$18,000
$16,000
$14,000
$12,000
$10,000
$8,000
$6,000
$4,000
$2,000
$0
0
1000
2000
3000
4000
5000
6000
7000
8000
9000
10000
Total cleaning area (sq. ft.)

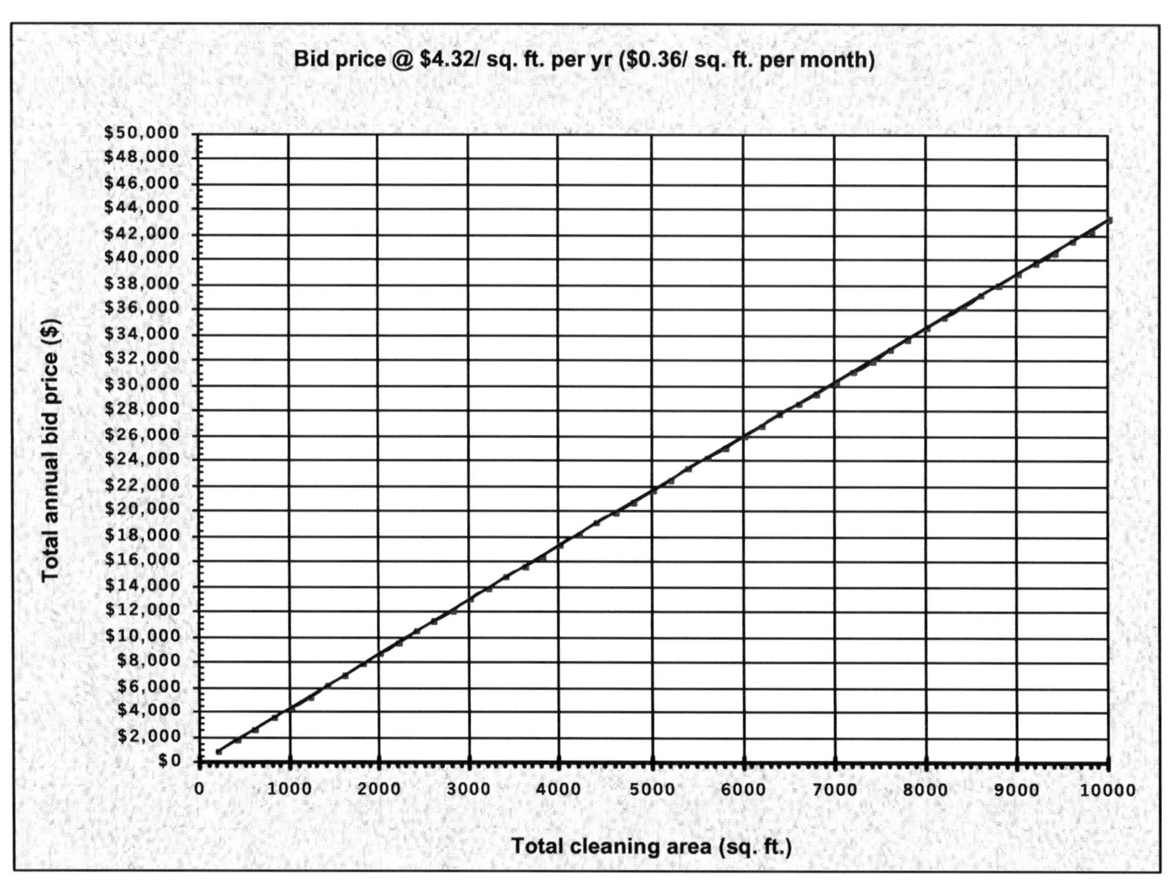
Bid price @ $4.32/ sq. ft. per yr ($0.36/ sq. ft. per month)
Total annual bid price ($)
$50,000
$48,000
$46,000
$44,000
$42,000
$40,000
$38,000
$36,000
$34,000
$32,000
$30,000
$28,000
$26,000
$24,000
$22,000
$20,000
$18,000
$16,000
$14,000
$12,000
$10,000
$8,000
$6,000
$4,000
$2,000
$0
0
1000
2000
3000
4000
5000
6000
7000
8000
9000
10000
Total cleaning area (sq. ft.)

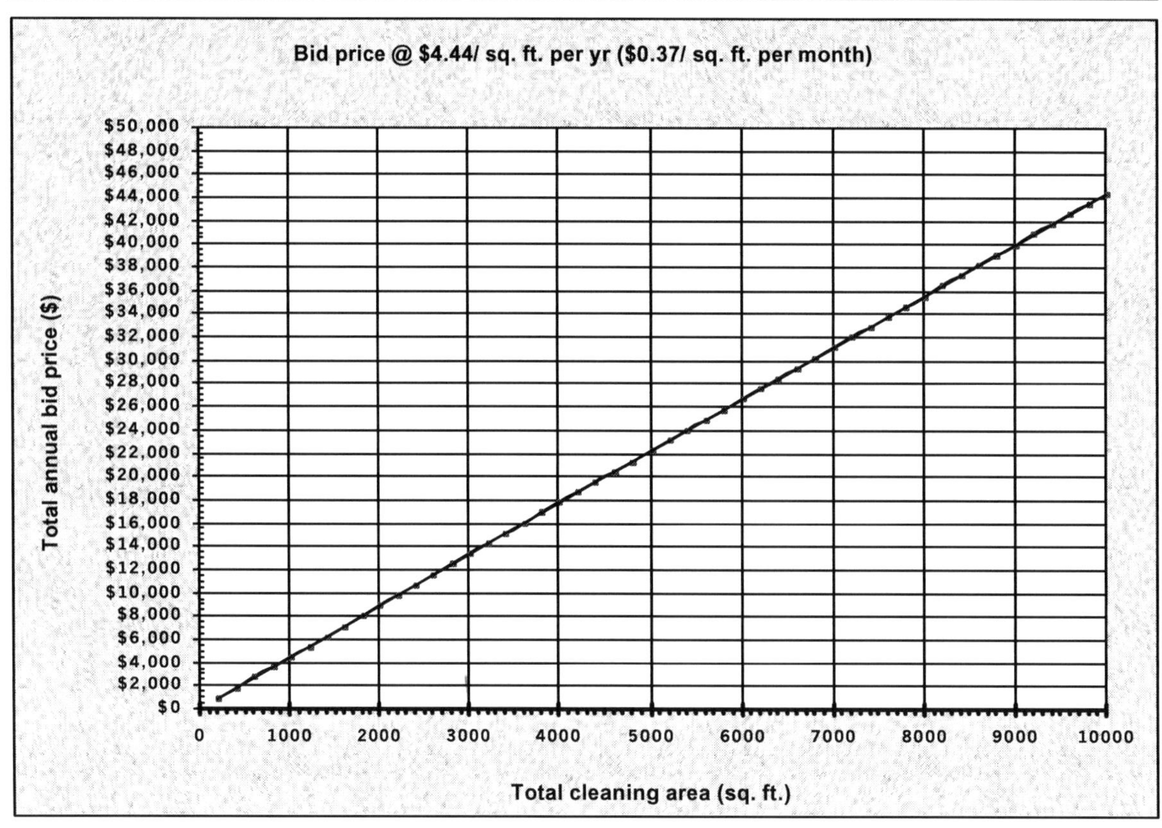
Bid price @ $4.44/ sq. ft. per yr ($0.37/ sq. ft. per month)
Total annual bid price ($)
$50,000
$48,000
$46,000
$44,000
$42,000
$40,000
$38,000
$36,000
$34,000
$32,000
$30,000
$28,000
$26,000
$24,000
$22,000
$20,000
$18,000
$16,000
$14,000
$12,000
$10,000
$8,000
$6,000
$4,000
$2,000
$0
0
1000
2000
3000
4000
5000
6000
7000
8000
9000
10000
Total cleaning area (sq. ft.)

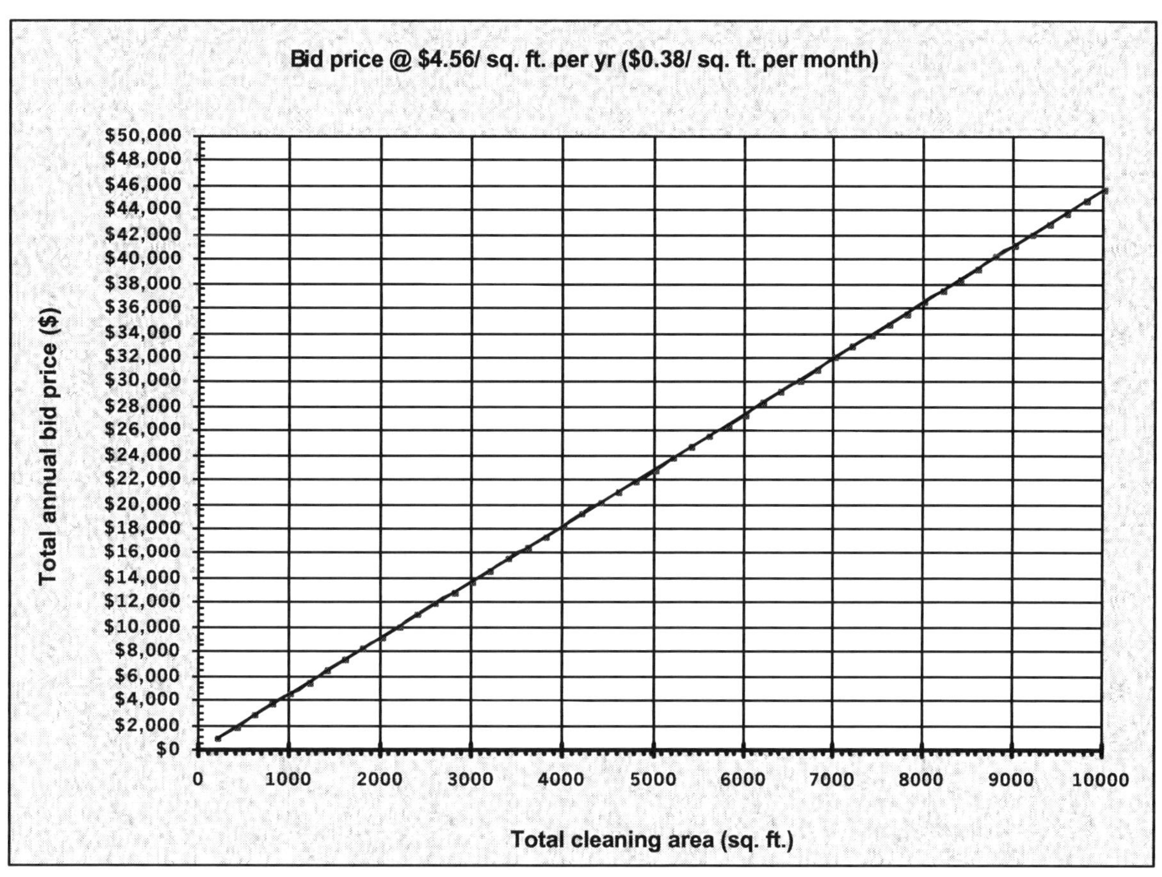
Bid price @ $4.56/ sq. ft. per yr ($0.38/ sq. ft. per month)
Total annual bid price ($)
$50,000
$48,000
$46,000
$44,000
$42,000
$40,000
$38,000
$36,000
$34,000
$32,000
$30,000
$28,000
$26,000
$24,000
$22,000
$20,000
$18,000
$16,000
$14,000
$12,000
$10,000
$8,000
$6,000
$4,000
$2,000
$0
0
1000
2000
3000
4000
5000
6000
7000
8000
9000
10000
Total cleaning area (sq. ft.)

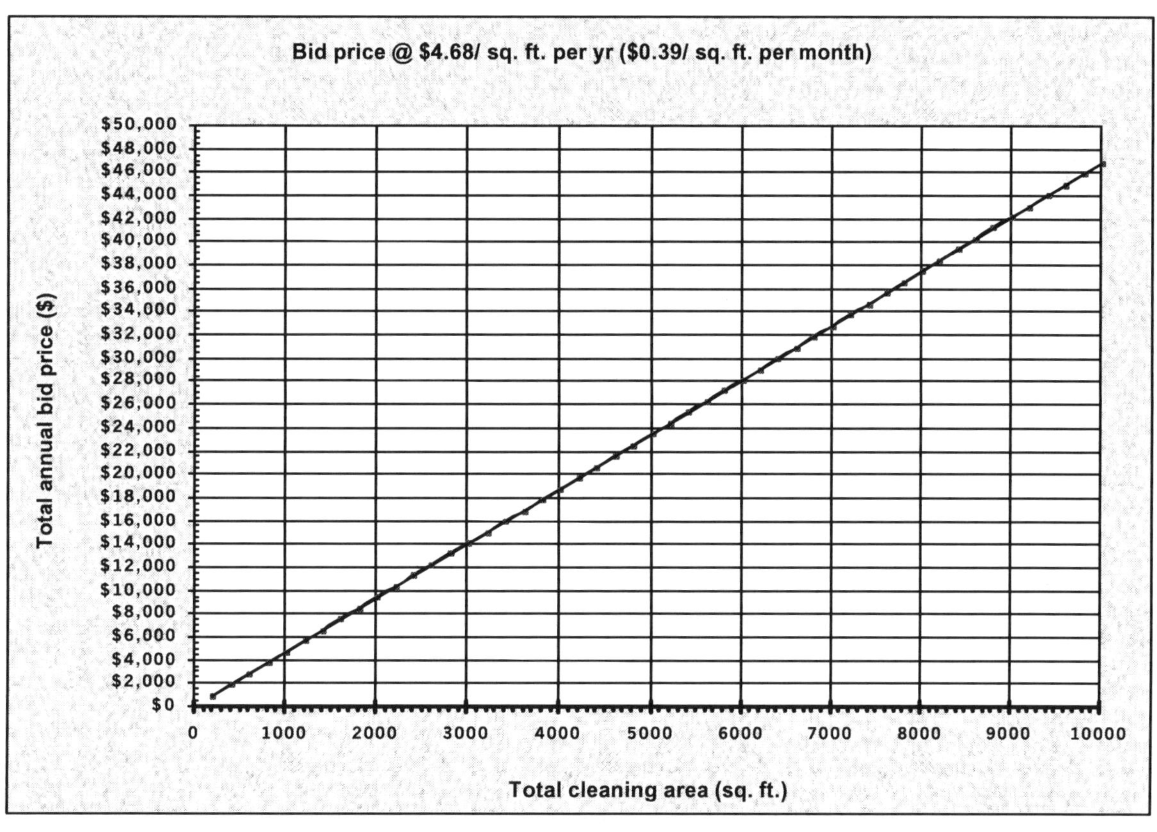
Bid price @ $4.68/ sq. ft. per yr ($0.39/ sq. ft. per month)
Total annual bid price ($)
$50,000
$48,000
$46,000
$44,000
$42,000
$40,000
$38,000
$36,000
$34,000
$32,000
$30,000
$28,000
$26,000
$24,000
$22,000
$20,000
$18,000
$16,000
$14,000
$12,000
$10,000
$8,000
$6,000
$4,000
$2,000
$0
0
1000
2000
3000
4000
5000
6000
7000
8000
9000
10000
Total cleaning area (sq. ft.)

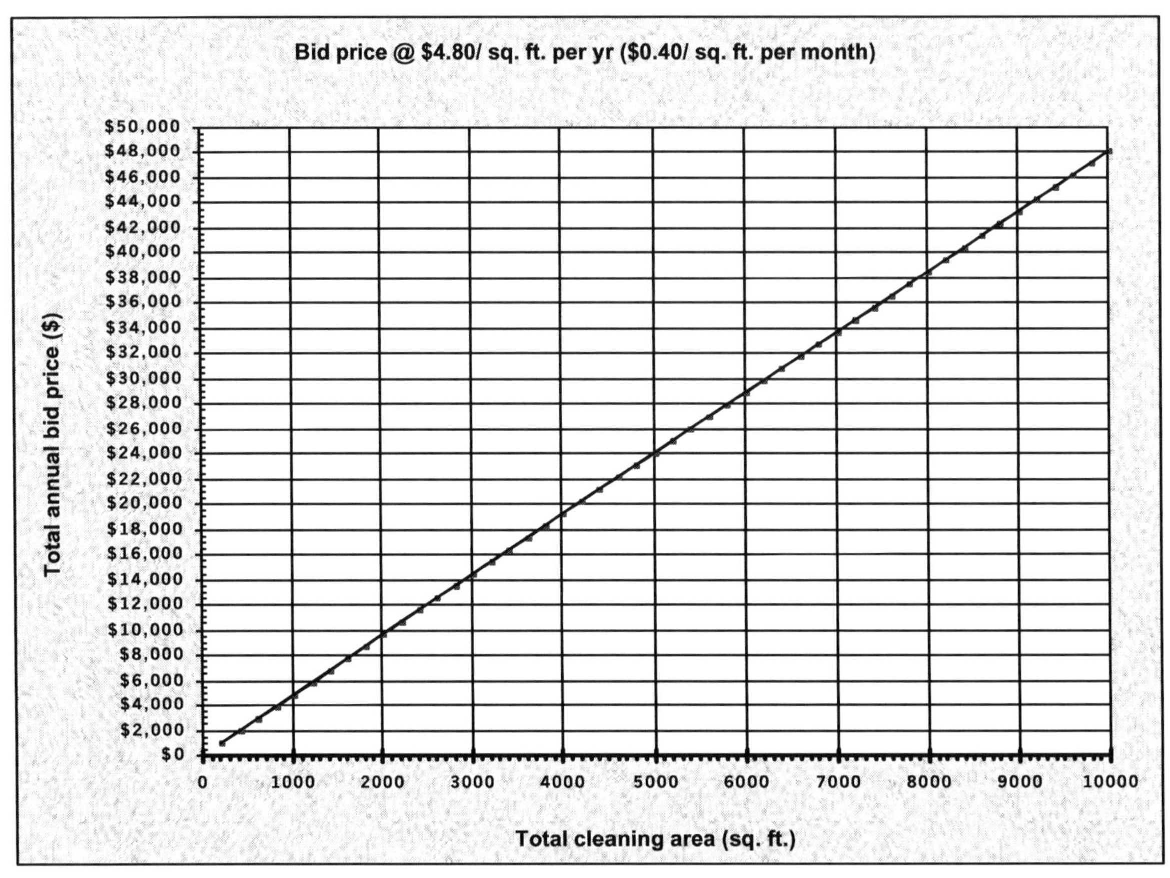
Bid price @ $4.80/ sq. ft. per yr ($0.40/ sq. ft. per month)
Total annual bid price ($)
$50,000
$48,000
$46,000
$44,000
$42,000
$40,000
$38,000
$36,000
$34,000
$32,000
$30,000
$28,000
$26,000
$24,000
$22,000
$20,000
$18,000
$16,000
$14,000
$12,000
$10,000
$8,000
$6,000
$4,000
$2,000
$0
0
1000
2000
3000
4000
5000
6000
7000
8000
9000
10000
Total cleaning area (sq. ft.)

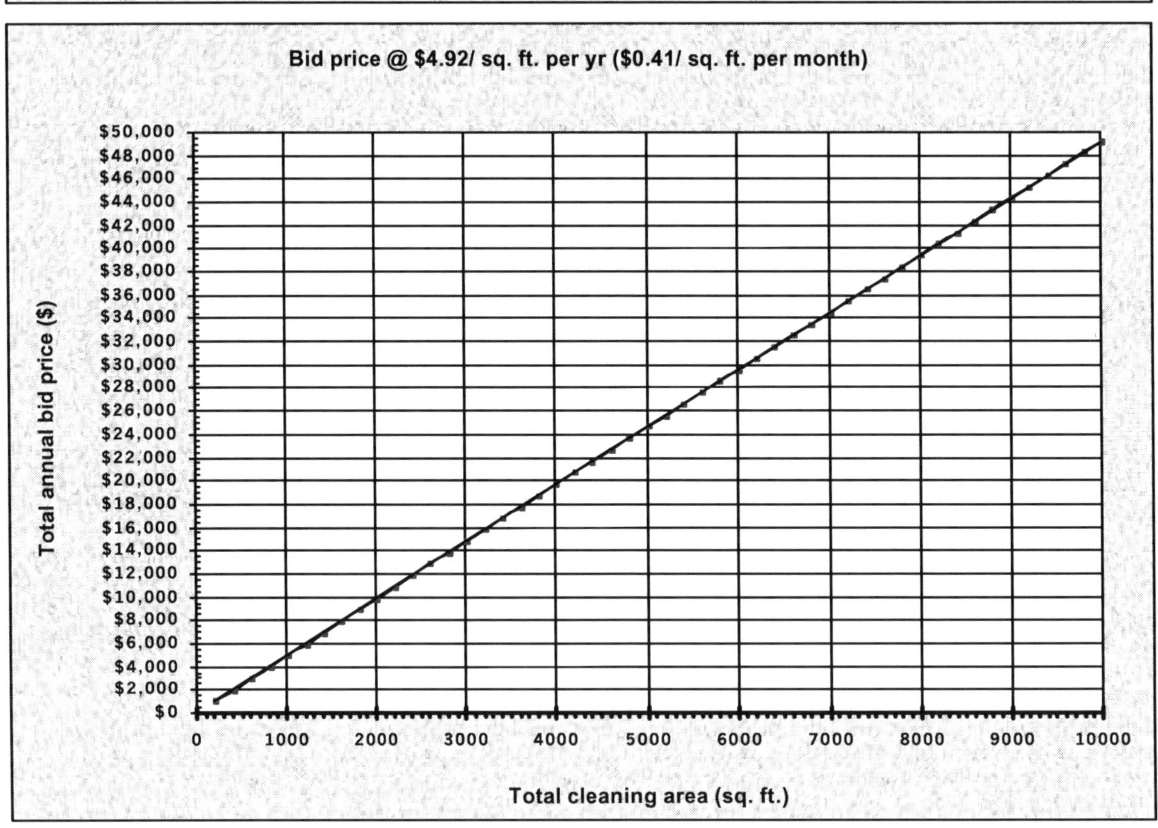
Bid price @ $4.92/ sq. ft. per yr ($0.41/ sq. ft. per month)
Total annual bid price ($)
$50,000
$48,000
$46,000
$44,000
$42,000
$40,000
$38,000
$36,000
$34,000
$32,000
$30,000
$28,000
$26,000
$24,000
$22,000
$20,000
$18,000
$16,000
$14,000
$12,000
$10,000
$8,000
$6,000
$4,000
$2,000
$0
0
1000
2000
3000
4000
5000
6000
7000
8000
9000
10000
Total cleaning area (sq. ft.)

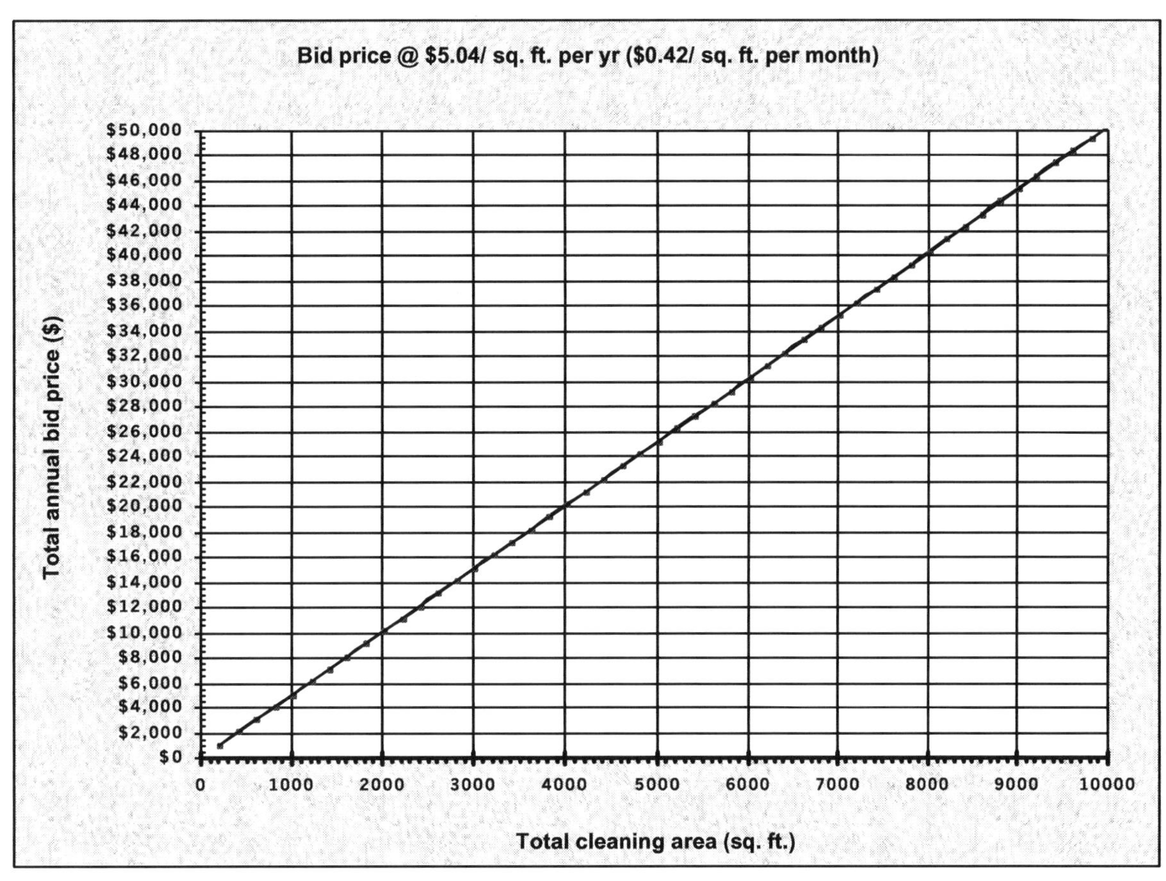
Bid price @ $5.04/ sq. ft. per yr ($0.42/ sq. ft. per month)
Total annual bid price ($)
$50,000
$48,000
$46,000
$44,000
$42,000
$40,000
$38,000
$36,000
$34,000
$32,000
$30,000
$28,000
$26,000
$24,000
$22,000
$20,000
$18,000
$16,000
$14,000
$12,000
$10,000
$8,000
$6,000
$4,000
$2,000
$0
0
1000
2000
3000
4000
5000
6000
7000
8000
9000
10000
Total cleaning area (sq. ft.)

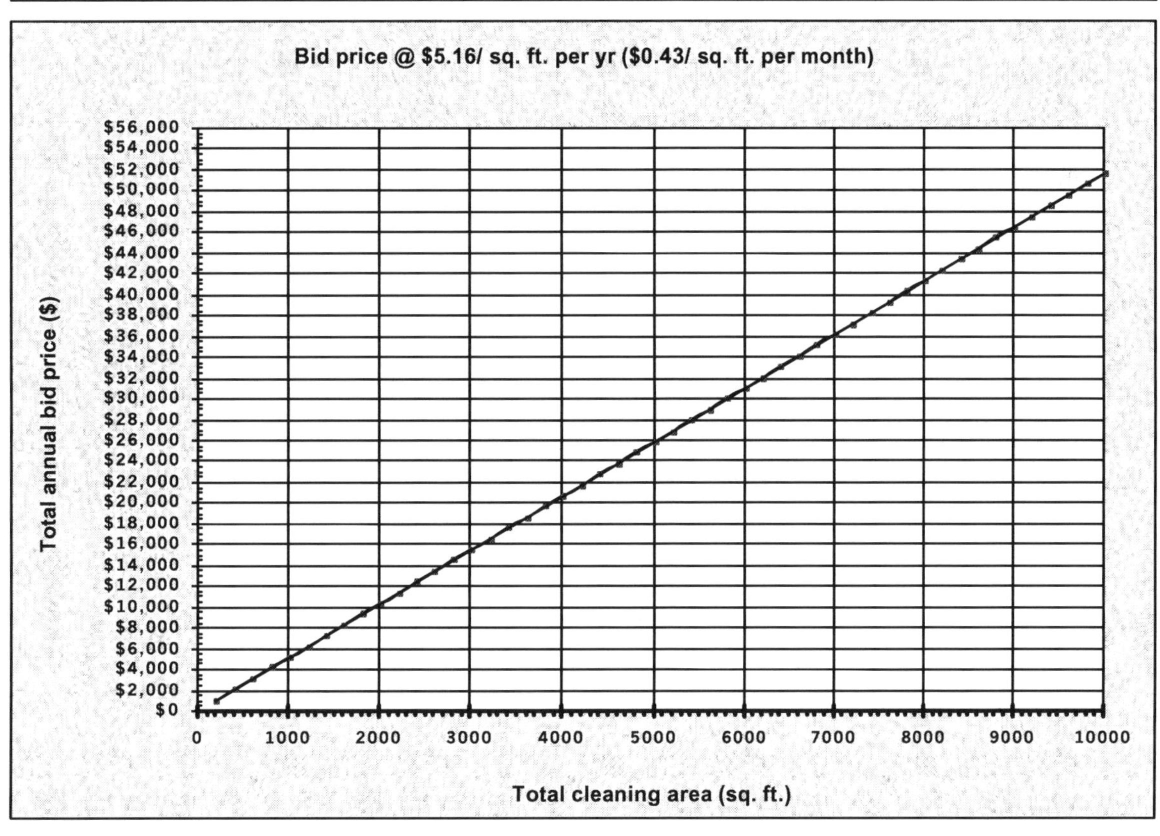
Bid price @ $5.16/ sq. ft. per yr ($0.43/ sq. ft. per month)
Total annual bid price ($)
$56,000
$54,000
$52,000
$50,000
$48,000
$46,000
$44,000
$42,000
$40,000
$38,000
$36,000
$34,000
$32,000
$30,000
$28,000
$26,000
$24,000
$22,000
$20,000
$18,000
$16,000
$14,000
$12,000
$10,000
$8,000
$6,000
$4,000
$2,000
$0
0
1000
2000
3000
4000
5000
6000
7000
8000
9000
10000
Total cleaning area (sq. ft.)

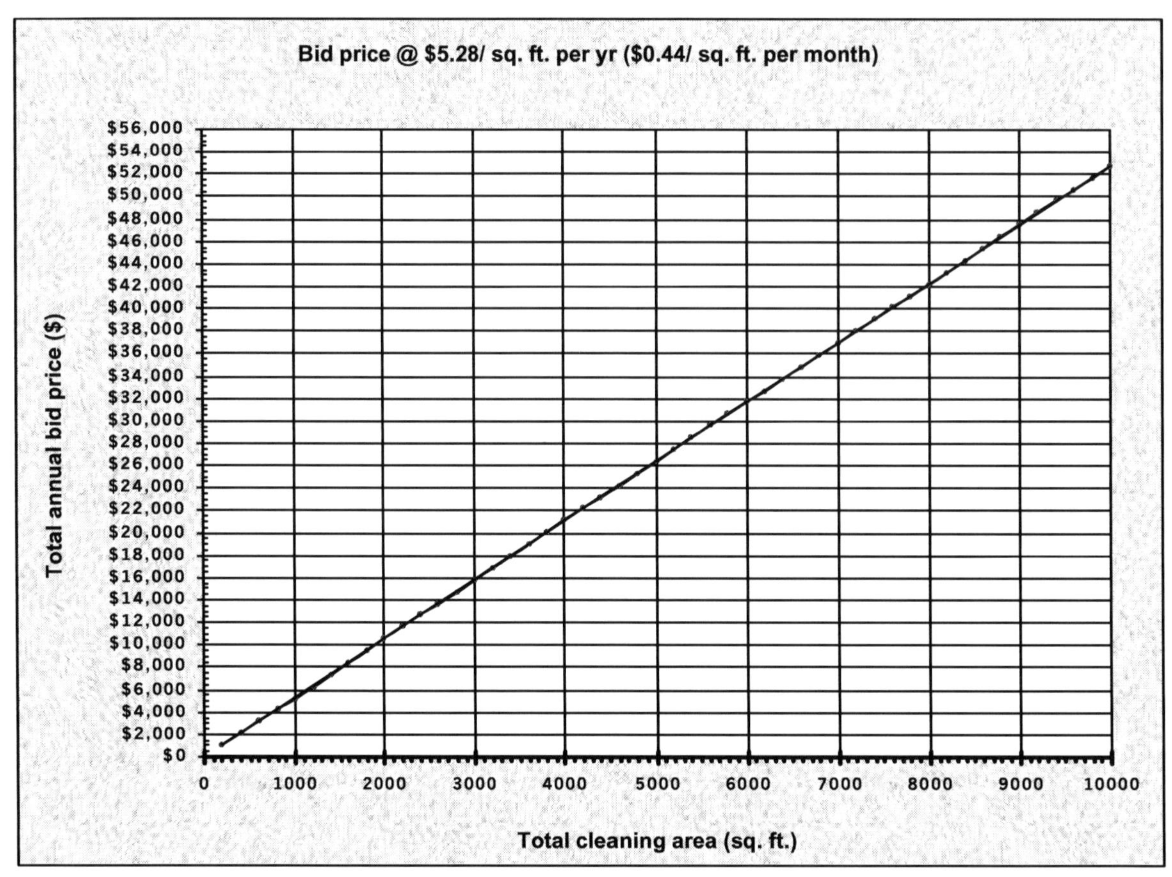
Bid price @ $5.28/ sq. ft. per yr ($0.44/ sq. ft. per month)
Total annual bid price ($)
$56,000
$54,000
$52,000
$50,000
$48,000
$46,000
$44,000
$42,000
$40,000
$38,000
$36,000
$34,000
$32,000
$30,000
$28,000
$26,000
$24,000
$22,000
$20,000
$18,000
$16,000
$14,000
$12,000
$10,000
$8,000
$6,000
$4,000
$2,000
$0
0
1000
2000
3000
4000
5000
6000
7000
8000
9000
10000
Total cleaning area (sq. ft.)

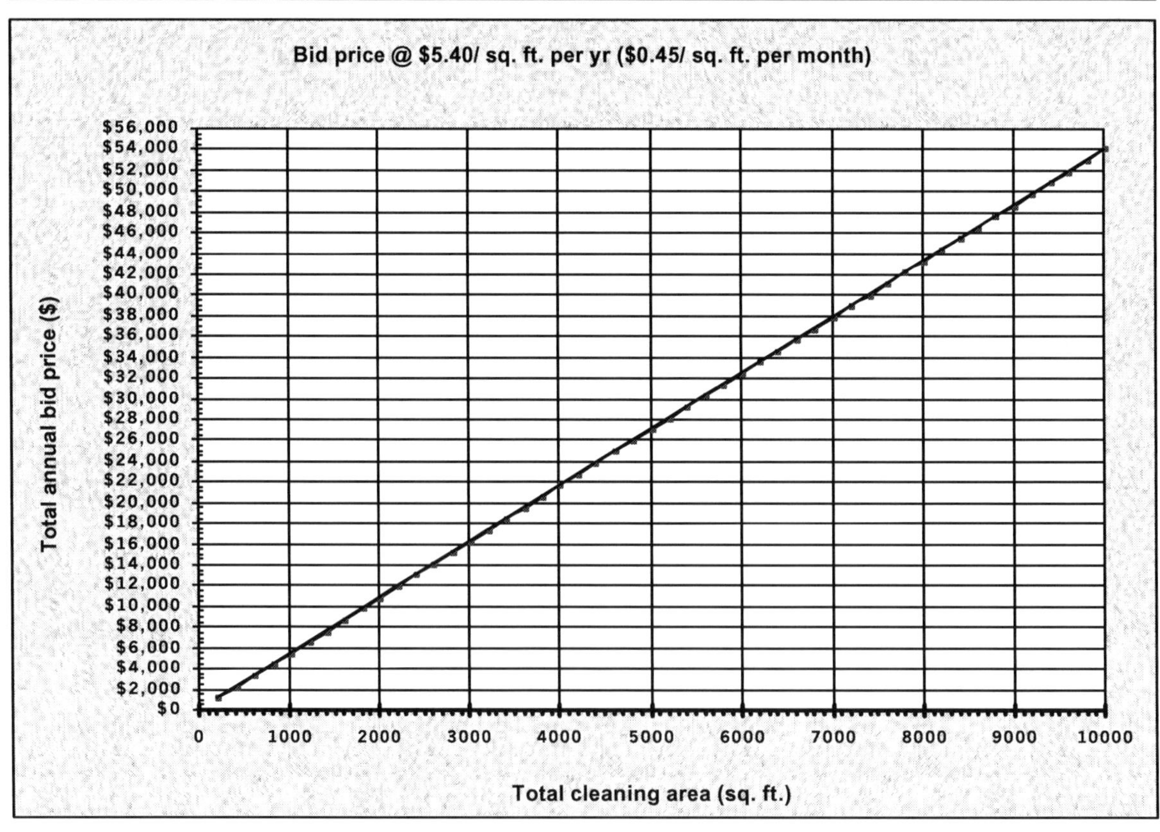
Bid price @ $5.40/ sq. ft. per yr ($0.45/ sq. ft. per month)
Total annual bid price ($)
$56,000
$54,000
$52,000
$50,000
$48,000
$46,000
$44,000
$42,000
$40,000
$38,000
$36,000
$34,000
$32,000
$30,000
$28,000
$26,000
$24,000
$22,000
$20,000
$18,000
$16,000
$14,000
$12,000
$10,000
$8,000
$6,000
$4,000
$2,000
$0
0
1000
2000
3000
4000
5000
6000
7000
8000
9000
10000
Total cleaning area (sq. ft.)

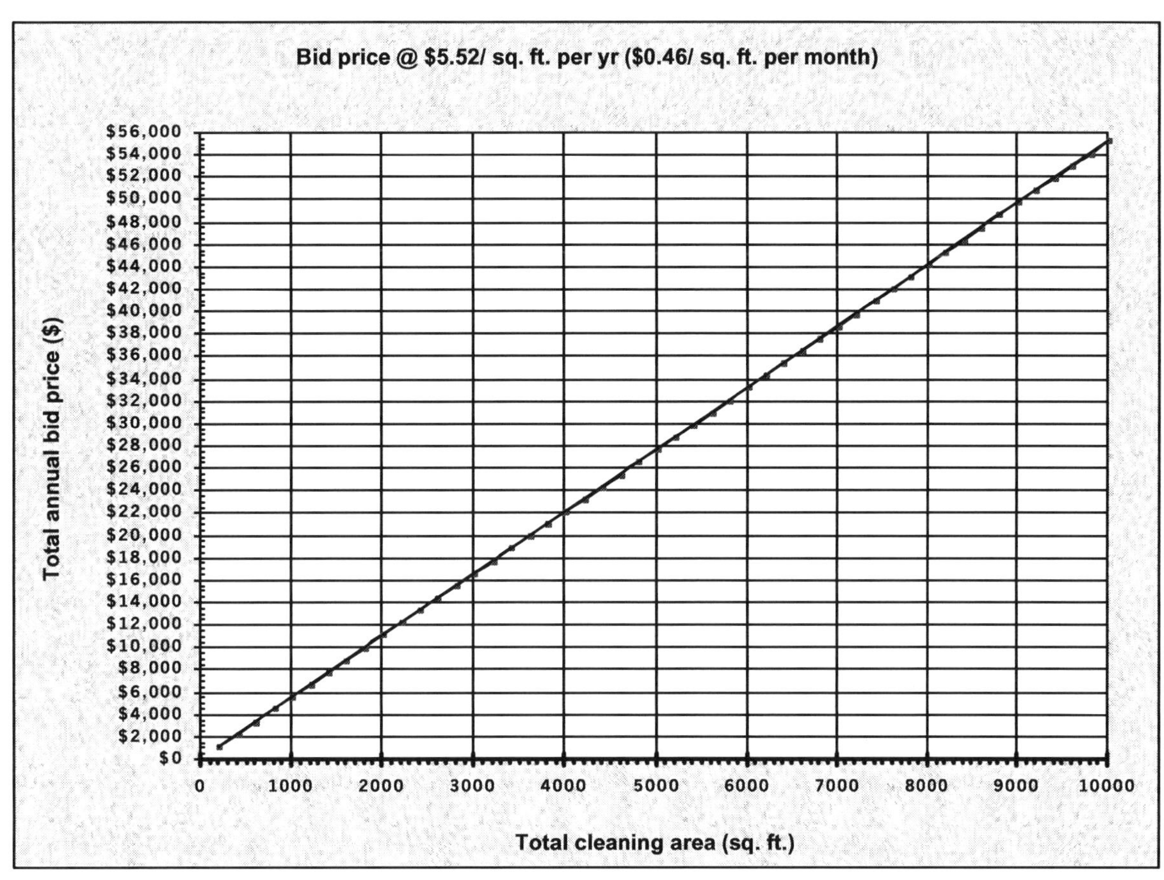
Bid price @ $5.52/ sq. ft. per yr ($0.46/ sq. ft. per month)
Total annual bid price ($)
$56,000
$54,000
$52,000
$50,000
$48,000
$46,000
$44,000
$42,000
$40,000
$38,000
$36,000
$34,000
$32,000
$30,000
$28,000
$26,000
$24,000
$22,000
$20,000
$18,000
$16,000
$14,000
$12,000
$10,000
$8,000
$6,000
$4,000
$2,000
$0
0
1000
2000
3000
4000
5000
6000
7000
8000
9000
10000
Total cleaning area (sq. ft.)

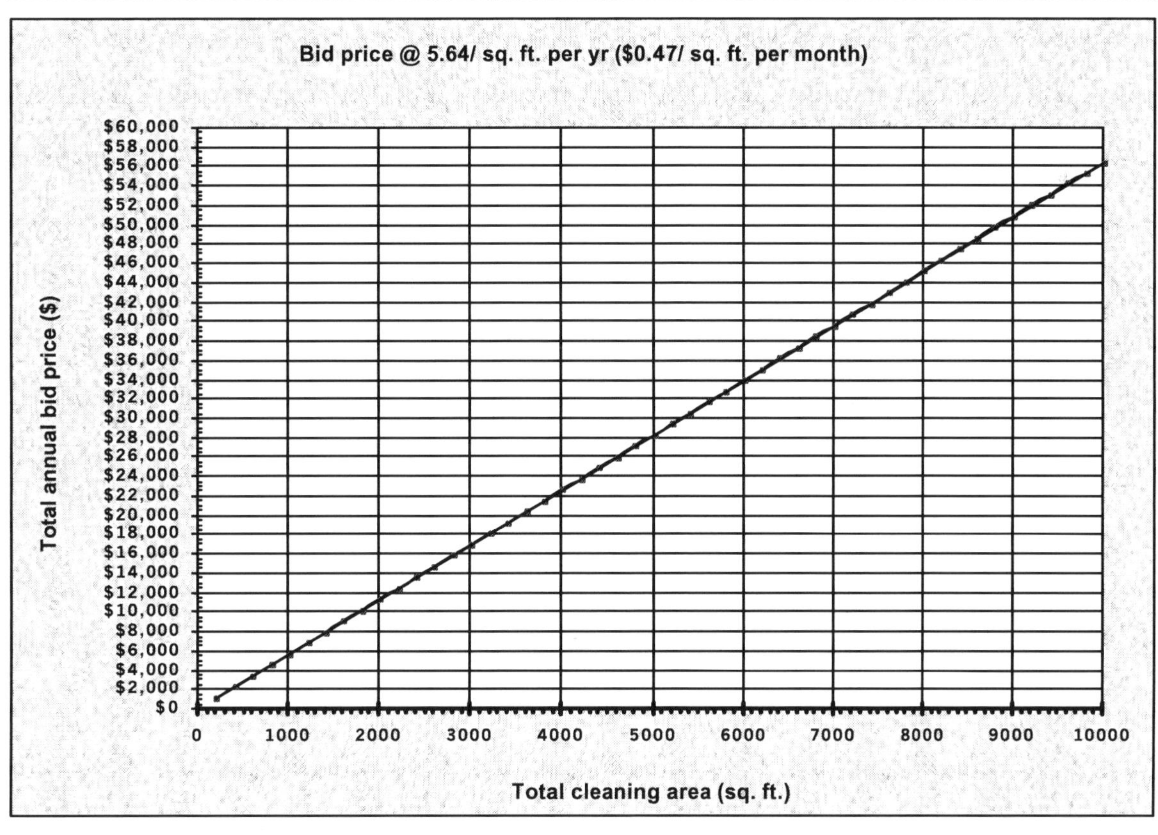
Bid price @ 5.64/ sq. ft. per yr ($0.47/ sq. ft. per month)
Total annual bid price ($)
$60,000
$58,000
$56,000
$54,000
$52,000
$50,000
$48,000
$46,000
$44,000
$42,000
$40,000
$38,000
$36,000
$34,000
$32,000
$30,000
$28,000
$26,000
$24,000
$22,000
$20,000
$18,000
$16,000
$14,000
$12,000
$10,000
$8,000
$6,000
$4,000
$2,000
$0
0
1000
2000
3000
4000
5000
6000
7000
8000
9000
10000
Total cleaning area (sq. ft.)

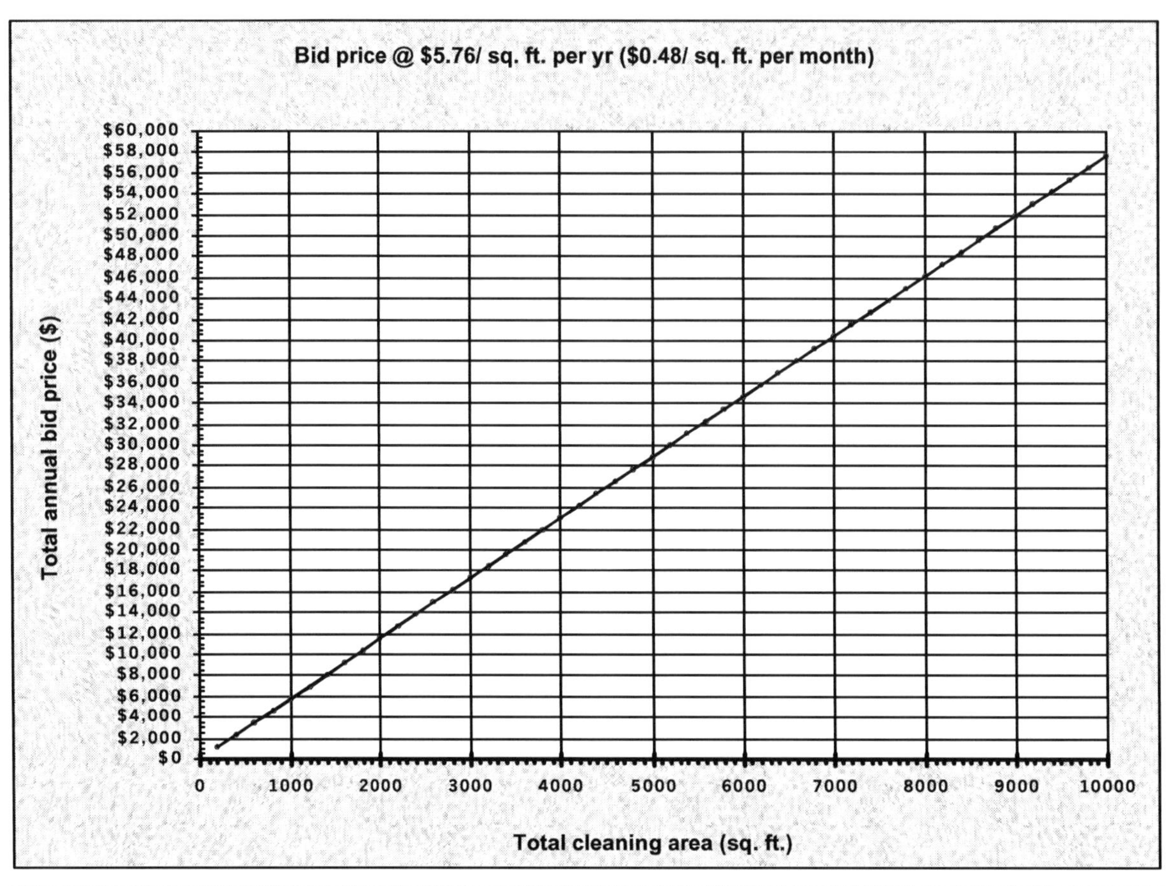
Bid price @ $5.76/ sq. ft. per yr ($0.48/ sq. ft. per month)
Total annual bid price ($)
$60,000
$58,000
$56,000
$54,000
$52,000
$50,000
$48,000
$46,000
$44,000
$42,000
$40,000
$38,000
$36,000
$34,000
$32,000
$30,000
$28,000
$26,000
$24,000
$22,000
$20,000
$18,000
$16,000
$14,000
$12,000
$10,000
$8,000
$6,000
$4,000
$2,000
$0
0
1000
2000
3000
4000
5000
6000
7000
8000
9000
10000
Total cleaning area (sq. ft.)

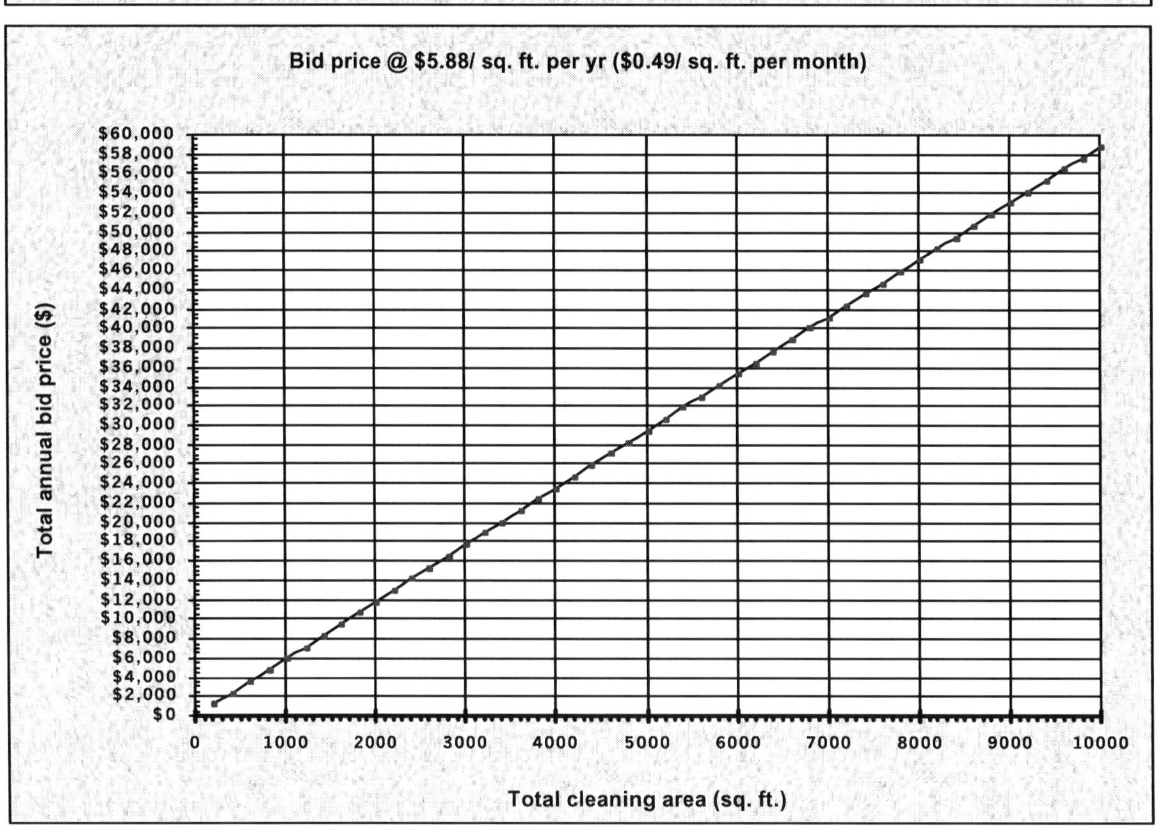
Bid price @ $5.88/ sq. ft. per yr ($0.49/ sq. ft. per month)
Total annual bid price ($)
$60,000
$58,000
$56,000
$54,000
$52,000
$50,000
$48,000
$46,000
$44,000
$42,000
$40,000
$38,000
$36,000
$34,000
$32,000
$30,000
$28,000
$26,000
$24,000
$22,000
$20,000
$18,000
$16,000
$14,000
$12,000
$10,000
$8,000
$6,000
$4,000
$2,000
$0
0
1000
2000
3000
4000
5000
6000
7000
8000
9000
10000
Total cleaning area (sq. ft.)

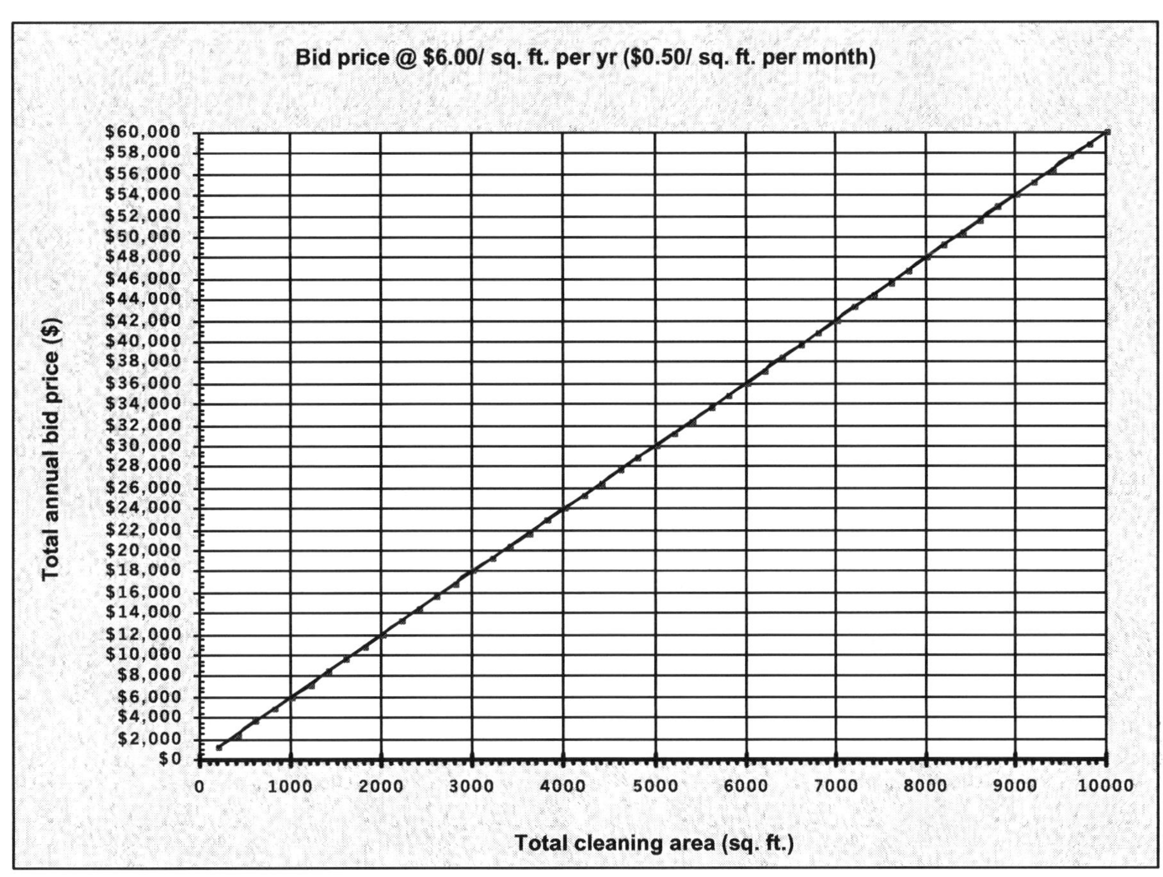
Bid price @ $6.00/ sq. ft. per yr ($0.50/ sq. ft. per month)
Total annual bid price ($)
$60,000
$58,000
$56,000
$54,000
$52,000
$50,000
$48,000
$46,000
$44,000
$42,000
$40,000
$38,000
$36,000
$34,000
$32,000
$30,000
$28,000
$26,000
$24,000
$22,000
$20,000
$18,000
$16,000
$14,000
$12,000
$10,000
$8,000
$6,000
$4,000
$2,000
$0
0
1000
2000
3000
4000
5000
6000
7000
8000
9000
10000
Total cleaning area (sq. ft.)

Chapter 9

Bid estimation, workload estimation and cost accounting worksheets

In this chapter, several forms that are useful as worksheets, in preparing bid estimations and workload determinations, are presented, along with a discussion of selected examples, to illustrate their potential uses. These forms are designed for use with a hand held calculator and where applicable, the charts and tables in this guide.

Overhead and total cost worksheets

The following overhead cost and total cost worksheet forms accompany this guide:

- ***cleaning services overhead cost worksheet*** *(short form);*

- ***cleaning services overhead cost worksheet*** *(long form);*

- ***cleaning services overhead distribution and total cost worksheet;***

Additionally, there are examples, with sample calculations, for the long form version of the *cleaning services overhead cost worksheet* and for the *cleaning services overhead distribution and total cost worksheet.*

The *short form of the overhead cost worksheet* is shown here, along with an example for the *long form of the overhead cost estimation worksheet*. Also shown here, is the form for the *overhead distribution and total cost worksheet*, along with a corresponding example.

CLEANING SERVICES OVERHEAD COST WORKSHEET

Period from: ______ to: ______ Date: ______

OVERHEAD CATEGORY	OVERHEAD ITEM	ANNUAL COST ($) (INPUT)	MONTHLY COST ($) (INPUT)	ANNUAL COST ($) (OUTPUT)	MONTHLY COST ($) (OUTPUT)
INSURANCE					
TAXES & LICENSES					
CAPITAL DEPRECIATION					
OFFICE RENT/ MORTGAGE					
UTILITIES					
MARKETING/ ADVERTISING					
LOANS/ LEASES					
INDIRECT LABOR & BENEFITS					
TRANSPORTATION					
SUPPLIES & EQUIPMENT					
MISCELLANEOUS/ OTHER					
Totals					

CLEANING SERVICES OVERHEAD COST WORKSHEET

Period from: ______ to: ______ Date: ______

Page 1

OVERHEAD CATEGORY	OVERHEAD ITEM	ANNUAL COST ($) (INPUT)	MONTHLY COST ($) (INPUT)	ANNUAL COST ($) (OUTPUT)	MONTHLY COST ($) (OUTPUT)
INSURANCE					
	general liability		75	900	75
	fidelity bond	120		120	10
	business automobile policy (BAP)	800		800	67
	workers compensation	1,200		1,200	100
TAXES & LICENSES					
	Advelorum tax: mil rate of 60 (0.5%)	58		58	5
	business license	100		100	8
	fictitious business name license	100		100	8
CAPITAL DEPRECIATION					
	All cleaning equipment & transportation	2,788		2,788	232
	office equipment	75		75	6

CLEANING SERVICES OVERHEAD COST WORKSHEET

Period from: ______ to: ______ Date: ______

Page 2

OVERHEAD CATEGORY	OVERHEAD ITEM	ANNUAL COST ($) (INPUT)	MONTHLY COST ($) (INPUT)	ANNUAL COST ($) (OUTPUT)	MONTHLY COST ($) (OUTPUT)
OFFICE RENT/ MORTGAGE					
	lease (sublet portion of a warehouse)	750		750	63
UTILITIES	(prorated portions of landlord's bills)*				
	electricity*		75	900	75
	gas*		45	540	45
	water *		15	180	15
	phone		55	660	55
	mobile phone		35	420	35
MARKETING/ ADVERTISING					
	yellow pages ad	400		400	33
	internet listing (preparation and submission)	500		500	42
	business cards	20		20	2

CLEANING SERVICES OVERHEAD COST WORKSHEET

Period from: ______ to: ______ Date: ______

Page 3

OVERHEAD CATEGORY	OVERHEAD ITEM	ANNUAL COST ($) (INPUT)	MONTHLY COST ($) (INPUT)	ANNUAL COST ($) (OUTPUT)	MONTHLY COST ($) (OUTPUT)
LOANS/ LEASES					
	interest on auto loan	90		90	8
	interest on 12 month loan	774		774	65
INDIRECT LABOR & BENEFITS	(employee benefits)				
	vacation & holiday employee 1*	1,321		1,321	110
	vacation & holiday employee 2*	1,321		1,321	110
	vacation & holiday employee 3*	1,321		1,321	110
	vacation & holiday employee 4*	1,321		1,321	110
	vacation & holiday owner/ supervisor*	3,850		3,850	321
	* 7.7% of wage or salary				
	(10 days holidays + 10 days of vacation)				
SUPPLIES & EQUIPMENT					
	uniforms**	900		900	75
	computer**	1,200		1,200	100
	floor machine**	750		750	63
	burnisher**	1,500		1,500	125
	carpet extractor**	1,800		1,800	150
	office supplies		25	300	25
	office furniture**	300		300	25
	** (acquired using 12 month loan)				

CLEANING SERVICES OVERHEAD COST WORKSHEET

Period from: ______ to: ______

Date: ______

Page 4

OVERHEAD CATEGORY	OVERHEAD ITEM	ANNUAL COST ($) (INPUT)	MONTHLY COST ($) (INPUT)	ANNUAL COST ($) (OUTPUT)	MONTHLY COST ($) (OUTPUT)
TRANSPORTATION					
	van (used, acquired with 3 year loan)	1,667		1,667	139
	maintenance	200		200	17
	gas	1,100		1,100	92
MISCELLANEOUS/ OTHER					
Totals				30,226	2,519

CLEANING SERVICES:
OVERHEAD DISTRIBUTION & TOTAL COST
WORKSHEET

TOTAL OVERHEAD ______

Date: __________

ACCOUNT IDENTIFICATION	ACCOUNT DIRECT LABOR	ACCOUNT MATERIAL COSTS	ACCOUNT (LABOR + MATERIALS)	ACCOUNT OVERHEAD	PERCENT OVERHEAD	ACCOUNT (TOTAL COST)
Totals						

CLEANING SERVICES:
OVERHEAD DISTRIBUTION & TOTAL COST
WORKSHEET

TOTAL OVERHEAD: 30,226

Date: __________

ACCOUNT IDENTIFICATION	ACCOUNT DIRECT LABOR	ACCOUNT MATERIAL COSTS	ACCOUNT (LABOR + MATERIALS)	ACCOUNT OVERHEAD	PERCENT OVERHEAD	ACCOUNT (TOTAL COST)
ACCOUNT 1	17,796	1,923	19,719	4,533.8	15.00	24,253
ACCOUNT 2	23,728	2,564	26,292	6,045.1	20.00	32,337
ACCOUNT 3	35,592	3,846	39,438	9,067.7	30.00	48,506
ACCOUNT 4	41,524	4,489	46,013	10,579.4	35.00	56,592
Totals	118,640.0	12,821.8	131,462	30,226.0	100.00	161,688

ACCOUNT TOTAL COST =
(ACCOUNT (LABOR + MATERIAL)
+ ACCOUNT OVERHEAD)

TOTAL LABOR + MATERIALS
FOR ALL ACCOUNTS

TOTAL COSTS
FOR ALL ACCOUNTS

Both the long and short form for the *overhead cost worksheet,* are used in the same manner. The only difference between them, is that the short form has only one line, for a single entry in each category, that summarizes all expenses or costs in that category and the long form provides for more detailed, multiple entries in each category.

The first two columns to the right of the *overhead item* column, provide for, either an annual cost input or monthly cost input (but not both). The worksheet is structured in this way, to provide for more flexibility, as various costs may be more familiar to the user, on either an annual or a monthly basis.

The last two columns, provide for two continuous columns of annual and monthly cost outputs, that are totaled at the bottom. Select either an annual or monthly input entry and then either divided by 12 (i.e., annual input entry/ 12), or multiply by 12 (i.e., monthly input * 12) in order to complete the last two columns (annual and monthly outputs). An annual and a monthly output are provided, so that overhead distribution and total costs, can be determined on either an annual or monthly basis (e.g., the overhead distribution and total cost worksheet example is calculated in terms of annual costs, it could also be calculated on a monthly basis).

Once the *total overhead cost* and the *direct labor* and *direct material* costs (i.e., cleaning supplies, cleaning equipment replacement parts, etc.,), have been determined, the ***overhead distribution*** and the ***total cost per account*** can be calculated, for over 20 individual accounts within a business (or, for up to 20 facilities within an account).

To use the *overhead distribution and total cost worksheet,* first enter the *account or facility ID's*, the *direct labor costs* and the direct *material cost,* into the first 3 columns. Then enter the *total overhead cost* into the single shaded cell or box at the top of the worksheet. Next, sum the 2nd and 3rd columns (i.e., *direct labor + material costs*) and enter the sum into the *"labor + materials"* column. The *"account overhead"* in the next column (5th from the left), is calculated in the following manner:

Weighted overhead distribution

$$\textbf{Account overhead} = \textbf{total overhead} \times \frac{\textbf{account (labor + materials)}}{\textbf{total (labor + materials)}}$$

For example: (account 1)

$$\textbf{Account 1 overhead} = 4{,}534 = 30{,}226 \times \frac{19{,}719}{131{,}462}$$

And (4,534 ÷ 30,226) x 100 = a 15% overhead rate for account 1

This is a weighted average approach to assigning overhead to individual accounts. The net effect is that the total overhead is more evenly distributed over all of the accounts in the business, or all of the facilities within an account, based on their relative cost. This is especially true when different accounts within the business (or different facilities within an account), have significantly different labor and or material costs.

The worksheet for *overhead distribution and total cost* shows the percentage of the total overhead applied to each account. This feature is useful for comparisons between various accounts, but it is not absolutely necessary to calculate this value, when using this worksheet form. Note that the example shown, calculates costs on an annual basis. It could have been calculated on a monthly basis as well. It should be pointed out, that all of the inputs must be in the same units (i.e ., monthly direct labor per account, material costs per month, and total overhead per month), in order for the calculations to be correct.

It may be noted by the reader who compares the ratio for the "*account (labor + materials)*" to the "*total (labor + materials)*", in this example, that it is the same ratio as for the individual *account overhead costs* versus the total *overhead* (i.e., the percentages are the same in each case). This would only be true in practice, <u>if</u> the ratio of labor to materials for each account, is always the same. In other words, it is possible to have identical labors cost for two different accounts, with significantly different material costs and visa versa.

When material costs (equipment parts, cleaning chemicals, etc.,) are a small fraction of the direct labor cost, a rough estimate of the overhead distribution can also be made, by ignoring the contribution from the direct material costs, altogether and multiplying the *total over head* by the ratio of the *account's direct labor* to the *total labor* for all accounts, to obtain an account overhead (i.e., TOH x (ADL ÷ TL) = AOH). However, the direct material cost must be included in the calculations for <u>total costs</u>, in order to prevent a low estimate for total costs in providing cleaning services, that will cut into profit margins.

In the above example for the *overhead cost worksheet*, "benefits" were included in the "*indirect labor*" category of the overhead cost worksheet, at a standard 7.7% of wage or salary (i.e., 2 weeks vacation and 10 holidays). It is possible to roll these expenses into the wages or salary associated with direct labor costs. Additionally, the direct labor includes the total compensation for the owner (minus benefits), as salary associated with direct labor for the accounts.

This is because he spends most of his time supervising his four employees and performing floor care services associated with each of his accounts. He has no secretary, performs his own bookkeeping, payroll, tax preparation, onsite consultations and bid proposals, but considers the time spent performing these administrative functions, small in comparison with the time he devotes to floor care services and management of the business.

In a larger concern, he would very likely delegate one or more of these *indirect labor* functions to employees or independent contractors and the cost for each of these functions would be accounted as part of the overhead. It would also be a legitimate approach, to assign a portion, of his salary under *indirect labor,* as an overhead expense. If he chooses to distribute his salary over both *indirect labor* and *direct labor* categories, the salary should be allocated proportionately, to reflect the relative amount of time he spends doing administrative versus onsite supervision and floor care services.

In these worksheet examples (although it is not evident from the information presented), the owner's salary of $50, 000, represents in practice, both the cost of his labor (direct and indirect, excluding benefits) and the total gross profit for his business. He is also paying four janitorial workers $8.25/ hr, plus $1320 in (holiday + vacation) benefits, for an effective wage of $8.89/ hr. The total direct labor cost for the four accounts is $118, 640.

The total cleaning area for the four accounts is ~95,000 sq. ft., and the total cost* of providing cleaning services for these accounts is $161,688. A quick search through the annual bid pricing charts in chapter 8, for a matching annual cleaning services rate, yields an average rate for the four accounts of $1.70/ sq. ft./ yr, or $0.14/ sq. ft./ mo,. Going forward, the owner could quote these cleaning services rates to prospective clients, for facilities of a <u>comparable</u> level of difficulty/ cost and be assured of making a reasonable profit.

As it happens, $1.70/ sq. ft./yr or $0.14/ sq. ft./mo., is a lucrative rate for the type of facilities being serviced and the market his business competes in. For the reasons mentioned earlier, the total cost of providing cleaning services for all four accounts, equals the <u>average</u> total fees charged for cleaning services (*i.e., **the profit margin is factored into costs, through the inclusion of the owner's entire salary as direct labor**).

Another approach the owner could have taken, would be to estimate fair market value for the various direct and indirect labor functions he is performing, then assign these costs as direct or indirect labor costs accordingly and distribute the balance of his salary as profit across each of his accounts. This approach is a more conventional way of estimating the cost of services and is easier to apply and understand (particularly in determining precise bid estimates for additional accounts).

The cleaning services owner's total compensation is effectively $53,850. He could for example, assign as direct labor, a salary of $24,500 + $1,887 in benefits (i.e., $26,387 total compensation), for his floor care services and onsite crew supervision. He could also estimate fair market value, for an independent contractor to perform essential indirect labor functions such as bookkeeping, payroll and tax preparation at $3,800$/ yr (e.g., $15.8/ hr for ~20 hrs/ mo). This leaves $23,663 as gross profit, or a profit margin of 14.6% based on his costs, not his customer's (i.e., (23,688 ÷ 161, 688) * 100 = 14.6%). Based on his customer's costs, the profit margin would be 12.7% (i.e, 23,688 ÷ (23,688 + 161,688) * 100 = 12.7%).

The latter approach to calculating a profit margin is ultimately more correct, based on the final price or rate that is offered or charged, both mathematically and from the customer's viewpoint. However, the profit margin based on the contractor's cost, is simpler to calculate and yields the same results, in regards to the final bid price or service rate that is offered, or charged to the customer.

The calculation of a profit margin, based on the contractor's total cost of services, can be expressed as a percentage, in the following way:

Profit margins as a percentage

% profit (profit margin) = (total gross profit ÷ total cost of service) * 100

Going forward, as this contractor's business grows, he may delegate most, or all of the functions that he is currently performing himself. Using the approach shown above, he can derive a profit margin for the cleaning services his company provides, that will yield reasonable compensation for his entrepreneurial efforts and allow him to grow his business, as well as provide growth for his employees.

A summary of the line calculations in the *Overhead distribution and total cost worksheet*, for a single account (or facility, if they are priced individually under the same account), goes as follows:

- **account direct labor + materials = account (labor + materials)**
- **account overhead = total overhead x** $\dfrac{\textbf{account (labor + materials)}}{\textbf{*total (labor + materials)}}$
- **percent overhead = (account overhead ÷ total overhead) * 100**
- **account total costs = account (labor + materials) + account overhead**

* i.e., the total (labor + materials) for all accounts, at the bottom of the worksheet. In order for the above calculations to be correct, all of the business's expenses for all accounts must be represented. All inputs must be either on a monthly or an annual basis, but not a mixture of annual and monthly inputs.

Work loading determination worksheets

As with the worksheets in the previous section, the worksheet forms for work loading determinations, are formatted and used in a similar manner. The W*orkload worksheet form*, can be used for estimating the labor requirements of a single room, cleaning area, facility or account. The worksheet form and an example are presented here.

WORK LOAD WORKSHEET

ACCOUNT OR FACILIT ______________________ Page 1

CLEANING AREA/ ROOM: ______________ Date: __________

CLEANING TASK	TOTAL No. units, or AREA (sq. ft.)	CLEAN TIME 1 ITEM (min) (INPUT)	CLEAN TIME 1 ITEM (hrs) (INPUT)	PROD. RATE hrs/ sq. ft. (INPUT)	FREQUENCY WEEKLY (INPUT)	FREQUENCY MONTHLY (INPUT)	CLEAN TIME 1 ITEM (min) (OUTPUT)	CLEAN TIME 1 ITEM (hrs) (OUTPUT)	TOTAL TIME WEEKLY (hrs)	TOTAL TIME MONTHLY (hrs)	TOTAL TIME ANNUALLY (hrs)
SWEEPING											
DRY MOPPING											
WET MOPPING											
VACUUMING											
EMPTY WASTE BASKET											
EMPTY TRASH CAN											
DUSTING											
WASH WINDOWS											
CLEAN OTHER											
CLEAN OTHER											
CLEAN TOILET S											
CLEAN URINALS											
CLEAN SINKS											
CLEAN MIRRORS											
MOP BATHROOM FLOOR											
REPLACE TISSUE PAPER											
REPLACE SANITARY NAPKINS											
REPLACE PAPER TOWELS											
REPLACE AIR FRESHENER											
REPLACE SOAP DISPENSER											
REPLACE/ CLEAN (OTHER)											
REPLACE LIGHTING											
CLEAN STOVE											
CLEAN MICROWAVE											
CLEAN OVEN											
CLEAN REFRIGERATOR											
CLEAN COUNTER TOPS											
CLEAN CUPBOARD DOORS											
CLEAN (OTHER)											

WORK LOAD WORKSHEET

ACCOUNT OR FACILITY ______________________ Page 2

CLEANING AREA/ ROOM: ______________ Date: __________

CLEANING TASK	TOTAL No. units, or AREA (sq. ft.)	CLEAN TIME 1 ITEM (min) (INPUT)	CLEAN TIME 1 ITEM (hrs) (INPUT)	PROD. RATE hrs/ sq. ft. (INPUT)	FREQUENCY WEEKLY (INPUT)	FREQUENCY MONTHLY (INPUT)	CLEAN TIME 1 ITEM (min) (OUTPUT)	CLEAN TIME 1 ITEM (hrs) (OUTPUT)	TOTAL TIME WEEKLY (hrs)	TOTAL TIME MONTHLY (hrs)	TOTAL TIME ANNUALLY (hrs)
SPOT CLEAN CARPET											
CARPET EXTRACTION											
BONNET CLEANING											
CARPET SHAMPOOING											
STRIP FLOOR (1 layer of finish)											
STRIP FLOOR (all finish layers)											
SCRUB FLOOR											
WAX/ APPLY FINISH (one coat)											
WAX/ APPLY FINISH (3 coats)											
BUFF FLOOR											
SPRAY BUFF											
BURNISHING											
EXTERIOR PRESSURE WASHING											
CLEAN GUTTERS											
OTHER TASKS											
Totals											

WORK LOAD WORKSHEET

ACCOUNT OR FACILITY ______________________ Page 1

CLEANING AREA/ ROOM: ______________________ Date: ____________

CLEANING TASK	TOTAL No. units, or AREA (sq. ft.)	CLEAN TIME 1 ITEM (min) (INPUT)	CLEAN TIME 1 ITEM (hrs) (INPUT)	PROD. RATE hrs/ sq. ft. (INPUT)	FREQUENCY WEEKLY (INPUT)	FREQUENCY MONTHLY (INPUT)	CLEAN TIME 1 ITEM (min) (OUTPUT)	CLEAN TIME 1 ITEM (hrs) (OUTPUT)	TOTAL TIME WEEKLY (hrs)	TOTAL TIME MONTHLY (hrs)	TOTAL TIME ANNUALLY (hrs)
SWEEPING											
DRY MOPPING											
WET MOPPING											
VACUUMING											
EMPTY WASTE BASKET											
EMPTY TRASH CAN											
DUSTING											
WASH WINDOWS											
CLEAN OTHER											
CLEAN OTHER											
CLEAN TOILET S	10	1.8			5		1.80	0.03	1.50	6.50	78.00
CLEAN URINALS	6	1.8			5		1.80	0.03	0.90	3.90	46.80
CLEAN SINKS	10	1.8			5		1.80	0.03	1.50	6.50	78.00
CLEAN MIRRORS	10	1.8			5		1.80	0.03	1.50	6.50	78.00
MOP BATHROOM FLOOR	1250			0.00025	5		18.75	0.31	1.56	6.77	81.25
REPLACE TISSUE PAPER	10	0.9			5		0.90	0.02	0.75	3.25	39.00
REPLACE SANITARY NAPKINS	2	0.9			5		0.90	0.02	0.15	0.65	7.80
REPLACE PAPER TOWELS	5	0.9			5		0.90	0.02	0.38	1.62	19.50
REPLACE AIR FRESHENER	10	0.9			5		0.90	0.02	0.75	3.25	39.00
REPLACE SOAP DISPENSER	10	0.9			5		0.90	0.02	0.75	3.25	39.00
REPLACE/ CLEAN (OTHER)											
REPLACE LIGHTING											
CLEAN STOVE											
CLEAN MICROWAVE											
CLEAN OVEN											
CLEAN REFRIGERATOR											
CLEAN COUNTER TOPS											
CLEAN CUPBOARD DOORS											
CLEAN (OTHER)											

Annualized monthly value e.g., (1.50 * 52)/ 12 = 6.50, not (1.50 * 4) = 6.00

0.00025 hr/ sq. ft., I.e., 1/ 4000 sq. ft./ hr = 0.00025hr/ sq. ft.

WORK LOAD WORKSHEET	ACCOUNT OR FACILIT ________ CLEANING AREA/ ROOM: ________ Date: ________										Page 2
CLEANING TASK	TOTAL No. units, or AREA (sq. ft.)	CLEAN TIME 1 ITEM(min) (INPUT)	CLEAN TIME 1 ITEM(hrs) (INPUT)	PROD. RATE hrs/ sq. ft. (INPUT)	FREQUENCY WEEKLY (INPUT)	FREQUENCY MONTHLY (INPUT)	CLEAN TIME 1 ITEM (min) (OUTPUT)	CLEAN TIME 1 ITEM (hrs) (OUTPUT)	TOTAL TIME WEEKLY (hrs)	TOTAL TIME MONTHLY (hrs)	TOTAL TIME ANNUALLY (hrs)
SPOT CLEAN CARPET											
CARPET EXTRACTION											
BONNET CLEANING											
CARPET SHAMPOOING											
STRIP FLOOR (1 layer of finish)											
STRIP FLOOR (all finish layers)											
SCRUB FLOOR											
WAX/ APPLY FINISH (one coat)											
WAX/ APPLY FINISH (3 coats)											
BUFF FLOOR											
SPRAY BUFF											
BURNISHING											
EXTERIOR PRESSURE WASHING											
CLEAN GUTTERS											
OTHER TASKS											
Totals							30.45	0.51	9.74	42.19	506.33

Annualized monthly value
e.g., (9.74 * 52)/ 12 = 42.19,
not (9.74 * 4) = 38.96

As with all of the worksheets in this guide, the workload worksheet forms are formatted and used in a similar manner. It should be noted that the cells or frames for the <u>outputs</u> in all of the worksheets in this guide (i.e., cells or frames containing the results of various calculations using two or more inputs), are <u>shaded</u> in order to distinguish them from input cells.

The best way of explaining the use of the workload worksheet presented here, is to look at the corresponding example that follows. The example shows workload calculations for a facility with 5 bathrooms, 3 men's bathrooms and 2 women's bathrooms.

On page one of the example, the inputs for the total number of "units" (i.e., items to be cleaned, or cleaning tasks to be performed), or the total cleaning area is entered into the first column. In this example the units entered consist of various bathroom fixtures to be cleaned, housekeeping supply replacement tasks and the total floor area for all 5 bathrooms (i.e., 1250 sq. ft.).

The second and third input columns contain the "clean time" for an individual cleaning task, in minutes or hours respectively. Either column may be used for calculating the workload for any individual cleaning task, but not both, at the same time. The fourth column provides for a production rate input, where appropriate.

In this example, the production rate for wet mopping the total floor area for all bathrooms is 0.00025 hr/ sq. ft., which can be found in the production rates for various cleaning tasks in chapter 3. It is possible to use a "clean time" input (i.e., columns 2 or 3), for floor areas or cleaning areas, if an estimate is available. However, only a single "clean time" or production rate can be used, in determining a workload for a single task.

The next two columns, provide inputs for the frequency with each task will be performed. Either a weekly or a monthly entry can be used, but not both, for any given cleaning task. In this example, all of the cleaning task frequency inputs are weekly (i.e., 5 times per week). For a task that is done quarterly, semiannually, or annually, use 0.33, 0.167 or 0.083 respectively, in the monthly input column.

The outputs for the worksheet are in the last 5 columns. They provide the total amount of hours and therefore the labor load, for any given cleaning task, at weekly, monthly or annual intervals. Based on weekly inputs, weekly, monthly and annual labor loads can be summarized. For monthly inputs, monthly or annual labor loads can be summarized.

It should be noted that the monthly and annual outputs in the example, are calculated on an ”annualized” basis from the weekly inputs. This is because, if the cleaning tasks are actually performed 5 times per week for an entire year, the total labor load for one year is, 5 x 52 weeks = 260 times per year, as opposed to 4 x 5 = 20 times per month for 12 months, or 20 x 12 = 240 times per year. This represents about an 8.33% difference.

A summary of the line calculations for this worksheet is shown here.

Line calculations for workload determination worksheet

Example: (clean commodes or toilets)

1.8 min ÷ 60 min/hr = 0.03 hr;

(10 items or tasks x 0.03 hrs/ item x 5 times/ week) = 1.5 total hours weekly;

(1.5 hrs/ week x 52) ÷ 12 = 6.5 hours monthly;

1.5 hours/ week x 52 weeks/ year = 78 hours annually

Example: (wet mop all 5 bathroom floors)

1250 sq. ft. x 0.00025 hr/ sq. ft. = 0.31 hours per task, or .031 x 60 min/ hr = 18.75 minutes per task;

(0.31 hrs/ item or task x 5 times/ week) = 1.563 total hours weekly;

(1.563 hrs/ week x 52 weeks/ year) ÷ 12 = 6.77 hours monthly;

1.563 hours/ week x 52 weeks/ year = 81.25 hours annually

Cleaning and housekeeping supplies cost estimation worksheets

As with the worksheets in the previous section, the worksheet forms for cleaning and housekeeping cost determinations, are formatted and used in a similar manner. The *Cleaning & housekeeping supplies worksheet forms*, can be used for estimating the cost of cleaning and housekeeping supplies for a room or area, or a facility, or an account. Both the short and long worksheet forms, as well as an example are presented here.

CLEANING & HOUSEKEEPING SUPPLIES
COST ESTIMATION WORKSHEET

Date:

CLEANING UNIT: FACILITY:______ AREA:______ ROOM:______

	no. of units:			no. of units:			no. of units:			no. of units:			no. of units:				
	FACILITY, ROOM, OR AREA ID: ______			FACILITY, ROOM, OR AREA ID: ______			FACILITY, ROOM, OR AREA ID: ______			FACILITY, ROOM, OR AREA ID: ______			FACILITY, ROOM, OR AREA ID: ______				
SUPPLY ITEM	quantity	cost/ item	total cost	quantity	cost/ item	total cost	quantity	cost/ item	total cost	quantity	cost/ item	total cost	quantity	cost/ item	total cost	Total monthly cost	Total annual cost
TOTAL COSTS (All supplies)																	

CLEANING & HOUSEKEEPING SUPPLIES
COST ESTIMATION WORKSHEET

Page 1

Date: **CLEANING UNIT:** **FACILITY:** ______ **AREA:** ______ **ROOM:** ______

	no. of units:			no. of units:			no. of units:			no. of units:			no. of units:				
	FACILITY, ROOM, OR AREA ID: ______			FACILITY, ROOM, OR AREA ID: ______			FACILITY, ROOM, OR AREA ID: ______			FACILITY, ROOM, OR AREA ID: ______			FACILITY, ROOM, OR AREA ID: ______				
SUPPLY ITEM	quantity	cost/ item	total cost	quantity	cost/ item	total cost	quantity	cost/ item	total cost	quantity	cost/ item	total cost	quantity	cost/ item	total cost	Total monthly cost	Total annual cost
GENERAL CLEANING SUPPLIES																	

CLEANING & HOUSEKEEPING SUPPLIES
COST ESTIMATION WORKSHEET

Date: CLEANING UNIT: FACILITY: AREA: ROOM: Date: Page 2

	no. of units:			no. of units:			no. of units:			no. of units:			no. of units:				
	FACILITY, ROOM, OR AREA ID: ______			FACILITY, ROOM, OR AREA ID: ______			FACILITY, ROOM, OR AREA ID: ______			FACILITY, ROOM, OR AREA ID: ______			FACILITY, ROOM, OR AREA ID: ______				
SUPPLY ITEM	quantity	cost/ unit	total cost	quantity	cost/ unit	total cost	quantity	cost/ unit	total cost	quantity	cost/ unit	total cost	quantity	cost/ unit	total cost	Total monthly cost	Total annual cost
REPLACEMENT PARTS & TOOLS																	

CLEANING & HOUSEKEEPING SUPPLIES COST ESTIMATION WORKSHEET

Date: CLEANING UNIT: FACILITY: AREA: ROOM: Date: Page 3

SUPPLY ITEM	FACILITY, ROOM, OR AREA ID: ______ no. of units:			FACILITY, ROOM, OR AREA ID: ______ no. of units:			FACILITY, ROOM, OR AREA ID: ______ no. of units:			FACILITY, ROOM, OR AREA ID: ______ no. of units:			FACILITY, ROOM, OR AREA ID: ______ no. of units:			Total monthly cost	Total annual cost
	quantity	cost/ unit	total cost	quantity	cost/ unit	total cost	quantity	cost/ unit	total cost	quantity	cost/ unit	total cost	quantity	cost/ unit	total cost		
HOUSE KEEPING SUPPLIES																	

CLEANING & HOUSEKEEPING SUPPLIES
COST ESTIMATION WORKSHEET

Page 4

Date: **CLEANING UNIT:** **FACILITY:** **AREA:** **ROOM:** **Date:**

	no. of units:			no. of units:			no. of units:			no. of units:			no. of units:				
	FACILITY, ROOM, OR AREA ID: ______			FACILITY, ROOM, OR AREA ID: ______			FACILITY, ROOM, OR AREA ID: ______			FACILITY, ROOM, OR AREA ID: ______			FACILITY, ROOM, OR AREA ID: ______				
SUPPLY ITEM	quantity	cost/ unit	total cost	quantity	cost/ unit	total cost	quantity	cost/ unit	total cost	quantity	cost/ unit	total cost	quantity	cost/ unit	total cost	Total monthly cost	Total annual cost
FLOOR CARE SUPPLIES																	
TOTAL COSTS (Cleaning supplies)																	
TOTAL COSTS (Replacement parts & tools)																	
TOTAL COSTS (Housekeeping supplies)																	
TOTAL COSTS (Floor care supplies)																	
TOTAL COSTS (All supplies)																	

CLEANING & HOUSEKEEPING SUPPLIES
COST ESTIMATION WORKSHEET

Date: 01/01/01 **CLEANING UNIT:** **FACILITY:** X **AREA:** ______ **ROOM:** ______

SUPPLY ITEM	no. of units: 1			no. of units: 1			no. of units: 3			no. of units: 1			no. of units: 1			Total monthly cost	Total annual cost
	FACILITY, ROOM, OR AREA ID: Acme Co. #1			FACILITY, ROOM, OR AREA ID: Acme Co. #2			FACILITY, ROOM, OR AREA ID: Acme Restaurants			FACILITY, ROOM, OR AREA ID: ______			FACILITY, ROOM, OR AREA ID: ______				
	quantity	cost/ item	total cost	quantity	cost/ item	total cost	quantity	cost/ item	total cost	quantity	cost/ item	total cost	quantity	cost/ item	total cost		
general purpose cleaner (1 qt.)	1.00	2.00	2.00	1.00	2.00	2.00	1.00	2.00	6.00							10	120
degreaser (1 qt.)	1.00			1.00			1.00	3.00	9.00							9	108
floor cleaner (1 gal)	1.00	5.00	5.00	1.00	5.00	5.00	1.00	5.00	15.00							25	300
mop heads (1)	0.33	4.00	1.32													1	16
scour pads (1 pack 3)	1.00	2.50	2.50	1.00	2.50	2.50	2.00	2.50	15.00							20	240
window cleaner (1 qt.)	0.50	2.50	1.25	0.50	2.50	1.25	0.50	2.50	3.75							6	75
vacuum bags (3/pack)	0.50	1.00	0.50	0.50	1.00	0.50	0.50	1.00	1.50							3	30
replacement belts (1)	0.25	1.00	0.25													0	3
back-up trash liners (box of 100)	0.33	5.00	1.65	0.33	5.00	1.65										3	40
floor stripper (1 gal)	1.00	15.00	15.00	1.00	15.00	15.00	1.00	15.00	45.00							75	900
floor finish (1 gal)	1.00	15.00	15.00	1.00	15.00	15.00	1.00	15.00	45.00							75	900
scrub pads	0.66	5.00	3.30	0.66	5.00	3.30	0.66	5.00	9.90							17	198
buff pads	0.66	5.00	3.30	0.66	5.00	3.30	0.66	5.00	9.90							17	198
TOTAL COSTS (All supplies)			51			50			160							261	3,127

The example shown, is based on the short form and is suitable for many small business applications. The long form works in the same manner, but allows for more entries and subtotals for cleaning supplies, housekeeping supplies, replacement parts and tools and floor care supplies.

The worksheets allow for the following types of calculations:

- **a monthly or annual cost estimate for a single supply item, across several rooms, areas, facilities or accounts**;
- **a total monthly cost estimate for all supplies required for a single room, area, facility or account**;
- **A total monthly or annual cost estimate, for all supplies across several rooms, areas, facilities or accounts**.

It should be noted here, that all entries for this worksheet are on a monthly cost basis. Daily, weekly or annual usage inputs (i.e., "quantity" entries), will result in inaccurate results. Also, It should be noted that the intent of this worksheet, is to estimate direct supply costs only (i.e., not for overhead supplies, such as office supplies, etc.,).

At the top of the sample *Cleaning supplies & housekeeping cost estimation worksheet form,* the "x" placed in the 'facility" cleaning unit check box, indicates that the supply costs are being determined for several facilities. Although a cleaning unit check box is not provided for the cost accounting of supplies for individual accounts, in this worksheet, it is possible to enter monthly supply cost inputs for entire accounts, rather than itemizing supply costs, for all of the individual facilities in an account, provided that cost inputs are available in that form. A review of the example will help make this feature, clearer.

In this example, the supply costs are calculated for all of the facilities in 3 accounts, the first two accounts, Acme Co.'s #1 & #2, have only one facility/ per account to clean. The third account, Acme Restaurants, is an account that has 3 identical restaurants, as shown by the number "3" in the "*no. of units*" input cell, in the header box over the *third block* of ["*quantity*", "*cost/ item*", "*total cost*"] columns (i.e., the 5th, 6th, and 7th columns on the worksheet). Each block of ["*quantity*", "*cost/ item*", "*total cost*"] columns, is highlighted in bold type.

An added feature of this worksheet, is the ability to calculate the supply cost of a single item for a single room, area or facility, or the cost for two or more cleaning units of the same type, requiring very similar or identical supply requirements. This feature can be particularly useful, in calculating the supply costs of a large facility with multiples of various room types, such as bathrooms, offices, cubicles/ work stations, break rooms, hallways etc.,. This feature is illustrated in this example, by the Acme Restaurant entries.

In the case of the Acme Restaurant, the "*quantity*" and "*cost/ item*" entries, represent the supplies required for a single restaurant. The "*total cost*" entry, represents the cost for all three restaurants (i.e., cleaning units), as indicated by the "3" in the "*no. of units*", input cell, in the header.

The inputs in each "*quantity*" column of the worksheet, are "unitless" and can represent the entire amount or quantity of a supply item, required for a "cleaning unit" (i.e., room, area, facility), or it can represent a single unit of the "*supply item*", or even a portion of a unit. For instance, in this example the "*quantity*" entry for window cleaner is "0.5". This represents a usage of 1/2 of the supply item (i.e., 1/2 quart of concentrate) per month.

The cost of a supply item can be distributed across all cleaning units, or it can assigned arbitrarily, to a single cleaning unit for the purposes of convenience, (e.g., a small expense for equipment replacement parts could be calculated in the first block of ["*quantity*", "*cost/ item*", "*total cost*"] columns, rather than distributing the cost across all cleaning units.

This is the case for mop head usage in this example. In the 1st "*quantity*" column, the entry for this supply item is "0.33" and is the only entry in the row. The contractor is changing his mop head every 3 months and is using that mop for all three accounts (i.e., or a total of 5 facilities).

So to record this expense in a single monthly entry, he calculates the reciprocal of the quantity he uses in 3 months (i.e., 1/ 3 = 0.33). If for example, he was using 5 mop heads in 3 months, he could calculate a monthly usage as follows:

(1 mo / 3 mo) x 5 items used for 3 months = 1.65 items/ month

Alternatively, if the cost of mop heads were large enough to affect the individual facility or account totals for all supply items significantly, he could have divided or distributed the cost over all 5 facilities (e.g., entries of 0.11, 0.11, 0.11/3 = 0.037, respectively).

The same approach is used for the replacement belts for his vacuum cleaner. A "*quantity*" value of "0.25" is the only entry in the row and represents a usage of ~ 1 belt every four months (i.e., 1/ 4 = 0.25).

"*Quantity*" entries, could also represent whole number quantities or amounts of a supply item as well. In our example, all of the whole number "*quantity*" inputs are a value of one. Values from 2 to 1,000 or more could also be used, depending on the usage of a given supply item.

The cost of each supply item is calculated and entered in the "*total cost*" input cell, for each "*cleaning unit*" block of three columns. At the end of each row, a total monthly and annual cost per supply item is tabulated across all of the cleaning units (i.e., facilities in this case).

In the bottom row, the total cost of all supplies for each cleaning unit is tabulated. Finally, in the last 2 output cells (i.e., bottom right corner), the total monthly and annual cost for all supplies, across all cleaning units is tabulated (i.e., total direct supply costs for the contractor's business).

Sample calculations for this example are shown here. They illustrate the cost and usage of "general purpose cleaner", for each of the 5 facilities, as found in the first row of the worksheet.

Acme Co. no.# 1:
1 qt. x $2.00/ qt. x 1 "cleaning unit" = $2.00

Acme Co. no.# 2:
1 qt. x $2.00/ qt. x 1 "cleaning unit" = $2.00

Acme Restaurants:
1 qt. x $2.00/ qt. x 3 "cleaning units" = $6.00

Total monthly costs:
$2.00 + $2.00 + $6.00 = $10.00

Total annual costs:
$10.00/ mo x 12 mo = $120.00

Calculations for the total cost of all supplies, used for a single cleaning unit (or multiples of the same type of cleaning unit with identical supply usage), is the sum of all of the total cost at the bottom of any given "total cost" column.

Housekeeping supplies are included as a category in these supplies cost estimation forms, for a couple of reasons. To begin with, customers will frequently require, that some or all housekeeping supplies be provided as part of overall cleaning services.

Therefore, one reason for the breakout of housekeeping supplies as a category, is to allow for an estimation of the quantities that may be required for any given account or facility. Secondly, it will be necessary to estimate the cost of these housekeeping supplies and subsequently the cash flow, that will be required to purchase them routinely.

How the cost of housekeeping supplies and the service costs, associated with providing this portion of the overall cleaning services (e.g., any labor involved in ordering and tracking, inventory storage, transportation or shipping to the customer, overhead, etc.,), figure into a bid estimate or proposal, is a matter that merits further discussion. One option is to separate the entire cost associated providing housekeeping supplies, from the costs of all other cleaning services and bill it as a separate charge.

This may include a breakout for the cost of the supplies and a service charge for the cost of providing them, or simply a charge for the cost of the supplies (in this way, you are selling the housekeeping supplies at cost and are therefore not required to charge and collect sales tax for these supplies). Any actual labor costs in providing these materials, could be rolled into direct labor or overhead costs for overall cleaning services, for example.

This approach to housekeeping supplies has a few advantages. First, it allows both you and the customer, to differentiate the cost of basic and specialty services such as general office cleaning and floor care, from the cost of the housekeeping supplies and any service charges for providing them. Secondly, it allows the customer the convenience of canceling the housekeeping supply service and sourcing their own supplies, should they wish to, without a disruption in the billing of other services.

Additionally, separating the billing for housekeeping supply services, prevents the customer from confusing variations in housekeeping supply usage and cost, with the price or rate they are paying for their primary cleaning services. It also avoids the trap of offering a set package price or rate for overall cleaning services (i.e., including housekeeping supplies), in which you have under-estimated the cost of these supplies, or the cost or usage, fluctuates upwards and your profit margin is significantly lowered.

Including a limited amount of housekeeping costs with direct material costs (e.g., such as back-up trash liners that you provide in a pinch when the customer's supply is interrupted), should present little or no problem however.

Bid estimation worksheets

The *Cleaning services bid summary worksheet form* discussed here, can be used for summarizing the service criteria and pricing for a one time job (e.g., floor care, pressure washing, make ready turnkey services, etc.,), or in establishing standard price structures for routine services, or to summarize the service criteria and bid rate, for any single room, cleaning area, facility or account. The worksheet form and an example are presented here.

CLEANING SERVICES BID SUMMARY WORKSHEET

ACCOUNT: ______________________

CONTACT: ______________________

ADDRESS: ______________________

PHONE: ______________________

E-MAIL/ FAX: ______________________

Date:

Cleaning services	Total sq. ft.	Frequency	Total labor (hrs)	Labor rate ($/ hr)	Direct labor cost	Direct material costs	Account overhead costs	Total account costs	Profit margin	Bid price (per job)	Bid price (monthly)	Price (per sq. ft./ month)	Price (per sq. ft. / year)
Basic services													
Special services													
Terms & conditions													

Zenith
Cleaning services
3300 3rd st
Any Town, USA
phone: xxx-xxxx; fax: xxx-xxxx
e-mail: email@zenclean.com

ACCOUNT: Acme Co.
CONTACT:
ADDRESS:
PHONE:
E-MAIL/ FAX:

Date: 01-Jan-01

CLEANING SERVICES BID SUMMARY WORKSHEET

Cleaning services	Total sq. ft.	Frequency	Total labor (hrs)	Labor rate ($/ hr)	Direct labor cost	Direct material costs	Account overhead costs	Total account costs	Profit margin	Bid price (per job)	Bid price (monthly)	Price (per sq. ft./ month)	Price (per sq. ft. / year)
Basic services													
general office cleaning: (monthly basis)	7,200	20/ mo	57.60	9.00	**518**	50	131	**699**	121	**820**	**820**	**0.11**	**1.37**
* all offices	4,500	12/ mo	21.60	9.00	**194**	30	55	**279**	49	**328**	**328**	**0.07**	**0.88**
* all restrooms													
* breakroom													
* warehouse													
* all hallways													
* receptionist area													
Special services													
Hard floor care:													
* Strip & wax (quarterly)	1,500	qrtly	17.00	22.10	**376**	75	59	**510**	90	**600**	**200**	**0.13**	**1.60**
* spray wax & buff (as needed)													
Non-routine cleaning maintenance				14.00									

Terms & conditions	
* Billing	1st of the month
* Payment	5th of the month, 10 day grace period, $25 processing fee following grace period
* Insurance/ bonding	Standard for all employees onsite, proof of ID at all times
* Quote period	Quote good for 30 days from the above date

Zenith Cleaning services 3300 3rd st Any Town, USA phone: xxx-xxxx; fax: xxx-xxxx e-mail: email@zenclean.com	ACCOUNT: Acme Co. CONTACT: ADDRESS: PHONE: E-MAIL/ FAX:							Date: 01-Jan-01		**CLEANING SERVICES BID SUMMARY WORKSHEET**			
			Customer copy										
Cleaning services	Total sq. ft.	Frequency	Total labor (hrs)	Labor rate ($/ hr)	Direct labor cost	Direct material costs	Account overhead costs	Total account costs	Profit margin	Bid price (per job)	Bid price (monthly)	Price (per sq. ft./ month)	Price (per sq. ft. / year)
Basic services													
general office cleaning: (monthly basis)	7,200	20/ mo								**820**	**820**	**0.11**	**1.37**
* all offices	4,500	12/ mo								**328**	**328**	**0.07**	**0.88**
* all restrooms													
* breakroom													
* warehouse													
* all hallways													
* receptionist area													
Special services													
Hard floor care:													
* Strip & wax (quarterly)	1,500	qrtly								**600**	**200**	**0.13**	**1.60**
* spray wax & buff (as needed)													
Non-routine cleaning maintenance				14.00									
Terms & conditions													
* Billing	1st of the month												
* Payment	5th of the month, 10 day grace period, $25 processing fee following grace period												
* Insurance/ bonding	Standard for all employees onsite, proof of ID at all times												
* Quote period	Quote good for 30 days from the above date												

The *Cleaning services bid summary worksheet* can be used in a variety of ways:

- ***as a hardcopy quote sheet, by itself, or as an attachment to a formally written bid proposal;***
- ***as a worksheet and documentation of record for bid estimation or price structuring calculations;***
- ***as a bidding worksheet for use in onsite consultations, or telephone inquiries;***

As with the other worksheet forms presented in this guide, most of the output or "results" cells (i.e., cells intended for entering the result of a calculation involving 2 or more input cells), are shaded for clarity and ease of use. It should also be noted, that it is also possible to abbreviate the calculations in the worksheet as needed, without providing every input, or performing a calculation for every output cell.

For instance, you can enter values taken from other sources (e.g., the price per sq. ft. (monthly and annual) charts in chapters 7 and 8), directly into selected output cells, without performing any additional calculations. A discussion of the example for this worksheet, should help to illustrate some of its potential uses and explain the math involved in the calculations.

To begin with, the *Cleaning services bid summary worksheet* example is presented in two forms, with and <u>without</u> cost figures (i.e., one form for internal use and one for release to customers, respectively). As a general rule, most businesses will <u>not</u> divulge cost accounting information to customers, under any circumstances. Additionally, the example shows the bid summary for <u>two</u> facilities. Each facility requires the same basic general office cleaning services, but at different frequencies. In addition, the larger facility requires hard floor care services quarterly. Non-routine maintenance is quoted at the same rate for both facilities.

Going across the top row of cells in the spreadsheet, a summary list of how each column may be used, includes but is not limited to the following options:

1.) The *"total sq. ft."* column, can be used, simply as an informational record of the size of the cleaning area, or as an input in conjunction with the input for the *"Bid price (monthly)",* to calculate a *"Price (per sq. ft./ month)"* or *"Price (per sq. ft./ year)"*. For example:

$804/ mo ÷ 7,200 sq. ft. = $0.11/ sq. ft./ mo, or

$0.11/ sq. ft./ mo x 12 mo = $1.34/ yr

Alternatively, you can look these rates up directly in the charts provided in chapters 7 & 8).

2.) The "*Frequency*" column, describes the frequency of the <u>inputs</u>. It is necessary to account for the frequency of the inputs when calculating the outputs (i.e., **conversions are needed for the last three outputs whenever they differ from the frequency of the inputs**, e.g., Bid Price (monthly) outputs are 1/3 of the Bid price (per job) when the input frequency is quarterly).

3.) The *"Total labor (hrs)" column,* requires an input value from the aforementioned workload worksheets, or some other source. It is intended to be used in conjunction with an input for *"Labor rate ($/ hr)"*, to calculate the *"Direct labor cost"*. For example:

57.6 hrs x $9.00/ hr = $518

Alternatively, the direct labor costs could be entered directly from some other source, such as the *Over head distribution and total cost* worksheet .

4.) The *"Direct material cost"*, *"Direct labor cost"* and *"Account overhead cost"* columns, are intended to calculate the *"Total account cost"*. For example:

$518 + $50 + $131 = $699

Alternatively, the *"Total account cost"* could be entered directly from some other source, such as the *"Overhead distribution and total cost"* worksheet, presented in a previous chapter.

5.) The *"Total account cost"* and *"Profit margin"* columns, are intended for calculating either the *"Bid price (per job)"* , or in this case *"Bid price (monthly)"*. For example:

$699 + 105$ = $804

6.) As shown in 1.), the *"Bid price (monthly)"* column can be used along with the *"total sq. ft."* column, to calculate the *"Price (per sq. ft./ month)"* or *"Price (per sq. ft./ year)"*. Alternatively, you can look these rates up directly, in the charts provided in chapters 7 & 8) and enter them directly into the last two columns.

7.) The *"Labor rate ($/ hr)"* column, can also be use to record a standard labor rate for all non-routine maintenance, going forward, as show in the "Special services" section, (e.g., $14.00).

8.) After completing a more detailed bid summary, a copy of the form can be made for the customer's perusal, without proprietary figures. As shown in the example marked ***"customer copy"*** (i. e., without labor & material costs listed).

Bid proposals and bidding requirements for cleaning services contract

An example of a formal bid proposal (with comments to the reader of this guide inserted) and a NOA (Cleaning services contract, notice of award), are provided here, for readers that may be unfamiliar with these types of documents, as well as those who simply wish to learn more about them.

The bid proposal example presented here, shows how a contractor can communicate an offer to provide specific and unique solutions to a potential customer's needs, with a "one to one" correspondence with the customer's requirements, as set forth in the initial onsite consultation. This approach ensures that the customer can see that each of his/ her problems, needs or requirements, have been carefully considered by the contractor and addressed with viable solutions.

The NOA example shows how a large company or government entity might detail their cleaning services contract bidding requirements (in particular cleaning specifications), as reflected in the content of the NOA, or alternatively, in pre-bid specifications. This may provide some insights for contractors seeking to expand their business, with large private or government contracts.

Acme Janitorial, Inc.
XXX Any street,
Any town, Any state/province
zip or mailing code: xxxxxx
Phone: xxx-xxx-xxxx
e-mail@acme.com
www.acme.com

Date: xx/xx/xx

To: "Responsible facility contact"
Customer/ Business's name
Customer/ Business's address

Re: bid proposal for cleaning services

Dear Mr./ Ms. "Responsible facility contact",

It was a pleasure meeting with you recently (*actual date optional*), to discuss your cleaning needs, during our free inspection and onsite consultation (*you may reference a recent phone conversation, or other type of meeting instead of an onsite consultation, as well here*). As you requested, Acme janitorial, Inc., has prepared a quote for cleaning and services, that we feel is very competitive for the services to be provided and will best meet your cleaning needs for the foreseeable future.

We have prepared our proposal with special consideration for the following cleaning needs that you have expressed, as well as the problems that you are currently experiencing with your present service:

Cleaning needs:

- Routine general office cleaning
- Hard floor care maintenance program
- Carpet care maintenance program

Problems or concerns:

- Spotty or inconsistent general office cleaning
  (e.g., waste baskets left full, carpets left un-vacuumed)
- Dust build-up and waste container overflow
- Doors left unsecured
- Lights left on or turned off, other than as specified by the customer
- Poor quality of hard floor care (e.g., low luster, slippery finish)
- Carpet stains allowed to stand and degrade the carpets

To address these issues we are recommending the following services and practices to most effectively meet your cleaning needs and minimize or eliminate the problems you are currently experiencing.

Routine general office cleaning:
3 times weekly (Tuesday, Thursday, weekend)

- Vacuum, or damp mopping of all floor surfaces
- Dusting of all desks, chairs, cabinets, tables and ledges
- Clean and disinfect bathroom toilet and sink fixtures
- Clean bathroom mirrors and wet mop bathroom floors
- Empty all ashtrays and trash receptacles as specified by the customer
- Clean front door glass and adjoining windows (inside and out)

Monthly deep clean to include:

- Wet mopping of all hard floors

- Spot cleaning of carpets and hard floors and for deep scuffs and stains
- Detailed cleaning of break room appliance surfaces as specified by the customer
- Thorough dusting of all surfaces as specified in routine office cleaning, as well as conspicuous or problem build-up area as specified by the customer (via instructions left at the front desk)

Quarterly hard floor care maintenance to include;

- an initial stripping and refinish of all hard floors, using a high luster finish formulation with anti-slide additives (the use of a special formulation coupled with the use of a high speed burnisher, will ensure a near "wet look" luster or finish)
- Monthly maintenance of hard floor surfaces to include cleaning or scrubbing of high traffic or problem areas
- Monthly spray buffing of reception area, break room, as well as high traffic or problem areas, susceptible to delustering, as needed.

Carpet maintenance program to include:

- Monthly, or as needed, spot cleaning of high traffic or problem areas
- Quarterly carpet extraction of all high traffic and problem areas
- Semi-annual carpet extraction with deodorizer treatment

Cleaning and housekeeping supplies:

- Acme janitorial will provide all cleaning supplies and trash can liners needed to perform the cleaning services to be provided
- Extra liners will be placed at the bottom of each trash receptacle to provide for in-house trash removal, between regularly scheduled cleaning services, in the event of potential overflow (should the problem persist, larger waste containers, or a move to daily cleaning service is recommended)
- All other housekeeping including, but not limited to, toilet paper, paper towels, hand soap, deodorizers, etc., will be provided by the customer

In addition, the attending general cleaning and floor care technicians will complete and initial a daily checklist, to include routine cleaning tasks performed as well as a check to insure that all doors are secured and the lighting is left as specified by the customer. A copy will be left for the facility contact at the front desk and their attending supervisor. This will help to monitor our performance and help to ensure that your existing cleaning service problems are minimized or eliminated.

Acme janitorial, Inc., provides complete window washing , Venetian blind washing, exterior pressure washing and gutter cleaning services as well. A brochure describing all of our standard services is provided with this proposal (attaching a brochure is *optional*).

We are pleased to offer these services to you at the competitive rates listed below. The prices quoted are good for 30 days from the date of this proposal. Billing is on the 1st of the month, unless otherwise requested by the customer, and is payable by check within 30 days. There is a $25 service charge for processing all returned checks (*billing stipulations* are *optional, they may be listed in the service agreement, as well*).

Routine cleaning services: **$ XXX. XX/ mo**

Carpet care maintenance program: **$ XXX. XX/ mo**

Hard floor care maintenance program: **$ XXX. XX/ mo**
Emergency or non-routine services: **$XX/ hr**
(includes all labor and basic cleaning supplies)

A copy of the proposed services and price quotes, as well as terms and conditions, are attached with a general service agreement that we provide to all of our customers.

Acme Janitorial, Inc., is an equal opportunity employer, serving our community since XXXX. Each of our technicians is professionally trained, fully bonded and insured, wears a uniform with an identifiable Acme janitorial logo or insignia and carries personal identification and proof of insurance at all times. We are also proud member of such prominent profes-

sional cleaning industry associations, as the NAPC, BCSAI and the IICRC.
We would like to thank you for your interest in Acme, at this time. To enter into a service agreement, complete the attached billing information form and provide an authorized signature on the general service agreement. Then phone or e-mail our offices and one of our account representatives will call on you within 2 business days, to pick-up copies of the contract, receive building access instructions, and answer any questions you may have regarding our services, at that time.

If you have any questions regarding our company, or you wish to discuss additional services, or changes to our proposal, please don't hesitate to call.

Sincerely,

Your Name, owner/ operator

Acme Janitorial, Inc.
XXX Any street,
Any town, Any state/province
zip or mailing code: xxxxxx
Phone: xxx-xxx-xxxx
e-mail@acme.com
www.acme.com

Sample Notice of Award
for a janitorial services contract
(with service agreement specifications)

Building specifications:
Total cleanable square feet: 24,000 sq. ft.

- Carpeted area: 22,000 sq. ft.
- Vinyl area: 500 sq. ft.
- Restroom area: ceramic tile, 1,500 sq. ft.

Restrooms: total 6; 3 male, 3 female

- Sinks: 12
- Urinals: 3
- Toilets: 12

Windows: 120

Cleaning specifications:
Cleaning hours:

- All work to be done between the hours of 5PM and 6AM the following morning

Maximum cleaning rate:

- 2500 sq. ft. per person per hour
  (maximum production rate per person allowed)

Daily:

- <u>Dust</u> all of the following surfaces with chemically treated dust cloth or mop: stairwells, floors, chairs, cabinets, tables, pictures, fire extinguishers ...)
- <u>Sweep or mop</u> all hard floor surfaces
- <u>Vacuum</u> all carpeted surfaces
- <u>Empty all trash receptacles</u> daily and remove to dumpsters
- Empty or consolidate all recyclables (m, w, f)
- <u>Clean and sanitize</u> bathroom fixtures, drinking fountains as needed

Weekly:

- Damp mop stairwells
  Buff hard flooring

- Wash bathroom fixtures and floors
- Spray wax and buff ceramic tile with wax, that has a non-slide formulation

Monthly:

- Remove all smudge marks from applicable surfaces such as door casings, floor moldings or skirts

Quarterly:

- Strip and wax vinyl floors, to a high luster, using a non-slide finish
- Clean interior and exterior windows, (except front door and windows, to be done weekly)

Semi-annual:

- Wash Venetian blinds, return within two days of removal
- Wash the interior of all windows with Venetian blinds

Quality Assurance:

- Contractor will provide written record of monthly and quarterly quality checks to facility contact

CLEANING SERVICES BID ESTIMATION CHARTS AND TABLES

Supplies:
All items necessary to maintain quality cleaning and housekeeping is to be provided by the contractor including:

- Hand towels, multi-folded and roll type
- Toilet tissues, standard roll count of 1000 sheets per roll 4.5" x 4.5"
- Liquid hand soap
- Sanitary napkins
- Trash bags

Employee requirements:
- All employees must wear contractor's uniforms onsite, log-in daily and maintain proof of identification , bonding and insurance at all times.

Removal of employees:
- Contractor will remove any employee as requested by the facility administrator within 24 hrs of proper notice

- General business liability: NA
- Fidelity bond: NA
- Business automobile insurance (BAP): NA
- Surety bond: NA

Safety:
- Contractor will comply with all federal, state and local regulations including OSHA safety requirements
- Contractor will provide employees with proper PPE and safety training and ensure that safety signs are posted onsite as applicable.
- Contractor will provide MSDS's for all cleaning chemicals to be used, with the written bid proposal and as necessary, to the facility administrator, in advance of all substitutions

Terms:
Contract period:
- 1 year

Emergency maintenance rate:
- $10/hr for all non-routine cleaning work at the discretion of the facility administrator

Contracted cleaning rates:
- $0.08 per square foot per month
- $0.96 per square foot per year
- $1920 per month

Payment:
- Prices valid for life of contract
- Billing, 1st week of each month
- Payment within 30 days
- $25 processing fee on all returned checks

Performance based incentives*:
- Failure to perform all weekly and monthly services satisfactorily, and as scheduled, will result in a 10% deduction monthly, per occurrence.
- Failure to perform all monthly, quarterly and semi-annual, services satisfactorily, and as scheduled, will result in a 35% deduction, per occurrence per time interval.

Contract extension:

- Service agreement may be extended for the period of 1 year, at the option of the facility administration and following completion of a service agreement extension and signatures from both the authorized facility management and the cleaning contractor's owner/ management.

Cancellation:

- The service agreement is subject to cancellation, at any time for lapse in performance of its terms and specification, by the contractor, as determined by the authorized agent of the "facility", or as warranted by unusual circumstances such as employee behavior or theft, substantive damage to facility personnel or property etc.,.

---

*These are performance based contract, terms and conditions. They are usually found in large business and government contracts. They are less common in small business service agreements.

Conclusion

It should be pointed out, that alternative approaches to calculating overhead and overhead distribution, total costs, workloads, supply costs and bid prices/ rates, which differ from those presented in this guide, can be used. Ultimately, they will lead to similar, if not identical estimates or endpoints.

Regardless of the approach used, you should strive for an optimum of:

- ***detail***;
- ***organization***;
- ***uniformity of approach***;
- ***accuracy***; and
- ***documentation and record keeping***,

in all of your bid estimation, work loading and cost accounting efforts.

In addition to preparing future bids, the worksheets in this guide can be used to quantify and analyze the direct and indirect costs and price structures of existing accounts, which may have not been carefully cost accounted thus far. This may present an opportunity to identify areas, where costs can be cut and where pricing and profit margins should be adjusted going forward. It is also a good idea to document the costs, profit margin, pricing and workloads for existing accounts, so that accurate values for overhead, direct costs, and routine workload estimates, etc., are available for use in the preparation of future bids.

Timing, is generally a critical constraint in preparing and submitting a competitive bid. The urgency of a customer's needs or requirements, or a limited, passing interest on the part of potential customers shopping for a better rate for cleaning services, or the need to ensure for fair and adequate review and consideration, relative to the bids of competitors, are all potential reasons, for the need of prompt preparation and submission of a price quote or bid proposal. A prompt response also sends a great signal to potential customers, which indicates that your company is eager to provide their cleaning services and helps to demonstrate your company's competency, in preparing an accurate assessment of their needs, as well as providing competitive solutions to meet them.

The forms at the end of this book have been compiled for convenient removal and reproduction by the reader. The complete set of forms can be found, following the index section of this guide. The reproduction of these forms is intended for the private use of the reader. Any reproduction of these forms, or any other material in this guide, for use in a commercial endeavor such as resale, training seminars, advertisements, derivative works, etc., is expressly prohibited and constitutes copyright infringement.

Index

CLEANING SERVICES OVERHEAD COST WORKSHEET

Period from: ______ to: ______

Date: ______

OVERHEAD CATEGORY	OVERHEAD ITEM	ANNUAL COST ($) (INPUT)	MONTHLY COST ($) (INPUT)	ANNUAL COST ($) (OUTPUT)	MONTHLY COST ($) (OUTPUT)
INSURANCE					
TAXES & LICENSES					
	needs 2nd proofing & printout				
CAPITAL DEPRECIATION					
OFFICE RENT/ MORTGAGE					
UTILITIES					
MARKETING/ ADVERTISING					
LOANS/ LEASES					
INDIRECT LABOR & BENEFITS					
TRANSPORTATION					
SUPPLIES & EQUIPMENT					
MISCELLANEOUS/ OTHER					
Totals					

CLEANING SERVICES OVERHEAD COST WORKSHEET

Period from: ______ to: ______

Date: ______

OVERHEAD CATEGORY	OVERHEAD ITEM	ANNUAL COST ($) (INPUT)	MONTHLY COST ($) (INPUT)	ANNUAL COST ($) (OUTPUT)	MONTHLY COST ($) (OUTPUT)
INSURANCE					
TAXES & LICENSES					
CAPITAL DEPRECIATION					

CLEANING SERVICES OVERHEAD COST WORKSHEET

Period from: ____ to: ____

Date: ____

OVERHEAD CATEGORY	OVERHEAD ITEM	ANNUAL COST ($) (INPUT)	MONTHLY COST ($) (INPUT)	ANNUAL COST ($) (OUTPUT)	MONTHLY COST ($) (OUTPUT)
OFFICE RENT/ MORTGAGE					
UTILITIES					
MARKETING/ ADVERTISING					

CLEANING SERVICES OVERHEAD COST WORKSHEET

Period from: ____ to: ____

Date: ______

OVERHEAD CATEGORY	OVERHEAD ITEM	ANNUAL COST ($) (INPUT)	MONTHLY COST ($) (INPUT)	ANNUAL COST ($) (OUTPUT)	MONTHLY COST ($) (OUTPUT)
LOANS/ LEASES					
INDIRECT LABOR & BENEFITS					
SUPPLIES & EQUIPMENT					

CLEANING SERVICES OVERHEAD COST WORKSHEET

Period from: ______ to: ______

Date: ______

OVERHEAD CATEGORY	OVERHEAD ITEM	ANNUAL COST ($) (INPUT)	MONTHLY COST ($) (INPUT)	ANNUAL COST ($) (OUTPUT)	MONTHLY COST ($) (OUTPUT)
TRANSPORTATION					
MISCELLANEOUS/ OTHER					
Totals					

CLEANING SERVICES:
OVERHEAD DISTRIBUTION & TOTAL COST
WORKSHEET

TOTAL OVERHEAD

Date: __________

ACCOUNT IDENTIFICATION	ACCOUNT DIRECT LABOR	ACCOUNT MATERIAL COSTS	ACCOUNT (LABOR + MATERIALS)	ACCOUNT OVERHEAD	PERCENT OVERHEAD	ACCOUNT (TOTAL COST)
Totals						

WORK LOAD WORKSHEET

ACCOUNT OR FACILITY: ______________________

CLEANING AREA/ ROOM: ______________________ Date: ____________

CLEANING TASK	TOTAL No. units, or AREA (sq. ft.)	CLEAN TIME 1 ITEM (min) (INPUT)	CLEAN TIME 1 ITEM (hrs) (INPUT)	PROD. RATE hrs/ sq. ft. (INPUT)	FREQUENCY WEEKLY (INPUT)	FREQUENCY MONTHLY (INPUT)	CLEAN TIME 1 ITEM (min) (OUTPUT)	CLEAN TIME 1 ITEM (hrs) (OUTPUT)	TOTAL TIME WEEKLY (hrs)	TOTAL TIME MONTHLY (hrs)	TOTAL TIME ANNUALLY (hrs)
SWEEPING											
DRY MOPPING											
WET MOPPING											
VACUUMING											
EMPTY WASTE BASKET											
EMPTY TRASH CAN											
DUSTING											
WASH WINDOWS											
CLEAN OTHER											
CLEAN OTHER											
CLEAN TOILET S											
CLEAN URINALS											
CLEAN SINKS											
CLEAN MIRRORS											
MOP BATHROOM FLOOR											
REPLACE TISSUE PAPER											
REPLACE SANITARY NAPKINS											
REPLACE PAPER TOWELS											
REPLACE AIR FRESHENER											
REPLACE SOAP DISPENSER											
REPLACE/ CLEAN (OTHER)											
REPLACE LIGHTING											
CLEAN STOVE											
CLEAN MICROWAVE											
CLEAN OVEN											
CLEAN REFRIGERATOR											
CLEAN COUNTER TOPS											
CLEAN CUPBOARD DOORS											
CLEAN (OTHER)											

WORK LOAD WORKSHEET

ACCOUNT OR FACILITY: ______________________

CLEANING AREA/ ROOM: ______________ **Date:** __________

CLEANING TASK	TOTAL No. units, or AREA (sq. ft.)	CLEAN TIME 1 ITEM (min) (INPUT)	CLEAN TIME 1 ITEM (hrs) (INPUT)	PROD. RATE hrs/ sq. ft. (INPUT)	FREQUENCY WEEKLY (INPUT)	FREQUENCY MONTHLY (INPUT)	CLEAN TIME 1 ITEM (min) (OUTPUT)	CLEAN TIME 1 ITEM (hrs) (OUTPUT)	TOTAL TIME WEEKLY (hrs)	TOTAL TIME MONTHLY (hrs)	TOTAL TIME ANNUALLY (hrs)
SPOT CLEAN CARPET											
CARPET EXTRACTION											
BONNET CLEANING											
CARPET SHAMPOOING											
STRIP FLOOR (1 layer of finish)											
STRIP FLOOR (all finish layers)											
SCRUB FLOOR											
WAX/ APPLY FINISH (one coat)											
WAX/ APPLY FINISH (3 coats)											
BUFF FLOOR											
SPRAY BUFF											
BURNISHING											
EXTERIOR PRESSURE WASHING											
CLEAN GUTTERS											
OTHER TASKS											
Totals											

CLEANING & HOUSEKEEPING SUPPLIES
COST ESTIMATION WORKSHEET

Date:

CLEANING UNIT: FACILITY: ______ AREA: ______ ROOM: ______

	no. of units:			no. of units:			no. of units:			no. of units:			no. of units:				
	FACILITY, ROOM, OR AREA ID: ______			FACILITY, ROOM, OR AREA ID: ______			FACILITY, ROOM, OR AREA ID: ______			FACILITY, ROOM, OR AREA ID: ______			FACILITY, ROOM, OR AREA ID: ______				
SUPPLY ITEM	quantity	cost/ item	total cost	quantity	cost/ item	total cost	quantity	cost/ item	total cost	quantity	cost/ item	total cost	quantity	cost/ item	total cost	Total monthly cost	Total annual cost
TOTAL COSTS (All supplies)																	

CLEANING & HOUSEKEEPING SUPPLIES
COST ESTIMATION WORKSHEET

Date:

CLEANING UNIT: FACILITY: ______ AREA: ______ ROOM: ______

	no. of units:			no. of units:			no. of units:			no. of units:			no. of units:				
	FACILITY, ROOM, OR AREA ID: ______			FACILITY, ROOM, OR AREA ID: ______			FACILITY, ROOM, OR AREA ID: ______			FACILITY, ROOM, OR AREA ID: ______			FACILITY, ROOM, OR AREA ID: ______				
SUPPLY ITEM	quantity	cost/ item	total cost	quantity	cost/ item	total cost	quantity	cost/ item	total cost	quantity	cost/ item	total cost	quantity	cost/ item	total cost	Total monthly cost	Total annual cost
GENERAL CLEANING SUPPLIES																	

CLEANING & HOUSEKEEPING SUPPLIES
COST ESTIMATION WORKSHEET

Date:

CLEANING UNIT: FACILITY: AREA: ROOM: Date:

	no. of units:			no. of units:			no. of units:			no. of units:			no. of units:				
	FACILITY, ROOM, OR AREA ID: ______			FACILITY, ROOM, OR AREA ID: ______			FACILITY, ROOM, OR AREA ID: ______			FACILITY, ROOM, OR AREA ID: ______			FACILITY, ROOM, OR AREA ID: ______				
SUPPLY ITEM	quantity	cost/ unit	total cost	quantity	cost/ unit	total cost	quantity	cost/ unit	total cost	quantity	cost/ unit	total cost	quantity	cost/ unit	total cost	Total monthly cost	Total annual cost
REPLACEMENT PARTS & TOOLS																	

CLEANING & HOUSEKEEPING SUPPLIES
COST ESTIMATION WORKSHEET

Date: CLEANING UNIT: FACILITY: AREA: ROOM: Date:

	no. of units:			no. of units:			no. of units:			no. of units:			no. of units:				
	FACILITY, ROOM, OR AREA ID: ______			FACILITY, ROOM, OR AREA ID: ______			FACILITY, ROOM, OR AREA ID: ______			FACILITY, ROOM, OR AREA ID: ______			FACILITY, ROOM, OR AREA ID: ______				
SUPPLY ITEM	quantity	cost/ unit	total cost	quantity	cost/ unit	total cost	quantity	cost/ unit	total cost	quantity	cost/ unit	total cost	quantity	cost/ unit	total cost	Total monthly cost	Total annual cost
HOUSE KEEPING SUPPLIES																	

CLEANING & HOUSEKEEPING SUPPLIES
COST ESTIMATION WORKSHEET

Date:

CLEANING UNIT: FACILITY: AREA: ROOM: Date:

	no. of units:			no. of units:			no. of units:			no. of units:			no. of units:				
	FACILITY, ROOM, OR AREA ID: ______			FACILITY, ROOM, OR AREA ID: ______			FACILITY, ROOM, OR AREA ID: ______			FACILITY, ROOM, OR AREA ID: ______			FACILITY, ROOM, OR AREA ID: ______				
SUPPLY ITEM	quantity	cost/ unit	total cost	quantity	cost/ unit	total cost	quantity	cost/ unit	total cost	quantity	cost/ unit	total cost	quantity	cost/ unit	total cost	Total monthly cost	Total annual cost
FLOOR CARE SUPPLIES																	
TOTAL COSTS (Cleaning supplies)																	
TOTAL COSTS (Replacement parts & tools)																	
TOTAL COSTS (Housekeeping supplies)																	
TOTAL COSTS (Floor care supplies)																	
TOTAL COSTS (All supplies)																	

CLEANING SERVICES BID SUMMARY WORKSHEET

ACCOUNT: ____________________

CONTACT: ____________________

ADDRESS: ____________________

PHONE: ____________________

E-MAIL/ FAX: ____________________

Date:

Cleaning services	Total sq. ft.	Frequency	Total labor (hrs)	Labor rate ($/ hr)	Direct labor cost	Direct material costs	Account overhead costs	Total account costs	Profit margin	Bid price (per job)	Bid price (monthly)	Price (per sq. ft./ month)	Price (per sq. ft. / year)
Basic services													
Special services													
Terms & conditions													

About the Author:

Walter Fenix is a veteran of several business start-ups with over 20 years experience in business and technical management. Mr. Fenix develops business tools including guides, manuals and software for use by small businesses and independent contractors. Other titles by Walter Fenix offered through the Knouen Group include:

Commercial & Residential Cleaning Services:
A Resource Guide To Developing And Maintaining Your Own Janitorial Or Home Cleaning Business
(Suggested retail price $34.95 US, $52.95 Canada)

Janitorial & Home Cleaning Services:
Bid Estimating Worksheets For Microsoft Excel*
(Suggested retail price $29.95 US, $44.95 Canada)
*** Software CD**

To learn more about these titles and how to order them individually, or at deep discounts through special package offers visit:

www.janitorial-and-home-cleaning-business-systems.com

or send an e-mail to:

email@janitorial-and-home-cleaning-business-systems.com

Book and software publications from the Knouen Group can also be purchased through many major on-line book retailers